Volume 12

The Broadman Bible Commentary

EDITORIAL BOARD

BROADMAN PRESS • Nashville, Tennessee

The Broadman Bible Commentary

Volume 12

General Articles
Hebrews - Revelation

The Bible text in this publication is from the
Revised Standard Version of the Bible, copy-
righted 1946 and 1952 by the Division of
Christian Education of the National Council
of Churches, and is used by permission.

Dewey Decimal Classification: 220.7
Library of Congress catalog card number:
78–93918
Printed in the United States of America

Preface

THE BROADMAN BIBLE COMMENTARY presents current biblical study within the context of strong faith in the authority, adequacy, and reliability of the Bible as the Word of God. It seeks to offer help and guidance to the Christian who is willing to undertake Bible study as a serious, rewarding pursuit. The publisher thus has defined the scope and purpose of the COMMENTARY to produce a work suited to the Bible study needs of both ministers and laymen. The findings of biblical scholarship are presented so that readers without formal theological education can use them in their own Bible study. Footnotes and technical words are limited to essential information.

Writers have been carefully selected for their reverent Christian faith and their knowledge of Bible truth. Keeping in mind the needs of a general readership, the writers present special information about language and history where it helps to clarify the meaning of the text. They face Bible problems—not only in language but in doctrine and ethics—but avoid fine points that have little bearing on how we should understand and apply the Bible. They express their own views and convictions. At the same time, they present alternative views when such are advocated by other serious, well-informed students of the Bible. The views presented, therefore, cannot be regarded as the official position of the publisher.

This COMMENTARY is the result of many years' planning and preparation. Broadman Press began in 1958 to explore needs and possibilities for the present work. In this year and again in 1959, Christian leaders—particularly pastors and seminary professors—were brought together to consider whether a new commentary was needed and what shape it might take. Growing out

of these deliberations in 1961, the board of trustees governing the Press authorized the publication of a multivolume commentary. Further planning led in 1966 to the selection of a general editor and an Advisory Board. This board of pastors, professors, and denominational leaders met in September, 1966, reviewing preliminary plans and making definite recommendations which have been carried out as the COMMENTARY has been developed.

Early in 1967, four consulting editors were selected, two for the Old Testament and two for the New. Under the leadership of the general editor, these men have worked with the Broadman Press personnel to plan the COMMENTARY in detail. They have participated fully in the selection of the writers and the evaluation of manuscripts. They have given generously of time and effort, earning the highest esteem and gratitude of Press employees who have worked with them.

The selection of the Revised Standard Version of the Bible text for the COMMENTARY was made in 1967 also. This grew out of careful consideration of possible alternatives, which were fully discussed in the meeting of the Advisory Board. The adoption of an English version as a standard text was recognized as desirable, meaning that only the King James, American Standard, and Revised Standard Versions were available for consideration.

The King James Version was recognized as holding first place in the hearts of many Christians but as suffering from inaccuracies in translation and obscurities in phrasing. The American Standard was seen as free from these two problems but deficient in an attractive English style and wide current use. The Revised Standard retains the accuracy and clarity of the American Standard and has a pleasing style and a growing use. It thus enjoys a strong advantage over each of the others, making it by far the most desirable choice.

Throughout the COMMENTARY the treatment of the biblical text aims at a balanced combination of exegesis and exposition, admittedly recognizing that the nature of the various books and the space assigned will properly modify the application of this approach.

The general articles appearing in Volumes 1, 8, and 12 are designed to provide background material to enrich one's understanding of the nature of the Bible and the distinctive aspects of each Testament. Those in Volume 12 focus on the implications of biblical teaching in the areas of worship, ethical duty, and the world mission of the church.

The COMMENTARY avoids current theological fads and changing theories. It concerns itself with the deep realities of God's dealings with men, his revelation in Christ, his eternal gospel, and his purpose for the redemption of the world. It seeks to relate the word of God in Scripture and in the living Word to the deep needs of persons and to mankind in God's world.

Through faithful interpretation of God's message in the Scriptures, therefore, the COMMENTARY seeks to reflect the inseparable relation of truth to life, of meaning to experience. Its aim is to breathe the atmosphere of life-relatedness. It seeks to express the dynamic relation between redemptive truth and living persons. May it serve as a means whereby God's children hear with greater clarity what God the Father is saying to them.

Abbreviations

ASV – American Standard Version
CBQ – *Catholic Biblical Quarterly*
IB – *Interpreter's Bible*
IDB – *Interpreter's Dictionary of the Bible*
Int. – Introduction
JBL – *Journal of Biblical Literature*
KJV – King James Version
LXX – Septuagint
MT – Masoretic Text
NEB – New English Bible
RSV – Revised Standard Version
TDNT – *Theological Dictionary of the New Testament*
TEV – Today's English Version

Contributors

Clifton J. Allen, Baptist Sunday School Board (retired): *General Article*

Morris Ashcraft, Midwestern Baptist Theological Seminary: *Revelation*

G. R. Beasley-Murray, Spurgeon's College, London: *2 Corinthians*

T. Miles Bennett, Southwestern Baptist Theological Seminary: *Malachi*

Reidar B. Bjornard, Northern Baptist Theological Seminary: *Esther*

James A. Brooks, New Orleans Baptist Theological Seminary: *General Article*

Raymond Bryan Brown, Southeastern Baptist Theological Seminary: *1 Corinthians*

John T. Bunn, Campbell College: *Song of Solomon; Ezekiel*

Joseph A. Callaway, Southern Baptist Theological Seminary: *General Article*

Ronald E. Clements, University of Cambridge: *Leviticus*

E. Luther Copeland, Southeastern Baptist Theological Seminary: *General Article*

Bruce C. Cresson, Baylor University: *Obadiah*

Edward R. Dalglish, Baylor University: *Judges; Nahum*

John I Durham, Southeastern Baptist Theological Seminary: *Psalms; General Article*

Frank E. Eakin, Jr., University of Richmond: *Zephaniah*

Clyde T. Francisco, Southern Baptist Theological Seminary: *Genesis; 1, 2 Chronicles; General Article*

D. David Garland, Southwestern Baptist Theological Seminary: *Habakkuk*

A. J. Glaze, Jr., Seminario Internacional Teologico Bautista, Buenos Aires: *Jonah*

James Leo Green, Southeastern Baptist Theological Seminary: *Jeremiah*

Emmett Willard Hamrick, Wake Forest University: *Ezra; Nehemiah*

William L. Hendricks, Southwestern Baptist Theological Seminary: *General Article*

E. Glenn Hinson, Southern Baptist Theological Seminary: *1, 2 Timothy; Titus; General Article*

Herschel H. Hobbs, First Baptist Church, Oklahoma City: *1, 2 Thessalonians*

Roy L. Honeycutt, Jr., Midwestern Baptist Theological Seminary: *Exodus; 2 Kings; Hosea*

William E. Hull, Southern Baptist Theological Seminary: *John*

Page H. Kelley, Southern Baptist Theological Seminary: *Isaiah*

J. Hardee Kennedy, New Orleans Baptist Theological Seminary: *Ruth; Joel*

Robert B. Laurin, American Baptist Seminary of the West: *Lamentations*

John William MacGorman, Southwestern Baptist Theological Seminary: *Galatians*

Edward A. McDowell, Southeastern Baptist Theological Seminary (retired): *1, 2, 3 John*

Ralph P. Martin, Fuller Theological Seminary: *Ephesians*

M. Pierce Matheney, Jr., Midwestern Baptist Theological Seminary: *1 Kings*

Dale Moody, Southern Baptist Theological Seminary: *Romans*

William H. Morton, Midwestern Baptist Theological Seminary: *Joshua*

Barclay M. Newman, Jr., American Bible Society: *General Article*

John P. Newport, Southwestern Baptist Theological Seminary: *General Article*

John Joseph Owens, Southern Baptist Theological Seminary: *Numbers; Job* (with **Tate** and **Watts**); *Daniel*

Wayne H. Peterson, Golden Gate Baptist Theological Seminary: *Ecclesiastes*

Ben F. Philbeck, Jr., Carson-Newman College: *1, 2 Samuel*

William M. Pinson, Jr., Southwestern Baptist Theological Seminary: *General Article*

Ray F. Robbins, New Orleans Baptist Theological Seminary: *Philemon*

Eric C. Rust, Southern Baptist Theological Seminary: *General Article*

B. Elmo Scoggin, Southeastern Baptist Theological Seminary: *Micah; General Article*

Burlan A. Sizemore, Jr., Midwestern Baptist Theological Seminary: *General Article*

David A. Smith, Furman University: *Haggai*

Ralph L. Smith, Southwestern Baptist Theological Seminary: *Amos*

T. C. Smith, Furman University: *Acts; General Article*

Harold S. Songer, Southern Baptist Theological Seminary: *James*

Frank Stagg, Southern Baptist Theological Seminary: *Matthew; Philippians*

Ray Summers, Baylor University: *1, 2 Peter; Jude; General Article*

Marvin E. Tate, Jr., Southern Baptist Theological Seminary: *Job* (with **Owens** and **Watts**); *Proverbs*

Malcolm O. Tolbert, New Orleans Baptist Theological Seminary: *Luke*

Charles A. Trentham, First Baptist Church, Knoxville: *Hebrews; General Article*

Henry E. Turlington, University Baptist Church, Chapel Hill, North Carolina: *Mark*

John D. W. Watts, Serampore College, Serampore, India: *Deuteronomy; Job* (with **Owens** and **Tate**); *Zechariah*

R. E. O. White, Baptist Theological College, Glasgow: *Colossians*

Bible Books and Writers

OLD TESTAMENT

Volume	Book	Writer
1, Revised	Genesis	Clyde T. Francisco
	Exodus	Roy L. Honeycutt, Jr.
2	Leviticus	Ronald E. Clements
	Numbers	John Joseph Owens
	Deuteronomy	John D. W. Watts
	Joshua	William H. Morton
	Judges	Edward R. Dalglish
	Ruth	J. Hardee Kennedy
3	1–2 Samuel	Ben F. Philbeck, Jr.
	1 Kings	M. Pierce Matheney, Jr.
	2 Kings	Roy L. Honeycutt, Jr.
	1–2 Chronicles	Clyde T. Francisco
	Ezra-Nehemiah	Emmett Willard Hamrick
4	Esther	Reidar B. Bjornard
	Job	John D. W. Watts
		John Joseph Owens
		Marvin E. Tate, Jr.
	Psalms	John I Durham
5	Proverbs	Marvin E. Tate, Jr.
	Ecclesiastes	Wayne H. Peterson
	Song of Solomon	John T. Bunn
	Isaiah	Page H. Kelley
6	Jeremiah	James Leo Green
	Lamentations	Robert B. Laurin
	Ezekiel	John T. Bunn
	Daniel	John Joseph Owens
7	Hosea	Roy L. Honeycutt, Jr.
	Joel	J. Hardee Kennedy
	Amos	Ralph L. Smith
	Obadiah	Bruce C. Cresson

Jonah	A. J. Glaze, Jr.
Micah	B. Elmo Scoggin
Nahum	Edward R. Dalglish
Habakkuk	D. David Garland
Zephaniah	Frank E. Eakin, Jr.
Haggai	David A. Smith
Zechariah	John D. W. Watts
Malachi	T. Miles Bennett

NEW TESTAMENT

Volume	Book	Writer
8	Matthew	Frank Stagg
	Mark	Henry E. Turlington
9	Luke	Malcolm O. Tolbert
	John	William E. Hull
10	Acts	T. C. Smith
	Romans	Dale Moody
	1 Corinthians	Raymond Bryan Brown
11	2 Corinthians	G. R. Beasley-Murray
	Galatians	John William MacGorman
	Ephesians	Ralph P. Martin
	Philippians	Frank Stagg
	Colossians	R. E. O. White
	1–2 Thessalonians	Herschel H. Hobbs
	1–2 Timothy	E. Glenn Hinson
	Titus	E. Glenn Hinson
	Philemon	Ray F. Robbins
12	Hebrews	Charles A. Trentham
	James	Harold S. Songer
	1–2 Peter	Ray Summers
	1–2–3 John	Edward A. McDowell
	Jude	Ray Summers
	Revelation	Morris Ashcraft

Contents

Hebrews   *Charles A. Trentham*

Introduction   1
Commentary on the Text 14

James   *Harold S. Songer*

Introduction 100
Commentary on the Text 106

1 Peter   *Ray Summers*

Introduction 141
Commentary on the Text 149

2 Peter   *Ray Summers*

Introduction 172
Commentary on the Text 175

1–2–3 John   *Edward A. McDowell*

Introduction 188
Commentary on 1 John 194
Commentary on 2 John 225
Commentary on 3 John 228

Jude   *Ray Summers*

Introduction 232
Commentary on the Text 235

Revelation   *Morris Ashcraft*

Introduction 240
Commentary on the Text 257

General Articles

Worship in the Bible   *Charles A. Trentham* 363
Ethics in the Bible   *William M. Pinson, Jr.* 373
The Mission of the People of God   *E. Luther Copeland* 383

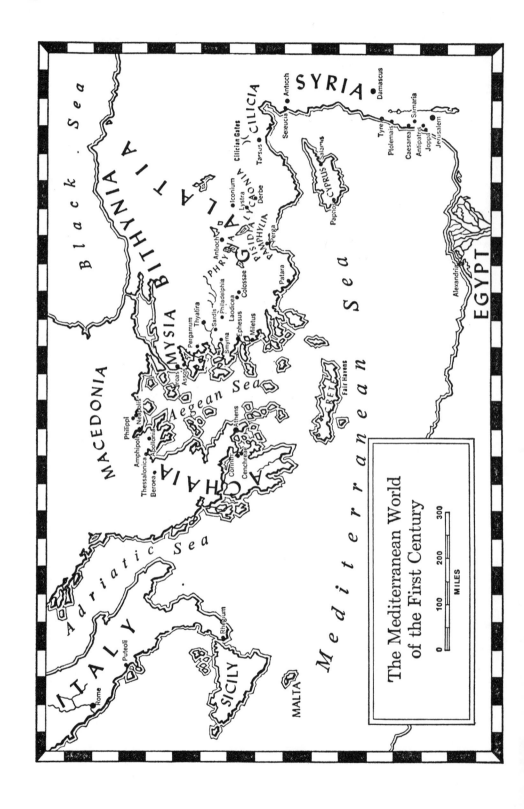

The Mediterranean World
of the First Century

Hebrews

CHARLES A. TRENTHAM

Introduction

Should you ask why anyone would try to add to the already voluminous research on the book of Hebrews, it would be enough to reply that the publication in 1965 of the new material on Melchizedek, derived from the Dead Sea Scrolls, has quickened the interest of the Christian community in the reexamining of the book of Hebrews. It has also provided some clues for identifying those to whom this document was originally addressed. James A. Sanders, Auburn Professor of Old Testament at Union Theological Seminary, now believes that they were people who had some affinity with the Essene sect, which had taken refuge in the Qumran community. But scholars are divided on the importance of the Qumran material as it relates to Hebrews. Feine-Behm-Kümmel summarize the situation:

Further, certain scholars recently, and in various ways, have attempted to establish that the intellectual world of Qumran influenced Hebrews (Schnackenburg, Betz), or at least that Hebrews is an appeal to former members of the Qumran sect of Essenes whose theological proclivities were similar to those of the author (Kosmala, Yadin). Coppens, on the other hand, has convincingly demonstrated that no specific parallels between Hebrews and the intellectual world of Qumran appear; rather, distinctive Qumran language has no analogy in Hebrews.[1]

1 Feine-Behm-Kümmel, *Introduction to the New Testament* (Nashville: Abingdon Press, 1966), p. 278.

Nevertheless, this document takes on enormous new life when viewed as addressed, in part at least, to converts to the Christian community from the Essenes, who were still clinging tenaciously to Essene doctrines and refusing to move on into a mature Christian faith.

When the Dead Sea Scrolls were first discovered, many a scholar's pulse was quickened as he faced the possibility of relinquishing many of the precious presuppositions which have been a part of our traditional belief. The person, who dared carry his flickering taper into the ominous darkness of the caves of Qumran, did so with considerable trepidation. He knew that the winds of truth might blow out his taper and require him to start with data that was hitherto unknown by the best of scholars and thus require reinterpretation of the Christian faith from older and more reliable manuscripts and from materials that give much clearer descriptions of the circumstances to which the first heralds of Christ addressed themselves.

This consideration is particularly pertinent to the study of Hebrews since so much that has been said about this document in the past is so negative and conjectural that it remains the most enigmatic book in the New Testament. Its long battle for a place in the New Testament canon is in itself so intriguing as to commend its study to the serious student of Christian origins.

As we attend to the major introductory matters, we shall be asking what form this

1

manuscript originally took: Was it a letter, a sermon, or both? Can we say anything for certain about who wrote it? Can we assign a date to its writing? To whom was it first addressed and why was it written?

I. Letter or Sermon?

What we now call the book of Hebrews may very well be the earliest Christian sermon recorded in our New Testament. Some scholars object to this view on the grounds that no one sermon could carry such involved theology, nor could any congregation be expected to assimilate so much profound and intricate thought at one hearing. Of course, it is true that this discourse bears little resemblance to the brief, single, pointed homilies of our time. Nevertheless, the preaching in the pulpits of the Reformation and Puritan periods would resemble Hebrews, both in richness of content and in length of composition. At the same time, it cannot be denied that, as Dinkler argues, Hebrews may be a combination of several sermons collected and combined by the author in this one volume.[2]

The beautifully balanced continuity of discussion argues, however, for the unity of this work. The author calls his work a "word of exhortation" (13:22), and there is nothing in the document itself to indicate that it is a letter until the personal salutation in this verse. The word "letter" does not appear in the manuscript. The translation "I have written a letter unto you" (13:22, KJV) is better read "I have written to you.")

Hebrews does not begin as a letter. It is launched with two ringing adverbs. It is possible that the opening paragraph was worn off of the original manuscript. It might even have been removed deliberately. For example, Harnack argued that it is quite likely that, if a woman wrote it, the first paragraph would have been deleted because of the low estate of women at the time.

[2] E. Dinkler, "Letter to the Hebrews," IDB, Vol. E-J (Nashville: Abingdon Press, 1969), p. 572.

At any rate, Hebrews sounds like a sermon. Notice how often the writer refers to speaking: "For it was not to angels that God subjected the world to come, of which we are speaking" (2:5). "Though we speak thus, yet in your case, beloved, we feel sure of better things that belong to salvation" (6:9). "And what more shall I say?" (11:32).

The long debate concerning whether this work is a letter or a sermon might be resolved in the possible conclusion that it was, first of all, a sermon to a particular congregation of Palestinian Christians and later sent by the author as a letter to the church at Rome.

If it is accepted as a sermon, it gives us rich insight into the high literary merit of some early Christian preaching, for it is a masterpiece of first-century Christian prose. It contains the purest and best Greek of the New Testament. The rhythmical cadences and marvelous bursts of sheer eloquence have earned the author the title, "The Isaiah of the New Testament."

Edmund Gosse, distinguished British man of letters, wrote of the impact which his father's reading of Hebrews made upon his sensitive, young mind when he was a child (quoted by James Moffat, p. xxx).

The extraordinary beauty of the language—for instance, the matchless cadences and images of the first chapter—made a certain impression upon my imagination, and were (I think) my earliest initiation into the magic of literature. I was incapable of defining what I felt, but I certainly had a grip in the throat, which was in its essence a purely aesthetic emotion, when my father read, in his pure, large, ringing voice, such passages as "The heavens are the work of Thy hands. They shall perish, but Thou remainest, and they shall all wax old as doth a garment, and as a vesture shalt Thou fold them up, and they shall be changed; but Thou art the same, and Thy years shall not fail."

II. Authorship

The next question concerns who wrote Hebrews. The oldest manuscripts do not name an author. The first traces of the letter appear in the Western church when, in A.D. 95, Clement of Rome wrote to the church at Corinth and quoted the passage in Hebrews concerning the superiority of Christ to the angels. Although Clement is writing to Corinth from Rome, Clement gives no indication that it was written by Paul. In the first, second, and third centuries, the Western church did not claim it for Paul. Both Clement and Hermas of Rome, writing just before and after the close of the first Christian century, knew this book, respected it most highly, and quoted from it; but neither assigned a title nor an author to it. It was not until the fourth century that Hilary became the first in the Western church to claim it for Paul. If the congregation at Rome was the first to receive it as a letter, it would seem that this Western church would have been the first to acknowledge it as Pauline.

The earliest claim for the Pauline authorship comes from the Eastern church, from Pantaenus of Alexandria in A.D. 180. Some discount the testimony of Pantaenus on the grounds that he was very zealous for the Eastern church. The Alexandrians were great Christians. They desired a letter from Paul to be addressed personally to them. When Peter wrote to the churches of the Dispersion in Asia Minor to encourage them in faithfulness in view of the return of the Lord, he said: "Our beloved brother Paul wrote to you" (2 Peter 3:15). Pantaenus claimed that Hebrews is that letter. If Hebrews is not that letter, then the letter is lost. We now know that some of Paul's letters were lost.

Clement of Alexandria, a student of Pantaenus, writing early in the third century, contended that Paul wrote this book in Hebrew and that Luke translated it into Greek, for he could readily recognize that the Greek of this author was different from that of Paul.[3] To support his argument he pointed to the similarity between the Greek of Hebrews and that of the Gospel of Luke and the book of Acts. Clement explains that Paul did not mention his own name at the beginning of the epistle because he did not wish to renew the antagonism of the Jews against him since he was known as the "Apostle to the Gentiles."

As a whole, the Eastern church accepted Paul as the author and it was received into their canon as such. Still, it must be remembered that the community in Alexandria was not without its doubts concerning the authorship of Hebrews. Among the doubters was Origen, a man of considerable stature, who lived in Alexandria between A.D. 186 and 253. He wrote: "For not without reason have the ancients handed it down as Paul's."[4] But he noted that the style is not Pauline. He said that it was most likely written by an unknown disciple of Paul. He is the author of the most quoted conclusion, which is often misread because it is taken out of context. Here is what he really said:

If I gave my opinion, I should say that the thoughts are those of the apostle, but the diction and phraseology are those of some one who remembered the apostolic teachings, and wrote down at his leisure what had been said by his teacher. Therefore if any church holds that this epistle is by Paul, let it be commended for this. For not without reason have the ancients handed it down as Paul's. But who wrote the epistle, in truth, God knows. . . . The statement of some who have gone before us is that Clement, bishop of the Romans, wrote the epistle, and of others that Luke, the author of the Gospel and of Acts, wrote it.[5]

It is significant to remember that, in the Western church, the Pauline authorship was not accepted until the fourth century. Hebrews is not listed in the Muratorian Fragment (the collection of the New Testament books by Muratori—one of the earliest collections of Scripture), or in the canonical lists through the time of Eusebius, who did the outstanding work on New Testament criticism through the Patristic period. This father of church history

---

3 Eusebius, *Church History* VI. 14. 2–3 (see IB, XI, 581).

4 *Ibid.*, 13–14, p. 582.
5 *Ibid.*, 13–14, pp. 581–582.

says that the book was questioned at Rome because it was not written by Paul. Irenaeus (A.D. 130–200) and Hippolytus (A.D. 150–222) knew the letter but denied that Paul wrote it. Tertullian, the first great latin father, ascribed it to Barnabas.

From the middle of the fourth century on, the Western canon assimilated the Eastern canon and Hebrews was included. However, Augustine admitted that he accepted Hebrews as a concession to Eastern opinion, and it was not until the early fifth century that an official synod of the Western church could bring itself to speak of the fourteen letters of Paul (Hebrews being the fourteenth).

The uneasiness over this work broke out again during the Reformation. Erasmus, one of the leaders of the Reformation, doubted it on literary grounds. He claimed that Clement of Rome wrote it. His claim was based on the statements in 1 Clement to the church at Corinth, which are identical with statements in Hebrews.

Luther doubted the Pauline authorship on doctrinal grounds and was the first to suggest that Apollos—the friendly rival of Paul and the eloquent man who was powerful in the Scriptures—was the author. This view is currently espoused by no less a modern scholar than T. W. Manson. Calvin suggested that Luke was not merely the translator but the writer of Hebrews.

The theological arguments against the Pauline authorship are quite convincing. There are some superficial similarities in the Christology of the two writers, i.e., the writer of Hebrews, whoever he was, and Paul. Christ's preexistence, the intercession of Christ, and the atonement and redemption through death might claim a Pauline derivation. The writer's eschatology also is very similar to Paul's. However, the writer's principle concern is with the priesthood of Christ. Not a mention of this is made in the known letters of Paul. Paul's major emphasis is upon the risen Christ. Hebrews 13:20 is the only specific reference to the resurrection in the entire document.

The doctrine of salvation also is stated quite differently. In Galatians Paul contends that, by the death of Christ, Christ redeemed us from the curse of the law; and in Romans, he emphasizes redemption from the power of the flesh. Neither of these is found in Hebrews. Paul's strong emphasis on justification by faith does not appear in Hebrews. In Hebrews the great object of sacrifice is that we may draw near to God (10:22).

The concept of faith differs quite markedly. In Paul, faith is self-commitment to Christ, at the foot of the cross, in the power of the resurrection. In Hebrews, faith is seen as a conviction of the reality of the unseen world and as a corollary to that loyalty to the unseen world which is made known in Christ.

The absence of the "in Christ" passages, the mystical passages which compose the heart of the Pauline gospel, led Martin Luther to conclude that Hebrews 2:2–3 could not possibly have been written by the same man who wrote Galatians 1:1,12. Calvin agreed with Luther on this.

The careful syntax of the author of Hebrews differs radically from the bursting spontaneity of Paul. Paul was like a rushing mountain torrent, plunging over the rocks with no time for watertight syntax, rhythm, or polished innuendo. Paul's style was extreme freedom in the matter of style. It is almost psychologically impossible for Paul to have written Hebrews.

It is far easier to say who did not write Hebrews than it is to say anything for certain about who did. There are, nevertheless, certain things we know about this author. First, we know he was a Hebrew. He had a thorough knowledge and understanding of Judaism and of Jewish history. He was a master of the Midrash, the exegesis of the Jewish Scriptures.

The writer was more Jewish than Paul, on one hand, and more Greek than Paul, on the other. That brings us to the second thing we know about him. He was a Hellenistic Jew. His affinity with Philo, who synthesized the revelation of God to Moses with Greek philosophy, is often implied. His affinity for Plato's doctrine of two worlds, which leads him to see this world as a shadowy reflection of the real world above, is evidence of this. Beyond this, we cannot go. The suggestion of Apollos as the writer has its strong points. Still, it is exceedingly hard to understand why no one before Luther appears to have suggested this possibility.

Tertullian wrote: "For there exists also a writing of Barnabas to the Hebrews." [6] Then he goes on to quote Hebrews (ch. 6) on the impossibility of a second repentance. Tertullian claims that there was a unified tradition concerning the authorship of Barnabas. We know that Barnabas was a Levite, which would fit with this writer's thorough knowledge of Levitical worship. Barnabas was from Cyprus, which was Alexandrian in its culture. His very name meant "son of consolation," which reflects the necessary gifts for writing a composition noted for its comfort and encouragement. Barnabas was a friend of Timothy and a companion of Paul, which might account for some of the Pauline flavoring of the document. The fact remains that we have not one line from Barnabas by which we may judge his style or thought.

Harnack, G. H. Moulton, and Randall Harris hold to the joint authorship of Aquila and Priscilla, the teachers of Apollos. If Priscilla had a part in writing it, we could account for the omission of her name by remembering Paul's aversion to women being leaders or speaking in the church. The edict of Claudius, in A.D. 49, made Aquila and Priscilla refugees and banished them from their homeland.

Whoever wrote it was a pilgrim upon the earth. The passages, "For here we have no lasting city" (13:14) and "I urge you the more earnestly to do this in order that I may be restored to you the sooner" (13:19), show the displaced-person complex of the writer (13:14,19). The use of many nautical metaphors is further evidence of a wandering kind of life: "We who have fled for refuge" (6:18). "Lest we drift [be swept away from anchorage]" (2:1). "Draw back" is a technical term for shortening the sail (10:38, KJV).

The fact that we cannot identify the author does not diminish the value of this work. Instead, it speaks positively of the richness of the early Christian community in talent and culture. It tells us that Paul was not the only great master in the early church. There was enormous talent reflected in this writer, whose chief concern seemed to be to encourage the thoughtful people of the Christian community to retain their faith and hope in Christ.

III. Time of Writing

There is no clear historical evidence within the body of Hebrews to assist us in setting the exact date of its composition. We can, however, draw the outer limits by saying that it could not have been written later than A.D. 95, for by that time Clement of Rome had quoted from it in his epistle to Corinth. If one holds that it was written by Paul, then it must have been composed before A.D. 64, when the martyrdom of Paul likely took place. Timothy is mentioned in the writing; therefore, it must have been written before his martyrdom, which probably occurred during the Domitianic persecution in the late eighties or nineties. There is a tradition, however, that Timothy died a natural death in Ephesus.

All we can say for certain is that the letter was written during a time of persecution. Still, it is not easy to prescribe that period of persecution. Several possibilities are open to us. The Neronian persecution in Rome in A.D. 64 is one. If Hebrews was written originally to Christians in Rome, the Neronian persecution would fit. This date would not fit, however, if, as we have contended above, this was first a sermon to Palestinian Christians and later mailed as a letter to Rome, because the Neronian perse-

---

6 *Ibid*, p. 582.

cution was limited to Rome. The difficulty with the Neronian date is the word of the writer: "You have not yet resisted to the point of shedding your blood" (12:4). In the Neronian persecution, many were put to death. They were covered with pitch and burned in Nero's gardens. The Neronian date is not very satisfactory.

Another choice might be the Domitianic persecution, from A.D. 81 to the late nineties. The problem with this date is that the supposed persecution under Domitian was an attempt to enforce the worship of Domitian. There is no mention of such in Hebrews. The persecution of these people seemed to take the form of taunting because of their belief in the Parousia, such as is found in 2 Peter 3:4: "Where is the promise of his coming?"

A major factor to be considered in setting the date is the absence of a reference to the fall of Jerusalem and the destruction of the Herodian Temple by the Romans in A.D. 70. A reference to such an event would have so strengthened the writer's argument concerning the reality of the heavenly sanctuary as over against the shadowy, insubstantial nature of the earthly sanctuary that it is inconceivable that such a calamity would have been omitted from his discussion. Some of the force of this argument might be removed by the fact that this writer makes no mention of the Temple. His concern is with the tabernacle, which was the center of Israel's worship before arriving in Canaan.

It must be conceded that the author's argument—"Here we have no lasting city, but we seek the city which is to come" (13:14)—might well be a reference to the fall of Jerusalem. It might also be a description of a people who are on the outside of the established religion of the Holy City—a pilgrim people who are "outside the camp" (v. 13). At the same time, we must admit that the appeal of the heavenly city would probably be far greater to a people who had seen what they once considered to be an inviolable city sacked by the Romans.

To say, "Here we have no lasting city," to people who could still see the sacred walls of Zion intact and who believed that God himself was the defender of the Holy City, would not be a very convincing argument. For the writer to have explained in greater detail what he meant by "here we have no lasting city," to people who walked among the burned-out ruins of Jerusalem, would have been the belaboring of the obvious and a reopening of the wounds that were still too tender to touch.

Another significant date, which heretofore has been either unknown or ignored in the search for the time of writing, is June of A.D. 68, when the Qumran community was destroyed by the Romans. Since some of the first hearers of this sermon may have been recent converts from the Essene sect of the Qumran community, they might very well have undergone dual persecution. First, it could have been for their Essene faith, which contended that the Essenes alone were the true Israel to whom the Davidic promise of a Messiah was made and to whom a high priest, like Melchisedek, would come. Now that they have been converted to Christianity, they are facing not only the persecution of the Roman military forces, which began because of the Jewish revolt in A.D. 66, but also the sufferings imposed upon them at the hands of the Jews, who were desperately attempting to revive the smoldering fires of Judaism. This, combined with the delay of the Parousia, was beginning to tell on their Christian morale. Their hands were drooping. Their knees were beginning to tremble.

Marcus Dods contends, from the passage, "Every priest stands daily at his service" (10:11), that the Temple was still standing, which would place its writing before A.D. 70. Westcott holds to the date of the Neronian persecution, between 64 and 67, while Harnack and Holtzmann prefer the time of the Domitianic persecution of 90–96. Of course, the enormous prestige of these scholars cannot be denied. Still, it must be remembered that they had no access to the Dead Sea Scrolls and to the light which they have shed upon first-century Palestinian Christianity.

To me, it seems most satisfactory to choose a date between A.D. 68 and 70, when the Qumran community had been destroyed and the sacking of Jerusalem had begun. It would have required massive pressure to dampen the burning enthusiasm of the early Christian community, and these events would have provided such pressure as this document describes.

IV. Destination

The only positive indication of the destination of Hebrews comes from the ambiguous statement in 13:24, "Those who come from Italy send you greetings"; which may mean either those residing in Rome, or those of Rome who were then residing elsewhere. The manuscripts, Sinaiticus and Vaticanus, list the title of the letter simply as *"Pros Hebraious."* Of course, this was written in later. Nevertheless, it tells us that Christians very early considered it as addressed to Jews in a community that was threatened with extinction. The writer summons the recipients to make an absolute break "outside the camp" (13:13). A. S. Peake believed this could only mean an absolute break with Judaism. A. B. Davidson also held this view.

James Moffatt and E. F. Scott held an opposite view, that the recipients were Gentiles. They contended that the writer was not referring to apostasy from Judaism but apostasy from the living God. The frequency of the Old Testament quotations would not necessarily argue that Jews were the original hearers, for this writer believed that the Old Testament was for all Christians. Paul evidently believed this also, for he filled his letter to Corinth with Old Testament quotations.

A relevant passage, at this point, is 6:1-2—"Therefore let us leave the elementary doctrines of Christ and go on to maturity, not laying again a foundation of repentance from dead works and of faith toward God, with instruction about ab-

lutions, the laying on of hands, the resurrection of the dead, and eternal judgment." This passage is not necessarily addressed to Jews, but rather refers to doctrines which all Christians were taught at the time of their entrance into the Christian community. In fact, repentance, faith, resurrection from the dead, and eternal judgment were already in the Old Testament, and Jews knew of them.

Furthermore, the faults, referred to in Hebrews, were more likely to be true of Gentiles than of Jews. "Do not be led away by diverse and strange teachings; for it is well that the heart be strengthened by grace, not by foods, which have not benefited their adherents" (13:9). What is seen here is not a timorous drawback from Jewish orthodoxy, but an open break with gnosticism. James Moffatt contends that this betrays no trace of Judaism as a competing attraction. Perhaps he goes too far.

Others combine the above view, suggesting that Hebrews was written to Christians with no view to Jews or Gentiles, but rather to the temptation, common to all Christians, to grow cold, lose interest, and become religious vagabonds. These view the title, *"Hebraious,"* as symbolical. The word means pilgrims or sojourners. In Genesis 14:13 (LXX) Abram, the Hebrew, meant "the man from across the river." This view agrees with the etymological meaning of the word "Hebrew"; but overstress on this meaning is a bit farfetched.

We know that the recipients were a second generation of hearers. The original message had been "attested to us by those who heard him" (2:3). They had not stood in the bright dawn of the Christian faith. They were losing some of the early enthusiasm and were growing lax in their faith, perhaps, because of the delay of the Parousia. The strain was beginning to tell. "You have need of endurance" (10:36). The drift was finding expression in their antipathy to the church. Therefore, the writer calls them not to forsake assembling (10:25). William Manson, in his Baird lectures, sees them as Jewish Christians forgetting the command to evangelize the world. The writer's main thrust is to call Christians, who are disposed to linger in their Jewish origins, to move out into the greater freedom of Christ.

If Hebrews is viewed, as earlier suggested, in the dual role of sermon and letter, then we must attempt further to identify the original hearers, who would have understood its meaning best and who can, therefore, help us to understand it as it was originally delivered.

Let us begin with the assumption that, as a letter, it was mailed to Rome. The evidence for this is in the familiarity which both Clement and Hermas of Rome had with the letter shortly before and after A.D. 100. The epistolary close, "Those who come from Italy send you greetings," also accords with this. This is the only substantial evidence we may offer.

If it was first delivered as a sermon, it is far more important to identify the original hearers if we are to make much meaning out of the intricate and involved theological arguments. Many locations of this original congregation have been offered, including Jerusalem, Samaria, Antioch, Caesarea, Colossae, Ephesus, and Alexandria, as well as Rome.

The Dead Sea Scrolls have compelled us to face the obvious affinities between the hermeneutics and Christology of Hebrews with the thought forms of the sect of Essenes at Qumran. The recently published Qumran material, about the Old Testament figure of Melchisedek, gives us a clue to a fuller understanding of the person and work of Christ as the great High Priest in the heavenly sanctuary. This is the heart of the Christology of Hebrews. This encourages us to believe that the hearers of this sermon may have been in a Christian congregation in a city of the Decapolis, perhaps, Gerasa, modern Jerash. In the congregation, perhaps, were recent converts from the Essenes.

Against this view, some have maintained the strong Hellenistic tone of the writer's argument. To counter this, it may be mentioned that there is nothing in this document so exclusively Hellenistic that it could be called non-Palestinian. Indeed, Palestine was not walled in from the world around her. She was as much a part of the culture of the Mediterranean basin as any other geographical part. There is much in Hebrews to suggest Palestinian thought forms and nothing conclusively against Palestine as the location of the original congregation of hearers.

It might be argued that the fact that the author is not at home in the Hebrew language might militate against this view. Let me reply that there were many Jews in Palestine who could neither read nor speak Hebrew, just as it was true in the fifth century B.C. that most Jews could not understand Hebrew when Ezra read the law to them as recorded in Nehemiah 8.

We know that the hearers did understand the Old Testament in the manner in which it was customarily expounded in the synagogues and in the Essene cults. They were also most familiar with the Jewish sacerdotal system. They were also amenable to Greek thought forms and rhetoric. Some of them, at least, were familiar with Platonic, Philonic, and Gnostic ontology. They were sufficiently Hellenized as not to be antagonized by the combination of Old Testament eschatology with more Hellenistic views. This has led many to favor Alexandria as the site of this original congregation, a view which certainly cannot be dismissed.

It is now known that there was a Christian congregation which was largely converted from the Essenes of Alexandria and was called the "Therapeuti." It seems to me, however, that it is more likely that the congregation to which Hebrews was addressed was like that group, described in Acts 6—8, which had in its membership such notable Christians as Stephen (the first Christian martyr), Philip, Prochorus, Nicanor, Parmenas, Nicolas, and Timon.

There is a passage in Ecclesiasticus (44—50), which was greatly beloved by the Essenes of Qumran and which describes the history of the faithless and faithful in ancient Israel. It is very analogous to the content of Hebrews 3, 4, and 11. The Ecclesiasticus passage and the Hebrews material both bear a remarkable resemblance to the sermon of Stephen, the Palestinian Hellenist and the first Christian martyr. This sermon is recorded in Acts 7.

V. Purpose

What did the author have in mind for his readers? He is concerned with the problem of religious drift, the waning enthusiasm, and the loss of courage and zeal on the part of this primitive Christian congregation.

At this juncture, let us look in depth at this problem. Can we trace the causes of this drift? [7] Look, first, at three general causes:

1. The first was religious formalism. The writer of Hebrews describes true worship as a drawing near to God, but these people had allowed it to degenerate into the fulfillment of certain acts, rites, and ceremonies. So the author jars them out of their complacency by asking, in effect, "Have you ever actually seen the majesty of the God to whom you are supposed to be drawing near? Do you really know what it means actually to speak to the Lord of hosts, the King of glory? Can you do this and be routine and casual about it? Who would ever have any awareness of God's presence and not cry out, 'Who is sufficient for these things?' " •

All worship is inappropriate unless it helps people to draw near to God. The only valid question after a service of worship is, "Did I meet God?"

2. The second cause of their drift was familiarity with divine truth. Nothing can be deadlier. Hebrews 5:12 tells us that these people had been handling the truth of God in a perfunctory way so long that

it had lost its grip. They knew it so well that, by this time, they should have been "teachers."

Hebrews 6:1,12 tells us that they were spiritually and intellectually sluggish. The truth of God" when handled casually, becomes the savor of death unto death. The remedy for such deadly familiarity is found in realizing the inherent splendor of the gospel. The writer magnifies the romance of primitive religious orthodoxy and the essential excitement of Christian faith.

Thus he asks his hearers, to paraphrase, "Have you realized who Christ is? Go back to the founder of your faith and think about him until you are gripped by the reality of what God is trying to say to us." Look again at that magnificent prologue (1:2–4). Can such claims ever become commonplace? If you begin to drift, go back and ponder again the sublime Christology of the Christian faith.

Think also of your soteriology. Have you grasped what was done by God in Christ for salvation? If you would come back from your drifting, then remember that you are a citizen of two worlds, not one, and that you are anchored already in the world to come (6:5).

Take another look, says the writer, at the real meaning of Christian faith as "the substance of things hoped for" (11:1, KJV). If religious familiarity removes the sheen from your religion, then "give the more earnest heed to" it (2:1, KJV). Arouse yourself out of your stupor and unconcern. Above all, "consider him" (12:3). Lest you lose the splendor of the gospel, go back to Bethlehem where the Word was made flesh to dwell among us (John 1:14), and to Galilee where he lived for us, and to Calvary where he died for us, and to the empty tomb, and to the Mount of Olives where we are lifted up with him in heavenly places (Eph. 1:20). Let not a day pass without deliberately standing in wonder before that which has become so familiar that you now take it for granted.

3. The third general reason for this religious drift was complacence. "For though

---

[7] Years ago, I sat in a class on the theology of Hebrews at New College in Edinburgh and heard James Stewart discuss this problem. He cited six causes for this drift, three of them general and three of them specific. I am indebted to him for the list.

by this time you ought to be teachers, you need some one to teach you again the first principles of God's word" (5:12). So the preacher hammers home to his hearers, "You are drifting. You must press on to a fuller maturity." He makes large use of the term *teleis*, i.e., *teleiōn* (mature or fully grown, 5:14); *teleiōtēta* (maturity or full growth, 6:1); *teleiōsai* (make perfect, 2:10).

The Law was never able to produce perfection. Neither is there such a thing as a perfect Christian. We must have an eschatology toward which we are moving. A Christian must live in that dynamic tension between what he is and what he is to become.

Look, now, at three specific causes of this religious drift and how the writer deals with them.

1. There was severe persecution. In 10:32–33 our attention is called to the great hardships and afflictions which characterized the apostolic age. The Christians were not indifferent, but a terrific storm had snapped their moorings, and they were at the mercy of the waves of persecution.

At first, Rome was the friend of the church, defending it against the Jews, but eventually this policy was reversed. In A.D. 49 there was a riot in Rome and Claudius delivered an edict expelling all Christians and Jews.

Furthermore, the Christian community had reached a decision that Gentiles did not have to be circumcised in order to become Christians. Since they did not have to be circumcised, they had no connection with the established religion of the Jews. They were, therefore, subject to the judgment of Rome which forbade all but established religions.

Rome's wrath was also kindled against Christians by what she considered foreign superstitions. Rome was puzzled about the practices behind closed doors where the Lord's Supper was observed. The religion of Isis and Cybele practiced immorality behind closed doors. Were Christians guilty

of the same? Christians talked about the end of the world in fire. Did this mean that they intended to start the fire? Christians had been accused of starting the Neronic fire, according to the fifteenth book of the Annals of Tacitus.

In A.D. 64, when the persecution began under Nero, thousands and thousands of nameless Christians died, and two died who were not nameless, Paul and Peter—likely about this time. Now the Christians are faced with another period of persecution. In the face of such persecution, the preacher reminds them that they have need of patience (10:36—12:1). "Therefore let us go forth to him outside the camp, bearing abuse for him" (13:13).

The preacher encourages fortitude in the face of persecution by quickening the memory of his hearers. He calls them to remember three things: (1) Remember your noble past (6:9–10). (2) remember your leaders who have gone to death and imitate their fortitude (10:32; 13:7), also faithful heroes of Israel (11:1 ff.). (3) Above all, remember the sufferings of Jesus —"Jesus who, for the sake of the joy that lay ahead of him, endured the cross, making light of its disgrace, and has taken his seat at the right hand of the throne of God" (12:2, NEB). "Jesus also suffered outside the gate, to consecrate the people by his own blood" (13:12, NEB). Let us also go outside the camp. It is enough for the disciple that he be as his Master and the servant as his Lord.

2. The second specific cause of their religious drift was the delay of the "Parousia. There was now no sign of the second advent. The believers were disillusioned. They were now asking, "Why wait any longer?" Thus they began to lose interest and to drift away from the faith.

How does the preacher deal with this? He begins with an affirmation of the certainty of the second advent. Its delay does not mean that it will not come. "Christ . . . will appear a second time" (9:28). It has been observed that this is the only time in the New Testament that the words, "a second time," appear to describe the final coming of Christ. Whatever may be made of that, the *eschaton* loomed large in all New Testament thought.

The preacher says, "He who is to come will come" (10:37, NEB). Therefore, he calls his hearers to "hope until the end" (6:11). He assures them that they can live even now in the power of a realized eschatology. That is the meaning of: "Faith gives substance to our hopes, and make us certain of realities we do not see" (11:1, NEB). He tells us that Christians have already actually tasted the "powers of the age to come" (6:5).

3. The third specific cause of this religious drift was ethical compromise. Some in the Christian community were imagining that they could continue to be identified with Christ while conforming to the patterns of a pagan society.

The criticism and contempt of their neighbors was beginning to tell. Christians were ostracized by their own family circles with such disdain that there were left with none to support them. They were also exposed to public abuse (10:33)—"a gazingstock" (KJV) and a "spectaculum" (Vulg.). Paul wrote, "We are made a [theatrical] spectacle unto the world" (1 Cor. 4:9, KJV). The lure of strange doctrine was taking hold on them (13:9). The preacher also speaks of certain people who were profane or completely secularized (12:16).

The preacher also tells them what their compromise is doing. He makes the most staggering charges. They are crucifying the Son of God afresh. They have "trodden under foot the Son of God, and hath counted the blood of the covenant, wherewith he was sanctified, an unholy thing" (10:29, KJV). He calls them out of their compromise to make a clean break of self-commitment. They must make a clean break and go outside the camp.

The entire message of Hebrews, as I see it, is concentrated in two verses: "Jesus also suffered outside the gate in order to sanctify the people through his own blood. There-

fore let us go forth to him outside the camp, bearing abuse for him" (13:12–13). These practical passages must not be viewed as digressions from the author's argument, as some view them. On the contrary, these practical passages are the center. The preacher's theology is for the sake of reinforcing these practical demands.

In the demand, "let us go forth to him outside the camp," James S. Stewart sees three factors: (1) the iron camp, a secure religious bulwark; (2) an alien force, the world; and, (3) a tiny band of brave, intrepid souls, getting outside the bulwark into the alien world and pressing further on with their warfare.

The preacher sees the church in the setting of the Exodus. The stage is set between Egypt, the land of bondage, and Canaan, the land of promise. Leviticus tells us that the camp was the sacred place, the one abode of light in a dark wilderness. Exodus tells us of the perils outside the camp. To get outside was not to return.

In those days, the people of God were a people on the march. They were neither culturized, nor institutionalized, nor secularized. When they reached an oasis in the wilderness, the majority would always say, "Let us abide here." The leaders would always prod them on.

From Abraham to John the Baptist, this was the story of Israel—the camp of God terrified by the secular world. The prophets of God were the intrepid souls who moved beyond the people outside the camp. For this, they were tormented and afflicted.

The preacher of Hebrews says that this related to the church of his day. The church was static. To break up that static camp, he sees an expeditionary force composed of one, solitary person. It was Jesus, who went outside the gates of the camp and was crucified. He thus began the eschatological journey. He became the conscience of his church, demanding that his redeemed follow. There can be no turning back, no drifting. We must get on with the eschatological journey. The cry is, "Onward, on to the city of God!"

In the light of these influences toward drifting, there is, then, a fourfold summons: First is the summons to self-commitment, to complete commitment with no attempt to conciliate those who would make faith more compatible with society. The symbol of Christianity is a cross—death to self, death to all that impedes the journey.

Second is the summons to advance. This rings like a bell through this sermon. Nothing is more devastating to Christian faith than the thought that we have arrived at perfection and must, therefore, spend our best energies defending our doctrines and glorifying the present condition of the institutional church. The church at her best is a desert bivouac which must be taken down each generation and moved forward toward the abiding city.

Third is a summons to evangelize. Long ago, the hearers of the sermon should have been out in the world teaching others, seeking to claim an alien world for Christ (5:12). As it was, they were like children meekly trudging back to kindergarten, preferring milk to keep them mild, rather than meat to make them strong for battle.

Fourth is the final summons to a sturdy belief in the reality of the unseen world: "For here we have no lasting city, but we seek the city which is to come" (13:14). Most of our energy is consumed by our endeavor to fortify our brief encampment in the flesh with health and financial security. God has deliberately made this journey precarious. He makes the way perilous that we might pause and remember that we are pilgrims here and to remind us that we are in the end time. We must, therefore, get on with the "eschaton."

The writer of Hebrews is concerned with countering the syncretism which was threatening the Christian community because of the influence of Essene sacerdotal ideas. He therefore goes to great length to demonstrate that everything, which was true to the Old Testament pattern, was completely fulfilled and superseded in Jesus Christ—the Son of God, the royal Servant, and the great, eternal High Priest. He insists that only the Christian commu-

nity is the true Israel, who will enter the final, sabbath rest of God in the heavenly sanctuary. A Christian's whole life must be lived as though, at any moment, he may be called to face the final truth. The final truth is that the one, overruling reality is that God alone is man's judge and that he is also the God of all. There is no comfort in this, for the preacher goes on to remind us that "our God is a consuming fire" (12:29). The church of the first century was no bulwark of separation and no haven of rest. It was a part of the establishment. It was a community of outsiders "outside the camp" (13:13), where its communicants are continually reminded that they are not protected from all perils. They are moving toward a place and a time where all theories must face the consuming fire of truth made known in God's Son. It is a fire that cannot be dampened by any backlog of good works, but only by the grace of God made known to us in the One in whom God and man actually met. He is the One who is already in charge in the heavenly sanctuary, interceding, pleading his sacrifice, and who is already enthroned in majesty at the right hand of the most high God.

Ultimate truth is and always has been his. Because this is true, we strive for peace with all men, and for a life of brotherly love with all men, because our judge is their God. Also because of this, there is strength for the drooping hands and trembling knees in the most perilous of times.

Outline

I. God's final word for the final age (1:1—3:6)
  1. Introduction (1:1–4)
  2. Above all angels (1:5—2:5)
     (1) Superior in his nature (1:5–14)
     (2) Word of Jesus *versus* the word of angels (2:1–5)
  3. Superior in redemptive work (2:6–18)
     (1) Necessity of incarnation (2:6–9)
     (2) Jesus: hero and priest (2:10–13)
     (3) Heart of the matter (2:14–18)
  4. Greater than Moses (3:1–6)

II. Finding the true rest of God (3:7—4: 13)
 1. Peril in unbelief and disobedience (3:7–19)
 2. Creative fear of God (4:1–3)
 3. The appointed day (4:4–8)
 4. Our final rest (4:9–11)
 5. Word of warning (4:12–13)
III. Our great High Priest (4:14—5:10)
 1. Nature of the High Priest (4:14–16)
 2. Qualifications of the true High Priest (5:1–10)
  (1) Human qualifications (5:1–6)
  (2) Moral qualifications (5:7–10)
IV. Application (5:11—6:20)
 1. Against sluggishness (5:11–14)
 2. Crucifying Christ again (6:1–12)
 3. Reassurance (6:13–20)
  (1) The promise (6:13–17)
  (2) Anchor of hope (6:18–19)
  (3) Forerunner and High Priest (6: 20)
V. Heart of the argument (7:1–28)
 1. Melchizedek (7:1–3)
 2. Superiority of Melchizedek (7:4–10)
 3. A divine priesthood (7:11–14)
 4. An effectual priesthood (7:15–19)
 5. An eternal priesthood (7:20–22)
 6. A perpetual priesthood (7:23–25)
 7. The perfect priesthood (7:26–28)
VI. The new tabernacle (8:1–6)
VII. The new covenant (8:7—9:28)
 1. Inward and effective (8:7–13)
 2. Place of the old covenant (9:1–28)
  (1) Ark of the covenant (9:1–5)
  (2) System of exclusion (9:6–10)
  (3) A superior tabernacle (9:11)
  (4) A superior sacrifice (9:12–23)
  (5) The superior hope (9:24–28)
VIII. The ultimate will of God (10:1–39)
 1. Failure of the law (10:1–4)
 2. Final sacrifice (10:5–10)
 3. Final forgiveness (10:11–18)
 4. The invitation (10:19–25)
 5. The warning (10:26–31)
 6. The encouragement (10:32–39)
IX. Meaning of faith (11:1–40)
 1. Substance and evidence (11:1–2)
 2. Belief in the Creator (11:3)
 3. The faithful of the Old Testament (11:4–34)
 4. Summary of horrors (11:35–38)
 5. Delay of the promise (11:39–40)
X. Words of encouragement and discipline (12:1–24)
 1. Call to complete the course (12:1–2)
 2. Need for discipline (12:3–17)
 3. The final arrival (12:18–24)
 4. The final warning (12:25–27)
 5. A call to gratitude and worship (12: 28–29)
XI. A call to virtue and sacrifice (13:1–16)
 1. Application of Christian virtues (13: 1–8)
 2. Sacrifices which God approves (13: 9–16)
XII. The conclusion (13:17–25)
 1. The appeal (13:17–19)
 2. The benediction (13:20–21)
 3. The prayer (13:22–25)

Selected Bibliography

BRUCE, A. B. *The Epistle to the Hebrews.* Edinburgh: T. & T. Clark, 1908.

CALVIN, JOHN. *Commentaries on Hebrews.* Edinburgh: Calvin Translation Societies, 1853.

DAVIDSON, A. B. *The Epistle to the Hebrews.* ("Bible-Class Handbook.") Grand Rapids: Zondervan Publishing House, 1950.

DAVIES, J. H. *A Letter to Hebrews.* ("The Cambridge Bible Commentary.") Cambridge: University Press, 1967.

DODS, MARCUS. *Epistle to the Hebrews.* ("Expositor's Greek Testament," IV.) London: Hodder and Stoughton, Ltd., 1917.

MANSON, WILLIAM. *The Epistle to the Hebrews.* London: Hodder and Stoughton, Ltd., 1951.

MOFFATT, JAMES. *A Critical and Exegetical Commentary on the Epistle to the Hebrews.* ("The International Critical Commentary.") Edinburgh: T. & T. Clark, 1924.

MONTEFIORE, HUGH. *A Commentary on the Epistle to the Hebrews.* ("Harper's New Testament Commentaries.") New York: Harper & Row, 1964.

NAIRNE, ALEXANDER. *The Epistle to the Hebrews.* ("Cambridge Bible.") Cambridge: University Press, 1957.

NEIL, WILLIAM. *The Epistle to the Hebrews, Ritual and Reality.* ("Torch Bible Commentaries.") London: Student Christian Movement Press, Ltd., 1955.

PEAKE, A. S. *Hebrews.* ("The Century Bible.") Edinburgh: T. C. and E. C. Jack, n.d.

PURDY, ALEXANDER C. and J. HARRY COTTON. "The Epistle to the Hebrews," *The Interpreter's Bible,* Vol. XI. Nashville: Abingdon Press, 1955.

SAPHIR, ADOLPH. *The Epistle to the Hebrews.* New York: C. C. Cook Company, 1902.

SCOTT, ERNEST F. *The Epistle to the Hebrews.* Edinburgh: T. & T. Clark, 1922.

WESTCOTT, B. F. *The Epistle to the Hebrews.* 3d. ed. London: Macmillan and Company, 1920.

YADIN, YIGAEL. "The Dead Sea Scrolls and the Epistle to the Hebrews," *Scripta Hierosolymitana,* IV. Jerusalem: Hebrew University, 1957.

Commentary on the Text

1. God's Final Word for the Final Age (1:1—3:6)

1. Introduction (1:1–4)

[1] In many and various ways God spoke of old to our fathers by the prophets; [2] but in these last days he has spoken to us by a Son, whom he appointed the heir of all things, through whom also he created the world. [3] He reflects the glory of God and bears the very stamp of his nature, upholding the universe by his word of power. When he had made purification for sins, he sat down at the right hand of the Majesty on high, [4] having become as much superior to angels as the name he has obtained is more excellent than theirs.

These stately lines of introduction constitute the most beautiful single passage in the New Testament. The two major emphases are: first, that God has spoken; second, that God has spoken for the final time.

The theology of this writer is thoroughly Hebraic. No Hebrew writer undertakes to defend the existence of God. Even the oft-quoted passage, "The fool hath said in his heart, There is no God" (Psalms 14:1; 53:1, KJV), is better translated, at the end, "No God is here." This is a denial of God's effective presence rather than of his existence.

Jeremiah speaks of those who "have spoken falsely of the Lord, and have said, 'He will do nothing'" (5:12). The prophet is thus speaking of the attempt of a wicked man to persuade himself that he can go on with his wickedness and still escape divine judgment.

Theoretical atheism is not recognized in the Bible. Even outside the Bible, the term "atheist" has not been so much a term which men used to describe their own opinions as one that has been used against them by their adversaries.

The two basic assumptions of Hebrew theology are that God is and that God has spoken. The writer of Hebrews saw the source of all authority in the voice of God. Every person believes in some authority. Either he believes in the authority of God, or he makes an authority of his own whims. Either he has an authority that is unshakeable, or he makes an authority of fleeting fads and fancies. Christianity begins with the affirmation, *God spoke.* For the writer of Hebrews, Christ was God's voice.

What God has said partially in the prophets, he said fully in Jesus. God spoke one central truth through each prophet. Through Amos, he spoke of justice. Through Isaiah, he spoke of holiness. Through Hosea, he spoke of forgiving love. But each of these was only a fragment of the total truth about God's character. In Jesus, the full-orbed truth was made known. Great, dramatic events in history and nature showed God's grandeur and concern for his people in the Old Testament; but Jesus revealed God by being incarnate.

Hebrews is best interpreted in terms of the *eschaton,* the end time. There is a rediscovery of this long-forgotten and underemphasized key to the understanding of the New Testament theology. Perhaps, the distortion of the gospel by some millenarians, which resulted in so much flamboyant and speculative preaching, has frightened away many from what was a very basic and exceedingly precious part of the thought of the New Testament writers. The end of the ages had come down in Jesus Christ: the end time had begun.

The Essenes of the Qumran community were greatly concerned with the end time. In this, they were like the earliest Christians. The Midrashic literature, which we have inherited from Qumran, bears a remarkable resemblance to Hebrews. This resemblance is in the manner in which Old

Testament passages are gathered at random, from many sections of the Hebrew Bible, and used to reinforce or prove a writer's point of view.

Furthermore, there is also a similarity in the manner in which both Hebrews and the Qumran literature interpreted the Old Testament texts, as speaking immediately to their own times. For both, God spoke to their contemporary situation through Old Testament passages. This was not true of later rabbinic Midrash literature, which chose not to contemporize, i.e., not to apply a particular point from the Old Testament to a specific political event in their day and time. Instead, the later rabbis chose to moralize rather than historize. They would discover what a particular Old Testament passage said about what God is like. From this profile of God, they would deduce what God expected from his people now, in this age. Both the Qumran writers and the writer of Hebrews had a greater sense of the immediacy of God as he spoke to their situation. It was not by deduction from an ancient analogy, but a living word.

The point at which the Essenes of Qumran and the Christians, addressed in Hebrews, were at variance was in their insistence that each, and not the other, was the true Israel whom God would use at the end of days to bring to man the only salvation. In those dreadful days, each community insisted that access to God would be available only through them.

Both of these communities insisted that the Old Testament Judaism had been fulfilled in them. It is, therefore, conceivable that the writer had this conflict in mind, when he opens his treatise with a discussion of how God has spoken in the past and how he brought his word to its final expression.

In many and various ways shows the richness and variety of God's approach to man. The many modes and means, by which God addressed himself to man, does not belittle the Old Testament revelation. Although it was fragmentary and temporal, it was, nevertheless, God who had

spoken. He spoke in many forms.

He spoke through theophanies, as with Jacob at Bethel (Gen. 28:10–17); through voices, as to Samuel (2 Sam. 3:1–18); through visions, as to Isaiah (Isa. 6); through oracles and signs. He spoke through the still, small voice to Elijah. He spoke through the weeping compassion of Jeremiah, and through the trumpet-toned denunciation of Amos. He spoke through famine, flood, drought, and pestilence. He spoke through the bountiful harvest, and through liberation from exile. He spoke through the soft light of the stars, the gentle winds of summer, and in the roaring sounds of many waters. God spoke in many parts. He spoke through the law, through the judges, and through the poets and prophets.

God spoke. Christianity is a religion of revelation. God, in his grace, takes the initiative. The "given," with which the gospel begins, is the word of God. God gives no vague intimations from which we may speculate about his meaning. God speaks to this person, about this matter, in this moment.

Of old means that the rabbis divided time by the periods before and after the Messiah.

With the words, **to our fathers,** the writer here brings the holy history of Israel to the fore in the first sentence of his sermon. Israel was not like any other nation. God had given his word personally to Israel and had made a covenant with his people, as he had not done with any other nation. The writer, in later emphasis on the supremacy of Christ, does not lose any of his enormous respect for the traditions of his fathers. He is a man with roots, set in a nation with roots. His concern is not to destroy roots, but to bring the vine of Israel to its full fruition.

By the prophets means that God speaks to people through people. God's means is a man. He spoke **by the prophets.** The age of the prophets is now drawing to a close, says the writer. The word *prophets* is not mentioned again until 11:32. There it describes the line of God's great men, including some priests in the Old Testament. This designation accords with the common, first-century meaning and is the meaning of the term in this passage.

The NEB has a better translation of *but in these last days.* It reads, "In this the final age."

He has spoken. This form of the aorist tense of the verb describes action in its entirety. Regardless of its duration, it gathers action into a single whole. This gathers the whole of Jesus' life and work, his birth, teaching, death, and resurrection into a single entity. Through him, God has given us this full and final word.

Carlyle Marney tells us:

We all remember how precious is the word of a loved one when it turns out to have been his *last* word. Letters are treasured and memorized. Words meant casually are given incredible meaning. Time and again the church grasps for some new word, but we are always driven to the last thing God said for sure.

This is what the New Testament is about: the last things they said God said. Looking back over their shoulder for a time when God was alive [on earth] they remembered he made a Testamentary—a Covenant—a Last Will and Deed—a Word—the last thing God said was Jesus who is the Christ. You may as well admit it. After Jesus comes on stage the subject of Holy Scripture is the Christ. This is what it means to call him the Word of God.

God had said other words, but not lately, and *Talmud* is but embroidery on a word already spoken. So is Christian history just embroidery. Church History has been our hearing and mishearing and refusing to hear the Son. And all our "denominations" represent some mishearing of God's last word. Even our precious unheard Holy Spirit, since the fourth century *filoque* clause was added, is heard to speak through and from the Son for it was of the Son that the Holy Spirit reminded us, taught us, rebuked us, and caused us to remember. Every distorted record is a distortion of the Son—for this is the last word from God we have heard.[8]

The uniqueness of this final revelation is that it is a *Son* kind of revelation. Jesus does not belong among the prophets. The

[8] Carlyle Marney, *The Carpenter's Son* (Nashville: Abingdon Press, 1967), pp. 9–10.

prophets message looked to the future for fulfillment. Christ, the Son, is God's message of fulfillment. No new revealer followed him. The prophets were men only. Christ was Son of man and Son of God.

Notice how these words stagger under the weight of these astounding claims, made by this early Christian preacher. Jesus is God's Son. He is no temperal being. He is the bearer of eternal salvation. He is the Lord of history, the inheritor of the ages. All that is said here is in full accord with the most primitive and cardinal Christian doctrine, as is witnessed in Mark 1:1. As the Son of God, he is the only valid avenue by whom we can draw near to God.

Seven sublime claims are made for the Son of God, in vv. 3–4. Four things are said about his nature, and three about his achievements.

(1) *Whom he appointed the heir of all things.* There were two ways of interpreting the relationship of Jesus to God in early Christian history. There were the adoptionists, who said that Jesus became in history the Son of God by God's appointment. There were others who believed that he was the preexistent Son and was with God in the beginning. On the surface, the writer seems to be fusing both points of view in this verse. This is not necessarily true. The appointment might have been made in the eternal intention of God before time began. As one scholar has insisted, creation was cast on redemption lines. Is this what Paul means when, in the Colossian letter, he contends that all things will be summed up in Christ (3:11)? He is the inheritor of the ages in the sense that God has been moving through all the past to bring his kingdom of redemption to its fulfillment in the Son who now stands in the heavenly sanctuary, applying his sacrifices, pleading our cause, and anchoring us with him within the veil.

(2) *Through whom also he created the world.* This is the one whom John calls the "Word" (1:1), the one who stood in creation's bright morning with the Father to call the whole created order into being.

This is the one who "knew what was in man" (John 2:25), not by Oriental intuition, but as the maker of man, who entered into our race through the door of flesh. This is the maker of man, who himself condescended to be made man in our behalf. He is not only the heir, he is the maker. And all things belong to him.

(3) *He reflects the glory of God.* He is the effulgence, the full shining forth of the Father's radiance. He is the one of whom it was said, "In him is no darkness at all" (1 John 1:5). Another way of saying this is that he *bears the very stamp of his nature.* He is the stamp of God's hypostasis, the exact image of his essence, an unalloyed emanation. The *stamp* means the clear-cut impression made by a seal, the very facsimile of the original. Our word character is a transliteration of the Greek word translated "stamp." The combining of the two words, effulgence and stamp, is a dual attempt to express the same thing, the exact likeness of the Son to the Father.

(4) *Upholding the universe by his word of power.* Christ is the Logos of God, the wisdom of God, the agent of God in creation, by whom all things are upheld and held together (John 1:1–5). Paul insists on this in Colossians: "In him all things hold together" (1:17).

Look, now, at the three achievements of the Son:

(1) *When he had made purification for sins.* Through his life, death, and resurrection, the purification of the sin of man was accomplished. Forgiveness was made possible and, with it, the reconciliation of man with God. He is now our great High Priest within the veil, offering his blood for our forgiveness and opening the way of access by which man may draw near to God.

If true religion is drawing near to God, as this early preacher contends, the great question becomes: how can sinful man ever hope to approach God? His answer is that man can do this because his sin has already been purged. In Christ's "once for all" (7:27) sacrifice of himself, he provided eternal cleansing for all who receive this by faith. Thus, by his sacrifice, the way of access to God was opened forever. Christ, then, is not only unique in his nature, he is also unique in his achievement.

(2) *He sat down at the right hand of the Majesty on high.* The uniqueness of Christ's achievement is further argued by the place he now occupies in the heavenly sanctuary. He sat down on the right hand of the most high God, in a position of majesty and unparalleled power, as one whose earthly work is finished and as one whose position in the new order can never be challenged.

(3) *Having become as much superior to angels as the name he has obtained is more excellent than theirs.* His name is "Son." The angels' name is "messenger."

We moderns, who are carried along in the mad momentum of our material world, may not have the psychological equipment to understand this passage in Hebrews. The world of the Bible is a world inhabited by angels. Students of the origins of religion, who believe that religion is but a chase of the evolution of man, may feel that angels belong exclusively to the dim beginnings of religion in the shadowy, impenetrable past. Were this true, you might expect fewer references to angels as the 4,000 years of man's pilgrimage in the Bible draws to an end.*

---

*NOTE: The truth is, angels were the constant companions of the Son of man and of the people in the early church. The writer of the Apocalypse says that time will come to an end, when the angel of God stands astride the earth and the sea to usher in the end time of man on earth (Rev. 10:1–6). Twelve angels wait to welcome the redeemed home to their rest in the holy city, one at each gate of the city of God (Rev. 21:12).

Job hears the angels shout for joy in the creation: "When the morning stars sang together, and all the sons of God shouted for joy" (38:7). When Adam and Eve disobeyed God, they were driven from their garden home. At the east of the Garden of Eden, God placed the cherubim and a flaming sword to guard the way of the tree of life (Gen. 3:24).

The story of Abraham, the father of the

faithful, is a story of a man who was visited by angels. It was the angel of God who halted the hand of Abraham when he held the knife above the heart of Isaac (Gen. 22:11–12). It was an angel who assured him that God would never forget his promise to him (22: 17–18). The writer of Hebrews admonishes us: "Do not neglect to show hospitality to strangers, for thereby some have entertained angels unawares" (13:2).

Angels were commissioned to destroy Sodom (Gen. 19:1). The grand encounter of Jacob with the angels of Bethel caused him to say, with breathless wonder: "Surely the Lord is in this place; and I did not know it. . . . this is none other but the house of God, and this is the gate of heaven" (Gen. 28:16– 17). In the burning bush, on the backside of the Midian desert, an angel spoke to Moses (Ex. 3:1–2; Acts 7:30). When Israel was delivered from bondage, it was with the assistance of the death angel, who struck the firstborn of every family (Ex. 12:12–13). When Moses was given the law, amid the thunders of Sinai, the law was delivered by the angels (Heb. 2:2).

When Israel was oppressed by the Midianites, it was an angel who appeared unto Gideon, under the oak tree at Ophrah, and said: "The Lord is with you, you mighty man of valor" (Judg. 6:12). It was an angel of the Lord that came to Elijah, under the juniper tree, and gave him back his courage and strength (1 Kings 18:5). When the Assyrian armies of Sennacherib encompassed the city of Jerusalem and Hezekiah laid his plight before the Lord in prayer, that night the angel of the Lord smote 185,000 Assyrians (2 Kings 19:35).

The psalmist saw God surrounded by 20,000 chariots and thousands of angels (Psalm 68:17). In the year that King Uzziah died, the youthful Isaiah went into the Temple and saw God, high and lifted up. Above his throne stood the seraphim, crying one unto another: "Holy, holy, holy is the Lord of hosts; the whole earth is full of his glory" (Isa. 6:1–3). The book of Daniel overflows with the winged servants of God. It was the angel of God that delivered the Hebrew children from the fiery furnace (Dan. 3:28).

It was the angel of God who announced the coming of the child of heaven to Mary and Joseph (Luke 1:26–35). The angels sang at his birth (Luke 2:9–11). Angels ministered to our Lord in the wilderness, after his forty days and nights of temptation (Matt. 4: 11). Jesus declared: "Every one who acknowledges me before men, the Son of man also will acknowledge before the angels of God" (Luke 12:8). "There is joy before the angels of God over one sinner who repents" (Luke 15:10). The angels carried the beggar to Abraham's bosom (Luke 16:22). Little children have guardian angels (Matt. 18: 10). Jesus spoke of the devil and his angels (Matt. 25:41). He said: "When the Son of man comes in his glory, and all the angels with him, then he will sit on his glorious throne" (Matt. 25:31).

At the time of his betrayal, Jesus said that he could ask the Father for twelve legions of angels for his defense (Matt. 26:53). The strengthening angel came to him in the garden of Gethsemane (Luke 22:43). Paul said that on the cross Jesus vanquished the dark angels (Col. 2:14–15). An angel rolled away the stone from the door of the tomb and announced the resurrection of Christ (Matt. 28:2–6).

Angels were not only the companions of Jesus but also of his people. In the book of Acts alone, angels did many things: An angel opened the prison doors for the apostles (5: 19); an angel directed Philip to the Ethiopian officer (8:26); an angel struck Herod dead (12:23); an angel directed Cornelius to send for Peter (10:3–7); an angel stood by Paul in that terrifying storm at sea (27:23).

The writer of Hebrews assures us that the angels of God are the servants of God and the servants of those who inherit salvation. As such they do three things: (1) they worship Christ (1:6); (2) they offer us adequate assistance for the service of God (12:22); (3) they are the ministering spirits sent forth to help us to enter into the fullness of salvation.

In Jubilees 11:2 we have an interesting account of the creation of angels:

"On the first day he created the heavens which are above the earth, and the waters, and all the spirits which serve him: the angels of the presence, the angels of sanctification, the angels of the spirits of the winds, and the angels of the spirit of the clouds, and of darkness, of snow, of hail, and of hoar frost, and the angels of the voices of the thunder and of the lightning, and the angels of the spirits of cold and of heat, and of winter and spring, and of autumn and of summer, and of all the spirits of his creatures which are in the heavens, and on the earth, the abysses and the darkness, eventide and light, dawn and day, which he hath prepared in the knowledge of his heart."

The Essenes of the Qumran community assigned a high place to the archangel Michael and to Melchizedek, whom they viewed as a heavenly redeemer. These were to play the chief roles in the drama of redemption in the end time.

This "NOTE" shows that it was very important for the writer to set forth carefully his case for Christ as being above all angelic intermediaries.

He moves swiftly and without equivocation in this introductory paragraph to his full identification of Christ with God. Instead of simply consummating the long line of Old Testament prophets, Christ is seen as exalted above all angels because he is seated at the right hand of the most high God himself. The writer devotes the remainder of chapter 1 to the quoting of seven Old Testament passages, which will establish in his manner the superiority of Christ over angels. He desires to prove the absolute superiority of Christ in order that, at the end of chapter 2, he may return to the figure which he uses in chapter 1 (v. 1) for Christ standing at the end of the prophetic line that he may not only suffer for man, but that he may conquer death through death, as he indicates in 2:9,14.

2. Above All Angels (1:5—2:5)

The Hebrews believed that God is surrounded by the heavenly hosts, his angels (cf. Isa. 6; 1 Kings 22:19). Millions upon millions of angels were in the army of God. The Hebrews believed that the angels were in control of the old age before the coming of the Messiah. The writer of Hebrews shows that, in the final age, Christ is in control, for he is the Son who *sits* beside his Father in majesty, while the angels stand to do God's bidding. He is the Son, while they are the servants. He is *begotten* of God, while they are the creatures of God. He is the firstborn, whom the angels worship.

Christ is master of the forces of nature and superior to the angels, who are obedient to his will. He is Lord of all life. He is that without which man cannot live. To deny him is to deny the anointed of God.

(1) Superior in His Nature (1:5–14)

5 For to what angel did God ever say,
"Thou art my Son,
    today I have begotten thee"?
Or again,
"I will be to him a father,
    and he shall be to me a son"?
6 And again, when he brings the first-born into the world, he says,
"Let all God's angels worship him."
7 Of the angels he says,
"Who makes his angels winds,
    and his servants flames of fire."
8 But of the Son he says,
"Thy throne, O God, is for ever and ever,
    the righteous scepter is the scepter of thy kingdom.
9 Thou hast loved righteousness and hated lawlessness;
    therefore God, thy God, has anointed thee with the oil of gladness beyond thy comrades."
10 And,
"Thou, Lord, didst found the earth in the beginning,
    and the heavens are the work of thy hands;
11 they will perish, but thou remainest;
    they will all grow old like a garment,
12 like a mantle thou wilt roll them up,
    and they will be changed.
But thou art the same,
    and thy years will never end."
13 But to what angel has he ever said,
"Sit at my right hand,
    till I make thy enemies
    a stool for thy feet"?
14 Are they not all ministering spirits sent forth to serve, for the sake of those who are to obtain salvation?

Ray Summers, whose scholarship has greatly enriched my own thinking, provided me with fresh and convincing material on the Dead Sea Scrolls and the epistle to the Hebrews by Yigael Yadin, a foremost authority on the Scrolls. In his article, Yadin stresses the decisive role of the archangel of light, Michael, in the eschatological era. He quotes from the Dead Sea Scrolls: [9]

"Today is His appointed time to subdue and bring low the Prince of the Dominion of Wickedness. And He will send eternal assistance to the lot to be redeemed by Him through the might of an angel: He hath magnified the authority of Michael through eternal light to light up in joy the (House) of Israel, peace and blessing for the lot of God, so as to raise among the angels (lit. gods) the authority of Michael, and the dominion of Israel among all flesh. And the righteousness shall rejoice in Heavens, and all sons of His truth shall be glad in eternal knowledge."

[9] Yighael Yadin, "The Dead Sea Scrolls and the Epistle to the Hebrews," *Scripta Hierosolymitana*, IV (Jerusalem: Hebrew University, 1957), 46–47.

The superiority of Christ over the angels is stressed in five arguments: First, Christ is declared a *Son,* an honor never accorded an angel (v. 5). James Moffatt (p. 10) points out that, while "sons of God" is not unknown as a title for angels in the Hebrew Old Testament (Gen. 6:2,4), in the Septuagint no individual angel is ever called *huios* (a son). Second, the angels are commanded to worship the *Son* (v. 6). Third, angels are servants. Christ is the sovereign in the universe (vv. 7–9). Fourth, Christ is creator, the angels are creatures (vv. 10–12). Fifth, the angels are ministers, while Christ is mediator (vv. 13–14). Angels are subordinated to servitude, even to the redeemed of God.

Four times in the first chapter, Christ is referred to as *Son:* once in v. 1, twice in v. 5, and once in v. 8. When human symbols are applied to God, it is well to remember that only God fully knows what these symbols mean. "No one knows who the Son is except the Father" (Luke 10:22). We must not marvel, then, that this ancient preacher compounds seven references from the Old Testament to tell us what he means by this term.

Thou art my Son, today I have begotten thee. Verse 5 quotes Psalm 2:7 and 2 Samuel 7:14 as evidence of Christ's divine sonship. These are messianic passages, the first finding its source in the second. They explain what the writer means by "the more excellent name" in v. 4. This same verse was cited in Romans 1:4 and applied to the resurrection of Jesus. Luke also makes the same interpretation of it in Acts 13:33 ff. *Begotten* is to be understood, not as having a beginning, but as being unique in relationship, the *only* Son.

In 2 Samuel the prophet Nathan came to David, when David was obsessed with the desire to build a house of God. David is told that he cannot build God's house but that his seed will build it. In other words, what David cannot do for God, God promises to do for David. God's promise to David is twofold: First, "Your [David's] throne shall be established forever" (2

Sam. 7:16). Second, to the one who sits upon that throne, "I will be his father, and he shall be my son" (v. 14). Peter, in his sermon at Pentecost, said that this was fulfilled in the resurrection of Jesus (Acts 2:30–31).

Let all God's angels worship him. This is a quotation from Deuteronomy 32:43 and Psalm 97:7. This, in its original setting, bears upon the worship that is due to God alone. This gives us insight into one of the writer's principles of Old Testament interpretation. He sees all passages which refer to God as being prophetic utterances concerning the Son's preexistent life with God.

First-born speaks of superiority. It is so used by Paul in Colossians 1:15, where Christ is called "the first-born of all creation," and Paul insists that Christ is superior to all angelic powers and spiritual mediators.

Who makes his angels winds, and his servants flames of fire. In the universe over which the Son reigns, the angels are the ministering spirits ceaselessly sent forth to do God's work. To the Hebrews, the winds and the lightnings and the thunderstorms were the servants of God. So the law, given in the thunder of Sinai to Moses, is viewed as ordained by the angels. A. B. Davidson (p. 48) says: "When His Angels are sent forth as messengers they are made winds (Ps. 104:4), when they minister before the throne of His glory they are flames of fire (Ex. 3:2)." This writer is in harmony with 2 Esdras 8:21–22: "Before whom the host of angels stand with trembling, and at whose bidding they are changed to wind and fire."

Thy throne, O God, is for ever and ever. This is a quotation of Psalm 45:6. It is pointed out that nowhere else in this epistle is the Son addressed as God and that this passage can be read, "God is thy throne." But, in the light of other high claims made for the Son, it is not out of place to address the second person of the holy Trinity as God. *The righteous scepter is the scepter of thy kingdom.* When Christ sat down at the right hand of God, his righteous life was fulfilled and became the pattern of his everlasting reign.

Therefore God, thy God, has anointed thee. Hugh Montefiore (p. 47) suggests: "The author must have been accustomed to the outright ascription of divinity to the Son, for he shows here not the slightest embarrassment [in addressing the Son as God]." It may be said that this is the only passage which addresses the Son outrightly as God. In John 1:1, the "Word" is called "God." But the direct addressing of the Son as God is used only by the writer of Hebrews. He is insisting that the Son's superiority to the angels is based on nothing less than his divine nature. This heavenly King is called to the highest possible life of joy *with the oil of gladness. Beyond thy comrades* means his comrades, in this instance, are the angels, not human beings.

Verses 10–12 are from Psalm 102:25– 27. The creative power and permanence of God are here applied to the Son. The Septuagint adds the introductory word, "And, Thou, Lord," to the original Hebrew version. The permanence of God is of primary importance because we cannot worship a transient process. Only that which is permanent is worthy of man's worship. The writer may have been familiar with Philo, who writes of the sky as being the mantle of God. This passage emphasizes the control of Christ, the Creator, over his creation. The world deteriorates, even the sky can be discarded and with it the lights of heaven; but the Creator is not a part of the perishable order.

Till I make thy enemies a stool for thy feet, from Psalm 110, emphasizes the character of the Messiah as conqueror. In this final age the angels are not in control, but the conquering Son of God himself. God now has highly exalted him. The reign has begun. One day every knee shall bow before him. The world to come will be one in which all things are under his control.

Are they not all ministering spirits sent forth to serve, for the sake of those who are to obtain salvation? The angels are continu- ally sent to help men to receive God's salvation, but they could never effect it. Only God could do that. As their name implies, angels are messengers of salvation. The Son's decisive action in history was all that was required for complete salvation.

Those who are to obtain salvation speaks of the eschatological dimension of salvation. Salvation has three dimensions: the initial act (Eph. 2:8), the continuing process (2 Cor. 2:15), and the final consummation (Rom. 13:11).

(2) *The Word of Jesus* Versus *the Word of Angels (2:1–5)*

[1] Therefore we must pay the closer attention to what we have heard, lest we drift away from it. [2] For if the message declared by angels was valid and every transgression or disobedience received a just retribution, [3] how shall we escape if we neglect such a great salvation? It was declared at first by the Lord, and it was attested to us by those who heard him, [4] while God also bore witness by signs and wonders and various miracles and by gifts of the Holy Spirit distributed according to his own will. [5] For it was not to angels that God subjected the world to come, of which we are speaking.

Chapter 2 introduces us to the major problem confronting this early community of Christians. The splendor of their faith was fading, and they were losing their fervor. The currents of their society were sweeping them away from Christ. Their problem was religious laxity.

Therefore is the preacher's means of bringing all the massive weight of his heavy theology in the first chapter to bear upon his concern over the lethargy of this early congregation. He has not been indulging himself in a display of exegetical skill in order that he might correct an aberration in doctrine. His concern is practical. His congregation is beginning to drift.

The emphatic position of the pronoun *we* points the specific object of the author's concern. He is not concerned about religious drift in general but about what is actually happening in his own congregation. *Must pay the closer attention* is a call to extreme care to cling tenaciously. *What we have heard* is another example of the fact that this writer never uses the word "gospel." Is it because he seems more concerned with a somber word of warning than with the good news? Good news ceases to be good news for people who can treat casually the most exciting word that ever came out of heaven.

Lest we drift away from it. Christ is the anchor and the rudder. He holds us to the truth and guides us by the truth. The ship of the soul may glide by the harbor as the current bears it on. The word "drift" literally means "to be carried past," and so to lose. The danger which threatens this Christian community is not that they should embrace some aberrant doctrine nor deliberately break the law of God. It was rather that they should heedlessly drift and be carried away by the tide of their times.

The message declared by the angels is the law. The angels were regarded as the mediators in the giving of the law. This is indicated by Paul (Gal. 3:19) and by Stephen (Acts 7:53; cf. Deut. 33:2). Josephus quotes Herod as saying: "The most excellent of our doctrines and the most sacred part of our laws we have learned of God through angels.[10]

The message . . . was valid. The argument is a fortiori, from the lesser to the greater. He does not minimize the law of Moses but calls it valid in its place.

Every *transgression or disobedience* join together to express a disregard for what they had heard, the former expressing the positive and the latter the negative. The former expresses indifference to the demands of the Christian message.

Received a just retribution indicates payment for wages earned. The writer describes this more fully in 3:17. The law of God carries certain unalterable consequences. When Israel disobeyed, she suffered 40 years for her disobedience. The austerity of the punishment for breaking the law of Moses is described in 10:28.

How shall we escape? An old Welsh

preacher called this a question which can never be answered. The wisest man of earth cannot answer it. The devils in hell cannot answer it. The angels of glory cannot answer it. God himself cannot answer it—for there is no escape from the consequences of neglect! *How shall we escape if we neglect such a great salvation?*

Escape means to find safety in flight. The psalmist said there is no getting beyond God: "Whither shall I go from thy Spirit? Or whither shall I flee from thy presence? If I ascend to heaven, thou art there! If I make my bed in Sheol, thou art there! If I take the wings of the morning and dwell in the uttermost parts of the sea, even there thy hand shall lead me, and thy right hand shall hold me" (139:7–10). There is no escape. That which is to be escaped is the consuming fire of judgment (10:26). If Christ's word is neglected, there is no escape from judgment. Indifference means certain downfall.

Salvation for this preacher was escape from the mortal condition of this world that is passing away and possession of the heavenly world which is to come.

Neglect is to "lose care for." Jeremiah said: "Cursed is he who does the work of the Lord with slackness" (48:10).

Such a great salvation. This qualitative superiority of the salvation of Christ is attested in four ways:

(1) *It was declared at first by the Lord.* The law was spoken by angels, but the word of salvation was spoken by the Lord himself. Our Lord's proclamation included everything he was and did and said—his life, teaching, death, and resurrection—especially the heart of it all (Mark 8:34–35; 10:45).

(2) *It was attested to us by those who heard him.* The word of salvation was confirmed by ear-witnesses of our Lord who had witnessed the historical events in Galilee and Jerusalem. *Attested* refers to the trustworthiness with which the witness of the word of salvation was passed on.

(3) God also bore witness. There were four ways by which God bore witness:

---

[10] *Antiq.,* XV. 5.3.

signs; wonders; various miracles; gifts of the Holy Spirit. Hugh Montefiore (pp. 53–54) distinguishes between signs, wonders, and mighty works:

A sign is a divine intervention manifesting God's nature and revealing his purpose, and a wonder is an extraordinary event the miraculous nature of which evokes awe and astonishment. . . . Mighty works may be distinguished from wonders and signs in as much as they manifest God's power rather than the miraculous nature or inner meaning of what he does.

By gifts of the Holy Spirit. The new age, of which Joel (2:28) spoke, dawned at Pentecost. The ecstatic atmosphere was proof that the Spirit had come. The *gifts of the Holy Spirit,* however, were not exclusively associated with excitement. Paul details them in Galatians 5:22–23 as "love, joy, peace, patience, kindness, goodness, faithfulness, gentleness, and self-control." The best proof of the presence of the Spirit's presence is in the quality of change which it brings to life. Paul discusses the relative merits of the gifts of the Spirit in 1 Corinthians 12—14. He concludes that the best gift of the Spirit is the ability to love others as Christ loved.

Distributed according to his own will means that spiritual gifts are not capriciously bestowed. They are given for the purpose of fulfilling the will of God. This is why each Christian's unique gift must be respected as a divine trust. It is also the reason each servant of Christ is unique. All imitation of others is out of place. For a preacher to attempt to conform too rigidly to the pattern of another is to disregard the unique gift which God has given him to equip him for his special calling.

In the phrase *his own will* the pronoun is in the emphatic position and enforces what has been said above, that spiritual gifts are for the purpose of serving God's will and not our own.

(4) This is the eschatological word—*for it was not to angels that God subjected the world to come.* Salvation for this preacher would be consummated in the world to come. He was saying that those who lose their grip on the ultimate reality that is in Christ have no hope of final salvation.

The Christian view of salvation has often been impoverished by those who dwell exclusively on one phase of salvation, as if that were all that God has in mind for us. Some dwell only on the initiation of salvation in the first confession of faith. Others dwell only on the developmental or educational aspect of Christian nurture. Others dwell exclusively on the *eschaton.* We are not entitled to reduce the full deliverance of God to the phase which appeals most to us.

This writer describes the richness of complete salvation and places it far above anything that even the angels can provide.

The end of salvation, nevertheless, is the primary concern of this early preacher. He sees Christians, whom he addresses, as dwelling too much on their Jewish heritage and refusing to move on to their eschatological calling.*

---

* NOTE: Cf. William Manson sees the eschatology of Hebrews bound up with the sermon of Stephen in Acts 7. The announcement of the world mission of the Christian community, in the book of Acts, came after this question had been put to Jesus by the disciples: "Lord, will you at this time restore the kingdom to Israel?" (Acts 1:6). They seemed to be preoccupied with Israel's role in the final establishment of God's kingdom. Jesus thus thrust them out beyond the borders of Jewry to the ends of the earth with their mission (Acts 1:8).

Stephen encountered the hostility of Jews who said: "This man never ceases to speak words against this holy place and the law; for we have heard him say that this Jesus of Nazareth will destroy this place, and will change the customs which Moses delivered to us" (Acts 6:13–14).

We are not obligated to take their charges at face value to see some truth in them. While not attacking the true purpose of the Temple and of the law of Moses, Stephen showed them that they had diverted its offerings and its sanctuary to idolatrous purposes. At the end of the long review of Israel's history (Acts 7), his adversaries were so in-

Is this not a word for the contemporary church, when so many seem so panicky about institutional religion? The church would do well to pattern her life after the tabernacle, not after the Temple. The church is a desert bivouac which, in her forms and organizations, must be taken down and restructured by each succeeding generation.

The church must be mobile and must not drift from her purpose. The children of Israel, at their worst, were desert drifters attempting to establish a beachhead in a wilderness. At their best, they were seekers of a land of promise.

The NEB translates *of which we are speaking,* "which is our theme." *The world to come* was considered the subject of absorbing interest which culminates the *such a great salvation.*

The salvation, which we are warned not to neglect, can be summed up as being superior to any word of angels because (1) it was announced through the lips of the Lord himself (NEB); (2) it was confirmed by ear-witnesses; (3) it was accompanied by the wondrous works of God; (4) it has its destiny in the world to come. This eschatological thrust must undergird the

evangelistic fervor of the church, for the word of God to his church is, "Lead on!"

3. Superior in Redemptive Work (2:6–18)

(1) Necessity of Incarnation (2:6–9)

6 It has been testified somewhere,
"What is man that thou art mindful of him,
　or the son of man, that thou carest for him?
7 Thou didst make him for a little while lower than the angels,
　thou hast crowned him with glory and honor,
8 putting everything in subjection under his feet."
Now in putting everything in subjection to him, he left nothing outside his control. As it is, we do not yet see everything in subjection to him. 9 But we see Jesus, who for a little while was made lower than the angels, crowned with glory and honor because of the suffering of death, so that by the grace of God his might taste death for every one.

The intention of God was to subject *the world to come* to man, not angels, and to crown man, not angels, *with glory and honor.* How could this be done? In the mysterious ways of God, man must be made for a *little while lower than the angels.* This must also include the representative man through whom God would bring about the subjection of all things to man.

---

censed that they ground their teeth in fury. "But Stephen, filled with the Holy Spirit, and gazing intently up to heaven, saw the glory of God, and Jesus standing at God's right hand. 'Look,' he said, 'there is a rift in the sky; I can see the Son of Man standing at God's right hand'" (Acts 7:54–57, NEB)! This is the only time in the New Testament that the apocalyptic title, "Son of man," is found on any other lips than those of Jesus. Stephen was here grasping the truth of which Daniel spoke; that the Son of man, who was to have a kingdom of all peoples, nations, and languages, had arrived in the presence of God and was now King of that kingdom (Dan. 7:13–14).

All religious institutions were now transcended; including the law, the Temple, and its sacrifices.

Stephen thus indicts Israel in the past for her resistance to God. He reminds them that God was always seeking to lead his people out of themselves. "The God of glory appeared to our father Abraham . . . and said to him, 'Depart from your land and from your

kindred and go into the land which I will show you'" (Acts 7:2–3). Abraham's posterity were all pilgrims seeking a land of promise. When Moses encountered the angel of God in the burning bush, he was called to lead forth the people of God from Egypt (Acts 7:22–36).

The tabernacle was fashioned for mobility, according to the pattern of God for a people who were supposed to be on the move. The Temple came when Israel, under David, desired a permanent dwelling for the Most High. Stephen is careful to point out Solomon's words at the dedication of the Temple: "The Most High does not dwell in houses made with hands; . . . 'Heaven is my throne, and earth my footstool'" (Acts 7:48–49).

Stephen is incensed by the blindness of Israel to this truth in becoming idolatrous in their attitude toward the Temple. He points up the persecution of the prophets and the murder of Jesus and insists that what Israel has always resisted is what is called the suprahistorical purpose which God has had for his chosen people.

We see this victory not yet complete, *"But we see Jesus.* This is the major emphasis of this paragraph. He was crowned because of his redemptive suffering. He was exalted to God's right hand as the "forerunner" (6:20) and as the "perfect pioneer" (2:10) who has led the way.

The central concern of the preacher is to show how the death of Christ is related to man's salvation. To lift man up to God, it was necessary for God to come to man. The incarnation must, therefore, be interpreted as an integral part of salvation. Christ was superior to angels, not in spite of the incarnation but because of it.

To the Jews, the suffering of Jesus was a stumbling block to their faith in him. They asked why it was necessary for Christ to suffer death. The preacher answered, because it was the purpose of God to bring men, not angels, to glory and because there is but one way by which man may reach that destiny, and that is by suffering. It was befitting that their leader should act as a pioneer on the path of suffering. Moreover, his suffering accomplished two things: It made him sympathetic and thus qualified him as High Priest; and, by his death, he broke the power of death which had kept man in fear.

The word of salvation spoken by the Lord was superior to that of angels because it spoke of the painful passion of the Son of God on earth. His patient suffering and faithful endurance of death not only taught him sympathy, it enabled God to invest him with power which he could use on behalf of his fellow men.

It has been testified somewhere. This was a familiar Alexandrian manner of introducing Scripture. The absence of the name of a human author enforced the theory of inspiration which the author held. The name of the human speaker was not as important to him as was his belief that it was God who was really speaking.

What is man that thou art mindful of him? Psalm 8 speaks of the greatness of man and of his divinely appointed authority over creation. These words are not unlike the words of Shakespeare: "What a piece of work is man! how noble in reason! how infinite in faculty! in form and moving how express and admirable! in action how like an angel!" (*Hamlet,* Act II, Sc. 2, 1. 263). The preacher of the Hebrews, however, writes these words with a certain awareness of man's high origin; thus his words breathe with gratitude to God.

Or the son of man is a Hebrew parallelism meaning the same as ordinary man.

Thou didst make him for a little while lower than the angels. This is a temporal concept rather than a qualitative one.

Thou hast crowned him with glory and honor, putting everything in subjection under his feet. This speaks of man as God intended him to be, not as he actually is. It was the intention of God to make man the master of all things and to crown him at last with glory and honor. Although it was the divine intention, it has not been realized. Man's frailty is seen in the fact that he lives in terror of death with his spirit enthralled by the devil (2:15).

Now in putting everything in subjection to him, he left nothing outside his control. As it is, we do not yet see everything in subjection to him. It is very obvious that this has not been fulfilled in man in general. Nor has it yet been fulfilled in Jesus, for the world to come has not yet come. But it has begun in his death, resurrection, and ascension. He has his place at the right hand of the most high God, and at his second coming all of his enemies will be vanquished.

But we see Jesus, who for a little while was made lower than the angels, crowned with glory and honor. In Jesus, God's representative man, all things are fulfilled. He was made for a little time, from his birth to his resurrection, lower than the angels. He was crowned with glory and honor. All things have been potentially put under his feet.

His present exaltation is the guarantee that, in God's time, all things will be put in subjection to him at his second coming (9:28). The kingdom of Christ is present.

It is growing, and it will come to a consummation.

Because of the suffering of death, so that by the grace of God he might taste death for every one. To the question, Why did Jesus suffer? one decisive answer is given: He suffered for the sake of all mankind.

So that by the grace of God means that it was in keeping with the very moral nature of God that Christ should suffer death. Only thus could he be a true brother to his brothers. Only thus could he share the full measure of incarnation. The Saviour must be identified with his people. He must be a sufferer. It was by God's grace that this was offered. Man had no rightful claim on God.

Taste death refers to the bitter cup of his Gethsemane agony (Mark 10:38–39), also the terror and desolation of the cross.

(2) Jesus: Hero and Priest (2:10–13)

[10] For it was fitting that he, for whom and by whom all things exist, in bringing many sons to glory, should make the pioneer of their salvation perfect through suffering. [11] For he who sanctifies and those who are sanctified have all one origin. That is why he is not ashamed to call them brethren, [12] saying,
  "I will proclaim thy name to my brethren,
   in the midst of the congregation I will praise
     thee."
[13] And again,
  "I will put my trust in him."
And again,
  "Here am I, and the children God has given
     me."

The desire of God is to bring *many sons* to share his glory. Therefore, by his grace, he gave us himself in his Son. He came to be flesh of our flesh, to taste death—not simply to see what death is like, but actually to experience for everyone. By this gift of immeasurable grace, God took firmer hold and laid heavier demands on us than the law, of which the angels were custodians, could ever make.

Man has not yet achieved his divine destiny, but Jesus has. Christ is presented as the *pioneer of their salvation* who was made *perfect through suffering.* He is the

completely adequate Saviour. He is already glorified. This is the ground of the believer's assurance, that we who follow him shall likewise be glorified. "We shall be like him, for we shall see him as he is" (1 John 3:2).

For it was fitting does not mean that man is entitled to judge what is appropriate or what is right or wrong for God to do. Instead, it means that it was in keeping with what God has revealed about himself. *In bringing many sons to glory* indicates that the *many sons* are in contrast with the one Son in glory.

Should make the pioneer of their salvation perfect through suffering. The title "pioneer" (*archēgos*) gives us a "hero Christology." Christ is the conqueror who goes forth to destroy the devil, who enslaves men in the fear of death. In his resurrection, he conquered death and thus set free those who live all their lives in fear of death. This idea of conflict, in which Christ met the evil one in desperate and final encounter, is often mentioned in the New Testament.

In 1 Corinthians 2:6–8 Paul insists that, if the *archonta* (the supernaturally conceived rulers) of this world order had known the wisdom of God, they would not have crucified the Lord of glory and thus sealed their own defeat. In Colossians 2:15 Paul speaks even more pointedly of the Christ of the cross disarming the powers and authorities, making a public spectacle of them, and triumphing over them on the cross.

The apostle John also has this concept of the conquering hero-Christ: "Now is the judgment of this world, now shall the ruler of this world be cast out; and I, when I am lifted up from the earth, will draw all men to myself" (12:31–32). It is also seen in John 14:30: "The ruler of this world is coming. He has no power over me." The same point of view is reflected in the Synoptic Gospels, in the triumphant encounter with the devil in the wilderness temptations. It is also in Luke 10:18, when Jesus says: "I saw Satan fall like lightning from heaven." He also warns Simon: "Satan demanded to have you, that he might sift you like wheat" (22:31). Christ is thus uniformly viewed as the heavenly hero-conqueror, who was made man that he might enter into the very arena of the flesh and do for man what man alone had never been able to do for himself.

How was the perfect *pioneer* made *perfect?* It was *through suffering.* Angels cannot suffer, only mortals can. But why was suffering necessary? The writer does not attempt a philosophical discourse on pain. He is exceedingly practical. He insists that *he who sanctifies and those who are sanctified have all one origin.*

To perfect him meant to make him completely adequate for his task. His task was not simply to show men how to die, but actually to die a redemptive kind of death that men might be brought near to God in his glory. He must be one with them in suffering. Suffering is a major part of human existence. One who did not suffer could never be like man. The perfect pioneer has broken open the road to God by his suffering.

That is why he is not ashamed to call them brethren. There was shame in his humiliation on earth. This writer calls us to remember this "pioneer and perfecter of our faith, who . . . endured the cross, despising the shame" (12:2). While his shame was real, he could still despise it. He, no doubt, was also often ashamed of his brethren, i.e., of their spirit and behavior, but he was not ashamed of what he was able to do for them. He was not ashamed that he was able to *call them brethren.*

The writer dwells upon the greatness of the Son, who condescended to be made man, and the reality of his humiliation. At the same time, he emphasizes the redemptive pride which the Son has in what he had done for man. He has sanctified them, i.e., he has made God's people his very own. He has brought them into the actual presence of God.

The solidarity of the Christian family in Christ is here emphasized. The perfect pioneer is one with his family. He was the Son of God in a sense in which they were not. He was of a higher rank. Still, he took supreme pride in being a brother to his brothers.

I will praise thee. The Son delights to join with his brethren in the praise of the Father. *I will put my trust in him.* The genuine humanity of Jesus is further established in the truth that he must trust in God. Philo made trustful hope toward God the essential mark of humanity.

Here am I, and the children God has given me. Our Lord is like a proud father, in this verse, displaying his children. The one who had no family of the flesh now has children whom God has given him. They are God's children and, as such, the Son has a fellow feeling toward them. This is the intimate fellowship of the family of God.

Returning to the earlier question—Why did the Son of God share fully in our human experience?—the answer given by the writer of Hebrews was that there was no other way to bring the *many sons* ultimately to God except as the one Son, who is perfect, sanctifies the *many sons.* He did this by becoming their great High Priest and by purifying them from their sins.

By his grace the purified are bound together into one family, having a common origin in God. Our shame is removed and we become the children of grace. We need not crawl cringingly into his presence. We can approach him with holy boldness. We can walk upright, with heads erect, as sons of God.

Still, a word of caution should be spoken. We must not press this metaphor too far. The writer of Hebrews carefully avoided identifying the nature of the Son with that of the *many sons.* We are one with Christ in that our sanctification comes from God. But we are not one with him by nature. Our sonship to God is derived by grace, whereas he has always been the Son of God. The writer of Hebrews was very careful not to blur this distinction.

The dignity of man is derived from what Christ has done for him. Today, when human depravity has such far-reaching implications, we should expect the evil of the human heart to be flashed before us constantly, not only from the pulpit, but from all mass media: the daily press, modern drama, television, and even scientific journals. The result has been that many a young person has been so often reminded of his depravity that he has forgotten other essential truths about himself.

Jesus of Nazareth did not beat people in the face and degrade them by continually reminding them of their sin and unworthiness. He knew that a person could be hit and hit so often that the very heart could be crushed out of him. Therefore, it was said of Jesus, "A bruised reed he will not break, and a dimly burning wick he will not quench" (Isa. 42:3). He did not come to discourage people, but to put the strong, royal courage of heaven in their hearts. He was not ashamed to call men *brethren.* Jesus always probed through man's depravity so that he might pull to the surface the amazing potentialities of the human spirit.

(3) Heart of the Matter (2:14–18)

14 Since therefore the children share in flesh and blood, he himself likewise partook of the same nature, that through death he might destroy him who has the power of death, that is, the devil, 15 and deliver all those who through fear of death were subject to lifelong bondage. 16 For surely it is not with angels that he is concerned but with the descendants of Abraham. 17 Therefore he had to be made like his brethren in every respect, so that he might become a merciful and faithful high priest in the service of God, to make expiation for the sins of the people. 18 For because he himself has suffered and been tempted, he is able to help those who are tempted.

He himself likewise partook of the same nature, that through death he might destroy him who has the power of death, that is, the devil. How Jesus vanquished the devil, the writer of Hebrews does not tell us. Gustaf Aulen, in his *Christus Victor,* saw the cross as the victor's chariot in

which the Saviour rode in triumph over everything the powers of darkness could do to break his love for man. "Having loved his own . . . he loved them to the end" (John 13:1). Nothing could make him stop loving man, not even the crucifixion.

Nothing more bracing and encouraging could ever be said about man than that God loves him. The heart of the Christian gospel is the inexhaustible power of God's love for man. It has often been said that God loves the unlovely. This is true if we mean by it that it is what is in God and not what is in man that makes God love us. It may also be true that God loves that which man regards as unlovely, but the very fact that God loves man means, in the nature of things, man is lovable. This appears strange to man because he has let so little of the divine love into his life. He is so distrustful that he must be cautious about loving too freely. The fact that God loves man should rekindle a wholesome self-respect within him and cause him to have the same respect for others, and to look upon them with love as God loves them.

By allowing nothing to break his love for us, Christ broke the bonds of the fear of death which had enslaved us. He who broke the bonds of death to come back from the grave to his own because of his love for them will surely come to us when we face the final hour.

In his incarnate life, death, and resurrection, Jesus accomplished four things: (1) he destroyed the work of the devil, v. 14; (2) he delivered his children from the fear of death, v. 15; (3) he became a merciful high priest, v. 17; (4) he became a helper of the tempted, v. 18.

(1) Obviously, it was an established belief in the community to which this sermon was first addressed that the devil somehow held man in the kind of bondage which ultimately would bring man down to death. The Wisdom of Solomon (1:13–14) clearly teaches that man was originally regarded as immortal and that it was not God's

original intention that man should die. It was the devil who introduced death into the world. Those who choose to follow the devil sin against God and thus bring death upon themselves. It was a part of the apocalyptic hope that the Messiah would crush the power of the devil.

(2) *Deliver all those who through fear of death were subject to lifelong bondage.* The fear of death has steadily enslaved even the most sophisticated of people. The Greeks labored hard to dispel this fear. Epictetus and Philo both declared that such fear was unworthy of a wise and good person. Still, fear persisted even for such noble souls as Seneca and Cicero, who felt that the fear of death was an almost universal emotion. The fear of death is one of the controlling emotions of life. Seneca argued valiantly against this fear. Still, he confessed: "If you take anyone, young, middle-aged, or elderly, you will find them equally afraid of death" (quoted by James Moffatt, p. 36).

But the preacher of Hebrews saw more than Seneca. It was what was beyond death that concerned him. "It is appointed for men to die once, and after that comes judgment" (9:27). Death is not the ultimate crisis, but the judgment. The Christian's hope could only be assured by Christ who will come a second time—the Christ who was offered for our sins—"not to deal with sin but to save those who are eagerly waiting for him" (9:28).

(3) *That he might become a merciful and faithful high priest in the service of God.* He is *merciful* because of his understanding which came through his experience. He is *faithful* in that he carries out the purpose of his sacrifice. He makes expiation for our sins.

Christ is now our merciful and faithful High Priest. He experiences our sufferings, knows our sorrows, and helps us to meet our temptations. He is not a remote or tyrannical judge, but a sympathetic reconciler of men to God.

(4) *He is able to help those who are tempted.* When we suffer, we are tempted

to turn away from Christ. These Christians, in Hebrews, were facing severe persecution for their loyalty to Jesus. The horror of death stood before them. They were tempted to shrink back and deny their allegiance to Jesus. The word translated "help" means literally 'to run to the cry." When the most severe temptation to renounce our faith confronts us, Jesus is able to run to our cry. He stabilizes us with the same strength which was his in Gethsemane when he too was tempted to shrink back. Christ knows all about our temptations— every fierce struggle when Satan tries to deceive and ensnare, to lead us into lust or dishonesty or jealousy or greed or malice or laziness or pride—and offers us his power to withstand them. One touch of his conquering Spirit will help us to overcome our temptations.

He is the unceasing intercessor. More than helping us withstand our many temptations, Jesus holds up hands of unceasing intercession before the mercy seat of God. He will not put them down until the last redeemed soul comes home to God. "He always lives to make intercession for them" (7:25). What assurance it is to know that our security is grounded in the constant intercession of Jesus!

4. Greater Than Moses (3:1-6)

1 Therefore, holy brethren, who share in a heavenly call, consider Jesus, the apostle and high priest of our confession. 2 He was faithful to him who appointed him, just as Moses also was faithful in God's house. 3 Yet Jesus has been counted worthy of as much more glory than Moses as the builder of a house has more honor than the house. 4 (For every house is built by some one, but the builder of all things is God.) 5 Now Moses was faithful in all God's house as a servant, to testify to the things that were to be spoken later, 6 but Christ was faithful over God's house as a son. And we are his house if we hold fast our confidence and pride in our hope.

For this early preacher, it was incredible that the Christian community, which had received so much from God, should allow their faith to burn so low. He thus seeks to rekindle the flame of Christian faith, ardor, and zeal. His primary question is: How can Christians rekindle their faith when it has burned low? His answer is, by concentrating on Jesus. The flame of faith is refueled, not by theological propositions, ideas, or doctrines; but by a person—even Jesus.

The word *consider* means here, not to evaluate in an academic sense, but to concentrate on Jesus in order to discern his true meaning and learn the lesson that he teaches. Why should they fix their attention on Jesus? The answer is twofold: The first is because of who they are. The second is because of who he is.

They are *holy brethren, who share in a heavenly call.* They have been purged of their sins and now belong to the household of God. The modern mind is repelled by the word, *holy,* because it is defined in terms of moral perfection. But this is not the New Testament meaning. The apostles regarded every Christian as being holy because he had been set apart by God, cleansed of his sins and called to fulfill the purpose of God for his life. We are told, in later passages in Hebrews, that there were many flaws in the lives of these early Christians. A holy person is not perfect. He is not one who has arrived where God wants him to be but one who has received a divine call to walk with his face toward God. Christians are called to remember their higher nature as holy people called to a high and heavenly destiny.

Brethren means this calling is not to achieve an impossible ideal but to share the warmth of a family relationship. Christ is already their brother. They are with him because he has sanctified and made them holy. They are members of a holy family.

Their call is *a heavenly call,* both from and to heaven. They are now citizens of a higher country. They are citizens of two worlds.

One of the keys to understanding this sermon is in the preacher's doctrine of two worlds. For him there are two worlds in which the Christian lives. There is the world of sense and, above it, the world of permanent reality. He seeks to convince his hearers that they are citizens of two worlds. This doctrine parallels the Jewish doctrine of two ages, namely, the present age and the age to come. There are, however, certain discernible differences between these two doctrines.

The coming age was associated with the coming of the Messiah and with resurrection and judgment. Jesus made it the framework of his doctrine of the kingdom of God in the sense that, with his coming, the kingdom came on earth. The apostolic church followed this teaching, that the *eschaton* had come in the person of Christ. Christians could actually feel the power of the *eschaton.* It was the final age (1:2). Christians had "tasted . . . the powers of the age to come" (6:5). This age would culminate in the second coming: "Christ . . . will appear a second time . . . to save those who are eagerly waiting for him" (9:28). There is the steady beckoning onward in 13:13–14: "Therefore let us go forth to him outside the camp, bearing abuse for him. For here we have no lasting city, but we seek the city which is to come." *

---

* NOTE: The basic thought of the doctrine of two worlds, however, is different. It is not Hebraic, but Hellenic. The world of reflection is a world of invisible reality. Theology, in this sense, is not so much concerned with the true sequence on the horizontal plane, dealing with past, present, and future. Instead, it is concerned primarily with the vertical, divine interpenetration in which this world is always interpenetrated by the higher world.

Alexandria was the home of this kind of thought and its best expression was in Philo. It was Philo who sought to synthesize the Hebrew doctrine of creation with the philosophy of Plato. For Plato believed that, before the divine architect could make this world, he had to have a pattern. That pattern was in the eternal world. So Plato contended that every lovely thing in this universe about us is a shadow of the unimaginable loveliness of God himself. We cannot get through to ultimate reality. We can see only the reflections. So Philo took over the thought from Plato's

Timaeus and, in his *De opificio mundi*, he undertook to work out a synthesis between the Old Testament and Plato.

This kind of thought is also found in the best of pre-Christian writing, which is found in the apocryphal book of the Wisdom of Solomon, written a century before the Christian era: "She [wisdom] is a breath of the power of God, And a clear effulgence from everlasting light, And an unspotted mirror [image] of the working of God" (7:25). The writer also speaks of how the pattern of the sanctuary was made according to the pattern in the heavens.

Philo was indebted not only to Plato, but also to the later Stoics, especially for their doctrine of the "logos." The problem of the Stoics was to explain how a holy God could come into contact with this base, material world. They found the answer in a mediator, whom they called the "logos."

The Philonic concept of the two worlds of substance and shadow runs persistently through Hebrews. This is seen in four basic doctrines: (1) The doctrine of creation (11:3). The visible was made out of the invisible. (2) The doctrine of law (10:1). The law was a shadow but not the very substance of the good things that were to come. (3) The doctrine of sacrifice (9:11). Christ is a priest of a greater and more perfect tabernacle. (4) The doctrine of man (2:8–9). Even man is a poor copy of true man.

Thus, using the doctrine of two worlds as his clue, the preacher lays down several conclusions:

(1) He insists that there are two worlds (9:24). This world is the vestibule. The other world is the inner shrine. The other world is already in existence. If we sometimes call it the world to come, it is only because it is not fully realized in time.

(2) The unseen world is the true world. The adjective "true" is found in this epistle in 8:2; 9:24; 10:1,22.

Francis Thompson expressed the reality of the unseen world in unforgettable lines from "The Kingdom of God":

"O world invisible, we view thee,

O world intangible, we touch thee,

O world unknowable, we know thee."

(3) Man is a citizen of both worlds (2:6–11). Plata expressed this in his belief that the soul belongs to genesis (birth) as it comes into time. Yet, in its natural nature, it has kinship with the realm of ideas. In this sense, it belongs to the ideal world. This kinship inspires the love of philosophy and a passion for reality, which explains the homesickness of the soul for its native country—the ideal world.

For the preacher of Hebrews, man is a citizen of two worlds by virtue of what God has done for him. He ideally put all things in subjection beneath his feet (2:8). He fulfilled his purpose and borught man into the real world in Christ (2:9).

(4) The tragedy and predicament of man is that he is caught in the tension between these two worlds. He lives in that borderland where he has been given a promise, but has not yet received the fulfillment of that promise. In truth, the best of God's servants have "all died in faith, not having received what was promised" (11:13). Man tries to find peace by retreating into one world or the other, but finds no peace. He tries to find peace in this world, but the world above haunts him. He tries to be in harmony with the world above, but this world continually drags him down.

Robert Browning expresses this tension in "Bishop Blougram's Apology." God looks down over his head, and Satan looks up between his feet.

(5) The preacher insists that there is only one way by which man's tension can be resolved. This is given in the prologue of his sermon. The invisible world must invade the visible and deal with man's limitations and sin. One from above must reach down to man and lift him up.

(6) The message of the preacher is that this has actually happened. It happened in a measure under the old covenant. God spoke to our fathers through the prophets (1:1). By the law, through the priests and their sacrifices, God did get through with his word for man. The invisible world actually sent its signals across the gulf into the visible world. But they were like smoke signals, containing only fleeting gleams and fragmentary truths; so that man remained in the grips of sin, and the cold terror of death held him in its unrelenting grasp.

(7) The invisible world stopped signaling and actually came into the visible world in Christ. "[You] have tasted" (6:5), said the preacher. Also, "you have come" (12:22). Jesus Christ bridged the gap because he belongs to both worlds. By his sinless life, he takes human life and wraps his strength around it. By his complete surrender to the will of God, he broke the power of this present world once for all. By reason of his exaltation, he is able to infuse his power into those who come to him. By reason of this intercession, he is able to keep his people anchored within the veil—that world of final reality (6:19).

(8) The grand conclusion of this preacher is that, through Jesus, man can live the life

The preacher calls his hearers to *consider Jesus*, to concentrate on Jesus because of who he is. He is the *apostle*, one sent forth as an ambassador of God. This is the only time in the New Testament that Jesus is referred to as an apostle. An apostle is one who is sent with a message. He is an ambassador who carries the power and authority of his country with him. Jesus is the ambassador of the high country of heaven. He merits our attention because of the country he represents and also because of the authority which is vested in him.

For this preacher, Christianity is the confession (*homologia*), and Jesus is the *high priest of our confession*. For him to say that Jesus is our High Priest was a confession of faith, just as important as the confession, "Jesus is Lord" (Rom. 10:8–9), was for Paul.

He is also our High Priest. This is one of the primary emphases of Hebrews. This writer is the only New Testament writer who called Jesus a high priest. What did he mean? The Latin word for priest (*pontifex*) means a "bridge builder." Christ is the bridge between God and man. He speaks for God to man, and he speaks for man to God. He is fully identified with God and man. He is able, therefore, to cross the barrier built by our sins and to bring us near to God.

The preacher discusses the priesthood of Christ more fully in 4:14. At this point, he is building up his argument. Beginning with Christ as superior to the prophets (1:2), he proceeds to Christ as an apostle who is superior to angels (2:4–9) and superior to Moses (3:1–6). In 4:14 he finally comes to his great declaration that Jesus is the "great high priest who has passed through the heavens."

Jesus has been counted worthy of as much more glory than Moses. It should be remembered that the converts from the Essene sect of the Qumran community, who may have been among the hearers of this sermon, had been taught to expect a messianic prophet, like Moses, to appear at the end of days. This belief played a great role in Essene religion.

The claim is made that Jesus was greater than the greatest man Israel had ever known. Moses towered like a mountain peak over Israel. Had he not delivered them from the land of bondage? Had he not led them through the wilderness and molded a heterogeneous multitude of slaves into a great and mighty nation? Had he not seen God face to face? Had Moses not received the law from God? Who could conceivably be greater than Moses?

---

of the eternal world here on earth. He is, to be sure, still under the limitations of this world. He is still a pilgrim and a sojourner. He is still seeking an invisible city. Nevertheless, he is anchored in that other world by his relationship to Christ and the invisible world has taken control of his life.

The preacher to the Hebrews, at this point, greatly transcends the thought of Plato and Philo. Their thought was that man at birth was brought into the vestibule of the real world and by education he could be led into the inner shrine. Plato insisted that man must think thoughts divine and, insofar as it lies in human nature, to possess immortality. He believed that the wise man could possess immortality, but not perfectly. Aristotle said that you should put on immortality as far as you can by following wisdom. The Greek philosophers said that the possession of eternal life is for those who follow wisdom. On the contrary, Jesus had taught that the passport to eternal life is not wisdom but the child-heart. Hebrews is in accord with that.

The preacher places strong emphasis on "the power of an indestructible life" (7:16). He merges the apocalyptic with the present. He insists that "you have come . . . to the city of the living God, the heavenly Jerusalem" (12:22). He speaks of those who do enter God's rest (4:3). He insists that faith makes the future present, the unseen visible, and the ideal actual.

The permanent importance of this preacher's doctrine is in his insistence that, while the Christian may be a sojourner and pilgrim at the same time, he is not waiting for eternal life. For the believer, the great transition from death unto life does not come at the end of life but at the beginning of his reception of Christ. When this happens, he is possessed by something which death cannot touch: "the power of an endless life" (7:16, KJV). He has passed from death unto life.

A more staggering claim could not be made than that anyone could be greater than the man whom God had chosen to receive his law and hand it on to his people. Still, the writer of Hebrews, with clear and lucid logic, proceeded to show the superiority of Jesus over Moses.

It should be remembered that the writer intended no denigration of Moses. He held him in the highest esteem. His major concern was to show that, without a greater leader than Moses, the fate of the Christian community would be similar to that of those who fell in the wilderness under Moses. They never reached the Promised Land and never entered into God's rest.

The superiority of Christ over Moses is shown in three ways:

(1) Christ is one with God in the building of a redeemed nation. Moses was a part of the nation which God was building (3:1-4). No matter how magnificent a house may be, the one who is both builder and architect is greater.

(2) Christ is superior to Moses in the capacity in which he serves (3:5-14). Christ is the Son over the house (v. 6). Moses is a servant in the house (v. 5). He is a free servant, an important and a faithful servant; but, however faithful and important a servant may be, he never has the status of a son in the household.

(3) Christ is superior in his achievements (3:15—4:13). The writer is asking in effect: "Why will you insist on choosing Moses above Jesus when Moses failed?" It took colossal courage to ask Jews a question like that. But his argument is clear and irresistible. He states two ways in which Moses failed: He failed to keep his people together (3:15—4:2). His mission was to lead 3,500,000 people into the promised land. But many fell short because of unbelief. Moses also failed to achieve the ultimate goal, which was to bring his people into rest (4:3-13).

Moses also was faithful in God's house. The faithfulness of Moses to his people was supremely set forth in his total identity with their plight. Even in their rebellion he would not forsake them. He cried out to God for their forgiveness and placed himself on the altar for them, as he prayed: "But now, if thou wilt forgive their sin— and if not, blot me, I pray thee, out of thy book which thou hast written" (Ex. 32:32). But however faithful a servant may be, he never can have the status of a son in the family. Only Christ is the Son of God.

And we are his house if we hold fast our confidence and pride in our hope. The preacher reminded his hearers of their status. They may be in this household of God, of which Christ is the builder and over which he is the Son and in which Moses is a servant. They may be in this family where the light, warmth, food, and fellowship of heaven are known; but there is a condition. They must hold fast their confidence firm to the end.

Should you ask, "What is Christian faith?" the preacher would answer, "It is confidence held firm to the end." It is the boldness which belongs, by nature, to the children of God. It is forthright assurance, with neither arrogance nor apology. It is a proper pride in who we are by the grace of God and, above all, a pride based on the hope of God's final triumph over sin and death. Christian people are those who put their confidence in God and find their highest pride in the hope that he holds before them.

God's house is often used as a figure of the church (cf. 1 Peter 4:17; 1 Tim. 3:15). But the church is not the house of God unless it meets the conditions. We are the house, the dwelling place of the Eternal if we hold fast our confidence and hope.

When is the church the house of God? It is not when we have large and prestigious memberships and imposing buildings, superb music and superlative preaching. We are God's house when, as a church, we hold fast our confidence in God and when the hope we have in God holds us fast until the end. In this house, our faith is nourished by God, and we share in all the benefits our Lord brings—the cleansing of our sins, the restoration of our lost humanity, the sympathy of our great High Priest, and an open access to God.

The call which this preacher gives to his church is to remind them of their heavenly call to move on toward their goal. The call is, "Onward, Christian Soldiers!"

II. Finding the True Rest of God
(3:7—4:13)

1. Peril in Unbelief and Disobedience
(3:7–19)

7 Therefore, as the Holy Spirit says,
"Today, when you hear his voice,
8 do not harden your hearts as in the rebellion,
   on the day of testing in the wilderness,
9 where your fathers put me to the test
   and saw my works for forty years.
10 Therefore I was provoked with that generation,
   and said, 'They always go astray in their hearts;
   they have not known my ways.'
11 As I swore in my wrath,
   'They shall never enter my rest.' "
12 Take care, brethren, lest there be in any of you an evil, unbelieving heart, leading you to fall away from the living God. 13 But exhort one another every day, as long as it is called "today," that none of you may be hardened by the deceitfulness of sin. 14 For we share in Christ, if only we hold our first confidence firm to the end, 15 while it is said,
"Today, when you hear his voice,
   do not harden your hearts as in the rebellion."
16 Who were they that heard and yet were rebellious? Was it not all those who left Egypt under the leadership of Moses? 17 And with whom was he provoked forty years? Was it not with those who sinned, whose bodies fell in the wilderness? 18 And to whom did he swear that they should never enter his rest, but to those who were disobedient? 19 So we see that they were unable to enter because of unbelief.

Man is as restless as the wayward wind. Man away from God is destined always to be restless. Long ago Augustine made that discovery, which is expressed in one of the most frequently quoted passages: "Our hearts are restless until they rest in thee." Long before Augustine, the writer of Psalm 95:11 heard God saying to his rebellious people: 'Therefore I swore in my anger that they should not enter my rest." The

writer of Hebrews borrows these lines as words of warning and calls his generation to hear what the Holy Spirit is still saying. That which happened to Israel during her 40 years in the wilderness will happen to all who refuse to hear the voice of God (v. 7), who harden their hearts (v. 8), who grieve God, and who always go astray (v. 10). God's wrath, his steadfast, implacable opposition to unrighteousness causes him to swear that "they shall never enter my rest" (v. 11).

Hebrews is addressed to Christians who are in a crisis comparable to that of Israel in her 40 years in the wilderness. The preacher views the Christian life as a new "exodus," at the end of which the faithful will come, not to an earthly promised land, but to a heavenly rest.

The Holy Spirit says. The preacher hears the voice of the Holy Spirit, in Psalm 95:7–11, who insists that the people of the first Exodus fell short of their goal because they refused to listen to God. The penalty of such refusal was the loss of what God had promised them if they would be obedient. They began the march in faith, but they did not persevere.

Today another "exodus" has begun. Jesus himself called his death an exodus or a "departure" (Luke 9:31). The ultimate sin is the refusal to accept what Christ offers in this deliverance. The final journey has begun in him. Now God has declared again an ultimate chance, a final "now," a critical last "today" of salvation.

Do not harden your hearts as in the rebellion, on the day of testing in the wilderness. This recalls Massah and Meribah in Exodus 17:1–7 and Numbers 20:1–13. In their burning thirst, the children of Israel lamented leaving Egypt, rebelled against Moses, and lost their trust in God. God told Moses to speak to the rock and water would flow from it. In his anger, Moses struck the rock. For his disobedience, he was forbidden to enter the land of promise. Great as Moses was and marvelous as were his achievements, his unbelief barred his entrance into rest. For 40 years he and his people wandered in frustration. At last, he came to view the land flowing with milk and honey. He may have pleaded: "O God, let me now tread this good land. Forty years have I lingered and labored with these people in the wilderness." But the response of God would have been: "Speak no more of this. Thou shalt not enter" (cf. Deut. 34:1–8). And Moses died in frustration and was buried in Nebo's lonely veil, hard by the land of his dreams which he never entered. His disobedience cost him the promised land. We, who have so much greater a leader than Moses, are under even greater peril if we are disobedient.

They shall never enter my rest. We are frantic people, who are not ruled by sweet reason but are caught up in the compulsion to do all things for ourselves, and we despise that weakness which depends on anything or anyone outside of ourselves. We are swept along in the merging tide of ceaseless activity and go farther and farther from God and never find rest because we refuse to obey him.

But what is God's rest? What the Christian is promised is more like the rest of God after the six days of creation than like the entrance of the Israelites into Canaan. It is the rest which comes in the wondrous satisfaction of achievement, the peace which is the result of the assurance that we have continual, open access to God. This is not temporary relaxation, but God's own perfect and continuing rest. This is not cessation from creative activity, but the removal of the anguish which accompanies the labor of a person who has only his own meager resources to draw from. God needs no rest to recover his energy. Are we not told, "He who keeps Israel will neither slumber nor sleep" (Psalm 121:4)? God's strength is never diminished. He never ceases his creative activity. He has an abiding sense of rest, into which by faith we are called to enter.

Isaiah said: "The wicked are like the troubled sea; for it cannot rest" (57:20, ASV). Those who rebel against God are like a person swimming against the tide.

His fatigue causes every muscle to cry out for rest. His nerves are tangled and drawn. His sanity is threatened. How can he survive this ceaseless round of duties— meeting so many who are also in a state of nervous exhaustion—and the long hours of toil until he cannot think clearly? How can he endure the terrific strain of wondering how much longer he can hold on and meet the dreadful competition of an aggressive and hostile economy, wondering what will happen to his family when he can no longer produce and will be replaced by a machine or a computer?

The restless person is full of half-covered fears which he cannot quiet. His uneasy days are full of aimless wandering, and his nights bring him to the realization that he has no sense of direction or fulfillment. He trembles lest his dishonesty be discovered or that his inadequacy should come out into the open. Life has become an oppressive burden. Where can he find rest?

The preacher answers that man's predicament is the result of the *deceitfulness of sin.* His spiritual collapse progresses, as Marcus Dods (p. 276) has described it: The heart becomes unbelieving when it is hardened through sin. Thus, the psychological order becomes: sin, followed by a deceived mind, then a hardened heart, unbelief, and finally apostasy.

In other words, the decline and fall of man is the result of his deliberate transgression against the will of God. This is followed by his mental confusion, in which good seems evil and evil seems good. Then the heart is hardened until it is no longer sensitive to the call of God to come back to the good life. Since the mind is deceived and the heart is hardened, how can he believe? What is left for him save to desert the living God and to wander restlessly in a spiritual wasteland?

Hardened describes the condition of a stiff, unbending stick. Sin blinds a person to the significance and attractiveness of God's offer of mercy.

Exhort one another every day. Because of the great and grievous peril, Christians are called to exhort one another daily.

As long as it is called today means while the opportunity is still open. No one's faith is a private possession, nor a solitary experience. Faith must be nurtured by others. We need continual encouragement to *hold our first confidence firm to the end*. Christian faith is not merely an initial experience of believing in Jesus. It is a steady, persistent trusting in him and an obedience of him to the very end of life.

It is easy to misplace the emphasis of the New Testament. Some Christians prefer to emphasize the security of the believer in terms of an absolute guarantee at the beginning of Christian pilgrimage, that he will be preserved in the faith forever. So their slogan is: "Once saved, always saved." Other Christians prefer to emphasize the precariousness of the Christian pilgrimage by insisting that one can be saved today and lost tomorrow. The New Testament does not put the problem in quite these terms. Instead, it insists that the emphasis belongs both on the grace of God and on the performance of the believer. In other words, if he holds fast to the end, this is the evidence that he received the grace of God in the beginning. The only visible proof of Christian conversion is the course of a Christian's life. *Leading you to fall away from the living God* should be interpreted in the light of the thrust of the entire book, which is a stern word of warning.

Verses 12–13 point the importance of the fellowship of the church in which every member has an urgent concern for the spiritual welfare of every other member. This is a part of the plan of God to hold us true to him and to one another. The church is always the community of the concerned—first, for one another, and then, for others. This is one of the important values of the church relationship.

If only we hold our first confidence firm to the end, this is the proof that *we share in Christ*. There may be *an evil, unbelieving heart* in those who see themselves as God's people (vv. 12–14). The preacher

of the Hebrews does not express the Christian's relationship to Christ in the same terms as Paul. There is nothing here of Paul's mystical emphasis on union with Christ. He does not talk about our being in Christ, or about Christ being in us. Instead, he calls us to concentrate objectively on Christ. He does not magnify inward contemplation, but calls us to look outside of ourselves to one whom he calls the "pioneer" (2:10), the "forerunner" (6:20), and the "perfecter of our faith" (12:2). We share with Christ to the degree we are loyal to him and follow him into the life of the world to come.

Those who were disobedient. The tragedy of Israel was spelled in two words, *unbelief* and *disobedience*. Three times the preacher calls our attention to the truth that it was unbelief that robbed Israel of the rest which God wanted to give her. So he appeals for a steady, open belief in God, which brings the heart to rest in him.

Twice the preacher hears the Holy Spirit pleading that we hear God's voice and give up our unbelief (vv. 7,15). God speaks in manifold ways, but we allow so much confusion and clamor to come in that God's voice cannot be heard. God speaks in the laughing eyes of little children which show us the purity and gladness of God. The memory of a mother's prayers call us back to childhood's clean ideals, before the world became too much a part of us. The quiet grandeur of the evening sky speaks of how God brings all things in nature to their rest. If we listen, he will bring our hearts to rest in him, for we shall see that it makes more sense to believe in him than in our own ingenuity or in our capricious neighbors or in the sudden turn of circumstances.

2. Creative Fear of God (4:1–3)

¹ Therefore, while the promise of entering his rest remains, let us fear lest any of you be judged to have failed to reach it. ² For good news came to us just as to them; but the message which they heard did not benefit them, because it did not meet with faith in the

hearers. ³ For we who have believed enter that rest, as he has said,
"As I swore in my wrath,
'They shall never enter my rest,' "
although his works were finished from the foundation of the world.

Let us fear lest any of you be judged to have failed to reach it. The creative fear that God wants in the Christian life is the fear, not of what God will do to us, but of what we may do with the promise of God. We need have no fear that God will not keep his promise. We, however, may have much fear that we shall come short of meeting the conditions on which God's promises are made.

While the promise of entering his rest remains. There are more references to the promises of God in Hebrews than in any other book in the New Testament. These promises are personal. In this day, when so many are known by a number instead of as a person, God still knows our names. So the writer of Hebrews spoke not of humanity in mass but of *us* and *any of you.* Into these personal pronouns, you can write your own name.

Good news came to us. The promise of God is in the good news that ample rest has been provided. God's rest stands ready. The door to spiritual repose has been opened. It was opened for Israel, but they deliberately closed it by their lack of faith, *because it did not meet with faith in the hearers.*

His works were finished from the foundation of the world. When God made the world, he made provision for spiritual rest. His rest from all his works on the seventh day is the symbol of the truth that he made a world in which rest is provided. From the calm steadiness of our God, who works without the devastating tensions which plague our human labors, we may take our cue.

Jesus said, "Come to me, all who labor and are heavy laden, and I will give you rest" (Matt. 11:28). He did not mean, "I will show you the way to cease all your striving," for even on the sabbath he could

say, "My Father is working still, and I am working" (John 5:17). The good work of God must never cease lest our universe collapse into the nothingness out of which it was formed. Rest does not mean cessation of activity but the peace which comes from open access to God.

3. The Appointed Day (4:4–8)

⁴ For he has somewhere spoken of the seventh day in this way, "And God rested on the seventh day from all his works." ⁵ And again in this place he said,
"They shall never enter my rest."
⁶ Since therefore it remains for some to enter it, and those who formerly received the good news failed to enter because of disobedience, ⁷ again he sets a certain day, "Today," saying through David so long afterward, in the words already quoted,
"Today, when you hear his voice,
   do not harden your hearts."
⁸ For if Joshua had given them rest, God would not speak later of another day.

God made the sabbath as a day of rest, a day to contemplate our Creator and the wonders of his creation. This day marked the end of the original creation. The promise of the new creation would come when Christ broke the bonds of death and arose from the grave to bring in a new age and a new order. The apostle Paul wrote: "If then you have been raised with Christ, seek the things that are above" (Col. 3:1). There are some Christians who enjoy the blessings of this new age and of this new order, in which spiritual values are to hold their supreme allegiance; yet they use the very day, which symbolizes this new age, as a day for business as usual.

So long afterward speaks of the interval of time between the desert wanderings of Israel and the writing of Psalm 95:7–8. Unbelief had robbed those, who first heard of God's promised rest, of entering into it. Now God appeals, through David, that we not miss this rest because of the hardness of an unbelieving heart.

For if Joshua had given them rest, God would not speak later of another day. Jesus in Greek is the name for Joshua. What appears to have happened, at this point of the preacher's argument that Moses failed to bring rest to the people of Israel, is that someone replied, "But Joshua accomplished what Moses failed to do. He brought the people into the promised land of rest."

But the writer of Hebrews contended that it was not the land of Canaan that God had in mind as the ultimate destination of his people. Canaan was the type of a more perfect rest which God provides for the total person. The final rest of God includes the result of the quieting of our half-covered fears, deliverance from aimless wanderings, and forgiveness for that which has pierced our burning hearts with pain. The preacher speaks of God as calling this *my rest.*

4. Our Final Rest (4:9–11)

⁹ So then, there remains a sabbath rest for the people of God; ¹⁰ for whoever enters God's rest also ceases from his labors as God did from his.
¹¹ Let us therefore strive to enter that rest, that no one fall by the same sort of disobedience.

So there remains a sabbath rest for the people of God. A clue to the meaning of the words *sabbath rest* may be found here:

Philo, in *De Cherubim* (26), explains why Moses calls the sabbath . . . the "sabbath of God" in Ex. 20:10 etc.; the only thing which really rests is God—"rest . . . meaning not inactivity in good . . .—for the cause of all things which is active by nature never ceases doing what is best, but—an energy devoid of laboriousness, devoid of suffering, and moving with absolute ease" (Moffatt, p. 53).

This is the kind of rest which God offers his people.

The people of God have thought of the Lord's Day as a foretaste of heavenly rest. This is a day for spiritual renewal. God intended this day to be a time for lifting the human family up into the rapture of worship of the living God, whose endless activities bring to him no exhaustion. He offers to lift us above the darkness of human deceit that we may see the clear, painful, but healing light of God's right-

eous judgment upon our frenzied activities. He would thus remind us that to labor in the fellowship of God brings us through our enervating frustrations with the assurance that "in the Lord your labor is not in vain" (1 Cor. 15:58).

Strong and urgent words are used here, urging all who have heard God's word to remember that disobedience brought the destruction of God's people, who were originally delivered from Egyptian bondage. The unbelieving heart still bars the gates to the spiritual Canaan.

Let us therefore strive to enter that rest. The rest that was promised to the Israelites was entrance into the promised land. But the preacher to the Hebrews used the term to foreshadow the entrance into the heavenly sanctuary (10:9) and into the city of the living God (12:22). In a sense, God's rest is bound up with man's rest, just as his work is bound up with man's work. Could God have so structured life that neither he nor we can have perfect rest until we rest together? Could this be the reason there must be labor and striving if we are to enter into the rest which he has promised? Is there any rest known to man comparable to that which follows hard toil and worthy achievement?

The word *strive* means to make haste, also to bend every effort, for the same peril is before the disobedient as that which befell the generation that died in the wilderness on the very borders of Canaan.

5. Word of Warning (4:12–13)

¹² For the word of God is living and active, sharper than any two-edged sword, piercing to the divisions of soul and spirit, of joints and marrow, and discerning the thoughts and intentions of the heart. ¹³ And before him no creature is hidden, but all are open and laid bare to the eyes of him with whom we have to do.

We have been given a clear word of warning from God and this word has three characteristics:

(1) *For the word of God is living.* This is not a word stored away in some dust-covered manuscript, buried in the ancient

archives of Israel. It is a word that is alive with the very life of God. The Spirit of God conveys the living word to the people of God. The Holy Spirit singles us out, one by one, and speaks the personal word to us in an immediate conversation.

(2) It is *active.* This word is capable of doing what God intended. This is the assurance which we find so powerfully set forth in Isaiah 55:11: "So shall my word be that goes forth from my mouth; it shall not return to me empty, but it shall accomplish that which I purpose, and prosper in the thing for which I sent it."

(3) It is *piercing* and penetrating. Some scholars see this two-edged sword as a surgeon's scalpel, which lays everything open to the eyes of the divine Surgeon. God sees clearly into every corner of the *soul,* which is the life-principle of every person. He also sees the *spirit,* which sets man apart from all other living things. By his spirit, man reasons and reaches beyond the visible verities to the God in whose image he was made. God then is able to see everything about the physical and spiritual life of man.

The word of God sits in judgment upon *the thoughts and intentions of the heart.* The word *thoughts* also means desires. Actually, it refers to the emotional side of life, that part of a person which is controlled by his passions and feelings. *Intentions* refers to the intellectual and volitional side of life. The preacher of Hebrews is saying: Remember that your thoughts and feelings are clearly seen by God.

Before him no creature is hidden. The preacher sums up this passage by assuring his hearers that they are compelled to meet the eyes of God. The insistence that *all are open and laid bare* carries the thought that all the garments in which we masquerade before men are stripped away when God turns his gaze upon us. Our disguises are destroyed, and we are compelled to meet the eyes of God just as we are.

Laid bare is a colorful word which the author apparently learned from Philo, who used it to portray a wrestler "downing" his opponent by seizing his throat. It was also used in wrestling circles to designate seizing an opponent by the throat in such a manner that he could not move. We may evade God for a time, but, at the last, we will be gripped and held fast by divine hands. We will be forced to look into his all-seeing eyes. The only thing that finally matters is what God sees in us.

III. Our Great High Priest (4:14—5:10)

1. Nature of the High Priest (4:14–16)

14 Since then we have a great high priest who has passed through the heavens, Jesus, the Son of God, let us hold fast our confession. 15 For we have not a high priest who is unable to sympathize with our weaknesses, but one who in every respect has been tempted as we are, yet without sinning. 16 Let us then with confidence draw near to the throne of grace, that we may receive mercy and find grace to help in time of need.

Very likely, many of us today would look upon the priesthood as a part of the ancient paraphernalia of Israel's religious system, which passed out of being with the tabernacle and the Temple. To see our present need of priesthood, we would do well to remember that a principle function of the priest was to hear the confession of sin.

Unless our sins are confessed, they weigh down our spirits with heavy burdens, dissipating the energy with which we should be serving God. To suppress or to cover our sins, or to pretend that we have not sinned, consumes our energy so that there is little left for serving God and helping others.

Unacknowledged sin also becomes a moral malignancy which spreads to consume our holy ambitions and aspirations. The flimsy pretense, that we make before God and man, becomes an iron curtain which we must hold up day and night, never daring to let it down for a moment. What a relief it is to be able to confess our sins, to receive the forgiving grace of God, and to know that we do not have to pretend any longer! The priest is the one who receives our confession. We need and have a great High Priest in Jesus Christ.

We have a great high priest. He is great in nature. A perfect high priest must be one who, by nature, is in full communion with God and man. He must bring God to man and man to God. To do that, he must be in touch with God by nature. The writer of Hebrews insisted that Jesus does precisely that. He has not been given his status with God as a personal reward. He has it by nature. He is the Son of God. By being who he is, he brings God himself to man.

He *has passed through the heavens.* He is highly exalted. He has also done something to make our access to God possible. As the ancient priests passed through the veil of the Temple on the great Day of Atonement, so Jesus passed through the ultimate veil into the very presence of God in heaven. Various meanings have been assigned to this phrase, *passed through the heavens.* This Hebrew preacher most assuredly believed in the resurrection, but his emphasis was upon the exaltation of Jesus in his ascension. God raised Jesus from the dead that he might sit down on the right hand of the Majesty on high. *Passed through the heavens,* then, might refer to the ascension and exaltation of Jesus.

Some writers place the emphasis in this passage on the word *through.* They conclude that Jesus passing through the heavens meant that heaven could not hold him; that Jesus is so marvelous and great that not even heaven could circumscribe him. It seems more in keeping with the context and with the typology of this book to see the passage as meaning that Christ has now entered the heavenly holy of holies, the ultimate and eternal presence of God. Thus, he is the ultimate and final High Priest, before whom all may bring their confession.

One of the powerful works of the sculptor, Lorado Taft, is entitled "The Blind." The figures are from an almshouse, and all are either insane or blind, except one—a child. Twilight has come and they are lost. A blind mother has hoisted the child, her sane and seeing little one, to her shoulder to guide the helpless multitude to safety.

Even so, God has hoisted his Son above our blind, insane generation to be the priest and to bring us to sanity and light. With this assurance, we have arrived at the final religious reality. We need never even hope that God can surpass what he has already provided in Jesus. This is one of the solid realities to which we may hold fast forever.

Let us hold fast our confession. These hortatory words sum up the preceeding two chapters (cf. 3:1,6,14).

For we have not a high priest who is unable to sympathize with our weaknesses. Hebrews does not leave our High Priest exalted so high above us that he would appear to be inaccessible. This is the same man of Nazareth who bore our infirmities in his own body during the days of his flesh.

One who in every respect has been tempted as we are. He suffered every kind of temptation known to man. He knew stronger temptations than any one of us has ever known. Jesus knew by experience every kind of temptation we shall ever know. He was like us in all ways save one, he knew no sin. The reference, *yet without sinning,* pertains primarily to the sin of disobedience to the will of God.

Let us then with confidence draw near to the throne of grace. The Christ who chose to bear such temptation and to suffer such anguish is the Christ who now sits upon the throne of grace. It was for us that he did this. Therefore, with holy boldness and confidence, we may come to the throne of grace with the full assurance that we will find help for our personal needs.

With confidence is a call to resoluteness, the resolution which results from the assurance that we can rely on the sovereign mercy and compassion of God.

Throne of grace means grace is now enthroned. To draw near the royal throne of supreme authority would bring nothing but trembling were we not assured that God's authority is grounded in his grace.

Note the progression in this passage—the terrifying picture of God's all-seeing eye, then the tender compassion of one who is our Maker and who also has walked our difficult road. Finally, we are called to concentrate on our only hope—his throne of grace.

2. Qualifications of the True High Priest (5:1–10)

(1) Human Qualifications (5:1–6)

¹ For every high priest chosen from among men is appointed to act on behalf of men in relation to God, to offer gifts and sacrifices for sins. ² He can deal gently with the ignorant and wayward, since he himself is beset with weakness. ³ Because of this he is bound to offer sacrifice for his own sins as well as for those of the people. ⁴ And one does not take the honor upon himself, but he is called by God, just as Aaron was.

⁵ So also Christ did not exalt himself to be made a high priest, but was appointed by him who said to him,
"Thou art my Son,
   today I have begotten thee";
⁶ as he says also in another place,
"Thou art a priest for ever,
   after the order of Melchizedek."

At this point, the preacher, for the first time, explains what it is that makes a true high priest: (1) His humanity must make him humane (vv. 1–3); (2) a true high priest cannot appoint himself (vv. 4–6).

He can deal gently with the ignorant and the wayward, because he too is encompassed with infirmity. He was vulnerable to the same temptations which they knew. The word translated *deal gently* was coined by moral philosophers to describe the golden mean between extravagant grief and hard apathy. This was exhibited by Abraham in his sorrow over the death of his wife. It is appropriate grief. The Hebrew preacher takes this word and makes it describe moderation of anger in a person who has been provoked.

Our great High Priest deals gently with *the ignorant and wayward,* those who sin because of the weakness of human nature. These were the only people whose sins were dealt with on the Day of Atonement. This preacher knew no pardon for deliberate presumptuous sinners (3:12; 10:26). The people for whom pardon is possible are those who err because of ignorance and those who truly repent. The ritual of sacrifice in the Old Testament did not cover deliberate, willful sins (cf. Num. 12:11). Only unintentional sins were pardoned (Lev. 4:2; 5:17–19; Num. 15:22–31; Deut. 17:12).

This preacher takes an exceedingly serious view of sin. Søren Kierkegaard called sin "a sickness unto death." A church without a robust doctrine of sin has nothing to say to a world like ours.

Because of this he is bound to offer sacrifice for his own sins as well as for those of the people. Because of human weakness, the high priest was required to sacrifice for himself, his household, and then for the people. And *one does not take the honor upon himself* means that he does not take the office or the position.

Thou art my Son, today I have begotten thee is this preacher's favorite text. It is taken from Psalm 2:7. In v. 6 he quotes from Psalm 110:4 and links the divine sonship with the role of the high priest. In the beginning of the sermon (1:2–3), he spoke of the mission of the Son as the purifying of men from their sins.

Thou art a priest for ever, after the order of Melchizedek meant that he was a Melchizedek kind of priest. The genealogy of the priestly order was carefully preserved, but there was no known record of Melchizedek. He did not, according to the common impression, receive his priesthood from his earthly genealogy, nor did he pass it on to his descendants. He was a priest, appointed in a special way, of God.

No earthly prototype, however, was adequate to describe Christ for this Hebrew preacher. He, therefore, was most careful to insist that Christ was too large to be contained in any earthly category. The preacher is, therefore, very meticulous in his insisting that Christ was not required to offer sacrifice for himself, for he was without sin.

(2) Moral Qualifications (5:7–10)

7 In the days of his flesh, Jesus offered up prayers and supplications, with loud cries and tears, to him who was able to save him from death, and he was heard for his godly fear. 8 Although he was a Son, he learned obedience through what he suffered; 9 and being made perfect he became the source of eternal salvation to all who obey him, 10 being designated by God a high priest after the order of Melchizedek.

Jesus, by rigid, moral discipline, qualified himself to be the great High Priest. Four things stand out in his qualifications: (1) He qualified himself by prayers (v. 7); (2) he qualified himself also by agony and tears (v. 7); (3) he qualified himself by faith in him who is able to save (v. 7); (4) he qualified himself by obedience (v. 8).

In the arena of moral combat, Jesus qualified himself to be the source of eternal salvation to all who follow his example of obedience, and thus he actually became what God designated him to be—High Priest (vv. 9–10). The appointment of God was primary, but it was not an unqualified appointment. It involved a response of faith and obedience which involved suffering.

In the days of his flesh, Jesus offered up prayers and supplications, with loud cries and tears. Luke stressed the tears of Jesus (22:44). This preacher of Hebrews was deeply impressed with the human life of Jesus, lived out in history. What impressed him most was the intense faith and courage of Jesus in the face of his cross. He sees this anguish as redemptive.

Rabbinic piety stressed the value of penitential tears. Three kinds of prayers were described by the rabbis: entreaty, crying, and tears. A quiet voice was used in entreaty. The voice was raised for crying, and tears represented the highest form of prayer.

He was heard for his godly fear. The reverential submission to the will of God,

his Father, was the basis for the answer to our Lord's prayers.

Although he was a Son, he learned obedience through what he suffered. This sonship did not immunize him from the necessity of learning as every genuinely human being must learn. The deepest lessons of life are learned through anguish. The learning of Jesus was not an exception to this.

Being made perfect means, not that he was not at every given moment perfect, but rather, that his moral perfection ultimately depended upon his response to each challenge presented to him. This was especially true as this challenge intensified, as his cross drew nearer and became not an eventual but a grim, present reality.

He became the source of eternal salvation to all who obey him. Salvation was conditioned on loyalty to Christ. To disobey him is the evidence of disbelief (3:18; 4:6,11). To disobey him is the practical denial that he is God's appointed High Priest (v. 10).

IV. Application (5:11—6:20)

1. Against Sluggishness (5:11–14)

11 About this we have much to say which is hard to explain, since you have become dull of hearing. 12 For though by this time you ought to be teachers, you need some one to teach you again the first principles of God's word. You need milk, not solid food; 13 for every one who lives on milk is unskilled in the word of righteousness, for he is a child. 14 But solid food is for the mature, for those who have their faculties trained by practice to distinguish good from evil.

The high knowledge of the Son of God as High Priest is given only to those who have taken the elementary foundations of the faith seriously enough to master them. Only the mature can grasp the sublime significance of the high priesthood of Jesus. The preacher fears that his hearers are still too immature to grasp this.

About this refers to the high priest according to the order of Melchizedek (v. 10). *We have much to say* was a customary literary form of the day. *Which is hard to explain* means the fault is with the hearer, not with the subject. *Since you have become dull of hearing.* The word translated *dull of hearing* is a common ethical term for sluggishness. When used with hearing it denotes dullness—which can become a besetting and destructive sin for the Christian.

For though by this time you ought to be teachers, you need some one to teach you again the first principles of God's word. It was time for them to be mature; and when a person is mature, he should have enough Christian knowledge to qualify him to teach others. The writer was using this manner of chiding to prod his hearers into learning what should be familiar to every Christian. There should come a time in the life of a mature Christian when he would not require being reminded of the fundamentals of the faith. Cyrus told the Persian chiefs that he would be ashamed to give them advice on the eve of battle. So this Hebrew preacher insists that his hearers have had the fundamentals of their faith long enough to have mastered them.

You need milk, not solid food. They have slipped back into a second spiritual childhood. The contrast between milk and solid food was a popular device in Greek ethical philosophy. Origen used this passage to answer Celsus, who had charged Christians with being afraid to address an educated and intelligent audience. The mature Christian, who is ready for solid food, is one who is ready to understand the priesthood of Christ.

For every one who lives on milk means one whose only food is milk (cf. 1 Cor. 10:17). *Unskilled,* means without experience and, therefore, unskilled. *In the word of righteousness* was a phrase frequently used in moral philosophy as the equivalent of moral truth. The final moral truth had come in him who is now the great High Priest. Mature people cannot ignore this or defer facing it. *For he is a child* means it is childish to face final moral truth.

But solid food is for the mature, who are those capable of decisive commitment and

of making up their minds. *For those who have their faculties trained by practice to distinguish good from evil* indicates that, for the Hebrew preacher, there were only two kinds of pupils—the mature and the immature. The mature are those who have the senses exercised for distinguishing both good and evil.

Faculties does not describe the mental faculties, but the powers that make one a person. The Stoics used this term to describe an organ of the sense, but it later acquired a moral significance and became the equivalent of the power of moral discrimination. That which distinguishes the mature person from a child is the power to make moral judgments and to be morally responsible.

2. Crucifying Christ Again (6:1–12)

¹ Therefore let us leave the elementary doctrines of Christ and go on to maturity, not laying again a foundation of repentance from dead works and of faith toward God, ² with instruction about ablutions, the laying on of hands, the resurrection of the dead, and eternal judgment. ³ And this we will do if God permits. ⁴ For it is impossible to restore again to repentance those who have once been enlightened, who have tasted the heavenly gift, and have become partakers of the Holy Spirit, ⁵ and have tasted the goodness of the word of God and the powers of the age to come, ⁶ if they then commit apostasy, since they crucify the Son of God on their own account and hold him up to contempt. ⁷ For land which has drunk the rain that often falls upon it, and brings forth vegetation useful to those for whose sake it is cultivated, receives a blessing from God. ⁸ But if it bears thorns and thistles, it is worthless and near to being cursed; its end is to be burned.

⁹ Though we speak thus, yet in your case, beloved, we feel sure of better things that belong to salvation. ¹⁰ For God is not so unjust as to overlook your work and the love which you showed for his sake in serving the saints, as you still do. ¹¹ And we desire each one of you to show the same earnestness in realizing the full assurance of hope until the end, ¹² so that you may not be sluggish, but imitators of those who through faith and patience inherit the promises.

A house must have a foundation or it will be shaky and insecure, but a foundation is not a house. It would be absurd to build a foundation on top of a foundation and to repeat this process and never get on to building the superstructure. The writer of Hebrews tells us that we, who spend so much thought and energy on the elementary principles of the Christian faith, are like a builder who repeats the laying of the foundation and never moves on to build the house of life. A foundation is important to the house, but it is not the house.

We, who continue in the kindergarten of religion, who never move on to a mature expression of what we have learned, are like children who lay one block on top of another—each like the previous one. Or, we are like educational vagabonds, who haunt the hall of learning year after year because they have not the basic courage to thrust out into life and practice what they have learned.

You have only to look at the doctrines which compose the foundation of the Christian life, to know that no Christian superstructure can be built without these. The writer lists six doctrines:

(1) The first is repentance from dead works, which means turning away from deeds which bring death. The doctrine of repentance is a chief concern of this writer. He remembered the words of his Master: "Unless you repent you will all likewise perish" (Luke 13:3). (2) Next is the doctrine of the high priesthood of Jesus. (3) The doctrine of faith comes next. This inward openness toward God permits God to come into our lives. (4) Then there is baptism, which is a part of Christ's commands. Even then a debate about baptism was apparently going on. The laying on of hands symbolized the transference of a blessing. It was customary to place the hands on a Christian's head and pray that he might be anointed by the Holy Spirit. (5) The doctrine of the resurrection is a part of the foundation because Christianity is a religion of eternal life through the living Lord. (6) Finally, the doctrine of judgment constantly reminded Christ's people that they must face God at the end of life. They knew that what God judged them to be was far more important than what people thought of them.

Now, each of these doctrines is basic to historic Christian faith. But the mastery of these was not the full intention of Jesus for his followers. So often we permit theological debate, over the nuances of doctrine, to divert us from God's intention for our lives. Actually, the writer shows us that Christians, even in his day, dwelt too long on these elementary doctrines and refused to go on to the maturity of robust disciples, who no longer survive on milk but require meat for vigorous energy to do the work of God in the world.

Are we, in the modern church, spending so much time trying to add members to our religious institutions and train them in the first principles of the faith that we have no energy left to cultivate the maturity which has a dynamic magnetism about it, which would draw people to the Saviour more than all of our organized activities can hope to do?

Under the heavy pressure of persecution, the Christians confronted in Hebrews were considering escaping their suffering by repudiating their faith in Jesus. Therefore, the writer reminds them of what they have at stake. He speaks of five things which have happened to those who are considering turning their backs on Jesus: (1) First, they have *been enlightened.* There was an ancient saying, "When Jesus comes, the shadows depart." Their darkness had been shattered and the everlasting light had shone for them. (2) They *have tasted,* which means they had experienced *the heavenly gift.* God had given himself to them in his Son. (3) Furthermore, they *have become partakers of the Holy Spirit,* without which no one can be born from above (John 3:5). (4) They *have tasted the goodness of the word of God.* They had discovered the truth in the word of God. (5) They had experienced a foretaste of what it was to live in eternity. They *have tasted . . . the powers of the age to come.*

Could such people, who had experienced such things, ever desert the Redeemer?

To begin with, it must be clear that discerning and devout students of Scripture will not always arrive at the same answer to this question, depending on how they relate the warning of Hebrews to their whole view of the gospel. Each person is obligated to seek the answer which best harmonizes with his understanding of God's grace in Christ and the freedom and relationship involved in Christian salvation. I would add further that I doubt that the passage before us was intended in the purpose of the Spirit to be the sole basis for the formulation of a doctrine of either apostasy or spiritual security. I take the position that the writer sought to instruct Christians in the context of a specific situation, and I have sought to state my understanding of the meaning and application of the truth to Christian experience. This passage and others (3:12–14; 10:26–39; 12:16–17) are best understood, I believe, in relation to the central purpose of Hebrews.

To come back to the question raised, there can be no doubt that they were considering it; therefore, this writer warns them of what would happen should this take place. If they should desert Jesus, they would *crucify* him again. They would be reopening his wounds. They would be casting their lot with those who said, "He deserves death" (Matt. 26:66). They, therefore, would *hold him up to contempt,* to let the mocking laughter of those who railed at him on the cross ring out again. In effect, they would be saying, "We have tried him and found him false. He did not do what he promised."

During the reign of the Emperor Diocletian, the Christians were apprehended and ruthlessly persecuted. After the persecution subsided, one test applied to every surviving member of the church for the retention of his membership was, "Did you deny Christ and so save your life?" If he had denied his Lord, he could not continue in the Christian church. If he had held his own life to be dearer to him than Jesus, then Jesus was not his Lord.

A legend tells us that, during the days of Nero, Peter was caught in Rome. When his courage failed, he fled out of the city for his life. As he sped down the Appian Way, a figure suddenly blocked his path of light. Peter lifted his eyes and looked into the searching eyes of Jesus. *"Domine,"* said Peter, *"Quo vadis?"* "Lord, where are you going?" The somber reply was, "I am going back to Rome to be crucified again, this time in your stead." The instant sense of shame turned Peter around. His courage returned and carried him back to Rome to die a martyr's death. Peter saw that his denial and cowardice were again opening the wounds of the Saviour. Though this may be a legend, it serves for helpful illustration.

To bring a person who has finally denied Jesus back to salvation would be impossible, for it would be saying that the "once-for-all" death of Jesus was insufficient. A new foundation would have to be laid. So we face the question: Could God ever do more for us than he did in Jesus? Could he ever speak more clearly and with greater finality than he spoke in Jesus? Could his heart ever be opened in more tender compassion and love than it was on Golgotha? Could a high priest ever come with more sympathy for us than Jesus had? Could God ever offer fuller grace in the forgiveness of our sins than he offered in Jesus? Could there ever be more open, immediate access to God than has been opened up for us in Jesus? With his clear, shining light for our darkness, with his adequate strength for our weakness and the Holy Spirit to be our guide, we have full and complete salvation. If we refuse this or renounce this, there could be nothing more God could do to renew us to repentance.

For land which has drunk the rain that often falls upon it, and brings forth vegetation useful to those for whose sake it is cultivated, receives a blessing from God.

To illustrate this point, the preacher shows that all land receives some rain. Some land brings forth fruit, and it is blessed of God. That land which does not bring forth fruit *is worthless and near to being cursed.* Those who are children of God prove this by their fruit.

Yet, in your case, beloved, we feel sure of better things means: "You are the kind that should bring forth good fruit." The great hope for these people is that, despite their obsession with the elementary things of religion and despite their wavering under the pressures of their persecution, they were still doing some work of love for God and man. The promise is that God will not forget this. He is a just God, therefore, every good deed will be duly compensated in God's own way and time.

This is God's way of saying to us in our day: "You may not be perfect in your attitude toward others, nor in your performance of the work I have given you to do. Nevertheless, do not lose heart, for I am aware of the good that you are doing. Work on, then, with courage, patience, and hope until the very end. Do not let the meager results beat you down into apathetic cynicism, which produces that deadly lethargy that robs us of the harvest."

Having shaken those who were contemplating apostasy back into their senses, the writer adds a word of comforting assurance. He uses a term of endearment and encouragement. *Beloved* he calls them. This is the only time he uses this term. There is no sentimental romanticism in this writer. Yet, the strong words of warning are now softened by the assurance that, while they have contemplated departing from Jesus, they actually have not done so. They have not fallen, even though they have remained too long in the Christian primer. There have been times when they have broken out to do their work for God and their labor of love in ministering to God's people.

There are things which must necessarily accompany salvation. What are they? Essentially, they are love for God and labor for God's people. The true servant of the Saviour is the person who has such confidence in the foundation of his faith that he does not have to examine and defend it constantly, nor debate about it. With quiet assurance, he grounds his life in this and proceeds to love God and to show that love by laboring to help people.

Things that belong to salvation might be the heroic defense of a man, marked for persecution, caring for the children of the needy, and helping the jobless find greater dignity than they can ever have on a government dole.

To get on to the maturity which Christ offers involves self-forgetfulness, even the forgetting of the egocentric schemes of religion, which cause some to look upon Christianity as a poor man's psychiatry and a rich man's conscience soother. A little boy asked his grandfather, "Granddaddy, can people get along without religion?" "Yes, son," replied the grandfather, "and people can get along without eyes, but they cannot see."

Notice how personal this appeal is. *We desire each one of you to show the same earnestness in realizing the full assurance of hope until the end.* The God of the Bible is still the personal God of the people. To Moses, God said, "I know you by name" (Ex. 33:17). To Cyrus, God said, "It is I, the Lord, the God of Israel, who call you by your name" (Isa. 45:3). This is what Paul Tournier is calling the personalism of the Bible. So important are names to God that entire chapters of the Scripture are devoted to genealogies.

The hope of the Christian church is that every member of the church will maintain such zeal in serving God that all, even all that God hopes for, will come true at last. This hope, of course, is grounded on the fact that God works in and through Christians by his living Spirit. Faith has a forward dimension. If it does not hope for something better in the future, it is not genuine faith. Christian maturing is growing in faith, hope, and love. Faith has a historic foundation of abiding realities. It is by faith that we pull these realities into the living present. Love is the power by which we serve our day and generation in the spirit of Jesus. Hope is the means by which we taste the power of the age to come.

We do not walk the way of faith, love, and hope as solitary pilgrims. Others have gone before to show us the way. We have not only the Holy Spirit within us to guide us, but also the objective example of those who have resisted the temptation to remain *sluggish* and slothful and have, by faith, walked with steady, strong endurance and have found God's *promises* to be true. The writer says that God has made his promises and faithful men have found his promises to be true. The way you are called to walk, then, is not solely a way of faith. There is empirical evidence that this is the right way and the rewarding way.

3. Reassurance (6:13-20)

Since the Christian pilgrimage is made by faith and not by sight, there is constant need of assurance and encouragement. In the first paragraph of chapter 6, the preacher issued both chiding and warning (vv. 1-8). The second paragraph is a word of encouragement (vv. 9-12). Works of love and service to the saints are recommended (v. 10). Then, he tells his hearers that his desire for them is that they shall realize the full assurance of hope until the end (v. 11).

The final paragraph (vv. 13-20) undergirds this assurance. To accomplish this, the hearer is carried all the way back to the father of the faithful, Abraham, and to the promise which God made to him. When God makes a promise, it is not a casual word to be forgotten. It is the ground of eternal assurance. Notice what strong words enforce this preacher's attempt to bring assurance to his hard-pressed and persecuted people. He fills this brief paragraph with such words as *surely* (v. 14). Twice he speaks of an *oath* (vv. 16-17). He speaks of *final confirmation* (v. 16). He says that **God desired to show more con-**vincingly** (v. 17). Twice he uses the word *unchangeable* (vv. 17-18). He speaks of a *sure and steadfast anchor of the soul* (v. 19). He speaks of a *hope* which is already anchored behind the veil in the eternal, invisible world (v. 19); and of a *forerunner* whose race is over, who has already entered the world of eternal reality, and who has already become a *high priest for ever* (v. 20). Nothing can divest him of his priesthood and nothing can change the promise of God in which our hope is finally vested. Thus, in eight verses, this preacher packs words of permanent assurance for all who believe in the great High Priest.

Look more carefully, now, at these symbols of hope and assurance. There are four of them: the promise (6:13-17); the anchor of hope (6:18-19); the forerunner and the high priest—the culminating symbol in which all of these are fulfilled (6:20).

(1) The Promise (6:13-17)

13 **For when God made a promise to Abraham, since he had no one greater by whom to swear, he swore by himself,** 14 **saying, "Surely I will bless you and multiply you."** 15 **And thus Abraham, having patiently endured, obtained the promise.** 16 **Men indeed swear by a greater than themselves, and in all their disputes an oath is final for confirmation.** 17 **So when God desired to show more convincingly to the heirs of the promise the unchangeable character of his purpose, he interposed with an oath,**

Philo was embarrassed by the concept that God should have to reinforce his word by an oath. Is not the word of God assurance enough? Did not Jesus warn us against oaths (Matt. 5:34-37)? Did he not encourage us not to swear by anything in heaven or on earth, but to let our yes be yes and our no be no? Did he not imply that the character of the person behind the spoken word was ground of the trustworthiness of the word and not the colorful oaths which supported it, no matter how multiplied they might be? Did not James further warn us: "But above all, my brethren, do not swear, either by heaven or by earth or with any other oath, but let your yes be yes and your no be no, that you may not fall under condemnation" (5:12)?

What possible meaning, then, could we find in the oath of God? If human character is the basis for believing in a promise made by a person, how much more should the divine character be the basis for believing in his promise? This may sound like a very noble and idealistic argument to the contemporary mind. But the preacher of Hebrews apparently did not have such high-flown scruples against oaths. Further, each of the admonitions against making an oath, referred to above, is to be interpreted in its context. The major concern of the preacher was to reinforce the hope and assurance of his people. How could he better do that than by saying to them, in effect: "God's promise is incontrovertible. He has done everything to assure you that he will never break his promise." While his promise should never be doubted, we continue to doubt it every day. Our human dullness and the dimness of our faith cause the promise of God to lose its gripping power. God, therefore, puts every reminder before us of the permanent validity of his promise. Men should have believed God's spoken promise never again to destroy the world with a flood. But God chose the dramatic symbol of the rainbow to enhance his reminder to his people of his perpetual favor toward them.

Beyond this, the Hebrew preacher had an Old Testament Scripture with which he was required to reckon. Abraham was the prime example of steadfast faith in God's promises. He had taken Isaac, the son of his old age—the only visible proof that God was keeping his promise to multiply him and bring out of his loins a great nation—and at the command of God had placed him on the altar of sacrifice and was ready to plunge the knife into his heart when his hand was stayed by the hand of heaven (Gen. 22:12). Then it was that God said: "By myself I have sworn, says the Lord, because you have done this,

and have not withheld your son, your only son, I will indeed bless you, and I will multiply your descendants as the stars of heaven and as the sand which is on the seashore" (Gen. 22:16–17).

The point is that the Hebrew preacher had before him this word from Genesis concerning the oath which God swore by himself. Was it God's way of saying that, by his name, that is by everything that made him God, his promise would be kept? Was this what made the promises of God so exceedingly precious to early Christians? Fourteen times the Hebrew preacher speaks of God's promise (cf. 4:1; 6:12,15, 17; 7:6; 8:6; 9:15; 10:36; 11:9,13,17,33, 39).

The apostle Peter was so enamored with the promises of God that he called them "precious and very great promises" (2 Peter 1:4).

So when God desired to show more convincingly . . . he interposed with an oath. It was God's great desire to give man confidence in his promise that occasioned God's oath. This oath guaranteed the promise of God. This seems a very quaint analogy to modern man, but it was very real to primitive man. Do we not need some jarring event in our own experience to cause us to take God's promises more seriously and to make him the ground of our hope?

(2) Anchor of Hope (6:18–19)

18 so that through two unchangeable things, in which it is impossible that God should prove false, we who have fled for refuge might have strong encouragement to seize the hope set before us. 19 We have this as a sure and steadfast anchor of the soul, a hope that enters into the inner shrine behind the curtain,

The reference to the *anchor of the soul* reminds us that there are only four references to an anchor in the Bible. Three of them occur in Luke's unforgettable account of the storm at sea (Acts 27:29–30,40), and the other appears in v. 19. The anchor cross was one of the signs used by the early Christians to signify their faith and hope. Should you visit the catacombs—the underground tombs beneath the city of Rome where early persecuted believers worshiped—you would find the anchor cross as one of the signs on the walls indicating that Christians once carved their symbol of hope on the walls of tombs.

The transverse bar gives the anchor the appearance of a cross. This may have influenced its being chosen by the early Christians. It is said to have been the emblem of Clement, Bishop of Rome, who, according to tradition, was bound to an anchor during the persecutions, under the Emperor Trajan, and cast into the sea.

Originally, the anchor symbolized hope. When a ship was securely anchored, it could not be wrecked. Because of its similiarity in appearance to a cross, it came to be the symbol of the hope of salvation through the cross.

The anchor was a symbol of Christian hope not only in the Western church but also in the Eastern church. Clement of Alexandria, while condemning the extravagant use of Christian symbols, still approved the use of a ship's anchor as a Christian seal.

But what did the *anchor* mean specifically in this passage? The preacher refers to *we who have fled for refuge.* These pilgrims are under the pressure of persecution. They have been compelled to take flight, if not physically then spiritually. Where can they find refuge? It is not in hope as a psychological state of mind. As in Colossians 1:27 ("the hope of glory"), this is the *hope* which God gives us, not the hope that springs from the human heart. They are not told to be hopeful that their condition will improve or that the pressure will lessen. It was not that they were encouraged to believe that things were bound to brighten and get better. The hope that was set before them had positive content. Hope was defined as the object of expectation. The content of their hope was the assurance that they were moored to an immovable object. They were not destined to sail the wild seas at the mercy of the storms forever. They were already anchored if they, by faith, would accept it.

So the preacher joins the promise of God and the blessed hope together. The *unchangeable promise* of God encourages us to seize the hope.

This suggests decisive, completed action. It does not mean to continue to cling to, but in one tremendous act to lay this hope up in our hearts. It is not a vague and vapory dream. It is a reality which we can grasp by faith.

God has given *the hope set before us.* In the same active manner, we are called upon to seize, to take hold of this hope. This hope is God's work. It is offered by God to man. We are invited to anchor our souls in what God has provided for us. The full, unfolding of what we hope for is in the invisible, eternal order. Nevertheless, we can lay hold on it by faith. *

---

* NOTE: The hope, in which we are called to anchor our souls, is described by James Stewart in the example of the criminal who had a little daughter, who was the image of her dead mother. She was all the world to her father. One day, he was arrested by the authorities and taken to prison. During his imprisonment, the child died. He did not learn about it until the day of his release from prison. It was a shattering blow, for without the bright-faced, little girl, life held no meaning for him.

His world came to an end. Accordingly, he decided that, when nightfall came, he would take his life by jumping off the Dean Bridge.

When the evening shadows gathered, he climbed high upon the parapet. He gazed down at the dark, murky waters and was just ready to leap and end it all when, suddenly, there flashed before his memory the opening words of the Christian Creed: "I believe in God, the Father Almighty." He knew little about God, but he did know something about fatherhood. He suddenly found himself thinking that, if God is like that, if that is the kind of being God is, then I can trust him with my child. In that moment, death receded and life began anew. In the very last gasp the anchor of his hope in God had held. He had entrusted himself also to the Father.

The anchor is *sure and steadfast* because it is cast in eternity in *the inner shrine,* in the world of permanent reality. The hope of a Christian is anchored in the truth that Christ has carried the values of his earthly sacrifice, the values of his earthly cross into the eternal world.

This is the moral force which springs from Christian hope. For as James Stewart has said, "Hope is not a continual, pathetic waiting for something to turn up." Instead, it is the source of the energy that moves us to work for a righteous order on earth.

A thoroughgoing secularist may tell us that it is God's business to build heaven, so he has no concern with that. It is man's business, says he, to build an established order of justice and righteousness on earth. That sounds very noble indeed. It also sounds very arrogant, for perfect justice and righteousness always evade us here; and the only source which sustains us in our moments of overwhelming frustration is the hope that, in the future, sometime, somewhere, God will bring our imperfect efforts to fulfillment.

Our anchor is not cast in the ever-changing waters of this world, but in a world which only the eyes of faith can see. Our hope is immediately grounded in what Christ has already done on his cross and in the intercession which he continually offers for us in the very presence of God.

He is now *behind the curtain.* The preacher carries an analogy from the tabernacle into the courts of heaven. This ritual is described in Leviticus 16:2 ff., where Aaron passed through the curtain, or veil, which screened the innermost shrine.

(3) Forerunner and High Priest (6:20)

20 where Jesus has gone as a forerunner on our behalf, having become a high priest for ever after the order of Melchizedek.

The third symbol of assurance is seen in Jesus as the *forerunner,* who has already finished the race. We are encouraged to be assured that we too shall finish the course

set before us (12:1), because Jesus has gone before as the pathfinder and as one who blazed the trail before us and set the example for us.

It was *on our behalf* that he did this. This forerunner has passed into the heavenly world, carrying with him the anchor to which the soul of every believer is firmly fixed. The forerunner also carries the idea that Christians neither passively wait for deliverance, nor do they run away from reality. Instead, they run toward the forerunner, who is already at home in the believer's final home.

With this fourth symbol, *high priest,* the preacher reaches the culminating argument of the sermon. The foremost concern of the preacher is that his hearers should understand that Christ is their High Priest. Their supreme need is for doctrinal renewal which will anchor them in the uniqueness of Christ. He is the High Priest who has offered himself for his people, who continually intercedes for them, and who is present in the eternal world—not to make sacrifice, but to be present as the one whose sacrifice has already been made once for all.

V. Heart of the Argument (7:1-28)

Few passages are clothed more in the regalia of an ancient, religious ritual than is the seventh chapter of Hebrews. Intricate and antiquated modes of thought carry us into the faraway, shadowy days of Abraham. There we trace the heritage of God's chosen people and see demonstrated the superiority of the great High Priest, whom God has set in the eternal sanctuary to serve humanity forever.

1. Melchizedek (7:1-3)

1 For this Melchizedek, king of Salem, priest of the Most High God, met Abraham returning from the slaughter of the kings and blessed him; 2 and to him Abraham apportioned a tenth part of everything. He is first, by translation of his name, king of righteousness, and

then he is also king of Salem, that is, king of peace. ³ He is without father or mother or genealogy, and has neither beginning of days nor end of life, but resembling the Son of God he continues a priest for ever.

Here we have one of the writer's long sentences. He did not practice the modern staccato of short sentences. Although his sentences are long, they are beautifully balanced, both in form and substance. The entire sermon is so neatly structured that exactly six chapters precede the seventh chapter, which is the doctrinal heart of the sermon, and six chapters follow it.

The heart of the Christian hope reposes in the truth that Jesus, the High Priest, stands now in the heavenly sanctuary, in the presence of God, behind the veil. This hope is not composed of the stuff that dreams are made of. It is solidly based on the truth that the priestly work of Jesus is just as superior to that of Aaron as his relationship to God as Son is superior to the position of the angels.

This hope is securely based on the oath of God. Just as he swore to keep his promise to Abraham, he also took an equally binding oath when he invested Christ as High Priest: "This one was addressed with an oath, / 'The Lord has sworn / and will not change his mind, / "Thou art a priest for ever" ' " (7:21).

Already the preacher had made allusions to Christ as High Priest (cf. 2:17; 3:1; 5:5–10). No other New Testament writer uses this designation for Christ. The writer of Hebrews explains in part what he means by it when he calls Jesus a "faithful high priest in the service of God" (2:17), and "the apostle and high priest of our confession" (3:1). He goes on with chapters 3 and 4 before he discusses the relationship of the high priesthood with Christ's sonship (5:5–10). Then he does not elaborate on this again until the last verse of chapter 6. At this point he presents the concept of Christ, as the High Priest, as the culmination of everything he had previously said.

It is as though the author realizes that he must approach the colossal conclusion very cautiously. He dares not bombard his hearers with the full development of such a new concept without giving them a few preliminary allusions and without giving them time to ruminate on these allusions. Therefore, he alludes to Christ's priesthood and his being of the order of Melchizedek four times before his careful and complete analysis of its meaning in chapter 7.

With the words *for this Melchizedek* the preacher begins a careful exposition of Genesis 14:18–20 and Psalm 110:4, the only two references in the Old Testament to Melchizedek.

The understanding of the identity of Melchizedek provides the clue for understanding this chapter. He is *king of Salem,* which is identified with Jerusalem, in the Dead Sea Genesis Apocryphon on Genesis 14:18. He is also *priest of the Most High God,* which probably refers to the High God worshiped by the Canaanites in Jerusalem before the Israelites took it over.[11] He is thus a king, who exercises both royal and priestly prestige, towering over all the other people mentioned in chapter 7. He was the supreme authority in the city which was destined to become the holy capital of Israel.

Abraham acknowledged his authority when he bowed before him and offered him tithes. In Psalm 110, Melchizedek is regarded as a prototype of the Davidic Messiah, who is God's adopted Son. This ideal king will establish *righteousness* (*zedek*) and *peace* (*shalom*).

This letter does not allegorize, but it is steeped in typology. Here Melchizedek, since he is above Abraham the patriarch and Aaron the priest (vv. 11–17), is the type of Christ. One of the major emphases of Hebrews is the truth that Christ is above all Old Testament figures and above all other mediators. A part of the preacher's argument, in insisting on the royal high

11 Cf. BBC, I, p. 175.

priesthood of Christ, is to say that his priesthood transcends all others because it is "after the order of Melchizedek" (5:6). He exercises both kingly and priestly authority.[12]

This seventh chapter may be broken into seven parts. Verses 1–3 are the first part and contain an exposition of Genesis 14: 18–20: "And Melchizedek king of Salem brought out bread and wine; he was priest of God Most High. And he blessed him and said, / 'Blessed be Abram by God Most High, / maker of heaven and earth; / and blessed be God Most High, / who has delivered your enemies into your hand!' / And Abram gave him a tenth of everything." Compare this passage now with Hebrews 7:1–2. You see at once, also, that the Genesis passage does not contain the poetry in 7:3—which appears here in prose form, but is really a little poem. It is surmised that the preacher of Hebrews is quoting poetry about Melchizedek which cannot now be located.

He is without father or mother or genealogy, and has neither beginning of days nor end of life, but resembling the Son of God he continues a priest forever. It is noteworthy that the author quotes this little "poem" as though he assigns the same authority to it that he assigns to Old Testament Scripture. It would appear, therefore, that the writer is quoting from a very acceptable and well-known tradition concerning Melchizedek, which would certainly have been familiar to his hearers. There was a large body of literature which was accumulated in intertestamental times and which elaborated on incidents which were barely mentioned in Old Testament passages. For example, the story of Enoch is barely mentioned in Genesis 5:18–24, but an enormous story about him appears in the book of Enoch.

In the Genesis account, no reference is made to Melchizedek's being without father or mother. No reference to his ancestry is made. Therefore, the preacher leans heavily on the silence of Genesis, which was an acceptable and popular method of argument in his day.

Resembling the Son of God is believed to have meant, originally, resembling an angel or a heavenly being. At this point, it is helpful to remember that the Seputagint always translated the Hebrew phrase "son of God" as "angel of God." The original story about Melchizedek probably said that he resembled a son of God or a heavenly being and, therefore, remains a priest forever.

It is noteworthy, however, that the preacher of Hebrews goes beyond this original story. He applies the title, "Son of God," only to Christ. So he makes the story of Melchizedek, in this verse, to refer to the one Son of God, Christ himself. This reinforces his argument because he can now insist that it was Melchizedek who was like the preexistent Son of God, and not Christ who was like Melchizedek. Such an argument permitted the preacher to maintain that Christ was like Melchizedek in that he was above both Abraham and Aaron and, in that sense, Melchizedek was a type of Christ. At the same time, it was the preexistent Christ from whom even Melchizedek derived his pattern. It was in this ideal sense, in his resembling Christ, that Melchizedek *continues a priest forever.*

This preacher apparently goes as far as he can in honoring Melchizedek, of whose order the Essenes of the Qumran community claimed they were the priests. These Essene covenantors saw Melchizedek as an angel. The Hebrews' preacher says to them: "Very well, granted that he was an angel, and granted that he was a priest above all other priests, he was still inferior to the true, unique Son of God."

2. Superiority of Melchizedek (7:4–10)

4 See how great he is! Abraham the patriarch gave him a tithe of the spoils. 5 And those

---

12 Cf. The preacher's expository method resembled, in every aspect, the typical Jewish Midrash; but it was even more notably analogous to an Essene Midrash from Qumran Cave 4, in a document called 4 Q ("florilegium").

descendants of Levi who receive the priestly office have a commandment in the law to take tithes from the people, that is, from their brethren, though these also are descended from Abraham. 6 But this man who has not their genealogy received tithes from Abraham and blessed him who had the promises. 7 It is beyond dispute that the inferior is blessed by the superior. 8 Here tithes are received by mortal men; there, by one of whom it is testified that he lives. 9 One might even say that Levi himself, who receives tithes, paid tithes through Abraham, 10 for he was still in the loins of his ancestor when Melchizedek met him.

Now the preacher offers his specific proof that Melchizedek is superior to Levi and Abraham. It is a strange argument, but completely acceptable to the Semitic mind of the first century. He contends that when Abraham gave tithes, Levi also gave the same tithes, for Levi *was still in the loins of his ancestor* (Abraham, his father) at the time of the offering. It was the Israelite law that all the people of all the tribes should pay tithes to the tribe of Levi, the priestly tribe.

It is the prerogative of the priest to bless others because his position is superior to that of an ordinary man. Therefore, since Melchizedek had blessed Abraham, he was considered superior to Abraham. In like manner, the one who receives tithes is regarded as superior to the one who pays tithes.

Here tithes are received by mortal men; there, by one of whom it is testified that he lives. The superiority of Melchizedek to Aaron and Levi is here again argued on the basis that he belongs to the eternal order of the angels. While Aaron and Levi are mortal, Melchizedek lives. This is the culmination of the preacher's argument and his highest claim for Melchizedek.

3. A Divine Priesthood (7:11–14)

11 Now if perfection had been attainable through the Levitical priesthood (for under it the people received the law), what further need would there have been for another priest to arise after the order of Melchizedek, rather than one named after the order of Aaron? 12 For when there is a change in the priesthood, there is necessarily a change in the law

as well. 13 For the one of whom these things are spoken belonged to another tribe, from which no one has ever served at the altar. 14 For it is evident that our Lord was descended from Judah, and in connection with that tribe Moses said nothing about priests.

Now if perfection had been attainable through the Levitical priesthood refers to a completely adequate relation to God.

What further need suggests that someone in the congregation was contending that Melchizedek's priesthood was succeeded by the Aaronic priesthood. If this is the case, the preacher points to the Psalter and reminds his hearers that it was written after the Pentateuch, and that, in Psalm 110:4, God had promised by an oath to set up a priesthood after the order of Melchizedek. Why, he asks, should God have made such an oath and such a promise if the Levitical priesthood had accomplished all that he desired? Thus he stresses the inferiority of the Aaronic priesthood.

For when there is a change in the priesthood, there is necessarily a change in the law as well. The emphasis on the inferiority of the Aaronic priesthood is further argued on the ground that the law of Moses, which appointed the Levitical priesthood, has been superseded. The message declared by angels (2:2), the law of Moses, was inferior to the word of Christ. Therefore, when the priesthood was changed, the law was changed. The supremely important agent is the priest, not the law. The Mosaic law was just as effective as the priesthood which administered the law. The personal character of the priest, who interpreted the law and dealt with the lawbreakers, was far more important than the letter of the law.

For the one of whom these things are spoken refers to Melchizedek.

Belonged to another tribe, from which no one has ever served at the altar indicates that the new priesthood is so radically different that it originates in a tribe from which no priest had ever come and concerning which *Moses said nothing.* A higher law than that of Moses must invest this new priest with his authority. The preacher insists that the law of Moses was not eternal but changeable, and he offers as incontestable proof the fact that Jesus, the High Priest, who fulfilled the prophecy of Psalm 110:4, came out of the tribe of Judah and thus began a new kind of priesthood no longer governed by the Mosaic law.

4. An Effectual Priesthood (7:15-19)

15 This becomes even more evident when another priest arises in the likeness of Melchizedek, 16 who has become a priest, not according to a legal requirement concerning bodily descent but by the power of an indestructible life. 17 For it is witnessed of him,
"Thou art a priest for ever,
after the order of Melchizedek."
18 On the one hand, a former commandment is set aside because of its weakness and uselessness 19 (for the law made nothing perfect); on the other hand, a better hope is introduced, through which we draw near to God.

Here, the preacher's point is that the high priesthood of Jesus is validated, not by the law of Moses, but by something infinitely greater—*the power of an indestructible life.* Other human priests received their office by *bodily descent,* that is, by their natural lineage in the tribe of Levi. They received this at birth and relinquished it at death. No such mortality applies to the high priesthood of Jesus.

While this writer attacks the law of Moses for its imperfection, he is not to be regarded as an antinomian. The only point of the law which he questions concerns the adequacy of the priesthood which was appointed by the law of Moses. He makes it abundantly clear that he regards the oath of God and the power of an indestructible life, by which the priesthood of Christ was established, as being superior to the law.

Before the writer of Hebrews could establish his argument concerning the superiority of Jesus, he had to counter the argument of his Jewish opponents. They looked in pious horror upon anyone who insisted that there could be a greater priestly order than the Levitical order.

Therefore, the writer showed that there

was one such priest. His name was Melchizedek, the priest to whom Abraham paid a tithe and from whom Abraham received a blessing. Moreover, since Melchizedek had no recorded lineage, he typified a priest who did not receive his office from a system of earthbound rules. The Levites were required to trace their lineage from Levi with exceeding care. Over against that there stood a man who neither received his priesthood from his ancestors nor passed it on to his descendants. Melchizedek was, therefore, a type of a perpetual high priest.

How was the superiority of the priesthood of Christ established by the power of an indestructible life? When a ruthless religious order nailed him to a cross and when his last breath lay silent, the Levitical priests breathed more easily. They said, in effect: "This troubler of Israel is done with; this destroyer of our glorious Temple, this wrecker of our religion is finished." But he came out of the grave by the power of an indestructible life.

Is it not worth remembering that some of the priests in the days of Jesus were Sadducees who did not even believe in the resurrection of the dead? It was the resurrection of Jesus that put the seal of triumph on our Christian gospel. This High Priest is King forever of the world in which the spirits of just men made perfect are to reside forever (12:23).

A better hope is introduced, through which we draw near to God. What does it matter if the authority of the Mosaic law is impaired, if a better hope is the result? A healthy religion is not essentially expressed in trembling before the law, but rather in a bright hope which enables us to draw near to God. For this Hebrew preacher, religion was essentially drawing near to God. It was not trembling on the other side of the veil, through which only the high priest could go only once a year on the Day of Atonement. Instead, it was personally drawing near to God.

Some have seen in this concept of nearness not only a spatial nearness, but also a temporal nearness. That is to say, in Christ, the world of spiritual reality had entered time; and in his resurrection and ascension, he carried our humanity into the eternal world, thus breaking down all spatial barriers and enabling us to draw near to God. Moreover, with this achievement, he also brought the end time into being so that he may come at any moment and consummate the kingdom of God.

This was a constant source of hope to early Christians. This priest from the tribe of Judah is the conquering Lion of Judah, who may come as a "thief in the night" (1 Thess. 5:2; cf. Matt. 24:43; Luke 12:39; 2 Pet. 3:10.) He may surprise an indifferent world, just as a thief takes advantage of the element of surprise (cf. Matt. 24:27). The world will behold his coming. Then the wealth and glory of the world will fade before his splendor and the profane, deluded order—saturated in mirth and frivolity, mocking and jeering at the holy ways of God—shall see the sudden destruction that shall come and shall not escape. But to the faithful this word is given: "Blessed are those servants whom the master finds awake when he comes" (Luke 12:37). "And when the chief Shepherd is manifested you will obtain the unfading crown of glory" (1 Peter 5:4).

5. An Eternal Priesthood (7:20–22)

20 And it was not without an oath. 21 Those who formerly became priests took their office without an oath, but this one was addressed with an oath,
"The Lord has sworn
and will not change his mind,
'Thou art a priest for ever.'"
22 This makes Jesus the surety of a better covenant.

The writer brings this long sentence to a close by placing Jesus in an emphatic position (in the Greek), thus stressing his superiority.

6. A Perpetual Priesthood (7:23–25)

23 The former priests were many in number, because they were prevented by death from continuing in office; 24 but he holds his priesthood permanently, because he continues for

ever. **25 Consequently he is able for all time to save those who draw near to God through him, since he always lives to make intercession for them.**

The inferiority of the Levitical priesthood lay in the mortality of the ministering priest, so they *were many in number.* No one could be certain of appearing before the same priest twice. The permanence of the priesthood of Jesus is assured in the truth that *he continues for ever. Consequently he is able for all time to save.* It is his permanence which makes his perpetual saving activity possible.

Those who draw near to God through him. As previously noted, drawing near to God was what vital religion meant to his author. It was a Greek term which described worship in its formal aspect, but it could also mean that pressing forward to the end time, when the pilgrimage of life would end and man would actually stand in the real presence of the High Priest in the heavenly sanctuary. He has already prepared the rest for those who press on to that city. No one need doubt that he shall be welcomed there, for Christ is the High Priest of that city.

Since he always lives to make intercession for them. Here, the preacher tells us what our High Priest does in heaven. He is behind the veil. We cannot see him, but our faith may assure us that he continues forever the unchangeable intercessor. God will never change his mind about this appointment and this purpose (v. 21).

The purpose of his ministry there is to *make intercession.* Does this not lift prayer up to a higher plane? If Christ has no higher work in heaven than to pray for others, what greater work can man do on earth than to pray for others?

Christ carries the blood of humanity into the heavenly sanctuary as a sympathetic High Priest and brings to us a perfect access to God. We can now *draw near.* He supersedes even Michael, whom the Jews believed to be the angelic guardian of Israel. Christ is no mere angel, but a man who shed his blood for men. He is now the one and only mediator of God and man—the man Christ Jesus (cf. 1 Tim. 2:5; Heb. 8:6,9,15; 12:24).

7. The Perfect Priesthood (7:26-28)

26 For it was fitting that we should have such a high priest, holy, blameless, unstained, separated from sinners, exalted above the heavens. 27 He has no need, like those high priests, to offer sacrifices daily, first for his own sins and then for those of the people; he did this once for all when he offered up himself. 28 Indeed, the law appoints men in their weakness as high priests, but the word of the oath, which came later than the law, appoints a Son who has been made perfect for ever.

The perfect adequacy of Christ in his moral qualifications as High Priest is emphasized in *such a high priest*. *Holy* sums up the perfect piety of Jesus including his possession of such virtues as obedience, faith, humility, loyalty, and reverence. *Blameless* denotes his perfect innocence. He not only had no harmful attitudes toward others, he practiced no evil deeds against them. *Unstained* carries the picture of the essential moral goodness of Jesus in contrast with the ceremonial purity of the Levitical priests, who were required to separate themselves from all people for seven days before the Day of Atonement, that no defiling touch might disqualify them to offer a pure sacrifice. In contrast, Jesus was so essentially good that he did not have to be hypersensitive about mingling even with sinners.

These phrases, *separated from sinners, exalted above the heavens,* unite to show that, when Jesus sacrificed himself for the sins of men once for all, he had no further contact with sin in the priestly sense. The only vital contact he ever had with sin was in his perfect resistance of its temptation and in his perfect sacrifice for the sins of others. Now that such a sacrifice has been completed, his work for sinful men is over. He does not have to sacrifice repeatedly as did the Levitical priests. He now resides in a higher sphere, immune to the contagion of human sin.

The chapter lends itself to a sermon of seven points to show how, through this greater High Priest, God offered to man a better hope (7:19). The law made nothing perfect, said the preacher. But this better hope offers us perfect access to God and perpetual cleansing for our sins. Jesus, the High Priest, is greater in seven ways:

(1) He is greater because of his divine appointment (7:14-15). The Levitical priesthood rested on the authority of the law. This priesthood failed, so God appointed a priest out of Judah.

(2) He is greater because of his indestructible life (7:16-19). He was nailed to a cross and then lay silent in the tomb; but not for long, for God reversed the verdict that accounted him worthy of death, raised him up to life, and exalted him to his own right hand.

(3) He is greater because of the oath of God (7:20-21). The oath of God established the priesthood of Christ. In Psalm 110:4 it is written: "The Lord has sworn and will not change his mind, 'You are a priest for ever after the order of Melchizedek.'" This made the priesthood of Christ superior to the Levitical priesthood because no such oath supported it. God's solemn pledge was that the priesthood of Christ would be permanent. It would never pass away as other priesthoods had.

(4) He is greater because his work is based on a better covenant (7:22). The old covenant was the agreement between God and his chosen people described in Exodus 24:1-8. Moses read the law to the people and the people responded by saying: "All that the Lord has spoken we will do, and we will be obedient" (Ex. 24:7). God had promised that, if the people obeyed him, they would always have access to him. The old covenant was based on obedience to the law. Because man could not keep the law, priests were required to make sacrifices for every breach of the law, so that the way of access to God might be kept open.

But the writer of Hebrews said that Jesus was the guarantor of a better covenant, a new kind of agreement between God and man. This new agreement was not based on law and obedience, as was the old. Instead, it was based on love and the perfect sacrifice of Jesus. The new covenant was not based on man's righteousness, but on God's love.

(5) He is greater because his priesthood is perpetual (7:23–24). The Levites were temporary priests because they were subject to death and had to be replaced. Their work was very brief. But since Jesus lives forever, he is able to be a permanent priest.

(6) He is greater because he offers absolute salvation (7:25). He is able to save the worst of sinners and to save them completely. This is possible because his intercession is ever ascending before God in our behalf. He becomes our representative in heaven, lifting up arms of endless intercession. He will not let them down until the last redeemed soul comes home to God. What assurance there is in the truth that every child of God is continually in the prayers of Jesus!

He saves us by the sacrifice of himself and sustains our salvation by his intercession. Salvation is no mechanical transaction. It is the continuous activity of God. Even faith must be sustained by the activity of God.

What do we mean when we say a person is saved? A part of what we mean is associated with danger and peril. Whether salvation has significance for us or not depends upon how real we consider our danger to be and on how seriously we consider our peril.

Do we believe that life separated from God is lost? Do we believe that the person who has lost his guiding light is in danger? The New Testament teaches that such a person is lost and needs to be rescued. He needs to find the white light of God's cleansing power and guiding grace in Christ. To feel clean and to find life's right direction and to be identified with God's attitude and work is to be saved.

(7) He is greater because of his personal qualifications (vv. 26–28). Clear, vi-brant words mark the character of Jesus. He was priest by virtue of his character, not by his lineage. He was one in whom even God could see nothing but purity.

Jesus was a man with nothing but loving-kindness in his heart. There was nothing but good in him, so he could not hurt anyone. He was stainless. No defiling relationship, by which he exploited others, ever disqualified his sacrifice. Jesus was different from sinners in that he never succumbed to temptation. He was made higher than the heavens in the sense that he now dwells above the possibility of defilement. When he was exalted to God's right hand, he was in the realm where God cannot be tempted of evil.

Because of this timeless, undefiled, exalted superiority to all other priests, Jesus had no need to make a sacrifice for his own sins, as the high priest did once a year on the Day of Atonement. Instead, he can offer a sacrifice once for all—a perfect sacrifice—for it is himself which he offers. It is not that this sacrifice is made over and over, but that his presence with God is a perpetual reminder of what was accomplished once for all. Through his perfect and permanent sacrifice, the way of access to God is perfectly and permanently opened for us.

Jesus is the Son made perfect forever. In this emphasis, the Hebrew preacher pulls together the values of two Christologies, which have often been separated in Christian history, and such separation has deprived us of the full meaning of Christ for us.

One Christology majors on the preexistent status of Jesus as the Son of God and tends to play down the reality of his manhood, with all of the gory agony of his suffering. The other Christology is the adoptionist view, which magnifies the superior manhood of Jesus, by which he won his status before God and was, by virtue of his moral achievement, appointed of God as his Son. Our logic says to us that we must choose one or the other, but the Hebrew preacher felt no such compulsion. He chose both and saw them perfectly blended in the economy of God.

The preacher of Hebrews viewed Jesus —while he was on earth, in the days of his flesh—as totally vulnerable to all the temptations that man suffers and endures (2: 14–18). But, since he triumphed over every temptation, he has been made perfect forever and appointed or adopted because of his performance as the Son of God at God's right hand (1:3)

He was, prior to his earthly experience, the preexistent Son of God among heavenly beings. But now his experience on earth has accomplished something even for God which could not have been apart from his suffering. So he has now been given a position, in a kingdom of his own accomplishment, superior to that which he knew in his preexistent status.

As bewildering as this line of thought may appear to our contemporary mind, this uniting of the Christ of preexistence, who had always been, and the Christ of human experience, who accomplished the work of grace by which men draw near to God, is the heart of this writer's thought. This is why the seventh chapter is the most crucial in Hebrews.

This has been brought to light since 1965 with the publication of the Qumran Cave 11 Essene document. This document presents Melchizedek as the dominant figure in the drama of judgment and salvation in the end time. Melchizedek is seen as a heavenly redeemer. The Essenes believed that the end time, when Melchizedek would appear, was near.

Prior to the discovery of this document, chapters 8 and 9 were viewed as the heart of the sermon. It is now possible to see chapter 7 as the pivotal chapter, and what follows is a fuller exposition of what has been mentioned in the earlier chapter.

With this new structure, the Melchizedek after whose priesthood the priesthood of Christ is patterned, but over whom Christ is superior, is clearly seen as the heavenly savior figure in whom the Essenes at Qumran put their trust and around

whom they built their theology.

The Cave 11 document presents the old Jerusalem Zadokite priests as the leaders of the Essene community at Qumran. It appears that they believed themselves to be priests after the order of Melchizedek. This document gives an exposition on passages in Leviticus 24 and Deuteronomy 14, which insist that it would be: "Melchizedek who (6) will bring them back to them and he will proclaim liberty for them to set them free and (to?) make atonement for the sins . . . (8) to make atonement therein for all the children of light and for the men of the lot of Melchizedek." [13]

The Cave 11 document also speaks of Melchizedek as a god or an angelic figure, who will preside at the final assize at the end of days. We have seen previously that this preacher's argument about Christ being superior to angels may have been an answer to those in his congregation who were converted Essenes but who still clung to a kind of angel worship.

Moreover, the Essene belief in the role of angels and Moses and the prophets at the end time has been contradicted, as the preacher insists that Christ alone, who is superior to all, will be the king, the judge, and the priest at the end time.

Could it be that the great temptation of this congregation of early Christians was to escape persecution by identifying with an officially recognized sect—an Essene form of Judaism—by fusing the above mentioned Essene beliefs with the elementary doctrines of their own faith, mentioned in (6:1–5)? If so, we no longer have to wonder why this Hebrew preacher so belabors his argument to prove that Christ alone is the Son of God, King, Judge, and High Priest forever.

VI. The New Tabernacle (8:1–6)

[1] Now the point in what we are saying is this: we have such a high priest, one who is

[13] M. De Jonge and A. S. Van Der Woude, *11Q Melchizedek and the New Testament*, "New Testament Studies," Vol. 12 (London: Cambridge University Press, 1965/66), p. 303.

seated at the right hand of the throne of the Majesty in heaven, 2 a minister in the sanctuary and the true tent which is set up not by man but by the Lord. 3 For every high priest is appointed to offer gifts and sacrifices; hence it is necessary for this priest also to have something to offer. 4 Now if he were on earth, he would not be a priest at all, since there are priests who offer gifts according to the law. 5 They serve a copy and shadow of the heavenly sanctuary; for when Moses was about to erect the tent, he was instructed by God, saying, "See that you make everything according to the pattern which was shown you on the mountain." 6 But as it is, Christ has obtained a ministry which is as much more excellent than the old as the covenant he mediates is better, since it is enacted on better promises.

We are now on the other side of the watershed of chapter 7. This is the beginning of a passage which extends from 8:1 to 10:18 and which has, as its major concern, the description of the kind of work which Christ now does in the heavenly tabernacle. The crucial question is, How can Christ be both the ministering priest of the sacrifice and the sacrifice itself? No one else in the New Testament addresses himself to such a complex question. The Gospel of John has many similarities with Hebrews in its basic theology; but, even there, the writer of the Gospel makes no attempt to harmonize the problem which the writer of Hebrews poses for himself. The uniqueness of this problem has led some scholars, such as James A. Sanders, to contend that the necessity for facing it grew out of some very specific beliefs which had been carried over by some of his hearers from the Essenes. Such scholars contend that it is inconceivable that any writer would have set such a difficult problem for himself had it not been forced upon him by some actual doctrinal position which he was compelled to answer. For example, Yigael Yadin says that the readers expected the resumption of the Mosaic ritual of sacrifices under the direction of an Aaronic high priest at the end. Thus the writer stresses the one-time sacrifice of Jesus in offering up himself.

Chapter 8 falls quite naturally into two parts. The first part is composed of vv. 1–6 and compares the old order of priest-hood and the old earthly tabernacle with the new priesthood of Christ in the heavenly tabernacle. This passage thereby proves the inferiority of both the old priesthood and the old tabernacle. The second part of the chapter, composed of vv. 7–13, is concerned with comparing the new covenant with the old covenant and thus proves the inferiority of the old to the new.

This chapter opens with the positive emphasis on the main point of the preacher's argument that we have an adequate, permanent High Priest, now ministering in an eternal tabernacle of the Lord's own making. The remainder of the chapter is a negative emphasis upon the inadequacy of both the old priesthood and the old tabernacle.

Verse 5 introduces us to familiar battleground for scholars. Here the author appears to call upon the philosophy of Plato to help him establish the inferiority of the old tabernacle. He uses two familiar Platonic words when he calls the old tabernacle a *copy* and a *shadow* of the one in heaven. This is undeniably Platonic language. It cannot, however, be established that Plato was the source of this writer's thought, for one has only to go to Exodus 25—40 to find the writer's thought clearly embedded in the Old Testament. In this passage, Moses is commanded by God to build the tabernacle precisely according to the pattern revealed to him on the mountain.

The appearance of such words as *copy* and *shadow* have tempted some to link this author with Philo of Alexandria, who used the same words, and to insist that our author was a resident of Alexandria. It is now known that these words had been circulated very widely and were a part of the contemporary idiom, even of Palestine, and that the writer was using this to make what the Old Testament had already said more compatible with the language of his time. Platonic thought probably contributed nothing but a vehicle for expressing what was already in the preacher's mind and which had been in the Old Testament many centuries before Philo and Plato.

The terms, *copy* and *shadow*, are used to describe the sanctuary in 8:5; in 9:23 they are used to describe the priestly equipment. In 10:1 "shadow" denotes the content of the law as over against the pattern from which it was copied. The writer never uses those words in any other place. He clinches the argument he is making without using either the word copy or shadow, which shows that he was not a borrower of the content of his argument from either Plato or Philo. For example, in 9:11, instead of using the contrast between copy and pattern, he employs a thoroughly biblical argument when he insists that the heavenly tabernacle was not made with hands. He was emphasizing that it belonged to the order of the Creator and not to the order of creation.

What do you think about when you hear the words, New Testament? Some think of a book which contains a story recorded first in what we call the Old Testament, the story being continued after the intertestamental period.

You may be like a doctor who sat in a service which I conducted in a university church. When I said that war is never anything better than what some consider a necessary evil, he blurted out his objection: "Then what about those wars in the Old Testament in which God commanded his people to slaughter their enemies?" I suggested that the Old Testament is not the same as the New Testament. But he said, "It is the same God in both." "Yes," I replied, "but there was not the same understanding of God." The psalmist who said, "Happy shall he be who takes your little ones [children of his enemies] and dashes them against the rock" (137:9), did not have the same measure of light from God as Jesus, who said: "Love your enemies and pray for those who persecute you" (Matt: 5:44). He taught us that God is not the enemy of our enemies. He is not even the enemy of his enemies. His love goes out toward those who oppose him

most. But the point is that there are those who think of the New Testament merely as a continuation of the Old. They would see in both the common word, Testament.

If you should ask another person what he thought of when he saw the words, New Testament, he would probably underline the word New and see no continuity whatsoever. He is one who wants to doubt everything that is old. He never has realized that, if man could really accomplish what Descartes appealed for in radical doubt—that is, if it were possible for man to doubt everything—he would be reduced to imbecility.

Lesslie Newbigin said:

A rock climber makes progress by letting go a handhold or a foothold one at a time while he searches for a new grip. While he does so his whole attention is on the hand or foot which is groping for a new hold, but in fact he depends upon the other three holds to which for the moment he is paying no heed. If he were to try to let go of them all together, he would be lost. Just so the processes of doubting and rethinking by which we advance in understanding depend upon beliefs which for the moment we do not doubt but simply take for granted.[14]

Even so, to repudiate all man's religious past is self-destructive nihilism.

Would it not be wiser to put the emphasis neither on the words Old or New, but upon the word Testament, and ask, What does it mean? It means a covenant which God made with his people simply because men cannot be united unless they share some common bond. The bond that bound God's people with God and with one another was the covenant.

Our age has been secularized because the new unification of man is not on a common religion nor even in a common ideology, but on a shared secular terror and a shared secular hope. The shared secular terror is enough to unite us in despair. The

[14] From *Honest Religion for Secular Man*, by Lesslie Newbigin. Published in the U.S.A. 1966, by The Westminster Press. © SCM Press, Ltd., 1966. Used by permission.

shared secular hope is not enough to unite us in hope.

VII. The New Covenant (8:7—9:28)

1. Inward and Effective (8:7-13)

7 For if that first covenant had been faultless, there would have been no occasion for a second.

8 For he finds fault with them when he says:
"The days will come, says the Lord,
  when I will establish a new covenant with
    the house of Israel
  and with the house of Judah;
9 not like the covenant that I made with their
    fathers
  on the day when I took them by the hand
  to lead them out of the land of Egypt;
  for they did not continue in my covenant,
  and so I paid no heed to them, says the
    Lord.
10 This is the covenant that I will make with
    the house of Israel
  after those days, says the Lord:
  I will put my laws into their minds,
  and write them on their hearts,
  and I will be their God,
  and they shall be my people.
11 And they shall not teach every one his fellow
  or every one his brother, saying, 'Know the
    Lord,'
  for all shall know me,
  from the least of them to the greatest.
12 For I will be merciful toward their iniquities,
  and I will remember their sins no more."
13 In speaking of a new covenant he treats the first as obsolete. And what is becoming obsolete and growing old is ready to vanish away.

What can unify us in hope if not the new covenant of God? Look at what it promises: It promises that God will take the initiative. Notice the repeated emphasis on the personal initiative of God: the personal promise of God: *I will establish a new covenant . . . I will put my laws into their minds, and write them on their hearts, . . . I will be their God, . . . I will be merciful . . . I will remember their sins no more.* This is a God who promises to blot our sins out of his memory and give us a new beginning. Not that he looks lightly upon sin. A church that has no serious view of sin has no serious sense of mission. The hope is that God looks compas-sionately on the sinful plight of his people.

The old covenant was based upon the obedience of man to the law of God. The new is based on the realization that never has there been a man who could perfectly obey the law of God. So the new covenant was based upon the grace of God and upon the perfect sacrifice of Christ, who covers man's transgressions forever and draws him back to receive the forgiveness of God and restores his hope that, one day, he shall awake in the likeness of his God, in whose image he was created. That image has been fatally flawed by himself and by his society, and only God can restore it.

Verses 7-13 are really the delineation of the "better promises" (8:6) on which the new covenant is enacted. The Hebrews preacher is impressed with the truth that even the old covenant itself promises a new covenant. With the exception of vv. 7 and 13, this entire passage is a quotation from Jeremiah 31:31-34, which is the uppermost reach of Old Testament prophecy and the greatest anticipation of the saving work of Christ. The new covenant has Christ as its mediator, just as Moses was the mediator of the old covenant. The writer sees this new covenant as "more excellent" than the old because it is underwritten or legally secured by "better promises" (8:6). This security is Christ himself for, in 7:22, Jesus is called the "guarantor" (NEB) of a better covenant.

This passage (Jer. 31:31-34) was often used by Paul (cf. 2 Cor. 3:6; Gal. 4:24; Eph. 2:12). Jesus mentioned it in Matthew, Mark, and Luke. The word *covenant* is used more than 30 times in the New Testament. A covenant is a pact between persons, as the covenant between David and Jonathan. Genesis 6:18 and 17:2 are examples of a covenant between God and men.

When Abraham went out of Ur of the Chaldees at God's command, God bound his people to him in a great covenant. He demonstrated his keeping power when he intervened in Egypt to break the power of the Pharaoh, to liberate his people from bondage, and to bring them out of a land flowing with milk and honey. Then came the prosperous days of the kingdom and, later on, the corruption of idolatry, the perversion of justice, and the mockery of empty worship. The people went after strange gods. Divine judgment fell, the old covenant was broken, and captivity came.

The prophets of the Old Testament recognized that a wholesome religious order must provide three things: a moral standard to challenge the will, a divine fellowship to satisfy the spirit, and an inward cleansing to soothe the conscience. The old covenant partially met these needs. It met the need for a moral standard by providing the law. It met the need for fellowship with God by providing the priesthood which would speak to God for man. It met the need for the cleansing of the conscience by an annual Day of Atonement.

The problem was that these did not work, for man continued to sin. The law failed to keep him from sinning. So also did the priesthood and the Day of Atonement. They were shadows without substance. Only the substantial sin-breaker, Christ himself, could cancel the power of sin and cleanse the conscience forever.

So the word of the Lord came to Jeremiah promising a new covenant and assuring him that God would do a better thing for man. Jeremiah showed the people that ancestral religion was not enough, Sinai was not enough, animal sacrifices were not enough. In the grace of God a new covenant was provided. Some passages which look forward to a new covenant to supersede the old are not only Jeremiah 31:31–34, but also Ezekiel 36:25–26 and Isaiah 59:21.

The new covenant would be a permanent covenant. Notice the personal quality of this covenant presented in the first-person singular pronoun: God said, "I will establish a new covenant." "I will put my laws into their minds." "I will be their God." "I will be merciful toward their iniquities." "I will remember their sins no

more." The three outstanding features which mark this new covenant are inwardness, immediacy, and the initiative of God.

(1) *I will put my laws into their minds, and write them on their hearts.* The inwardness or internal nature of the new covenant is seen in the fact that the law was no longer recorded on tables of stone but on the fleshly tablets of the heart. Does this not mean that, by the entrance of Christ into a person by his Spirit, he guides him into the knowledge of the truth? It is his voice that now whispers, "This is the way, walk in it" (Isa. 30:21).

(2) *And they shall not teach every one his fellow.* This second characteristic, the immediacy of the new covenant, means that no longer are we dependent upon a body of traditional testimony for our religious guidance. Another interpretation of v. 11 might be, "No man shall say to his neighbor or to his brother, know the Lord; for everyone shall know me, from the least of them to the greatest." It is the privilege of those who come under the new covenant to have a knowledge of God which is not confined to hearsay or to the testimony of others. This knowledge grows out of the personal communion of the soul with God. To know God is not simply to have a book of information about him, but to have a personal relationship with God that grows out of obedience to him. God's greatest concern is not to impart information about himself to satisfy our speculative curiosity. He is interested in building a kingdom of right relationships between people. He gives himself to those who obey him. This obedience brings a vital, immediate knowledge of God himself, which is infinitely better than a knowledge of facts about him.

(3) Finally, there is the divine initiative in the forgiveness of sin: *I will remember their sins no more.* Here is permanent forgiveness. Under the old covenant, man would offer his sacrifice, but the very next moment he would have an uneasy feeling of anxiety, for he would wonder if he had committed a new sin for which he must make an additional sacrifice. He would be

bowed down almost constantly by the burden of guilt.

In the Saviour there is personal, permanent, and perpetual forgiveness from God, who promises to remember our sins no more. This is seen in Jesus' attitude of love, in his teaching of forgiveness, and in his tremendous respect for people. He loved people, not because of what they owned, not because of what they had achieved, not even because of what they were in a moral sense. He loved them because they were people. If they had failed in everything they undertook, if they had broken every commandment and had lost their conscious communion with God, they were still people; therefore he loved them. He refused to measure values in terms of moral achievements.

When Christ personally forgives, he causes us to be personally forgiving. The only way we can know that we have been forgiven is that we are now forgiving toward others. Is there anything more healing than forgiveness? Because we have a much greater covenant, we are constrained to be that much more loyal to our God who has, in the life of Jesus, provided a moral standard to challenge our wills. He has also provided a continual personal fellowship to nurture our spirits, and a permanent cleansing to put our consciences to rest.

This passage from Jeremiah was of paramount importance to the Essenes at Qumran. It was emphasized in their scriptures. They believed, as did the Christians who came after them, that God had made them the new Israel—the elect within the elect. They called themselves "a holy house for Israel," and "a most holy assembly for Aaron." They felt that they were ordained to make atonement for the guilt, rebellion, and sinful disloyalty apart from the burnt offering and the fat of sacrifices and thus to obtain favor for the land. But the point of variance between the Essene theology and that of the writer of Hebrews is that the Essenes believed that the necessity of sacrifice was suspended only temporarily. Their great hope was that, at the end of

the age, God would drive the Hasmonean priesthood out of Jerusalem and reinstate them, for they regarded themselves as the true heirs of David's priest, Zadok.

The Hebrew preacher had a much more radical doctrine. To him the new covenant meant that all sacrifices were put away forever, because Christ, in his suffering and death, offered a perfect sacrifice once for all. It may very well be that one reason the Hebrew preacher lays such heavy emphasis upon this new covenant is to counter the Essene concept of their own new covenant.

2. Place of the Old Covenant (9:1-28)

The new covenant tells us that vital worship is standing in the presence of God with all our defenses down, in order to experience communion with God. Worship is a feeling of amazement and unworthiness, and, at times, it is an attempt to probe a mystery and to understand what God did for us in Christ.

The preacher of the Hebrews sought to tell his congregation what Christ meant to them by using all the priestly paraphernalia of the ancient tabernacle as symbols which were fulfilled in Christ. He sees Christ as the one in whom God and man became one. He gives strong emphasis to the humanity of Jesus but also to his divinity. Consider three reasons for his stressing the essential deity of Christ:

(1) The first is because there is a veil which only God can remove (cf. 6:19; 9:3; 10:20). This veil hangs like a polluted smog between this world of shadows and the bright world of ultimate reality where God dwells. By his coming into the world, Christ shattered that veil and brought the shining light of God's presence to man. In his face we see the light of the knowledge of the divine glory.

(2) Second, he stressed the divinity of Christ because he saw a sin which only God could forgive. If sin is only against man, then man can forgive it; but if it is against God, then only God can forgive it. No priest or ritual can do anything more

than to announce or symbolize the terms by which God forgives sin. Jesus does more than forgive. He puts sin away (9:26). He cleanses us from "dead works" (9:14), the deeds that bring death, and he brings the renewal of life.

(3) Finally, there is a city which only God can build (cf. 11:10,16; 12:22; 13:14). "You have come to Mount Zion and to the city of the living God" (12:22). The city of God is built on the foundation of the truth that Jesus came forth from God. "He has prepared for them a city" (11:16) means that the solid reality of the unseen world is no dream of bards and seers and heroes of the faith, but a reality now in existence, built by Christ.

(1) Ark of the Covenant (9:1–5)

¹ Now even the first covenant had regulations for worship and an earthly sanctuary. ² For a tent was prepared, the outer one, in which were the lampstand and the table and the bread of the Presence; it is called the Holy Place. ³ Behind the second curtain stood a tent called the Holy of Holies, ⁴ having the golden altar of incense and the ark of the covenant covered on all sides with gold, which contained a golden urn holding the manna, and Aaron's rod that budded, and the tables of the covenant; ⁵ above it were the cherubim of glory overshadowing the mercy seat. Of these things we cannot now speak in detail.

In the ninth chapter of Hebrews, the preacher presupposes that his hearers are thoroughly familiar with the forms of worship practiced in the tabernacle. Since we cannot make such a claim for a modern congregation, we do well to go back and familiarize ourselves with a description of the primitive place of worship, which was built according to the pattern which God gave Moses on the mountain.

There was, first, the court of the tabernacle, which was 150 feet long and 75 feet wide. It was covered with a curtain of white linen, symbolizing the wall of holiness that surrounded the presence of God. In this court stood the altar of acacia wood sheathed in brass. On that altar the sacrifice was laid. There also stood a laver where the priests cleansed themselves before performing their sacred duties.

Within the court stood the tabernacle. The tabernacle proper was composed of the holy place, covering two-thirds of the whole; and the holy of holies, covering one-third of the whole. A veil of fine linen —colored blue, purple, and scarlet— separated the holy of holies from the holy place. Only the priests could stand in the holy place, and only the high priest could stand in the holy of holies; and he could go there only once a year, on the great Day of Atonement.

In the holy place there were three items: (1) the golden lampstand, fueled with pure olive oil, which was always burning; (2) the table of shewbread, with 12 loaves of bread, which were changed every sabbath; (3) the altar of incense, with its sweet savor rising morning and evening, symbolizing the prayers of the people going up before God.[15]

Within the holy of holies stood the ark of the covenant containing the golden pot of manna, Aaron's rod that budded, and the two tables of stone containing the law and the covenant which God had made with Moses. The lid of the ark was called the mercy seat. On the mercy seat, made of solid gold, stood two cherubim with overarching wings (Ex. 25:22). Each of these appurtenances in the Temple has been used as a type of some greater reality to be realized in Christ.

Look now at the ark of the covenant. In this ark reposed the most sacred mememtos of God's dealings with his people. So sacred were these that no man dared touch the ark.

(1) First, there was within the ark the golden pot of manna, recalling the miraculous provision of God for his people in the wilderness (Ex. 16:32–34).

Israel must never forget that it was God who, out of his bounty, provided their

---

[15] Cf. James Moffatt, pp. 114–115, for a full discussion on the controversy over the actual location of the altar of incense.

bread. Christ likened himself to that bread (John 6:33–35). It is this which has caused the Christian church to sing with Reginald Heber:

"Bread of the world, in mercy broken,
    Wine of the soul, in mercy shed,
By whom the words of life were spoken,
    And in whose death our sins are dead.
And be Thy feast to us the token
    That by Thy grace our souls are fed"

(2) The second item in the ark of the covenant was the rod of Aaron, which recalled another wondrous intervention of God on behalf of his people (cf. Num. 16:21–17:11). The people of Israel had murmured against Moses and Aaron, making the incredible charge: "You have killed the people of the Lord" (Num. 16:41). The wrath of heaven fell, and such a plague spread through the congregation that 14,700 died and Aaron made an atonement and "stood between the dead and the living; and the plague was stopped" (vv. 47–48). Then the Lord commanded Moses that 12 rods, one for each of the heads of the house of their fathers, should be brought to the tabernacle. The one that God chose would blossom. On the morrow, Aaron's rod blossomed. This was the sign that God had chosen Aaron. "And the Lord said to Moses, 'Put back the rod of Aaron before the testimony, to be kept as a sign for the rebels, that you may make an end of their murmurings against me, lest they die' " (Num. 17:10).

This ark of the covenant then reminded the worshipers of the priest who must be respected and who alone could remove the plague of death. Christ, who now stands as the great High Priest forever in the heavenly sanctuary, is one who delivers us from murmuring against God, which brings death.

(3) The third object in the ark of the covenant was the law of Moses and the covenant of God based thereon. Christ now stands with the new and better covenant, based on his grace and his perfect sacrifice.

(2) A System of Exclusion (9:6–10)

⁶ These preparations having thus been made, the priests go continually into the outer tent, performing their ritual duties; ⁷ but into the second only the high priest goes, and he but once a year, and not without taking blood which he offers for himself and for the errors of the people. ⁸ By this the Holy Spirit indicates that the way into the sanctuary is not yet opened as long as the outer tent is still standing ⁹ (which is symbolic for the present age). According to this arrangement, gifts and sacrifices are offered which cannot perfect the conscience of the worshiper, ¹⁰ but deal only with food and drink and various ablutions, regulations for the body imposed until the time of reformation.

The common man could come only to the gate of the tabernacle and stand in wonder before its mystery and majesty. He could not personally draw near to God. For all of its magnificence, the preacher to the Hebrews still called the tabernacle a shadow of the divine realities (8:5). He said that Christ had provided a greater and more perfect tabernacle "not made with hands" (9:11). In Christ there would be open access for all to draw near to God (10:22).

(3) A Superior Tabernacle (9:11)

¹¹ But when Christ appeared as a high priest of the good things that have come, then through the greater and more perfect tent (not made with hands, that is, not of this creation)

But when Christ appeared carries the idea of a dramatic arrival on the scene of the great High Priest, who changed everything. To arrive in the very presence of God, he had to pass through the upper heavens, not through a man-made court *made with hands.*

The good things that have come relate to Christ's present priesthood. Christ is our true tabernacle. He is the very presence of God. Ultimately all that matters in life is God, oneself, and one's neighbor in close personal, proper relationship. No cultic or credal point is permanently important— only relationships.

(4) A Superior Sacrifice (9:12–23)

12 he entered once for all into the Holy Place, taking not the blood of goats and calves but his own blood, thus securing an eternal redemption. 13 For if the sprinkling of defiled persons with the blood of goats and bulls and with the ashes of a heifer sanctifies for the purification of the flesh, 14 how much more shall the blood of Christ, who through the eternal Spirit offered himself without blemish to God, purify your conscience from dead works to serve the living God.

15 Therefore he is the mediator of a new covenant, so that those who are called may receive the promised eternal inheritance, since a death has occurred which redeems them from the transgressions under the first covenant. 16 For where a will is involved, the death of the one who made it must be established. 17 For a will takes effect only at death, since it is not in force as long as the one who made it is alive. 18 Hence even the first covenant was not ratified without blood. 19 For when every commandment of the law had been declared by Moses to all the people, he took the blood of calves and goats, with water and scarlet wool and hyssop, and sprinkled both the book itself and all the people, 20 saying, "This is the blood of the covenant which God commanded you." 21 And in the same way he sprinkled with the blood both the tent and all the vessels used in worship. 22 Indeed, under the law almost everything is purified with blood, and without the shedding of blood there is no forgiveness of sins.

23 Thus it was necessary for the copies of the heavenly things to be purified with these rites, but the heavenly things themselves with better sacrifices than these.

Two things made Jesus' absolute sacrifice superior to the sacrifices of ancient Israel. First, it was *his own blood* which was offered. It was his own life. As the life of God is infinitely superior to that of animals, so is the sacrifice which Jesus offered infinitely superior to the sacrifice of animals. There was finality in his sacrifice (9:25–26). It was once for all (9:26). Second, it offered eternal redemption (9:28).

Behind the Jewish sacrifice for sin lay the authoritative axiom: *"Without the shedding of blood there is no forgiveness of sins."* For all of our modern knowledge of chemistry in this scientific age, we still stand appalled before the mystery of the

blood. Imagine then how awesome was the feeling of primitive man when he stood in the presence of blood. The blood carried the mysterious substance by which God brought life into being. They said that life is in the blood. A part of the power of God lay in the blood. To offer blood was to offer the ultimate gift of life itself. The sacrifice was not a superstitious, magical ritual, but the offering of the best that man knew to his God when he offered blood. Blood was precious, for when the blood was shed, life was gone.

Peter said: "You know that you were ransomed from the futile ways inherited from your fathers, not with perishable things such as silver or gold, but with the precious blood of Christ, like that of a lamb without blemish or spot" (1 Peter 1:18–19).

The shedding of blood denoted the seriousness of sin and the great difficulty with which sin was forgiven. It was not God's anger which was abated by the offering of blood. Instead, it was God's own perfect love that made sin so difficult to forgive. The more you love, the harder it is for you to forgive the people who harm those you love.

Even so, God cannot easily forgive our sins. An easy forgiveness is not forgiveness at all, for it does not see the seriousness of the sin which causes others to suffer. For God to forgive, he must not only love, he must maintain his moral integrity. He must be "wounded for our transgressions" (Isa. 53:5). He must feel deeply and suffer. This God did in the superior sacrifice he offered for our sins in his only begotten Son.

How much more shall the blood of Christ, who through the eternal Spirit offered himself without blemish to God, purify your conscience from dead works to serve the living God. The ancient ritual had one major flaw. It did not cleanse from sin that was committed with a presumptuous heart and a high hand. The ritual could cleanse a man's body and, at the same time, leave his heart black with brooding and anxiety. It did not lift the load of guilt from his conscience. It left the sinner depressed and exhausted. Jesus' sacrifice is superior.

The contrast is between the outward pollution, which comes from touching dead bodies, and the inward pollution, which comes from dead works. Ceremonial cleansing may cleanse the former, but only the redeeming energy in the blood of Christ can cleanse one from dead works. With the cleansing of the conscience, the worshiper may then draw near to worship and serve God.

To the writer, worship was supremely important. For him the sole purpose of religion was to gain access to God. Forgiveness was essential to that access. Therefore, he saw the forgiveness, which Christ made possible through his blood, as the opening up of the road of access to God.

When Christ forgives, our energy is no longer drained off by carrying an enormous burden of past guilt. With forgiveness there comes renewal and a fresh burst of energy which comes from our nearness to God. With this energy, we may serve by doing God's work of lifting burdens from the heart of humanity. Isaiah knew this long ago when he wrote: "Trust in the Lord for ever, for the Lord God is an everlasting rock" (26:4). The purpose of true religion is *to serve the living God.* Christ not only purifies for service, he also empowers us for it.

There is one emphasis which we must not overlook, the reference to *the eternal Spirit.* It was by virtue of the third person of the Trinity that Jesus was enabled to walk without spot or *blemish* through this world, and it was by virtue of the Spirit's power that he arose from the dead. Through that same Spirit, Christ cleanses us and empowers us *to serve the living God.*

Since a death has occurred means that a sacrifice involving death is essential to put the testator's will in force. How could the will of the living Jesus be in force? It was because he once had died. His death had retroactive power, cleansing the ac-cumulated offenses of the past.

The author never works out a rationale of sacrifice. He does not ask why this was necessary. *Which God commanded you* was all the reason he needed.

But the heavenly things themselves with better sacrifices than these indicates that nobler sacrifices than those used for the cleansing of the earthly tabernacle must cleanse the heavenly sanctuary.

How could heaven itself require cleansing? James Moffatt suggests that the constant work of forgiving sinners in the heavenly tabernacle "rendered even that in some sense defiled" (p. 132). The cosmic power of sin to defile must never be taken lightly. Is this what the Revelator meant when he said: "But nothing unclean shall enter it, nor any one who practices abomination or falsehood, but only those who are written in the Lamb's book of life" (21:27)? Whatever cleansing was required was adequately accomplished in the sacrifice of Jesus.

(5) *The Superior Hope (9:24–28)*

24 For Christ has entered, not into a sanctuary made with hands, a copy of the true one, but into heaven itself, now to appear in the presence of God on our behalf. 25 Nor was it to offer himself repeatedly, as the high priest enters the Holy Place yearly with blood not his own; 26 for then he would have had to suffer repeatedly since the foundation of the world. But as it is, he has appeared once for all at the end of the age to put away sin by the sacrifice of himself. 27 And just as it is appointed for men to die once, and after that comes judgment, 28 so Christ, having been offered once to bear the sins of many, will appear a second time, not to deal with sin but to save those who are eagerly waiting for him.

Our High Priest, who has entered into the heavenly tabernacle, will come again for his own. He wants his people to be ready for his coming. Christ's people are to live under the awareness that they must one day give an accounting to God. After death there is the reality of judgment. For those who are ready, the Judge is also the Saviour. The early church never forgot that, beyond death, every man has a rendezvous with God. For the enemies of God, this thought is full of terror. For the friends of God, it is full of hope for his appearance will mean salvation.

Christ, having been offered once to bear the sins of many, will appear a second time. Much has been made by those who would "demythologize" the gospel of the argument that the actual words, "second coming of Christ," do not appear on the pages of the New Testament. Still, what the preacher of Hebrews says is that Christ will appear the second time.

Few things were more exciting to us in our childhood than the approaching event which was announced with the words, "Christmas is coming!" There was a similar delirious kind of ecstasy among the early Christians as they whispered with breathless wonder, "The Lord is coming!" Despite the delay, this hope did not die. At the end of the New Testament (after at least 60 years had passed between the time Christ made his promise and the vision of John on Patmos) the entire Christian story came to a close with the promise of Jesus: "I am coming soon" (Rev. 22:20). All the desires of the Christian community were concentrated in one prayer: "Come, Lord Jesus!"

A careful look at the New Testament leaves us with the unshakable assurance that the early Christian community was carried forward by what has come to be called the blessed hope of the return of Jesus. There is widespread disagreement about what this meant, but there is little disagreement that it was an integral part of the faith of the first followers of Jesus.

In one of the most sophisticated, contemporary Bible dictionaries, under the subject of "Parousia," the writer says: "In general the New Testament writers expected an imminent, dramatic, visible return of Christ to usher in the New Age." [16] He asserts that, while twentieth-century Christendom has no definite pattern of interpretation of this event: "It may be as-

sumed, however, that the main line of the Christian tradition will interpret the Parousia to mean, at least, that God will bring to perfect completion the work begun through Christ, and that the same Christ who stands at the center of Christian faith will also stand at the final boundary of human experience in time, in space, and in eternity."

The Christ still has not been divested of his royal dignity as King of angels and King of the ages. So it was that the Hebrew preacher saw him as one who "appeared as a high priest of the good things that have come" (9:11). These good things include: (1) the "greater . . . tent [tabernacle] (not made with hands)" (9:11); (2) his own blood (9:21–22) which secures eternal redemption through the eternal Spirit (9:14); (3) a purified conscience (9:14); (4) the mediator of a new covenant (9:15); (5) The promised eternal inheritance (9:15).

The same one he sees appearing a second time, *to put away sin by the sacrifice of himself. . . . will appear a second time, not to deal with sin but to save those who are eagerly waiting for him.*

After that grim procession wound its way up a hill called "Calvary," and the Son of man laid down his life in unrelieved agony, the world saw him no more. But those who believed in him saw him. To them he manifested himself for 40 days, showing himself alive by many infallible proofs (Acts 1:3). At the end of that time, he ascended into heaven and they saw him no more. But theirs was not a mood of grief and despair. Instead, they "were continually in the temple blessing God" (Luke 24:53). What was the secret of their joy? It was their belief in him and in his promise to return to them (cf. John 14:3; Matt. 16:27; 25:13; 26:64). When the disciples met one another on the street, their word of greeting was "Maranatha!" ("Our Lord, come!").

This hope kept them on their guard against sin, sustained them in their sorrows, and undergirded them in their conflict with

16 H. K. McArthur, "Parousia," IDB, Vol. K-Q (Nashville: Abingdon Press, 1962), p. 659.

an evil world. It was the lamp shining for them in the darkened world until the morning star, their Lord and Saviour, should appear.

Has the church forgotten this? Not entirely. We never pray the Lord's prayer without praying, "Thy kingdom come" (Luke 11:2), which is an appeal for the coming of the King. We never celebrate the Lord's Supper without saying, "For as often as you eat this bread and drink the cup, you proclaim the Lord's death until he comes" (1 Cor. 11:26).

Our sin is not that we do not mention the Lord's return. Our sin is that we mention it but do not deeply believe it. For if we believed it as we should, we would put it in the forefront of our Christian proclamation: "Awaiting our blessed hope, the appearing of the glory of our great God and Savior Jesus Christ" (Titus 2:13). This was the unyielding hope of early Christians.

That Christ will return is said more frequently in the New Testament than anything else about him. His coming is mentioned some 500 times. It is spoken of as a visible, personal coming for "every eye will see him" (Rev. 1:7). It is to be a sudden coming, like "as the lightning comes from the east and shines as far as the west" (Matt. 24:27). It is to be an unexpected coming. Men will not believe in it, just as they refused to believe in the flood in Noah's day. It is to be an unpredictable coming, as a thief in the night (1 Thess. 5:2) and as the bridegroom who came while the virgins slept (Matt. 25:1–13).

There were scoffers in the days of Peter who asked: "Where is the promise of his coming? For ever since the fathers fell asleep, all things have continued as they were from the beginning of creation" (2 Peter 3:4). To them it was unthinkable that the continuity of history should ever be broken by such an apocalyptic intervention as the coming of Christ. Peter's answer was that the world had a beginning and it will have an ending and the ending will be in the same hands as was the beginning. "Blessed are those servants whom the master finds awake when he comes" (Luke 12:37). That word "blessed" describes the mood of those who cling to the blessed hope.

One of the grandest of the Puritan preachers was Richard Baxter. In his *Saints' Everlasting Rest,* he takes those golden words of Jesus and makes them live one by one. You have heard them sung to the music which deeply moves the soul: "Come, O blessed of my Father, inherit the kingdom prepared for you from the foundation of the world" (Matt. 25:34). It is easy for us to so accentuate the passages which come afterward as a panacea for our social ills and to lose the grandeur of the opening promise. "Come," says our Lord at the end of days. His golden scepter is extended, indicating that we are welcome. We have once approached his throne of grace. Now we may approach his throne of glory.

VIII. The Ultimate Will of God (10:1–39)

This chapter may be divided into six parts: Verses 1–6 describe the failure of the law to make perfect people. Verses 5–10 describe the ultimate will of God in terms of the one who took a body and, through moral obedience, did the will of God. Verses 11–18 describe the final forgiveness which puts away sin and makes a sin offering no longer necessary. Verses 19–25 contain words of invitation to draw near to God, which is what religion is all about. Verses 26–31 contain a solemn warning concerning the punishment of those who deliberately sin after receiving a knowledge of the truth. Verses 32–39 bring the chapter to a close with words of encouragement to hold on just a little longer and not throw away the reward which will soon be granted at the judgment.

1. The Failure of the Law (10:1–4)

¹ For since the law has but a shadow of the good things to come instead of the true form of these realities, it can never, by the same sacrifices which are continually offered year after year, make perfect those who draw near. ² Otherwise, would they not have ceased to be

offered? If the worshipers had once been cleansed, they would no longer have any consciousness of sin. ³ But in these sacrifices there is a reminder of sin year after year. ⁴ For it is impossible that the blood of bulls and goats should take away sins.

For since the law has but a shadow indicates its inadequacy. A shadow may intimate an approaching presence, but it has no substance of itself. It cannot, therefore, do the work which God intended in the perfecting of his people. *The good things to come* arrived in Christ who gave substance to God's promise.

It can never . . . make perfect those who draw near. Here the preacher gives his final evaluation of the Levitical cultus. The reason the law cannot make people perfect is because *it is impossible that the blood of bulls and goats should take away sins.*

Otherwise, would they not have ceased to be offered? Three things prove the inadequacy of the old system: (1) their constant repetition of sacrifices showed that their effect was only temporary; (2) the fact that the consciousness of sin remained proved the cleansing was imperfect; (3) the old sacrifices were continual reminders of guilt, when God desired that even the memory of sin should be forgotten (10:17).

The writer dwells on the defectiveness of the Old Testament system by stressing one verb in v. 4, translated *to take away* sins. This verb is never used anywhere else in the New Testament. However, the implicit purpose of Christ's work is stated as "the putting away of sin" (9:26).

2. The Final Sacrifice (10:5–10)

⁵ Consequently, when Christ came into the world, he said,
"Sacrifices and offerings thou hast not desired,
but a body hast thou prepared for me;
⁶ in burnt offerings and sin offerings thou hast taken no pleasure.
⁷ Then I said, 'Lo, I have come to do thy will, O God,'
as it is written of me in the roll of the book."
⁸ When he said above, "Thou hast neither desired nor taken pleasure in sacrifices and offerings and burnt offerings and sin offerings"

(these are offered according to the law), ⁹ then he added, "Lo, I have come to do thy will." He abolishes the first in order to establish the second. ¹⁰ And by that will we have been sanctified through the offering of the body of Jesus Christ once for all.

Consequently means the inadequacy of animal sacrifices made the new sacrifice—the self-sacrifice of Jesus—necessary.

When Christ came into the world, he said. In vv. 5–7 the preacher puts Psalm 40:7–9 on the lips of Christ. The point of the psalmist is that God had given him "an open ear" (Psalm 40:6) to hear that what God delights in is not sin offerings but in the doing of his will.

But a body means that, in order to do God's will, it was necessary for Christ to have a body. What the law could not accomplish was accomplished in the single self-sacrifice of Christ which required a body. For him to practice willful obedience to God, a body was required. For this willful obedience put his sacrifice infinitely above all animal sacrifice in which animals had no choice as to their destiny.

Lo, I have come to do thy will, O God. The will of God, in this instance, was that Christ should die for the sins of men and thus establish a new covenant. Does this indicate that what Jesus did at Golgotha was to gather up "from the foundation of the world" (9:26) what God has always been—one whose way is the way of self-sacrifice over against our way of self-destruction through self-assertion? "Christ did not come into the world to be a good man; it was not for this that a body was prepared for him. He came to be a great high priest, and the body was prepared for him that by the offering of it he might put sinful men forever into the perfect religious relation to God." ¹⁷

He abolishes the first in order to establish the second. Jesus came into the world fully aware of the inadequacy of animal sacrifices to put away sin. He came willing to give himself for the sins of men and thus

---

¹⁷ James Denney, *The Death of Christ* (New York: George H. Doran Company, 1907), p. 234.

to bring them near to God (2:10). What the law failed to do, Christ did by suffering once for all in his body. He abolished temporary sacrifices and established an eternal sacrifice.

3. The Final Forgiveness (10:11–18)

11 And every priest stands daily at his service, offering repeatedly the same sacrifices, which can never take away sins. 12 But when Christ had offered for all time a single sacrifice for sins, he sat down at the right hand of God, 13 then to wait until his enemies should be made a stool for his feet. 14 For by a single offering he has perfected for all time those who are sanctified. 15 And the Holy Spirit also bears witness to us; for after saying,
16 "This is the covenant that I will make with them
    after those days, says the Lord:
    I will put my laws on their hearts,
    and write them on their minds,"
17 then he adds,
    "I will remember their sins and their misdeeds no more."
18 Where there is forgiveness of these, there is no longer any offering for sin.

And every priest stands daily at his service. The futility of the old process for cleansing sin is seen in a repetition of a ceremony which can never do what the new covenant can do—*take away sins.*

But when Christ had offered the finality of Christ's offering is underscored in three phrases: (1) *Christ had offered for all time,* being of the order of eternity. What he did had eternal consequences. (2) *A single sacrifice* emphasizes the uniqueness of what Christ did. It need never be repeated. (3) *He sat down at the right hand of God.* His sacrificial work is ended. He can behold its saving efficacy forever. There is nothing more he can do, nor is there any more he need do in opening up the way of access to God.

Then to wait indicates that it is as if the preacher is saying that Christ sits, saying to himself with perfect assurance, "Now, let it work!" Here the preacher quotes from his favorite psalm (110:1). In this God promises to bring all foes into submission to him. Christ had now completed all that is necessary for his ultimate triumph. He can now confidently await the time when this shall happen.

Verse 14 reiterates the qualities discussed above. *By a single offering he has perfected for all time those who are sanctified. The Holy Spirit also bears witness to us.* Now the Holy Spirit bears the assurance that the promises of the new covenant have been fulfilled. Verse 18 sums up the Christian truth: *Where there is forgiveness of these, there is no longer any offering for sin.* God now forgives sin on the basis of the sacrifice of Christ. No more sacrifice for sin is necessary.

Thus far, chapter 10 has described our Lord's perfect offering for sin. The writer has told us that the Old Testament law was only a shadow of the reality that came into our world in Jesus (10:1). The sacrifice of Christ is as superior to the Old Testament system as the substance is to the shadow; just as superior as the blood of Christ is to the blood of bulls and goats; just as superior as the spiritual world is to the material world; just as superior as eternity is to time.

No shadow could ever remove humanity's massive burden of guilt. Nothing less than the intervention of the living God himself could do this. So Christ came saying, "Lo, I have come to do thy will" (10:9). Great as human guilt is, the living God in Christ is greater.

Now, because of all that God had done for man in Christ, the writer of Hebrews laid down this magnanimous, comprehensive invitation.

4. The Invitation (10:19–25)

19 Therefore, brethren, since we have confidence to enter the sanctuary by the blood of Jesus, 20 by the new and living way which he opened for us through the curtain, that is, through his flesh, 21 and since we have a great priest over the house of God, 22 let us draw near with a true heart in full assurance of faith, with our hearts sprinkled clean from an evil conscience and our bodies washed with pure water. 23 Let us hold fast the confession of our hope without wavering, for he who promised is faithful; 24 and let us consider how to stir up one another to love and good works,

25 not neglecting to meet together, as is the habit of some, but encouraging one another, and all the more as you see the Day drawing near.

Since we have confidence means that the invitation is to have courage to draw near to God. Among the Jews there was a natural shrinking back from the presence of majesty. As the Jew went in before the king, who was an absolute monarch, he never knew whether or not he would be received. The story of Esther illustrates the point (ch. 4). The respect which the Jews had for their king, they had in far greater measure for their God. This is highly commendable. Never can there be irreverent arrogance in the heart of a true worshiper. Reverence and holy confidence are companions in the soul of one who has met the God whom Christ made known to us. This is a repetition of the appeal for confidence, found in 4:16.

By the blood of Jesus means that this confidence is grounded, not in our personal worthiness, but in the sacrifice of Jesus.

By the new and living way which he opened for us is a living way because of our *great priest*—"since he always lives to make intercession for them" (7:25). It is also a living way in the sense that the blood of Christ affords a continual fellowship with God. Jesus has opened a way to God, and we are to travel that same way —the way of self-sacrifice. The cross saves us when it becomes our cross. Christ saves us by transforming us, not by making a transaction with the Father.

Through his flesh is used allegorically to represent the veil of the tabernacle which shut man out of the presence of God. When the flesh of Christ was pierced on the cross, the very heart of God was laid open to our view. Now we know his infinite love, so we need have no doubt about his disposition toward us. When the Saviour died, the veil of his flesh and the veil of the Temple were torn into. Then God and man stood face to face.

Let us draw near. The main thrust of this invitation is to draw near to God. What is it that prevents man's drawing near to God? It is the veil. Between this world and the world of permanent reality there hangs a veil. Man's predicament is that he is unable of himself to penetrate that veil. This preacher sees the greatest good in life as unhindered fellowship with God; but the veil precludes that fellowship. What is that veil and how can man ever get through it?

The veil is composed of man's sin. The veil, in a sense, was a merciful recognition of the truth that man, in his sin, is too blinded to bear the full beam of the light of God's presence and still live. The Old Testament taught that no man could see God and live (cf. Ex. 20:19; Lev. 16:2,13; Judg. 6:22–23; 13:23). When the veil was temporarily removed for Saul of Tarsus, on the Damascus road, he was made blind for three days (Acts 9:1–19).

The supreme purpose of God is to remove that veil. Man has always sought to remove it for himself by three ways:

(1) He has undertaken to remove the veil by metaphysics or philosophy. Socrates said, "Know thyself!" The Greeks said, "Orthodoxy—right thinking is the way to God." If man could only be straight in his thinking, he could break through the veil. But straight thinking includes far more than the ability to assimilate and arrange the facts. Man's thinking is always influenced by his moral and spiritual condition. Straight thinking must also include his ability to discern values. For example, straight thinking must lead us to see that "two plus two is four" is not as great a conclusion as that a person must do right.

(2) Man has also sought to remove this veil by means of mysticism. There are two kinds of mysticism. The first is given over to emotionalism—the belief that if one could get outside of himself in ecstasy, he would thereby be closer to God. The Greek mystery religions had some of this. One of the central ceremonies was the "Tauroboleum," which was accompanied by mad ecstasy. Paul warned against such unrestrained excitement. He contended that God is a God of order (1 Cor. 14:33,

Phillips). There is a place for emotion in religion, for emotion is a basic part of life. But let it be the emotion that arises out of truth, not the emotionalism that is artificially induced.

The second type of mysticism is that which contends that the veil between God and man may be removed by self-cultivation, by probing into the depths of our souls. This is the practice of the person who is always looking within and becoming a thoroughgoing introvert. The soul is not cultivated in that way. Such probing ends in self-induced morbidity. So the man who looks to God and to others finds greater growth in the things of God than the recluse who is concerned only with his own miserable little soul. He becomes so thoroughly introspective that he gauges himself by his own deluded imagination rather than by the pattern that is in Christ. Growth comes not through frenzied introspection, nor through mad activism; but through trusting surrender to God and his ways.

(3) There are also those who attempt to remove the veil by moralism or sheer self-righteousness, or by identifying their own morals with the will of God. Such a person asks and expects an affirmative answer to the question, "If we do the best we can, will we not be all right?" But the New Testament emphasizes that no man has the resources within himself to lift himself above the veil. Even his moral judgment and moral will belong on this side of the veil in the world of shadows.

Man cannot help himself. The question then becomes: Will God help him? If the veil is shattered, it must be from the other side. Is this what was meant by the veil in the Temple being torn from top to bottom? It was torn, not from the bottom to the top by the hand of man, but from top to bottom by the hand of God.

In his dilemma, man began to look around him and to ask, "Who will deliver me and bring me to God?" It had never occurred to him to ask, "Who will bring God to me?" Thus the writer of Hebrews reminds us that man looked in four historic directions before God finally broke through the veil in his Son:

(1) Man looked, first, to the prophets (1:1–3). God really spoke in the prophets, but a voice is not an abiding presence. It may bring a fragment of truth, for a prophet could speak or write only what he was capable of hearing or seeing. The prophet was a kind of candle in the darkness, for the real sun had not risen.

(2) Man looked also to the angels (1:4–2:7). Jewish theology contained an elaborate system of angelology. Angels were regarded as the powers of God and as the strange, subtle forces in the universe. They are engaged in the adoration and service of God. But they do not really know by experience human nature in its nobility and shame.

(3) Man has also looked to Moses and the law to get him through the veil. The preacher to the Hebrews insists that Moses, as compared with Christ, was only a servant in the house of God and not a son over the house (3:5–6). Moses was identified with a legal system that was merely preparatory. It could not bring people to the rest of God, for the whole system of legalism was on the wrong side of the veil. In fact, it caused men to draw back, not to draw near to God.

(4) Man, finally, looked to the priests to penetrate the veil and take him to God. The major part of this epistle is concerned with Aaron and the system with which he is identified. To the people of the Old Testament, the priest was far more important than the prophet. But the priests were inadequate. They were sinful (7:27–28) and mortal (7:23). The sanctuary was inadequate (9:11). The sacrifice was inadequate (9:10,12; 10:4,6). It was impossible for the blood of bulls and goats to take away sin. This was evidenced in the fact that they were always having to be repeated.

The access to God had to be opened by one who came from the other side of the veil. He came from eternity into time and brought an eternal sacrifice which could be offered once for all. He brought God to man. Thus through him, there is perpetual access to God.

The condition of one who would draw near to God is described in v. 22. Fullness of faith, purity of heart, and a clean life are the prerequisites. We cannot blunder into the presence of the Almighty and All Holy on our own terms. God has described the attitude and the condition in which this approach must be made.

We are to draw near *in full assurance of faith.* God must be approached wholeheartedly, with no doubtful reservation. We are to believe that God exists and that "he rewards those who seek him" (11:6). We are to believe that God is always in a receptive mood to welcome us as we come. He delights to receive our worship and to answer our faithful prayers. Jesus said, "According to your faith be it done to you" (Matt. 9:29). How often we lose the blessings of God because our faith is not what it ought to be!

Again, we are to draw near to God with pure hearts, *with our hearts sprinkled clean from an evil conscience.* "If I had cherished iniquity in my heart, the Lord would not have listened" (Psalm 66:18). One reason most of us do not pray is that we are uncomfortable in the presence of God. Our first prayer, therefore, must be, "Create in me a clean heart, O God, and put a new and right spirit within me" (Psalm 51:10). Christ's sacrifice is regarded as providing inward cleansing of the total inner life—the heart.

Clean living must also accompany our approach to God. We must draw near with *our bodies washed with pure water.* For the Jew, the ceremonial washing of the body was symbolical of moral cleansing. The clean life is one of the clear evidences that the Holy Spirit is in residence there. Sin will mar the beauty of the body as well as the soul. Everywhere we see man and women who are living monuments to the disfiguring power of sin. God, who loved beauty so much that he painted the lily with its dreamy white, gave the rose its blushing charm, and threw around the evening sun its drapery of a thousand colors, expects the life of the highest of his creatures to be a "thing of beauty and a joy forever."

After the appeal to draw near to God, there is another appeal to *hold fast the confession of our hope.* Again, this preacher's emphasis on the *eschaton* comes to the fore. The Christian hope is anchored in Christ within the veil of the heavenly sanctuary. It is the hope that beckons us onward and buoys us when we are tempted to lose faith. We are called, therefore, to hold it fast. Hope is a part of the Christian confession of faith which we make at the time of our baptism. We are buried with Christ in baptism. We are raised to walk in newness of life (Rom. 6:4). We confess at that time that not only have we been raised with Christ in newness of life (Col. 3:1), but we shall be raised with him in the last day (1 Thess. 4:16).

The third appeal is that we *stir up one another to love and good works.* This completes the grand triumverate of Christian graces: *faith* (v. 22), *hope* (v. 23), and now *love* (v. 24). Where one of these graces appears in the New Testament, the other two usually will not be far away. These are the graces which are inevitably produced by nearness to God and are the inevitable products of the new open access to God.

Notice how *good works* is bound up with faith, hope, and love in this passage. This preacher does not separate what belongs together in dynamic Christian behavior.

The translation *consider* is rather bland and low-key. The preacher is talking about a kind of rivalry which is constructive and productive. His thought may be translated "let us rival one another." There are many kinds of rivalry which are unworthy of Christians. Some rival others to see how much money they can make, how much more popular they can be, how much more luxury they can enjoy, how much better cars they can drive, and how much better clothes they can wear. But Christian rivalry does not belong in that category. It has its own unique excitement. It is a spiritual rivalry which causes us to call up all of our spiritual resources as we seek to rival one another in love and good works. What a community ours would be if each of us pledged all of his spiritual, physical, and material resources to see who could do the most good works for others!

Not neglecting to meet together is clearer in the KJV, "not forsaking," which urges us not to do to one another what God has promised never to do to us. "I will never fail you nor forsake you" (13:5).

The call of the preacher to his Hebrew congregation could be implemented only where common worship and fellowship are maintained. Therefore, he issues solemn warning against setting a bad example by abandoning public worship. The active good life, inspired by love, is kept alive by people who care enough for one another to assemble together.

Encouraging one another reminds us that one must consider the discouragement he brings to the Christian church when he deliberately absents himself from its service. We are called to be encouragers. Black moods of discouragement come to us swiftly and constantly. Even John the Baptist, intrepid layer of the axe at the root of the tree, was plunged into despondency after being imprisoned. He had had enough courage to stand before Herod to denounce his adultery, but his imprisonment plunged him into a mood of doubt. He sent his disciples to ask Jesus, "Are you he who is to come, or shall we look for another?" (Matt. 11:3).

True religion was meant to put courage into the soul. Moses was the most towering man of the Old Testament, partly because he was often heard saying to his faltering people: "Be strong and of good courage, do not fear or be in dread of them: for it is the Lord your God who goes with you; he will not fail you or forsake you" (Deut. 31:6). David also could encourage Saul the king with his sweet singing because he "strengthened himself in the Lord his God" (1 Sam. 30:6).

God's people are to receive courage from one another by gathering together in worship. Many are defeated in the Christian life because they abandon the assembly where they might see the shining examples of dedicated men and women who hold fast to their faith and live out their days in the splendor and courage of Christ himself.

Who were these who had forsaken the fellowship of worship, *as is the habit of some?* Were they those who had begun to feel the stigma attached to such a despised sect; people who could not bear to be unpopular; people who began to see firsthand the terrifying dangers involved in following the crucified Christ; people who grew weary of the hardships and sacrifice involved in their identity with the Christian church? Whoever they were, this preacher warns them of the dangers of extreme individualism, suggesting the perils of being a pious particle when God offers us the solidarity of a fellowship to help us to withstand the massive pressure and criticism of a hostile society.

It is revealing to find that, even in the earliest days, there were those who were tempted to separate from their fellow Christians. Some felt themselves superior to the common horde of worshipers. Some were always on a quest for something better. They were incapable of full commitment, for they imagined that each new discovery was but a temporary resting place until fuller and clearer light came. This was especially true of the devotees of the mystery cults. The sooner they withdrew from a cult, the more superior they felt themselves to be.

You can see that, in such a climate, with such an attitude, it was exceedingly difficult to proclaim a religion which required holding fast forever. Anyone who forsook the common body of Christ's worshipers denied the very finality of Jesus as the full revelation of God. Any attitude or action which indicated disloyalty was regarded as exceedingly serious.

When the way to God was fully and finally opened by Jesus, it was a grave offense not to draw near and not to hold fast gratefully and loyally to what had been given them in Christ. This accounts for the gravity of the warning which follows.

5. The Warning (10:26-31)

26 For if we sin deliberately after receiving the knowledge of the truth, there no longer remains a sacrifice for sins, 27 but a fearful prospect of judgment, and a fury of fire which will consume the adversaries. 28 A man who has violated the law of Moses dies without mercy at the testimony of two or three witnesses. 29 How much worse punishment do you think will be deserved by the man who has spurned the Son of God, and profaned the blood of the covenant by which he was sanctified, and outraged the Spirit of grace? 30 For we know him who said, "Vengeance is mine, I will repay." And again, "The Lord will judge his people." 31 It is a fearful thing to fall into the hands of the living God.

No New Testament preacher spoke stronger words of warning than did the writer of Hebrews. Sin, to him, was the most terrible of enemies, and disloyalty was the deadliest of sins. The person who deliberately sins, after receiving full knowledge of truth, is guilty of a sin as heinous as though he had trampled underfoot the Son of God.

In the early days of World War II, a book appeared entitled *Out of the Night*. It was written by Jan Valtin, who told of an old and feeble Jewish man, arrested by the gestapo and accused without any evidence of an assault on a German girl. He was beaten until he could stand no longer. He was thrown into the prison court that people passing by might show their contempt by treading upon him until his life was literally stamped out. This puts into a modern setting the despicable contempt which one shows toward Christ when he repudiates his commitment to him.

What could a holy God say in such circumstances save, "*Vengeance is mine, I will repay.*"

In some theological circles, the God of righteous wrath is thought to be confined to the Old Testament. The God of the New Testament is said to be pure compassion, who is lenient toward the sins of men. Over against this stands the preacher to the Hebrews saying, *It is a fearful thing to fall into the hands of the living God.*

Blasphemy against God is steadily regarded throughout both Old and New Testaments as a heinous sin. One form of blasphemy was the deliberate withdrawal from the Christian community. This amounted to an avowed repudiation of what the Christian community espoused. It was a disowning of the covenant relationship which Christ came to offer his people and which he made possible with his own blood. To repudiate such a covenant was to destroy the very ground on which God now forgives sin. To abandon Christ and his people is to give public testimony that one considers the Christian gospel inadequate.

Nothing was more offensive to this preacher to the Hebrews than taking God's mercy and loving-kindness for granted. The greatness of his mercy made the sin against that mercy all the more heinous. The person who takes his loyalty to Christ lightly is such an easygoing, relaxed person that he imagines God also to be easygoing. Because he has never taken his promises to God seriously, he thinks God does not take them seriously.

Moses argued for the extreme penalty for the willful rejection of God's law (cf. Deut. 17:2-13). Here the Hebrew preacher brings out his most powerful argument toward those who are contemplating turning away from Christ.

This is a crisis situation in the early church. It is questionable whether the preacher of Hebrews had in mind structuring a doctrine in this passage around which theologians, for all time to come, might debate the issue either of the possibility of falling from grace or the doctrine, "once saved, always saved." Let us, nevertheless, take solemn warning from the fact that there is enough said about falling away in the New Testament that no serious student dare take it lightly (cf. Matt. 7:21; 10:22; 24:10; Gal. 5:4; Heb. 3:12–14; 4:11; 6:4–6; 10:38–39; 2 Peter 1:10).

6. *The Encouragement* (10:32–39)

32 But recall the former days when, after you were enlightened, you endured a hard struggle with sufferings, 33 sometimes being publicly exposed to abuse and affliction, and sometimes being partners with those so treated. 34 For you had compassion on the prisoners, and you joyfully accepted the plundering of your property, since you knew that you yourselves had a better possession and an abiding one. 35 Therefore do not throw away your confidence, which has a great reward. 36 For you have need of endurance, so that you may do the will of God and receive what is promised.
37 "For yet a little while,
   and the coming one shall come and shall
      not tarry;
38 but my righteous one shall live by faith,
   and if he shrinks back,
   my soul has no pleasure in him."
39 But we are not of those who shrink back and are destroyed, but of those who have faith and keep their souls.

Now, the preacher to the Hebrews turns from solemn warning to helpful encouragement. He reminds his hearers of the valor they had shown in the days immediately after their conversion. They knew at that time that, if they renounced Christ, their persecution would cease. However, like strong wrestlers, they had stood up to the persecution, content to be the object of popular contempt and hatred while they bravely assisted their fellow sufferers.

They had relieved their brethren who were thrown into prison. They had borne the confiscation of their property with joy, in the assurance that they had wealth of another kind which made them far richer than those who robbed them.

Faith is never held without struggle. This writer, therefore, reminded his readers that character is made in conflict and struggle. We are to hold fast to our faith in the most difficult and trying times, knowing this: *For you have need of endurance, so that you may do the will of God and*

receive what is promised.

But my righteous one shall live by faith. Endurance is a necessary requirement for salvation. "He who endures to the end will be saved" (Matt. 10:22).

The encouragement of the hearers comes both from a memory and from a hope. The delay of the coming of Christ had been one cause of the church's loss of faith and general apathy. Therefore, the rallying cry goes forth: *For yet a little while, and the coming one shall come and shall not tarry.* True faith makes no provision for the relaxation of loyalty. It perseveres in hope. So the preacher speaks his reassuring word: *But we are not of those who shrink back.*

To *shrink back* was unpardonable, for it amounted to abandoning Christian faith as we approach the day of judgment. To shrink back was to be *destroyed.* The day of judgment is drawing near, says this preacher. Jesus had gone before in our behalf. Our faith is to be not in our own works and obedience to the law, but in the person and work of Christ. To shrink back from that is to lose everything.

Verses 37–38 are quoted from Habakkuk 2:3–4. This was a passage which was very familiar both to early Christians and to the Essenes. Paul, as well as this Hebrew preacher quotes this passage. There is also a treatment of this passage in a Qumran commentary. In the Essene community, Habakkuk's *righteous one* was regarded as the one who was scrupulously loyal to the laws and bylaws of the sect and also to the minutiae of Essene doctrine. On the other hand, the *righteous one* for a Christian was one who lived by faith in Christ.

Christianity was distinguished from all early Jewish sects by its emphasis on the nature and work of Christ, while the sects emphasized faith by one's own ability to keep the law and to do good works of righteousness.

Both Christians and Jews emphasized faith in God and both emphasized obedience and good works. They differed in the fact that, while the Jewish sects placed their primary emphasis upon obedience to the law and good works, the Christians placed their primary trust in Christ.

IX. Meaning of Faith (11:1–40)

1. Substance and Evidence (11:1–2)

¹ Now faith is the assurance of things hoped for, the conviction of things not seen. ² For by it the men of old received divine approval.

Here is the classic definition of Christian faith. The rhythmical balance and beauty of this translation actually rob it of some of its robust meaning. A casual reader might conclude that faith creates the things we hope for. But the entire argument of the writer of Hebrews is designed to convince us that the unseen realities of religion have independent and objective validity. Faith does not turn life into a daydream of wistful longing. Instead, faith brings the things which God has already prepared for us in the future into the living present and makes them real now. Faith is not a blind plunge into the dark. It is based upon the clearest light that God can give to man and upon his unshakable promises.

The word translated *assurance* actually means "things put under." So faith is the foundation of the Christian life. The life of a Christian rests on the faith that he has in God.

For a clue to the meaning of the substance of faith, we may return to a passage in which Christ is called the character of God's own substance or "hypostasis" (1:3). Could we then go so far as to say, "If you want to see what faith is, look at Christ"? It is Christ who is the object, who calls forth our faith; and it is Christ who is the subject, who gives substance to our faith. It is Christ who pulls our future hope into the present, and it is Christ who will bring the realization of our hope when he comes again. He is the "pioneer and perfecter" of our faith (12:2). He is the Alpha and Omega of the Apocalypse.

Faith as a certain assurance is also seen in 3:14: "For we share in Christ, if only we hold our first confidence firm to the end."

The conviction of things not seen means Christian faith is not a whimsical, transitory mood. It rests on the bedrock conviction that the great realities of life are the things which are unseen. Thus, conviction gives us the steady assurance that God's best blessings are still in the future. While we have grasped a part of the divine reality in Christ, there is more to be enjoyed than we have yet dreamed of. Therefore, the future for the Christian is not uncertain. Christian faith is always certain of one thing—the future belongs to God.

Here again, let it be emphasized that the unseen realities are not made real by faith. On the contrary, it is the conviction that God has prepared a city which justifies our faith. Moreover, the conviction of things unseen is not the proof of faith. Instead, it is the fact that the future is in the hands of God which gives faith the reality to behold. Faith does not give substance. It gives assurance because the substance is already a reality. Faith takes its stand upon the promise of God and eagerly anticipates the future. The preacher to the Hebrews thus uses faith in almost the identical way that Paul uses hope.

For by it [faith] *the men of old received divine approval.* The preacher is here reminding his hearers that in the interim, before the return of Christ, they must live as the faithful in Israel lived, that is, by faith in God's promises.

This noun *faith* occurs 23 times in this passage. Eighteen times it occurs in the dative form and stands at the beginning of each sentence for emphasis.

2. Belief in the Creator (11:3)

³ By faith we understand that the world was created by the word of God, so that what is seen was made out of things which do not appear.

The Christian is to have no doubt about the ultimate source of his universe. *The world was created by the word of God.* This does not mean that the process of creation did not remain a vast mystery to him. But the writer of Hebrews was certain that, in God's own way, he created this world and all other worlds. We do not begin our Christian faith, however, with our belief in the Creator. We begin with faith in the Redeemer. Our faith in him carries us back to the origin of all things and forward to a future which is also in his hands.

When the writer of Hebrews declared, *What is seen was made out of things which do not appear,* he was refuting an argument which was current in his time. This view insisted that the world was made of imperfect material which was already in existence. According to this view, the world was inherently evil; therefore man could not be personally responsible for its evil. The preacher of Hebrews refutes this argument by contending that God made this world of no preexisting material. This is God's world. Man is responsible for the evil which his disobedience introduced into God's world.

Faith is called forth by revelation and the first revelation which God made to man was the creation of the world. Thus Paul insisted, in Romans 1:20: "Ever since the creation of the world his invisible nature, namely, his eternal power and deity, has been clearly perceived in the things that have been made."

The most impressive of all examples is the author's insistence that, by faith, we understand the universe itself was created by the word of God. Thereby, he underscores his emphasis that everything man sees can be understood only faith.

3. The Faithful of the Old Testament (11:4–34)

4 By faith Abel offered to God a more acceptable sacrifice than Cain, through which he received approval as righteous, God bearing witness by accepting his gifts; he died, but through his faith he is still speaking. 5 By faith Enoch was taken up so that he should not see death; and he was not found, because God had taken him. Now before he was taken he was attested as having pleased God. 6 And without faith it is impossible to please him. For whoever would draw near to God must believe that he exists and that he rewards those who seek him. 7 By faith Noah, being warned by

God concerning events as yet unseen, took heed and constructed an ark for the saving of his household; by this he condemned the world and became an heir of the righteousness which comes by faith.

8 By faith Abraham obeyed when he was called to go out to a place which he was to receive as an inheritance; and he went out, not knowing where he was to go. 9 By faith he sojourned in the land of promise, as in a foreign land, living in tents with Isaac and Jacob, heirs with him of the same promise. 10 For he looked forward to the city which has foundations, whose builder and maker is God. 11 By faith Sarah herself received power to conceive, even when she was past the age, since she considered him faithful who had promised. 12 Therefore from one man, and him as good as dead, were born descendants as many as the stars of heaven and as the innumerable grains of sand by the seashore.

13 These all died in faith, not having received what was promised, but having seen it and greeted it from afar, and having acknowledged that they were strangers and exiles on the earth. 14 For people who speak thus make it clear that they are seeking a homeland. 15 If they had been thinking of that land from which they had gone out, they would have had opportunity to return. 16 But as it is, they desire a better country, that is, a heavenly one. Therefore God is not ashamed to be called their God, for he has prepared for them a city.

17 By faith Abraham, when he was tested, offered up Isaac, and he who had received the promises was ready to offer up his only son, 18 of whom it was said, "Through Isaac shall your descendants be named." 19 He considered that God was able to raise men even from the dead; hence, figuratively speaking, he did receive him back. 20 By faith Isaac invoked future blessings on Jacob and Esau. 21 By faith Jacob, when dying, blessed each of the sons of Joseph, bowing in worship over the head of his staff. 22 By faith Joseph, at the end of his life, made mention of the exodus of the Israelites and gave directions concerning his burial.

23 By faith Moses, when he was born, was hid for three months by his parents, because they saw that the child was beautiful; and they were not afraid of the king's edict. 24 By faith Moses, when he was grown up, refused to be called the son of Pharaoh's daughter, 25 choosing rather to share ill-treatment with the people of God than to enjoy the fleeting pleasures of sin. 26 He considered abuse suffered for the Christ greater wealth than the treasures of Egypt, for he looked to the reward. 27 By faith he left Egypt, not being afraid of the anger of the king; for he endured as seeing him who is invisible. 28 By faith he kept the Passover and

sprinkled the blood, so that the Destroyer of the first-born might not touch them.

²⁹ By faith the people crossed the Red Sea as if on dry land; but the Egyptians, when they attempted to do the same, were drowned. ³⁰ By faith the walls of Jericho fell down after they had been encircled for seven days. ³¹ By faith Rahab the harlot did not perish with those who were disobedient, because she had given friendly welcome to the spies.

³² And what more shall I say? For time would fail me to tell of Gideon, Barak, Samson, Jephthah, of David and Samuel and the prophets—³³ who through faith conquered kingdoms, enforced justice, received promises, stopped the mouths of lions, ³⁴ quenched raging fire, escaped the edge of the sword, won strength out of weakness, became mighty in war, put foreign armies to flight.

This section has been called the Westminster Abbey of the Old Testament because here the great Hebrew giants of the ages assemble to hear their massive witness to their faith in God. Here is the story of gallant men and women who went forward toward goals they did not clearly see and toward ideals that lay beyond the reach of humanity. The entire passage gathers around the response of faith to the revelation of God.

Beginning with v. 4, the preacher draws incidents from Genesis, Exodus, Joshua, and Judges to illustrate the primary importance of faith. The importance of this passage is seen in the truth that it goes beyond the Old Testament pattern which never uses men as models of faith to be praised. Instead, the heavy emphasis in the Old Testament is on man's sin and his dependence upon God's forgiving grace.

Abel, Enoch, Noah, Abraham and Sarah, Abraham and Isaac, Jacob and Esau, Joseph, Moses and the Exodus, the escape across the Red Sea, the fall of Jericho, and the help of Rahab the harlot are used as examples of the kind of faith the preacher is calling for in the Christian community. He indicates that there is not sufficient time to describe the faith of Gideon, Barak, Samson, Jepthah, David, Samuel, and the ·prophets.

The writer passed over Adam and Eve and came to *Abel* because he was the first person to receive the divine approval. We are not told why God preferred Abel's offering to Cain's. We are simply told that Abel's offering was made in faith. His outward gift revealed his inward faith and righteousness for subsequent ages to see.

By faith he is still speaking. His example of faith speaks in every generation, not simply as an immortal memory, but it stimulates faith in others so that God speaks through him and through our faith in the living present.

It is interesting to know that God still speaks through the grim story of a slaughtered brother at the beginning of the biblical pilgrimage. The examples of faith, chosen by the preacher to the Hebrews, were not designed to glorify Israel, but to tell the bad along with the good and to show that, even if the worst comes to a man as a result of his faith, now as it did to Abel, God still is on the scene. All is not lost. Abel still speaks as one whose faith in God has been rewarded and as one who is in the keeping of God forever.

By faith Enoch walked so close to God that, when the end came, there was no shocking detour in his pilgrimage. He simply kept on the same path that brought him nearer to his God. Just as the preacher used the most grim story of Abel to illustrate faith, he now takes the most exalted story—the story of a man who did not die—to illustrate faith. This preacher did not shun deathbed stories. He spoke openly of death—of death by murder and of an exodus from this world without death.

He was attested as having pleased God. Enoch thus received the highest accolade. To satisfy God, Enoch had to have faith. Remember the following reference to the fact that *without faith it is impossible to please him.*

True religion means drawing near to God. Those who would draw near to God must believe two things: first, *that he exists;* second, *that he rewards those who seek him.*

But it is not merely belief in God which forms the core of Christian faith. It is belief in a God who cares. When Jesus said: "Set your troubled hearts at rest. Trust in God always; trust also in me" (John 14:1, NEB); was he not saying: "Many people believe in God, but what matters is your belief in the God whom I have known: the God who cares, the God who is involved in the human situation, and the God who cares enough to reward the faithful"? Did he not go on and talk about the house of many mansions?

Some of us have been taught that we are most spiritual when we never think of the rewards of religion. "Goodness for goodness' sake" is the motto of such people. Goodness brings its own reward, we are told. In a sense, this is undoubtedly true, and it is indeed very noble to enjoy goodness for its own sake. But the writer of Hebrews said that those who draw near to God must believe, not only that he exists, but also that he rewards those who seek him. To practice goodness for goodness' sake may be very commendable, but it may also be an egocentric philosophy which enhances human pride so much that it is tantamount to saying: "I have no need of the blessings of God. I will earn my own blessings and turn my own behavior into the only kind of blessing I will ever expect. I will behave in such a manner that it creates its own blessing." That may be good and noble ethics, but it is poor and flabby religion.

Faith for this preacher always received its reward. True faith never seeks God in vain. For the very fact that a person is in search of God is evidence itself that God is in search of him; for no one ever turned his face toward God until, first of all, God had moved upon his heart. God stands as the instigator and the rewarder of faith. The fear of punishment and the hope of reward may be a good motive for beginning the service of God, but it could never be the highest motive. The most faithful servant forgets about the reward in the joy of serving the God of his love.

Noah was the champion of nonconformists. What a mark of madness it must have seemed to the mocking bystanders to see a man building a mammoth ark so many miles from the nearest body of water! When they asked him why he was building the ark, he replied that God had informed him that the world would be destroyed by a flood and that he must be ready. Every man who takes God seriously is considered mad by those who take him lightly.

The radical obedience of Noah condemned the unbelief and disobedience of those about him. His faith enabled him to save his family and to know the deliverance of God. Noah believed when all appearances were encouraging unbelief. Ultimately, the unseen was manifested and his faith was vindicated in his own lifetime.

The father of the faithful was *Abraham,* the man who dared by faith to venture into the unknown. He heard the call of God and obeyed. Faith for Abraham was never a placid thing. It was a disturbing force compelling him to venture into the unseen. Faith that does not involve risk is not faith. True faith can never be based on conclusive evidence or upon carefully calculated profits. Faith acts upon that which is unseen, yet real. Faith feels the pull of the beyond.

By faith he sojourned in the land of promise, as in a foreign land. When he arrived at the place promised to him, Abraham found it still in the hands of others. He was compelled to live in this land, which God had promised to him, as a foreigner. He, nevertheless, retained his patience and hope.

For he looked forward to the city which has foundations, whose builder and maker is God. His patience was maintained by the assurance that God's promise would be fulfilled to him. His hope was not centered altogether in the family which God had promised him, but even more in a future life in the unseen world (11:1).

God had promised to give Sarah a child. She was far past the age of childbearing and felt this to be an impossible promise. However, because of her firmly-founded faith in God, she was given strength, even in her elderly years, to conceive and to bear a child. For her faith in the unseen became rewarded in that which was seen—a child (Gen. 17:15—21:7).

This passage is remarkable because of the low estate of women in the first-century world. Nowhere previously had a woman's faith been mentioned.

On the surface the author does not appear to recall the skeptical laughter of Sarah (Gen. 18:12). This would seem to deny her faith. Could it be that skepticism and faith often dwell side by side, as in the case of one who said, "I believe; help my unbelief" (Mark 9:24)? The great question is, which will be the stronger and which will finally win, skepticism or faith?

Verses 13–16 speak in general of the faith of the patriarchs, especially Abraham, Isaac, and Jacob. All of these not only lived in faith, they died in faith, believing in life beyond the grave. Their far-off vision of what they had been promised was embraced with delight. They knew it was no daydream. *They desire a better country, that is, a heavenly one.* Their true home was in the high country of heaven.

God is not ashamed to be called their God, for he has prepared for them a city. Here God is presented as taking pride in what he has prepared for those who have faith in him. The inference is that, had God not prepared adequately for his people after promising them that he would, he would then be ashamed to call himself their God.

He had already built the city. He was the "builder and maker" (11:10). And in that city which is the homeland of the faithful, God takes pride.

By faith Abraham, when he was tested offered up Isaac. Abraham's most severe trial came when he received a command from God which appeared to contradict what God himself had promised—that through Isaac his seed should be multiplied. *Of whom it was said, "Through Isaac shall your descendants be named."* Not only was he willing to go against everything in his father-heart in order that he

might obey his God; he was also willing to go against his own understanding of the promise of God (v. 18).

He considered that God was able to raise men even from the dead. This is the high water mark of patriarchal faith. This is Abraham's complete faith, that what is placed upon God's altar can never be finally lost. *Figuratively speaking, he did receive him back.* This was a parable on the resurrection, for Abraham received his own son back. The word translated "received" means "to get back what belongs to you."

Isaac, Jacob, and *Joseph* are listed as examples of how faith made possible the continuance of the race which God had chosen as his instrument of salvation. Isaac's promise to Jacob is recorded in Genesis 27:28–29. Joseph's promise to Jacob is recorded in Genesis 47:29–31. The confidence of Joseph that God will fulfill his promise to Israel is reflected in Genesis 50:24–25, where Joseph insists that, for all the glory he knew in Egypt, the greater glory lay ahead in a land which God had chosen.

The writer records five times when faith made an enormous difference in the life of *Moses.*

(1) It was his parent's faith which preserved him in infancy. Their's was a faith which defined the edict of Pharoah.

(2) Moses *refused to be called the son of Pharaoh's daughter.* The word translated "refused" means a deliberate choice. The sin which he was tempted to enjoy would have involved him in disloyalty to the people of God. Therefore, his faith defended him against disloyalty. Disloyalty was a most heinous sin for this writer. Concerning the phrase, *abuse suffered for the Christ,* James Moffatt points out: "By identifying himself with God's people in Egypt, Moses encountered the same [abuse] as their very messiah afterwards was to endure. He thus faced what the writer, from his own standpoint, does not hesitate to call [the abuse of Christ]" (p. 180). *For he looked to the reward*—he had

his eyes on the future. This described the attitude of one whose eyes are withdrawn from everything else and focused on one single thing.

(3) Moses' flight from Egypt to Midian is regarded as an act of faith (Ex. 2:14 ff.). Despite the fact that Moses' fear is recorded in the Old Testament narrative, this author sees the real motive in his flight as his faith that he is on God's mission. Despite his murder of the Egyptian and the fact that his life was in jeopardy, he continued to have faith in God's purpose for him. At times it requires stronger faith to leave a place where there is danger than it does to remain there. For some people would prefer danger to the unknown.

(4) Moses' belief in God's final preservation of his people is another act of faith. The obedience of Moses concerning the Passover was prompted by his faith.

(5) Moses' faith is now shared by his people as they cross the Red Sea (Ex. 14:16 ff.). This venture in obedience to God's command is the evidence of faith.

In v. 30 we have the writer's commentary on Joshua 6:1–20. The solid faith of the people by which they crossed the Red Sea is now seen as the force which brings down the walls of Jericho.

In v. 31 the writer turns from the faith of the community to concentrate on the faith of one woman. The story is recorded in Joshua 2:1–21; 6:25. Her lack of character does not disturb this writer. It is her faith which caused her to assist the spies. She believed that the God of Israel was to be respected. Therefore, she was saved while her fellow citizens, who did not respect the God of Israel, perished.

The writer assumes the familiarity of his congregation with the great sagas of the book of Judges, the book of Kings, and the prophets. The mere mention of names is sufficient to stir memories of valor.

Gideon's triumph over the Ammonites was often told in Israel (cf. Isa. 9:4; 10:26; Psalm 83:11). The achievements of the faithful were well enough known that the

reference to *conquered kingdoms* immediately called to mind the conquests of David. *Stopped the mouth of lions* recalled the work of Daniel (Dan 6:18,23). *Quenched raging fire* referred to the three friends of Daniel (Dan. 3:19–23). *Escaped the edge of the sword* referred to deliverance from murder, as in the case of Elijah (1 Kings 19:1 ff.), and Elisha (2 Kings 6:14 ff.). *Won strength out of weakness* could possibly refer to Hezekiah's recovery from illness and other similar instances. *Became mighty in war* and *put foreign armies to flight* could refer to the Maccabean struggle (1 Mac. 2:7).

4. Summary of Horrors (11:35–38)

35 Women received their dead by resurrection. Some were tortured, refusing to accept release, that they might rise again to a better life. 36 Others suffered mocking and scourging, and even chains and imprisonment. 37 They were stoned, they were sawn in two, they were killed with the sword; they went about in skins of sheep and goats, destitute, afflicted, ill-treated—38 of whom the world was not worthy—wandering over deserts and mountains, and in dens and caves of the earth.

Women received their dead refers to incidents such as 1 Kings 17:17 ff. and 2 Kings 4:8–37. James Moffatt thinks the word *tortured* refers to: "A punishment probably corresponding to the mediaeval penalty of being broken on the wheel. This dreadful punishment consists, says Scott in a note to the thirtieth chapter of *The Bethrothed*, in the executioner, with a bar of iron, breaking the shoulder-bones, arms, thigh-bones and legs of the criminal, taking his alternate sides. The punishment is concluded by a blow across the breast, called the *coup de grâce*, because it removes the sufferer from his agony" (p. 187). It is known that the Maccabean martyrs suffered horrible torture.

Refusing to accept release means that, in order to obtain release, they would have had to be disloyal to their convictions. Rather than dishonor their religion, they chose to suffer and put their trust in the resurrection, *that they might rise again to a better life.* It required a powerful hope to sustain the loyalty of believers against such torment.

Others suffered mocking and scourging. Second Maccabees 7 describes beatings which were not immediately fatal but which caused great shame. *And even chains and imprisonment* may refer to the prolonged sufferings after such beatings.

They were stoned. Stoning was the traditional punishment, which took the life of Jeremiah in Egypt. *They were sawn in two* may refer to the tradition which holds that, during the reign of Manasseh, Isaiah was sawn in two with a wooden sword. *They were killed with the sword.* First Kings 19:10 and Jeremiah 26:23 tell of such a fate for the prophets whom the people disliked (cf. Moffat, p. 188).

It is known that the faithful followers of Isaiah, who defied the idolatry of Manasseh and fled to the hills, were clothed in garments of hair, *in skins of sheep and goats.* Goatskins were rougher than sheepskins. Both were regarded as the garb of a prophet (1 Kings 19:13–19). They were *destitute, afflicted, ill-treated.* People treated them as though they were not fit to live.

These were people *of whom the world was not worthy.* There are some people who are too good for the company of those who would slaughter all who differ from them.

There is a class of whom the world is always worthy and more than worthy: it is worthy of those who watch for, reproduce, exaggerate its foibles, who make themselves the very embodiment of its ruling passions, who shriek its catchwords, encourage its illusions, and flatter its fanaticisms. But it is a poor role to play, and it never has been played by men whose names stand for epochs in the march of history.[18]

Some of the loyal escaped death, but they knew a living death in a fearsome flight. They were found *wandering over*

18 H. L. Stewart, *Questions of the Day in Philosophy and Psychology* (New York: David McKay Company, 1912), p. 133.

deserts and mountains, and in dens and caves of the earth. They were hunted like animals. Mattathias and his sons may have been in the author's mind (1 Mac. 2:28).

5. Delay of the Promise (11:39–40)

39 And all these, though well attested by their faith, did not receive what was promised, 40 since God had foreseen something better for us, that apart from us they should not be made perfect.

The writer sees the delay of the reward of the faithful as a part of the divine plan. It was no failure in their faith which caused this postponement of reward. Neither had God failed them. Instead, it was a part of God's long-range plan. Now the writer uses this to encourage the followers of Christ to hold on a little while longer because the end is near. God has delayed the coming of Christ in order that we may share in it (1 Peter 10:20).

That apart from us they should not be made perfect. The perfect reward of those who served God faithfully in the Old Testament is seen as being made possible through Christ who worked out perfection for all his faithful. All of God's people are included in what Christ has accomplished. All are enrolled among the "spirits of just men made perfect" (12:23) at last.

X. Words of Encouragement and Discipline (12:1–24)

1. Call to Complete the Course (12:1–2)

1 Therefore, since we are surrounded by so great a cloud of witnesses, let us also lay aside every weight, and sin which clings so closely, and let us run with perseverance the race that is set before us, 2 looking to Jesus the pioneer and perfecter of our faith, who for the joy that was set before him endured the cross, despising the shame, and is seated at the right hand of the throne of God.

The smooth, exalted style of the Greek classicists is employed by the author. *Therefore,* in this sentence, means "for that very reason let us also." Then he describes the kind of patience which is required to finish the Christian course of life, by introducing two metaphors from the familiar

Greek contests—one from footracing (vv. 1–2,11); the other from the battlefield (vv. 3–4,12).

Since we are surrounded by so great a cloud of witnesses. We are people surrounded. The race of life is not run in isolation. We are not alone. Loneliness is the one burden a person cannot continue to carry. A person who is left alone in life soon loses all incentive for courageous endeavor. When no one else cares whether or not we are well or whether or not we succeed in our undertakings, there is little to sustain us in our work. When no one offers to share the burden or to speak an encouraging word, life loses its zest. But in the Christian life we are never alone. A great cloud of witnesses surrounds us. The writer of Hebrews called the roll of the heroes of the faith in the eleventh chapter. In chapter 12 he called on his readers to remember that these who have gone before bear their witness that faith in God brings life to its highest fulfillment.

The members of this preacher's congregation are called upon to view themselves as runners in a footrace while all the Old Testament saints, who have been described in chapter 11, are seated in the stadium cheering them on as they view the contest. Performers are often inspired when great athletes of former days are known to be in the stands observing them. The memory of their valor cheers the runner on. It is what the runner sees in the witnesses, not what the witnesses see in the runner, that inspires him. He knows that he has a pattern of superior performance to emulate.

Research has established that this reference is the first time the Greek word for *witnesses* (*martur*) was used in the sense of the word "martyr." In other words, the word known to us as "martyr" did not originally mean one who died for the faith. It originally meant a witness. It came to mean one who died for the faith when our author so used it for the first time in this passage. Could it not then be said that he was the one to whom it was revealed that witnessing in the Christian sense involves patient endurance unto death?

Normally, we think of a witness as one who has, in his own experience, seen something which he is able to share. This is the sense in which the word witness (martyr) is used in 10:28.

When the writer of Hebrews uses this word to describe the Old Testament heroes, he means more than "eye witnesses." He is talking about people who, through the eyes of faith, were able to see the unseeable and thus, through faith and hope, lived out lives which now bear witness to the worthwhileness of patient endurance.

The writer also sees them as witnesses in the sense of observers of the contest in which Christians are now engaged. He sees them surrounding us in history, past and present, and in the eternal future. A clue to his meaning may be found in what Emil Brunner wrote: "We live in the past by faith; we live in the future by hope; we live in the present by love." [19] Thus man fulfills his transcendent nature.

The word witness (martyr) then may have these dimensions of meaning: First, our preacher may have been saying that, by their faith, the Old Testament heroes were actually able to witness or declare what would finally happen to many of the people of God.

In the second place, the writer sees the final race actually taking place. The young church was running that race, and what the saints of old once saw in the future is now taking place in the present, and they are now looking on as actual spectators. Their faith would be fulfilled now as they witness the final triumph of the people of God. To feel the effect of this on that young church, ask yourself how you would live if you were actually in the company of these great witnesses. We are to live worthily of our heritage. This is the final race. It is also the battle of all battles upon which all the people of God in the past had staked their very lives.

The Hebrew philosophy of history is

[19] Emil Brunner, *Faith, Hope and Love* (Philadelphia: The Westminster Press, 1956), p. 13.

seen here. The Hebrew believed in the solidarity of history, that is, in the fact that the past is a part of the present. The hearer of this preacher of Hebrews would have no difficulty, then, in thinking of all the saints of old sharing in the race and in the conflict of the church in the final age. The people of the past were present to witness God's promise; they will also be present to witness the fulfillment of that promise.

Let us also lay aside every weight. The fleet-footed contender in the Olympic games knew the folly of carrying excess weight. He dared not carry anything that would encumber him. His one goal was to win the race, no matter how great the self-denial.

And sin which clings so closely may refer to stripping off the robe which the athlete wore to keep his limbs warm before the race, that it might not catch the wind, impair his limbs, and slow his speed. He divested himself of any habit which would handicap him or diminish his endurance. Sin is here regarded as a garment which would encumber the movement of the runner. Sin trips us in the moral race as the folds of a long-flowing garment would trip a footracer.

The one great lesson a racer must learn is self-denial. Jesus, if he taught anything, taught self-denial. He taught the joy of giving, not the joy of getting. He taught the joy of giving your best to the race of life.

Now, the preacher does not specify what the encumbrances are. He implies that one who runs the course appointed for him will soon discover for himself what encumbers him, what it is that would disqualify him for the race.

The writer was not talking about deliberate transgressions, for the person who continues to sin deliberately is disqualified from running this race at all. This reference is to the sins that overtake us so subtly that we are not aware of them until we are already in the race. Some such sins are: spiritual sluggishness, which saps our

vitality and causes us to lose interest in doing our best; inattention to prayer and reading the Word of God; impatience, which causes us to run at top speed for awhile, but to drop out of the race when the muscles tire and the breathing is hard. The Christian's race must be run with resolution.

Let us run with perseverance. Perseverance is a strong word which refers to the ability to keep up the stride when the competition is the hardest and the road the roughest. "He who endures to the end will be saved" (Matt. 10:22).

The race that is set before us means we are on a course that has been chosen for us. We are to please the one who appointed us a place in life. Christian pilgrims are not in this world on a leisurely tour in which we go sightseeing by day and return to our same lodging at night. We are on a racetrack, a place that calls for utmost exertion. We did not choose to be there. The race was chosen for us.

Looking to Jesus the pioneer and perfecter of our faith. What keeps a runner going is what he sees at the end of the race. The preacher warns the runner to have eyes for no one but Jesus. All the saints of the past are strong examples, but only Jesus was the perfect example. All the world around them would divert them from their appointed course. Only Jesus is the pioneer of perfect faith, who by his own life showed us for the first time the perfect pattern of faith. From the beginning to the end of the course which God appointed him, he showed the way of true faith.

The *perfecter* is the one who does and will fulfill the promises of God to us. His Spirit in us makes possible the fulfillment of his purpose for us.

Who for the joy was set before him endured the cross. The joy here described is the result of the self-renunciation mentioned in 2:9. The sacrifice which Christ made was not sacrifice for the sake of sacrifice, but sacrifice for the object of his love. His joy stemmed out of his faith that, beyond his sacrifice, lay a kingdom of redemption in which his beloved would share, a kingdom over which he would reign, *seated at the right hand of the throne of God.*

The saintly writer urged Christians to follow the example of Jesus' *despising the shame.* He urged Christians to despise the world, to despise themselves, and to despise the fact that they were despised. Could anything have been harder for Jesus than the experience of bearing on his sensitive soul the contempt of those whom he loved?

If you have a low opinion of another and he despises you, you are not greatly grieved. But if your son or daughter, whom you love with all your heart, despises you; this is as heavy a burden as you will ever be called upon to bear. If, in your sorrow, you are tempted to give way to self-pity, think of Jesus. Do you imagine that you have ever suffered anything comparable to his suffering? He loved everyone who despised him with all his heart. This made their despising all the more bitter for him.

2. Need for Discipline (12:3–17)

3 Consider him who endured from sinners such hostility against himself, so that you may not grow weary or fainthearted. 4 In your struggle against sin you have not yet resisted to the point of shedding your blood. 5 And have you forgotten the exhortation which addresses you as sons?—
"My son, do not regard lightly the discipline of the Lord,
  nor lose courage when you are punished by him.
6 For the Lord disciplines him whom he loves, and chastises every son whom he receives."
7 It is for discipline that you have to endure. God is treating you as sons; for what son is there whom his father does not discipline? 8 If you are left without discipline, in which all have participated, then you are illegitimate children and not sons. 9 Besides this, we have had earthly fathers to discipline us and we respected them. Shall we not much more be subject to the Father of spirits and live? 10 For they disciplined us for a short time at their pleasure, but he disciplines us for our good, that we may share his holiness. 11 For the moment all discipline seems painful rather than pleasant; later it yields the peaceful fruit of righteousness to those who have been trained by it.
12 Therefore lift your drooping hands and strengthen your weak knees, 13 and make straight paths for your feet, so that what is lame may not be put out of joint but rather be healed. 14 Strive for peace with all men, and for the holiness without which no one will see the Lord. 15 See to it that no one fail to obtain the grace of God; that no "root of bitterness" spring up and cause trouble, and by it the many become defiled; 16 that no one be immoral or irreligious like Esau, who sold his birthright for a single meal. 17 For you know that afterward, when he desired to inherit the blessing, he was rejected, for he found no chance to repent, though he sought it with tears.

Few things are more pathetic than the undisciplined life. We are in the midst of a generation which has been misled by a superficial psychology. It has deified desire, abhorred inhibitions, and proclaimed a freedom which releases our impulses to find gratification at any price. The fear of frustration has made us slaves of our desires. We have overlooked a very simple but fundamental fact of life. We cannot perform the most elementary task of life without discipline. If we allowed the allurements which distract us to take control, we would never get to work in the morning. We would never complete any assignment or meet any obligation. God has so structured life that every joy we know is the product of a painful discipline. So the writer of Hebrews reminds us that *the Lord disciplines him whom he loves.*

The Christian life is a life of hardship. How are the hardships to be regarded? They are to be taken as the process of discipline which ultimately will produce *the peaceful fruit of righteousness.*

The preacher reminds these hearers that, since they are the new Israel, they are the sons of God who are described in the third chapter of Proverbs. This passage assures us that those who are closest to God receive the special discipline of God. The Jews explained the chastising of God here as a means of lessening their punishment at the final day of judgment.

In your struggle against sin you have not yet resisted to the point of shedding your blood. They had suffered painfully (10:32 ff.), but these sufferings were not comparable to those who had died for their faith. He calls them out of self-pity to remember the valor of those who laid down their lives for the faith.

If you are left without discipline, in which all have participated, then you are illegitimate children and not sons. A father designs his discipline to enable his children to be comfortably integrated into the family for the mutual benefit of every member of the family. The illegitimate child, who is not to be a member of the family, receives no such discipline. Therefore, any kind of punishment which causes us to conform to the pattern of family behavior must be viewed as being motivated by love. Of course, the discipline imposed upon a child by a brash temper of the father does not honor God nor produce Christian character.

Because discipline leads us to be partakers of God's holiness and of the fruit of righteousness, we are to lift our drooping hands, strengthen our weak knees, and walk in straight paths. It is harder to walk the straight path of our daily routine with steady courage than it is to run in a glamorous race, with a crowd to cheer us on. But this too is a part of the preparation for holiness, without which no man shall see the Lord.

This serves as a corrective to the notions of "cheap grace," which have taken over much of the church. The belief in transactional atonement, which is little more than "juggling the books," leaves little place for existential holiness. Note, however, that the *holiness without which no one will see the Lord* is coupled with grace (v. 15). Salvation is God's work of making us new. "Salvation is a new man," said Frank Stagg, "not a new label."

Therefore lift your drooping hands and strengthen your weak knees. This passage is most picturesque. The drooping hands convey the same idea as the attitude of the people of Israel when they desired to abandon the rigors of the wilderness and return to the flesh pots of Egypt. Nothing is accomplished by drooping hands. *Make straight paths for your feet,* said the writer. "If you wobble and wander, your crippled leg will not be healed. It will be put out of joint." The undisciplined life makes our drooping hands and wobbly knees permanent disabilities. As we lift up our hands and walk straight, we encourage others. Courage comes by contagion.

Drooping hands and weak knees were familiar phrases found in a number of Old Testament passages. They were also found in familiar Essene writings, so that the Essene converts to this Christian community would know at once what the preacher meant.

What is lame could refer to those who are ready to collapse in their faith. Christian endurance is necessary, not only for personal salvation, but also for the sake of weaker Christians who need a strong, encouraging example. The crippled members of the church draw courage from the strong. If despair is an attitude that can spread like a plague, courage is also highly contagious.

Strive for peace with all men. Was strife threatening to destroy this congregation? A quarreling church dissipates her energies and robs her members of the proper climate for developing deep consecration. *And for the holiness.* Contentious people, who are more concerned about winning in argument than they are with living in harmony, make it difficult to work effectively for purity, goodness, and the holiness which makes possible the vision of God: "Blessed are the pure in heart, for they and they alone] shall see God" (Matt. 5:8).

See to it that no one fail to obtain the grace of God. This should be the supreme concern of each member of the Christian community, and it should be the corporate concern of the community. *That no "root of bitterness" spring up and cause trouble.* It is interesting to observe that this word ("root of bitterness") was used by Peter in his denunciation of Simon Magus, who tried to buy the gift of the Holy Spirit with money (Acts 8:23). The writer may be referring to the passage in Deuteronomy 29:18: "Beware . . . lest there be among you a root bearing poisonous and bitter fruit." Here the warning is against one who assures himself that he is in the covenant relationship, even though he continues to keep a stubborn heart.

The preacher to the Hebrews, however, is not thinking of stubbornness as the cause of the poisonous influence, but rather those people who are like Esau, who value immediate gratification of sensual desire above the final approval of God (Gen. 25: 28–34; 27:1–39).

That no one be immoral or irreligious like Esau, who sold his birthright for a single meal. The major concern of the preacher to the Hebrews is with those who are deserting his congregation. He likens them to Esau. Why should he choose Esau? His was the sin which "clings so closely" (12: 1). Esau was also an example of a wicked person who grew up among good people (Isaac and Rebekah) but refused to follow the pattern of their lives.

It has been pointed out that it was not overpowering hunger that motivated Esau. Had it been, he would hardly have been guilty. His guilt lay in his calculated decision that the satisfaction of his hunger was more important to him as a person than the appreciation of his birthright.

Are we wrong when we insist that anyone who wants to repent can? The Scripture teaches us that Esau could not repent. *For you know that afterward, when he desired to inherit the blessing, he was rejected, for he found no chance to repent, though he sought it with tears.*

There is another possible translation of this passage which, on the basis of the gender of the pronoun "it," makes the antecedent "the blessing." In other words, it was the blessing which Esau sought and not a place of repentance, according to the ASV.

However, the insistent concern of the author seems to be to bring every possible argument to bear upon his hearers who are contemplating defection from the Christian community. Therefore, he lifts this appalling story of Esau up as an example of what they are contemplating. For the third time (cf. 6:4–8; 10:26–31), he emphasizes his doctrine that, if one repudiates the truth made known in Christ, there is no possible repentance which can reconcile such an offender with God. But again it is recognized that there will be different interpretations of this passage, depending on one's view of the purpose of the Esau analogy.

The word translated *rejected* was often used to describe officials who had been disqualified for office. Here God is described as acting to carry out his law that certain deliberate choices carry irrevocable and fatal consequences. The reason for this seems to be that certain choices either reflect or lead to a condition in which, however much one may desire to repent, he cannot. It seems that God rejected Esau by leaving him to the consequences of his own choice. The tears of Esau paint a vivid picture and issue a strong warning to all who would deliberately choose to turn away from Christ. A. B. Davidson said (p. 242): "Those tears of Esau, the sensuous, wild, impulsive man, almost like the cry of some 'trapped creature,' are among the most pathetic in the Bible."

3. The Final Arrival (12:18–24)

[18] For you have not come to what may be touched, a blazing fire, and darkness, and gloom, and a tempest, [19] and the sound of a trumpet, and a voice whose words made the hearers entreat that no further messages be spoken to them. [20] For they could not endure the order that was given, "If even a beast touches the mountain, it shall be stoned." [21] Indeed, so terrifying was the sight that Moses said, "I tremble with fear." [22] But you have come to Mount Zion and to the city of the living God, the heavenly Jerusalem, and to innumerable angels in festal gathering, [23] and to the assembly of the first-born who are enrolled in heaven, and to a judge who is God of all, and to the spirits of just men made perfect,

[24] and to Jesus, the mediator of a new covenant, and to the sprinkled blood that speaks more graciously than the blood of Abel.

The preacher sees his hearers as being on the very verge of entering the city of God. In fact, by faith they have come to it. They are like the Israelites, on the eastern bank of the Jordan, ready at any moment to go into their promised land. So he is saying to them, in effect, "Do not draw back now that you are about to cross the threshold into the very presence of God in the heavenly Jerusalem." When people have worked and hoped and dreamed of some glorious fulfillment, as the time to enter in draws near, there is often an emotional depression for fear that it will not be all they expected or that it may be so much more than they expected. The reaction is almost more than they can bear.

Now, it should be stressed that what Christians apprehend by faith and finally receive is not less awesome than that which confronted the Israelites in the blazing fire, darkness, gloom, and tempest which made Moses tremble at Sinai. On the contrary, it is all the more terrifying for they enter the very presence of God himself. Look carefully now at the appalling scene:

For you have not come to what may be touched. In other words, you have come to the ultimate spiritual reality, to the city which remains for those who know that the sum total of reality does not reside in the things our eyes behold, our ears hear, and our fingers touch. This is the world of those who know that the bedrock reality of life is spiritual.

A blazing fire, and darkness, and gloom, and a tempest, and the sound of a trumpet, and a voice were physical manifestations which caused the strongest to tremble, but God himself seemed to be remote and unapproachable. So terrified were the leaders of Israel that they appealed to Moses to go up on the mountain for them and take God's messages (Deut. 5:23 ff.).

Notice that the writer does not say in v. 22, "You *shall* come" but *you have come.* By faith this actually occurs. Thus, we see again his view of the solidarity of history held together by faith. By faith the believer actually enters the city of the living God.

"He has prepared for them a city," the writer has said, in 11:16. Now they may enter. He is also using familiar Old Testament language. Isaiah referred to "Mount Zion, the place of the name of the Lord of hosts" (18:7; cf. Amos 1:2; Mic. 4:1 ff.).

And to innumerable angels in festal gathering. Psalm 68:16–17 speaks of the "mount which God desired for his abode, yea, where the Lord will dwell for ever. With mighty chariotry, twice ten thousand, thousands upon thousands." Daniel 7:10 also said, "A thousand thousands served him, and ten thousand times ten thousand stood before him; the court sat in judgment, and the books were opened." Angelic hosts thronging in glad worship around the living God was a familiar part of Israel's concept of heaven. Jesus said, "There is joy before the angels of God over one sinner who repents" (Luke 15:10).

And to the assembly of the firstborn who are enrolled in heaven. The firstborn were those with a title to God's blessing (Ex. 4:22). The concept of the heavenly books, in which the names of the heirs of salvation are recorded, gave steadfast assurance to the people of God. Since they are enrolled in heaven, they are not yet there, so this is a reference to the whole body of Christ on earth.

And to a judge who is God of all is the heart of the whole matter, says the preacher. You are to enter the presence of the Judge who will say whether or not you have been faithful and disciplined. He is no easygoing God. He is the Judge of all: all men, all angels, "the living and the dead" (Acts 10:42).

The major point is that he is not only our God, he is also the God of every other person whose life we have touched, the God of everyone we have wronged. We cannot feel that he will champion our cause against any other human being. As the God of all the earth, he is impartial. That is a far more sobering prospect than anything that confronted Israel at Sinai.

And to the spirits of just men made perfect were those who were made righteous by faith and, afterwards, received the fullness of perfection in the presence of God (11:40).

And to Jesus, the mediator of a new covenant, and to the sprinkled blood means that those contemplating entering the presence of God may take courage. They will not be there alone, nor to plead their own performance, but to plead the perfect sacrifice of Jesus and the grace of God made manifest in the new covenant.

That speaks more graciously than the blood of Abel contrasts the blood of Jesus with the blood of Abel. In the Genesis narrative (4:10), after Cain slew his brother, God came to walk in the cool of the garden and to say, "What have you done? The voice of your brother's blood is crying to me from the ground." Said this preacher, by implication, "When the blood of our guilt cries up before God, the blood of Christ cries louder." The blood of the murdered Abel was the blood of guilt crying for vengeance (11:4). But the blood of Christ was reconciling blood. The blood of guilt shuts the door of access to God. The reconciling blood opens that door for all who will draw near.

The blood of Jesus is "gracious" blood because it is the blood of him who ever intercedes for us and pleads his sacrifice as the ground of our forgiveness.

4. The Final Warning (12:25-27)

25 See that you do not refuse him who is speaking. For if they did not escape when they refused him who warned them on earth, much less shall we escape if we reject him who warns from heaven. 26 His voice then shook the earth; but now he has promised, "Yet once more I will shake not only the earth but also the heaven." 27 This phrase, "Yet once more," indicates the removal of what is shaken, as of what has been made, in order that what cannot be shaken may remain.

The final voice of God has now spoken and must not be refused. *His voice then shook the earth* is a reference to God's action at Sinai when God warned Israel to obey him. When the preacher says, *but now he has promised, "Yet once more I will shake not only the earth but also the heaven"* he is referring to the prophet Haggai's word: "Once again, in a little while, I will shake the heavens and the earth and the sea and the dry land" (2:6). The contrast is between the human voice of Moses, who was the divinely instructed messenger of God on earth, and the very voice of God himself, speaking in the blood of Jesus as the final sacrifice for sin.

This phrase, "Yet once more," indicates the removal of what is shaken, as of what has been made, in order that what cannot be shaken may remain. The purpose of cosmic catastrophe, which will shake all things, is that we may see that kingdom which alone is permanent. The book of Enoch tells of a convulsion which will shake not only heaven but the nerves of the angelic hosts as a premonition of the last judgment (60:1). Perhaps the preacher is using this to say, "The end time is very near." They are arriving at the end, though they have not yet arrived.

5. A Call to Gratitude and Worship (12:28-29)

28 Therefore let us be grateful for receiving a kingdom that cannot be shaken, and thus let us offer to God acceptable worship, with reverence and awe; 29 for our God is a consuming fire.

Therefore let us be grateful for receiving a kingdom that cannot be shaken. The Christian pilgrim is called to be grateful for that one unshakable reality, the kingdom of God to which he is now drawing near. Such gratitude leads to worship: *And thus let us offer to God acceptable worship, with reverence and awe.* Worship is impossible until we feel the grandeur, the majesty, and the wholly otherness of God. When we dwell on these qualities, a reverent awe will fall over our souls.

For our God is a consuming fire. Despite the fact that it is God's own Son who is our High Priest, who intercedes for us, there is no softening of the punitive side of God's nature. He is no easygoing God who winks at unfaithfulness. He is a "consuming fire," before whom no man can stand at all unless he stands in awesome reverence and holy fear.

XI. A Call to Virtue and Sacrifice (13:1–16)

1. Application of Christian Virtues (13:1–8)

¹ Let brotherly love continue. ² Do not neglect to show hospitality to strangers, for thereby some have entertained angels unawares. ³ Remember those who are in prison, as though in prison with them; and those who are ill-treated, since you also are in the body. ⁴ Let marriage be held in honor among all, and let the marriage bed be undefiled; for God will judge the immoral and adulterous. ⁵ Keep your life free from love of money, and be content with what you have; for he has said, "I will never fail you nor forsake you." ⁶ Hence we can confidently say,
"The Lord is my helper,
I will not be afraid;
what can man do to me?"
⁷ Remember your leaders, those who spoke to you the word of God; consider the outcome of their life, and imitate their faith. ⁸ Jesus Christ is the same yesterday and today and for ever.

Some authorities believe that the formal part of Hebrews ends here and that the thirteenth chapter is a postscript, containing counsel on Christian ethics, personal references, and a benediction. It should be noted also, however, that such a position was held by those who felt that the primary concern of this letter was with the confession of Christian faith and not with Christian conduct and behavior. Contemporary scholars, who recognize that confession and conduct were closely joined in early Christianity, consider the thirteenth chapter a vital part of the epistle and not an afterthought, nor an addendum.

In this passage Christian duties are carefully delineated. There is a fervent call to practice Christian morality and to worship and work with an unchanging Christ in a changing world.

Let brotherly love continue. This passage warns us that the breakdown of Christian faith begins with the cooling of our ardor and affection for our fellow Christians. When barriers are built between us and our fellow believers, they are also built between us and God.

Strong emphasis is placed on the word "continue." Our preacher has consistently emphasized the importance of endurance. Endurance is holding fast to proper doctrine, and with equal tenacity the Christian must endure in behavior which is consistent with his belief. The Christian must continue to endure as one who, at any moment, may cross the threshold into the very presence of God in the heavenly city. The specific point stated here at which he must endure is in brotherly love.

Do not neglect to show hospitality to strangers. The brotherly love of v. 1 must extend beyond the borders of the immediate community and embrace even strangers. Zenophobia has plagued mankind through all of his earthly pilgrimage. It is noteworthy that the ancient Hebrew took note of this and placed strong emphasis upon the proper attitude toward strangers in his religion. To be hospitable toward people with whom we are not very comfortable is a special duty, carried over from primitive religion. In the light of fuller Christian insight, it is made all the more imperative for the followers of Christ. Brotherly love must be more than an emotion. It must be put into practice. What better way can we express the unmerited love which Christ had for us than by caring for those whom we have never seen before and may never see again? We cannot be indebted to them for any previous favors, nor can we reasonably expect payment from them.

For thereby some have entertained angels unawares. The writer probably had in mind Abraham and Sarah (cf. Gen. 18: 1 ff.), and perhaps Manoah (Judg. 13: 8 ff.). There is an ancient legend that Abraham planted a tree at Beersheba (cf. Gen. 21:33) as a place of refreshment for strangers. Hospitality to strangers was considered by the Jews as one of the six things for which a person would be rewarded in the world to come.

There were special Christian incentives for such hospitality. Christian heralds, going over the ancient world, could not depend upon lodging in the public inns which were often little better than brothels. They were neither clean nor safe. Temptation lay everywhere in such inns. Innkeepers were often extortioners; Christian evangels were often too poor to be admitted for lodging. A Christian was obligated to take such a stranger into his home and provide lodging that the proclamation of the gospel might be furthered.

Moreover, the Christian had an even higher incentive than those who felt that, by entertaining strangers, they might be entertaining angels unawares. Jesus had given them the highest incentive, in Matthew 25:40, when he assured us that a service performed for "one of the least of these my brethren" is a means of entertaining Jesus.

Remember those who are in prison. Since the earliest days of the Christian church, caring for people in prison has been a Christian duty. There were numerous instances of the generous sacrificial care of imprisoned Christians by their fellow Christians. They would feed the prisoners and raise money to ransom them.

The preacher may not have been above a utilitarian approach to this matter, when he said, *as though in prison with them.* He knew that all Christians were candidates for imprisonment. Therefore, he warned them that they were *also in the body.* The implication was that they might be imprisoned at any moment and would then be dependent upon the mercy of their fellow Christians, as those who were already in prison were now dependent upon them for help.

It can be said, however, that a nobler motive for identifying with prisoners would be that it is in character for a Christian to be with the oppressed, not for what he will get out of it, but because his Lord is always identified with the oppressed.

Seneca stressed the nobility of the true friendship which is not self-centered, when he declared that a wise man befriends the sick, not because he hopes that the sick man will return the favor, but that he may have an outlet for pure compassion (cf. Moffatt, p. 226).

Let marriage be held in honor among all, and let the marriage bed be undefiled. The sanctity of the marriage vows implies two things: the marriage bond is honorable and not to be despised; and the cause of Christ is honored or dishonored by a Christian's sexual behavior.

All are thus called to sexual purity. The word translated *marriage bed* means sexual intercourse. *Undefiled* means sincere, pure. A distinction is drawn between "fornicator" and "adulterers." Fornicators are guilty of unlawful sexual intercourse. Adulterers are guilty of unlawful sexual intercourse with another's mate. Moffatt (p. 227) says of fornicators and adulterers: "In the former case, the main reference is to the breach of another person's marriage; in the latter, the predominating idea is treachery to one's own marriage vows." In other words, fornicators are guilty of breaking another person's marriage vows, while the adulterers break their own marriage vows. The preacher warns that all such illicit relationships *God will judge.*

Keep your life free from love of money. Greed of gain and sexual impurity are often joined in life, for one aids and abets the other. Paul, therefore, warned that "the love of money is the root of all evils" (1 Tim. 6:10). He linked immorality with greed (1 Cor. 5:10 f.). The possession of wealth often opens opportunity for sensual indulgence which otherwise might not be present. The love of money also has its own inherent perils in varied ways.

Be content with what you have. A Christian can never be satisfied with himself, but he can be content with what God has given him. Paul said, "There is great gain in godliness with contentment" (1 Tim. 6:6); not "godliness is great gain," for there are many godly people who are never truly content. They are always wanting more and become incapable of enjoying what they have because they are more conscious of what they do not have than of what they have.

Paul also said: "I have learned, in whatever state I am, to be content" (Phil. 4: 11). He was never content with himself. He said: "Not that I have already obtained this or am already perfect; but I press on" (Phil. 3:12). He said he was not content with his physical condition: he prayed over and over and over again that God might remove his "thorn . . . in the flesh" (2 Cor. 12:7). But he was content with what God had given him in Christ.

I will never fail you nor forsake you. Since a Christian is promised the presence of God, what more should he desire? The person, who wants the things which God can provide more than he wants God himself, puts himself above God; for he is more concerned with the things that will please and comfort him than he is with what service he can give to God. Our sufficiency is in God, who has promised never to leave us nor forsake us. What more can we ask? Hence, we can confidently say: *The Lord is my helper, I will not be afraid; what can man do to me?* The preacher quotes this passage from Psalm 118:6, and thus supports his unshakable confidence in the adequacy of his God.

In the setting of Hebrews a Christian's property was constantly in jeopardy. Instead of being anxious about it and bending his efforts to protect it or to recover it from those who had seized it, he should rest on the confidence that he has something better—a God who will never abandon him, but will supply his needs.

Remember your leaders, those who spoke to you the word of God—foremost, surely, the apostles and other faithful pastors. The primary function of early apostles was to preach the gospel in the power of the Holy Spirit. The declaration of the divine word was their mission. The Christian church is a community of memory. We owe much to those without whom we never could have heard the word of God.

Consider the outcome of their life, and imitate their faith. The word "outcome" is a metaphor for death. Their leaders laid down their lives for their faith. The blood of the martyrs is the seed of the church. The strong faith of others buoys us and carries us on. Three strong words are found in this verse around which a sermon may move to challenge and inspire Christians: remember, consider, and imitate.

Jesus Christ is the same yesterday and today and for ever. It is difficult to trace just how this sublime Christological affirmation fits into the writer's argument. Its magnetic euphemy indicates that it might well have been a frequently quoted formula in early Christian worship. If so, it would not necessarily have to apply at every point of the writer's argument. It might have been one of those sayings which preachers delight to introduce into sermons for the sake of style as well as substance. It might well have formed a part of an early Christian confession of faith meaning that, while human leaders come and go, the Christian's true leader remains.

The eternity of Christ, which is stressed in this verse, is in accord with the Christology of preexistence which, we have noted earlier, was such a vital part of this preacher's view of Jesus. All earthly leaders must come and go, but there is one who has permanent preeminence for a Christian. He is the Lord over all, blessed forever. Ours is an age that worships change. But without some invariable, it is impossible to evaluate change. Unless God's forgiveness and mercy are constant, we have no ground for permanent hope. The continuity of our communion with Christ is based upon our belief in his constancy. He "is the same yesterday and today and for ever." The many doctrines that bid for our allegiance must be judged by the truth revealed to us in Christ. Any teaching that would take us away from him must be refused.

2. Sacrifices Which God Approves
(13:9–16)

⁹ Do not be led away by diverse and strange teachings; for it is well that the heart be strengthened by grace, not by foods, which have not benefited their adherents. ¹⁰ We have an altar from which those who serve the tent have no right to eat. ¹¹ For the bodies of those animals whose blood is brought into the sanctuary by the high priest as a sacrifice for sin are burned outside the camp. ¹² So Jesus also suffered outside the gate in order to sanctify the people through his own blood. ¹³ Therefore let us go forth to him outside the camp, bearing abuse for him. ¹⁴ For here we have no lasting city, but we seek the city which is to come. ¹⁵ Through him then let us continually offer up a sacrifice of praise to God, that is, the fruit of lips that acknowledge his name. ¹⁶ Do not neglect to do good and to share what you have, for such sacrifices are pleasing to God.

These *diverse and strange teachings* might well have referred to the dietary laws of the Jews or the Essenes. It was exceedingly difficult for converts to Christianity to discontinue their belief that God bestowed special favor through certain foods. In writing to the Romans, Paul insisted that "the kingdom of God does not mean food and drink but righteousness and peace and joy in the Holy Spirit" (14:17). Paul also met this temptation in his Colossian letter, in chapter 2.

The preacher of Hebrews insists that *the heart* of a Christian is *strengthened by grace, not by foods.* The heart is the total inner life of a person. It is not food that sustains such life, but the grace of God. Ascetic abstinences do not strengthen the heart. Only the grace of God can.

The same word, here translated "grace," is translated "gratitude" in v. 28. The writer is saying that grace is God's gift to man, while the proper response is gratitude, which is man's gift to God. God's grace is a dynamic gift, which disposes its recipient to be gracious to others because of his gratitude to God. Where there is no gratitude, there is no evidence that God's grace has been bestowed.

We have an altar from which those who serve the tent have no right to eat. The true Christian sacrifice, on which our fellowship with God depends, has nothing to do with eating. Instead, it is a sacrifice in which we vow to do gracious, charitable deeds for others. Before this spiritual altar of sacrifice, we ask one question: "What may I offer to God?" The answer is: "I must offer praise to God and I must share with others what God has provided."

The sacrifice of praise was considered to be a purer form of worship than a sacrifice for sin because a sacrifice for sin would be an act of influencing God to grant forgiveness. It would be, in that sense, a self-centered act, while the sacrifice of praise would be offering God an unconditional offering in recognition of what God is and of what he has already done. The act of sharing with others was considered, by ancient rabbis, as a sacrifice which replaced the Temple ritual and which was pleasing to God. We communicate the spirit of the gospel by sharing.

The rabbinic saying, quoted in Tanchuma 55.2, reinforces this: "In the time of messiah all sacrifices will cease, but the sacrifice of thanksgiving will not cease; all prayers will cease, but praises will not cease (on basis of Jer. 33:1 and Psa. 56:13)" (quoted by James Moffatt, p. 237).

There are three superlative references to Christian service and worship in the New Testament. They are Hebrews 13:16, Romans 12:1–2, and James 1:27. For all the theological involvement and emphasis of this writer, let it not be forgotten that this preacher emphasizes that true worship is concentrated on compassion and charity toward man.

The permanence of Christ, emphasized in v. 8, calls us to remember that the primary obligation of the Christian is to identify with Christ's sacrifice and thus be with him. To go to him involves willingness to go *outside the camp, bearing abuse for him.* Here the Christian commitment of faith is described in three graphic pictures:

(1) *Outside the camp* means where the cross is. Jerusalem was the sacred city. No

crucifixion could occur within her walls. Therefore, the Son of God was taken outside the walls of the city to the rugged brow of Golgotha. If we go to him, according to the writer of Hebrews, we too must go outside the Holy City, outside the comfortable sanctuary, and be willing to walk the road of the cross. Because Christ died for us, we must die to those things that caused his death.

(2) *Outside the camp* means also to be on the march. The camp, referred to in Leviticus, was the one abode of light in a dark wilderness; but the Land of Promise lay beyond. Only those who ventured out of the known light into the darkness by faith could hope to find the Land of Promise. In the book of Exodus, the camp was the only place of safety. To venture outside the camp was often not to return. But Jesus walked that perilous road outside the safety of the camp into a world that did not know him, in order that the light of God might shine through earth's darkness. He walked as the trailblazer, the pioneer of our faith.

(3) To go *outside the camp* means that we must believe in an unseen world. We must believe in the city of God more than we believe in anything on earth. Nothing is more destructive of Christian faith than building an organization and imagining that it is an abiding city to be equated with the city of God. The kingdom of God is already built. Never in the New Testament is it said that the kingdom is built.[20] The kingdom (rule of God) builds the church, but the church does not *build* the kingdom.

For here we have no lasting city, but we seek the city which is to come. Christ is always out beyond any established city, beckoning to us, warning us not to be conformed to any worldly pattern (cf. Rom. 12:2). The writer here emphasized what he has previously said, in 11:10, 14–16: The final rest for a Christian lies in that city toward which we must by faith be always moving.

XII. The Conclusion (13:17–25)

1. The Appeal (13:17–19)

17 Obey your leaders and submit to them; for they are keeping watch over your souls, as men who will have to give account. Let them do this joyfully, and not sadly, for that would be of no advantage to you.
18 Pray for us, for we are sure that we have a clear conscience, desiring to act honorably in all things. 19 I urge you the more earnestly to do this in order that I may be restored to you the sooner.

Christian pastors are solemnly charged with the responsibility of caring for every person whom God has placed in their care and for seeing that none is lost. Therefore, the preacher appeals to his hearers: *Obey your leaders and submit to them.*

Because of the heavy responsibility which the preacher carries, he includes himself (cf. v. 18) among these leaders and asserts his right to be obeyed, not because of his prestige, but because of what he does. He keeps *watch* over their souls. The word translated "watch" actually means to be sleepless. A good pastor keeps constant vigil, like an alert shepherd over his flock. And obedience is to be accorded to Christian leaders, not to enhance their position, but to grant them the assurance that they have not lost those whom God has committed to their care. If a rebellious, hostile member of a congregation consumes his pastor's time and energy, as he tries to reconcile him to the rest of the flock, then the pastor has that much less energy to devote to those who have never met the Saviour.

In this light, such strong words, as *obey* and *submit,* are justified. It is not that a pastor desires to be a demigod, but that he faces the overwhelming responsibility of one, who at last, must *give* an *account* to the great Shepherd of us all.

Furthermore, the pastor has the responsibility to proclaim the word of God, which is an authoritative word. The major dif-

---

20 Frank Stagg, *New Testament Theology* (Nashville: Broadman Press, 1962), pp. 152 f.

ference between a Christian pastor and any other kind of leader of men is that the Christian holds in his hands a book inspired of God, through whom God speaks. The conversation is not merely between the pastor and his hearer. But there is a third Person speaking to and through the pastor. Therefore, with unbending firmness, the preacher may say, "See that you do not refuse him who is speaking" (12:25).

Insubordination in the Christian congregation leads to disastrous collapse to morale and fellowship. A watchman who keeps watch over the camp through the night has a right to sound an authoritative alarm and to be obeyed.

Let them do this joyfully, and not sadly. This preacher cannot conceive of a Christian pastor neglecting his duty and having to grieve over his negligence of his flock. He sees a pastor's sadness stemming from the disobedience and insubordination of those who should be making the service of Christ joyful for him. Again, the pastor is not giving way to self-pity in this passage. His sadness is not over his plight, but over that of his communicants.

For that would be of no advantage to you. Not only would the pastor be grieved, but the disobedient and insubordinate would lose most of all if they failed to enter into the fullness of life into which the pastor was seeking to lead them (cf. 6:9; 10:39).

Pray for us. The pastor now makes his appeal in behalf of himself, for he knows that God's work must be done in the power of God. Hence the plea for support through prayer.

For we are sure that we have a clear conscience. He knows that his motives are worthy and that those who pray for him may have the assurance that what he wants, through their prayers, is that God's will may be done and, therefore, their best interests will finally be served.

Desiring to act honorably in all things. Had his hearers been murmuring against him because of his absence? Is he here reassuring them of his abiding concern for them even though he is absent from them?

That I may be restored to you the sooner. This preacher believed that the time of his coming to them was dependent upon their prayers (cf. Philem. 22)

2. The Benediction (13:20-21)

20 Now may the God of peace who brought again from the dead our Lord Jesus, the great shepherd of the sheep, by the blood of the eternal covenant, 21 equip you with everything good that you may do his will, working in you that which is pleasing in his sight, through Jesus Christ; to whom be glory for ever and ever. Amen.

There was a mutual prayer pact between the preacher of Hebrews and his congregation. He asked for their prayers, now he breathes a prayer for them. So beautifully balanced and euphonious is this benediction that it might well have been a formal part of early worship, often quoted, just as was the Christological formula in v. 8. Had the author been concerned primarily with praying in accordance with a logical sequence, based on what he had said in his letter, you would expect that he would have addressed Christ as the great High Priest, rather than *the great shepherd of the sheep.* Nowhere else in the epistle is there a reference to Christ as the "shepherd." However, when prayer is made, the soul is often lifted above any logical sequence; and we sometimes employ language not our own, but language which has been hallowed by others whose prayers we have heard.

Prayers, however, are not so ecstatic that they cannot be analyzed, at least in part. Look, then, at the components of this prayer:

Now may the God of peace. He addresses the God who makes peace possible by his triumph over evil, the God who brings transcendent tranquility to his children, the serenity of the saints who have come into fellowship with God and have achieved it through the painful process of rigorous discipline. Beyond that discipline, the soul is in harmony with God. They know the bliss of those who are perfectly reconciled with God. The cross of the Conqueror has provided peace. The discipline of the pilgrim people of God has now made that peace a present experience for them.

Who brought again from the dead our Lord Jesus. This was the final triumph. As Bach put it: "Christ lay in death's dark prison." But Peter said: "But God raised him up, having loosed the pangs of death, because it was not possible for him to be held by it" (Acts 2:24). And Paul tells us why: "The sting of death is sin" (1 Cor. 15:56). The Christ who conquered sin could also conquer the consequences of sin which is death. And he stands assuring us, who share his triumph over sin, that we shall also share his triumph over death; that we too can mock the power of death: "O death, where is thy victory? O death, where is thy sting" (1 Cor. 15:55)?

The great shepherd of the sheep. The immortal shepherd breaks the bonds of death to stand by his own, to lead them at last into the final fold of God. He will never leave them. Not even death can finally separate him from his own. Peter makes much of the role of the divine shepherd (cf. 1 Peter 2:25; 5:4).

By the blood of the eternal covenant. The God of peace, that is, the God who has triumphed over evil in the life, death, and resurrection of Jesus and thus brought spiritual serenity to his people, had a cosmic purpose in the resurrection. God reversed the judgment of evil men who put the Saviour on the cross. God vindicated Christ by raising him from the dead, saying in effect: "He is not worthy of death. He is worthy of life eternal!"

The purpose also was that he might present his blood in the heavenly sanctuary as the full and permanent atonement for the sin of man, thus making possible an eternal covenant. Through this new covenant, the redeeming energy of heaven is released into the soul of man (cf. 9:11, 24 ff.; Zech. 9:11; Isa. 55:3).

Equip you with everything good that you may do his will. It is by this blood of the eternal covenant that God equips his people to do his will. Man does God's will in the special energy of God. God's tender grace not only makes his will known to man, but also enables him to do his will.

Through Jesus Christ; to whom be glory for ever and ever, Amen. And all of this is through Jesus Christ. Through Jesus, God's word came to us. Through his sacrifice, we were brought to Mount Zion (12:22–24), that is, to the heavenly Jerusalem, the true tabernacle on high, the world of spiritual reality. In the constant grace of Jesus, we find guidance for our wandering feet, love to put down the hostilities which develop in our interpersonal relationships, and abiding hope that we, one day, shall be made perfect when we come into his presence.

3. The Prayer (13:22–25)

22 I appeal to you, brethren, bear with my word of exhortation, for I have written to you briefly. 23 You should understand that our brother Timothy has been released, with whom I shall see you if he comes soon. 24 Greet all your leaders and all the saints. Those who come from Italy send you greetings. 25 Grace be with all of you. Amen.

This kind of conclusion—*I have written to you briefly*—as a part of the pattern of those who apparently were so aware of how much more could be said on such momentous themes. There is a parallel in 1 Peter 5:12, where the writer insists: "I have written briefly to you."

You should understand that our brother Timothy has been released. We cannot say for certain that this implies that Timothy has been in prison, because the word translated "released" may mean nothing more than that he is free or that he has started on the journey. The writer hopes to meet Timothy at the church which he is addressing.

Greet all your leaders and all the saints. The writer includes both leaders and members in his concern. Could the reference to *all* imply that they were too numerous to be named? The writer could then be wishing not to omit anyone.

Those who come from Italy send you greetings. The corporate witness of the Christian community is always kept in mind by this preacher. The church is a community of sharing.

Grammatically, *those who come from Italy* can mean either those who were then residing in Italy or those whose original home was Italy but who were at the time living outside of Italy. However, it would seem rather strange for the author to make such a broad and general greeting if he were writing from Italy. It would be more natural for him to be saying, "Your fellow Italians who are now with me outside of Italy join in sending greetings." The author had called himself a "refugee," in 6:18. He probably was planning a trip to the church in Rome to which this writing may have been addressed as a letter after it was first preached as a sermon.

Grace be with all of you. Amen. Since this work probably was first read aloud as a sermon (it can be read aloud in an hour), it closes with a benediction and an amen. Both 2 Timothy and Titus close in a similar manner (cf. 2 Tim. 4:22; Titus 3:15). *Grace* is the great and final word of the Christian gospel, the grace of God, who gave us our great High Priest, who has offered his own blood for us and now stands in the heavenly sanctuary interceding for us, until we too shall come into the full and final presence of God to be among the just men made perfect (12:23).

James

HAROLD S. SONGER

Introduction

James is a magnificent literary monument to the moral sensitivity and concern of the early church. For James the ethical implications of following Jesus extend to every aspect of the Christian life; and what it means to be a Christian is illustrated by concrete examples from a wide variety of situations ranging from personal disappointment to business planning.

But in spite of its lofty ethical perspective, James is neglected by many modern Christians. One reason for this seems to be the contagious hostility that Martin Luther expressed toward James. In the context of his dispute with the Roman Catholic Church, Luther took his stand on "justification by faith." In the Leipzig debate of 1519 Luther's opponent, Johann Maier of Eck used "So faith by itself, if it has no works, is dead" (2:17) as his trump card; and Luther's feeling against James mushroomed. In his introduction to James in the first edition of the Geneva Bible (1522), Luther depreciates James as nonapostolic, unorganized, and Jewish; and he gives it the now well-known designation of "a right strawy epistle" in comparison with such New Testament books as Paul's Romans or John's Gospel (Ropes, pp. 105–108).

Since Luther's rather harsh, but historically understandable, judgment regarding James, biblical scholars have pinpointed other features of the epistle which seem to justify Luther's view. Many distinctive doctrines of the Christian faith are not present. James does not mention the ne-cessity of the death of Christ for man's salvation; he does not speak of the Holy Spirit as the source of Christian strength; he does not refer to the miracles of Jesus; and he does not clearly affirm the incarnation.

When these doctrinal deficiencies are realized and the strong Judaistic flavor and apparently disorganized thought of the epistle are added, James does begin to appear "strawy." But this apparent inferiority vanishes when the purpose and literary character of the book are understood.[1] The solid contributions of James to the faith and life of the church need to be recovered, and the first step is a clear understanding of his purpose.

I. The Purpose of James

Stated simply, the epistle is intended to confront members of the church with the responsibilities of the Christian life. A fuller statement of the purpose of James thus involves an exploration of the audience he addresses and the message he articulates.

1. The Audience James Addresses

No doubt exists that James writes to persons who are already members of the Christian community. He repeatedly calls his readers "brothers"; he refers to matters

· [1] For the explanation of the doctrinal deficiencies, see the discussion of "The Purpose of James" and "Literary Relationships"; for the Judaistic flavor, see the section on "Literary Relationships"; and for the disorganization, see the discussion of "Paranetic Organization."

within the church such as the treatment of poor persons (2:1-7) and the responsibilities of teachers (3:1-12); and he considers himself along with his audience as being regenerated (1:18).

James is included among the so-called "catholic" epistles, and the term catholic in this usage means general or universal and is appropriately applied to James because it is addressed to Christians everywhere (1:1). Rather than having written to a local situation and spoken to the specific problems of a single congregation, James addressed the church as a whole and dealt with what he felt should be of major concern to all Christians.

2. The Message James Articulates

James apparently faced a situation in which persons were professing faith in Christ and participating in the Christian community without realizing the vast ethical and moral implications of such involvement (2:14-26). For James, being a member of a Christian community meant living in a dedicated struggle against sin (1:12-15,19-21), immorality (4:1-10), and injustice (4:13—5:6). Many of the Christians to whom James wrote had made some progress in Christian life; but they were not struggling enough with the larger implications of faith in Christ such as endurance in trials, consistency in Christian perspective, overcoming prejudice, economic responsibility, and planning one's life in reliance upon God. With magnificent insight, James summons Christians to consider the meaning of their profession of faith in Christ in terms that include one's personal life and his responsible involvement with others in society.

James does not stress social action in such a way that personal righteousness is sacrificed, but he insists on ethical involvement which is broader than struggling with personal sin and which seeks to carry out the implications of the gospel in society.

Unfortunately the theological debates of the reformation resulted in the epistle's being used in a way the author never intended, and some of the affirmations of James became suspect to Protestants. The letter continues to be misused by those who stress works in relation to man's becoming a Christian, and 2:14-26 is frequently used to insist that baptism is necessary for salvation. But James did not intend to address either the issue of the reformation or of baptismal regeneration—his basic concern was ethical. James considered the problem of faith and works simply because some persons were utilizing a profession of faith as a refuge from ethical responsibility. His concern was to maintain that Christian faith involves enduring moral responsibility.

II. The Literary Character of James

An understanding of James from the perspective of its literary character is the most crucial matter of all for adequately interpreting the epistle, and it also exposes the fact that those who stress the so-called deficiencies of the book have an inadequate grasp of its literary nature.[2]

1. Literary Type

James consists mainly of general ethical exhortations on a wide variety of subjects, and this type of literature is known as paranetic. Paranesis is general ethical instruction and exhortation. It is the kind of material that could be used to instruct all Christians, and the exhortations are not applied to a specific community. Unlike Paul's ethical teaching which is usually directed to a particular problem situation in a local church, the pleas of James are general and calculated to inspire Christian conduct in a wide variety of circumstances.

The type of literature known as paranesis flourished in the first Christian century in both the Jewish and Greco-Roman cultures to the extent that what amounted to a literary tradition was formed (Dibelius and Greeven, pp. 13-23). The uniqueness of the literary character of James in the New Testament is in its reflection in such

---

2 See the author's discussion of "The Literary Character of the book of James" in the *Review and Expositor*, 66 (1969), 379-89.

an unmixed way of this paranetic tradition with its peculiar features of organization and style.

(1) *Paranetic Organization.* It was characteristic of paranesis to place together in loose organization a series of exhortations without any concern to develop one theme or line of thought in the entire writing.

The most common method of joining materials in paranetic literature was to utilize catch or key words which tied paragraphs or sayings together. In 1:2–4 for example, the need to realize joy in suffering is dealt with, and in the conclusion (v. 4) the term "lacking" appears. This term forms the bridge to the discussion of wisdom where the term "lack" recurs (1:5). The linkage of the units of material (1:2–4 and 1:5–8) is more literary than logical; and in some cases in paranesis no logical connection for the placing of materials can be discovered.

Another frequently used method of organizing the material in paranetic literature was that of gathering various maxims under a topic as James does in 5:13–18 where prayer is discussed from various perspectives. At times the topic which the author uses is so general that a section hardly seems to have unity and appears as a collection of various exhortations. James 4:1–10 has defied all attempts to outline it or explain its progression of thought, and it is probably best seen as a collection of imperatives around the general theme of calling persons to consecration.

(2) *Paranetic Style.* The basic paranetic unit is the imperative sentence, and James includes about 60 imperatives in 108 verses. In the course of the development of paranetic literature, the imperative sentence was expanded into a short paragraph or brief moral essay which explained, illustrated, or applied the exhortation. James consists more of these brief paragraphs of ethical exhortation than of isolated imperatival sentences, although the latter are present. James 1:5–8 is a typical paranetic paragraph: man is exhorted to ask God for wisdom without doubting; the

doubter is described by an illustration from nature; and the conclusion warns the unstable man that he will receive nothing from the Lord.

Another feature of paranetic style is the listing of vices or virtues. Paul utilized this literary form in listing the works of the flesh and the fruit of the Spirit (Gal. 5:19–23); and a similar paranetic list of vices and virtues appears in James 3:13–18.

Paranetic literature also frequently incorporated a style of writing developed by Cynic and Stoic Greek philosophers and representing the literary crystallization of features of oral communication. This style, known as diatribe, is characterized by writing as if one were debating with an individual in the presence of an audience. James 2:14–26 is an excellent example of this diatribe style employed in paranetic literature. The statement, "You have faith and I have works" (2:18), is posed by the author as representative of his opponent and is constructed so as to further the argument. The quotation is introduced with a formula, "But some one will say," which was stylized in the diatribe; and the identification of the opponent as "you foolish fellow" (v. 20) was typical of diatribe style (for a discussion of diatribe style, see Ropes, pp. 6–18).

(3) *Conclusions.* A consideration of James from the perspective of its literary type makes it clear that James belongs to the category of first century literature known as paranesis. The author of James used a literary form and method of ethical instruction current in his own day to meet the needs of Christians; and it is the use of this form that explains both the variations in style and the peculiar organization of the letter. This recognition that James is paranesis makes it unnecessary to hold that the letter was written to a single church as some scholars do, e.g., Elliott-Binns.

2. *Literary Relationships*

Much of the material in the book of James is similar to sections in Jewish, Greek, or other Christian literature that existed when James was written. James 5:12, for example, is quite like Matthew 5:34–37; but James does not assign it to Jesus. This similarity between James and other literary materials raises the problem of the literary relationships of James.

(1) The Quest for Sources. In an effort to explain the literary relationships between James and other materials, some scholars have viewed James as incorporating an earlier document. Massebieau and Spitta, working independently, arrived in the 1890s at the theory that James was originally a Jewish document and that a Christian editor made minor additions to it, consisting basically of the name of Christ in 1:1 and 2:1. This theory gained little acceptance because of the undeniable Christian assumptions throughout James (see 1:18,21,25; 2:7; 5:8,12) and the fact that 2:14–26 reflects a Christian rather than a Jewish debate.[3]

The idea of a Jewish source recurs in the work of Arnold Meyer who affirmed that James is a Christian revision of an original Jewish letter of Jacob to the twelve tribes in which each tribe was referred to allegorically by the special vice or virtue which characterized it in Jewish tradition.[4] Meyer's position is devastated by the fact that no traditional characterization of the sons of Jacob existed in first-century Judaism, but his theory continues to be influential. It is in fact the basis of B. S. Easton's approach in *The Interpreter's Bible* (Vol. XII) in which the Jacob document is reduced and the Christian editing increased.

Many other suggestions regarding sources for James have been proposed, but none has gained acceptance for two reasons. First, the fact that agreement cannot be reached with regard to the nature and extent of the sources indicates how subjective such research with regard to James

is; and second, the recognition that James is paranesis provides the most adequate explanation for the similarities between materials in James and other literature.

(2) Paranesis and Literary Relationships. Many of the sections of James are quite similar to passages in Jewish, Greek, or other Christian literature. This literary similarity is characteristic of paranesis because it was customary in the paranetic tradition to use ethical materials from many sources which the author felt were appropriate for his purposes.

James utilizes the contemporary and customary Hellenistic illustrations of influence (3:3–5) in speaking of the tongue's power and reflects Stoic philosophical terminology in the expression "cycle of nature" (3:6). Yet the section that denounces economic exploitation (5:1–6) is reminiscent of the Jewish prophetic tradition, and the concerns of Judaism clearly emerge in the reference to the law in the condemnation of malicious speech (4:11–12). This feature of paranesis accounts for the affinity between James and the Jewish wisdom literature that has often been noted by scholars.

Although some paranetic literature is quite disjointed and represents more the work of a compiler than an author, James reflects the thoughtful utilization of a wide range of ethical materials in the context of his Christian perspective. The use of materials that ultimately reflect diverse perspectives was characteristic, and it was not the purpose of the authors of such material to challenge the religious or philosophical perspectives in which the material originated.

James, therefore, felt no need to discuss the characteristic and generally acknowledged Christian doctrines. He writes to Christians, assumes they are in basic agreement theologically, and uses the ethical materials that he feels are needed without any apology.

III. The Origin of James

Although the author identifies himself by name, the questions of who wrote James

---

3 For a discussion of this source theory, see Joseph B. Mayor, *The Epistle of St. James* (3rd ed. London: Macmillan and Co., 1910), pp. cxciii–ccv.

4 Arnold Meyer, *Das Rätsel des Jakobusbriefes,* "Beihefte für *Zeitschrift für die neutestamentliche Wissenschaft*" [Giessen: Töpelmann, 1930]).

and when and where it was written are difficult to answer.

1. Authorship

The author identifies himself simply as "James, a servant of God and of the Lord Jesus Christ" (1:1). Actually, the translation "James" is misleading because the Greek reads "Jacob." The name James is an English name which apparently comes from the Old Latin *Jakomus* which goes back to the Hebrew Jacob. The author of the book of James was actually named Jacob instead of James, but the English translators of the New Testament reserved the name Jacob for the Hebrew patriarch and translated the name of every other person called Jacob in the New Testament as James (Blackman, p. 38).

Of the several persons named James in the New Testament, the James known as the Lord's brother has been traditionally regarded as the author of the epistle. The simplicity of the author's self-designation implies an eminent and well-known person. The references to James the brother of Jesus in the New Testament (Acts 12:17; 15:13-21; 21:18-25; Gal. 1:19) demonstrate his status and provide information that fits in well with many of the concepts in the epistle. It is difficult to conceive that 1:1 refers to any other person than James the Lord's brother.

Many scholars who acknowledge that James the Lord's brother is designated as the author (1:1) feel that some unknown Christian wrote in the name of James, perhaps even incorporating many of the teachings of James. The reasons for this position are that there are some perplexing questions raised by affirming the traditional position on authorship. James was only slowly received into the canon, no very reliable early external evidence exists which assigns the epistle to the Lord's brother, and the Greek style seems too polished for a Palestinian Jew.

The difficulty of believing that some one wrote in the name of James is almost insurmountable when the reticence of the self-designation in 1:1 is considered, and this leads many scholars to hold that James was written by some Christian named James about whom nothing is known from the New Testament. In the later struggles of the church to set the limits of the canon, this James became identified with the Lord's brother; and the stage was set for the traditional assigning of authorship. This position does solve the problems of the traditional view, but it must remain hypothetical because it is basically an argument from silence.

In seeking to come to a position on this matter of authorship, it is clear that the scales are delicately balanced between the decision for James the Lord's brother and James the unknown Christian. The latter position does have the strength of solving nearly all of the problems of the slow acceptance of James into the canon; but what must not be overlooked is that James is in the canon of the New Testament and is authoritative for Christians apart from any decision about its writer. The authority of a book in the New Testament does not rest upon the precise identification of the author. The authority of the New Testament is in the reliability of its witness to Jesus Christ and his claims upon men. James is Christian Scripture and must be heeded and heard as authoritative for Christian faith regardless of one's theory of authorship.

2. Date and Place of Writing

The conclusion one accepts regarding the authorship of James determines the possibilities for both the date and place of writing of the epistle. Those who feel James the Lord's brother is the author locate the place of writing as Jerusalem and date it either in the forties or early sixties of the first century. As James was martyred in A.D. 62 and James 2:14-26 seems to reflect a Pauline controversy, a date around A.D. 60 seems the better choice of times from the traditional perspective.

Scholars who feel that the author was an unknown James or a Christian writing in the name of James usually place the epistle's date of writing at about the end of the first century. The place of writing is almost indeterminable for those who take these perspectives on authorship because of the general nature of the letter. Many suggestions for a place of writing have been made, but none is capable of convincing demonstration.

IV. The Distinctive Contribution of James

The book of James makes some distinctive contributions to Christianity, and these should not be ignored.

First, James is the purest type of paranetic literature to be found in the New Testament. The fact that a New Testament author employs methods of ethical exhortation that were being utilized with success in the first-century world is instructive for the church as it seeks to fulfill its educational task in the twentieth century. To be true to its heritage in the fullest sense, the contemporary church must be aware of and quite willing to adopt appropriate new insights and methods of instruction.

Second, the development of Protestant theology with its emphasis upon justification by faith creates a situation in which the grace and power of God are often stressed in such a way that Christians are sometimes in danger of loosening their grip upon the moral and ethical demands of the gospel. One of the outstanding distinctives of James is that he defines Christian life in terms of the moral and ethical behavior of those who profess faith in Jesus Christ. The measure of a Christian is taken by his ethical sensitivity and accomplishment.

Third, the epistle of James witnesses to the magnificent ethical perspective of an early Christian teacher and is instructive in terms of the balance maintained between personal spiritual development, responsible membership in the Christian community, and Christian action that is designed to be redemptive in the larger society of which the Christian is a part. The ethical injunctions of James call all Christians to ethical achievement which is both individual and social, including redemptive contributions to the church and the whole world.

Outline

James cannot be outlined in such a way as to indicate a logical development of thought because it is paranesis. All that can be done toward outlining is to indicate topically, by chapters, the paranetic sections of the letter.

I. Chapter 1
1. Epistolary greeting (1:1)
2. Joy in trial (1:2–4)
3. The secret of prayer (1:5–8)
4. Rich and poor (1:9–11)
5. Trial and temptation (1:12–15)
6. God and good gifts (1:16–18)
7. The importance of meekness (1:19–21)
8. Hearing and doing the Word (1:22–25)
9. Pure religion (1:26–27)

II. Chapter 2
1. Prejudice in action (2:1–7)
2. Prejudice and law (2:8–13)
3. Faith and works (2:14–26)

III. Chapter 3
1. The power of the tongue (3:1–5)
2. The misuse of the tongue (3:6–12)
3. The two wisdoms (3:13–18)

IV. Chapter 4
1. A call to consecration (4:1–10)
2. Evil speaking and the law (4:11–12)
3. The sin of presumption (4:13–17)

V. Chapter 5
1. The condemnation of the rich (5:1–6)
2. The need for patience (5:7–11)
3. Swearing (5:12)
4. The power of prayer (5:13–18)
5. Reclaiming the wayward (5:19–20)

Selected Bibliography

A splendid introduction to James, including additional bibliographical references is found in WERNER GEORG KÜMMEL, *Introduction to the New Testament*, trans. A. J. MATTILL, Jr. (Nashville: Abingdon Press, 1966), pp. 284–292, 390–391, 397–398.

BLACKMAN, E. C. *The Epistle of James.* ("Torch Bible Commentaries.") London: SCM Press, 1957.

BOWMAN, JOHN WICK. *Hebrews, James, Peter.* ("The Layman's Bible Commentary.") Richmond: John Knox Press, 1962.

DIBELIUS, MARTIN and HEINRICH GREEVEN. *Der Brief des Jakobus.* ("Kritisch-exegetischer Kommentar über das Neue Testament.") 11th ed. Göttingen: Vandenhoeck & Ruprecht, 1964.

EASTON, B. S. "James," *The Interpreter's Bible.* Vol. XII. New York: Abingdon Press, 1957. Pp. 3–74.

ELLIOTT-BINNS, L. E. "James," *Peake's Commentary on the Bible.* London: Thomas Nelson and Sons, 1962. Pp. 1022–1025.

MAYOR, JOSEPH B. *The Epistle of St. James.* 3rd ed. London: Macmillan and Co., 1910.

MITTON, C. L. *The Epistle of James.* Grand Rapids: Wm. B. Eerdmans Publishing Co., 1966.

MUSSNER, FRANZ. *Der Jakobusbrief.* ("Herders Theologischer Kommentar zum Neuen Testament.") Freiburg: Herder, 1964.

ROBERTSON, A. T. *Studies in the Epistle of James.* Ed. H. F. Peacock. Nashville: Broadman Press, 1959.

ROPES, J. H. *A Critical and Exegetical Commentary on the Epistle of St. James.* ("The International Critical Commentary.") Edinburgh: T. & T. Clark, 1916.

TASKER, R. V. G. *The General Epistle of James.* ("Tyndale New Testament Commentaries.") Grand Rapids: Wm. B. Eerdmans Publishing Co., 1956.

Commentary on the Text

I. Chapter 1

Eight carefully constructed paragraphs of exhortation, dealing with various themes but skillfully linked together, follow the stylized greeting (1:1) and demonstrate the author's mastery of paranesis (cf. "The Literary Character of James" in the Int.). The main perspective of each of these eight units and the ways James links them are discussed in the commentary as each section is introduced.

1. Epistolary Greeting (1:1)

¹ James, a servant of God and of the Lord Jesus Christ,
To the twelve tribes in the Dispersion: Greeting.

James begins with a greeting in the basic form of a first-century Greco-Roman letter. Nearly 80 percent of the books in the New Testament are in epistolary form— only the Gospels, Acts, and perhaps Revelation are exceptions—which the early Christian missionaries and teachers adapted for communicating with churches. Usually a distinction is made between a letter and an epistle. Although both utilize the same form, an epistle is less confidential in tone and directed to a wider circle of readers. James is more like an epistle than a letter. Although it begins with a greeting in the customary letter form (v. 1), it concludes more in the style of an

essay and does not have the personal references usually found in letters (cf. 1 Cor. 1:11; 16:1–20; 2 Cor. 7:13–16; Phil. 4:2–3) or at their conclusions (cf. 2 Cor. 13:11–14; Philem. 23–25).

The author designates himself simply as *James,* representing the Hebrew Jacob, and early Christian readers would most naturally identify him with that James (Jacob) who was prominent in the Jerusalem church (cf. Int. for a discussion of authorship).

In calling himself *servant* (slave) the author uses a term which was considered degrading by both Jews and Greeks in the realm of personal relationships because it implied bondage and the lack of freedom. The term was used, however, as one of respect in reference to man's relation to God in Judaism and indicated either all of Israel as committed to God or referred to some person of heroic faith, such as Moses (Mal. 4:4). For James to designate himself as *a servant of God* indicates an assurance in his relationship with God through Christ that surpassed the perspective of Judaism. The title implies both God's grace in relating to man and the author's commitment to obedience.

Other writers in the New Testament used this designation (e.g., Rom. 1:1; Phil. 1:1; Titus 1:1; 2 Peter 1:1; Jude 1:1; Rev. 1:1), and in later Christian literature "servant of God" became a synonym for a Christian (Hermas, Mandates 5.2.1). The author identifies his slavery as being *of God and of the Lord Jesus Christ*. Slavery to two masters was inconceivable (Matt. 6:24), and here is a clear indication of the author's understanding of the unity between God and Christ. For James, to serve Christ was to serve God and to serve God was to serve Christ.

The title *Lord Jesus Christ* represents the way in which Jesus was understood in Jewish and Gentile Christianity outside Palestine.[5] In the title, *Jesus* represents the name assigned by Joseph and Mary at angelic direction (Matt. 1:21; Luke 1:31); *Christ* is the Greek term for the Hebrew Messiah (anointed) which relates primarily to a Jewish context of fulfillment; and *Lord* (*kurios*) was used to refer to God in both Greek and Jewish literature.

James does not deal with the subject of who Christ is or what he accomplished in detail, but the use of the developed title for Jesus plus the fact that God and Jesus are coupled so as to imply equality indicates something of what his feeling is. The body of the letter assumes that the readers are committed to the Lord Jesus Christ and deals with what this implies for their lives.

To the twelve tribes in the Dispersion is an address indicating the Christian church as a whole (Mitton, p. 17). Originally, *twelve tribes* referred to the traditional groups in Israel; but by the first century an altogether accurate division into 12 tribes was no longer possible because of inadequate genealogical records. Some Jews were able to indicate their heritage with precision (cf. Luke 1:5 and Phil. 3:5), but it was expected that the Messiah would restore Israel correctly as 12 tribes when he appeared (Ropes, pp. 118–119). *Twelve tribes* could refer to all Israel as the people of God (Matt. 19:28), and thus in a Christian context it designated the true

people of God or the followers of Jesus. The reference *in the Dispersion* originally indicated the exilic situation (Matt. 1:17), but later was applied to all Jews outside Palestine (John 7:35).

Thus, by addressing his epistle *to the twelve tribes in the Dispersion* James simply means that he is speaking to the true people of God everywhere—that is the persons who believe in Jesus Christ as Lord without regard to the specific place where they live (cf. 1 Peter 1:1).

The term *greeting* was generally used in the first century in letters, and it marks the conclusion to the epistolary salutation (cf. Acts 15:23). Because letters were rolled instead of folded, the name of the sender and the identity of the person or persons addressed were customarily placed at the beginning of the letter as it is here.

2. Joy in Trial (1:2–4)

2 Count it all joy, my brethren, when you meet various trials, 3 for you know that the testing of your faith produces steadfastness. 4 And let steadfastness have its full effect, that you may be perfect and complete, lacking in nothing.

The skillful literary transition from the epistolary salutation to the first unit of exhortation is not apparent in an English translation, but the terms "greeting" (*chairein*, 1:1) and "joy" (*charan*) are almost equivalent in sound in Greek. Such linkage by alliteration is characteristic of paranesis.

Incredibly, James begins his exhortation with the directive that the Christian community is to regard its trials as an occasion for rejoicing. The imperative *count* means consider or understand it to be. The expression *all joy* means nothing but joy or supreme joy (Ropes, p. 129) and could appropriately be translated "ecstasy."

The term translated *trials* also means temptation (cf. 1:13–14), but it is misleading to render the term here as in the KJV because what is under consideration is afflictions, troubles, or difficulties. The trials are *various* or of every sort, and the implication of the verb used to describe one's

5 See Reginald H. Fuller, *The Foundations of New Testament Christology* (New York: Charles Scribner's Sons, 1965).

encounter with them is that *you meet* them unexpectedly or fall into them (cf. Luke 10:30, "he fell among"). *The testing of your faith* clarifies the basis for the exhortation to regard the tragedies of life as friends because the term *testing* indicates not the experience itself but the result of it; it implies that the difficulties of life can be the means or path to *steadfastness* and becoming *perfect* and *complete.*

Testing for the Christian is an opportunity or school for the development of *endurance,* and this is one of the hallmarks of authentic Christian existence for James. *Endurance* means continuing in one's reliance on God; it is constancy or persistence in faith. For James, Christian life matures as one endures, stubbornly trusting in God as the difficulties, tragedies, and problems of life are encountered. This enduring reliance is the context for one's progress in becoming *perfect and complete,* and the exhortation that the Christian is to see to it that *steadfastness have its full effect* implies that persistence in itself is not the final goal—the aim is to be perfect (mature) and complete (adequate). These terms occur frequently in paranetic literature and express in combination the concept of becoming fully what God requires and approves (cf. Mitton, pp. 23–26).

The concept of Christian growth through suffering is a part of the message of Jesus (Matt. 16:24–28), and its acceptance in the early church is clear (Rom. 5:3–5; 1 Peter 1:6–7). But James stresses it in a way that calls Christians to a magnificent reality—the tragedies and troubles of life are to be met with the joyful awareness that the path of Christian fulfillment is opened by endurance. The ultimate favor of God is not measured by deliverance from tragedy but by the Christian's being redeemed in it so that he will be *lacking in nothing* (cf. 1:12).

3. The Secret of Prayer (1:5–8)

⁵ If any of you lacks wisdom, let him ask God, who gives to all men generously and without reproaching, and it will be given him.

⁶ But let him ask in faith, with no doubting, for he who doubts is like a wave of the sea that is driven and tossed by the wind. ⁷,⁸ For that person must not suppose that a double-minded man, unstable in all his ways, will receive anything from the Lord.

If any of you lacks wisdom does not imply that some persons were sufficiently wise; the conditional statement probably assumes inadequacy and means "since you do lack wisdom." The perspective that wisdom comes from God is basically Jewish rather than Greek, but the concept that one should pray for wisdom is somewhat distinctive. The general perspective in Judaism in the first century was that the wisdom from God was contained in the Jewish Scriptures (Torah) and that man gained it by study. The relationship between wisdom and the Torah was so close that they were frequently identified (Sirach 24:1–29).

Wisdom in Judaism was religious and moral knowledge which enabled a man to serve God. This contrasts with the first-century Greco-Roman perspective of wisdom as ethical, scientific, or philosophical knowledge accumulated by human reason.

The Judaistic heritage of James shines through in his relating wisdom to God (cf. 3:13–18), but a distinct Christian emphasis emerges in the fact that wisdom is not related to study of the Torah but to prayer. James considers wisdom to be a supreme and direct gift from God to the Christian (cf. comment on 3:13–18) and uses it naturally as an example of what men should pray for.

Christians should pray with confidence because they address a *God who gives to all men generously and without reproaching.* The word *generously* carries the idea of sincerity or without reflection; God gives naturally and does not hesitate. The *without reproaching* clarifies God's giving further with the idea that he does not chide or remind one of previous gifts. The thrust of James is that God is a giving God.

This understanding of a God who gives to all men is the basis of the affirmation that when one prays *it will be given him.* The concern of the author is not only to encourage Christians to pray, but to stress that prayer must be in the context of unswerving and enduring reliance on God or *in faith, with no doubting.* The term *doubting* is explained by the illustration of the wind-driven *wave of the sea* and the vivid description *double-minded* which is literally "double-souled" (cf. 4:8) and means one who has two sets of loyalties. *Doubting* does not here mean questioning, confusion, or uncertainty about what one should pray for; it refers to indecision and applies to the person who wants both to rely on God and to go his own way—he is *unstable* (fickle or wavering) and hesitant in the face of what he knows he ought to do.

The essence of this section is that God is a giving and benevolent God who desires to help man, but the secret of prayer is that the Christian must be committed to God and willing to appropriate the gifts God gives. It is reading too much into this passage to affirm that all unanswered prayer indicates an insincere life. James returns to the subject of prayer in 5:13–18, and the passages should be understood in their mutual light.

4. Rich and Poor (1:9–11)

⁹ Let the lowly brother boast in his exaltation, ¹⁰ and the rich in his humiliation, because like the flower of the grass he will pass away. ¹¹ For the sun rises with its scorching heat and withers the grass; its flower falls, and its beauty perishes. So will the rich man fade away in the midst of his pursuits.

A consideration of the sections in which James refers to the poor and rich (1:9–11; 2:1–7; 5:1–6) shows that the term rich is used metaphorically or poetically to refer to the wicked or unrighteous, while poor is used to describe the pious or Christian person. For James, the term poor is not primarily economic, but spiritual—the poor man is the oppressed and downtrodden (2:6–7) who is rich spiritually because of

his faith (2:5) and looks forward to exaltation (1:9). The term rich refers to the exploiters (5:2–4), who persecute Christians (2:6–7) and who face terrible judgment (1:10–11; 5:1–5). This perspective which related pious with poor and wicked with rich represents a post-exilic Judaistic view which was quite popular in the first century (cf. Luke 16:19–30), even though it was rejected by the Pharisees who viewed wealth as a sign of God's favor (cf. Mark 10:23–26).[6]

The fact that James uses poor as the equivalent of pious, and rich in the same way to designate the wicked, is quite appropriate to his paranetic purpose and to the struggling and oppressed people he addresses. He does not intend to affirm that poverty is blessed and affluence a curse; he is using first-century perspectives to communicate: it is his message which should be heard, his medium should not be misunderstood.

The *lowly* (poor) is summoned to *boast in his exaltation;* and although the elevation of the poor can be taken in the sense of his present possession of the riches of faith (2:5), it is probably better to understand the whole section in the light of the final judgment (cf. Blackman, p. 51). The oppressed Christian should keep in mind the reversal of his fortune that judgment will bring, and he can glory in this.

Some scholars hold that the term "brother" should be inserted so that v. 10 would read *and the rich* "brother" *in his humiliation,* making it parallel to v. 9 (Ropes, pp. 145–146). It is, however, more consistent with the concept of the rich in James as a whole to understand the rich as the unrighteous and to interpret the verse as ironic: "the rich may boast *in his humiliation,* if he can!" (Dibelius, pp. 114–118). The destruction of the wicked rich is described in poetic language dependent on the Septuagint rendering of Isaiah 40:6–7 (cf. 1 Peter 1:24–25).

The thrust of this paranetic unit is to

---

6 Cf. Mussner, pp. 76–83.

encourage the oppressed by reminding them of their ultimate destiny. James is not addressing the rich, but the poor; and it is hardly appropriate to conclude that he had no compassion for the rich. The imagery is prophetic and traditional, and his reminder that all life stands under judgment is needed.

5. Trial and Temptation (1:12–15)

¹² Blessed is the man who endures trial, for when he has stood the test he will receive the crown of life which God has promised to those who love him. ¹³ Let no one say when he is tempted, "I am tempted by God"; for God cannot be tempted with evil and he himself tempts no one; ¹⁴ but each person is tempted when he is lured and enticed by his own desire. ¹⁵ Then desire when it has conceived gives birth to sin; and sin when it is full-grown brings forth death.

This section consists of two units with v. 12 dealing with trial which is to be endured and vv. 13–15 dealing with temptation which is to be resisted. The units are linked in paranetic style by the use of various forms of the same Greek word (*peirasmos*) which means both trial and temptation (cf. 1:2–4). It is possible to affirm that a unity of thought exists in the entire section because every temptation does pose a trial, but even from this perspective a literary seam exists between v. 12 and vv. 13–15.

The literary form of v. 12 is that of the Jewish beatitude which customarily consisted of a pronouncement of blessing followed by a definition of the blessedness (cf. Matt. 5:2–12). The first part of this verse follows this form in pronouncing *blessed* or that God looks with favor on the *man* (Christian) *who endures trial* (cf. 1:2–4), but the remainder goes somewhat beyond the beatitude form which would be completed in the conclusion *he will receive the crown of life*. The more elaborate conclusion of James further clarifies the first part of v. 12 and is, in fact, roughly parallel to it: the one who *endures trial* clearly *has stood the test*, and endurance is the mark of *those who love him.*

The crown of life (cf. 2 Tim. 4:8; 1 Peter 5:4; Rev. 2:10) is ultimate reward and could be paraphrased "crowned with life." The expression *those who love him* has its ultimate background in Judaism (cf. Deut. 7:9), but its use by James probably reflects the early church's tradition (cf. 2:5). In its entirety, v. 12 closely relates to 1:2–4 and carries the thought of that section beyond the earthly pilgrimage of the Christian.

James introduces a new thought with v. 13 and affirms that God is not the source of temptations to sin. Evidently he addressed a situation in which some Christians were either directly or indirectly blaming their failures on God. James focuses the responsibility for sin squarely on man, supporting his position negatively by affirming a current Hellenistic concept— *God cannot be tempted with evil and he himself tempts no one* (cf. Blackman, pp. 53–54). This seems to be opposed to the plea "and lead us not into temptation" (Matt. 6:13); but the Greek term there should probably be understood more as "trial" than "temptation."

James positively supports his position by describing the unfolding drama of evil from desire to death. The process leading to sin begins in *desire* (passion); and in graphic imagery James describes the power of lust with words which refer to fish or game being *lured* or *enticed* by bait to capture. In v. 15 the imagery shifts to the biological: *desire* is seen as conceiving and giving *birth to sin.* But the issue is not then completed—sin endures until it is *full-grown*, and at that point it appears as *death.* The horrible process demonstrates the deceptive power of sin. *Desire* may not resemble death, and *sin* may not at the moment of its birth, but *sin* finally appears as what it is—*death.* Man hardly understands what it means for him to sin until he confronts it as *death.* The *death* of v. 15 stands in sharp contrast to the *life* of v. 12; enduring leads to life, but yielding to temptation leads to death.

James is primarily concerned with the

point that man is responsible for his own sin; and this is valid because in the final analysis the individual himself decides to sin. This perspective should not be stressed so far as to overlook the evil forces and individual circumstances that contribute to one's decision to sin. James simply is discussing the matter from the perspective of man's responsibility rather than that of theology or philosophy and thus does not need to deal with the issue of cosmic evil or Satan.

6. God and Good Gifts (1:16–18)

16 Do not be deceived, my beloved brethren. 17 Every good endowment and every perfect gift is from above, coming down from the Father of lights with whom there is no variation or shadow due to change. 18 Of his own will he brought us forth by the word of truth that we should be a kind of first fruits of his creatures.

The connection in thought between the previous section is established by the author's warning *do not be deceived*—God does not send temptation (1:13–15); he sends good gifts.

The expressions *good endowment and perfect gift* define what James feels God gives against the claim that God gave temptation or some evil gift (1:13–15). James elaborates this by the affirmation that God never changes in his giving— *there is no variation or shadow due to change*. This description translates material which poses problems both in terms of what the better text is and what the terms mean. The textual alternative is represented by the RSV margin that some authorities read "variation due to a shadow of turning" and results in the omission of the *or* in the RSV text. The issue is thus basically whether this expression describing God's giving has two elements in it— *no variation* and no *shadow due to change* —or should be conceived of as a whole. Probably the best solution to the textual problem is the one represented by the RSV text, but the many suggestions proposed by scholars demonstrate that the text is at best quite difficult (see Ropes,

pp. 162–164, and Dibelius, pp. 131–132).

The precise meaning of the Greek terms is also difficult to determine and is bound up with other textual variations. The expression *no variation* probably refers to the constant alteration of the intensity of the light given by the sun and moon and means that God's goodness in giving does not change or wax and wane. The phrase *shadow due to change* is more difficult, and its exact meaning is determined by how far the astronomical imagery is pressed. It can mean that God is not "overshadowed in an eclipse" or that with God there is not "the slightest possibility of change." In either case the intent of the author is apparent: God is the *Father* (creator) *of lights* (heavenly bodies), and he does not vary as they do—God's gifts are always good.

James illustrates the good giving of God by pointing out that he regenerated us or *brought us forth by the word of truth* (the gospel). The reference to the *first fruits of his creatures* stresses that Christians supremely belong to God and demonstrate his goodness because the firstfruit of a tree both indicated the quality and was dedicated to God (cf. Deut. 18:4). Some scholars feel that the reference here in James is to Jews and creation rather than Christians and regeneration, but the use of the term *first fruits* in the Christian tradition makes the latter more likely (cf. 1 Cor. 15:20–23; Rev. 14:4).[7]

7. The Importance of Meekness (1:19–21)

19 Know this, my beloved brethren. Let every man be quick to hear, slow to speak, slow to anger, 20 for the anger of man does not work the righteousness of God. 21 Therefore put away all filthiness and rank growth of wickedness and receive with meekness the implanted word, which is able to save your souls.

The opening imperative *Know this* focuses attention on the importance of the three brief and poetically structured demands which follow—*quick (tachus) to*

---

7 See, for example, L. E. Elliott-Binns, "James I.18: Creation or Redemption?" *New Testament Studies*, 3:148–161, 1956.

hear, slow (bradus) to speak, slow (bradus) to anger. Although these counsels are valuable in human relationships, the author's point is to exhort Christians *to receive with meekness the implanted word* in its redemptive power. It is God's word to man that he should be eager to hear; and although it may come to him in the words of a friend, the primary reference is probably to hearing in worship (Mussner, p. 158). The word which the Christian needs may so challenge him that his reaction will be anger, but this will not work the *righteousness of God,* i.e., accomplish what God requires (cf. Matt. 6:1). A Christian should *receive with meekness the implanted word.* Meekness means basically self-control (cf. 3:13), not weakness. Here it means strength enough to be in control and not to evade the Christian teaching that is at first so challenging as to ignite a flare of emotion. Instead of rejecting instruction in anger, the Christian is *to put away all filthiness* (vulgarity or moral weakness) *and rank growth of wickedness* (all the evil around you) and receive the teaching God gives.

The term *implanted word* can mean natural, innate, or inborn (cf. Blackman, pp. 62–63); but in this context it probably means the word which is able to root itself deeply in your life and could be translated as planted (Mitton, pp. 64–65). The affirmation that the implanted word has the power *to save your souls* does not mean that the persons James addressed were not Christians because he calls them *beloved brethren.* The term *save* here refers to the redeeming of the Christian from the sins of his life as he grows and matures (cf. 1 Cor. 1:18). To become a Christian is to enter a relationship with God (1:12) that involves a continuing process of purification or being saved from sin (cf. 1:2–4).

8. Hearing and Doing the Word (1:22–25)

22 But be doers of the word, and not hearers only, deceiving yourselves. 23 For if any one is a hearer of the word and not a doer, he is like a man who observes his natural face in a mirror; 24 for he observes himself and goes away and at once forgets what he was like. 25 But he who looks into the perfect law, the law of liberty, and perseveres, being no hearer that forgets but a doer that acts, he shall be blessed in his doing.

The contrast between *doers of the word* and *hearers* which pervades this section reflects a situation in which persons had learned how to hear Christian teaching without really listening to it. Some Christians apparently felt that it was meritorious just to hear the word because James charges that they are *deceiving themselves.* Translated into modern terms, James is insisting that deception exists when Christians view attendance on worship and the hearing of a sermon as ends in themselves and do not consider how these experiences should lead to Christian action.

The illustration of the mirror (vv. 23–24) was common in paranetic literature where it usually served to stress the difference between the ideal and the existing person (Ropes, p. 176). Although it can be understood in James to indicate the difference between God's intention and man's condition (cf. Mitton, p. 70), it fits the context much better to view James as stressing the similarity between a person who forgets to perform the needed grooming the mirror revealed and the Christian who forgets to do what the word revealed as required. This application seems to be the correct view because James concludes with the phrase *no hearer that forgets but a doer that acts.*

The expression *looks into* which James uses in relation to *the perfect law* means literally "to bend over" in order to see better and hence "to inspect." The term appears in John 20:11 to describe Mary's careful inspection of the tomb of Jesus.

The object of the Christian's intense concern should be *the perfect law, the law of liberty* (cf. 2:12). The best representatives of Judaism could speak of the Jewish law in this way (cf. Ropes, p. 178), but the Christians often felt the Jewish law involved bondage (cf. Gal. 4:21—5:1). Probably James includes both the Old

Testament and the teachings of Christianity in his reference to *the law of liberty;* Christians did reject law in the sense of legalism, but did not reject the idea that God demands and deserves obedience.

The one who does *the word* is identified in the concluding verse with *the doer that acts* or the one who does the work. For James, Christian instruction was not indoctrination but an implementation of the message of Jesus in human life. The concluding beatitude (cf. 1:12) pronounces God's favor on the Christian *in his doings,* and this is consistent with the emphasis of James that being Christian means doing Christian deeds (cf. 2:14–26).

9. Pure Religion (1:26–27)

26 If any one thinks he is religious, and does not bridle his tongue but deceives his heart, this man's religion is vain. 27 Religion that is pure and undefiled before God and the Father is this: to visit orphans and widows in their affliction, and to keep oneself unstained from the world.

The relationship between this section and the preceding one is not close, but the motif of dividing persons into two categories is continued with "doers" (1:22) corresponding to the one who has *religion that is pure* and "hearers only" (1:22) to the one who *thinks he is religious.*

James is not addressing the hypocritical person who consciously wears a religious mask; he is speaking to the person who really thinks that *he is religious,* but is deceived. The possibility that a man can be so blind that he "deceives his heart" (cf. Matt. 7:21–23) should move every Christian to evaluate his relationship to God. For James this examination is an objective look at personal conduct because he is defining *religion.* This Hellenistic term, which seldom appears in the first Testament, was quite common in the first century to refer to the exterior or visible aspects of religious behavior. It could be used in a derogatory (cf. Col. 2:18) or in a good sense (cf. Acts 26:5) as it is here. James is not defining Christianity in its totality; he is giving a practical or working

definition of discipleship to expose self-deception.

Negatively, James affirms some religion is *vain* (worthless). The characteristics of it are revealed in one's speech which the person does not *bridle* (control or hold in check). James perhaps intends this to be amplified by his later discussions on speech (3:1–12; 4:11–12; 5:12); but the contrast here is a religion of unrestrained words (v. 26) over against one of intelligent action (v. 27).

Positively, there is Christian conduct which is *pure and undefiled.* These terms have a cultic association and indicate what is approved *before God and the Father* (cf. 3:9), i.e., God who is the Father. The Christian behavior that God accepts is described in two ways. First, it is conduct that implements Christian concern for others. *To visit* implies more than to call upon; it indicates the assumption of responsibility for and means to look after. *Orphans and widows* were without a base of power or support in the first-century community, and the grouping represents all the needy and oppressed (cf. Mark 12:40) in contemporary society. Second, Christian conduct has a personal as well as a social dimension; one is to be *unstained from the world.* Here *world* does not mean people (cf. John 3:16), but is almost synonymous with evil as it refers to the way of life of unredeemed humanity (cf. 4:4). *Unstained* is basically a cultic term, but coupled with *world* the entire expression means morally unblemished.

James stresses authentic Christian conduct as involving two dimensions—a personal struggle against sin and its pollution coupled with a responsible and redeeming relationship with others. From the Christian perspective, personal holiness without redemptive involvement with others is as revolting as social action without concern for personal righteousness.

II. Chapter 2

James utilizes the diatribe style throughout this chapter, writing as if he were in dialogue with an audience.[8] Imperatives are less frequent than in the preceding chapter; and the paranetic units are longer and more closely related.

1. Prejudice in Action (2:1–7)

[1] My brethren, show no partiality as you hold the faith of our Lord Jesus Christ, the Lord of glory. [2] For if a man with gold rings and in fine clothing comes into your assembly, and a poor man in shabby clothing also comes in, [3] and you pay attention to the one who wears the fine clothing and say, "Have a seat here, please," while you say to the poor man, "Stand there," or, "Sit at my feet," [4] have you not made distinctions among yourselves, and become judges with evil thoughts? [5] Listen, my beloved brethren. Has not God chosen those who are poor in the world to be rich in faith and heirs of the kingdom which he has promised to those who love him? [6] But you have dishonored the poor man. Is it not the rich who oppress you, is it not they who drag you into court? [7] Is it not they who blaspheme that honorable name by which you are called?

This section assumes the understanding of the rich and poor that appears at other places in James (cf. the comment on 1:9–11) and reflects the influence of the reception of the poor by Jesus in the exhortation not to show partiality in the church.

The first verse can be translated as either a question or a command, depending on how one understands the Greek negative particle (*mē*) which begins the clause. If the verse is translated as imperative, the negative may be taken with the verb as in the KJV ("have not the faith"), which is confusing; or it may be taken with the noun *partiality* as in the RSV, which is clear—but the noun must then be pressed so far as to translate it as a verb, *show no partiality*.

The most natural translation would take the negative to indicate a question which expected a negative answer, "You are not having faith in our glorious Lord Jesus Christ when you show partiality, are you?" Although this translation is rejected by most scholars on the ground that the style of James is more in keeping with an im-

perative (cf. Ropes, p. 186; Blackman, pp. 76–77), the recognition that James is using diatribe style makes it more likely that the verse is a question. In either case, the meaning of the verse is clear: prejudice and faith in Christ are incompatible.

Partiality is literally "to accept the face," and the Greek term was used in the translation of the Old Testament to represent a Hebrew expression (cf. Lev. 19:15; Psalm 82:2). The word indicates more than mere *partiality* and means improper partiality, favoritism, or prejudice. James affirms that such behavior is not appropriate for those who *hold* (have) *faith* or rely upon the *Lord Jesus Christ* (cf. 1:1).

The translation *the Lord of glory* attempts to communicate the force of the original which means either "our glorious Lord Jesus Christ" or "our Lord Jesus Christ who is the Glory" and stresses the relation of *glory* to the *Lord Jesus Christ* (cf. Ropes, pp. 187–188). Glory referred to the lofty majesty and visible splendor of God in Judaism, and the application of this term to Jesus indicates the resurrected Christ and Lord, who radiates the divine glory.[9]

James contrasts the magnificence of Jesus with the superficial glory of the rich man which consists of *fine* (white or brilliant) *clothing* and *gold rings.* Dress constituted a badge of status and vocation in the first century, and the contrast between rich and poor was quite conspicuous in one's clothing (cf. Luke 15:22; 16:19), as the poor man usually had only one work-stained garment. This *shabby* (dirty) *clothing* characterized a man as *poor;* and James illustrates the sin of prejudice by the way rich and poor are treated in the Christian assembly. The magnitude of the sin is heightened by the first-century understanding of the wicked rich and the pious poor (cf. 1:9–11). James is probably not reporting an actual incident, but construct-

---

[8] See the discussion of Paranetic Style in the Int.

[9] See the *Theological Dictionary of the New Testament* (Grand Rapids: Wm. B. Eerdmans, 1964), II, 232–255.

ing an example in diatribe style to expose sin.

The word translated *assembly* (*sunagogē*) is usually translated "synagogue" because it is the usual word for the Jewish place of meeting or the Jewish meeting itself. Three possibilities for its meaning here exist: First, the term may simply note the meeting place without implying any definition of the congregation. Second, it may be used as roughly equivalent to church, reflecting the situation before the division of the church from the synogogue. Or third, James may be using the term ironically to deepen his indictment of partiality in the church. In this quite likely view, James employs the word normally designating a Jewish congregation or place of worship because the prejudiced church had lost one of the major characteristics distinguishing it from Judaism.

The question posed in v. 4 is based on the situation described in vv. 2–3, and the Greek construction indicates that the answer should be affirmative. The fact that they had *made distinctions* (wavered or doubted, cf. 1:6) shows they were departing from the practice of Christ (v. 1) and demonstrates their relating to persons as *judges* rather than brothers (v. 1). They stand accused even as they act like judges because of the *evil thoughts* (sinful reasoning or motive) exposed in their partiality.

The verb *listen* is typical of diatribe style, and the expression *beloved brethren* marks a literary division which introduces a series of indicting questions (vv. 5–7).

The attitude of God to the poor posed a shaming contrast to the discrimination in the church. God has *chosen* (elected) *those who are poor,* but the Christians James addressed chose to dishonor them. God's election constitutes the poor as *rich in* (the realm of) *faith* (cf. 1:9–11) and as recipients *of the kingdom.* The correspondence between *kingdom* and "crown of life" (1:12) is strikingly portrayed by the parallel *which he has promised to those who love him* (cf. 1:12).

Further, the rich are said to *oppress* the poor, and this strong term is frequently used in the Greek version of the Old Testament for the persecution of the people of God. This oppression was both social and religious. The rich *drag* (force) the poor *into court,* and the implication is that the poor are exploited in the process. The rich *blaspheme* (act or speak irreverently or injuriously) the *honorable name.* This refers to the *name by which you are called* and means the name of the one you follow or Christ.

James' exhortation is relevant for a Christian's attitude in every situation in life. He pleads for an evaluation of persons that rests upon their essential worth from the perspective of God's love and the example of Jesus.

2. Prejudice and Law (2:8–13)

⁸ If you really fulfil the royal law, according to the scripture, "You shall love your neighbor as yourself," you do well. ⁹ But if you show partiality, you commit sin, and are convicted by the law as transgressors. ¹⁰ For whoever keeps the whole law but fails in one point has become guilty of all of it. ¹¹ For he who said, "Do not commit adultery," said also, "Do not kill." If you do not commit adultery but do kill, you have become a transgressor of the law. ¹² So speak and so act as those who are to be judged under the law of liberty. ¹³ For judgment is without mercy to one who has shown no mercy; yet mercy triumphs over judgment.

The challenge *if you really fulfil* probably reflects the author's answer to the plea persons might make when accused of discrimination: "We are not partial; we are trying to love the rich in the face of the current prejudice against them!" Some scholars feel that no such perverted excuse is implied, but the presence of *you do well* seems to call for it (cf. Ropes, pp. 197–198).

The *royal* (supreme or absolutely authoritative) *law* does not designate the one commandment to love your neighbor (Lev. 19:18) but the entire Old Testament law as summarized in it (cf. Blackman, p. 84). James interprets the directive to love one's neighbor in the context of Christian tradition (cf. Luke 10:25–37) as a law forbidding partiality, but the whole thrust of the indictment has Jewish presuppositions because the author is seeking to prove that they have committed *sin* by showing from the law that they are *transgressors*. Transgression means to step across the line or to disobey a specific directive, while *sin* means to fall short of what God desires or to miss the mark (cf. Rom. 5:12–21).

The affirmation that one who *fails in one point has become guilty of all* was taught in first-century Judaism (cf. Gal. 5:3), and this opens the way for the author's use of the Seventh and Sixth commandments (the Greek Old Testament has this reversed order) to deepen the blackness of the sin of partiality by associating it with adultery and murder.

The force of the argument against prejudice to this point would have been more powerful with Christians of a Jewish background because its premises are Judaistically oriented. Now James uses a basis of persuasion that would be forceful for all Christians, including those of a Gentile heritage. The Christians are to remember that they *are to be judged under the law of liberty*, which is the demand of Christ (cf. 1:25); both the law and the gospel summon Christians from prejudice to love. The appeal is now furthered by the argument that God's *judgment is* (will be) *without* mercy upon the Christian *who has shown no mercy*. The concept that mercy will receive mercy (*mercy triumphs over judgment*) was shared by both Jews (Sirach 28:1–4) and Christians (cf. Matt. 5:7) and is used here because *mercy* meant compassion, and prejudice can hardly be overcome without mercy. Some scholars feel that v. 13 is an isolated saying that does not fit too well in this context; but the theme of judgment is in the preceding verse and the linking of mercy with the commandment to love one's neighbor is in the earliest Christian tradition in the parable of the merciful Samaritan (cf. Luke 10:25–37).

The basic issue James faces in this section is instructive. He is trying to get Christians to recognize that what they are tolerating is sin. In the face of their apparent unwillingness to see sin as sin, James is forced to resort to legalistic absolutes (vv. 9–11) and to use common ground where he can find it (vv. 12–13) to drive home his point that partiality is sin.

3. Faith and Works (2:14–26)

This section constitutes a separate literary unit in diatribe style. The situation James addresses is clear, and a firm grasp of it is the best foundation for an adequate interpretation of this frequently misunderstood and hotly debated section of the epistle. James is dealing with a situation in the church in which persons professed faith (vv. 14,18) and considered themselves to belong to the Christian community (vv. 14–18) but did not feel that ethical or moral achievement was necessary (vv. 18 and 20). The persons James addresses had divorced faith from works (vv. 14,18,20) and were evidently maintaining that belief alone was sufficient (vv. 18–19).

At this point the question of the relationship between Paul and James emerges. James writes, "You see that a man is justified by works and not by faith alone" (2:24); but Paul affirms, "For we hold that a man is justified by faith apart from works of law" (Rom. 3:28).

The differences between these statements have been both heightened and distorted by theological controversy. Martin Luther chose Paul over James in the face of the apparent disagreement regarding justification, but this radical surgery on the canon has ominous implications for one's view of the authority of the New Testament (cf. Int.).

When James is approached with the assumption that he flatly disagrees with Paul on the matter of justification, the Christian interpreter is confronted by a dilemma before which it appears that either he must choose justification by faith and give up his belief in the authority of the entire New Testament (so, Luther) or he must maintain his belief in the authority of the entire New Testament and give up his belief in the centrality of justification by faith. But this dilemma is a false one. Two contrasting and apparently irreconcilable theological perspectives did clash, with Romans and James constituting part of the battleground; but it does not follow that the use of 2:24 in a sixteenth-century debate should control the interpretation of the entire section. It is actually misleading to approach 2:14–26 from the perspective of v. 24, because when the section is considered as a whole it is clear that the entire unit revolves around two basic concepts—faith and works—which are brought together ten times in the brief span of 13 verses. The two terms faith and works appear in vv. 14,17,18 (3 times), 20,22 (2 times),24,26. James is not stressing works in isolation from faith; he is discussing faith *and* works. The author states the fact that he is dealing with the relationship between faith and works three times in such a way that it is difficult to see how it has been overlooked. In vv. 17, 20,26 James pleads for *the inseparability of faith and works;* and in the context surrounding these verses, he seeks to illustrate and prove this inseparability.

The realization that James argues for the inseparability of faith and works makes it obvious that James is not in absolute disagreement with Paul. James does not affirm that a man is justified by works *apart* from faith, which would be the precise opposite to Paul's "justified by faith apart from works" (Rom. 3:28). James is stressing that faith and works must go together. But awareness of this does not remove all of the tension between him and Paul. Paul states that justification is "by faith apart from works" (Rom. 3:28), while James maintains it is "not by faith alone" but also by works (2:24). An understanding of this difference in stress is bound up with the different situations which Paul and James confronted.

¹⁴ What does it profit, my brethren, if a man says he has faith but has not works? Can his faith save him? ¹⁵ If a brother or sister is ill-clad and in lack of daily food, ¹⁶ and one of you says to them, "Go in peace, be warmed and filled," without giving them the things needed for the body, what does it profit? ¹⁷ So faith by itself, if it has no works, is dead.

James clearly addresses the Christian community as he terms his readers *my brethren.* That the persons James addresses as opponents in debate are also in the church is clear from the statement in v. 16 that one of you (i.e., one of "my brethren") says, from the illustration which portrays the needy Christian as *a brother or sister,* and also from the fact that faith is professed (vv. 14,18–20,24,26).

James is opposing persons in the church who profess to have faith but refuse to do what James feels a Christian should. The example of helping the needy Christian makes it clear what James intends by the term *works* (vv. 14–17): he means the deeds of the Christian life. This is in sharp contrast to Paul's use of the term; he speaks of "works of law" (Rom. 3:28) and means by works the fulfillment of legal requirements in order to earn favor with God and to procure ultimate salvation.

James thus addresses persons who are Christians and refers to works as what they should do in order to *be* Christians. Paul also writes to Christians, but he is dealing with works in relation to how a man *becomes* a Christian. In other words, Paul's "justification by faith" deals with how one becomes a Christian; but the "justification by works" of James deals with how one demonstrates that he is a Christian (cf. 2:24).

The sharp question—*Can his faith save him?*—is thus asked about the person who claims faith without engaging in Christian works. *Faith* here is used to mean the kind of belief in God that a profession without works involves (cf. vv. 18–20), and James says that such a *faith, by itself, if it has no works, is dead.* The term *save* probably refers to the final judgment here rather than to a past experience (cf. Matt. 24:13;

Rom. 5:9).

The illustration James chooses to expose the folly of faith without works not only reveals the poor situation of some early Christians—cold and hungry—and the inadequate response of some of their brothers; it is also instructive as to what constitutes a Christian response to basic human needs. The persons James opposes did do some things; they did wish them well, and even prayed for them. The *be warmed and filled* implies "may God warm and fill you." Yet this did not lead to *giving them the things needed;* and the refusal to take this step rendered their sympathy and prayer profitless. For James, to be a Christian is to do the Christian deed.

> 18 **But some one will say, "You have faith and I have works." Show me your faith apart from your works, and I by my works will show you my faith. 19 You believe that God is one; you do well. Even the demons believe—and shudder. 20 Do you want to be shown, you foolish fellow, that faith apart from works is barren? 21 Was not Abraham our father justified by works, when he offered his son Isaac upon the altar? 22 You see that faith was active along with his works, and faith was completed by works, 23 and the scripture was fulfilled which says, "Abraham believed God, and it was reckoned to him as righteousness"; and he was called the friend of God. 24 You see that a man is justified by works and not by faith alone. 25 And in the same way was not also Rahab the harlot justified by works when she received the messengers and sent them out another way? 26 For as the body apart from the spirit is dead, so faith apart from works is dead.**

This section begins in unmistakable diatribe style with the traditional *But some one will say.* The quotation which follows poses a problem which is difficult to explain satisfactorily.[10] One would expect "You have works and I have faith" to be the objector's claim, and this would fit the author's challenging response: *Show me your faith.* But the text reads *You have faith and I have works,* and this reverses the pronouns (*you* and *I*) because James stressed works and the objector faith.

One way to solve this difficulty is to take the quotation to be from a third party who is seeking to arbitrate the dispute by a compromise which would allow two groups in the church—a faith group and a works group. This solution, although widely held (cf. Mitton, pp. 108–109), is unacceptable for two reasons. First, the literary style of diatribe requires the quoted material to come from an objector in debate, not an ally or arbitrator. Second, the challenge of James—*Show me your faith*—identifies the speaker as an opponent.

A more satisfactory solution to this problem is to take the pronouns *you* and *I* in a general rather than a strictly personal way and to translate the sentence, "One person has faith and another has works" (Ropes, pp. 209–212).[11] When v. 18 is understood this way, the structure of thought in the entire section is clear. In the previous paragraph (vv. 14–17) James has challenged the view that faith can be held without works. He confronts those who profess without producing works with a compelling illustration (vv. 15–16) and concludes with a condemning affirmation: "So faith by itself, if it has no works, is dead" (v. 17).

This vigorous attack upon a dead faith prompts a defense which insists on a possibility of a separation between faith and works: "let one Christian stress faith and another works" (v. 18). James will not accept this; he insists on the inseparability of faith and works and faces the objector with three examples which demonstrate that faith and works cannot be separated in Christian existence: the demons, Abraham, and Rahab.

The first example relates closely to the first half of the reply James makes: *Show me your faith apart from your works.* Faith without works does exist, but not among Christians—among demons! The assertion that *the demons believe* (have faith) again

---

10 Ropes, pp. 210–214, gives a classic summary of the proposed solutions.

11 The solution that an early mistake in transmitting the text exists has been proposed, but is unlikely (cf. Dibelius, pp. 194–195).

shows that James can employ the term faith (cf. vv. 14,17) to mean that belief which is without works. The belief or faith that *God is one* alludes to the Shema or Jewish confession of faith (Deut. 6:4) which was repeated daily in the first century by faithful Jews. This stress on one God was also a Christian affirmation (cf. Mark 12:29–30), but not so distinctively such as the confession that Jesus is the Lord (Rom. 10:9). James' point is that even the demons are convinced of the power and reality of the one God. This proves the inadequacy of faith alone— demons have that much.

The reference to demons reflects the first-century understanding of the existence of demons (see Mark 3:20–27) and is an argument based on that understanding rather than an affirmation about it. The expression *and shudder* means basically to bristle, and this traditionally Jewish description of demonic reaction is a cutting reminder to those who argue for faith alone. *The demons believe—and shudder;* the Christians who profess faith without works do less work than the demons— they do not even so much as tremble.

The direct question *Do you want to be shown* casts further blame on the objector by questioning his willingness to confront the issue. The label *you foolish fellow* is harsh (cf. Matt. 5:21–22) but is characteristic of diatribe style (1 Cor. 15:36).

James uses Abraham to reinforce his position. This probably does not reflect a reaction to the use of Abraham in the Pauline tradition to prove justification by faith (Rom. 4) because James is not arguing that justification proceeds only from works as Paul's opponents apparently did (Rom. 4:2). James affirms that Abraham's example shows the inseparability of faith and works. James does not deny that *Abraham believed God, and it was reckoned to him as righteousness* (cf. Rom. 4:3; Gen. 15:6). But this pronouncement about his faith was *fulfilled* as his *faith was active along with his works* (lit., "faith worked with his works") and was

completed (or perfected) *by works* in the offering of Isaac.

The *justified by works* that James affirms occurs *after* Abraham's inclusion in the people of God, *not before*; and this focuses an important difference between Paul and James. Paul usually speaks of justification in the context of one's becoming a Christian, while James uses the term to apply to one's being a Christian. The use of the term in this latter sense involves being declared righteous at the final judgment, and Paul does occasionally speak of justification in this way (see Rom. 2:13; Gal. 2:17).[12]

The use of the term *justified* in reference to Abraham rises naturally from the Greek version of Genesis 15:6 because the Greek terms for righteousness (*dikaiosunē*) and justify (*dikaioō*) are from the same root. The conclusion James draws from the life of Abraham is that *You see that a man is justified by works and not by faith alone.* The disagreement between this affirmation of James and Paul's statement in Romans 3:28 is considerably reduced when the contexts of the two statements are considered and the different meanings of the key terms are recognized. Paul speaks to the issue of how a person becomes a Christian, and he means by "works" the deeds of the law performed by a Jewish legalist to gain favor with God; James speaks to the issue of how a person demonstrates that he is a Christian, and he means by "works" what the Christian should do in his faith.

James consistently makes one point: Christianity demands both faith and works. He faced a situation in which persons claimed faith without works and challenged it. Paul faced a situation in which men stressed the value of work without an emphasis on faith. Both points need to be made, and James is best heard after one has experienced the magnificence of the faith of Paul.

The third illustration James uses is that

12 For a superb discussion of this, see Joachim Jeremias, "Paul and James," *Expository Times* 66: 368–371, 1954–1955.

of Rahab. This example is not elaborated, and the author apparently assumes that the readers will understand the relevance of his reference. Rahab was a popular heroine in the first century (cf. Matt. 1:5; Heb. 11:31) and was extolled as an example of ideal conversion to Judaism. The point is, probably, that Rahab's faith was demonstrated by her works.

The concluding verse contains an argument from analogy in which the *body apart from the spirit* is compared to *faith apart from works*. The analogy is somewhat imperfect, as all analogies are, because James has been maintaining the inseparability of faith from works; and a body can be separated from the spirit. His point is clear however: *faith apart from works is dead.*

The relevance of James for contemporary Christianity is unavoidable. Christianity does not really exist when correct belief or statements of faith are of such concern that they can be substituted for moral obligations. Faith that does not lead to moral action and Christian involvement demonstrates its own character as profitless. Faith demonstrates its existence in obedience.

III. Chapter 3

One of the divisions in this chapter is difficult to determine. The first section consists of a discussion of the relationship between maturity and speech, including the illustrations of the bit and the rudder (vv. 1–4); and the following discussion of the evil capability of the tongue (vv. 6–12) constitutes a second and separate paranetic unit. The problem is in deciding which section v. 5 belongs to. Probably it should be taken with the paragraph that begins with v. 6 in the RSV because the illustration of the destructive forest fire is used to reinforce the following discussion of the tongue as an evil fire. Upon this solution, vv. 1–4 and 5–12 constitute separate units in which the author deals with the *tongue* from two perspectives.[13]

[13] For the alternative view, cf. Mayor, pp. 112–113.

The third unit in this chapter seems at first glance to be unrelated to the preceding discussion of the tongue, but some connection seems intended by the author in his question about "who is wise and understanding" (v. 13), which refers back to the teacher's role discussed in v. 1.

1. The Power of the Tongue (3:1–5)

[1] Let not many of you become teachers, my brethren, for you know that we who teach shall be judged with greater strictness. [2] For we all make many mistakes, and if any one makes no mistakes in what he says he is a perfect man, able to bridle the whole body also. [3] If we put bits into the mouths of horses that they may obey us, we guide their whole bodies. [4] Look at the ships also; though they are so great and are driven by strong winds, they are guided by a very small rudder wherever the will of the pilot directs. [5] So the tongue is a little member and boasts of great things. How great a forest is set ablaze by a small fire!

The term translated *teachers* appears as "masters" in the KJV, and this no longer adequate rendering dates back at least as far as Tyndale (1525).

What the author affirms is crystal clear: *Let not many of you become teachers.* The problem is in discovering what sort of situation prompted this command and made it necessary to remind his readers that teachers stand under heavy responsibility. The pronouncement that *you know* probably reflects an appeal to generally accepted church tradition (cf. Mark 12:38–40; Matt. 5:17–20) about judgment on teachers. This reminder that teachers *shall be judged with greater strictness* has suggested that a problem of false doctrine was in view, but James identifies himself as a teacher in the expression *we who teach* and does not raise the possibility of his abandoning this role or of anyone else doing that. This indicates that the issue is not heretical teachers who need to be removed from office. James is apparently addressing a situation that needs attention but is less than an ecclesiastical emergency.

The most likely occasion for his exhortation was the situation created by the opportunity for many persons to become teachers in the growing early churches coupled with the extremely high prestige a teacher commanded in the first century (cf. Matt. 23:2–8; John 3:2,10). Evidently some Christians were seizing the opportunity to be called teacher (rabbi) and rushing into the office without a solemn consideration of the responsibilities. James meets this by affirming that no man should be so eager to teach that he disregards the nature of the responsibility.

James evidently means by *become teachers* an official position in the church. This office was apparently among the highest in some of the earliest churches but later was included in the function of the pastor or bishop (cf. Acts 13:1; Eph. 4:11–12; 1 Tim. 3:1–2).[14]

The author's exhortation was not intended to discourage persons from sharing in the responsibility of instructing other persons in the context of the life of the church. James does not say "do not teach"; he is stressing that one should not be so eager to teach that he overlooks the responsibility.

In contemporary churches there is no problem with a surging crowd of eager applicants with superficial motivation for church responsibilities involving teaching. However, the basis of the exhortation of James is the awareness of the lofty responsibility and privilege of the teacher, and this perspective would not only lead to discouraging the thoughtless but also to encouraging Christians to be good stewards of their abilities in sharing the Christian faith.

James admits that *we all make many mistakes,* and this confession is stronger in the original than in the translation because *mistakes* is too weak for the Greek verb which means fail (cf. 2:10) or sin; the meaning is that we all sin (fail) over and over again (cf. Mitton, p. 122). What James stresses is that men's sins are prominent in their words; and that if a Christian

does not sin at this point, he has achieved maturity.

In affirming that he is a *perfect man* (mature person), *able to bridle the whole body also,* the author is assuming either that the tongue is so difficult to control that victory at this point assures it at every point or that the tongue so expresses a person's being that he can be viewed as led by what it says. The illustrations of the bit and the rudder can support either interpretation, but the author's claim that the man who controls his tongue is *able to bridle the whole body also* makes the first meaning more likely. He is assuming that the most difficult task a Christian faces is the mastery of his own speech. If control be achieved at this most crucial point, the struggle with sin will be victorious.

The illustrations of the *bit* and *rudder* stress that when one has control of these he has power over the horse or the ship. Just as the bit and the rudder constitute the basis of control, so a person should realize that speech (the tongue) is the crucial and controlling point in man's struggle with sin.

If v. 5 be taken with what precedes it, the implication of *So the tongue is a little member and boasts of great things* is that the preceding illustrations show the power of the tongue for evil; and this is possible if v. 2 is taken in the second of the two meanings mentioned. But this interpretation of v. 2 is unlikely, and the problem is solved if v. 5 be taken with the following section which deals with the misuse of the tongue (vv. 6–12).[15]

2. The Misuse of the Tongue (3:6–12)

6 And the tongue is a fire. The tongue is an unrighteous world among our members, staining the whole body, setting on fire the cycle of nature, and set on fire by hell. 7 For every kind of beast and bird, of reptile and sea creature, can be tamed and has been tamed by humankind, 8 but no human being can tame the tongue—a restless evil, full of deadly poison.

---

14 See P. H. Menoud, "Church, Life and Organization of," *The Interpreter's Dictionary of the Bible* (Nashville: Abingdon Press, 1962), I, 617–626.

15 Dibelius (pp. 226–232) maintains that the illustrations (vv. 3–4) were traditionally used to stress man's moral achievements and that they do not fit well into the context of James.

9 With it we bless the Lord and Father, and with it we curse men, who are made in the likeness of God. 10 From the same mouth come blessing and cursing. My brethren, this ought not to be so. 11 Does a spring pour forth from the same opening fresh water and brackish? 12 Can a fig tree, my brethren, yield olives, or a grapevine figs? No more can salt water yield fresh.

This section stresses the evil capability of the tongue and thus indirectly reinforces the affirmation of the previous section that one who can control his tongue will be "able to bridle the whole body also" (3:2).

The destructive power of the tongue is first stated and then illustrated by the graphic imagery of the forest fire (3:5),[16] and the discussion of the relation of the tongue to fire and evil continues in v. 6. Following this, argument from analogy is used to stress the tremendous power of the tongue (vv. 7–8); and in the concluding verses, the author pinpoints the evil inconsistency of the tongue (vv. 9–12).

The statement that *the tongue is a fire* is based on the preceding exclamation: "How great a forest is set ablaze by a small fire!" The illustration of a tremendous and destructive fire developing from a small spark or flame was common in Hellenistic diatribes where it was usually employed to portray the raging power of covetousness or passion (Dibelius, pp. 233–235). The term for "forest" can mean fuel or brush,[17] but forest is more consistent with the nonbiblical illustrations (Ropes, pp. 232–233). The point of the illustrative exclamation coincides with the statement that "the tongue is a little member and boasts of great things" and leads into the metaphorical affirmation that *the tongue is a fire.* James emphasizes the tremendously evil power of the tongue in the context of his view that this is the point where man's struggle with evil should be focused. The identification of the tongue with fire constitutes one among a series of

metaphors stressing the wicked and destructive capability of words: the tongue is called *fire* and *an unrighteous world;* and it is described as staining the whole body (v. 6), *setting on fire the cycle of nature* (v. 6), *set on fire by hell* (v. 6), *untamable* (v. 8), *a restless evil* (v. 8), and *as full of deadly poison* (v. 8). These images graphically portray the sinister power of the tongue, and this is their purpose. The force of the author's descriptive picture is in their successive portrayals, and a logical consistency does not exist between them. That the tongue is first fire itself and then viewed as having been set on fire (v. 6) constitutes no lapse in logic for the author; the descriptions stand in a loose complementary relationship.

The statement that the tongue is *an unrighteous world among our members* constitutes a difficult problem of interpretation. The phrase *an unrighteous world* poses two problems—what it means and what its relationship to the surrounding words is. Literally, the phrase would most naturally mean "the world of unrighteousness." The term *world* is often used to refer to the way of life lived by persons apart from God (see 1:27; 4:4); and the addition of the word *unrighteous* would make this meaning almost certain here. But the phrase *an unrighteous world* cannot easily be understood in this context, which has inspired attempts to understand the phrase to mean "the whole of evil" or "an ornament of iniquity." These meanings allow the phrase to be taken in apposition to *fire* in the first part of the verse and to translate "and the tongue is a fire, an ornament of evil (or, the sum of evil)." This solution strains the meaning of the text; and though problems do exist, it is probably best to understand the phrase naturally and to relate it to its following context as in the RSV: *The tongue is an unrighteous world among our members* (see comments by Ropes, p. 233). Taken in this way, the verse is understood as affirming that the tongue is a center or focal point of iniquity existing among the other members of one's

16 The reasons for construing the paranetic unit as beginning with v. 5 are given in the comment on the previous section.

17 See L. E. Elliott-Binns, *New Testament Studies,* 2:48–50, 1956.

body. The imagery is awkward because a person is viewed as consisting of units (*members*), and one of these is in itself a *world*. But in spite of the awkwardness, the meaning comes through: the tongue constitutes an evil force or center in man's life. This interpretation is substantiated by the following words *staining the whole body*, which refer to the tongue in the Greek text, rather than to *an unrighteous world* as the RSV translation might allow.

The term stain or defile is used by James in relationship to the world in 1:27; but here it refers to the power of the tongue to pollute human personality.

The sinister power of the tongue is now extended beyond a person to the entire realm of humanity as James affirms that the tongue kindles or sets afire *the cycle of nature*. A spark can ignite a forest (v. 5*b*), but the tongue is so powerful it can set all humanity ablaze. James probably employs this phrase in the popular sense of "human life" rather than in a technical way.

The source of the fire or destructive power that the tongue unleashes in human life is identified in the phrase *set on fire by hell*. The term translated *hell* (*geennes*) is a Greek transliteration of the Aramaic for the Hebrew Gehinnom (Valley of Hinnom). This valley was the location of the Jerusalem city dump and the traditional site for sacrifices made to Moloch (cf. 2 Kings 16:3); and in the pre-Christian Jewish literature the Valley of Hinnom had already come to be used to refer to the fiery abyss of final judgment. The statement of James that the fire of the tongue was kindled by *hell* communicates both the terrible wickedness of the tongue's power and the certainty of God's judgment on such sin. The meaning of James should not be pressed in terms of why he does not mention Satan because James is not giving a theory of the origin of evil—he is exposing it in the misuse of the tongue.

The author now turns to an analogy drawn from human experience to express the uncontrollable evil of the tongue. The

order of the listing as *beast and bird, of reptile and sea creature* reflects Judaistic tradition (cf. Gen. 1:20–26) and indicates the comprehensiveness of man's sovereignty as all of these creatures *can be tamed and has been tamed* (lit., is being tamed and has been tamed). The point of the analogy emerges in the statement that *no human being can tame the tongue*. This is not intended to stress the fact that man needs God's help to tame his tongue, even though this is true; the point is the contrast between man's ability to subdue creation and his inability to control his tongue. This exposes clearly the need for man to center his efforts on his speech (cf. 3: 1–4).

The evil capability of the tongue is further described in the terms *a restless* (unpredictable, impulsive, inconsistent; cf. 1:8) *evil, full of deadly poison*. The reference to *deadly poison* alludes figuratively to the venom of a poisonous snake which was associated with its tongue (see Rom. 3:13).

With v. 9 James explains more precisely what the sin and uncontrollability of the tongue is: *With it we bless the Lord and Father and with it we curse men*. The author's previous designations of the tongue as fire from hell and deadly poison would lead one to expect examples of totally evil uses of the tongue, but the very point James is stressing is that the depth of the wickedness of the tongue is to be found in its inconsistency.

To *bless the Lord and Father* is to praise God and probably reflects the Jewish expression "Blessed be he" which was customarily used when God was referred to. *Lord and Father* is similar to "God and the Father" (1:27) and emphasizes the relation of God to men because the God whom men bless is *the Father;* this perspective increases the sin in cursing men because the father and his household were viewed as one unit in the Judaistic perspective—to bless the father would also be to bless the children! James highlights this by his observation drawn from Judaism that the men cursed *are made in the likeness of God.*

To curse does not mean to use profanity; it refers to the Judaistic custom in the first century of expressing the hope that evil and tragedy would come to a person. Some curses were considered harmless while others were prohibited (cf. Prov. 11:26; 24:24; Ex. 21:17). *To curse* reflected an enduring hatred which eagerly longed for a person's misfortune and expressed itself in such words as, "May your children become idolators and your wife be unfaithful." The early Christians, following the teaching of Jesus, rejected all such cursing (cf. Rom. 12:14; Luke 6:28), and James reflects this position. The cursing that James condemns is seldom heard in modern life, but the spirit or attitude that produced it still exists and needs to be recognized as sin.

In the fashion of a Hellenistic teacher James cites examples from nature as arguments by analogy to demonstrate that such inconsistency as the tongue reveals is unnatural. A spring does not gush salt water and fresh from the same opening (v. 11) nor can olives come from a fig tree or figs from a grapevine (v. 12). In a similar vein, a spring that produced salty water is no place to draw fresh!

These illustrations reflect well-known realities in the author's world. Fresh and salt water springs were conspicuous because of the scarcity of fresh water and the use of some of the salt springs medicinally; and the fig, olive, and grape were widely cultivated. The author argues by analogy on the basis of these familiar realities, seizing on the consistency in them in contrast to the inconsistent behavior of the tongue.

In this section on the tongue, James clearly is dealing with the power of words. He recognizes that they can be destructive and calls for a realization of the evil and horrible power of the effect of what one says upon another person. James does not stress the other side of this reality—the redemptive use of words through which a person is able to express love, give advice, support, reflect judgment, and instruct others; but he does imply this in the next section. Paranesis was designed to inspire reflection, and the author's ultimate concern is to call Christians to realize that maturing demands speech which will have the effect of redemption and judgment appropriate to the needs of another person.

3. The Two Wisdoms (3:13–18)

13 Who is wise and understanding among you? By his good life let him show his works in the meekness of wisdom. 14 But if you have bitter jealousy and selfish ambition in your hearts, do not boast and be false to the truth. 15 This wisdom is not such as comes down from above, but is earthly, unspiritual, devilish. 16 For where jealousy and selfish ambition exist, there will be disorder and every vile practice. 17 But the wisdom from above is first pure, then peaceable, gentle, open to reason, full of mercy and good fruits, without uncertainty or insincerity. 18 And the harvest of righteousness is sown in peace by those who make peace.

Contrasting ways of life are portrayed in this section by the two kinds of wisdom; and although this perspective is basically Judaistic, the literary form is Hellenistic (see "Paranetic Style" in the Int.).

The opening question singles out the *wise and understanding.* Both of these terms can bear a general meaning; but when coupled they probably bear the more specific meanings of teacher and expert. The material in the section does apply to all Christians, however, because James measures the competence of the teachers and highly gifted persons in the church by demands for moral excellence required of all Christians. For James, the spiritual and ethical character of the leaders in the church was primary. The status of an official would not compensate for moral defects.

Wisdom is demonstrated by the *works* (cf. 2:12–26) of the *good life* (acceptable conduct). James stresses that this must be in *meekness of wisdom.* The accent here is not on wisdom because that needed no demonstration, having already qualified the person a teacher. What needed demonstration was *meekness* (cf. 1:21), which is basically discipline or control, and in this context it means utilizing *wisdom* under the Lordship of Christ for the purposes appropriate to the nurture of the Christian community. The alternative to *meekness of wisdom* is described in v. 14.

Instead of developing his discussion by posing an alternative such as "arrogance of wisdom," James employs the idea of two kinds of wisdom—demonic or earthly wisdom and wisdom from above (vv. 15–17). From this perspective, *meekness of wisdom* could be roughly equated with the *wisdom from above*. This use of two kinds of wisdom following the exhortation to *meekness of wisdom* finds its justification in the fact that the two wisdoms represent ultimate alternatives for conduct.

The description of the wisdom that *is not such as comes down from above* (is not from God) is given in terms of feelings or attitudes. *Bitter jealousy* describes fierce devotion to one's position coupled with an insensitivity toward the views of others. *Selfish ambition* refers to the spirit which greedily uses any means to support one's cause or program; it involves pride and personal ambition which will go to any length to be fulfilled.

The results of such *jealousy and selfish ambition* will be *disorder and every vile practice*. *Disorder* is closely related to the term rendered "restless" in v. 8; it connotes trouble, disorder, disruption, alienation, and anarchy. The final hallmark of the demonic wisdom is all inclusive—*every vile practice* or everything wicked.

James identifies the wisdom or way of life which he has portrayed as *earthly, unspiritual, devilish. Earthly* means human; *unspiritual* literally means natural, but in this context describes man's situation apart from God (cf. 1 Cor. 2:14). The term *devilish* means coming from an evil spirit and would be more accurately translated "demonic."

With this trilogy of terms with their mounting sense of distance and alienation from God, James portrays a force, spirit, or style of life which the Christian should recognize for what it is and abandon it. Such conduct is *false to the truth,* i.e., it is a betrayal of the Christian commitment.

James does not divide persons into groups with the non-Christians as the representatives of demonic wisdom; it is the Christian struggle with evil that is in view. That demonic wisdom for James approximates the Pauline expression "works of the flesh" (Gal. 5:19) is evident from the parallel terms in James 3:14–16 and Galatians 5:19–21.

In similar fashion, what James terms *wisdom from above* is described in terms parallel to Paul's "fruit of the Spirit" (Gal. 5:22–23). The *wisdom* from God (*from above* was a current Judaistic expression meaning from God) was *first* (preeminently) *pure* or holy and thus acceptable to God. The terms which follow amplify the character of this wisdom which is "first pure." It is *then peaceable* or productive of harmony between men in the highest sense; it does not pursue peace at the expense of purity or truth. It is *gentle* or reasonable, considerate, and kind. It is *open to reason* or compliant; it is *full of mercy and good fruits* or abounding in compassionate, helpful love and good works.

Two negative touches conclude the portrayal. The divine wisdom is *without uncertainty or insincerity* (lit., unhypocritical). The term translated *without uncertainty* can mean without partiality (cf. 2:4) or without doubting (cf. 1:6); the former meaning is probably better here and could be translated "without the spirit of partiality that disrupts."

In parallel with his discussion of demonic wisdom, James concludes his treatment of divine wisdom with a statement that describes the result of being controlled by such wisdom. The *harvest* (lit., fruit) *of righteousness* means the reward or result of doing what God demands—to follow divine wisdom is to be led to righteousness. The author employs a startling imagery—instead of the harvest being gathered, it is sown. This partly illogical metaphor according to agricultural life is eminently appropriate in spiritual experience because righteousness is not cultivated to be hoarded. The nature of Christian goodness is outgoing and has a social and communal aspect—the righteousness is sown or carefully bestowed in and on the community to contribute to its peace or redemption. The righteous are *those who make peace* (cf. Matt. 5:9); their deeds constitute a contribution to putting men in right relationship with one another as brothers. The righteous do not necessarily keep the peace, they may in fact actually disrupt the community for its ultimate good by declaring war on superficial compromises which pass for peace—the righteous *make* (accomplish or achieve) *peace.*

The correspondences between the works of the flesh and the fruit of the Spirit (Gal. 5:19–23) in Paul and the demonic and divine wisdom in James (3:13–18) make it clear that the same Christian realities are being described in different terms. For Paul, the works of the flesh represent the outcome of living under the dominion of sin; and the fruit of the Spirit is the result of living in reliance upon Christ. For James, the two wisdoms represent the same two possibilities of existence. James is not denying the Holy Spirit, he is simply reflecting a perspective in early Christian thought which conceived of the Christian life in different terms. Paul's perspective has become normative to explain the relationship of the Christian to Christ; but James, probably speaking from a much more Jewish perspective, prefers to speak of the power or help that God gives as wisdom from above.

To describe the Christian life as Paul does in terms of the Holy Spirit is to emphasize the grace of God, but to describe the way man relates to God in terms of divine wisdom as James does is to stress the Christian's responsibility for his existence. James consistently emphasizes man's responsibility and is perhaps best studied when one has already experienced and understood something of Paul's doctrine of the Holy Spirit.

IV. Chapter 4

A loosely connected series of imperatives begins this chapter. This collection of maxims (vv. 1–10) is followed by a brief paragraph, unrelated to the preceding material, which deals with evil speaking and the law (vv. 11–12). The chapter concludes with a rather tightly knit section in modified diatribe style which stresses the need for the recognition of God in the plans of life (vv. 13–17). Such rapid alteration of subject and style seems out of step with the literary artistry of much of the New Testament, but it was characteristic of paranesis.

1. A Call to Consecration (4:1–10)

¹ What causes wars, and what causes fightings among you? Is it not your passions that are at war in your members? ² You desire and do not have; so you kill. And you covet and cannot obtain; so you fight and wage war. You do not have, because you do not ask. ³ You ask and do not receive, because you ask wrongly, to spend it on your passions. ⁴ Unfaithful creatures! Do you not know that friendship with the world is enmity with God? Therefore whoever wishes to be a friend of the world makes himself an enemy of God. ⁵ Or do you suppose it is in vain that the scripture says, "He yearns jealously over the spirit which he has made to dwell in us"? ⁶ But he gives more grace; therefore it says, "God opposes the proud, but gives grace to the humble." ⁷ Submit yourselves therefore to God. Resist the devil and he will flee from you. ⁸ Draw near to God and he will draw near to you. Cleanse your hands, you sinners, and purify your hearts, you men of double mind. ⁹ Be wretched and mourn and weep. Let your laughter be turned to mourning and your joy to dejection. ¹⁰ Humble yourselves before the Lord and he will exalt you.

The first part of this section (vv. 1–6) condemns the desire for worldly pleasure by affirming it to be the cause of their hostility to one another and their distorted relationship with God in prayer. The remainder of the section consists of loosely related exhortations to consecration (vv. 7–10).

If the first two verses are taken literally and understood to reflect the actual historical situation in the early congregations, an appalling scene emerges: the Christians were in such open hostility that the state of things could be described as war (vv. 1,2). Some commentators do take this position (cf. Oesterly, pp. 456–457); but the recognition that James is paranesis leads to a comparison with similar literature which reveals that the terms *wars* and *fightings* were customarily used in such ethical discussions to refer to quarrels and disputes (Dibelius, p. 259). The term translated *wars* refers to quarrels that reflect a chronic hostility while the term rendered *fightings* refers to a dispute or clash that arises from a temporary or acute hostility.

This perspective on the *wars* and *fightings* bears on the interpretation of the accusation *so you kill*. Feeling that such an indictment of the church was impossible, many scholars have accepted the conjecture of Erasmus in the 1519 edition of his Greek text that a very early mistake in copying manuscripts resulted in the term for envy (*phthoneite*) being misspelled so that the text reads kill (*phoneuete*).[18] However no manuscript evidence supports this; and the accusation can be satisfactorily explained without such a radical procedure. The concepts of hostility and murder are frequently associated in the Christian tradition (Matt. 5:21–23; 1 John 3:15); and this awareness of hatred being tantamount to murder seems to be what James is assuming as he accuses his readers of terrible sin (cf. Ropes, pp. 254–256).

James thus assumes that his readers know that their disputes constitute horrible sin. His opening question—*What causes wars, and what causes fightings among you?*—is not posed so much to condemn the disputes as it is to expose the cause of the hostilities as the *passions that are at war in your members* (within you). The term *passions* is literally pleasures, and

James clearly means the desires or lusts for pleasure, hence *passions*. The unfulfilled longings and desires clash within them and lead to chaos in their personal relationships. James repeats his diagnosis of their situation in a couplet of Hebrew poetry: *You desire and do not have; so you kill* is followed by the parallel *and you covet and cannot obtain; so you fight and wage war*. The precise nature of the pleasure sought, the desire frustrated, and the coveting thwarted is not stated; and it is not the author's intent to identify these. With superb paranetic skill he evokes from his readers the question as to what they might be in order that they evaluate their own passions. The concern of James is that his readers realize that their own inner frustrations and covetousness must be faced because of the relationship between these and the quarrels, fights, disputes, and arguments among them.

With the observation that *you do not have because you do not ask*, the author takes another approach to the condemnation of their commitment to the pursuit of pleasure. Previously, the longing for pleasure was affirmed as the cause of hostile and distorted relationships with persons; now their longing for pleasure is viewed from the perspective of its effect on their relationship with God. This affirmation that they *do not ask* and that this is the reason they *do not have* must be understood generally in the context of this discussion and specifically in the light of the following verse. James is not suggesting that what they failed to get by fighting and coveting could be obtained through prayer. He is deftly showing how their intense desires for pleasure cannot be squared with their relationship with God. With sarcasm he suggests that they pray for what they have not been able to get. This stinging rebuke which exposes their sinfulness is followed by a diagnosis of the erosive effect of their lust for pleasure on their relationship with God in prayer. They do pray— *you ask*—but they *do not receive* because prayer is distorted by their intent to seek

18 A listing of the scholars adopting this solution may be found in Dibelius, p. 260, who favors it.

pleasure. The charge that *you ask wrongly* (with wrong motives) is explained by the phrase *to spend it on* (in the realm of) *your passions.* James is not accusing them of praying for sinful things, but with a selfish intent. They prayed to further their own interests and not to deepen their relation to God or to accomplish his will in the world. Apparently they were not really aware of the subtle way in which the influence of their inner desires had permeated their lives and distorted their spiritual existence. Their dedication to God was outwardly being maintained, but their hidden and secret dedication to pleasure and intense desire for it had put them in the position of trying to serve two masters (Matt. 6:24). They professed to want to follow God, but their other desires were controlling them.

In this discussion of the way in which inner desires can reveal themselves in distorted prayer, James should not be interpreted to mean that all unanswered prayer reflects an asking *wrongly.* What he says elsewhere regarding prayer (cf. 1:5–8,16–18; 5:13–18) must be taken along with his statements in this section.

Even though the persons James addresses are in the church, he calls them *Unfaithful creatures,* or literally, adulteresses. This harsh rebuke reflects a Judaistic background because sinful or idolatrous Jews were figuratively termed as adulterous (cf. Matt. 12:39; 16:4). The RSV translation correctly stresses the figurative aspect with *unfaithful,* but *creatures* is inappropriate and reads into James a derogatory implication. James means *unfaithful* ones or persons; no subhuman category is indicated as *creatures* suggests.

What justifies the description *unfaithful* is explained in terms of the impossibility of combining a right relation to God and *friendship with the world.* The term *world* does not mean persons, but the way of life or style of life of persons apart from God (cf. 1:27; 2:5). To long for this way of life is to want *to be a friend of the world,* and this desire is not compatible with the

desire to be loyal to God. The attempt to keep both options alive is to be *unfaithful,* for *whoever wishes* (desires or wants) *to be a friend of the world* is an enemy of God. James does not use the expression "friend of God" (*philos theou,* 2:23) as one might expect as the opposite of *friend of the world* (*philos kosmou*), but he stresses the ultimate and irreconcilable difference between what God requires and the world desires in the concept of *enemy of God.* James is trying to enable his readers to see that their deep longings for pleasure are unalterably opposed to their Christian commitment, and this incompatibility was dividing and distorting their entire existence.

But James quickly points out that even though they were taking the position of being *an enemy* of God, he had not abandoned them. *He yearns jealously* for us, and *he gives more grace.* James clearly intends these statements to encourage the Christians to realize God's concern and willingness to receive and help them. Even so, the verses do pose some difficult problems.

The indication that *the scripture says* (v. 5) prepares the reader for a quotation from the Old Testament as in the parallel *it says* (v. 6), but the quotation in v. 5 is not found in the Scriptures. The attempt to avoid the difficulty by holding that everything following *the scripture says* is parenthetical and that the quotation intended is in v. 6b is possible (see Ropes, pp. 262–265); but it is more likely that James is simply paraphrasing or summarizing Old Testament material such as is found in Genesis 6:3 or Exodus 20:5 (cf. Mitton, pp. 153–154).

But this does not end the difficulties. The quote itself is capable of many interpretations. Erasmus quipped: "There are waggon-loads of interpretations of this passage" (Mitton, p. 154). The problems are: (1) the term *spirit* may refer to man's spirit (RSV and TEV) or the Holy Spirit; (2) the term *spirit* may be either the subject (NEB and TEV) or the object (RSV) of the sentence; and (3) *jealously* may be either a good (RSV) or evil (NEB and TEV) description. The translation of the NEB—"The spirit which God implanted in man turns toward envious desires"— takes the verse to refer to man's constant inclination to evil and represents the major alternative to the translation of the RSV, which takes the verse to refer to God's concern for his rebellious people. Although either translation is grammatically possible, the RSV rendering fits the context of James better. In spite of the fact that man longs to be *a friend of the world*, God's love is such that *He yearns jealously* for our loyalty, and thus *he gives more grace*, i.e., he enables us to overcome the desire for pleasure that is destructive (cf. Ropes, p. 265). The quotation from Proverbs 3:34 (cf. 1 Peter 5:5) buttresses this interpretation as it affirms the availability of help from God for the wavering Christian.

On the basis of God's readiness to assist the Christians in their struggle to be loyal to him and to control their desires for pleasure, James gives a series of exhortations (vv. 7–10) which are roughly parallel and represent traditional paranetic calls to repentance.[19] Ten ringing commands peal out in four verses. Any one of them would be sufficient to bring the Christian to his God, but taken together they constitute an almost irresistible summons to loyalty.

The Christians are to be obedient (*submit*), stand opposed to (*resist*) the slanderer (*devil*), move close (*draw near*, cf. Mark 1:15) *to God*, clean up their conduct (*cleanse your hands*), purify their motives (*hearts*), get uncomfortable (cf. Rom. 7:24, *wretched*), be depressed (*mourn*), cry (*weep*), replace laughing with lamenting (*mourning*) and happiness with gloom (*dejection*), and subordinate themselves to God (*humble yourselves*). This massive call to emergency action in relation to God reflects the seriousness with

which James views their sin; and in calling them to repentance he terms them *sinners*, i.e., persons acting in opposition to God (cf. v. 4) and *men of double mind* (cf. 1:8) or persons with two loyalties (lit., "double-souled").

Only three promises are given along with these ten commands, but they are sufficient for the Christian: The devil *will flee from you*; God *will draw near to you*; God *will exalt* (lift up or help) *you* (cf. 1:9–11; Luke 14:11).

2. Evil Speaking and Law (4:11–12)

¹¹ **Do not speak evil against one another, brethren. He that speaks evil against a brother or judges his brother, speaks evil against the law and judges the law. But if you judge the law, you are not a doer of the law but a judge.** ¹² **There is one lawgiver and judge, he who is able to save and to destroy. But who are you that you judge your neighbor?**

This unit touches the subject of hostility in the community (cf. 4:1–2) but deals with it directly and from a fresh point of view. The condemnation of destructive speech (cf. 1:26; 3:1–12; 5:12) assumes a respect for the law which reflects a Jewish orientation.

The opening imperative can be taken to assume that the evil activity is in progress and to mean "stop speaking evil." To *speak evil* (lit., to speak down on) means to talk against a person in his absence; it indicates speaking about an individual in a malicious way in order to influence the opinion of others against him. It is the motive and purpose of the speaker that is being condemned because words are being used to spread hostility and erode the prestige or character of a person. Whether what is being communicated is true or not is not the issue—the focus is on the unspoken intent of the person speaking the words. The infectious maliciousness that *speak evil* indicates is clear in the use of the term to describe how non-Christians persecute Christians (1 Peter 2:12; 3:16; cf. Rom. 1:30).

James reinforces his prohibition by exposing the implications of evil speaking

---

[19] For the parallels in paranetic literature, cf. Dibelius, pp. 269–272 and Ropes, pp. 268–272.

and in the process sharpens his imperative by revealing the seriousness of such sin in an unforgettable way. James associates evil speaking with judging because the one who *speaks evil against a brother* puts himself in the position of judging his brother by his condemning speech against him. But such an evaluation of a person is the function of the law, and therefore one who speaks evil or judges his brother actually criticizes the law itself as inadequate and may be said to be speaking against or judging it. For Christians of a Jewish background, the supreme role of the law would make this argument a powerful and compelling one; to criticize, imply, or assume that the law was inadequate would be blasphemous.

Another approach to understanding the author's affirmation that evil speaking or judging one's brother is also to do this to the law is to understand law to mean the summarizing commandment to love one's neighbor (cf. 2:8). In the sin of speech James describes, this law is set aside and disparaged (Ropes, pp. 273–275). This approach is strengthened by the use of the term "neighbor" (v. 12), but is rendered less than satisfactory by the expression *doer of the law* and the unmistakable Jewish orientation in the view of the law and of God as *one lawgiver and judge,* who is *able to save and to destroy.* The basis of the argument is Jewish, and this is not out of character with paranesis or early Christian practice (cf. Gal. 3:6–18).

With regard to the remainder of this section, little disagreement exists. James affirms that to assume the role of one who would *judge the law* would thus be to challenge the one *lawgiver and judge,* i.e., God. The piercing question with which James concludes gathers up his entire argument—*But who are you that you judge your neighbor?* God is judge; the Christian who judges and pronounces sentence in his evil speaking against his brother is attacking God's law and even presuming to fill the role of the "one lawgiver and judge."

Most contemporary Christians do not have the Judaistic background which enables them to appreciate the force of the argument James uses to buttress his exhortation. They would be more impressed by an argument from the example of Jesus and his commandment that men should love one another. But the basic thrust of the thought of James is easily adapted to a Christian context. One who speaks evil against his brother does seize a right of judgment and does exercise action of condemnation that belongs to Christ and God (cf. Rom. 8:31–34; Eph. 4:30–32).

3. The Sin of Presumption (4:13–17)

13 Come now, you who say, "Today or tomorrow we will go into such and such a town and spend a year there and trade and get gain"; 14 whereas you do not know about tomorrow. What is your life? For you are a mist that appears for a little time and then vanishes. 15 Instead you ought to say, "If the Lord wills, we shall live and we shall do this or that." 16 As it is, you boast in your arrogance. All such boasting is evil. 17 Whoever knows what is right to do and fails to do it, for him it is sin.

This section is somewhat related to the following one (5:1–6) but not to the preceding. Such an abrupt change in subject was characteristic of paranesis, and neither author nor reader would have been uneasy with the radical transition in thought from a consideration of evil speaking to a treatment of how man should plan for the future.

The opening *Come now, you who say* (cf. 5:1) sounds harsher than this colloquial Hellenistic expression was in the first century, and the NEB translation, "A word with you, you who say," is more appropriate because the address is not argumentative but friendly. The persons addressed are industrious and ambitious small businessmen of the first century who are courageously planning future operations as traveling traders (cf. Acts 16:11–15). James is not objecting to their planning nor their desire for profit, but seeking to stress that men need to be aware of the reality of God and to consider him in their deliberations. This emphasis assumes that devotion to God is not confined to so-called religious acts and implies that Christians should bring their sense of God's presence and power into every area of life. The planning of those James addresses was not specifically religious, but he challenges the Christians involved in such pursuits to bring their faith and trust in God to such deliberations and to make their plans from the foundation of such faith.

James sharply confronts his readers with their limitations—*you do not know about tomorrow*—and with their mortality by challenging them with the question: *What is your life?* He answers for them in Judaistic imagery that stresses the transient and uncertain nature of existence by comparing life to a *mist* (puff of smoke or steam) *that appears* and *then vanishes*. The insecurity of life should lead the Christian to make all his plans with a recognition of his dependence on God. His counsel that *you ought to say* does not mean that the words he gives are to be repeated as a ritual of piety which validates the plans. The expression *If the Lord wills* is actually of pagan origin and was a feature of both superficial and genuine Hellenistic non-Christian piety (cf. Ropes, pp. 279–280). The expression may be used here with some irony: if the non-Christians said this, surely the Christian should bring his religion into every realm of life. But not only did the Christians fall short of even pagan standards, their spirit in planning was such that James charges they *boast* (exult or glory, cf. 2 Cor. 10:13–17) in their *arrogance* (presumption or pretension, cf. 1 John 2:16) and that this is *sin* (wrong).

The concluding maxim (v. 17) has a wide ranging application, but in this context it refers specifically to the refusal to relate faith to all of life. Now that James has exposed *what is right*, i.e., the need to make all of life's plans in the light of ultimate reality, the Christian *who fails to do it* commits *sin.* In modern terms, the separation of life into sacred and secular

categories so that one's faith in Christ is not a vital factor in all of existence and decision making is sin.

V. Chapter 5

This chapter consists of five units. The first two are closely related by the common theme of judgment (vv. 1–6 and 7–11), but the remaining three deal with topics that are only generally or loosely related.

1. The Condemnation of the Rich (5:1-6)

¹ Come now, you rich, weep and howl for the miseries that are coming upon you. ² Your riches have rotted and your garments are moth-eaten. ³ Your gold and silver have rusted, and their rust will be evidence against you and will eat your flesh like fire. You have laid up treasure for the last days. ⁴ Behold, the wages of the laborers who mowed your fields, which you kept back by fraud, cry out; and the cries of the harvesters have reached the ears of the Lord of hosts. ⁵ You have lived on the earth in luxury and in pleasure; you have fattened your hearts in a day of slaughter. ⁶ You have condemned, you have killed the righteous man; he does not resist you.

The first-century manner of expression which figuratively used the terms rich and poor to refer to the wicked and the righteous (cf. the comment. on 1:9–11) is the key to understanding this entire section which announces the doom of the wicked in a style reminiscent of the Old Testament prophet Amos. The first part of this unit announces the judgment (vv. 1–3), and the second gives the reasons for the condemnation of the wicked rich (vv. 4–6).

Even though the repeated address *Come now* (cf. 4:13) suggests a correlation with the previous section, the connection is superficial and confined to this one literary aspect. James has no ethical exhortations for those whom he addresses as the *rich* (the godless and the wicked, cf. 1:9–11 and Luke 6:24); he does not even call them to repentance (cf. 4:7–10) but to weeping and screaming in distress (*howl*) because of the sufferings (*miseries*, cf. Rom. 3:16) that are coming in the judgment of God.

James views the unrepentant wicked as existing so definitely under the shadow of the rapidly approaching judgment that he speaks of the things *that are coming* as already accomplished and present. This use of the Greek perfect tense is similar to the style of speech used by the Old Testament prophets who spoke of coming events as existing because of their faith in God's power (cf. Blackman, p. 142).

From the perspective of the judgment of God, James affirms that their *riches have rotted.* It is true that wealth in the first century usually consisted of hoarded or stored up materials rather than capital (cf. Luke 12:13–21), but a literal reference to rotten grain or foodstuffs and *moth-eaten* garments is not the point. James speaks from the bar of God's judgment; and his stress is the worthlessness of the things men have dedicated themselves to obtain, to protect, and to enjoy.

The realization that James is speaking figuratively provides the clue to understanding the statement that *gold and silver have rusted.* That this did not actually occur was well known in the first century (cf. Ropes, p. 285), but such imagery was traditional to affirm the ultimate worthlessness of wealth when compared with the value of loyalty to God (cf. Matt. 6:19–21). James expands the traditional imagery in two ways. First, he states that *rust will be evidence* (a witness) *against you;* and this is probably an accusation that they have used their wealth selfishly (cf. Sirach 21:10, "Lose your silver for the sake of a brother or a friend, and do not let it rust under a stone and be lost"). Second, James affirms that the rust *will eat your flesh like fire.* This poetic description combines the imagery of rust eating at metal with the traditional one of the consuming fire of judgment to create a terrifying picture of doom.

The final section of v. 3 summarizes the author's pronouncements of judgment on the wicked rich. Some scholars feel that the term *fire* should be in this sentence

rather than the preceding one (cf. Ropes, pp. 287–288) and that the verse should be translated as in the RSV margin ("since you have stored up fire"); but most scholars reject this because of the frequent use of the imagery of fire as eating flesh in connection with judgment (cf. Heb. 10:27; Judith 16:17) and the presence of the term "like" (Dibelius, p. 283). It is probably better to understand James as concluding his declaration of devastation by exposing the utter futility of their hoarding; the certainty of judgment means that they *have laid up treasure for* (in) *the last days* (cf. Rom. 2:5).

In vv. 4–6 James lays bare the basis of the terrible judgment he has announced (vv. 1–3) in three closely related accusations: they have exploited employees, lived selfishly, and oppressed the righteous.

James utilizes a Judaistic manner of expression in his charge that *the wages of the laborers* are crying out (cf. Gen. 4:10 for the crying out of Abel's blood). The charge that these wages were *kept back by fraud* refers to the refusal to pay the *laborers* at the end of each day's work as the Jewish law required (cf. Lev. 19:13; Matt. 20:8). This law was for the benefit of the poor whose need was so acute that they could not wait for their wages until merchandise or produce was sold by the employer. What is in view here is farm labor temporarily employed as *harvesters* of grain who had *mowed your fields* (estate or farms). The refusal to pay such workers promptly was frequently condemned in Jewish paranetic literature, and in Sirach 34:22 such sin is equated with murder. The workers who were denied their wages immediately had but little power to force payment, and James describes them as appealing to God and adding their cries to the voice of the wages.

This combined appeal is heard: it *reached the ears of the Lord of hosts.* This designation of God incorporates the Greek transliteration (*sabaoth*, cf. KJV) of a Hebrew term (cf. Isa. 5:9) which indicates God's power as the ruler of the hosts of heavenly powers or armies and could be better translated as "the Lord who rules all" or "the Lord of almighty power" (cf. Ropes, p. 289). This description of God reminds the readers that the rich who trample them do not have all power; *the Lord of hosts* is sovereign.

The refusal to give the workers what they had earned at the conclusion of the day's work is related to the next accusation. The exploiters lived *in luxury and in pleasure* because the delay in payment allowed the employer to use these funds for himself and then to replenish them and pay the workers when the harvest was sold. Not only were they violating the law of Judaism, they selfishly enjoyed *luxury* and *pleasure* in utter disregard for the desperate needs of others (cf. Luke 16: 25). Such greedy exploitation inspires James to utter a terrible sentence of condemnation; just as an animal is fattened for slaughter (cf. Luke 15:23), the luxury of these wicked persons is preparation for their doom in "the" (NEB, not "a" as in the RSV) *day of slaughter* (final judgment).

The oppression and disregard of the poor spelled out in vv. 4–5 are the basis of the culminating accusation in v. 6. By such conduct the wicked *have condemned* and so deprived the righteous that they may be said to *have killed* (cf. the comment on v. 4). Most modern scholars feel that *the righteous man* is a Hebrew expression meaning righteous men (cf. Blackman, p. 144 and Wis. of Sol. 2:10–12) and reject the sixth-century suggestion of Oecumenius that the reference is primarily to Christ. But even though the language is poetic, it is difficult to believe that the death of Christ was not also in the author's mind (cf. Ropes, pp. 291–292). While the statement that the righteous man *does not resist you* is applicable to the silence of Jesus during his trial (cf. 1 Peter 2:23), it probably refers primarily

to the inability of the poor man to offer resistance to the crushing oppression he faces.[20]

The purpose of this section which condemns the wicked needs to be kept in mind when an evaluation is made of the author's attitude toward sinful persons. James appears not to be speaking to the wicked; he seems to speak to the righteous who are discouraged and suffering under oppression. His purpose is to call the righteous to realize that God's judgment on such wickedness is sure and that the righteous should remain faithful to God. The entire section prepares the way for the exhortation to endurance in the next unit.

2. The Need for Patience (5:7–11)

7 Be patient, therefore, brethren, until the coming of the Lord. Behold, the farmer waits for the precious fruit of the earth, being patient over it until it receives the early and the late rain. **8** You also be patient. Establish your hearts, for the coming of the Lord is at hand. **9** Do not grumble, brethren, against one another, that you may not be judged; behold, the Judge is standing at the doors. **10** As an example of suffering and patience, brethren, take the prophets who spoke in the name of the Lord. **11** Behold, we call those happy who were steadfast. You have heard of the steadfastness of Job, and you have seen the purpose of the Lord, how the Lord is compassionate and merciful.

The condemnation of the wicked (5: 1–6) introduces and provides a part of the foundation for the exhortations to patience in this paragraph, and the close relationship between the sections is indicated by the use of *therefore* in v. 7.

The central affirmation of the need for patience is present throughout this section; it is stressed by arguments from analogy drawn from agriculture (vv. 7–8) and from examples drawn from Jewish tradition (vv. 10–11).

James calls the Christians to *be patient*. The term so translated (vv. 7,8,10) means

---

[20] The curious attempt of Ropes (p. 292) to make this a question relating to the witness of the poor at the judgment is generally rejected by scholars.

to submit without complaining or grumbling, and it is almost identical with the term translated *steadfast* (v. 11), which stresses the need for enduring or persisting. The distinction between the terms is that patience is more demanding; it is endurance without complaining, and it is this to which James summons the hard-pressed Christians. Patience need last only *until the coming of the Lord* (i.e., the appearance of Christ; cf. Ropes, pp. 293–294) because that event will shatter the bonds of hardship and bring reward (cf. 1:9–11).

Evidently the Christians James addresses felt that the time for the return of Jesus was overdue. James seeks to reassure them that the apparent delay should be met with patience, using an analogy from Palestinian agricultural life. The point of the illustration is in the climatic condition referred to in the expression *the early and the late rain* (lit., early and late; cf. Deut. 11:14). The two periods of rain were well known, and Jewish writings document the concern about these rains in Palestine in discussions about when prayer should begin for them in the event they were late (Mishna, Taanith 1:1–7). The early rain (October–November) was the occasion for sowing grain, and the late rain (April–May) stimulated the growth for the maturing of the crop. The Palestinian farmer depended on these two rains, and he could not harvest his crop until after the late rain.

James is arguing either that if a farmer can wait for grain with patience, they should be able to endure until the Lord returns, or that God like the farmer is waiting for harvest and Christians should be aware that the delay is out of God's concern and therefore should be patient. The latter meaning is to be preferred because James reassures the Christians that *the coming of the Lord is at hand*. The term *coming* (*parousia*) was used in the first century to refer to the arrival of kings or highly esteemed persons, and it was used by Christians to refer specifically to the return of Jesus in glory.[21] The affirmation that the coming *is at hand* means that it is very near. This expression is employed in the statement of Jesus that "the kingdom of God is at hand" (Mark 1:15). In the light of this sure reality that Jesus is to return, the Christians should renew their courage and confidence (*Establish your hearts;* cf. 1 Thess. 3:13).

With v. 9 James takes a slightly different approach to his theme. The discouragement of the Christians must not be allowed to express itself in grumbling and complaining. The term *grumble* means literally to groan. In association with *against one another* it refers to complaining which blames others for one's distress. The decisions about who is really at fault ultimately rest with the *Judge* (i.e., God or Christ), who *is standing at* (before) *the doors* (i.e., about to appear; cf. Mark 13:29; Rev. 3:20). The oppression and difficulties of the Christians may inspire grumbling, but these realities will not excuse them for it—they too, as the rich in 5:1–6, will *be judged*.

The exhortation to patience (vv. 7–8) is now reinforced by reminding the Christians that they were not in a unique situation because they suffered. Righteousness did not in the past exempt persons from life's difficulties. They should remember the prophets who were so privileged that they *spoke in the name of the Lord*. It is possible that James refers to Christian prophets (cf. Acts. 13:1), but the reference is more likely to the sufferings of the Jewish prophets which were catalogued and used to encourage others in first-century Judaism (cf. Heb. 11; Sirach 44:1—50:24; 1 Clement 4:1—19:3). James points the suffering and discouraged Christians to some models of conduct which they are to take *as an example of suffering and patience*. The Christians needed to be reminded that a mark of righteousness was in the displaying of patience in suffering (cf. 1:2–4).

21 See TDNT, II, 247–53.

James apparently refers to a currently used beatitude in the first part of v. 11, but the RSV obscures this by the translation of "we bless" or "we consider blessed" as *we call those happy.* The reference is stronger than mere happiness (RSV) and relates to the blessedness which issues from being favored by God. The first part of the verse could be translated: "we say 'Blessed are the ones who endured'" (cf. 1:12; Dan. 12:12). This reference to a well-known expression of blessedness summons the Christians to apply what they already knew to their own situation.

The classic example of Job was popular in the first century to illustrate God's blessings on the faithful sufferer. James easily assumes the reader's knowledge (*you have heard*) of Job from the Judaistic or perhaps even the Christian tradition (1 Clement 17:3; 26:3), although this is the only reference to Job in the New Testament. Quite accurately, James speaks of the *steadfastness* (endurance) *of Job* rather than his patience (cf. the comments on 5:7). Job did remain faithful to God in suffering; but he did complain and thus was hardly patient. In v. 9 James warns against grumbling; but the ultimate issue in suffering is to determine to endure and not to lose faith. Job grumbled, but he remained loyal and is an example revealing *the purpose* (goal) *of the Lord* as victory and blessing to the faithful.

The *purpose of the Lord* (cf. Job 42: 12) is ultimately not to oppress but to exalt (cf. 1:9–11), not to deprive but to bless (cf. 1:16–18); and this moves James to end his section with a statement of praise of God that is probably a paraphrase or summary of an Old Testament passage (cf. Ex. 34:6; Psalms 103:8; 111:4). The Greek terms are frequent in the translation of the Old Testament. The term for *merciful* used by James is quite common in the Septuagint, and the word *compassionate* is probably the equivalent of the Septuagint term meaning full of mercy (Ropes, pp. 299–300). The point James is making is clear. If they will remain faithful and not yield to the temptation to abandon God in the belief that he is less than a God of love and mercy, they will see for themselves the goodness of God as Job did and ultimately be able to praise him for his kindness and compassion.

3. Swearing (5:12)

12 But above all, my brethren, do not swear, either by heaven or by earth or with any other oath, but let your yes be yes and your no be no, that you may not fall under condemnation.

This brief unit of exhortation is closely related to the words of Jesus in Matthew 5:34–37; and it is difficult to resist the conclusion that James is quoting the words of Jesus as he had received them or is paraphrasing them. Against this view, it can be pointed out that many condemnations of the use of oaths can be cited in the contemporary Jewish and Greek literature (Sirach 23:9–11; Philo, *Decalogue*, 17–19; Pseudo Phocylides 16).[22] However, early Christian writers quote Jesus in almost the same words James uses here (cf. Justin Martyr, *Apology* 1:16:5; Clement of Alexandria, *Stromata* 5:99:1), which points unmistakably to the fact that what James includes was viewed as the words of Jesus. Added to this is the fact that the absoluteness of the prohibition in the words of Jesus is paralleled in the command of James, but not in the non-Christian sources (cf. Dibelius, pp. 295–299). The fact that James does not identify the exhortation as being the words of Jesus is paralleled in other Christian paranesis (cf. Rom. 12:14), and his introduction of the saying with the expression **But above all** indicates his awareness of its cruciality. Most convincingly of all, the literary form of the saying in James and the words of Jesus in Matthew are similar: both begin with an absolute prohibition of swearing and then conclude with specific examples.[23]

22 For many other references in contemporary literature, see Dibelius, pp. 295–296, and Ropes, pp. 301–303.
23 Dibelius (pp. 297–299) gives a full outline of the literary structure and even suggests that James is the more original paranetic form.

This specific use of the teaching of Jesus by James at this point and the apparent lack of its use elsewhere in the epistle does not pose a problem. James does not attempt to give his readers a collection of the teaching of Jesus; he assumes that they are Christians (1:1) and that they are in possession of Christian teachings—his purpose is to call Christians to obedience in practical ways, and he employs paranetic tradition from many sources to do this.

The relation of this section that prohibits swearing to the surrounding material in chapter 5 is general rather than specific. Probably the line of thought is that the suffering Christians (vv. 7–11) must guard their speech and not grumble (v. 9) or swear (v. 12). They should not swear (v. 12) but pray (vv. 13–18) and confess their sins (v. 16).

The command *do not swear* refers to the first-century practice of supporting one's speech by an oath such as "I swear that I will give up my children if this is not true" (Mussner, p. 214). The reference is not to cursing (cf. 3:9–12) or to the modern legal practice of swearing in a witness. What is condemned is the constant supporting of one's words by the use of oaths, which was very common in the first century (cf. Mussner, pp. 213–214; Mishna, Shebuoth, 1:1—3:11). To swear *by heaven* was to use some reference to God and to swear *by earth* was to refer to some reality of human existence. All oaths are condemned in the Christian tradition (cf. Matt. 5:33–37), and the Christian is to simply let his *yes be yes* and his *no be no*. The ultimate point is that the Christian's speech should be such that its truth and reflection of reality will not be suspect. The prohibition points more to the being of the speaker and the quality of one's communication than it does simply to refraining from the use of words that are oaths (cf. Mussner, pp. 211–212).

James writes much about the speech of persons, and what he says here should be taken in the context of his other instruc-

tions (cf. 1:19–21,26–27; 2:1–13,14–26; 3:1–12; 4:11–12,13–17; 5:9,13–18). This stress on the importance of what one says is underlined by the threat of judgment expressed here—*that you may not fall under condemnation* (judgment)—and is consistent with the warning of Jesus that "by your words you will be justified, and by your words you will be condemned" (Matt. 12:37).

4. The Power of Prayer (5:13–18)

[13] Is any one among you suffering? Let him pray. Is any cheerful? Let him sing praise. [14] Is any among you sick? Let him call for the elders of the church, and let them pray over him, anointing him with oil in the name of the Lord; [15] and the prayer of faith will save the sick man, and the Lord will raise him up; and if he has committed sins, he will be forgiven. [16] Therefore confess your sins to one another, and pray for one another, that you may be healed. The prayer of a righteous man has great power in its effects. [17] Elijah was a man of like nature with ourselves and he prayed fervently that it might not rain, and for three years and six months it did not rain on the earth. [18] Then he prayed again and the heaven gave rain, and the earth brought forth its fruit.

The main thrust of this section is the power of prayer and its appropriateness in every situation of life. Prayer is encouraged in times of distress (v. 13), elation (v. 13), sickness (v. 14), and sin (vv. 15–16a) and in assisting fellow Christians in striving for righteousness and spiritual health (v. 16a). The central theme of the entire section is summarized in v. 16b which affirms the power of prayer generally. The confusion and controversy over the meaning of *anointing with oil* (v. 14) has unfortunately diverted attention from the fact that James is calling Christians to realize the centrality of the importance of prayer in the Christian life.

The relationship between this section on prayer and the preceding one is not clear. Perhaps the line of thought is that men are not to swear but to pray. The following unit on the wayward brother introduces a new subject.

The first question James raises relates to

who is *suffering* (cf. v. 10). Although this term means basically to endure hardship, it is probably better to understand it here as the discouragement that hardship often inspires since the next question of James— *Is any cheerful?*—focuses so clearly on one's attitude (cf. Blackman, pp. 152–153). This perspective allows v. 13 to be translated: Is any one discouraged (depressed)? He ought to pray. Is any one elated (exulting)? He ought to sing praise (a hymn) to God.

These two extremes of attitude bracket all of life—James calls on men to pray when things go wrong and to pray when all goes so well that they are elated. Prayer is not to be just the spiritual moaning of the suffering; it is also the song of a jubilant and victorious faith.

The third question James poses apparently refers to a situation when the Christian is in such a condition that he feels he has not the strength to pray. When one is this *sick* (physically ill), prayer still is the prescription; and James discusses the power of the prayer of the *elders of the church* whom the Christian is to *call for* (summon).

The *elders of the church* probably refers to the eldest and most respected members of the congregation who also had a specific role in the church as its appointed officers (cf. Acts 11:30; 14:23; 15:4; 1 Tim. 5:1,17,19). Jewish communities also recognized elders, and the procedure James describes reflects Judaistic custom. The practice in the Jewish community was for the village elders to visit the dangerously ill person and to pray with him. If the person was able, he prayed with the elders; but if he were too ill to do this, they prayed for him while he prayed in his heart (cf. Ropes, p. 304).

The *anointing him with oil* was also a first-century custom (cf. Mark 6:13; Luke 10:34), but the medicinal use is not meant here in James because the person is only anointed (symbolically touched) with oil—it is not rubbed in, poured on, or taken internally as in medicinal utilizations.

This symbolic use of the oil to represent the healing power or presence of God is indicated by the fact that the *anointing is in the name of the Lord.* The use of *the name* along with the oil makes this a religious rite, not a medical one.

James is not so much instructing Christians as to what they should do in severe illness as he is illustrating his stress on the power of prayer by reminding them of their own use of prayer in connection with a symbolic ceremony of community concern in a moment of desperation. The early Christians were doing what James describes, and he is not instituting a procedure. His point is that prayer works— *the prayer of faith* (not the elders or the oil) *will save the sick man* (i.e., from death) because *the Lord will raise him up* (from his bed). The statement that the sins of the person will be forgiven probably refers to the fact that the illness in view was related to the person's sins (cf. John 9:1–2). Not all sickness was thought to be due to sin in the first century, but illness was often related to wickedness that was unforgiven (cf. Testament of the Twelve Patriarchs, Reuben 1:7, which has the idea that no sick person is cured of his disease until all his sins are forgiven him).

Unfortunately, this passage has been misused in the context of both faith healing and church ceremony. James does not intend to say that this procedure would cure every fatal illness for the Christian— this would make this passage absurd by forcing it to teach that Christians could escape death. God gives healing—according to his wisdom and mercy—through the means appropriate to the culture in which one lives; and this example in James is to be seen as reflecting procedures in the first century and not as a mandate for avoiding responsible medical care in modern life. The abiding value of James is his stress that man should depend on God in sickness; and the tragedy of many modern persons is that they call their physicians and do not also call on God.

The use of this illustration in James to

prove the validity of the sacrament of extreme unction is also misguided (cf. Ropes, pp. 306–307). The ceremony James describes was not for the Christian who was doomed to die; it was a ceremony to regain health. Extreme unction is thought to prepare for death; James describes a procedure which involves continued life.

The ceremony James discusses was of Jewish origin and was commonly practiced in the first century. As the early church made inroads into the Hellenistic world, the church used this passage to prohibit heathen remedies and incantations. Later, the oil came to be seen as magical and sacramental and as related to forgiveness of sins; and this made a contribution to the concept of extreme unction. The custom James describes belonged to the earliest Christian church in a Jewish setting; and although it is no longer a part of the culture of most persons, the ancient practice does have an abiding affirmation —man's life and health are ultimately in God's hands, and man should call on God and ask others to pray for him in his hour of need (cf. Sirach 38:9–15).

The *therefore* of v. 16 is based on the efficacy of prayer in all three of the situations James has mentioned in vv. 13–15. Because prayer is meaningful and effective in depression and exultation and sickness, Christians should *confess* their *sins to one another.* Forgiveness is not the chief issue here, but the confession of wrongdoing which points to flaws and weaknesses of character and personhood that can be the basis of praying *for one another that you may be healed.* The healing includes the concept of the sin that causes illness (v. 15) but is larger and refers also to the need for healing from the flaws that have produced sin. This interpretation seems demanded by the fact that the confession is not to the elders, but is seen as preparation for praying for one another.[24] This

view of the exhortation to confession of sin relates it to the healing and supporting fellowship of the Christian community in which both the sharing of one's life and the shouldering of responsibility for others in prayer are a part of the process of healing and maturing.

The latter part of v. 16 summarizes the theme of the entire section and is a general statement of the power of prayer. The term *prayer* means entreaty or petition, and it is the supplication of the *righteous* (Christian) *man* (person) that is considered. Such prayer *has great power* (is strong) *in its effects.* The term translated *in its effects* can be understood to mean "when God makes it effective" (cf. Blackman, p. 155), "when it goes into action" (*in its effects*), or as an adjective "effectual" which modifies prayer as in the KJV. The best understanding of this phrase is probably the one represented in the RSV translation because it is most consistent with the context in James. What James is affirming is that prayer has tremendous influence and that Christians should therefore pray.

The author illustrates his statement about the power of prayer by reference to Elijah, who was a popular example of the potency of prayer in the first century (Sirach 48:1–11). That James is drawing on first-century tradition is clear from his reference to Elijah's praying, which was a current Jewish interpretation of the passage in 1 Kings 17:1. In addition to this, James states that *for three years and six months it did not rain on the earth* (cf. Luke 4:25), which was a rabbinic estimate of the length of the drought based on 1 Kings 18:1 (cf. Ropes, p. 311).

The popular conception of Elijah in the first century was that he was almost superhuman (cf. Sirach 48:9–14) and that he would be a figure appearing at the end of time (Mark 9:11–13).[25] James makes his illustration forceful by stating that *Elijah was a man of like nature with ourselves*

---

[24] Ropes (p. 309) relates to the healing of v. 16 closely with the preceding section, but Dibelius, pp. 303–305, feels that vv. 16–18 are to be seen in a larger perspective.

[25] See Joachim Jeremias, TDNT, II, 928–941.

(i.e., a man like us); and the fact that his prayer altered the cycle of nature should encourage us to pray that the nature of our existence and that of others would be changed.

5. Reclaiming the Wayward (5:19–20)

¹⁹ My brethren, if any one among you wanders from the truth and some one brings him back, ²⁰ let him know that whoever brings back a sinner from the error of his way will save his soul from death and will cover a multitude of sins.

The concluding paragraph to the epistle constitutes another unit of exhortation. The ending of the epistle seems abrupt from the perspective of the style of the first-century letter which usually ended with a doxology (cf. 1 Cor. 16:23–24; Gal. 6:18; Phil. 4:23; Jude 24–25) or personal greetings (cf. 1 Cor. 16:1–20; Phil. 4:21; 2 John 13; 3 John 15), but it was characteristic of paranetic epistles to end as James does (cf. Sirach 51:30). The fact that this exhortative unit was placed at the conclusion does emphasize it and indicates the importance it had for the author.

What James has in view in the statement *if any among you wanders from the truth* is the possibility of a Christian living in a way which is inappropriate and opposed to the standard of the Christian community. This meaning of *wanders from the truth* is the only one that is appropriate to the following description that such a person needs to be brought *back* (lit., turned around or converted as in KJV) and that he is a *sinner* whose problem is *the error of his way. Truth* here thus means right conduct more than right doctrine, although both are probably in view. The person under consideration is the Christian who is involved in sinful conduct, and James terms such a person a *sinner.* James does not employ the term *sinner* here to mean a person who has never experienced salvation (cf. Rom. 5:8); he is using it as descriptive of a per-

son's behavior—the person is sinning and may appropriately be called a sinner (cf. Gal. 6:1; Matt. 18:15).

James does not exhort the Christian to help such persons. He assumes that they will feel responsible (cf. Gal. 6:1; Matt. 18:15), and praises the *one* who *brings him back* by pointing out what has been accomplished—this *will save from death* and *will cover a multitude of sins.*

The precise nature and relationship of these two accomplishments are debated. The first reference—*will save his soul from death*—seems clearly to apply to the *soul* (life or personality) of the erring brother; and it is the helping Christian who *will save* (be instrumental in delivering, cf. Rom. 11:14; 1 Cor. 7:16) his brother *from death.* How *death* is understood here determines one's interpretation of what James is affirming. It seems better to take James to mean *death* in the sense of what sin does to human life (cf. 1:15; 5:14–16; 1 Cor. 11:27–30) rather than to relate *death* to ultimate destruction or lostness (cf. Eph. 2:1; Rev. 2:11). This section of the verse could thus be: he shall deliver such a wayward Christian from the deadly result of his sins. What James is stating is that the destructive power of sin will be thwarted because the wayward Christian will turn away from the *error of his way* (cf. Mitton, pp. 212–213).

The second portion of the verse—*and will cover a multitude of sins*—is more debated. The meaning of *cover a multitude of sins* is clear; *to cover* sins means to obtain forgiveness or to make them to be forgotten. The problem is whose sins are referred to. If they are taken to be sins of the Christian who brings back his sinful brother, then James is affirming that redeeming a wayward Christian is so meritorious an act that it earns or accomplishes forgiveness for the one who does it. The idea that good works earned forgiveness was current in Judaism (cf. Oesterley, p. 476; Dibelius, pp. 307–308). That James here reflects such a Jewish idea is the position of many Protestant and

Roman Catholic scholars (cf. Mitton, pp. 213–217; Mussner, pp. 232–233).

Another possibility is to understand the sin referred to as those of the wayward Christian. On this view, James is affirming that the one who brings back his wayward brother will *cover a multitude of sins* because the wayward will abandon his sinful ways and receive forgiveness for those he has been involved in (cf. Robertson, pp. 198–199). This interpretation is more in line with the view of forgiveness that James expresses elsewhere (cf. 4:8; 5:15), but the language of James in itself would allow either interpretation.

In any case, James is not dealing with the problem of how one is forgiven; his concern is with encouraging Christians to assume responsibility for helping and restoring one another. Most of his exhortation has been addressed to Christians in their struggles as individuals, but he chooses to close his letter with a missionary and evangelistic note. Christians are to help one another in the struggle against sin; and they are not to allow the sinful conduct of others to be an excuse to ignore them. In the spirit of Jesus who died for men, they are also to give their efforts to save the erring.

1 Peter

RAY SUMMERS

Introduction

The first epistle of Peter has had a secure place in the New Testament canon from the earliest period of Christian history. It met both the tests by which the early Christians made up the approved list (canon) of writings by which Christian doctrine, Christian practice, and other Christian writings would be checked. The tests were: (1) Did the book bear the name of an apostle? (2) Did the book prove its intrinsic value as Scripture in the use of the Christians?

Traces of the language of 1 Peter are in the first Corinthian epistle of Clement of Rome about A.D. 97. While some scholars (Wand, p. 9) interpret these traces as examples of a common vocabulary of the day, others (Bigg, p. 8) are convinced that they are quotations from 1 Peter. The use of 1 Peter by Papias, about A.D. 125, has the unchallenged authority of Eusebius (*Eccles. Hist.*, III.39.17). Eusebius referred also to the use of the epistle by a group of Asian teachers whom he called presbyters. He stated that they made frequent use of the epistle as an undisputed work (*Eccles. Hist.*, III.1.3).

Clear quotations from the epistle are in Polycarp's letter to the Philippians about A.D. 125. While he did not name the writer of his source, he used parts of 1:8,15,21; 2:21,22,24; 3:9,13; 4:7. Other second-century writers quoted the epistle and attributed it to Peter. Some of these writers were Basilides (A.D. 125), Theodotian (160), and Irenaeus (180). By the time of

Origen and Tertullian in the first half of the third century, the epistle was widely known and used as authoritative. From the witness of external evidence, it has as strong support as one could desire.

I. Authorship

The salutation of the epistle clearly ascribes it to "Peter, an apostle of Jesus Christ" (1:1). While no other name has been advanced to replace the name of Peter, some scholars have regarded the authorship as pseudonymous. This has been due in part to problems of Petrine authorship which will be developed in the next paragraphs. Others have regarded the entire salutation (1:1–2) as an interpolation and not an original part of the text. Both ideas have been inadequately argued. There is not one shred of textual evidence to support the idea that the salutation is an interpolation. On the surface, the argument for pseudonymous authorship does appear convincing. Careful examination, however, reveals a superficial quality which leaves the objection to Petrine authorship unconvincing.

Four basic arguments summarize the case against Petrine authorship.[1] (1) Would Peter, a Jew, write a book which totally excluded any reference to the Mosaic law or to any distinctive ideas and practices of

[1] For two differently organized but excellent treatments of the entire introduction to 1 Peter, see the works of Guthrie (pp. 95–136) and van Unnik (pp. 758–66).

the Jewish religion? In response one must bear in mind that the writer was not addressing himself to problems in Jewish life and practice. He was addressing himself to problems in Christian life and practice and in a very specific setting of persecution. It is not at all certain that the recipients were predominantly Jews.

Too, one must bear in mind that Paul, a Jew, wrote some works which minimized the role of the Mosaic law in the life and practice of the Christian. Indeed, the atmosphere of 1 Peter is so similar to Pauline thought that some scholars have suggested a Pauline follower as the author of the epistle. Why a Pauline follower would write a book and ascribe it to Peter rather than to Paul is not clear. The epistle is not clearly enough addressed to Jewish Christians to demand the authority of the apostle to the Jews (Peter) rather than the apostle to the Gentiles (Paul). Mitton [2] has concluded that the similarities are due to 1 Peter's use of Ephesians. Selwyn's (pp. 363–466) examination of the Pauline similarities led him to attribute them to common patterns for the instruction of converts in the early church.

Further attention to this idea of dependence and similarities will be given in the exposition of parts of the text (particularly 2:11—3:12). Whether or not dependence can be established, the existence of common material in first-century teaching and preaching must be taken into account in considering what Peter or any other man may or may not have written.

(2) Would Peter, a disciple of Jesus Christ, omit all references to the life of Christ except the death and resurrection? Also, would he have omitted references to his own personal association with Jesus Christ and his own personal knowledge of Jesus' life? The writer's own purpose must determine the answer to these questions. The second question is not particularly impressive when one considers the fact that the presence of references to a personal re-

[2] C. L. Mitton, *The Epistle to the Ephesians* (Oxford: The Clarendon Press, 1951), pp. 176–197.

lationship to and a knowledge of Jesus' life in 2 Peter is used as an argument *against* his authorship. The answer to the first question must be made in regard to the author's purpose in stressing the significance of the crucified and risen Christ and the new life situation which that event introduces to men who commit themselves to Christ. References to the situation of the life of disciples before the cross and the resurrection would not be of primary value in expressing that purpose.

(3) Would Peter, a Palestinian Jew, not have quoted the Old Testament from the Hebrew (Masoretic Text) rather than from the Greek translation (Septuagint)? This objection assumes that Peter's text *was* the Masoretic Text; the Qumran Scrolls have revealed that there were other texts. Van Unnik (p. 764) has suggested that if Peter was using the Hebrew text, it may have been one more like the Septuagint than the Masoretic Text. He has indicated also that the part of Silvanus as Peter's scribe in writing the letter (5:12) would qualify the force of the argument that if Peter wrote the book, he would have quoted from the Hebrew text of the Old Testament. The Septuagint was unquestionably the Old Testament text of the Greek Christians, among whom Silvanus had worked since he joined Paul for the second missionary journey.

(4) Could Peter, a Galilean Jewish fisherman, have written such excellent Greek? In Acts 4:13 he is described as an "uneducated" man, i.e., an unlettered man. The objection is supported by Papias' statement that John Mark served as Peter's interpreter when he preached in the Greco-Roman community. This has been regarded as a reflection of a deficiency in Peter's Greek. Beare (p. 28), who argues against the Petrine authorship at every point, is most emphatic in his view that Peter could not have written such Greek.

The excellent Koine Greek, the near-literary style, and the sophisticated vocabulary of 1 Peter cannot be minimized. It is doubtful if one of Peter's background could have written it alone. It is at this point that the work of Silvanus as scribe becomes most important. He was a Greek Christian who had traveled with Paul on the second missionary journey (Acts 15:40—18:22). He had been associated with Paul in the writing of 1 Thessalonians (1:1) and 2 Thessalonians (1:1). The expression "by Silvanus" (1 Peter 5:12) means precisely "through Silvanus." Silvanus appears to have been far more than the bearer of the letter. It was a well-known policy for a first-century writer to give a competent scribe a very free hand in the writing of what was dictated to him. If this was true in this case, the argument against the Petrine authorship loses its force. Some have suggested that Silvanus' part in the production of the letter may account for the numerous similarities to Pauline writings (see the exposition of 2:11—3:12).

The case against the Petrine authorship is never strong and sometimes very fragile. Beare (p. 29) has certainly overstated his case in holding that the evidence against Peter is overwhelming. The internal witness of the claim to Petrine authorship (1:1) is textually secure. The external witness of the early church is as strong as any could desire. In the light of all this, one can accept the authorship by Peter with confidence and integrity.

II. Date

In a recent introduction to the New Testament, three authors [3] have classified 1 Peter with Hebrews and Revelation as "The Literature of Persecution." The term is accurate. To these might be added the epistle of James. Its recipients were facing oppression which was severe and tending to become critical. A major theme of the epistle is that of comfort and exhortation in the midst of trials. Uncertainty as to the nature of the persecution has left uncertainty as to the time of the persecution.

Three periods of Roman persecution of Christians have been suggested. They are briefly treated here. For a fairly complete discussion of the question, read Guthrie's treatment as previously cited.

The three periods of persecution which have been proposed are those of Nero (*ca.* A.D. 62–64), Domitian (*ca.* A.D. 90–97), and Trajan (*ca.* A.D. 111). If, as we believe, Peter wrote the letter, the persecutions under Domitian and Trajan are ruled out. Peter's death is safely fixed in the middle to late sixties (A.D. 64–67). If, however, the letter was not written by Peter, all three periods are possibilities.

The period of Domitian seems the least likely. Until recent years, twentieth-century scholarship has generally held that Domitian did persecute the Christians during the last years of his reign. The charge was that they were enemies to the Empire since they refused to worship Caesar as Lord and insisted on their confession "Christ is Lord." The persecution, however, was focused on Asia Minor where the heart of the Christian resistance was located. There is no evidence that the persecution was general throughout the Empire nor that it reached the countries named in 1 Peter 1:1. For a review of the literature on the Domitianic persecution see this author's book on Revelation.[4]

It must be noted as another evidence against the Domitianic period, that some writers deny that Domitian persecuted the Christians at all.[5] While the view has not been widely accepted, it would, if valid, be an argument against this date for 1 Peter.

The period of Trajan is the one most often accepted by those who reject the Petrine authorship. Beare (p. 13 f.) has endorsed this period. The case is based on the

---

3 Robert W. Crapps, Edgar V. McKnight, and David A. Smith, *Introduction to the New Testament* (New York: The Ronald Press, 1969), pp. 417–427.

4 Ray Summers, *Worthy Is the Lamb* (Nashville: Broadman Press, 1950).

5 See Wand, p. 16, and his citation of E. T. Merrill's *Essays in Early Christian History*. See also B. M. Newman's hypothesis that the background of Revelation is not one of Roman persecution of the Christians, but Gnosticism—*Rediscovering the Book of Revelation* (Valley Forge: The Judson Press, 1968).

similarity of the situation of the Christians as reflected in 1 Peter and in Pliny's letter to Trajan. Pliny was governor of Bithynia (one of the provinces named in 1:1) under the Emperor Trajan about A.D. 110. He wrote a letter to Trajan asking for a clarification of the status of those who were called Christians and were being charged as "wrongdoers," i.e., enemies to the Empire. He desired information as to what policy he should follow in the prosecution of these people.

The same word, as in Pliny's letter, is used in 2:12, "in case they speak against you as wrongdoers." Further, 4:12–16 is understood by some to mean that it was a crime against the state for one to bear the name Christian—"if you are reproached for the name of Christ" (v. 14); "if one suffers as a Christian, let him not be ashamed, but under that name let him glorify God."

The similarity is striking, but the case for identity is not strong. Neither Pliny's request nor Trajan's response makes it clear that Christians were being punished *because they were Christians* rather than for other reasons related to the odium in which they were held by the Romans. Too, Pliny and Trajan both reflect a policy which was already in progress and related to a clarification as to its continuance. First Peter appears to point to some pending future persecution which threatened the Christians. The case for the Trajan period is not adequate for rejecting the strong case for Petrine authorship which requires a much earlier date.

The *time* of the Neronian persecution (A.D. 62–64 and perhaps beyond) fits better, but the *situation* may not fit any better. There is little doubt about Nero's having persecuted the Christians. Only the strong "debunkers" of history deny this.[6] His persecution, however, was restricted to the area of Rome. There is no evidence that it got out into the provinces—certainly not to the provinces on the shore of the Black Sea and in Central Asia Minor. The only way the

Neronian persecution of Christians in Rome could become a problem for faraway Pontus, Galatia, Cappadocia, Asia, and Bithynia would be for it to be extended into an Empire-wide policy. While the same reason for the persecution in Rome (punishment for the charged crime of burning the city) would not have existed, Peter could well have feared such an extension. If so, a word of warning mingled with his words of instruction and comfort would have been in order.

There is a fourth persecution situation which may fit better than either of the above. It is a persecution situation which could have antedated the Neronian period or could have existed for Christians apart from either government persecution or prosecution. As early as 1937, Dana[7] argued for a persecution which was not by the Roman Empire and which was, indeed, without government sanction. His argument was that the pagans were coming to look with growing distrust and even jealousy upon the young Christian religion. It was making rapid and dangerous encroachments upon their own religion. Paul's experience with the shrine makers of Ephesus is an example of such fear. People were becoming Christian in such numbers that the business of selling silver shrines for the worship of Artemis was falling off. The pagan worshipers were ready to heap every indignity upon the despised Christians.

It may well be that those of whom Peter wrote were trying to get government sanction for the persecution. First Peter 2:12 reflects a possible charge by the pagans that the Christians were enemies of the Empire, "wrongdoers." Peter encouraged them to live in such way that when they were brought to trial ("on the day of visitation" was a term meaning at the time of court trial), their life of good works would both refute the charge and glorify their God. On this basis, Dana dated the book about A.D. 63.

While they do not appear to be ac-

---

[6] See Arthur Weigall, *Nero, the Singing Emperor of Rome* (New York: G. P. Putnam's Sons, 1930).

[7] H. E. Dana, *Jewish Christianity* (New Orleans: Bible Institute Memorial Press, 1937), p. 132.

quainted with Dana's work, both Guthrie (p. 107) and van Unnik (p. 762) favor a type of persecution that was not government sanctioned. They interpret the persecution as one that could have been experienced by Christians from their non-Christian townsmen anywhere in the Empire. Van Unnik is emphatic in the opinion that the persecution was not one which could have been brought about by state measures. He writes, "It had more the nature of a pogrom, which can be nerve-racking and hardly less difficult than open, official persecution." He holds that the letter fits well into the missionary situation of the middle of the first century as it is reflected in Acts. He concludes that the letter was written by Peter and probably about A.D. 60 (p. 765).

Guthrie follows a somewhat similar argument as to the nature of the trials which are reflected in the epistle. He sees them as generally related to reproaches but not martyrdoms. There is little that is distinctive in the persecutions which was not experienced by the Christians from the beginning of their separation from the Jewish religion. Guthrie holds for a date in the early sixties but not beyond A.D. 64. He cannot imagine Peter's urging honor to the Emperor (2:17) after the bloodbath under Nero in A.D. 64 (p. 120).

This situation and date appear best to fit the situation reflected in 1 Peter. It was a time of persecution in which the persecutors may have been trying to secure government sanction but had been unable to do so. That remained a threat. It was a time before the actual bloodbath which Nero unleashed on the Christians in Rome. In other words, anywhere in the area of A.D. 60–63. Dana was specific on A.D. 63 because of his view that Paul had been released from prison in Rome, that he was in Spain and, hence, Peter felt free to write to "Paul's churches"—Galatia and Asia.

III. Place of Writing

The place of the writing of the letter must be determined by the meaning of 1 Peter 5:13, "She who is at Babylon, who is likewise chosen, sends you greetings; and so does my son Mark." The term "she" is generally understood as a reference to the church in the place from which the author wrote. But what is the meaning of "Babylon"? Two interpretations have been advanced—a literal one and a symbolic one.

If the meaning is literal, there is no serious doubt but that the reference was to Babylon in Mesopotamia; the existence of an insignificant town named Babylon in northern Egypt hardly deserves to be mentioned. Arguments for the literal Babylon are along these lines: (1) The provinces addressed are on a generally east to west cycle—Pontus, Galatia, Cappadocia, Asia, and Bithynia. A messenger bearing the letter from Babylon in the east would naturally follow that route. (2) Peter was the apostle to the Jews (Gal. 2:7) and, while the ancient city of Babylon was in ruins, there remained a colony of Jews there. (3) Nowhere else does Peter use the cryptic or symbolic language which would be required if by "Babylon" he meant Rome.

If the meaning is symbolic, the reference is unquestionably to Rome. The argument for Rome as the place of writing is along these lines. (1) In other Christian and Jewish writings, Babylon was a cryptic reference to Rome (Rev. 16:19; 17:18; 18:2,10; Sibylline Oracles V. 143, 152; Baruch IX. 1). To both Jews and Christians of the first century, Rome came to be the supreme anti-divine world power that Babylon had been in the ancient history of Israel. (2) It is easy to understand how Peter, Silvanus, and Mark (Col. 4:10) would be together in Rome. It is difficult to imagine how they would have been together in Babylon.

(3) Peter engaged in westward missionary travels. His presence as one of the preferred preachers in the disputing of the Corinthians (1 Cor. 1:12) suggests the strong probability of his having been there. This is supported by Paul's reference in 1 Corinthians 9:5 to Peter's missionary travels accompanied by his wife. Apart from these

two references there is nothing known of Peter's movements after the Acts 15 conference in Jerusalem (A.D. 49) until the tradition of his residence and death in Rome in the sixties. Cullmann's [8] argument for Peter's residence and martyrdom in Rome is thorough and convincing. There is no early tradition of his residence anywhere outside of Palestine except that of the residence in Rome.

(4) A messenger carrying a letter from Rome to the provinces named would naturally disembark at a port in Pontus. Then he would move westward through the provinces named to the last one on the westward journey, Bithynia. Thence, he would return to Rome. This would depend on what part of "Asia" and "Galatia" he visited. Several possible routes could be projected unless the countries were to be visited in the order named.

There is no clearly demonstrated case for either Babylon or Rome. Much of the argument on both sides is conjectural. To this writer, the case for Rome is the more convincing.

IV. The Recipients

Geographically, the recipients of the epistle are clearly identified. They were residents of the five provinces named in the salutation (1:1): Pontus, Galatia, Cappadocia, Asia, and Bithynia. Of these there is evidence in Acts and Galatians of the planting of the Christian faith in Asia and Galatia. There is no record of the planting of the Christian faith in the other provinces. Jews and Gentile proselytes from Cappadocia, Pontus, and Asia were present in Jerusalem at Pentecost (Acts 2:9–11). It is possible that converts in those groups took the Christian faith back to their homes.

Ethnically, the identification is not so clear. The salutation, "To the exiles of the Dispersion" (1:1), immediately suggests that those addressed were Jews and the remainder of the letter makes it clear that

they were Christian converts. Dispersion is a translation of the Greek *Diaspora,* which for centuries had been a technical reference to the colonies of Jews dispersed throughout the Greco-Roman world, i.e., those living outside of Palestine. They were in every part of the Roman world as far south as North Africa and as far west as Spain. In 1 Peter, then, as in James 1:1, those of the Dispersion naturally suggests Jews rather than Gentiles.

Little help at identity is to be found in the Greek word translated "exiles" (RSV) or "sojourners" (ASV). The precise meaning of the Greek word is very difficult to determine. The determining matters must be the use of "Dispersion" and the character of the recipients as it is reflected in the epistle. The term "Dispersion," the apostleship of Peter to the Jews, and the very frequent use of Old Testament passages and terminology would appear to combine to settle the matter that the recipients were Christian Jews.

That long-accepted understanding is not without grave problems. Van Unnik (p. 761) can even refer to it as having been "abandoned" since the beginning of the twentieth century. There is an impressive list of evidences which point to the recipients as Gentiles who have been converted directly from paganism.

"Do not be conformed to the passions of your former ignorance" (1:14) sounds more like an address to former pagans than to former Jews. So does "you were ransomed from the futile ways inherited from your fathers" (1:18). The term "futile" is consistently used in the Old Testament for idol worship. "Once you were no people but now you are God's people; once you had not received mercy but now you have received mercy" (2:10) recalls Paul's application of the same passage from Hosea to the Gentiles who had come to Christian faith (Rom. 9:25–26; 11:31). "Let the time that is past suffice for doing what the Gentiles like to do" (4:3) is followed by a catalogue of sins associated with Gentile rather than Jewish life: licentiousness, pas-

8 Oscar Cullmann, *Peter: Disciple—Apostle—Martyr* (London: SCM Press, Ltd., 1958), pp. 89–152.

sions, drunkenness, revels, carousing, and lawless idolatry. Peter even suggests that the Gentiles are surprised that his readers (former Gentiles) do not join them in their "wild profligacy" and abuse them because they do not (4:4). He encourages them "to live for the rest of the time in the flesh no longer by human passions but by the will of God" (4:2). All this is overwhelmingly Gentile in flavor.

There are other passages which fit a Jewish people much more definitely than a Gentile people. Such a passage is 1:17, "And if you invoke as Father him who judges each one impartially according to his deeds, conduct yourselves with fear throughout the time of your exile." So is 2:9, "But you are a chosen race, a royal priesthood, a holy nation, God's own people, . . ." The last part of the verse, however, suggests that Peter may be assuring Gentile Christians of their new position and blessings, and their responsibility to "declare the wonderful deeds of him who called you out of darkness into his marvelous light."

Many passages could be listed which could apply equally well to Jewish or Gentile Christians. When one considers all the passages and considers what is known about the nature of the Christian church in the middle of the first century, the overpowering conviction is that this was a mixed congregation of both Jewish and Gentile Christians. If a majority group is to be named, the likelihood is for a church predominantly Gentile.

V. The Purpose

The purpose of the epistle must be considered in relation to its structure. That structure is complex enough to elicit varying views as to its basic nature. While it opens with the form of an epistle (1:1–2), the long section of 1:3—4:11 is not epistolary in form (Beare, p. 6). Guthrie (pp. 121–25) has a very helpful analysis of different views of the structure.

Some have regarded 1 Peter as a baptismal sermon. Reicke (p. 74) views the work

as two sermonic sections: one addressed to the newly baptized converts, the other addressed to the congregation.[8a] Beare (p. 8) argues for a combination of a baptismal formula set into an epistolary framework, possibly by a later editor but most likely by the original writer, himself. That the epistle has baptismal overtones cannot be questioned, even though baptism is mentioned only once (3:21) and possibly implied once (1:22–23). At the present state, convincing evidence that the epistle embodies a full baptismal liturgy is lacking.

The work is definitely sermonic in structure and catechetical in flavor. It is also without question a persecution document. If one is to choose between two views—a persecution document with references to baptism, or a baptismal document with references to persecution—the former has the weight of the evidence.

Two words stand out above all others in indicating the author's purpose in writing —assurance and exhortation. They were a people who, by faith in Jesus Christ, had come to be the people of God. But they were a people beset by persecution which promised to grow more rather than less severe. Words of assurance and exhortation address this dual situation.

The epistle, like Paul's letter to the Ephesians, opens with a long benediction which dwells on the assurance of the mercy of God by which the readers have been born anew. In this they can rejoice even in various trials because these trials demonstrate the quality of their faith (1:3–12). This passage of assurance is followed by a long series of exhortations beginning at 1:13. They are to gird up their minds and live as obedient children (1:14). They are to pass the time of their earthly sojourn in reverence for God (1:17). They are to love one

8a For other views, see B. H. Streeter, The Primitive Church (New York: Macmillan Co., 1929), p. 128; H. Preisker, Die Katholichen Briefe, 3rd ed. rev. of H. Windisch's commentary (Tübingen Mohr, 1951); F. L. Cross, I Peter: A Paschal Liturgy (London: A. R. Mobray and Co., Ltd., 1954).

another sincerely as people who have been born anew (1:22–23).

This is the pattern throughout the epistle. Blessings and exhortations to responsibility in relation to those blessings are recurring themes. The more severe the time of testing which they face, the more determined must be their commitment to the transcendent way of life into which they have come. This is the one unifying theme of the epistle—the transcendence of the Christian life above every other way of life. It is a theme to fan to a flame the joy of being a part of the people of God (1:8).

Outline of the Epistle

Salutation (1:1–2)
I. Life from God (1:3—2:10)
  1. Salvation through faith (1:3–12)
    (1) Born anew by God's mercy (1:3–9)
    (2) Born of grace promised by the prophets (1:10–12)
  2. Holiness through obedience (1:13—2:10)
    (1) Holiness modeled after that of God (1:13–21)
    (2) Holiness motivated by love of the brethren (1:22–25)
    (3) Holiness matured in union with Christ (2:1–10)
II. Life in society (2:11—3:12)
  1. Its civic responsibilities (2:11–17)
  2. Its domestic responsibilities (2:18—3:7)
    (1) On the part of servants (2:18–25)
    (2) On the part of wives and husbands (3:1–7)
  3. Its social responsibilities (3:8–12)
III. Life under trials (3:13—4:19)
  1. Encouragement in the endurance of trials (3:13—4:11)
    (1) By the occasion of the trials (3:13–22)
    (2) By the example of Christ (4:1–6)
    (3) By the imminence of the *eschaton* (4:7–11)
  2. Acceptance of trials (4:12–19)
IV. Closing exhortations and greetings (5:1–14)
  1. Exhortation to service (5:1–5)
  2. Exhortation to humility (5:6–11)
  3. Greetings and benediction (5:12–14)

Selected Bibliography

BEARE, F. W. *The First Epistle of Peter.* Oxford: Basil Blackwell, 1958.

BIGG, CHARLES. *A Critical and Exegetical Commentary on the Epistles of St. Peter and St. Jude.* ("The International Critical Commentary.") Edinburg: T. & T. Clark, 1902.

GUTHRIE, DONALD. *New Testament Introduction: Hebrews to Revelation.* Chicago: Inter-Varsity Press, 1964.

HORT, J. H. A. "The First Epistle General of Peter," *The Expositor's Greek Testament,* Vol. V. Grand Rapids: Wm. B. Eerdmans Publishing Company, n.d.

HUNTER, A. M., and Homrighausen, E. G. "The First Epistle of Peter," *The Interpreter's Bible,* Vol. 12. Nashville: Abingdon Press, 1957.

KELLY, WILLIAM. *The Epistles of Peter.* London: C. A. Hammond, 1923.

LEANEY, A. R. C. *The Letters of Peter and Jude.* Cambridge: At the University Press, 1967.

MASON, A. J. *The First Epistle of St. Peter.* ("Ellicott's Commentary on the Whole Bible," Vol. VIII.) Grand Rapids: Zondervan Publishing House, n.d.

REICKE, Bo. *The Epistles of James, Peter, and Jude.* ("The Anchor Bible.") Garden City: Doubleday and Company, Inc., 1964.

SELWYN, E. G. *The First Epistle of St. Peter.* New York: The Macmillan Company, 1958.

VAN UNNIK, W. C. "Peter, First Letter of," *The Interpreter's Bible Dictionary,* III. Nashville: Abingdon Press, 1962.

WAND, J. W. C. *The General Epistles of St. Peter and St. Jude.* ("Westminster Commentaries.") London: Methuen and Co., Ltd., 1934.

WILLIAMS, N. M. *Commentary on the Epistles of Peter.* ("An American Commentary on the New Testament," Vol. VI.) Philadelphia: The American Baptist Publication Society, 1888.

Commentary on the Text

Salutation (1:1-2)

¹ Peter, an apostle of Jesus Christ,
To the exiles of the Dispersion in Pontus, Galatia, Cappadocia, Asia, and Bithynia, ² chosen and destined by God the Father and sanctified by the Spirit for obedience to Jesus Christ and for sprinkling with his blood:
May grace and peace be multiplied to you.

Peter, an apostle of Jesus Christ identifies the author of the epistle as one of the twelve apostles. With some variations, the names of the twelve appear four times in the New Testament (Mark 3:13-19; Matt. 10:1-4; Luke 6:12-16; and Acts 1:12-13). The Acts account omits Judas Iscariot, whose previous suicide is a part of the chapter. In each list, the twelve are divided into three identical groups of four. Simon Peter is always named first. The impression is that of an organization for working purposes.

All four of the Gospels and the book of Acts reflect Peter's preeminent place of leadership in the life of the early church. In this salutation, there is a simple statement of his apostleship, no defense of it. Apparently it was never challenged as was that of Paul. Paul found it necessary to write vigorous defenses of his apostleship (Gal. 1—2; 1 Cor. 9:1-27; 2 Cor. 11:1—12:21). Peter's apostleship was universally accepted.

To the exiles of the Dispersion in Pontus, Galatia, Cappodocia, Asia, and Bithynia constitutes both an ambiguous and a clear identification of the recipients of the epistle. The geographical identity is clear (refer to discussion in the Intr.). The ambiguity in the identification relates to the terms *exiles* and *Dispersion*. The recipients are clearly Christians. Scholarly opinion is divided, however, over the question of the literal or metaphorical meaning of the two terms. If the meaning is literal, the reference is to Jewish Christians. If it is metaphorical, it is to all Christians, whether Jew or Gentile, in the designated provinces.

Exiles was commonly used for those who were staying for a while in a strange place, one foreign to their own homeland. For example, the Hebrew people were once *exiles* in Babylon. In this passage, the union of the term with *Dispersion* suggests strongly a Jewish people. *Dispersion* is a transliteration of the Greek word *diaspora*. It was a technical word for the Jews who were scattered abroad, dispersed, among the Gentiles (Deut. 28:25; 30:4; Jer. 41:17; Isa. 49:6; Psalm 147:2). In New Testament times, it was used for the Jews who were scattered in colonies throughout the Mediterranean world.

In the New Testament, the word occurs only three times. In John 7:35, "the Dispersion among the Greeks" clearly refers to the Jews residing outside of Palestine. In James 1:1, "to the twelve tribes in the Dispersion" seems to refer to the Jews residing outside of Palestine. The third reference here in v. 1 may do so. However, because both James and 1 Peter were circulated as Christian writings, and because some passages in 1 Peter appear clearly to reflect a Gentile way of life, many scholars understand the term to refer metaphorically to all Christians. For example, Arndt and Gingrich define *diaspora* as "Christians who live in dispersion in the world, far from their heavenly home." [9]

These exiles are addressed spiritually as ones who are *chosen and destined by God the Father. Chosen* is the word which is often translated "elect." *Destined* is the word often translated "foreknown." Both

[9] W. F. Arndt and F. W. Gingrich, *A Greek-English Lexicon of the New Testament and Other Early Christian Literature* (Chicago: The University of Chicago Press, 1957), p. 187.

ideas are familiar (cf. Eph. 1:4, elect; Rom. 8:29, foreknown). In his foreknowledge of the total persons, God has chosen these readers to be his own.

Sanctified by the Holy Spirit extends the doctrine of their being chosen by God. By the Holy Spirit they are set apart for holy service to God. All this foreknowing, choosing, and sanctifying points to *obedience to Jesus Christ* and *sprinkling* (cleansing) *with his blood.* This gathering up of so many doctrinal themes is rare in the salutation of an epistle. The Trinity (Father, Spirit, and Son) is bound together in the redemptive process of foreknowledge, election, sanctification, obedience, and cleansing. Hence, the end product of the Father's election is an obedient and cleansed servant of Jesus Christ, set apart by the Holy Spirit for sacred service.

Here is the first of numerous sermonic, poetic, or hymnic patterns in 1 Peter:

> According to the foreknowledge of God
> By sanctification of the Holy Spirit
> Unto obedience and cleansing of the blood of Jesus Christ

The salutation closes with the prayer, *May grace and peace be multiplied to you.* The same prayer is in 2 Peter 1:2. Jude 2 has a similar prayer for "mercy, peace, and love." All the letters of Paul have the prayer for "grace and peace," and 1 and 2 Timothy insert a third word, "grace, mercy, and peace."

The prayer was evidently widely used by the early Christians. *Grace* is a Greek concept. It relates to the unmerited favor of God as it works redemptively in the hearts of believers. *Peace* is a Hebrew concept. It relates to the condition of the heart when grace has done its work. In the prayer form, the two words are always in the same order. *Grace* must do its work before there can be *peace* in one's heart.

I. Life from God (1:3—2:10)

The theme of 1 Peter is the way of life of the Christian. Logically, the epistle opens with a presentation of that life as one which has its source in God. It consists of salva-tion through faith, and holiness through obedience to God in Christ.

1. Salvation Through Faith (1:3–12)

(1) Born Anew by God's Mercy (1:3–9)

³ Blessed be the God and Father of our Lord Jesus Christ! By his great mercy we have been born anew to a living hope through the resurrection of Jesus Christ from the dead, ⁴ and to an inheritance which is imperishable, undefiled, and unfading, kept in heaven for you, ⁵ who by God's power are guarded through faith for a salvation ready to be revealed in the last time. ⁶ In this you rejoice, though now for a little while you may have to suffer various trials, ⁷ so that the genuineness of your faith, more precious than gold which though perishable is tested by fire, may redound to praise and glory and honor at the revelation of Jesus Christ. ⁸ Without having seen him you love him; though you do not now see him you believe in him and rejoice with unutterable and exalted joy. ⁹ As the outcome of your faith you obtain the salvation of your souls.

Blessed be the God and Father of our Lord Jesus Christ calls to mind the identical beatitude in Ephesians 1:3. It is an expression of praise to God for what he has done. He has extended his *great mercy* with the result that we have been *born anew.* As grace is a concept which Peter holds in common with Paul, the new birth is a concept which he holds in common with John. It is a major theme in 1 John (e.g., 5:1–5), and its origin is unquestionably in Jesus' dialogue with Nicodemus in John 3:1–21.

In Peter's thought, this is birth *to a living hope.* It is not a forlorn and dead hope. Its very foundation is one of life. It is *through the resurrection of Jesus Christ from the dead.* As in all early Christian thinking, so here, the foundation of hope for a new life now and beyond death is the resurrection of Jesus Christ. In that resurrection the Christian sees the ultimate purpose of God for all the redeemed (1 Cor. 15:20–28).

This new birth is also birth *to an inheritance . . . kept in heaven.* The privileges of the Christian are great in this life, but the forward look of the Christian faith (cf. Eph. 1:14) envisions the greater riches of the future life. As an heir of God, the Christian has an inheritance which is *imperishable*, not subject to decay. Paul used the word in reference to the resurrection body (1 Cor. 15:52). It is *undefiled*, pure or unstained by filth in the spiritual or moral sense. It is *unfading*, unwithering as flowers wither, or as the celery leaf crown of the victorious Olympic athlete withers (5:4). Here is another touch of the sermonic or hymnic materials of 1 Peter. The Greek words for the three modifiers (imperishable, undefiled, unfading) all begin with the letter "a" imparting the kind of alliteration frequently used in sermons: *aphtharton, amianton, amaranton.*

This inheritance is in heaven awaiting those *who by God's power are guarded through faith.* It is a faith which commits one to the keeping power of God. It is not man's power but God's power which, like a watchman at the city gate, guards the security of the one who is trusting in him. *Salvation* is used in several ways in the New Testament. It may refer to the initial experience as in Luke 19:9, "Today salvation has come to this house." It may refer to a process by which one works a possession into a finished product as in Philippians 2:12, "Work out your own salvation." Or it may refer to the consummation of God's work of redemption at the second coming of Christ (Rom. 13:11; Heb. 9:28). That is the meaning in this passage. The full revelation of God's salvation will be seen only at the end, *in the last time.*

This confidence in the keeping power of God and the ultimate realization of this inheritance in heaven is ground for rejoicing now. The *now for a little while* is set over against the eternal nature of the inheritance. And the suffering of *various trials* is set over against the ultimate victory. The war is won even though the battle continues. Here is the introduction of the persecution theme in 1 Peter. In this passage there is no indication of the nature of the *various trials.* Many kinds of difficulties confronted the Christian in the non-Christian culture of the Roman world.

Peter encouraged the Christians to look upon the trials as a means of demonstrating the genuineness of their faith in their God. The word which is translated *genuineness* was commonly used for testing coins to determine whether they were genuine or counterfeit. As gold is purified by the fire which burns away the dross, so their faith would be purified by the fiery trials. Gold is fireproof, but it is perishable. A demonstrated faith is not perishable. And *at the revelation of Jesus Christ,* the second coming, that demonstrated faith will be an occasion of *praise and glory and honor.*

These tested Christians had not seen Christ, but they loved him without having seen him. They believed in him, and even under trials they experienced joy beyond their power to express it. The *outcome,* the end product, of their faith was that ultimate complete *salvation* of their *souls.* Soul in the New Tesament is most often descriptive of the total person. It is not just the "spirit" counterpart of the "body." It is the total being, and that total being is the objective of God's redemptive purpose in regeneration and resurrection.

In summary, this life from God is life now. It is life by God's mercy. It is life by birth. It is life which looks to life. It is life in union with the living Christ. It is life which is secure in God's power. It is life which is to be consummated at the coming of Christ.

(2) Born of Grace Promised by the Prophets (1:10–12)

10 The prophets who prophesied of the grace that was to be yours searched and inquired about this salvation; 11 they inquired what person or time was indicated by the Spirit of Christ within them when predicting the sufferings of Christ and the subsequent glory. 12 It was revealed to them that they were serving not themselves but you, in the things which have now been announced to you by those who preached the good news to you through the Holy Spirit sent from heaven, things into which angels long to look.

Continuing the theme of this new life from God, Peter assured his readers that it was the object of the interest of both prophets and angels. The prophets were the most honored people in the history of Israel. They *prophesied of the grace* which was to be the realized possession of the Christians. The *prophets* were the Old Testament spokesmen for God. To them God revealed that in his own time and in the Person whom he had chosen for the purpose, he would manifest in history his saving grace. *The Spirit of Christ within them* means that the agent of God's revelation to the prophets was the preexistent Christ who later became flesh (John 1:1–18; Phil. 2:5–11).

The prophets *inquired;* they sought diligently to understand *what person or time* it was of whom God spoke to them. Who would be that giver of grace? When would it become a matter of history? *It was revealed* to them that it would not become history in their day. It was to become history at some future day. That future day proved to be the time in which Peter's readers lived. The things which were foretold by the prophets came about in the life, death, and resurrection of Jesus Christ. In the past, prophets sought to know the details of God's redemption. Now, angels desire to look into it. The glorious fact is that the redeemed *experience* it. Those who were sent by the Holy Spirit *announced* that fulfillment as they *preached the good news,* the gospel, to these exiles.

That gospel contained such marvelous things that angels longed to look into and understand them. The Jewish people believed that the angels had greater knowledge than man. But in this matter, the redeemed experienced things which were beyond the understanding of the angels—God's salvation-bestowing grace.

2. Holiness Through Obedience (1:13—2:10)

(1) Holiness Modeled After That of God (1:13–21)

¹³ Therefore gird up your minds, be sober, set your hope fully upon the grace that is coming to you at the revelation of Jesus Christ.

¹⁴ As obedient children, do not be conformed to the passions of your former ignorance, ¹⁵ but as he who called you is holy, be holy yourselves in all your conduct; ¹⁶ since it is written, "You shall be holy, for I am holy." ¹⁷ And if you invoke as Father him who judges each one impartially according to his deeds, conduct yourselves with fear throughout the time of your exile. ¹⁸ You know that you were ransomed from the futile ways inherited from your fathers, not with perishable things such as silver or gold, ¹⁹ but with the precious blood of Christ, like that of a lamb without blemish or spot. ²⁰ He was destined before the foundation of the world but was made manifest at the end of the times for your sake. ²¹ Through him you have confidence in God, who raised him from the dead and gave him glory, so that your faith and hope are in God.

As this life from God is experienced by salvation through faith in God, it is characterized by holiness like that of God. The central idea in this section is expressed in v. 16 in the quotation from Leviticus 11:45, "You shall therefore be holy, for I am holy." In the Leviticus passage, the motivation for holiness on the part of God's people (Israel) was that he who had redeemed them from the bondage of Egypt was a holy God. They, as his people, were therefore to be a holy people—like God, like people.

Peter used the same argument for the Christians as the new Israel. The God who had redeemed them from their pagan life was a holy God. They, as the redeemed, were to be like their God—holy.

Gird up your minds is a figure of speech. Men wore long outer robes. When engaged in work with which the robes would interfere, they would tie the long robes up around their waists. Peter applied the figure in the intellectual realm. *Gird up your minds* meant to get out of their minds anything which would interfere with holy living. *Be sober* meant be levelheaded, think straight. *Set your hope fully* meant to focus on the coming consummation of God's redemptive grace at the coming of Christ. Such a focus would be conducive to holiness.

As obedient children imitate the life of the father whom they love, so these children of God were to emulate the character of their Father. *Conformed* related to the setting of a scheme or a system of life. Freely rendered it means, do not schematize your conduct according *to the passions of your former ignorance.*

It is possible that this admonition refers to Jews whose fathers had passed on to them erroneous teachings which they followed in ignorance of the true way of life. However, the expression *the passions of your former ignorance* much better fits a Gentile people who thought that life consisted of the indulgence of physical appetites. Compare Colossians 3:5–6 and Philippians 3:17–19 in which Paul speaks of those whose "god is the belly." See also Ephesians 4:17–20 in which the way of life of the Gentiles is identified with ignorance and the evil living which corresponds to that ignorance.

The theme of God's redemptive and holy character is introduced in v. 15 with the very strong adversative conjunction "but." *But as he who called you is holy, be holy yourselves in all your conduct.* The God who called them from their past ways of ignorance and sin is to be the model for their life as his people. The demand for holiness in man is predicated upon holiness in God. In so doing, it rejects any degree of moral relativism which too often characterizes society.

Basically, holiness means to be set apart. God is holy in that he is set apart from all others and from every thought or act which could be called sinful, unrighteous, unjust, etc. He calls for his people to be like him. The goal is absolute holiness. He cannot set a lower goal. Although that goal is never realized in this life, the tension of striving to reach it must always be there. The child of God must never be comfortable and satisfied short of reaching the goal.

God *judges each one impartially according to his deeds.* This realization inspires in the worshiper a motivation for right conduct. *Fear* means awe in face of the responsibility of pursuing holiness. *Throughout the time of your exile* means that as

long as one is in this world, he **is** to conduct his life with a sense of awe in realizing what his life is and what it should be.

Peter expressed the redemption of the Christians by using the figure of a price paid to ransom an object which is regarded as valuable. God looked upon these sinful people who, in their futility, were following the sinful ways of their fathers. He saw them as valuable. He paid the price for their freedom. The price was not *silver or gold.* It was something far more precious. It was blood; the *blood of Christ.*

This recalls the sacrificial system of the Old Testament. A lamb for the sacrifice had to be without blemish or flaw of any kind. John the Baptist pointed to Jesus as "the Lamb of God, who takes away the sin of the world" (John 1:29). Peter employs the same concept of the redemptive work of Jesus. Again, the language of vv. 18–19 has the alliteration of hymn or sermon. The price paid was not *silver;* it was *blood,* of a *lamb,* without *blemish* or *spot.* In the Greek text, each of these italicized words starts with the letter "a." The series ends with the climactic word *Christ*—"you were bought not by silver or gold, but by blood, the blood of a flawless, spotless lamb—Christ."

This was a part of God's redemptive plan *before the foundation of the world* (cf. Eph. 1:4), but it *was made manifest at the end of the times* for Peter's readers. That which God had planned before the creation of the world, he brought to reality at a point in history through the death and resurrection of Jesus Christ. Through Christ (v. 21) Peter's readers had fixed their *faith and hope* in God. It was *faith* that he had provided salvation and *hope* that they would realize that salvation as the fulfillment of his promise.

(2) Holiness Motivated by Love of the Brethren (1:22–25)

²² Having purified your souls by **your** obedience to the truth for a sincere love of the brethren, love one another earnestly from the heart. ²³ **You have been born anew, not of**

perishable seed but of imperishable, through the living and abiding word of God; 24 for
"All flesh is like grass
  and all its glory like the flower of grass.
The grass withers, and the flower falls,
25 but the word of the Lord abides for ever."
That word is the good news which was preached to you.

The holiness which comes by obedience to God and by modeling one's character after the character of God, points to one common bond which unites all the redeemed. That bond is sincere *love of the brethren.* The word *sincere* meant without false pretense, literally "unhypocritical." In the imperative *love one another earnestly from the heart,* the word translated *earnestly* meant constantly or with perseverance. The word translated *love* is agape, the crowning virtue of the Christian life. It is a word for rational goodwill, of desiring for its object the highest good, of putting highest value upon.

So is it to be with one who has been *born anew* v. 23). He has been born *not of perishable seed.* The term *seed* is used metaphorically of the physical basis for procreation. Man's *seed* is perishable and that which is born of it will perish, die. But the one who is *born anew* is born of God's *seed;* it is imperishable. One who is born of it is imperishable; he will not die. That *seed* of God is his *living and abiding word.* That which is born of man's *seed* is as perishable as the grass (v. 24, quoting Isa. 40:6–8). But that which is born of God's *seed* shall never perish. That *living and abiding word* (*logos*) is the spoken (*hrēma*) which was the means of evangelizing Peter's readers.

(3) Holiness Matured in Union with Christ (2:1–10)

¹ So put away all malice and all guile and insincerity and envy and all slander. ² Like newborn babes, long for the pure spiritual milk, that by it you may grow up to salvation; ³ for you have tasted the kindness of the Lord.
⁴ Come to him, to that living stone, rejected by men but in God's sight chosen and precious; ⁵ and like living stones be yourselves built into

a spiritual house, to be a holy priesthood, to offer spiritual sacrifices acceptable to God through Jesus Christ. ⁶ For it stands in scripture:
"Behold, I am laying in Zion a stone, a
    cornerstone chosen and precious,
and he who believes in him will not be put
    to shame."
⁷ To you therefore who believe, he is precious,
    but for those who do not believe,
"The very stone which the builders rejected
    has become the head of the corner,"
⁸ and
"A stone that will make men stumble,
    a rock that will make them fall";
for they stumble because they disobey the word, as they were destined to do.
⁹ But you are a chosen race, a royal priesthood, a holy nation, God's own people, that you may declare the wonderful deeds of him who called you out of darkness into his marvelous light. ¹⁰ Once you were no people but now you are God's people; once you had not received mercy but now you have received mercy.

As the birth of a baby promises growth to maturity, so *newborn babes* in the spiritual realm are to grow to maturity. The word *newborn* is related to the word which is translated *born anew* in 1:3 and 1:23. It differs from that word in that it has a prefix which emphasizes the newness of the experience, i.e., "just now born." All of the things which had characterized their lives before that birth are to be put off as one would put off an old or soiled garment. Those things are *malice . . . guile . . . insincerity . . . envy . . . slander.* All these are a part of the sins of the spirit (the disposition) in contrast to what we recognize as the sins of the flesh (murder, drunkenness, etc.). In the New Testament, both are presented as conduct which must be avoided by the Christian. One of our problems is that as we grow older the sins of the flesh burn themselves *out,* but the sins of the spirit seem to burn themselves *in.*

As "just now born" babies hunger for their mother's milk, so these *newborn babes* are to hunger for *the pure spiritual milk* which their Father supplies. The word which is translated *spiritual* is the one Paul used in Romans 12:1 to describe the service which redeemed men are to render to

God. From the Greek word, the English word "logical" is derived. The newborn baby longs for the food which is logically related to his growth requirement. In the spiritual realm, that logical food is spiritual in nature.

The word *pure* means undiluted. The spiritual milk which God supplies for his growing babies is whole milk of the most nourishing kind. The purpose of that milk is that the babies who drink it may *grow up.* The word indicates increase in stature. Paul urged the Ephesian Christians that they should be no longer children but that they should *grow up* to mature manhood (Eph. 4:14,15).

The expression *to salvation* further describes the kind of growth of which Peter writes. It is not growth which is related to the physical life, but growth which is related to the spiritual life. The term may be translated "with reference to salvation," i.e., the point of reference for the growth is a spiritual one. On the other hand, the term may be translated "looking to salvation." In this sense, it is salvation as the final and finished product which is the goal of growth. The physical person reaches a point at which growth stops. It would be abnormal for him if he did not stop growing. In contrast, the spiritual person is never to stop growing. His ultimate goal of growth is to come to approximate "the stature of the fulness of Christ" (Eph. 4:13).

For you have tasted is a grammatical construction which affirms the action which the verb indicates. Since it is a fact that you have tasted the graciousness of the Lord, *long for the pure spiritual milk* which produces growth as a child of God. Once the child of God has really *tasted* that food, his hunger can never be satisfied with substitutes.

The kind of holiness which Peter envisions for every child of God is one which moves toward maturity in union with the preeminent Son of God, Jesus Christ. In vv. 4–8, Peter employs the rejected stone theme of Isaiah 8:14; 28:16; Psalm 118:22. In his controversy with the Temple leaders,

Jesus applied the theme to himself (Matt. 21:42). They had challenged his authority to stop the flow of animals to the sacrificial altar by his cleansing of the Temple (Matt. 21:12–13,23). Jesus responded that he was a "stone" rejected by the builders of the Temple. He did not fit their plans. But God made him the most important "stone" in the entire structure. He was using a tradition that in the building of the Temple the builders had rejected an unusually shaped stone only to find later that they needed a stone of that exact shape.

Peter employed that idea. Christ was a *living stone.* He had been rejected by men, but to God he was chosen and precious. Now these children of God were as other stones. In union with Christ the *living stone* they are framed into a new *spiritual house,* a new temple as a dwelling place for God (cf. Eph. 2:19–22 for Paul's development of the same theme of the redeemed as God's new temple).

In this new temple the Christians constitute a *holy priesthood* for the purpose of rendering services to God. This is a basic passage in the cherished doctrine of the priesthood of all believers. Every believer is a priest for himself before God. Every believer is also a priest for every other believer before God. He pleads man's case with God and he pleads God's case with man. As such he offers *spiritual sacrifices.* The word for *spiritual* is different from the one in v. 2. This one relates to the nature of the sacrifices as adequate for the purposes of the worshiper's nature. He is spiritual; the service is spiritual. When this letter was written, the Temple in Jerusalem was still standing, and the priests offered up the sacrifices which the Temple service required. There was on the part of Christians, however, the growing awareness that those sacrifices were meaningless. Jesus Christ in his death had gathered up the total of sacrifice for sin. All of that to which the Temple sacrifices had pointed had become reality in his once-for-all sacrifice of himself (see the extension of this theme in Heb. 9).

Peter closed his use of the rejected stone theme by pointing to the dual nature of that stone. To those who believe and accept that stone which God has given, he is *precious.* As the Redeemer he becomes the foundation of God's new temple. But to those who do not believe and reject the stone, he becomes a stone of judgment. They stumble and fall when they come upon that stone in their path. Their stumbling and falling is *because they disobey the word.* The *word* which they disobey is the invitation of God to trust that *stone,* to make it the foundation for their lives.

As they were destined to do does not mean that those who rejected Christ were *destined* to do so apart from any choice to do otherwise. On the contrary, the offer was made to them; the choice was theirs. They could accept the offer or reject it. To accept it meant a destiny of blessed union with Christ. To reject it meant a destiny of judgment apart from such union. It was their refusal to accept the offer which determined their destiny.

In v. 9, Peter joins blessing and responsibility. The blessing is that his readers who had believed in Christ had come to be: *a chosen race, a royal priesthood, a holy nation, God's own people.* The statement bears the ring of a four-point sermon which Peter had preached many times. Examination of each of the four parts provides fruitful development (cf. Deut. 7:6; Ex. 19:6; Hos. 2:23).

A chosen race recalls God's choice of Israel as a people for his redemptive witness. *A royal priesthood* suggests a kingdom in which each citizen serves as a priest. *A holy nation* envisions a nation of people set apart to and bearing the nature of the holy God whom they worship and serve. *God's own people* is not a translation but a paraphrase of the last expression. The translation is "a people for his possession," or "a people for his cherishing." The word is used in Ephesians 1:14 for God's "cherished possession" which will be redeemed ultimately to the praise of God's glory.

Who were these people whom Peter described in such terms of blessed privilege? All the terms suggest people of Jewish culture. But when Peter wrote of the responsibility which grew out of their privilege, he used language which suggests people of a Gentile culture. They had become *a chosen race,* etc., in order that they might *declare the wonderful deeds* of the one who had called them *out of darkness* and *into his marvelous light.* Consistently in the Scriptures the Gentiles are referred to as a people who lived in darkness. Their coming to God was a coming to light.

The same impression comes from the reading of v. 10. Once they had not been a *people,* but now they had come to be *God's people.* Once they *had not received mercy,* but in their coming to union with Christ by faith in him they *have received mercy.* His reference is to Hosea 2:23. This theme Paul had used in Romans 10:14-20. He used it (quoting passages from Psalm 19:4, Deut. 33:21, and Isa. 65:1) in reference to the coming of the Gentiles to faith in the Redeemer whom God had provided. If Peter is doing the same thing here, he is dramatizing for Gentile Christians both the privilege into which they have come in Christ and their consequent responsibility for service.

II. Life in Society (2:11—3:12)

The second major section of this epistle links the theological emphasis of 1:3—2:10 to an ethical emphasis. In Christian thought, theology and ethics are inseparably joined. Where the *vertical* line of relation to God crosses the *horizontal* line of relation to man, there stands the Christian. So in 1 Peter, the doctrinal truth of redemption through new birth in a faith-union with Christ has its application in ethical truth as the expression of that redemption. Peter developed the theme of the Christian life in society in three areas: civic, domestic, and social responsibilities.

1. Its Civic Responsibilities (2:11-17)

¹¹ Beloved, I beseech you as aliens and exiles to abstain from the passions of the flesh that

wage war against your soul. ¹² Maintain good conduct among the Gentiles, so that in case they speak against you as wrongdoers, they may see your good deeds and glorify God on the day of visitation.

¹³ Be subject for the Lord's sake to every human institution, whether it be to the emperor as supreme, ¹⁴ or to governors as sent by him to punish those who do wrong and to praise those who do right. ¹⁵ For it is God's will that by doing right you should put to silence the ignorance of foolish men. ¹⁶ Live as free men, yet without using your freedom as a pretext for evil; but live as servants of God. ¹⁷ Honor all men. Love the brotherhood. Fear God. Honor the emperor.

In their relation to constituted government, Christians have a definite responsibility for good conduct. Peter addressed his readers as *aliens* and *exiles*, but he urged them to *maintain good conduct among the Gentiles.* The terms *aliens* and *exiles* may mean that these Christians were not Roman citizens. Or the terms may be a metaphorical reference to the fact that they are first of all heavenly citizens though they live in a world which is foreign to that citizenship. In either circumstance, they are obligated to upright conduct in relation to the state.

Peter urged them: *abstain from the passions of the flesh that wage war against your soul.* On the surface this appears to be a general statement concerning upright living in the struggle between good and evil. From this viewpoint, it would relate to the same kind of power struggle between flesh and soul (or flesh and spirit) which Paul discusses in Galatians 5:16–25. *Good conduct* on the part of the Christians will cause their Gentile neighbors to reflect on their *good deeds.* They will decide that the Christians are not *wrongdoers.* The result will be the conversion of the Gentiles; they will *glorify God* because of the Christian conduct. This is the interpretation which Selwyn (pp. 170–71) prefers. There is some difficulty in determining the meaning of *the day of visitation.* If Selwyn is correct, the term likely refers to the day in which God will search the hearts of the Gentiles; will bring them to conviction and conversion so that they *glorify God.*

If, however, vv. 11–12 relate directly to vv. 13–14, Peter is dealing with *good conduct* in relation to Roman law. Suetonius, a Roman writer in the time of the Neronian persecution, used the word "wrongdoers" to refer to the Christians in their bad attitude toward and resistance of the state. If that is Peter's meaning here, the expression *the day of visitation* relates to the time when the Christians would be brought to trial on the charge of resisting or disobeying state law. If they have maintained *good conduct,* the evidence will prove that they are not *wrongdoers* but that they are upright people. Their Gentile neighbors will give God credit for the conduct of the Christians. So understood, the passage reflects a persecution of the Christians which did not have government sanction but may have been seeking it.

There is no question about the meaning of vv. 13–17. They refer to the Christians in their relation to civic law. Similar passages are in Romans 13, 1 Timothy 2:1–7, and Titus 3:1–8. All these passages reflect a situation in which the state government was regarded as beneficial to the Christians and not hostile to them. They were, therefore, urged to obedience to civic law and prayerful support of the government. The situation in the book of Revelation was altogether different. There, the state was assuming the place of God and the Christians were urged to resist it even unto death.

In this passage in 1 Peter, civil authority stands for the same thing for which Christianity stands, i.e., the highest good for all men. Civil law, properly constituted and exercised, guarantees for all alike that which is good and protects all alike from that which is bad.

Be subject was a military or civic term meaning "be in subordination to." *For the Lord's sake* imparted to the imperative a Christian motivation. Because one belongs to Christ, he is under obligation to obey civic law. This involves obedience at all levels of governmental authority. *The emperor* was the *supreme* ruler. The *governors* were the agents of the *emperor* in enforcing the law. As just agents they were charged with the dual exercise of punishment for those who did wrong and praise for those who did right.

Peter looked upon the Christians' *doing right* as a matter of *God's will* for them. It was the desire of God that they do right in order to silence charges brought against them by uninformed and unthinking men, *the ignorance of foolish men.*

The lofty principle of conduct expressed in v. 16 is the very heart of the Christian life. Christians are *free men,* but they are never to use their freedom as an excuse for wrongdoing. Christian freedom grants no license for antinomianism—the idea that one is free, therefore he is not obligated to obey the law. Rather, the Christian is obligated to a higher controlling power, the realization that he is a servant of God. Paul argued in Romans 5—6 that love puts one under greater responsibility to right living than law can ever put him. This was Jesus' view as expressed in Matthew 5:20–48.

Therefore, in his total life the Christian is to exercise proper conduct in every relationship. He is to *honor all men,* to respect every man as a person. He is to *love the brotherhood,* to exercise a particular esteem for those who are his brothers in Christ. He is to *fear God;* the word denotes reverent awe before God. He is to *honor the emperor* as the one who is ultimately responsible for civil law and order. This most certainly reflects a time before Rome and some of her emperors became the enemies and persecutors of the Christians. Attention has been called earlier to Guthrie (p. 120) in his inability to imagine such an injunction to obedience to the emperor after the bloodbath under Nero in A.D. 64.

First Peter stands with Romans 13 in enjoining civil obedience as appropriate conduct for Christians. That assures that civil government is being conducted for the good of all. When it moves from this position, however, it is subject to challenge. The Christian citizen then becomes a conscience to the state to point out its error.

2. Its Domestic Responsibilities (2:18— 3:7)

For the Christian, life in society involves definite responsibilities in the realm of the home. Peter treated this in two areas: the responsibilities of servants to masters and the mutual responsibilities of wives and husbands.

(1) On the Part of Servants (2:18–25)

18 Servants, be submissive to your masters with all respect, not only to the kind and gentle but also to the overbearing. 19 For one is approved if, mindful of God, he endures pain while suffering unjustly. 20 For what credit is it, if when you do wrong and are beaten for it you take it patiently? But if when you do right and suffer for it you take it patiently, you have God's approval. 21 For to this you have been called, because Christ also suffered for you, leaving you an example, that you should follow in his steps. 22 He committed no sin; no guile was found on his lips. 23 When he was reviled, he did not revile in return; when he suffered, he did not threaten; but he trusted to him who judges justly. 24 He himself bore our sins in his body on the tree, that we might die to sin and live to righteousness. By his wounds you have been healed. 25 For you were straying like sheep, but have now returned to the Shepherd and Guardian of your souls.

Servants is the word for household servants or house slaves. Paul used a more general term for slaves (Eph. 6:5; Col. 3:22). Both words meant slave in contrast to a paid servant in our society. Slavery was a social institution of the first-century world. While the Christian leaders did not undertake to revolutionize the system by abolishing slavery, they did set into operation principles of freedom which meant that someday no man can be owned by another man. Paul may have suggested that slaves who had an opportunity to become free do so, and then use their freedom constructively as Christians (1 Cor. 7:20— 23).

Peter emphasized the duty of Christian slaves to show respectful submissiveness to their masters. This was to be their conduct in relation to masters who were *overbearing* as well as to those who were *kind and gentle.* The motivation which he suggested was that of the virtue of enduring unjust suffering. There is no virtue involved in patient acceptance of punishment if one deserves the punishment. On the other hand, if one patiently accepts mistreatment when he has done what is right, he has *God's approval.*

The approval comes because they are following the example of Christ who patiently endured mistreatment even when he had done no wrong. *He committed no sin.* He exercised no *guile,* no deceit. He did not return reviling for reviling nor threatening with threatening. Rather he committed himself to God *who judges justly.* When this conduct and submission brought him to his death, it was a vicarious death as a sacrifice on an altar built in the form of a cross—*He himself bore our sins in his body* and it was *by his wounds* that spiritual healing came to the sin-sick.

In this passage, Peter applied the Suffering Servant passage of Isaiah 53 to Jesus' experience on the cross. Jesus himself had understood his role as the Messiah to be patterned after the Suffering Servant of Isaiah (Luke 3:21–22; 4:16–27). The redemptive suffering of the entire nation of Israel came to a focus in the one person, Jesus. His death under sin meant that *we might die to sin.* The life which we now live beyond that death is a life related to *righteousness.* Like sheep that had strayed away from their shepherd, these Christians had come to Christ as the one who was the *Guardian* of their souls. Now, with patience they were to follow his example in suffering.

One may helpfully study this passage in parallel with Ephesians 6:5–9 and Colossians 3:22—4:1. Paul urged mutual responsibilities of Christian slaves and masters. Peter omits any reference to masters' responsibilities to slaves. In our society, there is no exact parallel for this problem. We have no slaves. There is, however, a principle of conduct involved which could go far in settling problems between employer and employee. That principle is a recognition of the responsibility for Chris-

tian conduct in *every* relationship of life. There is no relationship in one's life which is not touched by the fact that he is a Christian.

(2) On the Part of Wives and Husbands (3:1–7)

¹ Likewise you wives, be submissive to your husbands, so that some, though they do not obey the word, may be won without a word by the behavior of their wives, ² when they see your reverent and chaste behavior. ³ Let not yours be the outward adorning with braiding of hair, decoration of gold, and wearing of robes, ⁴ but let it be the hidden person of the heart with the imperishable jewel of a gentle and quiet spirit, which in God's sight is very precious. ⁵ So once the holy women who hoped in God used to adorn themselves and were submissive to their husbands, ⁶ as Sarah obeyed Abraham, calling him lord. And you are now her children if you do right and let nothing terrify you.
⁷ Likewise you husbands, live considerately with your wives, bestowing honor on the woman as the weaker sex, since you are joint heirs of the grace of life, in order that your prayers may not be hindered.

In any situation, the home involves one of the major segments of life in society. While the New Testament contains many brief references to home relationships, the three major ones are this passage in 1 Peter and the two Pauline passages in Ephesians 5:22–33 and Colossians 3:18–19. Because of their similarities and differences, the three should be studied together.

Likewise is a comparative word which points back to the injunction to servants. Just as servants subject themselves to their masters, wives are to subject themselves to their husbands. *Be submissive to* has the force of an imperative and involves continuing attitude and conduct. The verb is a strong one meaning to be subordinate to. In the Roman culture of the first century, a wife was the property of her husband. Even in the Hebrew culture in which she had a better position than in the Roman, a wife's social position was lower than that of her husband. The Christian religion was gradually bringing about the concept of the freedom of every person. The society, however, was not ready for the degree of equality of women with men, even of wives with husbands, which we know today. A Christian woman who insisted on pressing her new freedom was in danger of bringing hurt to herself and disrepute to the very religion which had given her that freedom.

The Pauline passages cited above issue the same injunction to wives to be submissive to their husbands. They do not, however, base the injunction on the motivation which Peter employed. He urged submission of a Christian wife as a means of winning her nonbelieving husband to Christianity. Even *though they do not obey the word,* by their observation of the conduct of their wives they *may be won without a word. The word* means the word of Christian proclamation or witness. It may extend even to a word of argument. Though the husband has not been moved to obedient response by it, he may be moved to obedient response by his wife's example.

That example is one of *reverent and chaste behavior.* The word *behavior* means one's manner of life. Here that manner of life is characterized by reverence and purity. *Chaste,* purity, was a religious word in both Christian and non-Christian use. Originally it was used as an attribute of the deity. Then it came to be used in a moral sense on the part of the worshiper. In Peter's use, a reverent and pure life on the part of the wife was an effective means of winning an unbelieving husband.

Peter extended his emphasis on the spiritual demeanor of the wife by urging that she not seek to be known for her physical or external attractiveness, but for her spiritual and internal attractiveness. The *outward adornment* which he named related to customs of grooming and dress, the braiding together of hair and gold chains, and the wearing of luxurious robes. They were customs which had no relation to religious devotion. Their relationship was to a society which was notably irreligious. Such adornment would suggest to all observers that the woman was a part of that irreligious society. It would not impress the observer with the woman's true inner character.

Peter recommended to wives that they seek to be known for the adornment of their inner spiritual character, *the hidden person of the heart.* For jewelry, he recommended an *imperishable jewel of a gentle and quiet spirit.* For the word *gentle,* Arndt and Gingrich (p. 705) suggest as synonyms "humble, considerate, . . . unassuming." *Quiet* is the word for silence in contrast to boisterousness. An unbelieving husband might more readily be won by *a gentle and quiet spirit* than by an argumentative one (compare v. 4 with v. 1). Such conduct is *very precious,* more precious than physical attractiveness, *in God's sight.* Peter used Sarah as an example of wives who related themselves submissively to their husbands as a part of their religious faith—*holy women who hoped in God.*

This submissiveness of wives was to have its counterpart in constructive attitude and conduct on the part of husbands. The same comparative word is used, *likewise.* The conduct of the wife involved a like conduct of the husband, the two mutually responding to one another. *Live considerately with your wives* involved two lines of consideration. One, the husband was to honor *the woman as the weaker sex.* Physically (perhaps) and socially (definitely), she was the *weaker sex.* Two, he was to honor her as a joint heir *of the grace of life.* While she was his *inferior* physically and socially, she was his *equal* in the realm of *grace.* Spiritually, they stood on level ground.

Peter joined to his instruction to the husbands a lofty spiritual motive for their so honoring their wives. That motive related to their sharing their devotional life. *In order that your prayers may not be hindered* means simply that the wrong attitude of the husband toward the wife can be hurtful to their prayer life together. How can they effectively pray together if attitudes of enmity and acts of resentment and disdain stand between them?

3. Its Social Responsibilities (3:8–12)

⁸ Finally, all of you, have unity of spirit, sympathy, love of the brethren, a tender heart and a humble mind. ⁹ Do not return evil for evil or reviling for reviling; but on the contrary bless, for to this you have been called, that you may obtain a blessing. ¹⁰ For
"He that would love life
   and see good days,
   let him keep his tongue from evil
   and his lips from speaking guile;
¹¹ let him turn away from evil and do right;
   let him seek peace and pursue it.
¹² For the eyes of the Lord are upon the righteous,
   and his ears are open to their prayer.
   But the face of the Lord is against those that do evil."

All of you gather into one group the total of Christian society—servants, wives, husbands, and all others who were a part of the community of Christians who were addressed in the epistle. Upon all of them Peter enjoined a oneness of spirit which would be realized in certain attitudes of relationship. *Sympathy* involved a sharing of the sorrows or troubles of another. *Love of the brethren* involved a life based soundly on what Jesus on his last night with the disciples had given as his commandment to his followers, "Love one another" (John 15:12,17). *A tender heart* involved the attitude of compassion. And *a humble mind* involved the humility of thought which does not look down upon any person as inferior.

Jesus had ruled out the law of retaliation (eye for eye, tooth for tooth) for his followers (Matt. 5:38–42). Paul had written to the Thessalonians, "See that none of you repays evil for evil, but always seek to do good to one another and to all" (1 Thess. 5:15). So Peter wrote, *Do not return evil for evil or reviling for reviling; but on the contrary bless.* These, and many other passages in the New Testament, rule out the "get even" attitude of life. Negatively, the Christian is not to respond to evil by returning evil. Positively, he is to respond to evil by returning good. The term "Christian retaliation" has a contradictory sound. What it means is that the only form of

retaliation open for the Christian is to return good for evil. It is a part of the proverbial vocabulary of Christianity that: to return evil for good is animal-like; to return evil for evil is human-like; to return good for evil is God-like.

To live in that way is to *obtain a blessing.* Such a life involves its own built-in blessing. Peter undergirded his instruction with a text from Psalm 34:12–16. The way for one to experience the good and enjoyable life is : (1) Clean speech, *keep his tongue from evil;* (2) honest speech, [keep] *his lips from speaking guile;* (3) upright life, *turn away from evil and do right;* (4) peaceful life, *seek peace and pursue it. The eyes of the Lord* are looking for those who live that kind of life. *His ears* are listening to catch the prayers of those who live that kind of life. But his *face . . . is against those that do evil.* He frowns with displeasure upon them. In Hebrew thought, the face of God meant his presence, his person. So, his entire person is against those who do evil.

III. Life Under Trials (3:13—4:19)

It has been noted repeatedly that 1 Peter is a part of the "persecution literature" of the Christians. The theme of hardship and persecution recurs throughout the epistle. While the exact nature of the persecution is difficult to determine, there is a constant encouragement of the readers to take a positive attitude and make a positive response to persecution.

1. Encouragement in the Endurance of Trials (3:13—4:11)

(1) By the Occasion of the Trials (3:13–22)

¹³ Now who is there to harm you if you are zealous for what is right? ¹⁴ But even if you do suffer for righteousness' sake, you will be blessed. Have no fear of them, nor be troubled, ¹⁵ but in your hearts reverence Christ as Lord. Always be prepared to make a defense to any one who calls you to account for the hope that is in you, yet do it with gentleness and reverence; ¹⁶ and keep your conscience clear, so that, when you are abused, those who revile

your good behavior in Christ may be put to shame. [17] For it is better to suffer for doing right, if that should be God's will, than for doing wrong. [18] For Christ also died for sins once for all, the righteous for the unrighteous, that he might bring us to God, being put to death in the flesh but made alive in the spirit; [19] in which he went and preached to the spirits in prison, [20] who formerly did not obey, when God's patience waited in the days of Noah, during the building of the ark, in which a few, that is, eight persons, were saved through water. [21] Baptism, which corresponds to this, now saves you, not as a removal of dirt from the body but as an appeal to God for a clear conscience, through the resurrection of Jesus Christ, [22] who has gone into heaven and is at the right hand of God, with angels, authorities, and powers subject to him.

Whatever the exact nature of the trials was, it was definitely related to their status as Christians. The expression *for righteousness' sake* indicates that their hardship was due to the life they were living as Christians. That is reflected again in v. 16, *those who revile your good behavior in Christ;* in 4:13, "you share Christ's sufferings;" and in 4:16, "if one suffers as a Christian."

In all of this there is an air of contingency about the sufferings. It is as if they were not yet suffering, but that suffering was a distinct possibility. It may have been distinct to the point of immediate threat. Peter expresses an attitude of joy in suffering that speaks almost of making light of them (v. 13). *If you are zealous* misses the contingent nature of the subjunctive mood which is employed, "if you should become zealous for what is right." The reference is to the good life envisioned in v. 11.

Here were Christians who were considering the risk involved in committing themselves to the kind of life which is described as ideal in vv. 10–11. They were wavering at the point of risking that life in their pagan surroundings. Peter chided them with the question, *who is there to harm you* and *have no fear of them.* He reminded them of Christ's blessing on those who suffer *for righteousness' sake* (cf. Matt. 5:10). Even in doing so, he viewed the suffering as only possible and not yet

taking place. The optative mood of v. 14 means "and even if you should suffer."

In addition to the negative command, *have no fear . . . nor be troubled,* Peter gave some admonitions regarding positive conduct in the face of any trial which might come. *Reverence Christ as Lord* is the fixed principle of approach to trials. Make his lordship in the heart absolute. Peter's term means precisely, "Set apart in your heart, Christ as Lord." With that settled, *always be prepared to make a defense* when challenged by those who want to know why you hold to your Christian hope. In the first-century Roman world that was a constant need. So is it in the twentieth century. There is a constant need for answering the challenge, "What is the basis for your Christian hope?"

Even the defense of one's faith in Christ must be done in the spirit of *gentleness and reverence.* Confidence in the faith one professes is not established by violence any more than the kingdom is established by violence. By such spirit of *gentleness and reverence* one will keep a clear conscience, and those who have been abusive of the Christian's faith will be *put to shame.* A good life is the best demonstration of one's Christian faith. Verse 17 recalls the words of 2:15. If it should prove to be within the will of God for one to suffer, it is better to suffer in a consciousness of having done what is right in defending one's faith, than to suffer in the consciousness of having done what is wrong in defending one's faith.

Christ suffered even to the point of death. The ancient manuscripts of 1 Peter differ in the wording of v. 18. That accounts for the difference in the KJV reading, "Christ also hath once suffered" and the RSV, "Christ also died." The Greek words for "he suffered" and "he died" are very similar. The RSV has the reading which is supported by the best manuscripts. Peter's words were to remind the Christians who were facing suffering that their Lord had suffered even to the point of death. Their suffering was because of their faith. Christ's suffering was redemptive. It made possible their faith.

His suffering was unto death. It was *for sins*. It was *once for all*. It was a never-to-be-repeated death as a sacrifice for sin. That *once for all* nature of his death is a frequently recurring theme in Paul and in the epistle to the Hebrews. Christ's death was like no other death in that it was *one* death for sins for *all time*. It was a vicarious death in that it was a death of *the righteous for the unrighteous*. He was *righteous*, upright, sinless, right with God. He did not deserve to die. He died for those who were *unrighteous*, sinful, wrong with God, deserving to die. The purpose of his death was *that he might bring us to God*. The expression translated *bring us to* was a word for introduction, as an introduction at a king's court. By his death, Christ presents us to God. He brings us to stand before God accepted and unafraid.

Peter appears to have introduced the suffering (death) of Christ to demonstrate the levity of any suffering of the Christians when compared with the gravity of Christ's suffering. He returned to extend that theme in 4:1–6. Before doing so, however, he turned aside to discuss the death of Christ in its relationship to man's salvation. In doing so, he penned one of the most debated passages in all of the New Testament, vv. 18–22, particularly vv. 18–20. Once in a more extensive research than is possible here, this author counted over thirty variations in interpretations of the passage.

Put to death in the flesh appears clearly to refer to his death as mentioned in v. 18. But there is debate about the meaning of *made alive in the spirit*. What is the meaning of the expression *in which?* What is the meaning of *he went and preached?* Where did he go? When did he go? What did he preach? Who were the *spirits in prison?* What is the correct translation of the expression which the RSV renders *who formerly did not obey?* Why was the preaching only to disobedient people of *the days of Noah?* How were the eight persons of

Noah's family *saved through water?* In what way does *baptism* correspond to that experience, and how is it that baptism *saves?* These are samples of the questions involved.

The most comprehensive single volume on the entire passage is a 275-page book by Bo Reicke,[10] professor of New Testament at the University of Basel. He traces the different interpretations of the passage from the time of Augustine to modern times. The many and varied interpretations may be summarized in the following views; no historical order is intended.

1. That Jesus between his death and resurrection went to the world of the dead as a part of his suffering for man's sins. It is difficult to see how his preaching to the imprisoned spirits fits this view, unless it was his proclaiming that he was suffering because of their sins.

2. That he went in order to proclaim his lordship even over the dead; to empty Hades of the righteous people who had died before that time; to manifest his glory as the Lord of life.

3. That he went to proclaim to the disobedient spirits that the redemptive work of God which had been offered to them and which they had refused had now become reality in his death on the cross. They, therefore, had been wrong in rejecting it and they were suffering only what they deserved to suffer. He was thus confirming their damnation.

4. That he went to proclaim salvation; to exhort the disobedient spirits to repent; to offer them a chance (or in some cases a second chance) at salvation. If this very widely held view is true, why was the preaching directed only to disobedient people of Noah's day?

5. That the passage does not relate to a descent of Christ to hell at all. Rather, it teaches that in the same eternal Spirit in which he was made alive (his resurrection), he had witnessed to disobedient men *at the time of their disobedience* while

10 Bo Reicke, *The Disobedient Spirits and Christian Baptism* (Copenhagen: Ejnar Munksgaard, 1946).

Noah was building the ark. Hence, the preaching took place at the time of their disobedience.

Space permits neither extended explanation of nor attempted refutation of the variant views. Because the last theory named (number 5) answers more questions than any of the others, it is the most satisfactory to this writer. It will, therefore, be used as the interpretation of the difficult passage. And let him who is without his favorite theory cast the first stone!

Put to death in the flesh expresses the realm or area of his death. *Flesh* is set over against *spirit* in the contrast *but made alive in the spirit.* In this view one is inclined to capitalize Spirit as the nature of his preincarnation being. *In which* indicates that it was in that Spirit that Christ went and preached to those who, as Peter wrote, were *spirits in prison* (imprisoned spirits), but who in Noah's day had been disobedient people who rejected the message of impending judgment. Whether the preaching was in some theophany type of appearance or whether it was the eternal Spirit (Christ) preaching through the message of Noah may be debated. It is more natural to think of Noah's preaching as the instrument through which Christ "preached." Every blow of Noah's hammer was a call to repentance in view of coming judgment. The call went unheeded even though *God's patience waited* for a response.

This view seems to be ruled out by the expression *who formerly did not obey.* Any translation is an interpretation. This translation indicates the view of the translators that the disobedience took place in Noah's time, but the preaching took place between Jesus' death and resurrection. Besides the biblical and theological difficulties involved in that view, there is a serious grammatical difficulty involved. The term which is translated *who formerly did not obey* is a Greek participle with no definite article.

In regular usage a participle *with* a definite article has the force of a relative clause which *identifies* the persons involved by telling *who* they were. If this participle

had the definite article, it would be accurately translated *who formerly did not obey,* or "he went and preached to imprisoned spirits, the ones who were disobedient . . . in the days of Noah," etc.

On the other hand, a participle *without* the definite article regularly has the force of a *temporal* clause telling *when* the action took place. That is the construction in this passage. Translated in that way, the passage reads "he went and preached to the imprisoned spirits when they were disobedient . . . in Noah's day," etc. The preaching took place at the time of the disobedience. Those who once were disobedient were imprisoned spirits in Peter's day waiting for the judgment of God who "knows how . . . to keep the unrighteous under punishment until the day of judgment" (2 Peter 2:9). This generally overlooked interpretation of the passage has had its sponsors throughout the period of New Testament study, from Augustine to Pearson and Williams ("An American Commentary").

The disobedient men of Noah's day were singled out as an example for two reasons. First, in Hebrew religious thought they were classic examples of people who were notoriously wicked. They ranked with the men of Sodom and Gomorrah in that regard. Peter so ranks them in 2 Peter 2:5-7. Second, Peter used them as a contrast to Noah who was an example of those who escaped God's judgment because they were obedient. Note that use again in 2 Peter 2:5. Too, it established his line of thought in relating salvation to the death (v. 18) and resurrection (v. 21) of Jesus Christ.

By means of the ark, which was the symbol of his obedience to God, Noah and his family were brought safely through the flood. As Peter expressed it, they *were saved through water.* It is more natural to speak of their being saved *from* the water *by* the ark. The only way the water can be spoken of as saving them is in its bearing up the ark in which they had taken refuge.

Peter's line of thought, however, demanded the expression *saved through water* because of his relating baptism to the total experience of his readers. The flood waters he called an antitype of baptism. The translation *which corresponds to this* is a rendering of the Greek word *antitupon,* which transliterates as antitype and which means image. The "saving" of Noah's family by the water of the flood was an image of the "saving" of the Christians by the water of baptism.

Baptism is not *a removal of dirt from the body.* It is not for the purpose of removing physical filth. No more is it for the removal of spiritual filth. Peter viewed baptism *as an appeal to God for a clear conscience.* Where the RSV has *appeal,* the KJV has "answer"; Goodspeed has "craving"; Moffatt has "prayer"; the ASV has "interrogation." The word may also mean "pledge" or "demand." In view of the New Testament teaching of baptism as something which Jesus commanded, the word "demand" seems to be the best expression of the idea which Peter presents. Baptism satisfied the "demand" of a good conscience before God.

Through the resurrection of Jesus Christ links directly with the act of salvation. When the explanatory clauses (*not as a removal of . . . but as an appeal to*) are left out, the direct line of Peter's statement is *Baptism . . . saves you . . . through the resurrection of Jesus Christ.* It is the power of the resurrection of Jesus Christ which effects salvation. In early Christian thought and practice, the experience of baptism was a very essential part of one's experience since it was the way one made his confession. This is seen clearest in Paul's interpretation of baptism in Romans 6:3–4. Identification with Jesus Christ in his death and resurrection means one's death to an old life and his resurrection to a new life. In the second century this became so emphatic that the candidate took off his old clothes, entered the water from one side of the pool, was immersed, went out on the other side of the pool, and put on new clothes. In baptism he interpreted the fact that he had died with Christ; he

had been buried with Christ; he had been raised with Christ to a new resurrection kind of life. Only that understanding of baptism can really answer the "demand" of a clear conscience before God.

The dramatic, if difficult, passage closes (v. 22) on the note of the triumph of Christ over that death which introduced the passage in v. 18. Having died once for all and having been raised from the dead, Christ has entered into a glorious destiny in which *at the right hand of God,* the position of honor and responsibility, he has *angels, authorities, and powers subject to him.* This supernatural hierarchy of rulers is frequently named in the New Testament as subordinate to the triumphant Christ (Eph. 1:21; 3:10; 6:12; Phil. 2:9–11; Col. 2:15; Rom. 8:38). These and other passages present the idea of both good and bad supernatural authorities and powers. Their nature is never made clear. Christ's triumph over them is made clear. And in Christ the believer triumphs over them (Rom. 8:38).

(2) *By the Example of Christ (4:1–6)*

¹ Since therefore Christ suffered in the flesh, arm yourselves with the same thought, for whoever has suffered in the flesh has ceased from sin, ² so as to live for the rest of the time in the flesh no longer by human passions but by the will of God. ³ Let the time that is past suffice for doing what the Gentiles like to do, living in licentiousness, passions, drunkenness, revels, carousing, and lawless idolatry. ⁴ They are surprised that you do not now join them in the same wild profligacy, and they abuse you; ⁵ but they will give account to him who is ready to judge the living and the dead. ⁶ For this is why the gospel was preached even to the dead, that though judged in the flesh like men, they might live in the spirit like God.

Therefore is a bridge word which spans the 3:19–22 passage and connects the suffering of Christ (3:18) with the suffering of those who follow him (4:1–3). In some manuscripts, *Christ suffered in the flesh* is followed by the phrase "for us." In other manuscripts the expression is followed by "for you." In the best manuscripts, neither phrase appears. Without it, however, the vicarious and redemptive nature of Christ's suffering is clear from 3:18, *the righteous for the unrigteous, that he might bring us to God.*

Arm yourselves is a command which uses a military term for taking up arms or equipment for battle. Paul frequently used the figures of war, fighting, and serving as a soldier to illustrate the life of the Christian as a war against evil (2 Cor. 10:4; Rom. 13:12; Eph. 6:10–20; 1 Tim. 6:12; 2 Tim. 2:3,4:7). *With the same thought* means with the same intent, and refers to the example of Christ's suffering. The Christian looks to the innocent suffering of his Lord. He sets his mind on one goal. If his own life in opposition to evil is to involve suffering, he will accept that suffering.

This commitment to suffering in one's opposing evil means that he *has ceased from sin* as a way of life. Sin no longer is the dominating force in his life. The rest of his life in this world is no longer under the dominion of *human passions,* but under the dominion of *the will of God.* His motive for life is not what man's desire dictates but what God's desire dictates.

Let the time that is past suffice points to the life of the Christian before he came to know Christ. It was a time of *doing what the Gentiles like to do.* As the Jews were the people who knew God, the Gentiles were the people who did not know God. They did not know the way of life which God desires for man. They gave themselves over to the practice of sexual impurity, drunkenness, and false religion. *Suffice* means enough—enough of that in the past; the future life is to be free of all such practices.

Verse 4 suggests that Peter's readers had once engaged in those practices. Their present refusal to do so was a surprise to their former companions in sin, who could not understand the change which had come over them. The former companions even abused and mistreated the Christians for not joining in *the same wild profligacy* which they had once shared. Two matters are important here. One is that the readers

who were addressed in this part of the epistle were Gentile Christians. The other is that the suffering, or persecution, which is under discussion here was not for political reasons. It was only because the Christians refused to continue to share with their Gentile neighbors the life of evil which they had formerly known.

The certain reckoning with God in judgment is affirmed. *They* refers to the Gentiles who continue their evil practices, and to them add persecution of the Christians who refuse to share the evil practices. *Give account* means that they are responsible to God and will answer to him for their total conduct. God is the judge of all, *the living and the dead.* This is true whether *him who is ready to judge* refers to God (v. 2) or Christ (v. 1). The latter may be more natural; it will be treated in the interpretation of v. 6. *The living,* men who are still in this life, are under his judgment. *The dead,* men who have passed from this life, are still under his judgment. Alike they all await that final reckoning when the creature answers to the Creator for what he has done with the trusteeship of life (Matt. 25:31–46; Rev. 20:11–15; and others).

The meaning of v. 6 is debated by interpreters. What is meant by the expression *the gospel was preached even to the dead?* Who are *the dead* in this passage? Selwyn (pp. 337–39) has a good review of the different views. He rejects the idea that *the dead* is a metaphorical reference to those who are "spiritually dead." He rejects alike, the idea that this passage is related to 3:18 ff. Regardless of whether the preaching to imprisoned spirits of 3:19 took place in Noah's day or between the death and resurrection of Christ, neither Jewish nor Gentile readers of Peter's day had any basis for thinking of "spirits" (3:19) as "dead" (4:6).

The dead must be understood literally. It must be identified with the same expression, *the dead,* in v. 5. Those who were *living* were still having the gospel preached to them. Those who were *dead* had had the gospel preached to them before they died.

The purpose of that preaching was that even though they would answer to God for the sins done *in the flesh,* they would live in a redemptive relationship to God *in the spirit.*

The expression *the gospel was preached* is ambiguous. It is a translation of one word which may be rendered very exactly "it was evangelized," that is, those who were dead as Peter was writing had been "evangelized" while they were living. On the other hand, it is possible that the subject of the verb is Christ, i.e., "Christ was preached" to them while they were living. The same one who was preached to them at that time now stands *ready to judge* them on the basis of that preaching and their response to it.

A weakness of many interpreters in treating this passage (vv. 5–6) has been their looking back to 3:19. This has been done in spite of two facts. (1) The words for the "preaching" in the two passages are different—"proclaim" in 3:19; "evangelize" in 4:6. (2) The words for the persons involved are different—"spirits" in 3:19; "dead ones" in 4:6. The passage should be interpreted, not by connecting it with the previous section (3:18–22), but with the following section (4:7–11)—the *end of all things* including the judgment of both *the living,* those still living at the coming of Christ, and *the dead,* those who have died prior to his coming. The entire section (4:5–11) is related to the eschaton, the end of the world order and the beginning of the eternal order.

(3) *By the Imminence of the* Eschaton (*4:7–11*)

7 The end of all things is at hand; therefore keep sane and sober for your prayers. 8 Above all hold unfailing your love for one another, since love covers a multitude of sins. 9 Practice hospitality ungrudgingly to one another. 10 As each has received a gift, employ it for one another, as good stewards of God's varied grace: 11 whoever speaks, as one who utters oracles of God; whoever renders service, as one who renders it by the strength which God supplies; in order that in everything God may be glorified through Jesus Christ. To him be-

long glory and dominion for ever and ever. Amen.

In the life to which Peter's readers had set themselves in their evil environment, suffering as Christ's people was inevitable. He encouraged them to endure the sufferings in the hope that they would soon be over. This was the hope that the present order of sin and suffering was to give way to the future glorious order which was to be realized in the coming of Christ.

The end of all things means the end of the present world order. *Is at hand* reflects the anticipation of the Christians that the consummation of the world order and the inauguration of the eternal order was to be in their lifetime. That anticipation was very general. It is reflected in the Gospels, particularly in Mark and Matthew; it is reflected in Acts; it is reflected in the Pauline epistles and in the general epistles—particularly Hebrews, James, 1 Peter; it is reflected in Revelation. That anticipation and its subsequent failure to be realized involve no problem in the inspiration and authenticity of the Scriptures. The time of the end is a matter which God concealed even from those whom he inspired to write about it.

In vv. 7–11 Peter followed a practice which was frequently employed by writers of the New Testament. He used the hope of the coming of Christ as an incentive for upright living and responsible service to God through service to one's fellowmen. *Keep sane* means to be sensible, to be reasonable, or to keep one's head. *Sober* means to be well balanced, to be self-controlled. It is instructive that Peter related them to the prayer life of his readers. Times of trial are times when even praying may be difficult. Praying can be effective if it is characterized by one's keeping his head and exercising self-control even as he prays.

Peter urged *love for one another* as an absolute essential, *above all,* in times which try men's souls. Such love *covers a multitude of sins* in that it does not look for the sins and weakness of others under stress. In love it passes up the temptation to point out the sins and weaknesses of others. It looks for opportunities to help others. So, whatever of the many functional services, *varied grace,* God gives to one, let him exercise that gift, or *grace,* in the spirit of love. The end product will be that God will be glorified. This is the way God's people are to spend the time of waiting for Christ's return.

2. Acceptance of Trials (4:12–19)

¹² Beloved, do not be surprised at the fiery ordeal which comes upon you to prove you, as though something strange were happening to you. ¹³ But rejoice in so far as you share Christ's sufferings, that you may also rejoice and be glad when his glory is revealed. ¹⁴ If you are reproached for the name of Christ, you are blessed, because the spirit of glory and of God rests upon you. ¹⁵ But let none of you suffer as a murderer, or a thief, or a wrong-doer, or a mischief-maker; ¹⁶ yet if one suffers as a Christian, let him not be ashamed, but under that name let him glorify God. ¹⁷ For the time has come for judgment to begin with the household of God; and if it begins with us, what will be the end of those who do not obey the gospel of God? ¹⁸ And
"If the righteous man is scarcely saved,
    where will the impious and sinner appear?"
¹⁹ Therefore let those who suffer according to God's will do right and entrust their souls to a faithful Creator.

Peter further explained the presence of trials as inevitable in the life of the Christian in a non-Christian world. *Do not be surprised* suggests that some of his readers were reacting with surprise that the Christian life involved suffering. Should not God's people be exempt from suffering? The answer is no. In a world of suffering, God's people share in the suffering. They were not, therefore, to think of the suffering as if *something strange,* something foreign to their status as Christians, had come upon them.

Fiery ordeal is indicative of the severity of the trials which they faced. The actual use of fire in the persecutions of the Christians cannot be ruled out. It does not appear likely, however, that burning at the stake which Christians in Rome faced under Nero had reached to these provinces. It may have been envisioned as a very real threat. Most likely the term *fiery ordeal* was a figurative expression of the severity of their trials.

Peter encouraged his readers to *rejoice* now at the privilege of sharing the sufferings of Christ in order that they might *rejoice and be glad* when their life of suffering ended with his glorious coming. The language of rejoicing at sharing Christ's sufferings recalls the beatitude of Jesus (Matt. 5:11–12) and the attitude of the Jerusalem Christians (Acts 5:41). They counted it a privilege to suffer for the name of Christ. So in the case of Peter's readers, their being *reproached for the name of Christ* was a blessing. It was a token of their being a part of the glorious people of God.

To suffer because of evil conduct, *as a murderer . . . thief . . . wrongdoer . . . mischief-maker,* was a shameful thing. It was to be no part of the life of the Christian (v. 15). On the other hand, to suffer *as a Christian,* because one belonged to Christ, was not a thing of which to be ashamed. It was a thing for which to praise God.

The very nature of the world in which they lived, and the time and circumstance in which they lived, inevitably involved judgment. God's judgment is upon all evil. Peter's readers had come to a time when God's judgment was to begin even *with the household of God.* There were those of God's family, Christians, who, under pressure of persecution and mistreatment, would be tempted to resort to striking back, to returning evil for evil, (death for death; stealing for stealing, etc., of v. 15). They were to know that this would incur God's punitive judgment upon them even though they were his children. As a wise and loving father disciplines a disobedient child, so God, in love, disciplines his disobedient children in order to bring them back to obedience (Heb. 12:5–11).

The fact that God will not spare judgment even where his own children are concerned—*it begins with us*—underlines the certainty and severity of his judgment upon those who reject the gospel. *What will be the end* emphasizes the severity of God's judgment. It is an argument from the lesser to the greater—since it is a fact that judgment *begins* with those who *accept* the gospel, how will it *end* with those who *reject* the gospel? Their prospect is dire indeed.

Peter enforced his argument by a quotation from Proverbs 11:31. The meaning is that salvation is a difficult thing for anyone to attain, even for one who tries to do right. The cross of Jesus Christ meant that it was not easy for God to save anyone. Since that is true, how can the *impious and sinner* hope for salvation. *Impious* means the ungodly, the condemned. *Sinner* means the irreligious, the one who has missed God's way. The emphasis of the passage is upon their hopeless state without God. The ultimate application of the Proverbs passage is a motivation for the Christians under suffering and trials to restrain themselves from evil, to give themselves to good conduct, and to commit themselves to a Creator who can be trusted to be faithful to them (v. 19).

IV. Closing Exhortations and Greetings (5:1–14)

1. Exhortation to Service (5:1–5)

¹ So I exhort the elders among you, as a fellow elder and a witness of the sufferings of Christ as well as a partaker in the glory that is to be revealed. ² Tend the flock of God that is your charge, not by constraint but willingly, not for shameful gain but eagerly, ³ not as domineering over those in your charge but being examples to the flock. ⁴ And when the chief Shepherd is manifested you will obtain the unfading crown of glory. ⁵ Likewise you that are younger be subject to the elders. Clothe yourselves, all of you, with humility toward one another, for "God opposes the proud, but gives grace to the humble."

The very personal element which was reflected in the "I beseech" of 2:11 appears again in the *I exhort* of 5:1. This closing ethical section contains a double exhorta-

tion. There is an exhortation to *elders* concerning their pastoral functions. There is an exhortation to those who are *younger* concerning their submission to the *elders*. That raises a question as to whether *elders* in v. 1 means the same as *elders* in v. 5 (see the comment on v. 5).

Essentially, the Greek word for "elder" meant exactly what the English word implies, an older person. In Christian usage, however, it came to be used as a title for the one who performed the function of pastoral leadership in the church (Acts 14:23; 20:17; 1 Tim. 5:17; Titus 1:5). The title was one which related largely to the respect in which the pastor was held. The title which related primarily to his functional service was "bishop", which meant overseer (Phil. 1:1; Titus 1:7, in which "bishop" appears to refer to the same persons as the preceding "elder" in v. 5).

Peter based his exhortation on several facts. (1) He was a *fellow elder*, hence, one who shared their concern. This should not be pressed since there is little if any evidence that Peter ever served in a capacity approximating that of a local pastor. His work appears to have more closely resembled that of a traveling evangelist or missionary. (2) He was a *witness of the sufferings of Christ*. As an eyewitness of the death of Christ, he was one whose exhortation would be respected by his readers. (3) He was also a *partaker in the glory that is to be revealed*. The word *partaker* meant one who shared. *The glory that is to be revealed* may refer to Peter's destiny as one who will share with his readers the consummation in the coming of Christ. More likely, however, it refers to his having shared with James and John the transfiguration of Jesus. Second Peter 2:17–18 contains a very clear reference to Peter's having witnessed the transfiguration of Jesus as something of a forecast of what his glory is to be at the second coming. Peter thus has witnessed both the *past* suffering and the *future* glory of Christ.

Tend the flock is a general expression for all necessary pastoral functions. As a shepherd is diligent to provide for every need of his flock, so the pastor is to provide for every need of his people. It is in reality *the flock of God* for which he provides responsible leadership. God has entrusted it to him. *That is your charge* is a translation of a Greek expression meaning precisely "among you." It refers to the multiple elders, each with his particular *flock of God.* His first responsibility is to that group. The method of his service is explained in three statements, each of which contrasts the negative and the positive aspects of that method:

Negative	Positive
not by constraint	*but willingly*
not for shameful gain	*but eagerly*
not as domineering	*but being examples*

Not by constraint means that the pastor is not to serve because he is compelled to do so. In many manuscripts *willingly* is modified by a phrase meaning "as God would have you to." The pastor's only *constraint* is to be God's will.

Not for shameful gain means that the pastor's motive is not to be the material gain involved in his service. In Titus 1:11 Paul refers to false leaders who engage in the work for material profit. He calls it "dishonest gain." *But eagerly* means "with enthusiasm," with a "burning readiness" to shepherd God's sheep.

Not as domineering means that the pastor is not to serve as one who "lords it over" the flock. *But being examples* means that the pastor is to be in front leading the flock rather than behind driving them.

The chief Shepherd refers to Christ. The term recalls the Good Shepherd allegory of John 10 in which Christ, as the Good Shepherd, dies for his sheep. *Manifested* is one of the terms regularly used for the second coming of Christ. His coming is to be a time of blessing for the faithful and punishment for the unfaithful. His award for the faithful shepherds will be *the unfading crown of glory. Unfading* reflects permanence in contrast to the perishable crowns given to victorious soldiers or athletes. These crowns were of ivy, or flowers, or vegetables. They withered quickly. *Crown* is not the diadem crown associated with royalty. It is the *stephanos* award for faithful service. This is to be the pastor's *gain* in contrast to the *shameful gain* (v. 2) which he is to avoid.

The second exhortation is to the *younger,* i.e., the younger members who are in the position of being followers rather than leaders. They are to submit themselves to the experienced and faithful leadership of the *elders.* In this case, as in v. 1, *elders* may refer to the pastors. On the other hand, it may be a simple reference to older Christians whose honorable lives warrant emulation. All members, young and old, are enjoined to *clothe* themselves *with humility* in their relationship to one another. Peter may be recalling Jesus' girding himself to render the humble service of washing the disciples' feet on the night of his betrayal—even Peter's feet (John 13:2–9). The motivation for the humility which Peter urged is that God sets himself against the *proud,* meaning the haughty, but gives *grace,* meaning favor, *to the humble.* The quotation is from Proverbs 3:34.

2. Exhortation to Humility (5:6–11)

⁶ Humble yourselves therefore under the mighty hand of God, that in due time he may exalt you. ⁷ Cast all your anxieties on him, for he cares about you. ⁸ Be sober, be watchful. Your adversary the devil prowls around like a roaring lion, seeking some one to devour. ⁹ Resist him, firm in your faith, knowing that the same experience of suffering is required of your brotherhood throughout the world. ¹⁰ And after you have suffered a little while, the God of all grace, who has called you to his eternal glory in Christ, will himself restore, establish, and strengthen you. ¹¹ To him be the dominion for ever and ever. Amen.

Continuing the theme of humility, Peter urged the Christians to humble themselves under the hand of God and leave to God the matter of their being exalted. He encouraged them to cast upon God all their anxieties in the realization that God cares for his people in all of their difficulties. On the other hand, he urged them to resist the devil as one would resist a roaring, devouring lion. It is the devil who opposes them and is responsible for all of the troubles they are experiencing. But those sufferings are not unique. They are the common lot of all the Christians. Too, they are only temporary. Beyond the suffering awaits eternal glory with God who called them in Christ.

3. Greetings and Benediction (5:12–14)

12 By Silvanus, a faithful brother as I regard him, I have written briefly to you, exhorting and declaring that this is the true grace of God; stand fast in it. 13 She who is at Babylon, who is likewise chosen, sends you greetings; and so does my son Mark. 14 Greet one another with the kiss of love.

Peace to all of you that are in Christ.

The identity of *Silvanus* as Peter's scribe, as Paul's traveling companion on his second missionary journey, and as Paul's scribe for 1 and 2 Thessalonians has been discussed in the Introduction. *Mark* is John Mark of Acts 12:12; 13:5; Colossians 4:10; Philemon 24; and 2 Timothy 4:11. He is known in the New Testament as one of the traveling companions of Paul. In early second-century Christian history he is known as a companion and interpreter for Peter's preaching among the Romans. Both Silvanus and Mark send greetings to the recipients of Peter's letter.

She who is at Babylon is a cryptic reference to the church in the city from which Peter wrote. The preponderance of opinion is that *Babylon* is a cryptic reference to Rome as that city (see the discussion in the Introduction).

The kiss of love was a kiss on the cheek or forehead. It was exchanged by members of the early church to indicate goodwill as they observed the Lord's Supper. It is the same as the "holy kiss" of 1 Thessalonians 5:26; 1 Corinthians 16:20; 2 Corinthians 13:12; and Romans 16:16. The prayer for peace which as a salutation opened the epistle is repeated as a benediction in closing the epistle, *Peace to all of you that are in Christ.*

2 Peter

RAY SUMMERS

Introduction

In contrast to the secure place of 1 Peter in the New Testament canon, the place of 2 Peter was insecure from the beginning. When Eusebius wrote his definitive history of the church about A.D. 325, he divided the Christian writings into three categories: the accepted books; the disputed books; the spurious books. The 27 books which ultimately came to be the approved list, our New Testament, were all in the first two categories. The second category, the disputed books, was made up of 2 Peter, Jude, James, 2 John, and 3 John. Eusebius indicated that while they were disputed, they were known to most of the Christian writers (*Eccles. Hist.*, III.25.3).

Three major reasons account for the hesitancy of the church to include 2 Peter in the approved list of writings by which all other writings would be checked. First, the book was practically unknown until early in the third century. Words and phrases which resemble 2 Peter in the writings of men of the second century are inconclusive. Their source may well have been in other books: for example, "with the Lord one day is as a thousand years, and a thousand years as one day." This was in several second-century writings, but most likely they took it from Psalm 90:4, the same source from which 2 Peter took it (3:8). The earliest clear reference to 2 Peter is in Origen (A.D. 217–251). In his commentary on John 5:3, he stated that Peter had left one acknowledged letter (our 1 Peter) and that there was a second, dis-puted one which bore his name (our 2 Peter).

Second, the differences between 1 Peter and 2 Peter and the universal acknowledgment of 1 Peter as the product of the apostle caused the early church to be slow to accept 2 Peter into their list. Those differences are so radical that Beker (p. 768) states categorically that "no theory of secretarial aid . . . can explain the differences in style and thought between I and II Peter."

Third, the identity of 2 Peter 2:1–19 with Jude 5–16 and their striking similarity at several other points (such as, 2 Peter 3:3 and Jude 18) caused the church to hesitate. Both books reflect a Gnosticism which appears to be later than the time of Peter. No definite identification of the writer, Jude, was possible. If, perchance, Jude preceded 2 Peter, would the well-known apostle have borrowed from a little-known or unknown writer? Because of these and other minor reasons, it was not until the 27 books were listed in the *Epistle of Athanasius* (A.D. 367) and approved subsequently by the Council of Carthage (397) that 2 Peter had a fixed place in the canon.

I. Authorship

Those who reject Peter as the author of this epistle do so on both external and internal bases. Externally, the evidence relates to the previously mentioned matter of the late appearance of the book in early

Christian use, for example, its first certain appearance in the writings of Origen, whose work was in the second quarter of the third century. It was not used by other major writers of the early period: Tertullian, Cyprian, or Clement of Alexandria. It was not in the earliest known collections of Christian writings: Marcion's collection (A.D. 145); the much more complete Muratorian collection (170). While it was accepted into the canon of the western church late in the fourth century, it was not accepted by the eastern church until the sixth century.

The internal evidence against Peter has also been mentioned. In language, grammar, and style it differs greatly from the accepted 1 Peter. While the Greek of 1 Peter is of a very high quality, that of 2 Peter is poor. Sentence structure is awkward. Hellenistic terms abound. Hellenistic thought forms are frequent. In vocabulary the two books have 100 Greek words in common. Of these, only five are distinctive enough to make a striking similarity. References to Peter's personal experiences with the Lord are regarded as overemphasized devices of the writer to make it appear that he was the apostle. The reference to an authoritative collection of the writings of Paul (3:15–16) is considered evidence for a late date.

While Gnosticism had its roots in the first century, it came to full expression in the second and third centuries. Definitely the heresy which is combated in 2 Peter is Gnosticism. Was it a Gnosticism which was so fully developed that it was too late for Peter, whose death was in the middle or late sixties? Many scholars think so. Jude also combated Gnosticism. Was it a later form so that Jude may have borrowed 2 Peter 2? Or, was it an earlier form so that 2 Peter 2 was borrowed from Jude? While this question will be more fully explored in the introduction to Jude, it must be indicated here that the majority of scholarly opinion holds that 2 Peter 2 was borrowed from Jude. Would the Apostle Peter have borrowed from the lesser known and lesser

authoritative Jude? Most scholars think not.

Those who accept Peter as the author of the epistle discount the above objections as having incontestable validity. They do so on both external and internal bases. Externally, they admit, 2 Peter does have little unchallenged use earlier than Origen in the second quarter of the third century. There are, however, possible reflections of 2 Peter in second century writings: 1 Clement (A.D. 95), 2 Clement (150), Aristides (130), Valentinus (130), Justin Martyr (165), Hippolytus (180), and Irenaeus (180). Soon after this other uses begin to appear. Then Origen quoted the book six times and showed no reluctance to accept it as genuine. There is no evidence that it was rejected outright by any of the early writers. Although Mayor (p. cxxiv) rejects the Petrine authorship on internal evidences, in his highly regarded commentary he concludes that if only the external evidence were available, scholars would be compelled to accept the book as having been eagerly espoused as useful by many early writers. That is a tribute to its acceptance as a genuine letter from Peter.

From the viewpoint of internal evidence, those who accept the letter as having come from Peter make much of the claim of the letter itself that it was from Peter (1:1). They challenge the validity of the idea that there was a widespread custom among Christians of the second century to circulate works pseudepigraphically. Too, they accept as genuine the author's claim to have been an eyewitness to the transfiguration of Jesus (1:16–18), that Jesus had predicted Peter's death (1:14), and that he had written an earlier letter to these readers (3:1).

These scholars recognize the difficult problem of the differences in vocabulary, style, and grammar in 1 and 2 Peter. The explanation is in terms of a different scribe for the two, a theory which goes back at least to Jerome (died A.D. 420). The good Greek of 1 Peter is attributed to Silvanus as scribe. The broken Greek of 2 Peter is attributed to some scribe unknown but less qualified than Silvanus. Since no scribe is mentioned in 2 Peter, as Silvanus is mentioned in 1 Peter 5:12, there has been conjecture that Peter himself penned 2 Peter. This is open to severe challenge in the light of the tradition that in his preaching among the Gentiles Peter used Mark as an interpreter.

With regard to the problem of the epistle's being addressed to the presence of Gnosticism, these interpreters point to the evidence for a mid-first century incipient Gnosticism in other New Testament books: Colossians and Ephesians, for example. Too, while the problem of the delayed Parousia is most pronounced in later works, the stage of development which it had reached in those works (Luke and John, for example) required a beginning several years earlier, as early as the last years of Simon Peter.

The only certain conclusion for one who works through the maze of arguments in many volumes on 1 Peter, 2 Peter, and Jude is simply this. The question of authorship, and hence date, of 2 Peter is open. It depends on how one weighs evidence and forms conclusions. If Peter wrote the book, the date must necessarily be placed in the middle sixties, shortly after 1 Peter (cf. 2 Peter 3:1). If Peter did not write it, the date must relate to the stage of development of the Gnosticism which is reflected in it. That could be from any time in the mid-sixties until the middle of the second century.

II. Purpose

One thing is abundantly clear. The book was written to combat heresy. Even in the salutation (1:2) the theme of true knowledge is introduced. That theme is developed in chapter 1. With that as a background, chapter 2 develops false knowledge as it is being promoted by false teachers. The false knowledge is that of Gnostic doctrine with its denial of Christ, its defiance of God's authority, and its inevitable failure under God's judgment. Chapter 3 develops a special problem, discouragement over the seeming delay of Christ's return. Peter affirms the certainty of that coming,

explains the "delay" in relation to the difference between God's way and man's way of reckoning time, and closes with a challenging presentation on how Christians ought to live in view of their hope in the second coming.

Outline of the Epistle

Salutation (1:1–2)
  I. Godliness through true knowledge (1:3–21)
    1. Knowledge which transforms (1:3–11)
    2. Knowledge which assures (1:12–21)
      (1) Peter's motive for assuring (1:12–15)
      (2) Peter's method of assuring (1:16–21)
 II. Ungodliness through false knowledge (2:1–22)
    1. Knowledge from false teachers (2:1–3)
    2. Judgment upon false teachers (2:4–10a)
    3. Character of false teachers (2:10b–16)
    4. Inevitable doom of false teachers (2:17–22)
III. The second coming of Christ (3:1–18a)
    1. Denial of his coming (3:1–7)
    2. Assurance of his coming (3:8–10)
    3. Living for his coming (3:11–18a)
    Conclusion (3:18b)

Selected Bibliography

BEKER, J. C. "Peter, Second Letter of," *The Interpreter's Dictionary of the Bible,* III. Nashville: Abingdon Press, 1962.

BIGG, CHARLES. *A Critical and Exegetical Commentary on the Epistles of St. Peter and St. Jude.* ("The International Critical Commentary." Edinburg: T. & T. Clark, 1902.

CRANFIELD, C. E. B. *I and II Peter and Jude.* ("The Torch Bible Commentaries.") London: SCM Press, Ltd., 1960.

GREEN, MICHAEL. *The Second Epistle General of Peter and the General Epistle of Jude.* ("The Tyndale New Testament Commentaries.") Grand Rapids: Wm. B. Eerdmans Publishing Co., 1968.

GUTHRIE, DONALD. *New Testament Introduction: Hebrews to Revelation.* Chicago: Inter-Varsity Press, 1964.

LEANEY, A. R. C. *The Letters of Peter and Jude.* Cambridge: At the University Press, 1967.

MAYOR, J. B. *The Epistle of St. Jude and the Second Epistle of St. Peter.* Grand Rapids: Baker Book House, 1965.

REICKE, Bo. *The Epistles of James, Peter, and Jude.* ("The Anchor Bible.") Garden City: Doubleday and Company, Inc. 1964.

SIDEBOTTOM, E. M. *James, Jude, and 2 Peter.* ("The Century Bible.") London: Thomas Nelson, 1967.

WAND, J. W. C. *The General Epistles of St. Peter and St. Jude.* ("Westminster Commentaries.") London: Methuen and Co., Ltd., 1934.

Commentary on the Text

This is a brief epistle which has a double purpose. The purpose is to warn the readers about the coming of false teachers and to assure them of the second coming of Christ, which the false teachers would deny. An interesting facet of the epistle is that of all of the books in the Bible this is one of the few in which the *chapter* divisions correspond to the *thought* divisions. In contrast to 1 Peter, this has been a neglected book. That is to be lamented because the book has a very remarkable message.

Salutation (1:1–2)

[1] Simon Peter, a servant and apostle of Jesus Christ,

To those who have obtained a faith of equal standing with ours in the righteousness of our God and Savior Jesus Christ:

[2] May grace and peace be multiplied to you in the knowledge of God and of Jesus our Lord.

Simon Peter establishes a claim of authorship. The pros and cons of that claim have been treated briefly in the Introduction. The double name embraces both his real Hebrew name, *Simon,* and the nickname which Jesus gave to him, *Peter,* that is, rock (John 1:42). He became the leader among the twelve apostles, and in the early years after the Lord's ascension he became the leader of the Jewish segment of the church.

There is no geographical or national identification of the recipients of the letter, as there is in 1 Peter. Those addressed are identified only in spiritual terms. They are *those who have obtained a faith of equal standing with ours.* The word *ours* may be a reference to Jewish Christians. If so, the readers who had obtained this *faith of equal*

standing were likely Gentiles. The nature of the heresy which is the focus of the epistle also suggests Gentile recipients. The unusual construction *our God and Savior Jesus Christ* may be an initial affirmation of the deity of Jesus Christ, a doctrine which the Gnostics denied.

The customary epistolary prayer for *grace and peace* is employed. In this instance it is linked with the *knowledge of God and of Jesus.* Moreover, the word which is translated *knowledge* is a compound form which means full knowledge. As such it represents a play on words. Peter prays for full knowledge, *epignōsis,* for his Christian readers in contrast to the knowledge, *gnōsis,* which was claimed by the Gnostics. He prayed for a multiplication of grace and peace in the realm of the full knowledge which has its foundation in God and the Lord Jesus Christ.

I. Godliness Through True Knowedge (1: 3–21)

1. Knowledge Which Transforms (1:3–11)

[3] His divine power has granted to us all things that pertain to life and godliness, through the knowledge of him who called us to his own glory and excellence, [4] by which he has granted to us his precious and very great promises, that through these you may escape from the corruption that is in the world because of passion, and become partakers of the divine nature. [5] For this very reason make every effort to supplement your faith with virtue, and virtue with knowledge, [6] and knowledge with self-control, and self-control with steadfastness, and steadfastness with godliness, [7] and godliness with brotherly affection, and brotherly affection with love. [8] For if these things are yours and abound, they keep you from being ineffective or unfruitful in the

knowledge of our Lord Jesus Christ. [9] For whoever lacks these things is blind and short-sighted and has forgotten that he was cleansed from his old sins. [10] Therefore, brethren, be the more zealous to confirm your call and election, for if you do this you will never fall; [11] so there will be richly provided for you an entrance into the eternal kingdom of our Lord and Savior Jesus Christ.

Peter's purpose in this paragraph is to give his readers the correct view of true knowledge and of what it does in the life of a Christian. *Knowledge* is a repetition of the word for full knowledge (v. 2), and undoubtedly he used it to contrast the results of the false knowledge of the Gnostics with the true knowledge which has its source in *him who called us,* i.e., our Savior and Lord, Jesus Christ.

All things that pertain to life and godliness indicates that there is no need for further revelations such as the Gnostics held to be essential. God in Christ supplies all that is needed to provide both *life and godliness,* both life and the acceptable kind of life. The Gnostics believed that salvation was totally spiritual and had no relation to the physical life. Knowledge which has its source in Christ indicates that salvation touches the entire person, both spiritual and physical.

By *his divine power* he has made it possible for us to share in *his own glory and excellence,* to partake of his very nature. Through the experiencing of that glory and excellence, he has given to us *precious and very great promises* which assure us that we may escape the controlling power of the world of corruption and evil. This means that we may actually enter here and now into the possession of the very spiritual nature of God.

For this very reason refers to the escaping of the world's corruption and the possessing of the divine nature. Because of that blessing, there is a corresponding responsibility for upright living. *Make every effort* means that the Christian is to work diligently at the task of conforming his practice to his nature. *To supplement* means to add to that which one already has. The

word introduces a series of desirable qualities for the Christian life. With his faith as the foundation, the Christian is to add these qualities, one upon the other, in an ascending scale until *love* crowns the whole. The framework suggests the constructing of a multi-floored building with faith as the foundation, and love as the roof. Or, in another apt figure, Green (pp. 57, 66–71) develops "the ladder of faith" with faith as its starting rung and love as its top rung.

Faith denotes personal trust in God's promises, and it serves as the foundation on which all else rests. To it is to be added *virtue,* which denotes moral excellence or vigor in Christian living. Next to be added is *knowledge,* which means practical understanding in order that the virtue will not be misdirected. Next in succession comes *self-control,* which, in this instance, relates particularly to the control of one's sexual impulses. It is to be supplemented by *steadfastness,* which is the basic New Testament word for patience; literally it means the ability to stay under a heavy load. To it is to be added *godliness,* which means God-likeness, to be well disposed toward the divine nature. That brings one to the twin qualities of *brotherly affection* and *love.* The two basic New Testament verbs for love are in these words. *Brotherly affection* is derived from *phileo,* meaning a warm personal affection for another. *Love* is derived from *agapao,* meaning to put supreme value upon. Fittingly they join to crown all the virtues of the life which begins with faith.

Verse 8 opens with a grammatical construction which is difficult to put into smooth English. The RSV translation suggests a conditional sentence, such as this: "If these things are in you . . . , they will keep you from being ineffective . . . ." Actually, the entire first clause serves as the subject of the second clause, such as this: "These things being and abounding in you keep you from being ineffective . . . ." In the Christian, the virtues of vv. 5–7 prevent *ineffective or unfruitful* living.

But what is to be said of the Christian

who lacks these virtues? His sad plight is described in v. 9. This verse, too, is very difficult to translate. A *translation* results in an awkward English sentence. The RSV here, as in v. 8, is a *paraphrase*. Let this interpreter try another paraphrase: "For in him in whom these things are not, there is blindness; he is myopic, having forgotten the cleansing of his former sins." This affirms that he has been cleansed of his former sinful life. It also affirms the tragedy of the emptiness of his present life. The lack of the virtues of vv. 5–7, *virtue* . . . *knowledge* . . . *self-control* . . . , etc., has resulted in a sort of spiritual nearsightedness which prevents his remembering his experience of having been cleansed. This is tragic emptiness.

Therefore (v. 10) is not the usual New Testament connecting word for "therefore." It is a strong contrasting expression—"wherefore, rather." Rather than living a careless life which results in the sort of blind emptiness described in v. 9, the Christian is urged to a zealous life which demonstrates the validity of his experience in Christ. *Be zealous* is the imperative form of the verb from which we get our English word hasten, hurry, or be speedy. It is a word which means to make every effort to do that which is being considered.

That which is being considered in this case is *to confirm your call and election.* *To confirm* is the translation of a verb meaning to make and an adjective meaning reliable or valid. The claim that one is called and chosen of God is to be validated by a life characterized by the virtues of vv. 5–7 rather than the nearsighted forgetfulness of v. 9. *If you do this* means precisely, "doing these things," i.e., validating one's call and election by right living. *You will never fall* means precisely, "You will never, never stumble over rocks in your path."

So is a comparative particle meaning thus or in this manner. Living in such way as to demonstrate the validity of one's claim to salvation causes one to walk life's rough road without stumbling over its rocks. It will

bring one to the *entrance into the eternal kingdom of our Lord and Savior Jesus Christ.* In this passage, *the eternal kingdom* refers to the ultimate destiny of the Christian, that which is at the end of this life's rough road. The word *entrance* is the exact word which one finds in Greece today marking the "way in," the entrance to a building.

The Christian who lives in the way which is set out in this passage will find that entrance *richly provided.* As a farmer is supplied all of the seed needed for sowing; as a member of a chorus is supplied all of the music needed for a performance; as a bride is supplied all of the contract needed to guarantee her marriage—so the Christian is *richly provided . . . an entrance* into that City Beautiful of Revelation 21—22.

2. Knowledge Which Assures (1:12–21)

(1) Peter's Motive for Assuring (1:12–15)

12 Therefore I intend always to remind you of these things, though you know them and are established in the truth that you have. 13 I think it right, as long as I am in this body, to arouse you by way of reminder, 14 since I know that the putting off of my body will be soon, as our Lord Jesus Christ showed me. 15 And I will see to it that after my departure you may be able at any time to recall these things.

I intend expresses Peter's intention that *always*, which means "every opportunity I have," he will remind his readers of the right way to live as Christians (vv. 5–7, 10). Even though they know the right way, and even though they are *established*, firmly fixed, in the truth which they have received, he will continue to remind them.

As long as he lives (v. 13) he will continue to remind them because he feels that it is *right*, the correct thing to do, for him to stir up their memory of God's way for his people to live. His motive for writing to them of the assurance which rests in the knowledge which comes from Christ is that he believes it is the correct thing for him to do.

Further, he is motivated by the knowledge that the end of his own life is near. He speaks of his death as the *putting off* of his body. The word for *body* is really the word meaning a tent, a temporary dwelling place. Paul wrote of death as the Christian's moving from a temporary "tent" kind of dwelling into an eternal "house-not-made-by-hands" kind of dwelling (2 Cor. 5:1–10). For Peter, too, to die meant to move out of a temporary tent and into the eternal kingdom. Most likely for both Peter and Paul the figure was drawn from the Exodus wilderness wanderings of their forefathers when for 40 years they lived temporarily in tents before entering into permanent residence in the land of God's promise.

As our Lord Jesus Christ showed me is unquestionably a reference to the experience of Jesus' prediction of Peter's death (John 21:18–19). That prediction was one which implied that Peter would die the death of a martyr, bound and led by the will of another rather than by his own will. It is not likely that this prediction can be used here as a certain way of dating the epistle, i.e., shortly before his martyrdom in Rome. While that cannot be ruled out, it is likely that Simon Peter lived out his entire life expecting at any time to share his Lord's death at the hands of enemies to the faith.

It is difficult to understand how Peter intends to see to it that even after his death he will continue to remind them (v. 15). The simplest answer may be the correct one—he will continue to remind them by means of this letter which he is sending for that purpose.

(2) Peter's Method of Assuring (1:16–21)

[16] For we did not follow cleverly devised myths when we made known to you the power and coming of our Lord Jesus Christ, but we were eyewitnesses of his majesty. [17] For when he received honor and glory from God the Father and the voice was borne to him by the Majestic Glory, "This is my beloved Son, with whom I am well pleased," [18] we heard this voice borne from heaven, for we were with him on the holy mountain. [19] And we have the prophetic word made more sure. You will do well to pay attention to this as to a lamp shining in a dark place, until the day dawns

and the morning star rises in your hearts. [20] First of all you must understand this, that no prophecy of scripture is a matter of one's own interpretation, [21] because no prophecy ever came by the impulse of man, but men moved by the Holy Spirit spoke from God.

Peter's method of assuring his readers of the right way of life which looks to that abundant entrance into Christ's eternal kingdom was to remind them of the cherished promise of Christ's second coming. The commonly used expression "second coming" is not a New Testament term. Its first use in Christian writings is in *The First Apology* of Justin Martyr about A.D. 150–60. In speaking of the two advents of Christ —one at his incarnation and the other at the resurrection and judgment of men— Martyr used the term "the second coming" to refer to the latter. It came to be a favorite expression of Christians in speaking of the cherished promise of his return (Acts 1:11). So, while the term is not a New Testament one, the doctrine is. The main New Testament term for the doctrine was simply the *presence*, a Greek word meaning his "being with" his people. That doctrine, mentioned here in chapter 1, will be the main theme of chapter 3.

Peter had not based his teaching regarding Christ's coming on *cleverly devised myths*. He based it on his having experienced the transfiguration of Christ (Matt. 17:1–5; Mark 9:2–7; Luke 9:28–35). He interpreted that transfiguration as something of a forecast of what Christ's appearance will be in his second coming (cf. 1 Peter 5:1). *Cleverly devised myths* was a reference to the method of the Gnostics in their teachings. Claiming a special revelation or knowledge (*gnosis*, from which they derived their name), the Gnostics thought of deity as a long series of "emanations" from the highest deity, for whom they had many names. An emanation was something like the fragrance of a flower going forth from the flower to form a lower class of flower.

In the Gnostic view, this highest deity sent forth from himself an emanation. Although a bit lower, it still possessed the quality of deity. This emanation, in turn, sent forth a lower emanation, still possessing the quality of deity but more removed from the highest deity. The Gnostics regarded Christ as one of the lowest in a long series of such emanations from deity. He was far from the majestic Christ whom Peter had seen in the transfiguration.

Peter based his teaching on his experience in sharing with James and John the transfiguration of Christ. They were *eyewitnesses of his majesty.* Refer to the Gospel accounts of the transfiguration. On that occasion Jesus *received honor and glory* when the voice out of the cloud spoke to them. The voice was that of the *Majestic Glory,* i.e., God himself. Christ in his transfiguration was seen as one who shared that *majesty* (v. 16). At his baptism the voice from heaven had spoken to Jesus, "Thou art my beloved Son; with thee I am well pleased" (Mark 1:11). At his transfiguration the voice spoke to the disciples, *This is my beloved Son, with whom I am well pleased* (v. 17; Matt. 17:5). That brilliant glorious appearance of Christ, Peter understood as a forecast of what Christ will be like at his second coming. The apostolic eyewitness of that glory is the *prophetic word* (v. 19) to which Peter's readers should give heed.

To that prophetic word Peter added the prophetic *scripture* (v. 20). To it Peter's readers should give heed *as to a lamp shining in a dark place.* The world was regarded as experiencing the darkness of night. In that darkness, God's word through his prophets was shining as a lamp. It would continue to shine until the light of morning. *Until the day dawns* refers to the second coming of Christ, which will end the world's darkness as the rising sun ends the darkness of night. *The morning star* in this passage is not likely a reference to Venus as it was used in ancient astronomy. Most likely in this case it means the sun which springs up to dispel the darkness of the night. The word is the one for the "source of light" rather than the regular one

for "star." A different word is used in Revelation 2:28 and 22:16 for Christ—the star which shines brightest in the early morning when it is the darkest. *The prophetic word* of his coming shines as a lamp in the dark night, but that lamp will be replaced by the coming of Christ himself to dispel the darkness as the rising sun dispels darkness.

Peter does not point to any particular *prophecy of scripture* concerning the glory of the coming of Christ. Early Christians interpreted Numbers 24:17 as a reference to Christ, "a star shall come out of Jacob." They understood Malachi 4:2 to refer to Christ, "the sun of righteousness shall rise, with healing in its wings." A part of the Song of Zechariah was based upon an ancient Hebrew prayer which Zechariah applied to the coming Messiah, "when the day shall dawn upon us from on high to give light to those who sit in darkness" (Luke 1:78). These are sufficient to reflect the fact that the Christians found in their Scriptures evidence for the glorious coming of the Messiah in consummation of God's redemptive purpose.

The interpretation of the prophetic scripture was important to Peter. The understanding of those scriptures is not *a matter of one's own interpretation.* Moffatt translates this, "no prophetic scripture allows a man to interpret it by himself." Williams translates it, ". . . is to be interpreted by one's own mind." What Peter is stressing is that the interpretation of the Scriptures requires more than human understanding. It requires the guidance of the Holy Spirit who gave it. The Scriptures did not come just *by the impulse of man.* They came as *men moved by the Holy Spirit spoke from* God. The word which is translated *moved* means literally "borne" or "carried." "Borne up" or "carried along" by the Holy Spirit, they spoke. What they spoke was in reality God's message.

Peter does not argue for the inspiration of the Scriptures. He assumes it. Clearly he is not defining the nature or method of inspiration. And surely he is not anticipating the verbiage of any given translation. The

Scriptures of which he wrote were, of course, the Hebrew Scriptures (our Old Testament). The New Testament as a body of approved writings was not in existence. It was in process of being written. What the Hebrews claimed for the Old Testament, Christians claim for the New Testament, that it was written by men who *moved by the Holy Spirit spoke from God.*

Peter's emphasis is that since the Holy Spirit moved men in the writing of the Scriptures, he must move them in the understanding of the Scriptures. The interpretation of the Scriptures is to be carried out in the community of faith. And any man of faith may interpret the Scriptures, but he cannot do it apart from the aid of the Holy Spirit who gave them. And the Holy Spirit aids all who seek to interpret the Scriptures. He gives no man a monopoly on interpreting them.

II. Ungodliness Through False Knowledge (2:1–22)

Chapter 2 is devoted entirely to a discussion of false teachers, their character, and their certain judgment and doom. Scholarly opinion has been almost unanimous that the false teachers were Gnostics who claimed to be a part of the Christian community, but in reality were destructive of Christian faith and fellowship.

The one major exception to that view is Reicke (pp. 160–172), who argues for a setting in the time of Domitian (A.D. 90–96). He interprets the false teachers as politically motivated representatives of Rome who were trying to elicit loyalty to Rome, which meant, in essence, a denial of Christ. His argument is forced, unconvincing, and completely lacking in the cogency which generally characterizes his exposition of the Scriptures. A far better detailed treatment of the chapter is that of Green (pp. 93–123).

1. Knowledge from False Teachers (2:1–3)

¹ But false prophets also arose among the people, just as there will be false teachers among you, who will secretly bring in destruc-

tive heresies, even denying the Master who bought them, bringing upon themselves swift destruction. ² And many will follow their licentiousness, and because of them the way of truth will be reviled. ³ And in their greed they will exploit you with false words; from of old their condemnation has not been idle, and their destruction has not been asleep.

Of old, the people of God had been troubled by *false prophets.* These were men who claimed to be authentic spokesmen for God, the basic meaning of the word prophet. Their messages, however, proved them false. In Numbers 22—30 there is the account of the false prophet Balaam, who caused so much trouble for Israel. He appears in 2:15 as one of Peter's examples of a false prophet. Deuteronomy 13:2–6 contains a warning from Moses about false prophets. A casual reading of Amos, Jeremiah, and Ezekiel reveals how numerous false prophets were.

Jesus predicted false prophets who would come in the days of trouble during the Jewish wars with Rome (A.D. 66–70) and would try to lead the people from the faith (Matt. 24:24). This is reflected in 1 Timothy 4:1–5 and 1 John 2:18–25 as a phenomenon to be anticipated in the last stages of God's redemptive work.

Just as means that, after the same pattern of false prophets in the old Israel, so *there will be false teachers* present and troubling the new Israel. The similarities between 2 Peter 2 and Jude will be considered at length in the subsequent commentary on Jude. It should, however, be noted at this point that in much of 2 Peter 2 the future tense is used as if pointing to anticipated future events: *there will be false teachers; they will secretly bring in; many will follow; the way of the truth will be reviled;* and others. There are exceptions, however, which indicate that some false teachers were already present—the present tense is being used in vv. 10b–19.

Who is a term which indicates character rather than identity; it speaks of their nature, such as: "who are of such nature that they bring in destructive heresies." Because they were false, their teachings were false.

Destructive heresies meant heretical teachings which were destructive of both doctrine and character. They extended even to a denial of *the Master who bought them.* This denial likely refers to the Gnostic denial of the deity of Christ (see the comment on 1:16). It could be a more practical matter, i.e., their lives are such that they are not true to the Master they profess. The passage may reflect the long-remembered grief of Peter over his own denial of his Master on the occasion of Jesus' trial and death. When they teach and live in such way as to deny the Master who died for them, they bring upon themselves their own *destruction,* a word meaning ruin.

The worst part is that they not only ruin themselves, but they also lead to the ruin of others. Others will *follow their licentiousness.* They would enter into the shameful indulgence of the passions of the flesh because the Gnostics were teaching that salvation was a spiritual process and what one did with his body had nothing to do with it. *The way of truth* was the Christian understanding that salvation relates to every area of life, spiritual and physical. To deny this and to live in sinful practices was to revile, to speak evil, of the truth. Theirs was the error of not understanding that freedom in Christ does not mean freedom from obligation to upright living. Life under love is far more demanding than life under law.

The false teachers combined their gross immorality (v. 2) with a spirit of greediness (v. 3). *Greed* means a covetous nature. *Exploit* was a commercial term for trafficking in merchandise. *False words* means false arguments. These were teachers who, out of a spirit of covetousness, spewed forth attractive but erroneous teaching in exchange for money from their victims.

Incensed by their false teaching and their leading the people into ruin, Peter voiced their certain judgment. He personified condemnation and destruction as agents of judgment. *Condemnation has not been idle;* it is as active as it was *of old* in the earlier Old Testament references to false prophets.

Destruction has not been asleep; it is wide awake and ready to pounce upon the false teachers.

2. Judgment upon False Teachers (2:4–10a)

⁴ For if God did not spare the angels when they sinned, but cast them into hell and committed them to pits of nether gloom to be kept until the judgment; ⁵ if he did not spare the ancient world, but preserved Noah, a herald of righteousness, with seven other persons, when he brought a flood upon the world of the ungodly; ⁶ if by turning the cities of Sodom and Gomorrah to ashes he condemned them to extinction and made them an example to those who were to be ungodly; ⁷ and if he rescued righteous Lot, greatly distressed by the licentiousness of the wicked ⁸ (for by what that righteous man saw and heard as he lived among them, he was vexed in his righteous soul day after day with their lawless deeds), ⁹ then the Lord knows how to rescue the godly from trial, and to keep the unrighteous under punishment until the day of judgment, ¹⁰ and especially those who indulge in the lust of defiling passion and despise authority.

The certain judgment which Peter proclaimed in 2:3, he illustrated in vv. 4–10a. He used three striking illustrations of God's responsible judgment on evil. The passage is one long conditional sentence in which the "if" clause extends from v. 4, *for if God did not spare . . . ,* through v. 8. The "then" clause finishes the sentence with vv. 9–10a, *then the Lord knows how . . . to keep the unrighteous under punishment until the day of judgment. . . .*

The grammatical construction is one which affirms the condition and may well be translated, "Since it is true that God did not spare . . . , then God knows how . . . ." The three illustrations are:

(1) *God did not spare the angels when they sinned.* These angels who sinned are not identified. Some interpreters think the reference is to "the sons of God" who entered into sexual union with "the daughters of men" to produce "the Nephilim" of Genesis 6:1–7. Some think the reference may be to the noncanonical book of 1 Enoch 10:4. Revelation 12:7–12 pictures

the archangel Michael and his angels fighting with Satan (the dragon) and his angels. The passage reflects the common view of the New Testament day that there were angels who had fallen from their once lofty place of service to God. (See comment on Jude 6.)

Here it is stated that God *cast them into hell*. The word translated *hell* is not the Gehenna of the Gospels but a Greek word Tartarus which in Greek mythology was the place of the abode of the wicked dead in contrast to the Elysian Fields which was the place of the abode of the righteous dead. *Pits of nether gloom* pictures their place of imprisonment as one of dense darkness while they wait for God's judgment. In 1 Enoch 10:12 the imprisonment of the wicked angels is to last until the day of judgment. Peter does not say that he is referring to the book of Enoch; Jude uses the same illustration, and he does indicate his source as Enoch (Jude 14).

(2) *If he did not spare the ancient world* is clearly a reference to God's judgment upon the world of Noah's day. The instrument of that judgment was the flood (Gen. 6:5—9:18). Hope is present even in the midst of judgment in that Noah and his family were spared. Noah is described as *a herald of righteousness*. A *herald* was a proclaimer, a preacher. While there is no Old Testament claim that Noah was a preacher of righteousness, there are frequent references to that intent in later writings.[1] As a righteous man in so wicked an environment, his *life* would have preached righteousness, and his *faith* in building the ark preached it whether or not he ever preached it by *words*.

(3) *If by turning the cities of Sodom and Gomorrah to ashes* is the third illustration of God's judgment on wickedness. Indeed, Peter wrote that God made the wicked people of those cities to be an example of judgment for later people *who were to be ungodly*. Again, in Lot there is a ray of hope in the midst of judgment. Lot is de-

scribed as a *righteous* man who was disturbed daily by the gross immorality of the people, a practice that has passed the name of their city as a name of shame on down through the ages. Salvation from the judgment fire and brimstone upon Sodom and Gomorrah came to Lot just as salvation from the judgment of the flood waters came to Noah.

Then the Lord knows how picks up the entire "if" clause and its double action of judgment and salvation. It is a note of hope that God can *rescue the godly from* trial (as Noah and Lot). By the same token it is a note of warning that he can *keep the unrighteous under punishment until the day of judgment*. The wicked who depart this life enter immediately into a state of punishment, but the final state of that punishment awaits the end and God's ultimate reckoning with man as to what he had done with the total trusteeship of life.[2] Peter states that this is especially true of those who in this life are guilty of the sin of *defiling passion* and who *despise* authorities. These evils he will develop in subsequent paragraphs.

3. Character of False Teachers (2:10b–16)

Bold and wilful, they are not afraid to revile the glorious ones, [11] whereas angels, though greater in might and power, do not pronounce a reviling judgment upon them before the Lord. [12] But these, like irrational animals, creatures of instinct, born to be caught and killed, reviling in matters of which they are ignorant, will be destroyed in the same destruction with them, [13] suffering wrong for their wrongdoing. They count it pleasure to revel in the daytime. They are blots and blemishes, reveling in their dissipation, carousing with you. [14] They have eyes full of adultery, insatiable for sin. They entice unsteady souls. They have hearts trained in greed. Accursed children! [15] Forsaking the right way they have gone astray; they have followed the way of Balaam, the son of Beor, who loved gain from wrongdoing, [16] but was rebuked for his own transgression; a dumb ass spoke with human voice and restrained the prophet's madness.

[1] For examples, 1 Clement 7:6; 9:4; Josephus, *Antiq.* 1.3.1; the Sibylline Oracles 1:128.

[2] For further development of this teaching in the New Testament see Ray Summers, *The Life Beyond* (Nashville: Broadman Press, 1959), pp. 24–29, 189–96.

These false teachers had no respect for religious authorities. *Bold* means presumptuous; they do not hesitate to defy man or God. *Wilful* means one who is determined to have his own way regardless of the result. *Revile* means to speak evil of; usually it is translated blaspheme. *The glorious ones* is ambiguous. It may refer to church leaders; the false teachers have no respect for them and revile them. On the other hand, it may refer to angels; even the higher creation of God, the unseen agents of God's will, do not escape the contemptuous words of the false teachers. In contrast, even angels do not accuse these teachers before God; they leave the accusing to be done by God. See the comment on Jude 8-9 in which reference is made to Michael's refusing to rebuke even an evil ruling authority, the devil; he left the rebuking to be done by God.

The character of these evil teachers is sketched out in a long series of illustrations. Each yields fruitful study, but space does not permit detailed exposition. In v. 12, they are compared to *irrational animals* which howl at things *of which they are ignorant.* In v. 13, they are compared to vile people who cannot wait for darkness to cover their shame but openly *revel in the daytime.* In v. 14, they are described as having eyes that can never be satisfied in looking for adulterous conduct. In v. 15, they are compared to the false prophet Balaam who for the sake of money taught Balak how to entice the people of God to sin. Even a dumb animal, the lowly ass, was intelligent enough to rebuke Balaam and to try to prevent Balaam from coming under God's judgment (Num. 22).

4. Inevitable Doom of False Teachers (2:17-22)

17 These are waterless springs and mists driven by a storm; for them the nether gloom of darkness has been reserved. 18 For, uttering loud boasts of folly, they entice with licentious passions of the flesh men who have barely escaped from those who live in error. 19 They promise them freedom, but they themselves are slaves of corruption; for whatever overcomes a man, to that he is enslaved. 20 For if, after they have escaped the defilements of the world through the knowledge of our Lord and Savior Jesus Christ, they are again entangled in them and overpowered, the last state has become worse for them than the first. 21 For it would have been better for them never to have known the way of righteousness than after knowing it to turn back from the holy commandment delivered to them. 22 It has happened to them according to the true proverb, The dog turns back to his own vomit, and the sow is washed only to wallow in the mire.

These false teachers are *waterless springs* and rainless clouds driven before the storm; i.e., they promise blessing, but they cannot deliver what they promise. They promise *freedom* to men who are trying to escape from evil, but they themselves are *slaves of corruption.* Slaves cannot provide freedom to others; they cannot even free themselves.

The false teachers are under a sentence of inevitable doom because of the hypocritical nature presented in the figures of waterless springs, rainless clouds, and enslaved promisers of freedom. That hypocritical nature is made all the more dramatic by two repulsive illustrations: a dog returning to eat his own vomit; a hog returning to her filthy wallow. The dog proverb is from Proverbs 26:11. The source of the hog proverb is uncertain; it is not in the Bible.

For if, after they have escaped introduces a concessive clause, one in which, for the sake of argument, the action is assumed as real. *Defilements* meant pollution or corruption. It was commonly used by both Christian and non-Christian writers to refer to moral pollution or crime. *Knowledge* is the word which Peter has used consistently for true knowledge as it is found in Christ.

They are again entangled in them and overpowered means simply that they return to their former sinful ways. They become *entangled* with them and are *overpowered* by them. This *last state,* being entangled again in that from which one was once free, is worse than *the first,* their evil state which had preceded their escape through the knowledge of Christ.

Peter considered their former condition of sin in a state of ignorance preferable to their present condition of sin in a state of having repudiated the Christ whom they had come to know as the only way out of sin. Peter's expression is almost identical with Jesus' words, "the last state of that man becomes worse than the first," in his strange fable illustrating the futility of reformation without regeneration. An evil spirit went out of a man in whom he lived. Having wandered about for some time and having found no more desirable place in which to live, the evil spirit returned to find that no good spirit had moved into the man in whom he had formerly lived; the man was like a freshly swept but empty house. Gleefully the evil spirit gathered together seven other evil spirits and they all moved into the man making his last state worse than his first (Matt. 12:45; Luke 11:24–26).

Now put all of the concessive argument together in paraphrase: Assuming for argument's sake that they (the false teachers) through the knowledge of Jesus Christ escaped the world's pollution and then repudiated that knowledge and went back to the world's pollution. What is their present state? It is worse than the former one. They have demonstrated their true nature. It is the nature of a dog which vomits up that which has made him sick and then goes back to eat it again. It is the nature of a hog, which, having been washed clean, goes back to her filthy mud wallow. The dog was not really "cured" by his vomiting. The hog was not really "clean" by her washing. Their dog and hog natures were still there.

These false teachers had heard the Christian message. They had lived for a while by its high standards. Their change had not been sufficiently radical to induce a continuation in that way of life. They repudiated it by returning to their former way of life. By the examples of two animals, both of which were loathsome to the Hebrew mind, Peter concluded that the teachers had simply demonstrated their true nature as sick (the dog proverb) and

filthy (the hog proverb). They were teachers to be avoided rather than followed.

III. The Second Coming of Christ (3:1–18a)

In chapter 3, Peter turns from his castigation of heretical teachers and directs his attention to the encouragement of his Christian readers. That he knows them well is reflected in his use of the word *beloved* three times (3:1,8,14). His encouragement relates specifically to their hope for the return of the Lord and their way of life as they wait for that return.

1. Denial of His Coming (3:1–7)

¹ This is now the second letter that I have written to you, beloved, and in both of them I have aroused your sincere mind by way of reminder; ² that you should remember the predictions of the holy prophets and the commandment of the Lord and Savior through your apostles. ³ First of all you must understand this, that scoffers will come in the last days with scoffing, following their own passions ⁴ and saying, "Where is the promise of his coming? For ever since the fathers fell asleep, all things have continued as they were from the beginning of creation." ⁵ They deliberately ignore this fact, that by the word of God heavens existed long ago, and an earth formed out of water and by means of water, ⁶ through which the world that then existed was deluged with water and perished. ⁷ But by the same word the heavens and earth that now exist have been stored up for fire, being kept until the day of judgment and destruction of ungodly men.

Opinion is divided as to the meaning of Peter's reference to a former letter which he had written to these readers. *The second letter that I have written to you* naturally suggests that it is 1 Peter. Interpreters who reject the Petrine authorship of 2 Peter understand this reference as a literary device of the unknown writer for the purpose of supporting his argument with the authority of the apostle Peter. Those who accept the Petrine authorship of 2 Peter think that the reference to a former letter may or may not be to 1 Peter. It may be to

1 Peter or it may be to a lost letter.[3]

If the matter of which Peter is reminding his readers (vv. 1–2) is a general one related to the difficulties and encouragements involved in the Christian life, 1 Peter fits the description. If, however, the matter specifically refers to the problem of scoffers at the doctrine of the second coming, 1 Peter does not fit the description. The 1 Peter references to the second coming are brief and hortatory (1 Peter 1:7,13; 4:7,13; 5:4). The idea of a lost letter is not foreign to the New Testament. In 1 Corinthians 5:9 Paul referred to a previous letter which he had written to Corinth. We do not have that letter unless some early hand "edited" it into our 1 and 2 Corinthians. Second Corinthians 2:1–4 and 7:8–9 may refer to still another "lost" letter from Paul to Corinth. The probability is that the apostles wrote many letters which we do not have.

Scoffers will come in the last days introduces the theme of Christ's return. It may be that Peter means that this fact was what they should remember from *the predictions of the holy prophets* as well as from *the commandment of the Lord* as it had been passed on by the *apostles.* It was very generally held by the early Christians that the final stages of God's redemptive work would be marked by opposition and false teachers (Matt. 24:3–5,11,23–26; Acts 20: 29–31; 1 Tim. 4:1 ff.; 2 Tim. 3:1 ff.; James 5:3; Jude 18; 1 John 2:18–29; 4:3).

The last days means that the redemptive process which God set in motion with the call of Abraham (Gen. 12) reached its final stages in the incarnation, death, and resurrection of Christ. Paul called it the "fulness of the time" (Gal. 4:4, KJV). Hebrews 1:2 designated it "these last days," and Hebrews 9:26 posited Christ's sacrificial death as being "at the end of the age"; the expression literally means "at the bringing together of the ends of the ages."

3 Space prohibits a desirable review of this entire question. Very honest and objective discussion of the question by two scholars sympathetic to the view that Peter wrote both epistles may be studied in Guthrie, pp. 143–71, and Green, pp. 13–40.

Christ's death and resurrection joined the end of the old age to the beginning of the new age. From that time, the world has been in *the last days* which will culminate in his second coming.

Scoffers refers to those who were denying the doctrine of the second coming. They were scoffing at the promise of his coming as an empty promise. The evidence is clear in the New Testament that the early Christians anticipated an early return of Christ. They lived in expectation of it. As that early return was not realized, problems of discouragement, perplexity, and doubt arose. Reflections of this condition are in 1 Thessalonians 4; 1 Corinthians 15; James 5; Hebrews 10. Luke's entire treatment of Jesus' discussion of his going away, the destruction of Jerusalem (A.D. 70), and his ultimate coming in judgment is organized to emphasize that the time between those events was to be a time, not of idle waiting, but of active witnessing (Luke 21:5–36). This is a part of his entire theological motif in Luke-Acts; the so-called delay of the Parousia was not to be a cause for discouragement but an opportunity for witnessing. Peter uses that theme in this passage (3:9, 15).

Those who were scoffing at the teaching of the second coming may or may not have been the false teachers of chapter 2. The matter is not clear. It is clear that they had rejected the Christian way of life and had determined their own sinful course—*following their own passions.* Their argument was that the world order was a stable one. It did not change. As it was in the old days (when *the fathers fell asleep,* i.e., died), so it was in their day—*all things have continued as they were from the beginning of creation.* Their view was the rejection of the idea that God would break into that stable world order by the return of Christ to end the order. It was a naturalistic view of the world order which left no place for the injection of the divine purpose. Hence, they mocked what they considered to be the naive faith of the Christians that Christ would return to consummate the world order and to inaugurate the eternal order.

Peter explained their error by three basic ideas. (1) They ignored the fact that God, who created the world and established its order, has remained active in that order and will continue to do so until his purpose is realized (vv. 5–7). (2) They ignored the fact that God is not limited by time, nor does he reckon time as men do (vv. 8–10). (3) They failed to see the forbearance of God in not ending the world order so that others may come to salvation and Christian maturity (vv. 9,11–18a).

By the word of God recalls the Genesis 1 account of creation. The creative word of God called order out of chaos in creating the world order. Note the unfolding ideas in vv. 5–7: The earth was called up out of the water (Gen. 1:9) as part of the work of the Creator. Also the work of the Creator caused the waters to arise over the earth again in the judgment of the flood (Gen. 7:11–24). The Creator is still at work in the world which was reclaimed from the flood water (Gen. 8:1–5). It is still within his purpose to judge the evil of the world. That judgment will not be by water, but by fire.

The Stoic philosophers of Peter's day believed in cycles of alternating destruction and renovation of the world by fire and water. Peter's view, however, does not appear to be related to that. His view is based on Hebrew religious thought. The most destructive natural forces known were water and fire. God had promised not to destroy the world again by water (Gen. 9:11–17). God was often spoken of as a consuming fire (Deut. 4:24; Mal. 4:1), and his judgment was to be as a consuming fire (Heb. 10:27). Hence, Peter's readers should ignore the scoffers. They should understand that God is still working out his purpose in his creation and that purpose included a consummative day of judgment and destruction of ungodly men.

2. Assurance of His Coming (3:8–10)

⁸ But do not ignore this one fact, beloved, that with the Lord one day is as a thousand years, and a thousand years as one day. ⁹ The Lord is not slow about his promise as some count slowness, but is forbearing toward you, not wishing that any should perish, but that all should reach repentance. ¹⁰ But the day of the Lord will come like a thief, and then the heavens will pass away with a loud noise, and the elements will be dissolved with fire, and the earth and the works that are upon it will be burned up.

Peter began his encouraging word by quoting Psalm 90:4. God is not limited by time as men are. With him one day is as a thousand years or conversely a thousand years as one day. The point is that temporal distinctions are not a part of God's consideration in working out his plans. He does not say, "I must do this in one day—I must do this in ten years, or a hundred or a thousand." What men consider as undue delay in fulfilling his promise that Christ will return is not to be explained as slowness on God's part. The verb which is translated slow (v. 9) meant hesitating—God is not hesitant about bringing the world order to judgment in the coming of Christ.

The delay is rather to be explained by God's mercy in not bringing it to an end sooner. Forbearing means that God bears long with man's weakness and sin. Not wishing that any should perish means that he desires all men to come to salvation and gives them ample time to do so. His desire is that all should reach repentance before that day of judgment comes. While he desires that all shall be saved, he can bless with salvation only those who come to repentance and the acceptance of his plan.

The day of the Lord will come is the strong affirmation of the certainty of it. Men may think that it is unduly long in coming. Men may give up hope in its coming. Men may even deny and scoff at the idea of its coming, but it will come. That certainty is a part of the entire New Testament teaching on the subject.

It will come like a thief means when men are not expecting it (Matt. 24:43; Luke 12:39; 1 Thess. 5:2). It will mean the end of the world order as men know it now.

The apocalyptic description of that end is not beyond the belief of twentieth-century man who lives with nuclear fission. "Total Hiroshima" is a very real prospect! *Loud noise* is from a word which means "a swishing sound." Imagine the "swish" of a rocket. With such a sound *the heavens* (i.e., the upper atmosphere of our earth) simply disappears. *The elements* may mean the basic materials of which the planet is made: water, soil, mineral, etc. Or it may refer to the heavenly bodies—planets, stars, moon, sun, etc. The meaning is their disappearance as they are *dissolved with fire.* So ancient man thought of the end of his world; so modern man fears the end of his world. Whatever is literal or symbolic, the language affirms the awesome fact that this present world order is not designed to last forever. The present sinful order is doomed. It awaits the time determined by the infinite purpose of God. Beyond it, man hopes for that "new kind of heaven and new kind of earth" (author's translation) into which sin can never enter (Rev. 21–22), *in which righteousness dwells.*

3. Living for His Coming (3:11–18a)

¹¹ Since all these things are thus to be dissolved, what sort of persons ought you to be in lives of holiness and godliness, ¹² waiting for and hastening the coming of the day of God, because of which the heavens will be kindled and dissolved, and the elements will melt with fire! ¹³ But according to his promise we wait for new heavens and a new earth in which righteousness dwells.
¹⁴ Therefore, beloved, since you wait for these, be zealous to be found by him without spot or blemish, and at peace. ¹⁵ And count the forbearance of our Lord as salvation. So also our beloved brother Paul wrote to you according to the wisdom given him, ¹⁶ speaking of this as he does in all his letters. There are some things in them hard to understand, which the ignorant and unstable twist to their own destruction, as they do the other scriptures. ¹⁷ You therefore, beloved, knowing this beforehand, beware lest you be carried away with the error of lawless men and lose your own stability. ¹⁸ But grow in the grace and knowledge of our Lord and Savior Jesus Christ.

Peter sees the certain end of the present world order as an incentive to *lives of holiness and godliness.* Throughout the New Testament, the coming of Christ is held out as a motive for right living. It is on that practical note that Peter concludes—*what sort of persons ought* we to be?[4]
(1) We should live holy lives, *without spot or blemish.* (2) We should live *at peace* with our fellowmen. (3) We should be diligent in evangelism, counting the time of waiting as an opportunity for *salvation* to come to others.

Peter emphasized this by a reference to Pauline letters which were known to his readers. The particular letters are not identified. According to Peter, they contained *some things* which were *hard to understand.* If Paul had had an opportunity to read 1 Peter 3:19–21 and 2 Peter 2:10–13, he might have countered with the same charge! Peter knew of cases in which *ignorant and unstable* men had twisted the meaning of Paul's writings as well as other Scriptures to their own ruin. The twisting meant that they misinterpreted Paul's letters intentionally and in such way as to support their own views. These persons may have been the false teachers and scoffers of whom he had been writing. His reference to Paul's writings as authoritative is one of the main starting places in the study of the formation of the Christian canon.

(4) We should beware of *the error of lawless men* (false teachers and scoffers) and not lose our own stability in standing up for truth. (5) We should continue to *grow in the grace and knowledge* which have their source in Christ. This growth looks to maturity as the people of God.

Conclusion (3:18b)

To him be the glory both now and to the day of eternity. Amen.

Fittingly, the epistle closes with a doxology to Christ—*To him be glory both now and to the day of eternity. Amen.*

[4] For more complete exposition of this passage see Summers, *op. cit.*, pp. 139–43.

1-2-3 John

EDWARD A. McDOWELL

Introduction

The First Epistle of John may be called more accurately a tract or homily. It does not have the form of an epistle. There is no formal salutation in which the author identifies himself, nor is there an identification of the persons to whom the writing is addressed. The customary farewell of an epistle is absent. Second and third John are brief personal letters, the former addressed to one church, the latter to an individual and through him to a church. The second and third epistles are of approximately the same length, and each was likely written on a single sheet of papyrus.

The three writings are strongly reminiscent of the Gospel of John in language and simple structure of sentences. Though simple in language, the first epistle, like the Gospel, is profound in thought. It is not as orderly in organization as is the Gospel. What appears to be its lack of order suggests that it may have been dictated to a scribe out of the author's memory of oft-repeated conversations and sermons. This apparent lack of logical order is caused by the repetition and overlapping of topics, but the overall effect of this pattern is to tie the topics together in a manner to give emphasis to their inseparable relationship.

1. Authorship

The second and third epistles are manifestly from the same hand. In v. 1 of each the author identifies himself as "The elder." In 2 John 1 the author addresses his readers as those "whom I love in truth." The author applies precisely the same words to Gaius, to whom the third epistle is addressed. In the conclusion of 2 John the author states that he had much to write but preferred not to use "paper and ink" (v. 12); in 3 John 13 the author uses the expression "pen and ink." In both letters he expresses the hope that he would see his readers soon and talk with them "face to face," in the Greek *stoma pros stoma,* "mouth to mouth." These similarities and differences, together with obvious likeness in form, style, and simplicity of language, are evidence that neither of these little letters was the work of a copyist but that both were written by the same individual. Internal evidence also suggests that the person who wrote these two letters wrote 1 John. The statements concerning the commandment of love in 1 John 2:7–8 and 2 John 5–6 are quite similar but sufficiently different to indicate that the same author expressed himself independently the second time concerning the same subject, as a copyist would not do. The same is true concerning the statement describing the false teachers who denied that Jesus had come in the flesh (1 John 4:1–3; 2 John 7). In both epistles these false teachers are branded as deceivers and as antichrists, but in 1 John it is the "spirit of antichrist" which refuses to make the right confession. Another and stronger illustration of independence in a second writing concerning the same idea is in the difference in the

Greek words for the coming of Christ in the flesh. In 1 John 4:2 the perfect participle is used and is rightly translated "has come," while in 2 John 7 the present participle is used and is correctly translated "coming."

The expression "walking in truth" (Gr.) is found in 2 John 4 and in 3 John 3-4. The idea of walking as descriptive of living the Christian life, or of living in sin, is prominent in 1 John (1:7; 1:6; 2:6; 2:11). In 1 John 1:7 the Christian life is described as walking "in the light," but this is coupled with "doing the truth" (Gr. v. 6).

The similarities in terminology and ideas that link the epistles so closely are reminiscent of the Gospel of John and suggest common authorship of all four writings. Among these are the emphasis on the coming of Christ in the flesh (John 1:14; 1 John 1:1–3; 4:2–3; 2 John 7); the contrast between walking in the light and walking in the darkness (John 12:35; 1 John 1:5–7); the new commandment of love (John 13:34; 1 John 2:7–8; 2 John 5–6) and others. A strong link between the Gospel and 1 John is the claim that each makes of being written by an eye witness to Jesus (John 1:14; 19:35; 21:24; 1 John 1:1–3). This is all the more significant because in no other New Testament writing is the claim made except in 2 Peter (1:16–18).

In the prologues of both the Gospel and 1 John "the Word" is identified as "the life." In both prologues there is no mistaking the identification of "the Word" and "the life" as Jesus Christ.

There are, however, differences in ideas and points of view between the Gospel and the first epistle. A. H. McNeile has summarized these in *An Introduction to the Study of the New Testament.*[1] Among the distinctives in the epistle are: no quotations from the Old Testament, no expression of hostility to the Jews, no reference to popular messianic ideas, more emphasis on eschatology, the conception of God

ethical rather than metaphysical, and stress laid on what Christ means for men rather than on his eternal relationship with the Father. McNeile sees a significant difference in the two writings in the epistle's use of the neuter, "That which was from the beginning" and the expression "concerning the word of life" (1:1), as contrasted with the Gospel's "In the beginning was the Word," and "in him was life" (1:1,4). McNeile concludes his summary (p. 305) by stating that the arguments for separate authorship on the basis of the differences have been subjected to very searching criticism and that "the verdict reached after careful linguistic analysis by R. H. Charles and A. E. Brooke that the Fourth Gospel and all three Johannine epistles were penned by the same person has not been overthrown."

James Moffatt[2] discusses at some length the differences between the Gospel and the first epistle. He concludes that "the characteristic traits of the Fourth Gospel and the First epistle betray a difference beneath their unity which is best accounted for by the supposition that while the writer of the epistle lived and moved within the circle in which the Fourth Gospel originated, he had an individuality and purpose of his own." Also he sees the theme of the Gospel as "Jesus is the Christ," while the theme of the epistle is "the Christ is Jesus."

The tradition that has come to us from the church fathers of the second century is that the apostle John was the author of 1 and 2 John, as well as of the Gospel. The tradition of the Johannine authorship of 3 John did not appear until the fourth century. Eusebius, who wrote his *Ecclesiastical History* after he became bishop of Caesarea in A.D. 313, preserved the tradition that came to him from the second century. He wrote (Book 3, chapter 24 of the *History*) that 1 John, as well as the Gospel, was acknowledged without controversy by

---

1 2nd. ed., rev. C. S. C. Williams (Oxford: The Clarendon Press, 1953), p. 303 ff.

2 *An Introduction to the Literature of the New Testament* (New York: Charles Scribner's Sons, 1911), pp. 589–593.

men of his own time, as well as by "the ancients," to be of the writings of John. By "John" he means John the apostle. At this same place, and in chapter 25, Eusebius reported that 2 and 3 John were among the disputed writings, but they are not in his list of spurious works named here.

The Muratorian Fragment, which gives a list of the accepted New Testament books, dated not much later than A.D. 170, identifies the author of the Gospel and the epistle (perhaps "epistles" from the Latin *epistulis*) as "of the disciples." It is impossible to determine whether or not the author includes 3 John in this statement. The author of the Fragment goes on to comment that John professes that he was not only an eye witness, but also a hearer of the wonderful works of the Lord in order. (He quotes from 1 John 1:1.)

Irenaeus (A.D. 135–200), bishop of Lyons, who as a boy knew Polycarp, who had known John (*Eccles. Hist.*, 5:20; Iren. *Against Heresies* III.3.4), quoted from 2 John II and identified the author of the words as "John the disciple of the Lord" (*Against Heresies* I.16.3; cf. III.16.8; 2 John 7,8). Irenaeus also preserves the tradition that the apostle John lived in Ephesus and remained with the church there until the time of the Emperor Trajan (A.D. 98–117).[3] Eusebius (*Eccles. Hist.*, 3.23) wrote that the "very disciple whom Jesus loved" returned to Asia from his exile after the death of Domitian (A.D. 96) and administered the churches there.

From these citations it is clear that the tradition of the second-century church fathers is that the apostle John was the author of 1 John and the Gospel of John, and that he was a resident of Ephesus in his latter years. Origen (A.D. 185–254) included 1 John among the canonical writings. Concerning the other two epistles, he wrote that John had left "perhaps also a second and third; but not all consider them genuine" (*Eccles. Hist.*, 6.25). Jerome (331–420) accepted the three epistles as

written by the apostle John but took note of the fact that others attributed 2 and 3 John to a different author, John the Elder (*De Viris Illustribus*, IX). As we have seen, there is some early patristic evidence that John wrote the second epistle. The language, style, and form of the third epistle so closely resemble that of 2 John that we are justified in bracketing together the two little letters as to authorship.

There is no general agreement among modern scholars that the apostle John was the author of either the Gospel or the epistles. James Moffatt has left this categorical statement: "The so-called 'first epistle of John' is neither an epistle nor is it John's— if by John is meant the son of Zebedee."[4] Moffatt's view is that 2 and 3 John were probably written by "John the presbyter," who was not the author of 1 John but was likely the author of the book of Revelation.[5] Moffatt's position with respect to the author of the Gospel is that he was unknown ("unless John the presbyter is brought in") and that nothing in the Gospel necessarily implies that he was an eyewitness.[6] C. H. Dodd's "tentative conclusion" was that the three epistles "were written in the Province of Asia, between A.D. 96 and 110 (or thereabouts), by one of the 'Presbyters' who are known to have lived in that province at that period" (Dodd, p. lxviii f.).

My own theory is that the apostle John wrote the Gospel with the assistance of a collaborator, who might well have been the man named Nicodemus, a brilliant Pharisee who was well versed in Jewish-Alexandrian philosophy. I hold that the apostle wrote the three epistles without assistance.

It seems reasonable, in the absence of positive evidence to the contrary, to accept the testimony of the early church fathers, who were closer to the scene by 1800 years than twentieth-century scholars. We may also conclude that whoever wrote 2

---

[3] *Against Heresies*, II.22.5 and III.3.4.

[4] *Op. cit.*, p. 594.
[5] *Ibid.*, p. 481.
[6] *Ibid.*, pp. 569 f.

John wrote 3 John and therefore attribute with a fair degree of confidence all three epistles to the apostle. It is true that the writer of 2 and 3 John calls himself "the elder" and that no such identification is made of himself by the author of 1 John, but this need not rule out the possibility that the apostle John in his later years might refer to himself as "the elder." It appears that Papias in his well-known statement referred to the apostles as elders (*Eccles. Hist.*, 3.39).

II. *Date of Writing*

Evidence from the church fathers discussed above, combined with the similarities in language and style which tend to link the writings in a common authorship, indicate that the epistles of John, as well as the Gospel, were written in the last quarter of the first century. This conclusion is confirmed in other citations from the church fathers that may be given. Polycarp, bishop of Smyrna, who suffered martyrdom in A.D. 156 at the age of 86, in his Letter to the Philippians (VII) quoted almost verbatim from 1 John 4:2–3. That letter was written between A.D. 107 and 116 near to the time of the martyrdom of Ignatius during the reign of Trajan (A.D. 98–117). Papias (*ca.* A.D. 140) used proofs from 1 John, according to Eusebius (*Eccles. Hist.*, 3.39.)

It is significant that the oldest fragment of the New Testament yet found is a piece of papyrus upon which is written a few verses of the Gospel of John (18:31–33,37–38).[7] Reliable authorities have dated it in the first half of the second century. Among the most important of New Testament manuscript discoveries is P[66], the Bodmer Papyrus II, a codex of the Gospel of John, dated around A.D. 200. (The earliest of the great uncial manuscripts, Codex Vaticanus and Codex Aleph, belong to the fourth century.)

Another of the important Bodmer manuscripts P[75] is a codex of the Gospels of Luke and John. The editors date this manuscript between A.D. 175 and 225.

The Dead Sea Scrolls have revealed that certain ideas found in the Gospel and epistles of John (such as the contrast between light and darkness) were current in some Jewish circles in the early first century.[8]

In a remarkable way recent papyri and archaeological discoveries have tended to confirm the tradition that the Gospel and epistles of John have come down to us from the last quarter of the first century.

III. *Purpose*

Three times in the first epistle John indicated his purpose in writing. He declared that he wrote (1) to make his joy complete (1:4), (2) to warn his readers not to fall into sin (2:1), (3) to assure the faithful among his readers that they possessed eternal life (5:13). It is necessary, however, to go beyond these expressions of purpose in order to set forth more comprehensively the several objectives, in addition to those stated, that John had in mind in sending out this letter to the churches. These objectives may be stated as follows:

1. John wrote *to warn against false teachers* whose twisted ideas concerning Jesus the Christ threatened to disrupt the *koinōnia*, the fellowship. In the prologue to his letter he makes plain the fact that the foundation of the fellowship is nothing less than the complete and unalloyed incarnation. He set out to proclaim to his readers "the eternal life which was with the Father and was made manifest to us . . . so that you may have ('go on having') fellowship with us; and our fellowship is with the Father and with his son Jesus Christ" (1:2,3). He would show in his letter the glory of this fellowship and how it could be enjoyed only by those who stood firmly upon the eternal foundation

---

[7] Now in the John Rylands Library of the University of Manchester, Manchester, England.

[8] See Raymond E. Brown, ch. XII, *The Scrolls and the New Testament*, ed. Krister Stendahl (New York: Harper and Bros., 1957), p. 206; cf. Millar Burrows, *The Dead Sea Scrolls*, (New York: The Viking Press, 1955), p. 83. Burrows believes that the manuscripts of the Scrolls are to be dated not far from the beginning of the Christian era.

of the incarnation.

So deeply does John feel about these false teachers that his indictment of them reminds us of the days when he lived up to the name "son of thunder," bestowed upon him by his Master. He brands a false teacher as the "liar" and "the antichrist" (2:22). These teachers are "false prophets" who are possessed "of the spirit of antichrist." He who is possessed of such a spirit does not confess "that Jesus Christ has come in the flesh" (4:1–3). These false prophets had deserted the fellowship. They were "antichrists" who "went out from us, but they were not of us; for if they had been of us, they would have continued with us" (2:18–19). It is plain that John has these same heretics in mind when he asks, "Who is the liar but he who denies that Jesus is the Christ?" and then proceeds with the declaration "This is the antichrist, he who denies the Father and the Son" (2:22–25).

Some of the false teachers, we observe, denied the humanity of Jesus—they refused to believe that the Christ had come in the flesh. On the other hand, there were those who denied his deity—they declared that the man Jesus was not Christ the Son.

The study of the Dead Sea Scrolls has confirmed the view, long held by some scholars, that these false teachers whom John attacked with such vehemence were the forerunners of the full-fledged Gnostics of the second century.[9]

This movement that culminated in second-century gnosticism was a philosophy based on the premise that matter is evil. When it invaded Christianity in the first century, its exponents adapted Christian beliefs to their own peculiar views concerning the universe and human existence. Their deadliest perversion of Christian doctrine was with respect to the person of Christ. They held that since matter was evil it was impossible that God, who was pure spirit and wholly good, could in any way be involved in matter. One group

held that Jesus was not in fact a man but only appeared to be (Docetists). This explains why John attacked the false prophets who denied that Jesus Christ had come in the flesh. Another group held that the Christ of God could not be involved in human suffering; therefore, they said, the Christ came upon the man Jesus at his baptism but left him before he suffered on the cross. This was an assault upon the deity of Christ and explains John's denunciation of anyone who denied that Jesus was the Christ.

These "pre-Gnostics" divided into two camps with respect to morals. One group taught that the way to overcome the evils of the flesh was by rigid asceticism. The other, in keeping with their dualistic interpretation of the universe, held that soul (or spirit) and body were separate and that once the soul was saved it was above contamination by the body and sin. Such a belief ran naturally into antinomianism and could become a serious menace to the moral and spiritual health of a church. The Balaamites and Nicolaitans who menaced the church at Pergamum (Rev. 2:14 f.) and the followers of the Jezebel in the church at Thyatira (Rev. 2:20–25) were doubtless representatives of this type of perverted Christian belief. These were the people who had "learned what some call the deep things of Satan" (Rev. 2:24). Having been initiated into the realm of the higher *gnōsis* they believed they could outwit Satan and enjoy the lusts and pleasures of the flesh without committing sin or involving the soul. Such teaching probably explains John's sharp attack upon those who said "we have no sin" (1 John 1:8).

The Gnostics taught that salvation was achieved through *gnōsis*, knowledge. Initiation into the higher realm of divine knowledge, they believed, won for them a place among the spiritually elite. It is understandable how such teaching within a Christian group would disrupt the fellowship by pitting a group of the elite against mere lowly believers. Further disruption of fellowship would occur when certain of

---

[9] See Stendahl (ed.), *ibid.*, ch. 2 by Oscar Cullmann, p. 19, and Burrows, *ibid.*, p. 252.

the elite would claim to be above sin and practice immorality in defiance of the Christian ethic.

The second epistle of John warns against these false teachers. The "elect lady and her children" are not to receive as guests any traveling evangelists who "will not acknowledge the coming of Jesus Christ in the flesh" or refuse to abide in the doctrine of Christ (vv. 7,9,10).

2. John wrote for *the sheer joy of sharing the marvelous experience* he had known of personal association with Jesus. This is the joy that overflows in the statement: "And we are writing this that our joy may be complete." He was now an old man, but time has accentuated the memories of the wonderful days in Galilee and Judea with the Master. "The word of life" incarnated in Jesus, John and the others had heard, had seen with their eyes, had looked upon, had touched with their hands! This was the overwhelming realization that had grown with the passing years. And now the supreme joy of his latter years was to share the experience he had had with Jesus, and interpret, as he was able, the meaning of that experience. Few years were left to him, and doubtless he was the last of the twelve remaining alive. He recognized his obligation to the churches. He had, with the help of a friend, written in his Gospel his memories of the ministry of Jesus. Now he must interpret in practical terms the test and rewards of discipleship and also sound warnings against ominous false teachings that threatened the life of the churches. And so he wrote his epistle. To share again the glory of experience with Jesus and its meaning for mortal men gave him overflowing joy.

3. John's purpose in writing his first epistle was also *to set forth some important tests of discipleship* and thereby provide criteria upon which his readers might base assurance of their salvation and possession of eternal life. The tests are these: (1) walking in the light, which is the same as obeying Christ's commandments (1:7; 2:3–6); (2) keeping the all-important commandment to love the brethren (2:9–11; 3:10,15–16; 4:7,20; 5:1–2); (3) having faith in Jesus Christ as the Son of God (2:23; 4:15; 5:1,5,10,12,13); (4) living a life of victory over sin (3:4–10; 5:18); (5) recognizing the presence of God's Spirit in the life (3:24; 4:13).

4. In the light of the tremendous emphasis in 1 John upon love (*agapē*) and the uniqueness of the statement "God is love" (4:8,16), it must have been within the scope of John's purpose to leave as a legacy to posterity *his interpretation of the love he had experienced in the life and teaching of Jesus.* The Greek noun for love—*agapē*—occurs in 1 John 18 times, more often than in any other book in the New Testament. It occurs in 2 John twice, in 3 John once. How much richer we are for the interpretation of love John has given us!

The purpose of the second and third epistles can be briefly stated. As has been indicated, 2 John was written to warn against hospitality to traveling missionaries who were carriers of the heresy which denied the humanity of Christ (docetism). The letter was also directed against entertaining those who repudiated the deity of Christ (v. 9).

The purpose of 3 John was to encourage hospitality to traveling missionaries (vv. 5–6), but there is no warning in the letter against heretics. In the letter the author castigated and warned Diotrephes because he had repudiated the Elder's authority and refused to entertain visiting brethren and was excluding from the church those who were welcoming them (vv. 9–10). The Elder contrasted the conduct of this arrogant church dictator with that of Demetrius who is highly commended (vv. 11–12).

IV. Destination

It is not known to what church or churches 1 John was directed. The author must have been on fairly intimate terms with the recipients because he addressed them as "My little children" (2:1), "Beloved" (2:7; 4:1,7,11), "little children"

(2:12,28), "Children" (2:18). Most likely these were the churches named in Revelation 1:11 and chapters 2 and 3, with the addition of the churches in Tralles, Magnesia, Miletus, Hierapolis, and Colosse. John was doubtless considered a sort of bishop or traveling overseer of these churches. By virtue of his apostleship he would be a welcome visitor and well beloved in all these churches.

"The elect lady and her children," to whom the second epistle is addressed, almost certainly describes a church, what church we do not know, but most likely one of the churches mentioned above.

The third epistle is addressed to Gaius, but it was probably intended to be read to the church of which Gaius was a member, and perhaps pastor. This church must have been one of those in the province of Asia mentioned above. It might very well have been the same church to which 2 John was addressed.

Selected Bibliography

ALEXANDER, NEIL, *The Epistles of John* ("Torch Commentaries.") London: SCM Press. 1962.

BARCLAY, WILLIAM, *The Letters of John and Jude.* 2nd ed. Philadelphia: Westminster Press. 1960.

BROOKE, ALAN E., *A Critical and Exegetical Commentary on the Johannine Epistles,* ("International Critical Commentary.") Edinburgh: T. & T. Clark. 1912. (Greek text.)

DANA, H. E., *The Epistles and Apocalypse of John.* Dallas: Baptist Book Store. 1937.

DODD, C. H., *The Johannine Epistles.* ("Moffatt New Testament Commentary.") New York and London: Harper & Brothers. 1946.

FINDLAY, GEORGE G., *Fellowship in Life Eternal,* An Exposition of the Epistles of St. John. Grand Rapids: Wm. B. Eerdmans Publishing Co. 1955.

LEWIS, GRENVILLE P., *The Johannine Epistles.* ("Epworth Preacher's Commentaries.") London: The Epworth Press. 1961.

LOVE, JULIAN PRICE, *1-2-3 John, Jude, Revelation* ("Layman's Bible Commentary.") Richmond: John Knox Press. 1960.

PLUMMER, A., *The Epistles of St. John.* ("Cambridge Greek Testament for Schools and Colleges.") Cambridge: The University Press. 1938. (Greek text).

STOTT, JOHN R. W., *The Epistles of John.* Grand Rapids: Wm. B. Eerdmans Publishing Co. 1964.

WESTCOTT, B. F., *The Epistles of St. John.* Cambridge and London: Macmillan and Co. 1886. (Greek text.)

Commentary on 1 John

Outline

I. Maintaining the fellowship (1:5—2:17)
Prologue (1:1-4)
I. Maintaining the fellowship (1:5—2:17)
 1. God is light (1:5-10)
 2. Christ our advocate (2:1-6)
 3. The old-new commandment (2:7-11)
 4. Victory over the world (2:12-17)
II. The antichrists (2:18-29)
 1. The antichrists described (2:18-25)
 2. Reliance upon the Spirit (2:26-27)
 3. Abiding in Christ (2:28-29)
III. The meaning of sonship (3:1—5:12)
 1. Glory of sonship (3:1-3)
 2. Sonship and sin (3:4-10)
 3. Love of the brethren (3:11-18)
 4. Assurance and obedience (3:19-24)
 5. Testing the prophets (4:1-6)
 6. God is love (4:7-12)
 7. Love and assurance (4:13-21)
 8. Love and faith in the Son (5:1-5)
 9. The three witnesses (5:6-12)
IV. Concluding counsel (5:13-21)
 1. Assurance and prayer (5:13-17)
 2. Victory with the Son (5:18-21)

Prologue (1:1-4)

[1] That which was from the beginning, which we have heard, which we have seen with our eyes, which we have looked upon and touched with our hands, concerning the word of life— [2] the life was made manifest, and we saw it, and testify to it, and proclaim to you the eternal life which was with the Father and was made manifest to us—[3] that which we have seen and heard we proclaim also to you, so

that you may have fellowship with us; and our fellowship is with the Father and with his Son Jesus Christ. 4 And we are writing this that our joy may be complete.

These remarkable words suggest at once the close relationship of the epistle with the Gospel of John. The two prologues have in common (1) the Word, (2) the life, (3) the Word as the life, (4) the Word as in the beginning, (5) the beholding of the Word. But the prologue of the epistle has a distinctive character of its own. It is much more personal in tone, and it is more vitally related with the body of the writing it is designed to introduce. There are two points of emphasis in the prologue of the epistle that stand out above all else: first, the personal experience of the author with *the word of life;* second, identification of believers with *the life . . . made manifest,* the source of *koinōnia,* the fellowship.

The epistle begins majestically with the words *That which was from the beginning,* and in this it is reminiscent of the Gospel. The *beginning* here can hardly mean less than "the beginning" means in John 1:1 where it denotes the eternity and timelessness of the Word. The Word in the Gospel is the Logos, the eternal intermediary between God and man and the agent of all creation. In the Gospel we read "in him was life"; in the epistle the expression is *the word of life,* by which is meant "the word which is life."

Both here and in the Gospel there is reflected the influence of Greek thought and the Logos concept propounded by the Jewish-Alexandrian philosopher Philo. But for Philo *incarnation* of the Logos was inconceivable—and this is just the difference between Greek philosophy and Christianity: a Logos which remains remote from man within the exalted supramundane realm as over against the preexistent Logos-Christ who enters human history as a man, Jesus of Nazareth. The incarnation for John in both the Gospel and this epistle is the foundation of authentic Christianity. In the epistle it is also the inescapable basis upon which the Christian fellowship rests.

We are not to assume that the influence of Greek thought dominates either the Gospel or the first epistle because John uses the Logos concept. As a matter of fact, the Gospel is basically Jewish or Hebrew in ideology. Insofar as the Logos or Word concept is concerned, we may relate this to the Old Testament idea of the *dabar,* or word, of God, as well as to Philo's Logos teaching. In the Old Testament a word was often conceived to be the projection of the character of the man who uttered it. So the word of God was the projection of the mind or the character of God and was inseparable from him. In a sense, the word of Jehovah was Jehovah himself among his people. When we meet, therefore, with the Word in the Gospel, or *the word of life* in the first epistle, we are to understand that the Hebrew background is here as well as the Greek. Jesus Christ as *the word of life* is the projection of the mind or character of God into the world of men and human affairs.

There is extraordinary emphasis in the prologue of the epistle on the personal experience of the author with the incarnate word. In the Gospel the one statement "we beheld his glory" (1:14, KJV) suffices, but in the epistle, John piles up words and repeats himself in an eloquent effort to express his feelings of amazement and wonder that he and his fellow disciples were companions of him who as *the word of life . . . was made manifest.* As if the Greek verb for *we have seen* were not sufficient to express his emotion at the recall of his memorable experience, John in the beginning adds *with our eyes* and twice repeats the word. This verb and the twice-used Greek verb for *we have heard* are in the perfect tense, which accentuates the vivid present reality of the author's past experience. To the aged apostle the days with Jesus were as real as if they were but yesterdays. But he adds yet another claim to reenforce the emphasis on personal experience with *the word of life.* It was not only *That which . . . we have looked upon* but

That . . . which . . . we have touched with our hands. The statement *we have touched* is the rendition of a Greek verb which emphasizes physical contact, and the stronger translation, "our hands have handled" (KJV), is better. It is the word used by Luke (24:39) to render the appeal of the risen Jesus to his terrified disciples to "handle" him.

The life was made manifest is a terse statement which in its few words comprehends the entire Christ event. *Life* is one of the key words of the Gospel. Its introduction here in John's opening words is another evidence of the close relationship between the Gospel and the epistle. *Life* here and in the Gospel has its source in God and is mediated to men by Jesus Christ the Son of God. It is eternal life, life above the common, life that transcends simple existence. Concerning the Logos, John had written "the Word was with God" (John 1:1). Here he declares *the eternal life* was *with the Father—pros ton patera.* The Greek in John 1:1 is *pros ton theon* (with or in the presence of God). In both instances the author is referring to the preexistent state of Christ as the Word or the Logos.

John declares that he is proclaiming this *eternal life* in order that his readers *may have fellowship (koinōnia) with us.* Thus he projects one of the chief objectives of his letter and forecasts the subject of the first main division of the epistle (1:5—2:17). This is not a denial of existing fellowship between the author and his readers. His purpose is to affirm the incarnation as the only true basis of Christian fellowship, for he declares *our fellowship is with the Father and with his Son Jesus Christ.* His meaning is clear: membership in the fellowship of believers is based upon union with God through Jesus Christ the Son. As the body of the epistle will show, John was concerned that the fellowship would not be disrupted by false teachers who, on one hand, denied the humanity of Jesus and, on the other, denied his deity. His proclamation therefore is a call to loyalty to the basic doctrine of the faith.

Since *koinōnia,* Greek for fellowship, is a major topic of interest in the first epistle, it is essential that we gain a clear conception of the content of the term as it is used here and in the New Testament as a whole. The idea expressed by the term in the New Testament is much more meaningful than the popular idea conveyed by "fellowship" as generally used. As stated above, the *koinōnia* projected in 1 John is based without equivocation upon the incarnation of God in Jesus Christ. This should remind us at once of its superiority to the friendship enjoyed in groups outside the church having common interests or of the fellowship enjoyed even by Christians in purely social gatherings.

The adjective upon which the term was built was *koinos,* which originally meant "common," i.e., belonging to several. The verb *koinōneō* meant to become a sharer, be made a partner, or to enter into a partnership. Koinonia in the New Testament was applied first to the community of disciples of Jesus which came into existence at Pentecost (Acts 2:41–47). But koinonia applied not only to the community but also to the experience of love enjoyed by these early believers. Basic to the love they shared and the existence of the community itself was their common experience with Jesus as Messiah and risen Lord. So real and deep was this experience that they held in trust their material possessions for the koinonia and sold them to provide food and clothing for the needy members of the church.

The author of 1 John does not depart from this original idea of the Christian koinonia. He simply expands and deepens the concept to show that the genesis and foundation of the Christian koinonia is the incarnation. He makes plain the fact that when men become partners of the Son of God through vital identification with him in his life, death, and resurrection, they become partners with and fellow workers of God. As such they share the mutual experience of divine love in the Christian fellowship and as partners in this fellowship.

The author closes his remarkable introduction with the statement: *we are writing this that our joy may be complete.* The Greek suggests his desire that his joy would be full to overflowing. The retelling of the oft-repeated story of his experience with Jesus and its meaning would give to him this overflowing joy.

I. Maintaining the Fellowship (1:5— 2:17)

1. God Is Light (1:5–10)

⁵ This is the message we have heard from him and proclaim to you, that God is light and in him is no darkness at all. ⁶ If we say we have fellowship with him while we walk in darkness, we lie and do not live according to the truth; ⁷ but if we walk in the light, as he is in the light, we have fellowship with one another, and the blood of Jesus his Son cleanses us from all sin. ⁸ If we say we have no sin, we deceive ourselves, and the truth is not in us. ⁹ If we confess our sins, he is faithful and just, and will forgive our sins and cleanse us from all unrighteousness. ¹⁰ If we say we have not sinned, we make him a liar, and his word is not in us.

In the prologue John introduced the fellowship which is to be the first subject of discussion. He has indicated that the earthly fellowship of believers exists only in their union with God through Jesus Christ. The source of the fellowship, therefore, is God, and the character of God determines the character of the fellowship. These truths account for the author's declaration of a great fundamental principle he and his fellow disciples had learned from Jesus: *God is light and in him is no darkness at all.*

Light and darkness as symbols of the contrasting spheres of good and evil are found frequently in the Old Testament and, of course, in the Gospel of John, providing evidence of the unmistakable tie between the Gospel and the epistle. The closest affinity of the New Testament with the Dead Sea Scrolls is found in the contrast between light and darkness that is made in both the Scrolls and the Johannine writings. The use in the Scrolls of these symbols and the concepts they represent shows that these ideas were current in Jewish circles in the early first century.[10]

In the prologue of the Gospel we see the contrast between light and darkness. The Logos is "the life" and "the life was the light of men." "The light shines in the darkness, and the darkness has not overcome it." The contrast then becomes a prominent concept in the Gospel (John 3:19–21; 8:12; 11:9–10; 12:35–36,46). The Old Testament background of the contrast may be illustrated from Isaiah's beautiful passage beginning: "Arise, shine; for your light is come" (60:1–3). Light as a symbol of God's being and presence may be seen in Psalms 4:6; 27:1; Isaiah 2:5; 60:20 ("the Lord shall be your everlasting light"), and elsewhere. Darkness as a symbol in the Old Testament of the realm of evil is found in Job 34:22 and Psalm 107:14. In the former it is the "deep darkness where evil doers may hide themselves."

Light, then, symbolizes in God primarily his holiness, although it represents his unapproachable glory and majesty as well. Jesus Christ is the "outshining" (Heb. 1:3) of God's character and as such creates the fellowship, the koinonia. Since God is light, the fellowship is in the realm of light. Abruptly, John begins to apply this principle: *If we say we have fellowship with him while we walk in darkness, we lie and do not live according to the truth* (Gr., "we do not the truth"). This is an inescapable conclusion to be universally applied, but the author is laying the foundation of the case he is to make against the disrupters of the fellowship who *walk in darkness* because of their claim to be without sin while living in sin. The implication is that even those who *walk in darkness* may claim to believe the truth without "doing" the truth. But there can be no genuine believing (*pisteuō*, trusting, having faith) apart from

---

10 See Burrows, *op. cit.,* pp. 338–340, and Brown, (ed. Stendahl), *op. cit.,* pp. 184–189.

practicing—living the truth.

Solid assurance is given concerning the fellowship of believers: *if we walk in the light, as he is in the light,* i.e., as God is in the light, *we have fellowship with one another.* This is equal to saying "if we live lives of holiness in keeping with God's holiness, we have fellowship with one another." Within the fellowship, founded thus upon the character of God, believers experience the solution of the problem of sin. In the fellowship *the blood of Jesus his Son cleanses us from all sin* (Gr., "continually cleanses us," present tense). The fellowship is a *holy* fellowship; it provides the continuous cleansing of its members, enabling them to live in union with God and one another.

The blood of Jesus is to be understood against the background of the blood of the animal offered in sacrifice in the Old Testament sacrificial system. The blood was thought to be the seat of life, the life itself (Gen. 9:4; Deut. 12:23). The life of the flesh was "in the blood" (Lev. 17:11), "and I have given it for you upon the altar to make atonement for your souls; for it is the blood that makes atonement, by reason of the life." The life of the animal in its blood was liberated by its death to represent the life of the individual or the congregation making the sacrifice. But the animal sacrifices of the Jewish sacrificial system were imperfect and inadequate. Of necessity they were repeated again and again. The animal was not a rational being, and there could be no fellowship between it and the person offering the sacrifice.

Jesus, by the pouring out of his life in his blood as the Son of God, provided the perfect sacrifice. With him, the true person, men may have fellowship, and in his life represented in his blood poured out on the cross they find the source of eternal life for themselves. The sacrifice offered by Christ was "once for all" (Heb. 9:12; 10:12), and by it he provided eternal redemption (Heb. 9:12), cleansing of conscience (Heb. 9:14), and sanctification (Heb. 10:10,14). Holiness in the fellow-ship is sustained through the cleansing power of *the blood of Jesus* because his blood is the unending life he continually gives to his own. The consciousness of forgiveness experienced by members of the fellowship is a powerful stimulant to love and brotherhood because love responds to love, and members of the fellowship know they are loved of God and have him as their common Father.

If we say we have no sin and *If we say we have not sinned* are conditions the author would have no cause to raise unless the danger of false teaching was present among those to whom he wrote. He is quite blunt in his characterization of this perfectionist doctrine, purveyed no doubt by those "pre-Gnostics" who taught that a saved soul was "pure" and above sin. Members of the fellowship who unwittingly believed such doctrine were victims of self-deception. But worse, they made God a liar—this is his meaning in the words *we make him a liar.* Why? Because God declared us to be sinners in sending his Son to save us from sin. God's *word is not in us* if we should in foolish pride or ignorance claim not to have sinned. The antithesis of such pride and ignorance is characteristic of members of the fellowship. They are people who instead of denying the presence of sin in their lives confess their sins. *If we confess our sins,* the result is forgiveness and cleansing. God's character is the guarantee of such result: *he is faithful and just.* The author has in mind both the initial confession accompanying conversion and the daily confession to God that the believer makes as a member of the fellowship. Daily confession as a duty of disciples was included by Jesus in the prayer he taught his disciples (Matt. 6:12; Luke 11:4).

Thus we learn that the fellowship is a cleansing and purifying fellowship. Its members are made holy not by the delusion of living above sin but by confession of sin and the power of the blood of Christ made continually available to them through their union with him in the fellowship.

2. Christ Our Advocate (2:1–6)

¹ My little children, I am writing this to you so that you may not sin; but if any one does sin, we have an advocate with the Father, Jesus Christ the righteous; ² and he is the expiation for our sins, and not for ours only but also for the sins of the whole world. ³ And by this we may be sure that we know him, if we keep his commandments. ⁴ He who says "I know him" but disobeys his commandments is a liar, and the truth is not in him; ⁵ but whoever keeps his word, in him truly love for God is perfected. By this we may be sure that we are in him: ⁶ he who says he abides in him ought to walk in the same way in which he walked.

The author does not wish his readers to presume upon their privilege of confessing sin and obtaining forgiveness. Addressing them in tenderness as *My little children,* he declares that he is writing to them *so that you may not sin.* John is careful with his tenses; here he uses the aorist and the meaning is "that you may not commit sin" or "fall into sin." He is not writing to keep them from going on in sin; he is writing to Christians, not to sinners. And so he uses the aorist again: *but if any one does sin,* not "if any one goes on sinning" (Gr., present tense). The present tense, denoting continuous action, is used in 3:4,6,8,9 to picture living in sin. In view of this usage we are justified in saying that John is careful with his tenses and that he uses the aorist (point or punctiliar action) in contrast with the present (durative).

For the Christian, the member of the fellowship (not for the nonbeliever), there is a remedy for the sin into which he falls: *we have an advocate with the Father, Jesus Christ the righteous.* The term used here for advocate is *paraklētos,* the same word used in John's Gospel by Jesus for the Holy Spirit. But Jesus thought of himself as the first Paraclete because he said, "And I will pray the Father, and he will give you another Counselor (*paraklētos*)" (John 14:16). The term means one called alongside another for purpose of help, counsel, or representation. Therefore the translations Comforter, Advocate, Counselor. Jesus Christ as our Advocate is *pros*

ton patera, with the Father, in close proximity to God, and yet ever by the side of him who is God's child. He has free access to the court of the great Judge and is accredited there. But he has standing on earth among men; he is *Jesus Christ the righteous.*

Our Advocate serves us in another capacity; *he is the expiation* ("propitiation," KJV) *for our sins,* and this is *for the sins of the whole world.* The word for expiation is *hilasmos.* It occurs only here and in 4:10. In the Septuagint the word is used to translate the Hebrew *kipurim,* which means a covering. The verb *hilaskomai* (Heb. 2:17; Luke 18:13) is used in the Septuagint to translate the Hebrew *kipur,* meaning to cover. The scriptural use of the terms is not to convey the idea of appeasing one who is angry toward another but of altering or removing the cause of alienation. The idea of propitiating or appeasing God is foreign to the New Testament. The sinner is reconciled to God, but God does the reconciling by providing in Christ the means of reconciliation. In Christ's death the cause of the sinner's enmity toward God is removed and his approach to God made possible through his union with Christ, who is the holy and righteous Advocate. It is in this sense that Christ is *the expiation for our sins, and not for ours only but also for the sins of the whole world.*

And by this we may be sure that we know him. The author now introduces the idea of obedience to Christ's commandments as evidence of the believer's assurance of his experience of Chirst. He expresses this as "knowing" Christ, but it is experience he has in mind. The assurance that *we know him* is equal to the assurance *that we are in him.* One meaning of the Greek verb *ginōskō,* to know, is to have an intimate experience with someone. The Gnostics claimed mystical knowledge of God and special revelations; thus, for them salvation was largely achieved through special knowledge.

John insists that knowledge of Christ

must be proven by obedience to Christ's commandments. And here for the first time he introduces the subject of love and the use of the Greek noun *agapē*. Later will be much elaboration of this subject (see comment on 2:15), but now he couples it with the idea of obedience to Christ: *whoever keeps his word, in him truly love for God is perfected.* The Greek here is simply "the love of God," meaning the love of which God is the source. It is this love which *is perfected,* that is, is brought to fruition or fulfillment in him who *keeps his* (Christ's) *word.* There is no such thing as *agapē* which is not expressed in obedience to Christ. As we shall see in greater ·detail later on, *agapē* transcends feeling and emotion and must be expressed in conduct and action. Assurance that we are in Christ should be subjected to this test: *he who says he abides in him ought to walk in the same way in which he walked,* which means that every member of the fellowship is to model his daily life after the life of Jesus.

3. The Old-New Commandment (2:7–11)

⁷ Beloved, I am writing you no new commandment, but an old commandment which you had from the beginning; the old commandment is the word which you have heard. ⁸ Yet I am writing you a new commandment, which is true in him and in you, because the darkness is passing away and the true light is already shining. ⁹ He who says he is in the light and hates his brother is in the darkness still. ¹⁰ He who loves his brother abides in the light, and in it there is no cause for stumbling. ¹¹ But he who hates his brother is in the darkness and walks in the darkness, and does not know where he is going, because the darkness has blinded his eyes.

Having introduced the subject of love and having identified it as belonging to Christ's commandments, the author proceeds to remind his readers of the old commandment of love *which you had from the beginning.* The author means that his hearers were possessors of this old commandment from the time they first heard and accepted the gospel, for he identifies it as *the word which you have heard.* But it is also *a new commandment.* Undoubtedly John is referring to the new commandment given by Jesus on the night before his crucifixion: "A new commandment I give to you, that you love one another; even as I have loved you, that you also love one another" (John 13:34). But John gives added meaning to the word *new;* he describes the old-new commandment as *true in him and in you.*

This is his way of expressing his conviction that time and experience have authenticated the commandment in the lives of Jesus and his followers. The "beloved disciple" and his fellow disciples came to an understanding of the words of Jesus in the upper room only after they had experienced the impact of his death and the descent of the Holy Spirit at Pentecost. In retrospect John now sees all the more clearly how Jesus' teaching concerning love was individualized, personalized, made alive in Jesus. It is *true in him* both as the Jesus of history and the eternal Christ. It is also true *in you,* i.e., in a group of believers in whom the Christ is alive as the eternal Word and the historical Jesus. The commandment is true in that it is real, for this is the meaning of *true* here. Because it comes alive and is real in persons, the commandment is always relevant, ever applicable to the ills and needs of humanity and society. So it is no dead statute laid away in a dust-covered book. Its reality can be seen in the result of its working: *the darkness is passing away and the true light is already shining.*

John saw the working of love even in the midst of the darkness of sin and evil of his own time. He is voicing here the continuing victory of the incarnate Word: "The light shines in the darkness, and the darkness has not overcome it" (John 1:5). The author is an optimist when he thus measures the power of love to overcome the darkness of evil. Is Christian love powerful enough to overcome the dreadful power of the atom bomb? If John were living in our time he would answer yes, but he would go on to say that the only way Christian love can be made relevant in any age is in individuals who incarnate Christ in their lives and are committed to his way of love.

The commandment of love in its application to human relationships is stated in terms of hatred of or love for a brother. *He who says he is in the light* (v. 9) is directed toward the professed member of the fellowship who *hates his brother* (v. 9). Who is the brother here? Is he any human being, or is he a member of the Christian fellowship? *Brother* in the epistle refers to a Christian brother, but certainly John would recognize hate as hate (next to unbelief the cardinal sin in the epistle), and therefore heinous sin, whether directed toward a Christian or an unbeliever. The inevitable conclusion is that one who *hates his brother is in the darkness still* and therefore outside the fellowship and without Christian brothers. Hating any person and walking *in the light* (v. 9) are mutually exclusive. It is he *who loves his brother* who *abides in the light* (v. 10). As light is the antithesis of darkness, so love is the antithesis of hate. Love and hatred cannot remain active together in the same person.

In it there is no cause for stumbling may better read "in him," etc. The translation *it* refers to the light. If the alternate translation is correct, "him" refers to the person who *abides in the light*. Both statements are true. Neither in the person who *abides in the light,* nor in *the light* itself, is there *cause for stumbling* (Gr., *skandalon*). Originally a *skandalon* was the device in a trap set for animals which when sprung caused the log or other heavy object to fall upon the victim. (Our word "scandal" started here and came through the Latin, *skandalum,* stumbling block.)

There is no middle ground between hate and love, no twililght zone where the light dimly shines. A man walks either in the light or in the darkness. He *who hates his brother* is devoid of sight *because the darkness has blinded his eyes.* The glories of the realm of light are unknown to him because he has no eyes to see them.

4. Victory over The World (2:12–17)

12 I am writing to you, little children, because your sins are forgiven for his sake. 13 I am writing to you, fathers, because you know him who is from the beginning. I am writing to you, young men, because you have overcome the evil one. I write to you, children, because you know the Father. 14 I write to you, fathers, because you know him who is from the beginning. I write to you, young men, because you are strong, and the word of God abides in you, and you have overcome the evil one.

15 Do not love the world or the things in the world. If any one loves the world, love for the Father is not in him. 16 For all that is in the world, the lust of the flesh and the lust of the eyes and the pride of life, is not of the Father but is of the world. 17 And the world passes away, and the lust of it; but he who does the will of God abides for ever.

John at this point breaks away from his stern tone and warnings against false brothers to address himself in endearing terms to the faithful members of the fellowship. His purpose is to remind his readers of their victories in the Christian faith and to assure them of his approval of their steadfastness. In addressing them he uses four terms, two of which, *little children* (*teknia*) and *children* (*paidia*), are general terms of affection which he applies in other places of the epistle to all his readers. The other two terms, *fathers* and *young men,* seem to have specialized meanings, the former referring to the members of the fellowship who have been longtime Christians, the latter to those who are younger in the faith.

Three times he uses the present tense *grapho: I am writing* (vv. 12,13), and three times the aorist *egrapsa: I write* (v. 14), which is normally a past tense, but there is no reference here to a former letter, for the "epistolary" aorist was frequently used in this way to refer to something written in the same letter. It appears that the author in his warm enthusiasm and sentimental attachment to his readers has cast what he has to say in a sort of poem of two stanzas, each line of the first stanza beginning with *graphō, I am writing,* and each line of the second stanza beginning with *egraspsa*, *I write* (or "I wrote").

Of more importance than the form of John's paean to his readers is its content. All readers (*teknia, little children*, v. 12) are reminded *your sins are forgiven*. John is a lover of the perfect tense, which is the tense used here and translated *are forgiven*. The tense emphasizes the present reality and finality of a past event. Here it might be translated "stand forgiven." In fact the perfect tense is used throughout the passage to describe the victories won by faithful believers. All readers (*paidia, children*, v. 13) are also reminded that they *know the Father*. (*Know* here is for the perfect *egnōkate*, "you came to know and still know").

The *fathers* are addressed twice and in each instance John gives as his reason for writing to them *you know him who is from the beginning* ("you came to know and still know"). This is a tribute to the older and more mature Christians on the strength of their knowledge of the eternal Christ, the Logos. Appropriately the *young men* (*neaniskoi*), those younger in the faith, are cited for their demonstration of strength: *you have overcome the evil one . . . you are strong*. But there is an added word of praise for the young in faith: *the word of God abides in you*.

Perhaps in John's rather delightful lyrical outburst of praise for his beloved *little children* we may trace a sort of progression in Christian experience: (1) forgiveness of sins, (2) knowledge of God as Father, (3) conquest of the evil one—realization of one's progress in holiness, (4) the indwelling in one of the word of God, and (5) knowledge of Christ as the one *who is from the beginning*.

John turns now to exhortation. He has reminded his readers that they have overcome the world, but he warns them not to rest upon their laurels. The world holds out its temptations even to faithful believers. So he writes *do not love the world or the things in the world*. The verb for *love* here is *agapaō*, which is not unusual, for it may be used of love of various objects as well as

for the expression of *agapē*, Christian love. The noun *agapē*, however, is always used of Christian love in the New Testament. The verb expresses choice, esteem, prizing, and lends itself naturally to the expression of *agapē* in action (see comment on 3:14–18). *Agapē* is used here for *love for the Father*. John is saying that it is impossible for one to choose or esteem the world and at the same time have in him *agapē* for God the Father. This should be a warning to those who use the term "love" loosely to describe as a Christian almost anyone who has a compassion for dispossessed people or a charitable attitude toward the poor. Sad to say, a person may possess these admirable qualities and at the same time *love the things of the world* and not have in him *love for the Father*.

World, as John uses it, is an ethical term referring not to the planet Earth, but to that segment of humanity, traditions, customs, things, and thought that belong to the "darkness," or that sphere of human existence that is alienated from God. John names some of the elements of *the world* as *the lust of the flesh, the lust of the eyes*, and *the pride of life*.

The third element here is particularly interesting. The Greek term for *pride* here is *alazoneia*. The verb form of this word means to act the *alazōn*: a boaster, a braggart, an empty pretender. *Pride* here is braggadocio, empty talk, the foolish presumption of one who trusts in his own resources and disdains the power of God and the rights of others.

The word for *life* here is appropriately *bios*, not *zoē*, thus emphasizing the temporal and material aspects of human existence. All this, declares John, *is of the world. And the world passes away* (lit., "is passing away"). Thus he focuses attention upon the transiency of *the world* and *the lust of it*, i.e., the fleshly desire that belongs to the world and drives men to crave the things of the world. Over against the transiency and temporality of the world and its elements is the indestructibility of him who does the will of God. He *abides forever*.

II. The Antichrists (2:18–29)

1. The Antichrists Described (2:18–25)

¹⁸ Children, it is the last hour; and as you have heard that antichrist is coming, so now many antichrists have come; therefore we know that it is the last hour. ¹⁹ They went out from us, but they were not of us; for if they had been of us, they would have continued with us; but they went out, that it might be plain that they all are not of us. ²⁰ But you have been anointed by the Holy One, and you all know. ²¹ I write to you, not because you do not know the truth, but because you know it, and know that no lie is of the truth. ²² Who is the liar but he who denies that Jesus is the Christ? This is the antichrist, he who denies the Father and the Son. ²³ No one who denies the Son has the Father. He who confesses the Son has the Father also. ²⁴ Let what you heard from the beginning abide in you. If what you heard from the beginning abides in you, then you will abide in the Son and in the Father. ²⁵ And this is what he has promised us, eternal life.

It is characteristic of John in his epistle that a subject discussed will touch a chord of memory diverting his attention to another subject which may or may not conform to logical sequence. This produces a kind of discourse such as old men often give. John was an old man and he doubtless dictated his epistle. His ideas and words flowed from a mind crowded with a vast accumulation of memories and convictions. Here we seem to have reached a break in the author's line of thought. With what seems to be abruptness he introduces the subject of antichrists.

It is altogether possible that this topic was suggested to John's mind by his immediately preceding meditation on the transient nature of the world. It is not necessary to think that when he wrote "the world passes away" in v. 17 his reference was to the imminent end of the world, but his thought would suggest the inevitable eschatological end. This would bring to mind and expression the teachings concerning last things he and his fellow disciples had learned from Jesus and which became a part of the eschatological tradition of the primitive church.

That this section of the epistle reflects the eschatological beliefs of the primitive Christian community is almost beyond question despite the ambiguity in John's reference to antichrists. This is significant in the light of the scarcity of eschatological teaching in John's Gospel and the insistence of some scholars that in the Gospel "realized" eschatology has displaced the primitive eschatology, the reason being that the promise of the Lord's return, the *parousia*, had failed to materialize. But here in the epistle, written by the same man who wrote the Gospel, we have an unmistakable reference to the appearing and *parousia* of Jesus (2:28). Or, for those who cannot accept the Johannine authorship of the epistle, we may say that the author reflects here the eschatological view of the Johannine circle. The references to antichrists in 2:18, 22 are almost certainly related to the warnings of Jesus concerning false Christs in Matthew 24:23–25 (Mark 13:21–23). The exhortation to confidence and readiness in prospect of the coming of the Lord in 2:28 is in keeping with the parables of watchfulness told by Jesus at the conclusion of the great discourse on last things (Matt. 24: 37—25:46; Mark 13:33–37).

As John begins the sober discussion of antichrists and the heretical nature of their beliefs, he addresses his readers with the endearing term **Children.** The statement *it is the last hour* is not in fact what John wrote in Greek; there is no definite article with *eschatē hora*, "a last hour." It appears that John deliberately cloaked his statement with' ambiguity by omitting the article in order that he might not be interpreted as predicting the imminent return of Christ.

The ambiguity is increased with the statement *so now many antichrists* (plural) *have come.* But the prediction had been *that antichrist* (not *antichrists*) *is coming.* The indefiniteness concerning *last hour* is increased with the knowledge that the terms *antichrist* and *antichrists* appear in the New Testament only here and in 2 John 7. This, of course, is not proof that the idea was absent from the primitive eschatological tradition. The *antichrist* of John's epistle might well correspond to "the man of lawlessness" (2 Thess. 2:3), who, according to Paul, would come before "the day of the Lord" arrived. The *antichrists* mentioned by John may have been derived from the "false Christs" (*pseudochristoi*) mentioned by Jesus in the "Synoptic Apocalypse" (Matt. 24:23–25; Mark 13:21–23).

It is to be remembered, however, that the appearing of these "false Christs" would *not* be a "sign" of the Parousia. Jesus warned against them because they and false prophets would "show great signs and wonders, so as to lead astray, if possible, even the elect" (Matt. 24:24). It should be observed that John's *antichrist* is identified as *he who denies the Father and the Son* (v. 22), and the antichrists are, like the false Christs, *those who would deceive you* (v. 26).

From these references and comparisons it is reasonable to conclude that there was in the early Christian church a fairly consistent eschatological tradition from which John drew here. John used it with a freedom that he was entitled to as a member of the twelve. His refusal to use the definite article with *last hour* seems to indicate that he is guarding against leading his readers to believe that he is predicting that the Lord's return is at hand. He will not violate the teaching of Jesus that "of that day or that hour no one knows, not even the angels in heaven, nor the Son, but only the Father" (Mark 13:32). His point is, then, that the *hour* to which he and his readers have come is a critical (one meaning of *last*) *hour;* it was an hour that indeed could be the last hour.

We turn now to John's chief concern, and that is that his readers shall recognize these *antichrists* by their beliefs and actions and that they identify them as enemies of the gospel and disrupters of the Christian fellowship. *They went out from us* tells in brief the story of their treachery to the fellowship. The words *they were not of us* reveal the character they bore as hypocrites within the fellowship. John goes on to show that they were actually not Christian disciples while in the fellowship because *if they had been of us, they would have continued with us.*

Who were these false disciples branded by John as *antichrists?* John identifies any one of them as *the liar . . . who denies that Jesus is the Christ . . . the antichrist . . . who denies the Father and the Son* (v. 22). This characterization of these men and John's severe condemnation of them indicate rather pointedly that they were leaders of a dangerous movement, which, if it had prevailed, would have overthrown the Christian faith. Their false doctrines were aimed directly at the person of Christ. The first heresy which invaded the church was a form of gnosticism that expressed itself concerning the person of Christ in two ways: it denied the deity of Christ on the one hand and denied his humanity on the other (see Int.). This is the heresy that John attacks here, and its protagonists probably believed sincerely in the beginning that they could advance the cause of Christ by importing the gnostic philosophy into Christian ranks and adapting it to Christian doctrine. But when they were opposed by the stalwart church leaders, John and others, and found themselves out of place in the Christian fellowship, they deserted the church. Leaders of the movement in the latter part of the first century and in the second century were Marcion, Cerinthus, and others.

But you have been anointed by the Holy One—"You have a *chrisma* from the Holy One." The verb *chriō* meant to anoint with oil; *chrisma* was the oil or ointment used, or the anointing itself. In the Old Testament period kings, priests, and prophets were anointed upon assuming their offices. With their anointing it was assumed that the Spirit of God came upon them (see 1 Sam. 16:13; Ex. 40:13; Isa. 61:1). The Messiah was *ho Christos,* the Anointed One. Jesus declared in the synagogue at Nazareth that he was the fulfillment of the prophecy in Isaiah 61, beginning "The Spirit of the Lord God is upon me; because the Lord has anointed me," etc. (Luke 4:16–21). The disciples were called *Christianoi* first at Antioch (Acts 11:26). In one sense they were "anointed ones," even as their Messiah and Saviour was the Anointed One.

In the passage before us John implies the close relationship existing between Christ and the readers, who as "anointed ones," recognize the truth and will not be misled by the *antichrists.* The *antichrists* are not only men who are against Christ, but they are liars who claim to be Christ. (The Greek preposition *anti* has both meanings, "against" and "in the place of.") On the other hand, believers are truly "little christs" in that they have been anointed by the same Holy Spirit who anointed Christ, and are in union with him. The reading *and you all know* (v. 20) is preferable to "you know everything," which is found in a number of manuscripts.

No one who denies the Son has the Father is an echo of Jesus' words, "He who hates me hates my Father also" (John 15: 23). The Jesus of the Synoptic Gospels, as well as of the Gospel of John, is inseparable from the God he revealed as Father. John was saying in effect that the antichrists were atheists. In later times there have been theologians who declared that God was dead, but they refused to give up Jesus. However, the Jesus they clung to was not *the Son.* Their heretical views of Christ separated them from the Jesus of the New Testament. John reinforces his idea of the inseparable relationship of Father and Son with the statement *He who confesses the Son has the Father also.* Again we are reminded of the close relationship of John's thought here with the words of Jesus as recorded in the Gospel (cf. John 10:30; 14:8–11; 17:20–23).

Let what you heard from the beginning is a call to the readers of the epistle to stand firm on the message of the gospel as it was originally preached to them. The heretics had departed from this message. If this message *abides* in them, remains inseparable from their daily lives, they *will abide in the Son and in the Father.* John is reminded that such unity is in keeping with

what he has promised us, eternal life. Again we are reminded of the words of Jesus in the Gospel, now concerning unity of Father, Son, and believers, and eternal life (John 17:3,20–23).

2. Reliance upon the Spirit (2:26–27)

26 I write this to you about those who would deceive you; 27 but the anointing which you received from him abides in you, and you have no need that any one should teach you; as his anointing teaches you about everything, and is true, and is no lie, just as it has taught you, abide in him.

The author makes a second appeal to his readers to rely upon what the Holy Spirit has done and does for them as they confront the antichrists and their false teaching. He has reminded them that the anointing they received by the Holy Spirit endowed them with the capacity to distinguish between truth and the lie invented by the heretics concerning Christ. Now he emphasizes the importance of the role of the Holy Spirit as teacher in the battle against heresy.

The words *but the anointing which you received* may be rendered more accurately, "but as for you—the anointing which you received," because the personal pronoun is in an emphatic position in the sentence. With this construction the *anointing* received by the Christian recipients of the epistle is made to contrast sharply with the "anointing" received by the false teachers —*those who would deceive you.* Here is evidence that in their ceremony of initiation into the mysteries of *gnōsis* the false teachers claimed to receive a spiritual anointing that bestowed upon them knowledge and prophetic insight superior to Christian truth and insight.

The *anointing* received by John's readers was *from him,* i.e., from Christ. By this interpretation the Holy Spirit is the agent of the anointing and is the One sent by Jesus as taught in Acts (2:33) and the Gospel of John (15:26; 16:7). John shows here the important relationship between the work of Christ and the work of the Holy Spirit. This is an inseparable relationship which expresses itself in sustaining and making ever relevant in the lives of believers the teaching of the historical Jesus. John writes *you have no need that any one should teach you.* He cannot mean that his readers have no need of the kind of teaching that he in his letter is imparting to them; he does mean that they have no need of teaching that adds to or conflicts with the fundamental elements of the faith contained in the original teachings of Jesus and the primitive Christian community. These were the teachings that were for John's readers a bulwark against heresy. The anointing from Christ by means of the Holy Spirit would keep alive these teachings in the minds and hearts of believers.

John's way of putting it is: *his anointing teaches you about everything, and is true, and is no lie.* This strongly implies that the anointing claimed by the false teachers inspired them to teach that which was a lie. The author writes here in perfect agreement with the promise of Jesus in John 14:26—"But the Counselor, the Holy Spirit, whom the Father will send in my name, he will teach you all things, and bring to your remembrance all that I have said to you." And when the author admonishes *just as it has taught you, abide in him,* we are reminded of the inseparable relationship between Jesus, the first Paraclete, the Holy Spirit, the second Paraclete, and the teaching of Jesus. Jesus had promised that the second Paraclete—the Spirit of truth— would be with his disciples forever (John 14:16 ff.). He declared "he dwells with you, and will be in you. I will not leave you desolate; I will come to you." To *abide in him* (v. 27), i.e., to abide in Christ, is to abide in what the Spirit teaches, which is the teaching of Jesus.

3. Abiding in Christ (2:28–29)

²⁸ And now, little children, abide in him, so that when he appears we may have confidence and not shrink from him in shame at his coming. ²⁹ If you know that he is righteous, you may be sure that every one who does right is born of him.

The idea of abiding in Christ is now brought into close relationship with the *Parousia,* second coming, of Christ (v. 28). The introduction of the term *parousia* here confirms the view that the author was thinking eschatologically in his reference to antichrists and a last hour (v. 18). This is the only appearance of the term in the Johannine writings (including the book of Revelation). It is evidence that real eschatology had not been displaced by realized eschatology in the Johannine interpretation of the gospel. Readiness for the Parousia was prominent in the eschatological teaching of Jesus and Paul, and such is the case here.

There is no separation of ethics from eschatology in the New Testament teaching. The believer who abides *in him,* that is in Christ, lives daily a life regulated by the criterion provided in the life and teachings of Jesus. He strives to live each day as if it were the day of the Parousia. John appeals to his readers to *abide in him, so that when he appears we may have confidence and not shrink from him in shame.* We are reminded by these words of the warning of Jesus: "For whoever is ashamed of me and of my words in this adulterous and sinful generation, of him will he the Son of man also be ashamed, when he comes in the glory of his Father with the holy angels" (Mark 8:38).

If you know that he is righteous is a condition fulfilled by those who abide in Christ; they know beyond doubt (because of their moral sensitivity) *that every one who does right is born of him.* There need be no objection to the conclusion that the author means born of Christ here. The context calls for this interpretation. The author has written of abiding *in him,* meaning abiding in Christ, and when he introduces the condition of knowing *that he is righteous,* Christ is the righteous one to whom he refers. The author knows that to be born of Christ is to be born of God, and to be born of God is to be born of Christ. Again we are reminded of the inseparable relationship between the Father and the Son as taught in the Gospel of John. "I am in the

Father and the Father in me" (14:11; see also 17:21).

This verse provides admirably a transition to the great discussion of sonship which follows, constituting the all important middle section of the epistle (3:1—5:12). The author will have many significant things to say concerning being born of God and the life of the children of God.

III. The Meaning of Sonship (3:1—5:12)

1. Glory of Sonship (3:1–3)

[1] See what love the Father has given us, that we should be called children of God; and so we are. The reason why the world does not know us is that it did not know him. [2] Beloved, we are God's children now; it does not yet appear what we shall be, but we know that when he appears we shall be like him, for we shall see him as he is. [3] And every one who thus hopes in him purifies himself as he is pure.

See what love the Father has given us provides a full measure of the author's feeling as he started this great section, and it should be punctuated with exclamation points. "Look!" he exclaims, "what *kind of love*," etc. The emphasis is upon the quality and distinctiveness of *agapē*. The great dissertation on love is yet to come (3:11–18; 4:7—5:5), but here we are given an example of the author's exalted conception of this kind of love. Appropriately the emphasis is on love's relationship to sonship, for sonship is now the subject in the forefront of John's consciousness. An analysis of v. 1 reveals these truths concerning love and its working: (1) its source is the God who is *Father*; (2) it is God's free gift to man, a gift that abides as his possession; (3) it confers sonship upon men who respond—the result is *that we should be called children of God*; (4) it produces in those who respond a confidence that they are the children of God—*and so we are* (the author's way of saying that this confidence of sonship was not a mere expression of doctrine but was a reality grounded in experience).

An echo of John 1:12 is worth noting here: "But to all who received him, who believed in his name, he gave power to become children of God." Those *called children of God* are named children of God because they receive and exercise this power.

The reason why the world does not know us can be found in the experience of Christ. The sons (or children) of God are rejected by the world even as the Son was rejected: he was in the world but not of the world (John 17:14). "He came to his own home, and his own people received him not" (John 1:11).

The author at this point reverts to his concern with last things and seeks to relate sonship to eschatology. He declares that *we are God's children now* but adds, *it does not yet appear what we shall be.* His conviction is that *when he* (Christ) *appears we shall be like him.* Sonship, in John's conception, is not a mere title or doctrine; it is not static but dynamic. A son grows, develops, matures. His goal of growth is maturity in the likeness of Christ himself. Every one who has the hope of seeing Christ at his second appearing *purifies himself as he is pure.* The process of purification is a day-by-day experience in the life of the child of God.

John's doctrine of sonship is in remarkable agreement with Paul's great discourse on sonship in Romans 8. (Did he read the copy of Romans to which Phoebe's letter of introduction to the church at Ephesus— chapter 16—became attached? Or is this agreement on the meaning of sonship between John and Paul simply an illustration of how two interpreters of the gospel drew from a common body of tradition and teaching?) These are the characteristics of sonship in Romans 8 that appear also in 1 John 3:1–3: (1) God is Father to those who receive "the spirit of sonship" (8: 15); (2) the children of God are blessed with the confidence that they are indeed the children of God (v. 16 f.); (3) there is an inseparable relationship between love and sonship (vv. 28,37–39); (4) sons are "called" (vv. 28–30); (5) sons are "conformed" to the image of the Son (v. 29);

(6) there is an eschatological fulfillment of sonship (v. 23). Paul uses the rare term *huiothesia* for sonship, but also the term *tekna* (children, v. 16 f.), the word used by John. Paul's word *huiothesia* should not be translated "adoption" (see Gal. 3:23—4:7) and should be omitted from Romans 8:23 in keeping with the better reading of some manuscripts. (We do not "wait for" that which we already possess—sonship—but for "the redemption of our bodies.")

2. Sonship and Sin (3:4–10)

⁴ Every one who commits sin is guilty of lawlessness; sin is lawlessness. ⁵ You know that he appeared to take away sins, and in him there is no sin. ⁶ No one who abides in him sins; no one who sins has either seen him or known him. ⁷ Little children, let no one deceive you. He who does right is righteous, as he is righteous. ⁸ He who commits sin is of the devil; for the devil has sinned from the beginning. The reason the Son of God appeared was to destroy the works of the devil. ⁹ No one born of God commits sin; for God's nature abides in him, and he cannot sin because he is born of God. ¹⁰ By this it may be seen who are the children of God, and who are the children of the devil: whoever does not do right is not of God, nor he who does not love his brother.

John's reference to the child of God's purifying himself in v. 3 opens the way for the discussion of sin which follows. Once again the author comes to grips with the doctrine of perfectionism purveyed by the false teachers and draws a sharp line between them and the true children of God.

Every one who commits sin may be more accurately rendered "Every one doing (*ho poiōn*) sin." As we have stated earlier, John is accurate in the use of his tenses, and the full force of the present tense as expressive of continuous action is to be insisted on here. Furthermore, the force of the participle as descriptive of the person involved in the action is to be applied. The result is that we have here the description of a person who continues to commit sin, or, as we say, one who lives in sin. The same principles apply to the use of the present tense and of the participle throughout this passage. Unless these principles are

applied we shall find ourselves interpreting John as teaching the perfectionism he is in truth combating, as, for instance, in the statement *No one born of God commits sin* (v. 9).

The term for sin, *hamartia*, is interesting in that it and the corresponding Old Testament word, *chattath*, have the same root meaning, "a failure to hit the mark." However, there was a significant difference in application of the idea in Greek and Hebrew thought. In classic Greek the idea of "missing the mark" was closely related to that of making a mistake or of committing an error, or of being guilty of a bad deed. There was not in the word and its corresponding verb the high ethical content that is present in the Hebrew term and its corresponding verb. The difference was that in the Old Testament sin was sin against Jehovah and was therefore both religious and ethical in its reference. The ethical and religious nature of the terms contribute to the even higher ethical and religious quality of *hamartia* and *hamartanō* in the New Testament. In John's Gospel and first epistle sin belongs to the realm of darkness as opposed to the realm of light.

In v. 4 John equates sin with lawlessness: *sin is lawlessness.* The term is *anomia*—without law, or no law, in other words, anarchy. The implication is that sin is violation of a moral cosmos sustained by law. Sin may be considered as contrary to and a revolt against the laws of this cosmos. Sin is anarchy because it is the sinner's expression of his willful determination to live according to the laws of his own choosing in disregard of the laws of the universal moral order.

You know that he appeared to take away sins. The author now appeals to the work of Christ as both evidence of the reality of sin and the antidote for sin. The very purpose of his appearing and life was to give to man the victory over sin. This purpose testifies to the fact that sin is no fiction. At the same time the life that he lived, the death that he died, and his victory over death, as John's readers *know* (by experience), destroyed the power of sin by taking away *sins* (plural). In the statement *in him there is no sin*, John projects the sinlessness of Jesus as essential to man's victory over sin. He who identifies with Jesus Christ, who participates in his life, shares in his sinlessness: *No one who abides in him sins.* The verb for *sins* is in the present tense, expressing durative or continuous action. The meaning is that the individual who abides in Christ does not go on sinning. The present participle follows and is translated *no one who sins* to describe the individual who lives a life of sin. That kind of sinner has never *seen him or known him.* The literal translation of v. 6 is: "Every one who sins has not seen (perfect tense) him, neither has known (perfect tense) him." The perfects show the abiding consequences of the sinful life: continuing blindness to Christ and ignorance of him.

Once more a warning against the false teachers: *Little children, let no one deceive you.* Jesus had warned against false prophets and declared, "You will know them by their fruits" (Matt. 7:16). John echoes the teaching of his Master; his word is *He who does right* (lit., righteousness) *is righteous, as he is righteous. He who commits sin* (the one doing sin, present participle) *is of the devil.* The test of the true believer is his life; the test of the sinner is his life; each is measured by his daily practice. The true believer practices righteousness, while the sinner practices sin—it is as simple as that. The criterion of righteousness is the righteousness practiced by Jesus; the child of God pactices righteousness *as he is righteous.* This must be a righteousness that "exceeds that of the scribes and Pharisees" (Matt. 5:20).

He who commits sin is of the devil. In thought the author is back again in the realm of cosmological contrast such as that alluded to in 1:5–7. The Dead Sea Scroll "The War of the Sons of Light and the Sons of Darkness" pictures a similar contrast involving the realms of light and darkness. Focusing attention on the inhabitants of the rival realms, the children of God and the children of the devil, John with unmistakable precision identifies both by their parentage. His thesis is "like father, like son." The sinner—*He who commits* (*ho poiōn*, present participle) *sin* is *ek* ("out of") the devil; he who does righteousness is born *ek* ("out of") God.

The sinner's ancestry is traced to the one who *has sinned from the beginning* (lit., the one who "sins from the beginning." In this manner he is identified as the primordial being who is the author of all sin and who never ceases to sin. His name is *diabolos* (Gr.), which means slanderer or accuser. His Old Testament name is *satan* (Heb.), adversary. He appears under both names in the New Testament; under both names he is the great adversary of Christ who tried in the temptations to destroy the work of the Messiah at its beginning (Matt. 4:1–10).

The reason the Son of God appeared. John accepts without question the dualistic interpretation of the moral order; the devil is the head of the realm of evil and is in mortal combat with God who heads the realm of good. God's response to Satan's design to corrupt and enslave man was to give his Son *to destroy the works of the devil.* Why the *works* and not the *devil* himself? Our answer must be that elimination of the devil from mankind's moral struggle would have done away with the struggle altogether by removing man's right of choice between good and evil. In such case man would no longer be man but some other kind of being. Man is richly endowed by God his Father in this moral struggle. *No one born of God commits sin; for God's nature abides in him.* A literal translation of this statement is, "Everyone born of God does not go on doing (present tense) sin, because his seed (*sperma*) abides in him."

God has armed his children for their warfare against Satan by implanting his own nature in them, even as an earthly father engenders in his children his characteristics by implanting his sperm (*spermatazoa*) in the ovum of the mother. Today we know that the spermatazoa carry from the father the genes, which combined with those of the mother, determine the characteristics of the child. We may say, therefore, in modern terminology that God's genes remain in his children and that sinning is contrary to their nature.

John declares that the child of God *cannot sin because he is born of God.* This is perhaps the primary proof text of those who believe in and teach perfectionism. But neither this statement nor any other in 1 John teaches perfectionism or sinlessness. The present infinitive is used here for *sin,* and it cannot express any other than durative or continuous action. We translate, therefore, as follows: "and he is unable to go on sinning, because he has been born (perfect tense) of God." The meaning is that the child of God is simply incapable of living a sinful life because the birth (begetting) from God experienced by him is an abiding reality. His character as God's child was fixed when God begot him. This character is devoid of the capacity to live in sin. The distinction between the children of God and the children of the devil is easily made on the basis of their conduct: *whoever does not do right is not of God.* But the author adds something by way of transition to what is to follow: *nor he who does not love his brother.* We are now on the *threshold* of a discussion of the greatest of all characteristics of the children of God: love.

3. Love of the Brethren (3:11-18)

¹¹ For this is the message which you have heard from the beginning, that we should love one another, ¹² and not be like Cain who was of the evil one and murdered his brother. And why did he murder him? Because his own deeds were evil and his brother's righteous. ¹³ Do not wonder, brethren, that the world hates you. ¹⁴ We know that we have passed out of death into life, because we love the brethren. He who does not love remains in death. ¹⁵ Any one who hates his brother is a murderer, and you know that no murderer has eternal life abiding in him. ¹⁶ By this we know love, that he laid down his life for us; and we ought to lay down our lives for the brethren. ¹⁷ But if any one has the world's goods and sees his brother in need, yet closes his heart against him, how does God's love abide in him?

¹⁸ Little children, let us not love in word or speech but in deed and in truth.

When John wrote in the preceding verse that one who does not love his brother is not of God, the reference was to a Christian brother. This is confirmed in v. 11 concerning *the message which you have heard from the beginning.* It is the reader's first acquaintance with the gospel to which the author appeals when he writes *from the beginning,* and the appeal echoes the new commandment "that you love one another; even as I have loved you, that you also love one another" (John 13:34). The new commandment belonged to the primitive teaching. It enjoined disciples of Christ to love one another, but this in no way exhausted the outreach of love that Christians were to practice. The love John teaches here does not nullify nor substitute for love of neighbor taught by Jesus (Luke 10:25-37), nor the love for enemies Jesus taught (Matt. 5:43-48). John's teaching here is to be interpreted in the context of his exposition of sonship and fellowship and the importance of love within the fellowship. He is thinking of the Christian group as the family of God, the members of which are the sons and daughters of a common Father.

Perhaps this is why he selected Cain as the tragic prototype of what Christian brothers are not to be. He *murdered his brother,* a member of his own family, the son of his own father. *He murdered* him *because his own deeds were evil and his brother's righteous.* Cain's foul deed was the natural expression of a sinful life: his *deeds were evil.* The deed of murder was in keeping with the other deeds of his daily life. Jealousy was in his heart. Cain looked with envy upon the deeds of his brother and his envy flamed into hatred. John's sober words are a warning that there is no place in the family of God for enmity between members of the family because murder, as in the case of Cain, is the natural expression of such enmity. This should be a warning to us in our own time of the peril of prejudice against our brothers of another race. Like Cain, we can have murder in our hearts that could lead to violence if we despise men of another race, even though they are Christians.

Hate is of the world, not of the children of God. This fact leads John to exhort his readers not to wonder *that the world hates you.* (Cf. John 15:18–19.) Hatred of those who love God is natural in those outside the family of God. On the contrary, love is a criterion by which the children of God may judge their membership in the family of God: *We know that we have passed out of death into life, because we love the brethren.* John gives us here not the only test of salvation but certainly one of the most important of all criteria by which an individual may judge as to whether or not he is a child of God. The test is: Does he love his Christian brothers? This brings us face to face with the question as to what love for *the brethren* is. By degrees, as we follow John's explanations of love's nature and working, we shall find the answer to the question.

In John's view, love is the determinative factor as to whether an individual lives in the realm of life or the realm of death. *He who does not love remains in death.* The present participle with the negative, *ho mē agapōn,* by inference may be translated "the non-lover." The author implies that one who is a "non-lover" remaining in the realm of death is an easy victim of hate, for his next statement is *Any one who hates his brother is a murderer.* As Jesus did, John traces the deed of murder to its source in the mind and heart (cf. Matt. 5:21–26), only John goes a step further and equates the thought and desire with the deed; he makes hatred of one's brother murder itself. It is a sobering thought, particularly in a time of violence when so many homicides are attributable to men's hatred of one another. Even the warning given here to a Christian group that hatred is murder is shocking.

By this we know love could be translated, because of the perfect tense, "we have known." It emphasizes experience as

important in giving to the individual an understanding of Christian love. Those who have experienced the love of God as revealed in Jesus Christ—*that he laid down his life for us*—are those who know what love is. The cross is the supreme expression of *agapē,* and he who experiences the cross is initiated into the mystery and power of love. Such experience must have its expression within the Christian fellowship: *and we ought to lay down our lives for the brethren.* The cross of Christ is inseparable from the cross of the believer; the disciple must be willing to follow his Master in death (cf. Matt. 16:21–26).

This commitment to the great cross principle within the fellowship gives reality to love and its redemptive power in the world. But such love is very practical in its application (vv. 17–18). It is expressed in care for the brother in need of food, clothing, and shelter: *the world's goods.* If a man has *the world's goods* and is aware of his brother's need but *closes his heart against him,* the pertinent question is *how does God's love abide in him?* Love is to be made real not *in word or speech but in deed and in truth* (cf. James 2:14–17).

The phrase *God's love* is *hē agapē tou theou* in Greek, literally "the love of God." It is obvious from the context that this does not mean love for God but love of which God is the author or source, or, as we might say, "God kind of love." At once this identifies the word as expressing love that is superior to natural or human love, love that man comes by as a human being.

4. Assurance and Obedience (3:19–24)

19 By this we shall know that we are of the truth, and reassure our hearts before him **20** whenever our hearts condemn us; for God is greater than our hearts, and he knows everything. **21** Beloved, if our hearts do not condemn us, we have confidence before God; **22** and we receive from him whatever we ask, because we keep his commandments and do what pleases him. **23** And this is his commandment, that we should believe in the name of his Son Jesus Christ and love one another, just as he has commanded us. **24** All who keep his commandments abide in him, and he in them. And by this we know that he abides in us, by the Spirit which he has given us.

John resumes here the subject of Christian assurance that was introduced in v. 14 in the statement about knowing we have passed from life to death because we love the brethren. But now it is assurance in spite of a bad conscience. *By this we shall know that we are of the truth* points back to the discussion concerning the duty of believers to love their Christian brothers to the point of laying down their lives for them and sharing their worldly goods with them. If such a high standard should arouse self-condemnation in the overly conscientious, *God is greater than our hearts, and he knows everything* (v. 20). The implication is that the child of God is not guilty of sin simply because his conscience condemns him. God is the one who passes judgment on our deeds; he sees all and knows us. Nevertheless, it is good to have a clear conscience because *if our hearts do not condemn us, we have confidence before God.* This enables us to be bold in prayer, so that *we receive from him whatever we ask* (cf. John 14:13). But this is true *because we keep his commandments and do what pleases him.* This being so, we shall not ask amiss or pray selfishly; we shall ask in his name, and to ask in his name is to ask in a way that *pleases him.*

Here John brings together the commandment *to believe in the name of his Son Jesus Christ* and the commandment *to love one another.* He harks back here to the great discourse of Jesus in the upper room: "A new commandment I give to you, that you love one another . . . believe in God, believe also in me. . . . Believe me that I am in the Father and the Father in me" (John 13:34; 14:1,11). Keeping his commandments is predicated upon union with Christ. All who keep them *abide in him, and he in them.* Now comes a statement providing a transition to a discussion of the work of the Holy Spirit in guiding believers to distinguish between true and false teachers: *And by this we know that he abides in us, by the Spirit which he has given us.*

5. Testing the Prophets (4:1–6)

¹ Beloved, do not believe every spirit, but test the spirits to see whether they are of God; for many false prophets have gone out into the world. ² By this you know the Spirit of God: every spirit which confesses that Jesus Christ has come in the flesh is of God, ³ and every spirit which does not confess Jesus is not of God. This is the spirit of antichrist, of which you heard that it was coming, and now it is in the world already. ⁴ Little children, you are of God, and have overcome them; for he who is in you is greater than he who is in the world. ⁵ They are of the world, therefore what they say is of the world, and the world listens to them. ⁶ We are of God. Whoever knows God listens to us, and he who is not of God does not listen to us. By this we know the spirit of truth and the spirit of error.

We have come now to the heart of John's assault upon the false teachers (see "Purpose" in Int.). The highly significant feature of John's renewal of his attack upon the heretics here is the manner in which he relates the work of the Holy Spirit to the Jesus of history. In the previous attack upon the false teachers, branded as antichrists (2:18–27), the emphasis was on their denial of the deity of Christ as the Son of God. Here it is on their denial that he was actually a human being.

Beloved, do not believe every spirit. This introductory term of endearment reflects John's deep concern for his readers in the critical temptation they faced. The Holy Spirit is not the only spirit bidding for control of their minds. John recognized the existence of other spirits. The false prophets *claimed* to be guided in their prophesying by the Spirit of God. How, then, could believers determine when a prophet was inspired by God's Spirit or by a false and lying spirit? There is an unfailing criterion of judgment to be applied by the believing community. The spirits must be put to the test *to see whether they are of God,* and the test is what they inspire the prophets to say about Jesus: *every spirit which confesses that Jesus Christ has come in the flesh is of God, and every spirit which does not confess Jesus is not of God.* Precisely at this point the false prophets would be exposed as the heretics they truly were, for they held the gnostic theory that Jesus was not actually human and only appeared to be a man. The basis of this belief about Jesus was the theory that all matter is evil, which would preclude the existence of the Son of God in human flesh since flesh is evil.

An interesting aspect of John's prescribed test is that he relates the spirit which inspires the prophet (whether false or true prophet) so intimately to the prophet himself that he represents the spirit as making the confession, and this is in keeping with the biblical idea of prophetic inspiration.

But the important matter here is John's insistence upon the actual humanity of Jesus and the inseparable tie between the Jesus of history and the work of the Holy Spirit. In the Jesus of history, the Jesus of flesh and blood, there is the objective criterion by which the inspiration of the Holy Spirit is judged. The Spirit works in keeping with and never contrary to the revelation of God in the man Jesus. This fact is highly important in separating false from true claims concerning the leadership of the Spirit. The Spirit at no time guides an individual to do or say that which is contrary to the work and teaching of the man Jesus. On the other hand, he who is sincerely committed to Jesus as Lord and who lives by the teaching of Jesus may be confident that his life is a Spirit-led life.

When John wrote *every spirit which does not confess Jesus,* he used the name *Jesus* deliberately, for it is the name designating Jesus the man, the human Jesus. There is a very interesting alternate reading which occurs in the Latin Vulgate here and which is attested to by Irenaeus, Origen, Tertullian, and Augustine, all Latin Fathers. It is, "every spirit which destroys [separates ?] Jesus." (The Latin verb of the Vulgate is *solvo* which here can mean either destroy or separate.) Whether the reading was the original or not, it shows that the ancient interpreters understood the seriousness of a doctrine that either "split" the human Jesus from the Christ or destroyed altogether the Jesus of history.

The apostle Paul apparently was confronted earlier with this same heresy which troubled the churches of the province of Asia. As early as A.D. 55, in the first epistle to the Corinthians, writing about spiritual gifts, he declared, "I want you to understand that no one speaking by the Spirit of God ever says 'Jesus be cursed (*Anathema Iēsous!*)' and no one can say 'Jesus is Lord (*Kurios Iēsous*)' except by the Holy Spirit" (12:3). The name Jesus here represents the man Jesus, as it does in this passage from 1 John. With Paul, as with John, the question is, What does a man inspired by a spirit say about Jesus? No one inspired by the Spirit of God would ever say, "Jesus be damned!" thus denying the reality of the Jesus who lived in the flesh. The Spirit of God, the *Holy* Spirit, inspires a man to confess the man Jesus as Jesus the Lord. In such a confession, and in the confession John insisted upon, the integrity of Jesus the Christ and the reality of the incarnation are preserved. John's way of putting the right confession: *Jesus Christ has come in the flesh* by its use of the perfect participle, emphasizes the fact that Jesus not only came in flesh, but that his coming in the flesh is an abiding reality.

This emphasis upon the humanity of Jesus is quite in keeping with the same emphasis in the prologue of John's Gospel: "And the Word became flesh and dwelt among us" (1:14). We should be impressed by this double assertion of the humanity of Jesus as indicating its importance for preserving the wholeness of the gospel. It was through the lips of the man Jesus that the Sermon on the Mount came to us; it was in the person of the man Jesus that the sublime example of a Godly life was given to us; it was the body of the human Jesus that was nailed to the cross. He who treats lightly the human Jesus is ever in peril of disregarding the authority of his teaching, the power of his example, and the meaning of his sacrifice.

This is the spirit of antichrist indicates that here and in 2:18–27 John is dealing with the same heresy, although in the former instance the charge against the false teachers was that they denied the sonship or deity of Christ (v. 22 f.). As we have seen, there were both expressions of the heresy, and the "antichrists" attacked by John may have been guilty of teaching both.

Little children, you are of God, and have overcome them. John seeks now to encourage the confidence of his readers that they are fully capable of resisting the blandishments and doctrine of the false teachers. He appeals to them to rely upon their inner resources as children of God to withstand the heretics. They are *ek tou theou,* "out of God," and their victory has already been won (perfect tense) and remains won. The same expression was used by Jesus as he faced the cross (John 16:33). This is true because *he who is in you,* i.e., God, *is greater than he who is in the world,* i.e., the devil incarnate in the false prophets. These false prophets *are of the world,* which puts them in sharp contrast with those concerning whom the author writes: *We are of God.* The realm to which both groups belong determines what they say and how they hear. What the false prophets say *is of the world, and the world listens to them.*

Associating all authentic Christian teachers with himself, the author declares, *We are of God;* therefore the conclusion: *Whoever knows God listens to us.* Contrariwise, *he who is not of God does not listen to us.* The actual test projected here comes to this: Who are the sympathetic hearers of a teacher? If they are people of the world, the teacher belongs to the world; if they are children of God, the teacher is of God.

6. God Is Love (4:7–12)

⁷ Beloved, let us love one another; for love is of God, and he who loves is born of God and knows God. ⁸ He who does not love does not know God; for God is love. ⁹ In this the love of God was made manifest among us, that God sent his only Son into the world, so that we might live through him. ¹⁰ In this is love, not that we loved God but that he loved us and sent his Son to be the expiation for our sins. ¹¹ Beloved, if God so loved us, we also ought to love one another. ¹² No man has ever seen God; if we love one another, God abides in us and his love is perfected in us.

Here we begin the greatest dissertation (4:7—5:12) on Christian love to be found in the New Testament with one exception, 1 Corinthians 13. Comparison of the two provides an interesting study of the working of the mind of each author—how they agreed, how they differed, but how both conceived of love as the paramount element of Christian experience. This latter truth Paul expressed in the memorable words: "So faith, hope, love abide, these three; but the greatest of these is love" (v. 13). John left no doubt of his conviction of the supremacy of love with his unique and daring declaration: *God is love* (4:8,16). The two men differed only in their manner of presentation; there was no disagreement between them on the nature of love and its essentiality to the Christian way of life; to both of them love was indispensable to Christian experience. Both had learned from Jesus what they knew and told about love; in him they had seen love incarnate; what they had seen in him and learned from him had been subjected to the severe tests of life and experience when they wrote, Paul in A.D. 55, John perhaps 25 years later.

In examining John's teaching concerning love and its relationship to sonship, it is profitable to give some attention to the terminology of love in the New Testament. We begin by referring to what was said in the discussion of "love of the brethren" (3:11–18) concerning *agapē* as meaning love of which God is the author, or the "God kind of love." Above all else *agapē* represents love that has its source in God. It is not to deprecate *erōs* to say that this word does not occur in the New Testament. As standing for romantic and erotic or human love, *erōs* has its place in the divine economy, but there was no use for the word in the proclamation of the gospel. *Erōs* is man's possession by his nature as a human being, whereas *agapē* is a special gift from God bestowed only upon those who are "born of God" and become children of God by the new birth.

Two or three occurrences of *agapē* have been found in secular literature belonging to the pre-Christian era.[11] But it was a word rarely used in secular literature. It was the term used by the translators of the Septuagint for erotic love (Song of Sol. 2:4,5,7; 3:5; 5:8; 8:4,6,7), doubtless because they interpreted the love poem allegorically or were loath to suggest by the use of *erōs* that the author glorified the kind of love suggested by this term with its pagan associations. Nevertheless, we may say that *agapē* was thoroughly "baptized into the Christian faith" by the early Christian writers! Paul was doubtless the Christian author who introduced the word into the Christian vocabulary. He used it as early as A.D. 50 when he wrote his first letter to the Thessalonians (1:3; 3:12; 5:8,13).

It is the distinctive term for Christian love and is never used for any form of love except Christian love (which cannot be said of its companion verb *agapaō*). It denotes the love which is the supreme mark of discipleship (John 13:35); which is climatically expressed in the death of Christ for sinners (Rom. 5:8); which binds us inseparably to Christ and God (Rom. 8:35, 39); which is the *sine qua non* of Christian experience (1 Cor. 13:1–3), and the "perfect thing" which matures personality (1 Cor. 13:8–12). The source of the love expressed by agape (now brought over into English) is in God (1 John 4:7), and it is written that God is agape, and he who lives in agape lives in union with God (1 John 4:16).

The companion verb *agapaō* is used 21 times in John's first epistle, twice in the second epistle, and once in the third epistle. It connotes the ideas of choosing, prizing, esteeming, and generally denotes the action of the will. It was the common verb in the New Testament for Christian love, but it does not always express agape, as is seen in Luke 6:32; 11:43; 2 Peter 2:15; John

11 See Liddell and Scott, *A Greek-English Lexicon*, ed. rev. Sir Henry Stuart Jones [Oxford: Clarendon Press, 1940], Vol. I).

3:19; 1 John 2:15, and in other places. Nevertheless, because of its meaning it was naturally capable of expressing Christian love in action.

The unique quality of agape is best illustrated in the teaching of Jesus concerning love of enemies (Matt. 5:43–48). Such love must be exercised by the will and the mind and cannot depend for expression upon emotion or feeling. Appropriately it is the verb *agapaō* which is used in this passage, not *phileō*. *Agapaō* denotes love by choice, love motivated by the will and implemented by action and conduct. The commandment of Jesus is to love in the way God our Father loves. He loves his enemies, those who do not love him. This is proven by the fact that "he makes his sun to rise on the evil and the good, and sends rain on the just and on the unjust." He who loves his enemy cannot rely upon his "feelings" or refrain from loving him because he cannot "feel right" toward him. He loves his enemy with agape when he sees him (with his mind) as a *person*, acts toward him (with his will) as a person, and trusts God to rectify his feelings toward him. He who loves with agape *wills the good* of all men. To love with agape is to achieve maturity that is divine in its nature—"you therefore shall be mature, full grown" (not "perfect," Matt. 5:48).

The other verb for love used in the New Testament is *phileō*, related to the noun *philos*, friend. It expressed friendly affection, mutuality, warm devotion. We are not to think of it as expressing a "lower" form of love than that expressed by *agapaō*. It is used for the highest form of love in John 5:20; 16:27; 21:15–17; 1 Corinthians 16:22, and Revelation 3:19, but it is also used to express love for one's life and the things of the world (Matt. 6:5; 10:37; 23:6; Luke 20:46; John 12:25; 15:19). It is not found in the Johannine epistles.

The noun *philadelphia* is used a few times in the New Testament. (See Rom. 12:10; 1 Thess. 4:9; Heb. 13:1; 1 Peter 1:22). Its meaning is brotherly love. The verbal adjective *agapētos*, used often in 1

John, means beloved, esteemed, dear. It is used of Christ as God's beloved Son (Matt. 3:17); Christians as beloved of God (Rom. 1:7); Christians as beloved of one another (Rom. 16:5,8). It is used often in salutations, as in 1 John 4:1. The word for friend, *philos,* is found occasionally in the New Testament. It is used in a higher sense of friends of Christ in John 15:14,15. The word for friendship, *philia* is found once in the New Testament, in James 4:4.

The exhortation *Beloved, let us love one another* (v. 7) opens the great discussion of love. The endearing term *agapētos* (*Beloved*) is the first word in the Greek; *agapōmen* (let us keep loving) is the second. The author proceeds to give three reasons for that appeal: (1) love is the distinguishing mark of the child of God; (2) the supreme expression of love is God's sending of his Son into the world; (3) God's children are duty-bound to love one another. The discussion which follows is conveniently divided under these headings.

(1) Love is the distinguishing mark of the child of God (vv. 7–8). *Love is of God* identifies the source of love; it is *ek tou theou,* "out of God," or "from God." This is always true of agape, even when it is in man. Of *erōs* it may be said it is *ek tou anthrōpou,* "out of man," or "of man," although it is an endowment given to man by the Creator. The point of difference is that *erōs* is the possession of all men as human beings while agape is the special gift of God to those human beings who become his spiritual children. The statement *and he who loves is born of God* adds weight to the point. Again we have the present participle for *he who loves,* which may be interpreted "the lover." It is the person whose daily life is characterized by love who was and still is (perfect tense) born of God. A child recognizes his father; so the individual who is a lover, whose life is governed by agape, recognizes God as his Father; more than simply recognizing him as Father, he *knows God,* knows him by experience. The loving child comes to some understanding of the hidden ways of

God and the mysteries of his being. Love is the bond that establishes rapport between the child and the Father.

Contrarywise, *he who does not love* (the "nonlover") *does not know* (aorist, "did not come to know") *God* (v. 8). Ignorance of God and, we may deduce, misinterpretations and misrepresentations of God are traceable to the absence of love in men's hearts. The person who loves with agape is the authentic interpreter of and spokesman for God, not the nonlover who has no true experience with God. The reason for this is that *God is love* (v. 8).

Perhaps no profounder statement was ever made than *ho theos agapē estin— God is love.* The author will repeat it in v. 16, but here is the place to comment on its meaning. The statement is not intended to be a "definition" of God. The author has written in another place (1:5) *God is light,* but neither these words nor *God is love* can be called a "definition" of God. Each says something concerning the character of God, and says it in a profound way. For instance, to say *God is love* is to say more than "God loves." One might say "man loves," and this would be correct, but one would not say "man is love." The reason is that the statement "God is love" declares that the very essence of God's character is agape, and therefore it is never absent as a factor in his every word and deed. Now to say *God is love* is not to reduce God to a power, a force, an energy called love. The statement cannot be reversed so that we could say "love is God." The syntax of the Greek sentence will not allow this, nor will reason and good theology permit it. The definite article occurs with *theos,* God, but not with love. God must remain the subject of the sentence and love the descriptive substantive in the predicate. If the article appeared also with love, we could say as a translation "love is God," in which case there would be a linguistic basis for a doctrine of pantheism. Such a doctrine would have no support whatsoever in any other part of the Bible.

As the statement stands, it speaks to us

eloquently of God as a person, for love does not exist apart from a person. It is the supreme characteristic of which a person is capable. *God is love* tells us the kind of person who presides over the universe. He is *the* person who through love begets children and implants in them the love that is the distinguishing characteristic of Father and children.

(2) The supreme expression of love is God's sending of his Son into the world (vv. 9–11). *In this the love of God was made manifest* points to what follows; this tells of the sending of the Son. It was a manifestation *among us*, one that could be seen and known in human experience. It was made not esoterically but openly, in a human being, a person who could speak to persons as persons and be understood. The person was God's *only Son.* The word *only* is the correct translation of *monogenē* (the same adjective used in John 3:16), the meaning actually being "only one of his kind," not "only begotten." There was and is none other like him. There are many sons but only one Son. The verb *sent* is perfect tense in Greek, which means that the Son was sent and remains sent.

The purpose of his sending was *that we might live through him* (v. 9). He came bringing life—God's greatest gift—to men. This is life that is eternal, life that is more than existence, life that conquers death, life *through* the ever-living Son. And so, *this is love, not that we loved* (perfect, "have loved") *but that he loved* (aorist) *us.* But now the author remembers the redemptive work of Christ and adds *to be the expiation for our sins.* (The word expiation translates *hilasmon;* see comment on 2:2.) The author seems to be saying that love cannot be known or understood in terms of man's feeble efforts to love God apart from agape, fully brought to light in the sending of the Son. It was the sending of the Son as an *expiation for our sins* that revealed love to the world and made it available in its fullness to man.

(3) God's children are duty-bound to love one another (vv. 11–12). *Beloved, if God so loved us.* Such love as that revealed in the sending of the Son calls for a worthy response: *we also ought to love one another. No man has ever seen God,* but he *has* seen his brother! The love of the unseen God is undeniable in the person and work of the Son; the response to that love can be made within the fellowship by practicing the same love toward Christian brothers. In loving one another we bring the invisible God into the realm of human experience—*if we love one another, God abides in us and his love is perfected in us* (v. 12). The perfect passive participle is translated by *is perfected.* The meaning is that God's love is brought to consummation, finds its appropriate expression and end in us. God's love, is made real, tangible, concrete in and through the Christian fellowship when the children of God practice love toward one another.

7. Love and Assurance (4:13–21)

13 By this we know that we abide in him and he in us, because he has given us of his own Spirit. 14 And we have seen and testify that the Father has sent his Son as the Savior of the world. 15 Whoever confesses that Jesus is the Son of God, God abides in him, and he in God. 16 So we know and believe the love God has for us. God is love, and he who abides in love abides in God, and God abides in him. 17 In this is love perfected with us, that we may have confidence for the day of judgment, because as he is so are we in this world. 18 There is no fear in love, but perfect love casts out fear. For fear has to do with punishment, and he who fears is not perfected in love. 19 We love, because he first loved us. 20 If any one says, "I love God," and hates his brother, he is a liar; for he who does not love his brother whom he has seen, cannot love God whom he has not seen. 21 And this commandment we have from him, that he who loves God should love his brother also.

In this section the author relates love to Christian assurance and prepares the way for the climactic affirmation of Jesus Christ as the Son of God in 5:1–12.

(1) Assurance through possession of the Spirit of God (v. 13): *By this we know . . . he has given of his own Spirit.* (See comment on 3:24.) The assurance is

of the indivisible unity existing between God the Father and his children: *we abide in him and he in us.* The assurance is based upon the knowledge that God has given (perfect tense) us of his Spirit and that the historic descent of the Spirit at Pentecost guarantees that the Spirit is a permanent gift to believers. The expression *of his own Spirit* emphasizes the fact that the Spirit belongs to the very person of God and when present in men is God himself in them. The resulting unity is that for which Jesus prayed: "that they may all be one; even as thou, Father, art in me, and I in thee, that they also may be in us . . . that they may be one even as we are one, I in them and thou in me" (John 17:21–23). Both in this great prayer and in the passage before us love is indispensable to this unity. The great prayer closes with these words: "that the love with which thou hast loved me may be in them and I in them" (v. 26).

(2) Assurance through recognition of the love of God in the sending of the Son (vv. 14–16a). *And we have seen and testify* made it a matter of apostolic record and witness that the Father had sent the Son. The apostles had beheld (perfect tense) him (cf. 1:1–2). The Father sent him, and he who was sent was *Savior of the world.* Union with God is effected through confession of the man Jesus as *the Son of God.* God *abides* in the person who makes this confession *and he in God.* The entire tenor of John's epistle demands that such confession be from the heart, sincere and vital, and accompanied by full commitment of the life to Christ. *So we know and believe* but v. 16 may be better translated: "And we have known (and still know, perfect) and have believed (and still believe, perfect) the love which God has among (*en*) us." The progression of thought is: confession of Jesus the man as the Son produces union with God which creates experience in which love becomes an object of knowledge and trust.

(3) Assurance for the judgment through love (vv. 16 b–18). *God is love* is a repeti-

tion of the great statement made in 4:8. Although meaning the same here, the accompanying truth is different: *he who abides in love abides in God, and God abides in him.* This is not pantheism since love is not God (see comment on 4:8). The meaning, in the light of what has gone before, is that an individual who abides in love (i.e., who lives a life controlled by love) possesses the Spirit of God and thereby partakes of the nature of God so that he is in union with God. *In this is love perfected with us* means love is brought to fulfillment (or completion) with us." In what is love brought to fulfillment in us? The *that* (*hina*) clause: *that we may have confidence for the day of judgment,* is explanatory of *In this* and what follows; the confidence of believers at the judgment, in other words, will be the fulfillment of love, the completion of love. Actually, *confidence* is boldness, the opposite of fear. The basis for this boldness which believers will have in (*en*, not *for*) the day of judgment is *as he is so are we in this world.* We are like him—like God (daring thought!)—*in this world;* he abides in us and we in him; we are his children; we love as he loves.

We shall have boldness at the judgment because *There is no fear in love.* This is true because *perfect love casts out fear.* This does not mean that there is a higher form of *agapē* called *perfect love* which *casts out fear.* Agape is *perfect love* wherever and whenever manifested. The author calls it perfect love here to emphasize the fact that in contrast with other expressions of love it has the power to cast out fear. In union with God through love in this life, we have no cause to fear to stand before him at the judgment. *For fear has to do with punishment* (lit., "Because fear holds punishment") means that fear and punishment go together. The person who looks toward the judgment with fear contemplates punishment and dreads the judgment. Not so the child of God who lives by love; he knows God in the intimacy of love, knows him as Father, and therefore has no cause to fear him. Fear is the enemy of love: *he who fears is not perfected* (perfect tense, "completed, matured") *in love.* The Greek present participle for *he who fears* describes the person who is habitually harassed by fear. It is such a person who does not attain maturity.

The author's view with respect to love and fear is psychologically sound. Experience teaches us that fear (a) paralyzes and inhibits human efforts, (b) separates individuals from one another and creates between them an atmosphere of suspicion, (c) creates conditions that encourage violence, (d) causes emotional and mental illness in individuals and groups. Love, on the other hand, motivates individuals to respect and accept one another and creates an atmosphere of good will in which they can live together in peace. Love matures individuals; fear impedes their growth toward maturity.

(4) The proof of love for God is love for one's brother (vv. 19–21). *We love, because he first loved us* means that our capacity for love originates in God's love for us. He is the author of and prime mover in agape. But no man who *hates his brother* can claim to have love for God. If a man says, *"I love God," and hates his brother, he is a liar.* The author wrote in 3:14 that a man who hates his brother is a murderer; now he declares he is a liar. Surely this categorizes hate as one of the most grievous of sins. It is interesting that both liars and murderers (as well as "the fearful," KJV) are classified in Revelation 21:8 as among those whose "lot shall be in the lake that burns with fire and brimstone." When a man *does not love his brother* it is clear evidence that he does not love God, *for he who does not love his brother whom he has seen, cannot love God whom he has not seen.* A person who has no love that can reach as far as the brother next to him is incapable of loving the unseen God. It is easy for a man to claim he loves the unseen God, but he must prove by his conduct his love for the brother who is so visible and near.

Love for God must express itself in love for the brother. *And this commandment we have from him, that he who loves God should love his brother also.* Jesus taught that love for God and love for one's neighbor are inseparable (Mark 12:28–31; Matt. 22:34–40). How much more imperative it is, then, that a child of God prove his love for God in love for his Christian brother!

8. *Love and Faith in the Son (5:1–5)*

[1] Every one who believes that Jesus is the Christ is a child of God, and every one who loves the parent loves the child. [2] By this we know that we love the children of God, when we love God and obey his commandments. [3] For this is the love of God, that we keep his commandments. And his commandments are not burdensome. [4] For whatever is born of God overcomes the world; and this is the victory that overcomes the world, our faith. [5] Who is it that overcomes the world but he who believes that Jesus is the Son of God?

John proceeds now to interweave the two subjects of love and sonship, so prominent in preceding discussions, with an emphasis upon the doctrine of Jesus Christ as the Son of God. In his unique manner he joins love, sonship, and faith in Jesus as the Son of God so skillfully that they are made to be inseparable. In accomplishing this blend of Christian doctrine and ethics the author no doubt has an eye on the heretical doctrines of the false teachers concerning the person of Christ, while at the same time formulating for his readers a synthesis of the most important elements of his teaching.

His opening statement bears a strong note of encouragement to those of his readers who are faithful to their original commitment to Christ: *Every one who believes that Jesus is the Christ is a child of God.* A more accurate translation is, "Every one who has faith that Jesus is the Messiah has been born (or begotten) of God." *Every one who believes* describes a person of faith, one who trusts. The verb *pisteuō*, which so often is rendered by the English verb "believe," should in many instances be translated "to have faith." Such is the case here. The corresponding Greek noun *pistis* is uniformly rendered faith, but since there is in English no verb "faith," the verb *pisteuō* is often weakened in translation to "believe." This places the emphasis upon intellectual assent, or assent to creed, in commitment to Christ, whereas it is faith or trust that is demanded by New Testament practice. Admittedly, belief is important in Christian commitment, but faith is primary and indispensable. In John's view it is the person who has faith that the man Jesus is the Messiah (Anointed One) of God who has been begotten of God.

This statement is joined with the declaration *every one who loves the parent loves the child.* In the Greek the literal declaration is unique: "Every one who loves the one who begot loves the one begotten of him," which is a way of saying, "Every one who loves God loves God's child." This amplifies what was said in 4:20–21. The test of one's love for God is love for his brother. John now reinforces what he has previously written (3:23–24) about the necessity of proving one's love by obeying the commandments, now referred to as God's commandments. Here he summarizes: *this is the love of God, that we keep his commandments* (v. 3). This makes it plain enough that *agapē* does not exist apart from its expression in conduct and action. Agape demands *doing,* whatever one's feelings or emotions may be. A person may not "feel right" toward a neighbor, a Christian brother, an enemy, and yet love him with agape by treating him as a person and doing right by him.

The author adds *and his commandments are not burdensome.* We are reminded of Jesus' criticism of the lawyers who laid upon the people "burdens hard to bear" (Luke 11:46) and of his invitation: "Come to me, all who labor and are heavy-laden, and I will give you rest. . . . For my yoke is easy, and my burden is light" (Matt. 11:28,30). Jesus said to the lawyers, "you yourselves do not touch the burdens with one of your fingers" (Luke 11:46). The common people of Jesus' day were helpless under the burden that commandments, traditions, and scribism had placed upon them. It was an entirely different day, brought in by Christianity, testified to here by John. The new commandments and the new power to keep them enabled him to write that God's commandments *are not burdensome* and then to give as the reason: *For whatever is born of God overcomes the world.* The word *whatever* is correct because it refers to something other than a person; it refers to *our faith* in the statement that follows; *our faith* is in the category of *whatever is born of God* and *overcomes the world.* It is *our faith* that gives us the strength to keep God's commandments and enables us to regard them as not *burdensome.*

What does John mean by *our faith* (*hē pistis hēmōn*)? He means the total response of the individual to God revealed in his Son Jesus Christ because he goes on to ask rhetorically, *Who is it that overcomes the world but he who believes that Jesus is the Son of God?* Of course he means that the person who does overcome the world is the person who believes that Jesus is the Son of God. Again we insist that *pisteuō* (the verb translated here "believes") means to have faith. The author has just declared *this is the victory that overcomes the world, our faith,* and *pistis* is the word that is translated *faith* and not "belief." The experience of the individual in responding by faith to the man Jesus as the Son of God is unique in that there is no other human experience like it. There has been no other person in history comparable to Jesus, and no other event comparable to the Christ event. John measured Jesus the Christ and his appearance among men against the background of the might of Rome, the deification of the emperors, and the challenge of the gnostic heresy, and he saw that the one victory over these conglomerate forces belonging to *the world* was faith in Jesus as the Son of God and conqueror of them all.

The faith of which he wrote involves the total commitment of the individual to Jesus

Christ as Lord and Saviour and to the way of life taught by him. Such commitment enables the believer to share in the victory of Jesus the Christ. John remembered that Jesus had said to his disciples on the eve of his crucifixion, "In the world you have tribulation; but be of good cheer, I have overcome the world" (John 16:33). The Greek perfect (*nenikēka*) means "I have conquered and the victory stands."

9. *The Three Witnesses* (*5:6–12*)

⁶ This is he who came by water and blood, Jesus Christ, not with the water only but with the water and the blood. ⁷ And the Spirit is the witness, because the Spirit is the truth. ⁸ There are three witnesses, the Spirit, the water, and the blood; and these three agree. ⁹ If we receive the testimony of men, the testimony of God is greater; for this is the testimony of God that he has borne witness to his Son. ¹⁰ He who believes in the Son of God has the testimony in himself. He who does not believe God has made him a liar, because he has not believed in the testimony that God has borne to his Son. ¹¹ And this is the testimony, that God gave us eternal life, and this life is in his Son. ¹² He who has the Son has life; he who has not the Son of God has not life.

John proceeds now to "call up" three "witnesses" to the messiahship and sonship of Jesus. No doubt his appeal to these witnesses is directed against the heretical doctrines of the false teachers; yet he must have realized that since the evidence provided by these witnesses belonged to the orthodox interpretation of Jesus and the gospel, it would have little weight in convincing the heretics of their errors in doctrine. The witnesses speak, therefore, to believers. Even so, it is necessary for believers to search for John's meaning of *the Spirit, the water,* and *the blood* as applied to the ministry of Jesus in the authentication of the man Jesus as the Son of God.

Our first step in interpretation here is to clarify the text. Those who use the King James Version will observe that v. 7 reads, "For there are three that bear record in heaven, the Father, the Word, and the Holy Ghost: and these three are one," and that v. 8 begins, "And there are three that

bear witness in earth." This reading is based upon an interpolation made in late manuscripts and is not a part of the most valid text. The Revised Standard Version correctly omits it.

The statement is that Jesus the Son of God is the one *who came by water and blood,* whereas with respect to the Spirit it is said *the Spirit is the witness.* How are we to interpret the three witnesses?

The *water* refers primarily to the baptism of Jesus, but there may be a secondary reference to the water which came from the body of Jesus when as he hung on the cross a soldier pierced his side with a spear (John 20:34). It is significant that *blood and water* came from his side. Each is a symbol here, as in the passage before us, where the two are again brought together. In search of the meaning of the symbolism of the water we call to mind the words of John the Baptist, "I myself did not know him; but for this I came baptizing with water, that he might be revealed to Israel" (John 1:31). Jesus literally *came by* (Gr., *dia,* through) water in order to reveal himself as the Messiah of Israel. The baptism of John was a part of the historical process and an event in holy history (the history of Israel) leading up to the revelation of the Messiah. John's baptism was designed to sift the people and identify among them God's Anointed. At the baptism of Jesus the Spirit with his witness confirmed the identification of him as Messiah. John declared, "I saw the Spirit descend as a dove from heaven, and it remained on him. . . . And I have seen and have borne witness that this is the Son of God" (John 1:32,34).

The water and the Spirit are brought together again in the conversation of Jesus with Nicodemus. The most reasonable explanation of Jesus' statement as to the necessity of being born of water and the Spirit (John 3: 5) is that water refers to the baptism of John and its requirement of repentance in preparation for the presentation by the Messiah of the kingdom of God to Israel. Jesus was saying to Nicodemus and to all the Jewish religious leaders (note the plural "You," *humas,* John 3:7) that they must repent (in obedience to the symbolism of John's baptism), thus "being born" of water, this in preparation for entrance into the kingdom of God as presented by the Messiah. But the birth from above was also essential (John 3:3,7). This was the birth of the Spirit (John 3:5) that acceptance of Jesus as Messiah would bring.

In what sense, then, is *water* a witness to the fact that Jesus is the Son of God as John claims in the passage before us? The water testifies to the fact that Jesus was a true historical being who joined hands with his forerunner John the Baptist in providing in the historical event of his baptism evidence that he was the Messiah of prophecy. The witness of the Spirit to the messiahship of Jesus was first given at the baptism, but it was a continuing witness in the work and words of Jesus and in the work and witness of all believers.

What of the *blood* as a witness to Jesus as the Son of God? As we have seen from the exegesis of 1:7, the blood of Jesus represents his life poured out for sinners, even as in the Jewish sacrifices the blood of the animal represented the animal's life given on the altar in place of the life of the one making sacrifice. The blood that Jesus shed in his death represented his utter self-giving and his complete identification with mankind. Also in the blood of Jesus the new covenant between God and his people was sealed (Matt. 26:28). The blood of Jesus is witness to the actual suffering and death of Jesus on the cross.

Concerning the witnesses John declared *these three agree.* The author insists on the wholeness and integrity of the gospel as it is based in the person and work of Christ. He will tolerate no denial of Jesus' deity— he is the Son of God as witnessed to by the Spirit; he will accept no denial of his humanity—he is the man Jesus who *came by water* and was revealed in his baptism as Israel's true Messiah; he will accept no denial of his actual suffering and death— he is the man Jesus who as the Son of

God actually suffered and died on a cross as testified to by his blood that was shed. In contradiction to *the testimony of men* (the testimony of the gnostic teachers) *the testimony of God is greater; for this is the testimony of God that he has borne witness to his Son.*

Added to God's testimony through the three witnesses is the testimony of the believer's inner experience: *He who believes in the Son of God has the testimony in himself.* What the three witnesses say concerning Jesus Christ becomes for the true believer not only objective historical reality but conviction of the mind and heart. What of the one who rejects *the testimony of God?* John's answer is *He who does not believe God has made him a liar.* Why? Because he refuses to believe God's testimony. What is God's testimony? It is that he *gave us eternal life, and this life is in his Son.* John's final affirmation concerning Jesus as the Son of God is that *He who has the Son has life.* By *Son* he means Son of God. His sober conclusion is that life from God is mediated to men not through one who was not truly human or not divine, but through one who was both human and divine.

IV. Concluding Counsel (5:13–21)

1. Assurance and Prayer (5:13–17)

[13] I write this to you who believe in the name of the Son of God, that you may know that you have eternal life. [14] And this is the confidence which we have in him, that if we ask anything according to his will he hears us. [15] And if we know that he hears us in whatever we ask, we know that we have obtained the requests made of him. [16] If any one sees his brother committing what is not a mortal sin, he will ask, and God will give him life for those whose sin is not mortal. There is sin which is mortal; I do not say that one is to pray for that. [17] All wrongdoing is sin, but there is sin which is not mortal.

As John moves toward the conclusion of his epistle, he seeks to leave with his readers one more reminder that his purpose in writing is a worthy one, and by implication he shares with them his conviction that they are sound in the faith. He writes to *you who believe in the name of the Son of God.* He assumes that his readers are persons who have faith in the character by which Jesus is known; he is the Son of God and by this name he is known. Central in his purpose in writing is that these faithful believers shall *know* (go on knowing, know out of a steady state of mind, *oida*) *that you have* (continually) *eternal life.* By eternal (*aiōnios*) life the writers of the New Testament mean life that is endless (as to time) and life that is God-breathed (as to quality).

The confidence which we have in him (in God) derives from the experience of true believers in prayer. That experience is that when God's children *ask anything according to his will he hears us.* If this is the faith believers have in prayer, the result is that *we know that we have obtained the requests made of him.* The true believer prays with such faith that he knows that what he asks for is his even before he receives the actual answer to his petition. The child of God with such faith keeps ever in mind the condition *according to his will.* Therefore he does not pray selfishly, and he accepts as the right answer to his petition whatever he receives. Indeed, his experience teaches him that when he does not receive what he specifically asks for, what he does receive is far better than what he asked for.

But there is an exception to the promise of answer to prayer. It pertains to prayer for persons who are guilty of *sin which is mortal,* literally, "sin unto death" (*hamartia pros thanaton*). John declares, *I do not say that one is to pray for that.* John goes on to explain: *All wrongdoing is sin, but there is sin which is not mortal* ("not unto death").

What does John mean by "sin unto death"? We observe first that, in John's view, a Christian brother can be guilty of *committing what is not a mortal sin* (a sin, or sin, not unto death). Prayer may be made for such a brother with expectation of an answer. But when John writes *God will give him life for those whose sin is not mortal,* he does not write "for those *brothers* whose sin is not mortal." In this manner he excludes the Christian brothers from those who would be guilty of committing "sin unto death." This leads us to express the belief that "sin unto death" was either the sin in which all unregenerate men live, or the sin of apostasy in which the gnostic false teachers (antichrists) lived. The latter are the people John likely had in mind as guilty of *sin which is mortal,* "sin unto death."

John would hardly discourage prayer for the unregenerate person, the ordinary, everyday sinner. But when we consider all he has said concerning the false teachers and the fact that he went so far as to label them antichrists, we need not wonder that he was of a mind that their sin was "sin unto death" and that prayer for them would be fruitless. It is to be observed that he does not command that prayer not be made for those who are guilty of "sin unto death." He had made a very strong statement concerning the certainty that God answers the prayers of true believers. He guards against going on record as claiming that God would answer prayer for those guilty of "sin unto death." He is confident, however, that if a brother prays for a brother who is not guilty of *a mortal sin God will give him life for those whose sin is not mortal.* Presumably the author means that in such case, the brother who is guilty of sin, will be "revived," as we say, and restored to life in the fellowship as an answer to prayer.

One additional point may be suggested: John may be reflecting here the teaching of Jesus concerning the sin against the Holy Spirit (Matt. 12:31–32). Blasphemy against the Spirit, Jesus taught, was unforgivable. The context (Matt. 12:22–37) shows that the Pharisees who charged Jesus with casting out demons by the power of Beelzebub were guilty of this sin against the Holy Spirit because they were so blind spiritually that they attributed the works of God to Satan.

2. *Victory with the Son* (5:18–21)

18 We know that any one born of God does not sin, but He who was born of God keeps him, and the evil one does not touch him.
19 We know that we are of God, and the whole world is in the power of the evil one.
20 And we know that the Son of God has come and has given us understanding, to know him who is true; and we are in him who is true, in his Son Jesus Christ. This is the true God and eternal life. 21 Little children, keep yourselves from idols.

We know that any one born of God does not sin. This is almost a repetition of what John wrote in 3:9 (cf. comment on 3:4–10). But the statement coupled with this declaration contains a new and stimulating idea: Jesus guards the child of God, and Satan does not hold on to him. This is the meaning of the statement *He who was born of God keeps him, and the evil one does not touch him.* The aorist passive participle (*gennētheis*) is rightly translated (with the definite article) as *He who was born* in contrast with the perfect passive participle and the article (*ho gegennēmenos tou theou*), translated *one born of God.* The latter is the common construction in the epistle for the true believer, the child of God. The aorist passive participle of this verb is used in the epistle only here and can only refer to Jesus as *He who was born of God.* In support of this interpretation is the fact that the object of *keeps* is *auton* (him), the third personal pronoun, not the reflexive *heauton* (himself), which would be the object of *keeps* if *He who was born of God* referred to a believer instead of to Christ.

From the exegesis, then, we derive a comforting conclusion, namely, the child of God, the *one born of God,* does not continue in sin (*hamartanei,* present tense) but has the continuous protection of the Son of God who was also *born of God* (as the Son in human flesh). The picture is of the Son guarding the sons of God. The Son is in contest with *the evil one* for the souls of the children of God, but the victory is continually won by the Son because, as

John writes, *the evil one does not touch him.* However, a better translation is "the evil one does not cling (present tense) to him."

We know that we are of God is an expression of confidence over against the depressing assertion that *the whole world is in the power of the evil one.* But there is no word in the Greek sentence for "power." The Greek actually says "the whole world lies in the evil one." The declaration is gloomy enough in the Greek without adding the idea that the whole world is in Satan's power. The Greek does allow that the whole world is the province of the devil's activity and is subject to the depredations of the evil one, but over against this dark picture is the grand assurance *that the Son of God has come.* The verb means "has come and is here." Furthermore, he *has given us understanding, to know him who is true* (v. 20). The idea is that by his coming and continuing presence the Son of God has given to the children of God insight that enables them to know God who is the true One (contrasted with the idols and false gods). *And we are in him who is true* is a declaration of the unity existing between God and the children of God, a favorite truth with John. It emphasizes the fact that the knowledge believers have of God is implemented by experience with God and is superior to the *gnōsis* claimed by the heretics. John assures his readers that they are also *in his Son Jesus Christ,* which is quite in keeping with the prayer of Jesus: "that they may all be one; even as thou, Father, art in me, and I in thee, that they also may be in us" (John 17:21).

This is the true God and eternal life refers to *him who is true* and affirms that union of believers with God and Christ is eternal life.

The final words: *Little children, keep yourselves from idols* is an appropriate exhortation in the light of John's exaltation of the God *who is true* and his Son Jesus Christ who *has given us understanding, to know him who is true.*

Commentary on 2 John

Outline

I. Salutation (1–3)
II. Exhortation to love and warning against false teachers (4–11)
III. Farewell (12–13)

In this letter and in 3 John we have samples of correspondence that was common in the first century, although the letter before us is more formal than the average letter among the thousands of papyrus letters and documents found in the sands and ancient garbage dumps of Egypt. The two little letters of John were doubtless written on papyrus sheets five by nine or eleven inches in size, these being the measurements of the average papyrus sheets of the time.

Papyrus, the paper of the Greco-Roman world, was the name of the plant from which the material was taken to make the sheets used for correspondence. Our English word paper is derived from the word. The plant flourished along the banks of the Nile River. The sheets were made from the pith inside the stalks. Thin strips of the pith were laid down as one layer, and another layer of strips was laid on top of this layer and at right angles to it. Then the material was dampened with water or perhaps with some thin liquid adhesive, and the two layers were pressed together. After being dried in the sun, the sheets were smoothed with a shell or bone. Later, the sheets were glued together to make rolls on which books were written. These rolls were usually 18 to 20 feet in length. (The Gospel of Mark was probably first written on a papyrus roll 19 feet in length).

The *ink* referred to in 2 John 12 and 3 John 13 was doubtless made from lamp-black (or soot), water, and gum. The *pen* (3 John 13) was either a reed brush or a quill pen (or something similar to a quill pen).

In the second century, or early third century, papyrus codices or books came into use. These were made in somewhat the manner that books are made today. Larger than average sheets of papyrus were folded and put together at the folds, each half-sheet making a page on each side. The most valuable of all biblical papyri are from a codex manuscript of the epistles of Paul. They are in two collections, one, P^{37}, the Ann Arbor Papyrus, the other, P^{45}, the London Papyrus (the Chester Beatty Collection). They are dated in the third century.[12]

I. Salutation (1–3)

1 The elder to the elect lady and her children, whom I love in the truth, and not only I but also all who know the truth, 2 because of the truth which abides in us and will be with us for ever:
3 Grace, mercy, and peace will be with us, from God the Father and from Jesus Christ the Father's Son, in truth and love.

The elder to the elect lady. Eusebius (*Eccles. Hist.*, 3.39) gives the famous quotation from the writings of Papias (early second century) in which he (Papias) seems to refer to the apostles as elders (*presbuteroi*), including among them John the apostle. But he goes on to mention an Elder (*presbuteros*) John who was alive, as we surmise from Papias' language, when he wrote, and from whom he learned much (through visiting teachers) concerning Jesus and the apostles and their teaching. Here, then, is evidence that the apostles were referred to soon after 2 John was

---

12 They have been described and reproduced in *A Third-Century Codex of the Epistles of Paul*, ed. Henry A. Sanders (Ann Arbor: University of Michigan Press, 1935).

written as "elders." Assuming that the apostle Peter wrote 1 Peter, he referred to himself as an elder (5:1). Papias' mention of this elder John, whom he distinguishes from the apostle John and implies to have been alive when Papias wrote, is the principal piece of evidence upon which some scholars rest the claim that this elder, and not John the apostle, was the author of the Johannine Epistles. But evidence which has come to us from the early church fathers, added to Papias' statement, plus Peter's reference to himself as a "fellow elder" with the elders of the churches to which he wrote, make a good case for the view that the Elder of 2 John was the apostle John and was the author of all three of the epistles, and most likely of the Gospel.

The *elect lady* was almost certainly a title applied to a church. The *children* of the elect lady were not only at home with their mother but apparently "scattered abroad" where the author had found *some* of them *following the truth.* The *children* are loved *in the truth* by the Elder, and also by *all who know the truth.* These statements do not sound as if they apply to one woman and her children. It would be in keeping with a usage of the time to refer to a group or a city as a lady. (We may compare this with our custom of designating a college as *alma mater,* "fostering mother.") One explanation worthy of consideration is that the author disguised the identity of the church in order to protect its members against persecution and arrest by government authorities. This explanation is based on the assumption that government persecution (under Domitian?) had already begun in the province of Asia. The church as the body of Christ is conceived of as his "bride" in Ephesians 5: 25–32 and in Revelation 19:7–8 and 21:2. (The very Greek word for lady here, *kuria,* is found in the salutation of a letter written in 1 B.C. by Hilarion to his wife Alis.[13] The

[13] *Oxyrhynchus Papyri,* 744, ed. Grenfell and Hunt, in George Milligan, *Selections from the Greek Papyri* (Cambridge: Cambridge University Press, 1912).

adjective *elect* here is more than an expression of respect or flattery. It bears the connotation of election as applied by Paul and Peter to the people of God as the chosen of God (Rom. 8:33; 1 Peter 1:2; 2:9). Observe that this *lady* has an "elect sister" (v. 13), who has "children" who send their greetings by the elder.

The term *children* applies to members of the churches. *I love in truth* is an affirmation that is more than formal, carrying with it the weight of the exhortation in 1 John 3:18, "let us love not in word or speech but in deed and in truth." Truth in both places has connotation of reality. It likewise refers in the three epistles to orthodox Christian doctrine as opposed to the heretical doctrines of the false teachers. It is this truth *the elder* refers to when he writes of all *who know the truth,* and *the truth which abides in us and will be with us forever.*

The opening benediction is noteworthy in that it is *in truth and love (agapē)* from *God the Father and from Jesus Christ the Father's Son.* In this brief compass the author brings together several of the major ideas that engage his attention in the first epistle: God is Father; Jesus is Son of God the Father; and the movement of God toward man is expressed in *truth* (reality) and *love (agapē). Love* and *truth (alētheia)* have the same force in 2 and 3 John as they have in the first epistle (as, for instance, in 2:4; 3:18 f.; 4:6; 3:1,16; 4:7 f.).

II. Exhortation to Love and Warning Against False Teachers (4–11)

[4] I rejoiced greatly to find some of your children following the truth, just as we have been commanded by the Father. [5] And now I beg you, lady, not as though I were writing you a new commandment, but the one we have had from the beginning, that we love one another. [6] And this is love, that we follow his commandments; this is the commandment, as you have heard from the beginning, that you follow love. [7] For many deceivers have gone out into the world, men who will not acknowledge the coming of Jesus Christ in the flesh; such a one is the deceiver and the antichrist. [8] Look to yourselves, that you may not lose what you have worked for, but may win a full

reward. ⁹ Any one who goes ahead and does not abide in the doctrine of Christ does not have God; he who abides in the doctrine has both the Father and the Son. ¹⁰ If any one comes to you and does not bring this doctrine, do not receive him into the house or give him any greeting; ¹¹ for he who greets him shares his wicked work.

I rejoiced greatly reflects the Elder's strong feeling concerning the heresy threatening the churches in that it reveals his gratitude for the loyalty of the faithful. The translation *some of your children* may cause the picture to appear darker than it really was. The Greek is *ek tōn teknōn,* "of your children." The author means simply that he found Christians who were members of the church to which he was writing *following the truth.*

The author's appeal to his readers to obey the commandment of love is quite similar to appeals in 1 John and, as was stated in the introduction, is evidence of common authorship of the two writings. (For interpretation that will apply to vv. 5–6 see comments on 1 John 2:7–11; 3:11–18; and 4:7–5:5.)

For many deceivers have gone out into the world introduces the main purpose of the letter, namely, to warn this church against the false teachers, who apparently were conducting a vigorous campaign in the province of Asia to win converts to their heretical views. They were the same teachers attacked by John in the first epistle: *men who will not acknowledge the coming of Jesus Christ in the flesh.* There is an interesting difference here in the form of the indictment against the false prophets, as compared with the way the charge is stated in 1 John 4:2. There the perfect participle is used in the Greek to describe the coming of Jesus Christ in the flesh, and the statement is properly translated "every spirit which confesses that Jesus Christ has come in the flesh is of God." Here, however, the present participle is used and the translation is properly *coming* (not *the* coming, however, as in the RSV). It is simply another way of describing the heresy

of the false prophets. The Elder was not accusing these heretics of denying the second coming of Christ; they were Docetists who denied that the body of Jesus was a real human body; they held that Jesus only *appeared* to be a man. Literally translated the Elder's statement (v. 7) is: "For many deceivers went out into the world, those not confessing Jesus Christ coming in flesh." The present participle ("coming") is descriptive of the person of Jesus in the course of his earthly life. He was one who could be described as a person "coming in flesh." Anyone denying that this was the character of Jesus is branded as *the antichrist* (v. 7). This was the name John gave the heretics in his first epistle (2:18; 4:2 f.).

The Elder expressed his concern that his readers would fail to recognize the false prophets for what they were and would open their homes to them in Christian hospitality. His concern was based upon the custom of first-century Christians of entertaining traveling evangelists and missionaries. His warning begins: *Look to yourselves, that you may not lose what you have worked for* (v. 8). Describing the visiting missionary who is one of the heretical teachers, he writes *Any one who . . . does not abide in the doctrine (didachē,* teaching) *of Christ does not have God.* By *the doctrine of Christ* he means not only the teaching of Christ but also the teaching about Christ. The latter would include the doctrine (or teaching) that Jesus was the Son of God. This is why the Elder wrote that any one who did not *abide in the doctrine of Christ* did *not have God.* The teaching that Jesus was the Son of God, God in the flesh, belonged to the *kērugma,* the primitive proclamation of the gospel, and it was this *kērugma* that John's correspondents had received. It was *he who abides in the doctrine of Christ* who had *both the Father and the Son* (v. 9), for Father and Son were inseparable in the teaching of Jesus. If a missionary of that time asked for entertainment in a Christian's home, his teaching was to be put to the test. If he *does not bring this doctrine,* warns the Elder, *do not receive him into the house or give him any greeting.* The Elder wrote in effect, "do not be at home to him."

The apparent harshness or even un-Christian nature of the prohibition testifies to the seriousness of the heresy and its inroads into Christian ranks. This is emphasized in the additional warning: *for he who greets him shares his wicked work.* This could mean that the host of one of the heretical teachers might not only be converted to the heretical doctrine brought by the false teacher, but that by entertaining him he would give approval to the work of the bearer of false doctrine. This hospitable treatment could influence the host's fellow church members to accept the false doctrine and could be reported in churches farther along in the false prophet's journey in an effort to bolster his cause.

III. Farewell (12–13)

12 Though I have much to write to you, I would rather not use paper and ink, but I hope to come to see you and talk with you face to face, so that our joy may be complete. 13 The children of your elect sister greet you.

The Elder has come in his writing to the end of the papyrus sheet. He had *much more* he would like to write, but he would *rather not use paper and ink.* His hope was *to come to see* his readers *and talk with* them *face to face* (*stoma pros stoma*, lit., "mouth to mouth"). By such a visit he wished to make complete *our joy,* as full to overflowing that it would be shared by both the Elder and the readers of his letter.

The children of your elect sister greet you is a farewell greeting in which the Elder included the members of the church to which he belonged at the time he wrote.

Commentary on 3 John

Outline

I. Salutation (1)
II. A good word for Gaius (2–4)
III. An appeal for Christian hospitality (5–8)
IV. Condemnation of Diotrephes (9–10)
V. Praise for Demetrius (11–12)
VI. Concluding words (13–15)

The letter could be a companion letter to 2 John in that it was supplementary to it, sent at the same time or later. In this case the statement "I have written something to the church" (v. 9) would refer to 2 John, and the "church" would be the "elect lady" of 2 John 1. Demetrius (v. 12) could have been the bearer of this letter, even of both letters. If the destination of both letters was one church and not two churches, we would have a more rational explanation of the preservation of what appear to be somewhat insignificant communications to individuals. Two letters addressed to a single church but dealing chiefly with a subject that was of concern to all the churches would be regarded as sufficiently important to be preserved by the receiving church and later to be included in a collection of letters. The common subject of both letters was the problem of hospitality to and entertainment of traveling missionaries. Second John was written to warn against hospitality to missionaries who were bearers of the gnostic heresy; the chief purpose of 3 John was to encourage hospitality to missionaries who were orthodox in their views. The letters therefore balance each other and taken together would serve as a guide to all the churches in their effort to follow the right course in the exercise of Christian hospitality.

I. Salutation (1)

1 The elder to the beloved Gaius, whom I love in the truth.

Three other men by the name *Gaius* appear in the New Testament, two of them being companions of Paul (Acts 19:29; 20:4), the other a man baptized by Paul at Corinth (1 Cor. 1:14; Rom. 16:23). Since the name was a common one, it is highly unlikely that the Gaius addressed by the Elder is to be identified with any one of the other three. It is possible that he was the pastor of the church mentioned in vv. 6,9,10, but it is also possible that Diotrephes, because of his unusual power as a leader in the church, was its pastor. However this may be, the Elder held Gaius in great affection; he numbered him among his *children* (v. 4), described him as *beloved* and addressed him as one *whom I love in the truth.* There being no definite article in the Greek before *alētheia* (truth), we may translate this clause "whom I truly love." However, we cannot rule out the possibility that the word here carries with it the weight that it has in 1 John 2:21, where it means the truth of the gospel of Jesus Christ the Son of God. If this be the meaning here, John is stressing the fact that Gaius is one of those persons whom he loves in the bonds of the gospel. The same may be said of the Elder's love for "the elect lady and her children" (2 John 1).

II. A Good Word for Gaius (2–4)

² Beloved, I pray that all may go well with you and that you may be in health; I know that it is well with your soul. ³ For I greatly rejoiced when some of the brethren arrived and testified to the truth of your life, as indeed you do follow the truth. ⁴ No greater joy can I have than this, to hear that my children follow the truth.

I pray that all may go well with you is the kind of formal wish which the letters of the time often contained. As as illustration, a letter of A.D. 22 from Sarapion in Alexandria, to his brother Dorin, has these words in the salutation: "greeting and continuing health." [14] The Elder expresses the wish that Gaius' spiritual health may keep

pace with his physical health: *as I know it is well with your soul* (*psuchē*). The Elder had occasion to rejoice at the reports the brethren had brought of the fidelity of Gaius. The phrase *the truth of your life* is literally "your truth." The man's character corresponded with his daily walk: *as indeed you do follow the truth.* This was a source of great joy to the Elder; he could have no greater joy than *to hear that my children follow the truth,* literally, "walking in the truth." Here we may be certain that John is referring to the truth as it is revealed in Jesus Christ the Son of God (1 John 2:21), and there can be little doubt that he measures the faithfulness of his children to the gospel against the background of the disloyalty of the false teachers.

III. An Appeal for Christian Hospitality (5–8)

⁵ Beloved, it is a loyal thing you do when you render any service to the brethren, especially to strangers, ⁶ who have testified to your love before the church. You will do well to send them on their journey as befits God's service. ⁷ For they have set out for his sake and have accepted nothing from the heathen. ⁸ So we ought to support such men, that we may be fellow workers in the truth.

Traveling philosophers, teachers, and lecturers were a common sight on the Roman roads in the first century. They were often entertained in the homes of their disciples or friends. Christianity was a missionary religion. This, together with the demand which arose early for teachers, led the Christian evangelists, missionaries, and teachers to follow the example set by their pagan counterparts by taking to the highways to propagate the faith and give instruction in its doctrines. The roads were excellent, busy with the traffic of commerce and pleasure, and often thronged with pedestrians of all descriptions. But the inns were questionable and often the centers of crime. They were shunned by Christians as places of disrepute.

Christian missionaries and teachers would naturally expect, therefore, to be enter-

---

14 Milligan (ed. Grenfell and Hunt), *op. cit.*, p. 34.

tained in the homes of Christians. It became a mark of true Christian charity for a family to open its home to visiting teachers and brethren. A widow who was worthy to be enrolled for the church's assistance must be one who had "shown hospitality, washed the feet of the saints" (1 Tim. 5:10).[15] By entertaining a visiting teacher or missionary the host bestowed upon him approval of his character and doctrine. This was the point at which the problem arose, and accounts for the stern warning in 2 John against entertaining a heretic.

Now if the destination of both letters was the same church, we can understand the better the reason for the admonition: *You will do well to send them on their journey as befits God's service.* In his first letter the Elder had spoken out strongly against entertaining heretics. Here he shows the other side of the matter: to entertain missionaries who were faithful to the gospel was a good practice. In this letter to his beloved Gaius he praises hospitality to strangers and trusts Gaius to explain his position to the church. In the other letter he had warned: "he who greets him (a traveling missionary) shares his wicked work"; in this letter he writes: *we ought to support such men, that we may be fellow workers in the truth.*

IV. Condemnation of Diotrephes (9–10)

⁹ I have written something to the church; but Diotrephes, who likes to put himself first, does not acknowledge my authority. ¹⁰ So if I come, I will bring up what he is doing, prating against me with evil words. And not content with that, he refuses himself to welcome the brethren, and also stops those who want to welcome them and puts them out of the church.

Diotrephes, who likes to put himself first was "the lover of pre-eminence." It was the character and activity of this man, no doubt, that led the Elder to address his letter to Gaius and trust him to present its

---

[15] The visitor removed his sandals upon entering a house, left them at the door, then accepted the host's sure mark of hospitality by allowing his feet to be washed.

---

contents in the right way to the church. Had the letter been addressed directly to the church, Diotrephes might have succeeded in having it suppressed. He must have been an obnoxious, unlovely person. He was guilty, according to the Elder, of not acknowledging *my authority.* This is probably what the Elder meant, although literally he wrote, "he does not receive us." If John the apostle was the author of the letter, as we have maintained, we are given here a glimpse of the widespread respect for his apostolic authority, in that this disrespect for his authority is something definitely contrary to what was expected. Furthermore, the apostle is confident he can "put him in his place" when he next visits the church, for he warns, *So if I come, I will bring up what he is doing;* he is not afraid to match his authority against the pretended authority of the self-inflated Diotrephes.

This man had made himself obnoxious to the Elder in opposing the entertainment of Christian brothers, a policy strongly advocated by the Elder. Diotrephes' power over the congregation must have been strong because he not only refused *himself to welcome the brethren,* but he stopped *those who want to welcome them and puts them out of the church.* It is difficult to understand how one man could exercise such authority, but apparently he did, because John's word for *puts . . . out* is *ekballei,* which means "throws out." He must have been the moderator of the congregation or chairman of the deacons. Could he have been the rich owner of a number of slaves who were members of the church?

V. Praise for Demetrius (11–12)

¹¹ Beloved, do not imitate evil but imitate good. He who does good is of God; he who does evil has not seen God. ¹² Demetrius has testimony from every one, and from the truth itself; I testify to him too, and you know my testimony is true.

Demetrius is one of a different stamp altogether, and the contrast between him and Diotrephes would not be lost on the congregation. *Beloved, do not imitate evil but imitate good* was addressed to Gaius, but its meaning to the congregation would be "do not imitate Diotrephes, but imitate Demetrius." Everyone, including the Elder, testified to the good character of this man who probably was the bearer of the letter. He also enjoyed testimony *from the truth itself*, which was high praise, meaning as it did that he bore the approval of the truth as revealed in the gospel of Jesus Christ the Son of God. The praise of the Elder would carry weight because, as he wrote, *you know my testimony is true.*

VI. Concluding Words (13–15)

13 I had much to write to you, but I would rather not write with pen and ink; 14 I hope to see you soon, and we will talk together face to face.

15 Peace be to you. The friends greet you. Greet the friends, every one of them.

The letter is brought to a close with customary words of farewell. The author had much more to write, but he *would rather not write with pen and ink.* His word for *ink* here (*melanos*) is the same used in 2 John 12, but he uses *kalamos* (pen), while in 2 John 12 he had used the word for paper, *chartēs*, related to the verb *charassō*, which meant to engrave. The word *kalamos* meant a reed, suggesting the plant from which the writing instrument was made. The expression *face to face*, literally "mouth to mouth" (*stoma pros stoma*) is the same as found in 2 John 12. It is a graphic description of intimate dialogue, for which in modern slang we might say "'eyeball to eyeball.'" *Greet the friends, every one of them,* is even more personal in the Greek; "Greet the friends by name" (*kat' onoma*).

Jude

RAY SUMMERS

Introduction

In a contest for the unenviable title, "Least Known and Most Neglected Book in the New Testament," Jude would have competition from 2 and 3 John alone. Many Christians know the expression "the faith which was once for all delivered to the saints" (v. 3). Fewer are familiar with the doxology (vv. 24–25), which stands as the most beautiful benediction in the New Testament. It is doubtful, however, if most of the Christians who know these passages know that they are in Jude.

It is unfortunate that the book is so little known. It is one of our most important documents from the period in Christian history when the lines between orthodoxy and heresy were being drawn. Its particular application is at the point of deciding that there *is* a relationship between profession and practice, between creed and conduct, between doctrinal belief and ethical behavior. No decision is of greater importance in the life of the church of our twentieth-century secular culture.

I. Authorship

The epistle bears the name of Jude as author. Further, this Jude identifies himself as the brother of James. Both names were common in the Hebrew community of the New Testament day. Jude is the short form for Judas and James is the English form for Jacob. In the New Testament there are several men by each name, Judas and James. There is only one combination of brothers by those names, however, the James and Jude who are listed as two of the four brothers of Jesus (Matt. 13:55; Mark 6:3). In 1 Corinthians 9:5 Paul wrote of "the brothers of the Lord" who, like Simon Peter and other apostles, were traveling evangelists who took their wives with them on their journeys. The reference may have been to James and Jude.

There is no other Jude in the New Testament who may have been well enough known to have identified himself in such a simple way. On the other hand, except for the above references, this Jude is unknown in the New Testament and practically unknown in early Christian history. In his *Ecclesiastical History* (III.19:1—20:6), Eusebius included a story of two grandsons of Jude, the brother of Jesus. Eusebius had the story from Hegesippus (about A.D. 180) that the two were accused before the Emperor Domitian. He dismissed them when, by their calloused hands, they proved to him that they were simple farmers and that they held no views which made them politically dangerous. According to the story, both of them later became bishops. There is no sound reason for rejecting the story. If it is a true story, Jude could well have lived long enough to have written this epistle.[1] Until more convincing evidence of a contrary nature is available, one can with intellectual integrity accept both James and

[1] Mayor, p. cxlviii, argues this convincingly in refuting those who argue that Jude could not have lived that long.

Jude as epistles from the Lord's half-brothers.

II. Date, Place, Recipients, and Purpose

The place of the writing of the epistle is entirely conjectural. There is no evidence available as to the area of Jude's ministry unless 1 Corinthians 9:5 indicates a ministry in that territory. Even if that is the meaning of the reference, it represents a ministry in the early fifties. Rome as a possible locale for the writing is tied in with many other conjectural matters related to 2 Peter, such as: Did Peter write 2 Peter? If so, did he write from Rome as he did in 1 Peter? If indeed he wrote 1 Peter from Rome! Did Jude use 2 Peter? Did 2 Peter use Jude? Did both use a common source with neither using the other? Conjecture as to the place of Jude's writing is idle; the matter is really of no importance.

All that can be said of the identity of the recipients is that they were beset by the same problems which vexed the recipients of 2 Peter. That suggests an identity of the two groups, but by no means proves it. The recipients were being threatened by false teachers who were likely Gnostics. Whatever the opinion of past scholarship, it is readily granted today that Gnosticism was an early and very widespread threat to the mainstream of Christian thought. Paul had contended with it at least as early as his epistle to the Colossians. By early in the second century it was firmly entrenched in the Mediterranean world—Palestine, Asia, Africa, and Rome. At any suggested date for the writing of Jude, it could have been addressed to Christians anywhere. With no particular line of argument, this writer inclines toward Syria or Asia.

The date of the writing is inevitably related to the date of 2 Peter and the question of the relationship between the two. Except for a few introductory verses and the closing doxology, almost all of Jude is common to 2 Peter, mostly 2 Peter 2. The material is common and the organizational approach is similar. As to the *amount* of the common material, compare: 2 Peter with Jude—1:2 with v. 2; 1:5 with v. 3; 1:12 with v. 5a; 2:1—3:3 with vv. 5b–19; 3:14 with v. 24.

As to the *nature* of the common material, note: (1) Both write to warn against false teachers. (2) Both use three illustrations of God's judgment, two of which are identical: judgment on angels; judgment on Sodom and Gomorrah. (3) Both use Balaam as an example of false teachers. (4) Both characterize the false teachers as men who are defiant toward divine authority. (5) Both use materials from apocryphal writings, though 2 Peter does not identify it as such; Jude does. (6) Both use the same strong metaphors to characterize the false teachers: rainless clouds; irrational animals; doomed to eternal darkness; spots and blemishes; loud-mouth boasters, etc.

Three theories stand out for explaining this similarity: first, 2 Peter borrowed heavily from Jude; second, Jude borrowed heavily from 2 Peter; third, both 2 Peter and Jude used a common source (oral, or more probably written) which has been lost. A fourth idea that the two are entirely independent has no value in explaining the minute details of common material.

Numerically, the majority of scholarly opinion favors the *first* view. While the arguments are long, tedious, and technical, the position is based almost completely on lines of probability of the nature of the following:

(1) It is more probable that the writer of 2 Peter would incorporate into his letter the entirety of Jude than that Jude would have lifted one chapter out of 2 Peter and presented it as a separate epistle. (2) The unknown writer of 2 Peter (another assumption based on probability) used the epistle from Jude, the brother of James and Jesus, to give authority to his letter. (3) The writer of 2 Peter removed from Jude the explicit references to apocryphal books (1 Enoch in Jude 6,14 and 2 Peter 2:4) and the identifiable materials of apocryphal books (The Assumption of Moses in Jude 9 and 2 Peter 2:11) to make his letter more acceptable to Christian

readers.

The *second* view is also supported by lines of probability of the nature of the following. (1) It is more probable that a writer (Jude) would lift out part of a previously written book (2 Peter) and present it as a separate letter than the reverse. Attention is called to Jude's situation. He was engaged in writing a treatise on "our common salvation" (v. 3) when disturbing news came of the inroads of Gnostic heresy in the churches. He felt compelled to change his intent and to write to warn them of the heresy. With 2 Peter at hand (and, perhaps, his recipients' acquaintance with it) he wrote, using the appropriate materials. (2) It is more probable that the lesser known Jude would have borrowed from a letter which bore the name of the apostle Peter than the reverse. (3) It is more probable that Jude would clarify the references to the apocryphal books involved than that Peter would obscure them. On this point Wand (p. 132) argues for the priority of Jude, and Bigg (p. 217) argues for the priority of 2 Peter! The two books were Jewish writings which were highly regarded and widely circulated books. There is evidence that some early Christians accepted at least Enoch as authoritative (e.g., Tertullian). (4) Much of 2 Peter uses the future tense as a warning that false teachers will arise, while Jude uses the past tense to indicate that they have already arisen and, in fact, have secured a large following. The "teachers" have gained "students." (5) The Greek of Jude seems to represent a smoothing out of some of 2 Peter's awkward constructions.

Because of despairing hopes of demonstrating either the first or the second views, the *third* view has arisen as a *via media*, i.e., perhaps both writers had a common source from which each borrowed. Guthrie (p. 246) presents the case for a possible written source, a "tract" in nature. Reicke (p. 190) presents the case for a possible oral source, sermonic in nature. The major objection to the view is that it tends to con-fuse if not to dodge the issue by positing a "lost document" source. It must be remembered, however, that the "lost document" hypothesis is not unknown in explaining common materials in two books. In spite of the fact that some scholars have given up on the theory of a common document ("Logia" or "Q") to explain the 272 verses of teaching material common only to Matthew and Luke, the theory is still alive and in good standing in the world of New Testament scholarship.

Out of all of the maze of argument on authorship and date, this writer emerges with the following recognizably vulnerable inclinations: The epistle was written by Jude, the half-brother of Jesus. It was written about A.D. 80 to warn against heresy and to encourage loyalty to a "faith" that had come to be rather firmly set as a body of belief. In issuing his warning and exhortation, Jude borrowed from the previously written 2 Peter as the best way to an acceptance by his heretic-harassed readers.

Outline

Salutation (vv. 1–2)
I. An appeal for orthodoxy (vv. 3–4)
II. A reminder of judgment (vv. 5–7)
III. A warning against heresy (vv. 8–16)
   1. Human propagation of heresy (vv. 8–13)
   2. Divine judgment on heretics (vv. 14–16)
IV. An exhortation to fidelity (vv. 17–23)
   Doxology (vv. 24–25)

Selected Bibliography

BEKER, J. C. "Jude, Letter of," *The Interpreter's Dictionary of the Bible*, **II**. Nashville: Abingdon Press, 1962.

BIGG, CHARLES. *A Critical and Exegetical Commentary on the Epistles of St. Peter and St. Jude.* ("The International Critical Commentary.") Edinburgh: T. & T. Clark, 1902.

CRANFIELD, C. E. B. *I and II Peter and Jude.* ("The Torch Bible Commentaries.") London: SCM Press, Ltd., 1960.

FEINE, PAUL and BEHM, JOHANNES, ed. by Werner Georg Kummel. *Introduction to the New Testament.* Nashville: Abingdon Press, 1966.

GREEN, MICHAEL. *The Second Epistle General of Peter and the General Epistle of Jude.* ("The Tyndale New Testament Com-

mentaries.") Grand Rapids: Wm. B. Eerdmans Publishing Co., 1968.

GUTHRIE, DONALD. *New Testament Introduction, Hebrews to Revelation.* Chicago: Inter-Varsity Press, 1964.

LEANEY, A. R. C. *The Letters of Peter and Jude.* Cambridge: At the University Press, 1967.

MAYOR, J. B. *The Epistle of St. Jude and the Second Epistle of St. Peter.* Grand Rapids: Baker Book House, 1965.

REICKE, BO. *The Epistles of James, Peter, and Jude.* ("The Anchor Bible.") Garden City: Doubleday and Company, Inc., 1964.

SIDEBOTTOM, E. M. *James, Jude, and 2 Peter.* ("The Century Bible.") London: Thomas Nelson, 1967.

WAND, J. W. C. *The General Epistles of St. Peter and St. Jude.* ("Westminster Commentaries.") London: Methuen and Co. Ltd., 1934.

Commentary on the Text

From its earliest written expression, the Christian faith has responded vigorously to heretical encroachment. In its first years, as represented in Acts and the earlier Pauline epistles, the encroachment was from the Judaizers who sought to impose their legal strictures upon Gentiles, who were becoming Christians.

The next major threat came from the Gnostics. Like the Judaizers, they claimed to be a part of the Christian community. Unlike the Judaizers, they contended for a freedom from legal restrictions which resulted in a life of license and corruption, a life which rejected all constituted religious authority whether human or divine. The epistle of Jude is one of the earliest which Christians addressed to that problem, the problem of determining the dividing line between doctrine true and false, and life true and false. The epistle is an indictment of heresy and a proclamation of orthodoxy in both doctrine and practice.

Salutation (vv. 1–2)

¹ Jude, a servant of Jesus Christ and brother of James,
To those who are called, beloved in God the Father and kept for Jesus Christ:
² May mercy, peace, and love be multiplied to you.

The writer designates himself *Jude* and identifies himself as *a servant of Jesus Christ and brother of James. Jude* is a Christianizing of the Hebrew and Greek Judas. The form Judas had a long and honorable history in Hebrew use but, for obvious reasons, not in Christian use. If this Jude was indeed the brother of Jesus (cf. the Int.), it was with becoming modesty that he did not stress it. He used the more humble *servant of Jesus Christ.* There appears to be little doubt that by **brother of James** he was referring to James the brother of Jesus, known in early Christian tradition as the leader of the church in Jerusalem (Acts 15) and the author of the epistle of James. *Those who are called* gives only spiritual identification to the recipients. *Called* is a New Testament concept for those who hear God's call to sonship and respond in obedient faith in Jesus Christ. Two other words characterize Jude's readers—*beloved* and *kept. Beloved* in the manuscripts is in the perfect tense, which expresses their state of being in the circle of God's love. *Kept,* in the same tense, means that they are in a state of being guarded from harm. Synonyms are "preserved," "watched over," "protected." The RSV translation *for Jesus Christ* implies that they are kept by God for Christ. If, however, the preposition *in* is to be understood with both God and Christ, the sense is that they are **beloved** in God and **kept** in Christ.

The familiar epistolary prayer for "grace and peace" (Paul's letter; 1 and 2 Peter) is different in Jude. His letter reflects a love for triple expressions. Here the triad forms a prayer for *mercy, peace and love* to *be multiplied* for them. This triad soon found its way into second-century writings, e.g., the epistle of Polycarp and the Martyrdom of Polycary (about A.D. 155).

I. An Appeal for Orthodoxy (vv. 3–4)

3 Beloved, being very eager to write to you of our common salvation, I found it necessary to write appealing to you to contend for the faith which was once for all delivered to the saints. 4 For admission has been secretly gained by some who long ago were designated for this condemnation, ungodly persons who pervert the grace of our God into licentiousness and deny our only Master and Lord, Jesus Christ.

"Our Common Salvation" was apparently the title of a treatise which Jude was in the process of writing. *Being very eager to write* is the translation of an expression which means exactly "while working with all diligence to write." The total impression is that he was actually engaged in the writing.

Our common salvation has been understood by some as a reference to Gentile Christians, whereas Jude was a Jewish Christian—hence the salvation we all have in common. This may be; it cannot be pressed. Vainly one wishes that Jude had been able to complete the treatise and that it had been preserved. How fascinating to have from the first century and the Lord's brother a theological essay on that theme!

I found it necessary means I had a necessity. He was interrupted by something which put upon him the necessity of dropping his treatise and of writing a sharp warning against heretical teachers. As he characterized the heretics, the sharpness of his warning at times became very heated. He wrote an impassioned appeal that his readers *contend for the faith.*

To *contend* means to agonize for. It was the word for military or athletic hand-to-hand wrestling with an opponent. That for which they were to fight was *the faith which was once for all delivered to the*

saints. In this instance *the faith* appears to be a body of doctrine, as we might say "the Christian faith." Such may be the meaning in Titus 1:4. It is a rare New Testament use. The word *delivered* was the word for the passing on from one to another of the teaching which began with Jesus and was continued by the apostles and missionaries. *Once for all* has a ring of finality about it. By Jude's time the teachings of Christ and his apostles had reached such a point of crystallization that loyalty to them meant orthodoxy and departure from them meant heresy.

Admission has been secretly gained indicates that, furtively, some who were not loyal to that faith had secured admission into the Christian circle. Jude characterized them as *ungodly*, irreligious. *Pervert* meant to turn into false channels. They twisted God's *grace* into perverse teachings which permitted *licentiousness*, lawless immorality. Either by their Gnostic doctrines or by their corrupt lives in serving other masters, they denied the *only Master and Lord, Jesus Christ* (see the comment on 2 Peter 2:1). Jude saw their condemnation as something which had been foretold *long ago*. This was likely a reference to prophetic and apostolic warnings that such teachers would come (2 Peter 3:2). Now they had arrived. Jude's readers must wrestle with them and maintain the faith.

II. A Reminder of Judgment (vv. 5–7)

5 Now I desire to remind you, though you were once for all fully informed, that he who saved a people out of the land of Egypt, afterward destroyed those who did not believe. 6 And the angels that did not keep their own position but left their proper dwelling have been kept by him in eternal chains in the nether gloom until the judgment of the great day; 7 just as Sodom and Gomorrah and the surrounding cities, which likewise acted immorally and indulged in unnatural lust, serve as an example by undergoing a punishment of eternal fire.

The idea of the condemnation of the heretics (v. 4) led the way to a strong reminder that God is a God of judgment on evil. Jude's readers *were once for all fully informed.* This appears to be a very exact reference to their having been informed by their reading of 2 Peter 2:4–10. Now Jude employs that passage to *remind* them of God's judgment. With another of his triads he illustrates; two of the three are identical with the 2 Peter illustrations.

Israel's history served as the first illustration. *He* is a reference to God. The ancient manuscripts have ten different readings, including "God," "the Lord," "Jesus," and "Christ." Whatever the reading, the RSV is correct in understanding the subject to be God who rescued Israel from Egypt. He saw to it that those who did not believe he could establish them in Canaan perished during the 40 years in the wilderness. Only those who did believe got into the land.

The second illustration parallels 2 Peter's use of the judgment of God on wicked angels. Jude's use is much more clearly a reference to 1 Enoch. In that book there is an account of 200 angels who entered into a conspiracy to leave heaven, descend to the earth, and enter into sexual union with women. This they did on Mount Hermon. Because of the evil they brought into the world, God sent the archangels Raphael and Gabriel down to the earth to bind the rebellious angels and to consign them to lower regions of darkness until the day of judgment. This use of an illustration from a non-canonical book constitutes no major problem. Some of the Jewish apocryphal books were widely used; 1 Enoch was one of the most popular. Jude used the story of the wicked angels to illustrate God's judgment on wicked men of his day.

The third illustration, too, parallels 2 Peter's use of God's judgment on Sodom and Gomorrah in the days of Lot. The disbelieving people of Israel were swallowed up by the wilderness; the wicked angels were swallowed up by darkness; the people of Sodom were swallowed up by fire. The total is a warning of judgment. Jude does not include the positive notes of 2 Peter in God's saving Lot from Sodom and Noah from the flood.

III. A Warning Against Heresy (vv. 8–16)

1. Human Propagation of Heresy (vv. 8–13)

⁸ Yet in like manner these men in their dreamings defile the flesh, reject authority, and revile the glorious ones. ⁹ But when the archangel Michael, contending with the devil, disputed about the body of Moses, he did not presume to pronounce a reviling judgment upon him, but said, "The Lord rebuke you." ¹⁰ But these men revile whatever they do not understand, and by those things that they know by instinct as irrational animals do, they are destroyed. ¹¹ Woe to them! For they walk in the way of Cain, and abandon themselves for the sake of gain to Balaam's error, and perish in Korah's rebellion. ¹² These are blemishes on your love feasts, as they boldly carouse together, looking after themselves; waterless clouds, carried along by winds; fruitless trees in late autumn, twice dead, uprooted; ¹³ wild waves of the sea, casting up the foam of their own shame; wandering stars for whom the nether gloom of darkness has been reserved for ever.

Yet indicates that, in spite of such examples of judgment, men still rebel against God. *These men* refers to the heretical rebels of v. 4. They *reject authority* is a general statement. In subsequent verses it is clear that they reject both God's authority and the authority of Christian leaders. *Revile the glorious ones,* too, is general and leaves room for their speaking rebelliously against both divine and human authority.

From the noncanonical Hebrew book, The Assumption of Moses, Jude took another vivid illustration. In that book there is an account of what happened when Moses died. The archangel Michael went to get the body. Satan arrived at the same time and for the same purpose. Michael insisted that Moses' body belonged to God. Satan insisted that Moses' body belonged to him because Moses had murdered the Egyptian. Because Satan was a ruler, though an evil one, Michael would not rebuke him, but simply said, *"The Lord rebuke you."* He left any reviling of rulers to God.

In contrast to Michael, *these men revile. As irrational animals* howl at *whatever they do not understand,* these heretical teachers spoke evil of all religious authority. That very religious authority would be their downfall.

Woe, God's judgment awaits them. Jude used another of his triads in illustrating their evil. Like *Cain* (Gen. 4) they *walk in the way* of rejecting true religion. Cain murdered his brother because his brother offered acceptable worship and Cain did not. Cain became a wanderer with the mark of God's judgment upon him. Their heresy is like his, judgment-bringing.

After the pattern of *Balaam's error* (Num. 22–25), these heretics *abandon themselves* to material gain at the cost of spiritual loss. Their heresy was the failure to recognize that nothing can be economically good if it is morally bad. This Balaam illustration, too, Jude shares with 2 Peter 2:15–16.

These men follow the heresy of Korah's rebellion (Num. 16:1–35). Korah organized 250 of the leading men of Israel to rebel against the authority of Moses and Aaron. In an earthquake Korah and all the men were literally swallowed up by the earth. Jude saw the false leaders of his day as men of the same character. With dramatic metaphors, he set out the peril of trifling with the power and judgment of God. They were self-seeking gluttons at the *love feasts* of the Christians. They were wind-driven *waterless clouds* (2 Peter 2:17) unable to deliver any promise of blessing. They were as dead as barren trees in the winter time. They were bare of leaves in winter, as they had been bare of fruit in the summer. Their destiny was to be uprooted and burned. They were like the uncontrolled *waves of the sea* that waste their power in futile dashing against the shore. They were like *wandering stars* with no controlled orbit and hence destined to purposeless tracks in the eternal darkness.

2. Divine Judgment on Heretics (vv. 14–16)

14 It was of these also that Enoch in the seventh generation from Adam prophesied, saying, "Behold, the Lord came with his holy myriads, 15 to execute judgment on all, and to convict all the ungodly of all their deeds of ungodliness which they have committed in such an ungodly way, and of all the harsh things which ungodly sinners have spoken against him." 16 These are grumblers, malcontents, following their own passions, loud-mouthed boasters, flattering people to gain advantage.

From 1 Enoch 1:9; 27:2; 60:8, Jude borrowed a majestic figure of God's judgment on the wicked. *Myriads* was a mystic word indicating an indefinite number of a tremendous size. In the KJV and the ASV it is regularly translated "ten thousand." The picture is that of a judgment scene in which God is assisted by his "holy ten thousand." They *execute judgment on all.* This is that solemn day when the creature answers to the Creator for what he has done with the trusteeship of life. *All* will answer; there will be no absentees from that court session.

Since the point of interest for Jude is the fate of the rebellious heretics, the focus is upon them. His understanding of their character is emphatic in his use four times of the word *ungodly.* It is like a reverberating proclamation of doom—*the ungodly . . . their deeds of ungodliness . . . committed in such an ungodly way . . . ungodly sinners.* Their action has been anti-God action. They *have spoken against him.*

In the Christian community they have rebelled against religious leaders. They have demonstrated that they are against everyone who does not agree with them. They are *grumblers,* murmurers; *malcontents,* complainers; *following their own passions,* self-willed; *loud-mouthed boasters,* speaking great swelling-with-importance words. They use flattery to gain a following. And they lead that following into false doctrine and corrupt life. They are under God's judgment.

IV. An Exhortation to Fidelity (vv. 17–23)

17 But you must remember, beloved, the predictions of the apostles of our Lord Jesus Christ; 18 they said to you, "In the last time there will be scoffers, following their own ungodly passions." 19 It is these who set up divisions, worldly people, devoid of the Spirit. 20 But you, beloved, build yourselves up on your most holy faith; pray in the Holy Spirit; 21 keep yourselves in the love of God; wait for the mercy of our Lord Jesus Christ unto eternal life. 22 And convince some, who doubt; 23 save some, by snatching them out of the fire; on some have mercy with fear, hating even the garment spotted by the flesh.

Jude's second purpose was made clear in terms of exhortation. From a passionate outburst against heretics, he turned to tender exhortation to the loyal. He reminded his readers of the apostolic warning of the coming of *scoffers.* This recalls 2 Peter 3:1 ff., but Jude gives no indication of the nature of their scoffing. In 2 Peter it was specifically scoffing at the doctrine of the second coming. If the scoffing is to be identified in Jude, it must be in their self-willed setting up of *divisions* or separations in the Christian fellowship. They were troublemakers who divided Christian against Christian. In so doing they demonstrated that they were *devoid of the Spirit,* who works for unity rather than disunity.

Verses 20–21 contain injunctions as to the inner personal devotion of the readers. He enjoined them to build themselves up on the *most holy faith,* i.e., be loyal to that faith which he had mentioned in v. 3. He enjoined them to *pray in the Holy Spirit—* as if immersed in the Holy Spirit and shut off from the world's evil. He enjoined them to keep themselves *in the love of God.* Let God's love be the area of their entire thought and life. Finally, they were to *wait for the mercy* of God. Their forward look was not to judgment, as was that of the

heretics. It was to *eternal life* in Christ.

Verses 22–23 contain injunctions as to how the readers were to deal with others. The last of Jude's triads is here. (1) *Some,* those who are doubters, they are to *convince,* lead them to strong convictions in the true faith. (2) *Some,* they are to *save,* and their rescuing them from error will be like *snatching them out of the fire*—saving them from the fiery judgment of God. (3) *Some,* they are to treat with *mercy* coupled with *fear* (reverential awe) lest they be contaminated even in the process of showing merciful consideration.

In summary: (1) Counsel for the doubters; (2) compassion for the unsaved; (3) caution for the contaminated. Honestly, the text for this third group is ambiguous. Many commentaries do not try to interpret it!

Doxology (vv. 24–25)

24 Now to him who is able to keep you from falling and to present you without blemish before the presence of his glory with rejoicing, 25 to the only God, our Savior through Jesus Christ our Lord, be glory, majesty, dominion, and authority, before all time and now and for ever. Amen.

This sometimes caustic and sometimes compassionate epistle closes with a doxology-benediction of great beauty. It is a tribute of praise *to him who is able to keep you from falling.* That is most meaningful when one considers the threat of heresy which threatened Jude's readers. That One is also able to present them *without blemish* and *with rejoicing* before his glorious presence.

The one to whom the tribute is made is identified as *the only God.* That, too, was meaningful in contrast to the Gnostics' long line of demigods. This God is *our Savior through Jesus Christ our Lord—* God-in-Christ, the only God whom we know. To him—*glory, majesty, dominion, and authority,* from eternity, *before all time,* to eternity, *and for ever,* but also *now. Amen.*

Revelation

MORRIS ASHCRAFT

Introduction

The book of Revelation is the strangest book in the New Testament. It is so difficult for most modern readers that they neglect it altogether. But many who do not ignore the book do something even worse: they misuse it. Sometimes the misuse is nothing more serious than an exaggeration of unimportant details. Sometimes, however, the central message is overlooked or obscured.

Bible students should not permit such neglect or abuse of the book to discourage them. The message of the book plumbs the depths of Christian faith and portrays in exalted terms the ultimate victory of Christ and his followers. Biblical scholars are in rather general agreement on the major ideas of the book. To be sure, there are enigmatic details in the book which defy explanation. But most students can grasp the central message of the book and, with persistence, can also penetrate much of the mystery surrounding that message.

The complex literary form of Revelation makes it more difficult to interpret than the other New Testament books. Galatians, for instance, is a genuine letter written by an identified individual to a known audience on a describable occasion about a specific problem. These details greatly assist the interpreter. Revelation, on the other hand, is a letter, a drama, a prophecy, and an apocalypse, all in one.

The author began with an address to a specific group (1:4) and ended with a conclusion similar to that of other New Testament letters (22:21). He included seven specific letters addressed to different churches within the general letter. He thought of himself as a prophet and his writing as a prophecy (1:3; 22:18). His frequent use of the Old Testament prophets shows not only his appreciation for them but also his desire to be reckoned with them. Also, the book is a great drama. Its plot, characters, scenery, and complex organization combine to create a moving drama filled with suspense. It is so clearly a drama that some commentators have accepted this as the primary clue for its interpretation. (Bowman; McDowell).

The author identified his writing as an apocalypse (1:1). Apocalyptic literature is not as well known today as are the other kinds mentioned. When John wrote, however, apocalyptic literature had been popular for almost three centuries and would have been one of the best-known literary forms among the Jews and early Christians.

I. Apocalyptic Literature

The two greatest apocalypses are the canonical books of Daniel and Revelation. But numerous apocalyptic passages appear in the Bible such as Isaiah 24–27, Mark 13, and 2 Thessalonians 2:1–12. The Gospels of the New Testament convey a strongly apocalyptic outlook. A number of noncanonical Jewish and Christian apocalypses provide a large and helpful literary source for understanding this kind of literature.

240

The origin of apocalyptic is somewhat obscure with roots in Egypt, Iran, Greece, and Israel. As a literary movement, apocalypticism is a product of later Judaism. It emerged with the decline or cessation of Old Testament prophecy and reached maturity in the second century before Christ. It did not fade until after A.D. 100.

In general, apocalyptic writings appeared in times of defeat and persecution. Their authors described the tragedies of their own times but assumed the names of revered saints of the distant past and wrote as if their works had been prophecies of things yet to come, and were now coming to pass. Jewish apocalyptic writers cited the history of Israel on occasions, but their primary concern was not historical. Their primary interest was theological even though couched in an elaborate scheme of world history. The authors, often with narrow nationalistic prejudice, sought to show that the tragedies, predicted long before, were happening according to some hidden plan. Some of the noncanonical apocalypses deserve the description "protest literature" with a "persecution complex." [1] But this is not the case with Revelation.

1. Characteristics of Apocalyptic [2]

It is hazardous but necessary to summarize the characteristics of this literature. The great danger in such a summary is that one may overlook the differences which exist among the apocalypses in his concern for their similarities. For instance, the theology of Revelation is vastly different from that of the noncanonical apocalypses. Revelation, like the other apocalypses, was written in a time of persecution, and has a pessimistic outlook on contempo-

rary culture, but not about God. Revelation is vibrant with faith and hope. It is filled with joyful singing and victorious expectation.

Apocalyptic had a pessimistic appraisal of contemporary culture. Evil had prevailed, at least temporarily. Either Antiochus Ephiphanes had desecrated the Temple or the Romans had destroyed it. In either instance, it appeared that evil had triumphed over God's people. Demonic powers seemed to be in control.

Apocalyptic offered a dualistic eschatological explanation. It was dualistic in that it saw events in relation to a cosmic conflict. The symbols included the primeval struggle between order and chaos, the fall of men and angels, and a present conflict of God with his forces against Satan with his forces. Wars in heaven and on earth were common. The eschatological element appeared as the only alternative when one considered the temporary triumph of evil against the conviction that God must ultimately prevail.

Apocalyptic writers spoke of two ages. The present age was evil, but a coming age would belong to God. The age to come was different not only in its futurity, but also in the sense that it already existed in heaven above. This led to the idea that human life now is somehow a shadow of a reality above.

In apocalyptic, God's transcendence approached remoteness. It seemed as if he had withdrawn from the world and its history. The writers spoke of him in terms of awe, and reported that he dealt with men only through his intermediaries.

A deterministic element permeated apocalyptic. The writers believed that history had been set in the dim past. Man was at the mercy of the inevitable.

Mystery and secrecy prevailed. The authors had received mysteries through visions, angelic messengers, or on conducted tours through the heavens. They had been commanded to write and seal their books. The enclosed mysteries could be known only by the initiated.

1 Stanley B. Frost, *Old Testament Apocalyptic* (London: The Epworth Press, 1952), p. 4.

2 M. Rist, "Apocalypticism," IDB, I, 157 ff.; S. B. Frost, *op. cit.,* pp. 3 ff.; D. S. Russell, *The Method & Message Of Jewish Apocalyptic* (London: SCM Press, 1964); H. H. Rowley, *The Relevance of Apocalyptic,* Rev. ed. (New York: Association Press, 1963); Gerhard von Rad, *Old Testament Theology,* II (New York: Harper & Row, Publishers, 1965), pp. 301 ff.; Robert W. Funk, ed., *Apocalypticism* (New York: Herder and Herder, 1969).

Apocalyptic was characterized by a strange view of history.[3] The prophets, for instance, had stood within history, had seen its meaning, and had foreseen its future from that standpoint. The apocalyptists, however, saw history as determined elsewhere. They divided history arbitrarily into schemes in accordance with their purposes. Actually, their concern was with the last generation of history rather than with history itself.[4]

There are some secondary characteristics found in some, but not all, apocalyptic works. Many of the writings were pseudepigraphical. The writers assumed the names of famous men of old such as Enoch, Moses, Isaiah, Baruch, and Ezra and presented their own works as if they were detailed predictions by these ancient men.

Angels and demons appeared frequently to explain what had actually happened behind the scenes. Visions were commonplace. Numerology was a sacred art in which numbers conveyed hidden meaning. Heavenly bodies had astrological influence on men.

The writers employed animal symbolism. They used the animals known to them and often created new animals by combining parts of existing animals. When the animals of nature were inadequate, they created new ones out of their wild imaginations.

They borrowed material without acknowledgment and modified it without restraint.

They expected catastrophic woes to fall on man before the end of time. Some of them expressed hope for a messiah, wrote of judgment, an abyss, and a lake of fire.

2. Examples of Apocalyptic

The book of Daniel is the most important single source of information for the interpretation of the Apocalypse of John, since it is the source of much of John's imagery. Daniel saw four beasts from the sea. Ani-

mals represented kingdoms and their horns were the kings. He featured angelic heavenly visitors and fell on his face before them. Daniel employed mysterious terms such as "time, two times, and half a time," "seventy weeks of years," and "a thousand two hundred and ninety days." He saw stars fall to the earth, witnessed great wars, and heard the meaning explained. He saw the drama of history, as if directed from an invisible throne.

The first six chapters of the book tell of Daniel and his friends who are exiles in Babylon. Daniel rises to political power because of his ability to interpret dreams. Although his interpretation of dreams for Nebuchadrezzar and Belshazzar bring him honor and power, both he and his friends suffer persecution because of their faithfulness to God (another apocalyptic theme). The three friends refuse to bow to the image of gold which Nebuchadrezzar had set up and are thrown into a fiery furnace. They were not even singed. When the king looked into the blaze, he saw a mysterious fourth person walking with them. Later, Daniel disobeys the edict of Darius which prohibited the worship of other gods; Daniel is seen praying to his own God. He is thrown into the pit with hungry lions, but God delivers him.

The second half of the book (chs. 7— 12) reveals the rapid sweep of history. Daniel receives the revelation through dreams and visions. He sees four great beasts come up out of the sea (7:3) representing the four great kingdoms of earth. The fourth beast has teeth of iron and ten horns. The horns represent kings. Daniel sees another vision of a ram and a he-goat (ch. 8). These are kingdoms. The he-goat, probably Greece, defeats the ram in battle; but its great horn is broken (Alexander) and is replaced by four other horns (Alexander's successors). Daniel's presentation of history covers the period through Antiochus Epiphanes. It has led many contemporary scholars to date the book in this stormy period of the second pre-Christian century.

The book of Enoch, known also as Ethi-

---

[3] For a contemporary discussion, see William R. Murdock, "History and Revelation In Jewish Apocalypticism," *Interpretation*, April, 1967, pp. 167–187.

[4] Gerhard von Rad, *op. cit.*, p. 304.

opic Enoch because it is extant only in the Ethiopic version, is usually designated 1 Enoch.[5] It is the most important of the noncanonical pseudepigraphical writings, since it had more influence on the New Testament than any other book outside the Old Testament. Though attributed to the ancient Enoch, it is a composite work written by unknown authors during the second and first centuries before Christ.

Enoch declares that God had given the revelation, and an angel had shown him a vision and had explained all that would come to pass in the future. Angels had lusted after the daughters of men and thus had fallen to earth and had caused evil among men. Enoch saw God's throne located on seven mountains. He saw the tree of life, the resurrection, and judgment. He saw into Sheol and discerned its divisions. An inordinate curiosity about the calendar led to a division of history into ten periods of which the seventh, characterized by apostasy, had arrived. The eighth period was expected soon and would be filled with righteousness. The wicked would be destroyed during the ninth age in preparation for the tenth, which would bring a new heaven and earth.

The Testaments of the Twelve Patriarchs was written in the period 109–107 B.C. Typically pseudepigraphical, it purports to have been written by the 12 sons of Jacob, whose names identify the individual "Testaments." It shows the typical characteristics of apocalyptic. It is particularly universal in outlook envisioning forgiveness for the Gentiles, as did some Old Testament works, but was in bold contrast to some of the other Jewish works of the period such as Jubilees, in which gentiles were loathed.

Of particular interest to us in this study is the rich variety of terms and ideas also found in Revelation. The Testaments speak of the messiah, the nations, paradise, the tree of life, the resurrection, rest in Eden, etc. A figure like Satan named Beliar appears. He wars against the messiah, but is defeated and is cast into the lake of fire forever. A new Jerusalem and an everlasting kingdom follow.

The Apocalypse of Ezra, known as 4 Ezra, is actually a part of 2 Esdras (3–14) of the Apocrypha. It consists of seven visions purportedly seen by Ezra in Babylon but is actually related to the latter part of the first Christian century. It portrays Jewish thought in the light of Jerusalem's fall to the Romans in A.D. 70. Chapters 11 and 12 appear to have come from the time of Domitian.

In typical apocalyptic fashion it has a series of seven. The end is near. Pessimism abounds in that it would have been better if Adam had not been created. There are two worlds, but the earthly one is drawing to a close. Widespread woes will precede God's intervention. Judgment is based on an opening of the books. Animal imagery prevails, and an eagle with 12 wings and three heads is particularly illuminating for Revelation's beasts. Behemoth and Leviathan, the two creatures, appear.

A messiah will appear and will reign for 400 years, after which all will die including the messiah. After a seven-year period of complete silence, there will be a general resurrection. After the judgment there will be a paradise of joy and a lake of torment.

One other significant sign in the book is a woman who symbolizes the heavenly Jerusalem, and suggests the woman of Revelation 12.

The Apocalypse of Baruch is also known as 2 Baruch. Although claiming to have been written by Jeremiah's scribe at the time of Jerusalem's fall to Babylon, it is pseudepigraphical and was written in the period of A.D. 70 about the time Jerusalem fell to Rome. Inasmuch as it was contemporary with the appearance of the New Testament writings and because its contents allude to Christian ideas, it is regarded as a

[5] R. H. Charles, ed., *The Apocrypha and Pseudepigrapha*, I (Oxford: The Clarendon Press, 1963), hereafter *Apoc. and Pseud.* The apocalyptic works reviewed appear in full in *Apoc. and Pseud.* A paperback edition of 1 Enoch is now available, R. H. Charles, *The Book of Enoch* (London: S.P.C.K., 1962).

Jewish apology in the light of Christianity.

The messiah is unlike the messiah of Revelation. This messiah is warlike and has a sword in his hand, whereas Christ in Revelation is armed only with the sword of his mouth which is the Word (1:16; 2:12; 19:15,21). Revelation has two beasts (ch. 13) and 2 Baruch features two monsters, Leviathan and Behemoth. Like Revelation's sea beast (13:1) Leviathan comes from the sea.

Baruch divided time into 12 periods and likewise predicted 12 woes, among which were famine, earthquake, sword, death, falling fire, etc. He portrayed the four world empires, the resurrection, the judgment, and a new world without end to replace the present world which was getting old.

The Secrets of Enoch is known also as Slavonic Enoch, but usually as 2 Enoch. Charles dated the work with confidence in the first half of the first Christian century, but other scholars have assigned a much later date.

The author claims that he is Enoch and that he has been given a guided tour through the heavens. In great detail he describes what he saw and what the angels explained to him. There is a tree of life which yields all manner of fruits. Hell is filled with murky fire and incredible torture. History is divided into periods of 1,000 years, parallel to the days of the week in such a way that the eighth period witnesses the end when time is no longer reckoned. This work has no messiah, but the scenery and actors are clearly apocalyptic.

3. Prophecy and Apocalyptic

The relationship between prophecy and apocalyptic is undeniable, but the border between the two has been blurred. Literary apocalyptic was the product of late Judaism. However, the antecedents appeared in the much earlier prophetic works.

Though he clearly recognized the diversity between the two, H. H. Rowley called apocalyptic "the child of Prophecy." [6] Ger-

hard von Rad said that this interpretation is "out of the question" [7] because their respective views of history are so incompatible. The similarity leads others to speak of apocalyptic as the "continuation" of prophecy in a new mode of expression [8] or a "substitute" which Judaism forged after the failure of prophetic inspiration. [9]

There is a noticeable difference between the two in form. As a rule prophecy was composed of brief, oral, and often poetic oracles which were proclaimed and only written later. Apocalyptic was literary in form from the beginning. Furthermore, it was long and prosaic in its schematic construction. Though visions appear in both kinds of literature, those of apocalyptic tend to be intentionally obscure leading to an esoteric emphasis. The prophets proclaimed in order to be understood, and they used visions and symbols to clarify. The apocalyptists not only wrote in very obscure terms, but declared they were ordered to seal their messages from others.

A different emphasis on ethics is detectable. The prophets had a profound appreciation for man's choices and behavior as factors in determining the future. The apocalyptists, believing the future had already been determined on other grounds, were amazingly lacking in exhortations of an ethical nature.

The greatest difference is in the respective views of history. The prophets stood in their own generation with an interpretation of the present in the light of Israel's past. Their predictions of the future grew out of the present. The apocalyptists were pessimistic about history. They took their stand in an age of the remote past and wrote as if they were predicting the future. They took the greatest liberties with the facts of the history they purported to predict. They earned a reputation for inaccurate restatement, forcing facts into their artificial

---

[6] Op. cit., p. 13.

[7] Op. cit., p. 303.

[8] Russell, op. cit., p. 92.

[9] Albrecht Oepke, "Apocalyptic," in Theological Dictionary of the New Testament, ed. Gerhard Kittel; trans. Geoffrey W. Bromiley (Grand Rapids: Eerdmans, 1966), III, 578; hereafter TDNT.

schemes, and confusing the characteristics of their own heroes.

The two worlds or two ages in apocalyptic writing replaced the prophets' one world. Apocalyptists are often given credit for a universal world-view or view of history, but the accuracy of the tribute is debatable. When the prophets spoke from the particular history of Israel, they often saw beyond to some implications of world history. The apocalyptists really began with the idea that the earthly scene was in some way a reflection of that real movement going on in the world above. Then the world kingdoms which were so characteristic were not really views of world history at all.

Many of the apocalyptic writers were fond of using the mythological motifs of the ancient world, but the prophets preferred historical thinking. Apocalyptists saw creation as the result of primeval conflict and therefore spoke in terms of dualism, fallen angels, wars in heaven, etc. The prophets had more confidence in history and God's role in it. The apocalyptists appeared only when that confidence had been shaken.[10]

Although apocalyptic literature is diverse, its main ideas are fairly clear.

II. Is Revelation an Apocalypse?

1. Similarities. John used the title "Apocalypse" and gave his work most of the characteristics of apocalyptic. Revelation is pessimistic about contemporary culture: John foresaw a horrible end in the near future. The dualistic-eschatological explanation is obvious. John also contrasts the present evil age with an age to come. God is transcendent. Determinism prevails. Mystery and secrecy are constantly displayed.

John employed the apocalyptic symbols of angels and demonic beings, heavenly bodies, animal imagery, numerology, and the great woes which would precede the end.

2. Differences. The differences between Revelation and the other apocalypses are more significant than the similarities. John's pessimism about man's history is overshadowed by his optimistic, confident expectation about the ultimate outcome of history.

John's dualistic language has been modified by his strong monotheism. The conflict takes place beneath God and there is never any question about his sovereignty. The transcendence of God in Revelation suggests awe and wonder, but there is no hint that God is removed from or disinterested in the world.

The deterministic element, though present in Revelation, never suggests man's helplessness, nor does it threaten man's freedom or responsibility. The letters to the seven churches show that John thinks that man's decisions and responses in the world do shape history as well as personal destiny.

The mystery and secrecy in Revelation are not the esotericism of the noncanonical apocalypses. John strives for understanding. He seeks to reveal, not to conceal. His message is not to be sealed up but to be read publicly and proclaimed.

Revelation is not pseudepigraphical. The author is John. Although other apocalyptists assumed names and wrote from the standpoint of the past, John used his own name, wrote to people who knew him and from the context of his own age. John's book is different from the other apocalypses.[11]

Revelation reveals a different idea of suffering. In other apocalypses, suffering results from the decrees and acts of evil powers and produces hopelessness. In Revelation, moral decisions can overcome suffering. Christ's suffering gained victory, and faithful disciples can gain ultimate victory through suffering.

John has managed to retain the tension between human history and eschatological hope characteristic of the prophets and obvious for its absence in the noncanonical apocalypses (Morris, p. 24).

In Revelation there is a Christian view of God and of history. Judaistic elements

---

10 Stanley B. Frost, "Historical and Mythological," *The Bible in Modern Scholarship*, J. Philip Hyatt, ed. (Nashville: Abingdon Press, 1965), pp. 98 ff.

11 Bruce W. Jones, "More About The Apocalypse As Apocalyptic," JBL, LXXXVII, Sept., 1968, p. 327.

sometimes almost obscure the Christian view of God, but the Christology is redemptive. History has meaning in Revelation. John's interpretation of history is not like that of Jewish apocalyptists.[12] His Christology of the Lamb is historical and is the focus of history.

3. *Prophetic-Apocalyptic.* Revelation has most of the characteristics of apocalyptic, but there are remarkable differences between Revelation and the other apocalypses. John preferred that his work be known as prophecy. The teachings of Jesus contain both apocalyptic and prophetic elements, and certainly Jesus did not share all of the views of the noncanonical apocalypses (Bowman, p. 235).

The prophetic element in Revelation is even stronger than the apocalyptic.[13] John's allusions to the Old Testament prophets add further evidence for seeing Revelation as prophecy.[14]

In the following interpretation, it is assumed that the Revelation to John has drawn heavily upon both the prophecies and apocalypses. John was a creative dramatist who took the forms and symbols of this literature and presented his drama with its distinctive Christian theology. The purpose of the author is decidedly Christian; his theology is Christian; his illustrations are often pre-Christian.

III. Authorship

The traditional view has been that John the apostle wrote not only Revelation but also the Gospel and the three Johannine epistles. This view has had to face many objections in the modern period. The objections have originated in the stylistic differences among the Johannine writings, lack of adequate identification of John in Revelation, and literary evidence suggesting another author.

The internal evidence is limited. The author claimed to be John, (1:1,4,9; 22:8), a brother, a servant, and witness of Jesus Christ who had been exiled to Patmos. No more! On one occasion he referred to apostles whose names were inscribed on the foundation stones of the wall of the New Jerusalem (21:14). Since he wrote without further identification and exercised a certain authority, it has been assumed that he was well known to the Christians of Asia.

The name John was a common name. Our evidence does not prove that the apostle ever went to Asia Minor. However, the name John without further qualification was naturally taken by the later church to mean the apostle. The assumption that he was so well known as to need no further identification only means that his intended readers did know him well. But this could have been the case if John had been one other than the apostle. His reference to the 12 apostles of the Lamb (21:14) suggests a time subsequent to that of the apostles and presents a question whether an apostle could write about himself in this way.

1. *The Case for John the Apostle.* The internal evidence is taken to identify John the apostle. His prestige as an apostle made further identification superfluous. He wrote with the authority of an apostle, and the 21:14 reference is general enough to have been written by an apostle. The logical inference is that of apostolic authorship.

The external evidence is strongly in favor of John the apostle, the son of Zebedee. Justin Martyr wrote before A.D. 166 that John the apostle had prophesied by means of a revelation which mentioned a thousand-year reign. Justin had lived in Ephesus about A.D. 135 and presumably would have had close acquaintance with the area of the Apocalypse.[15] Irenaeus, a student of Polycarp, wrote (*ca.* A.D. 185) that the apocalypse had been written by "John, the disciple of the Lord," evidently meaning the

---

[12] Mathias Rissi, "The Kerygma of the Revelation to John," *Interpretation*, XXII, No. 1, Jan. 1968, p. 5.

[13] See "Apocaluptō, Apocalupsis," TDNT, III, 589; F. B. Vawter, "Apocalyptic: Its Relation To Prophecy," *Catholic Biblical Quarterly*, Jan. 1960, pp. 33–46.

[14] George E. Ladd, "Why Not Prophetic-Apocalyptic?" JBL, LXXVI, Sept. 1957, 192 ff. Also "The Revelation and Jewish Apocalyptic," *Evangelical Quarterly*, 29:94–100, Apr.–June, 1957; John Wick Bowman, "The Book of Revelation," IDB, IV, 58 ff.

[15] Justin Martyr, *Dialogue with Trypho*, 81.

apostle (*Against Heresies*, V.30). Clement of Alexandria (*ca.* A.D. 215) wrote of the apostle John in exile on Patmos (*Miscellanies*, VI.13). Tertullian (*ca.* A.D. 200) agreed with these previous authorities on John the apostle (*Against Marcion*, III.14). Eusebius (*Church History*, VI.25), who did not agree, nevertheless cited Origen (*ca.* A.D. 220–225) as having written that John the disciple who had reclined upon Jesus' breast had written both the Gospel and the Apocalypse.

Other authorities are cited by advocates of apostolic authorship but they are secondary sources repeating the evidence cited.

2. The Case for John the Elder. The case for another author arose largely because of the inadequacy of the traditional view. The internal evidence establishes only that the author's name was John. Nowhere did he claim to have been either an apostle or a disciple. The 21:14 passage is understood as being against apostolic authorship. Stylistic and grammatical differences between the Gospel and the Apocalypse rule out common authorship (Charles, I, xxxviii ff.). Furthermore, Justin Martyr is the only source who could have been primary. The other authorities were probably citing his evidence, and he could have been wrong. Revelation contains no references to the personal life of Jesus as would be expected if the author had been an apostle. Revelation encountered objection to its being accepted into the canon. This is inexplicable if the author were an apostle.

Early literary evidence suggests that Revelation was written by a man from Ephesus known as the Elder or Presbyter John. Dionysius of Alexandria (*ca.* A.D. 265) was the first, to our knowledge, to reject the apostolic authorship because of the great differences in the Johannine writings. He conjectured that John Mark may have been the author, mentioned other men named John, and referred to the two tombs of John in Ephesus. Dionysius dropped the idea of John Mark, but left open the matter of the Elder John. Eusebius (*Church History*, VII.25) has repeated the conjectures of Dionysius in great detail.

Papias (A.D. 70–140) is the other authority whose remarks point to Elder John. It must be acknowledged that many scholars are very uncertain about the reliability of these remarks which we know only in the writings of Eusebius (*op. cit.*, III.39). Papias wrote five books but never claimed to have had personal acquaintance with eye witnesses of the Lord, even though Irenaeus referred to him as one who had known John personally and had been the associate of Polycarp. Papias claimed only that his information had come from elders. Papias wrote about two men named John, the Evangelist and the Elder. Eusebius conjectured that the author of Revelation was this other John, Elder John.

Tradition has preserved a number of hints that John the apostle died a martyr's death too early to have written Revelation. Regretably, the evidence is fragmentary and based on sources several centuries later (Charles, I, xlv ff.).

Although tradition has favored apostolic authorship, modern scholarship has largely rejected the idea. It is almost universally held that Revelation was written about A.D. 95. This is quite late for an apostle to have written it. The internal evidence does not specify John the apostle. On the other hand, Presbyter John is a shadowy figure whose very existence is uncertain. Our author was a Christian prophet named John, whose ministry in the province of Asia was prominent enough that he needed no further identification when he wrote the Apocalypse in the last decade of the first century.

IV. Occasion and Purpose

John believed a great persecution was about to begin. The demand for Christians to worship the emperor was the occasion for the persecution and posed a double threat: if the Christians refused to worship the emperor they would be put to death; if they complied they would abandon Christ.

1. The Persecution. The internal evidence is clear. John was writing from exile (1:9), and at least one Christian had already died a martyr's death in Pergamum (2:13). John warned those in Smyrna of suffering to come which would include prison and tribulation (2:10). He warned the Philadelphians of an hour of trial which was coming on the whole world (3:10). In a vision he saw under the heavenly altar those who had been slain for the word (6:9). The harlot Rome was drunk with the blood of the martyrs of Jesus (17:6). The great city had fallen partly because the blood of the prophets and saints was found within her (18:24). God's judgment on the harlot avenged the "blood of his servants" (19:2). In the resurrection "those who had been beheaded for their testimony to Jesus" would reign with Christ (20:4).

The external evidence in non-Christian sources is more difficult to find. Nevertheless, we are not without such evidence. Both Tacitus and Suetonius have told us of Nero's persecution of the Christians in A.D. 64. The longer account is that of Tacitus (*Annals*, XV.44). Suetonius (*Nero*, XVI; *Domitian*, V. and XV) tells us that Domitian was a devotee of the gods and built temples to them bearing his own name. Domitian had Flavius Clemens killed and his wife exiled for "atheism." Atheism was the charge against Christians who were "atheists" because they rejected the gods of Rome. Suetonius also recorded that Domitian levied a special tax on the Jews because of their exemption from emperor worship. He added that there was prosecution against those who did not publicly acknowledge the Jewish faith but lived in that manner (*Domitian*, XII), evidently meaning the Christians.

Pliny's letter to Trajan and Trajan's reply concerning the persecution of the Christians in Bithynia (*ca.* A.D. 112) give us our clearest insight into the nature of the persecutions of Christians by Roman governors,[16] though admittedly not in Domitian's time.

Numerous Christian sources cite or allude to Domitian's persecution of Christians. Clement of Rome (1 Clem. I, 1;V) wrote as early as A.D. 95 or 96 about "the sudden and repeated calamities and reverses which are befalling us" seemingly alluding to the persecution. He also mentioned Paul and Peter, who had been persecuted and had "contended even to death."

Tertullian (*Apology*, V) and Lactantius (*Of the Manner in Which the Persecutors Died*, III) spoke of Domitian's persecution of the Christians being like that of Nero's.

A modern work on the subject concludes that by the time of Domitian the identity of the Christians was more clear-cut and that "Domitian persecuted them for refusal to accept his divinity."[17]

2. Emperor Worship. The idea of worshiping the emperor sounds strange to modern ears, but it should not when one considers the totalitarian claims made by some modern states.

Rome had a tolerant attitude toward other religions because of the polytheistic nature of her own. Conquered peoples were allowed to keep their own religions and practice them as long as they did not violate Rome's laws.

The cult of Rome, deification of Rome into a goddess, *Dea Roma*, had begun long before the beginning of emperor worship. Peoples in conquered countries could affirm their loyalty to Rome by building temples to Roma and by maintaining religious practices in her honor. Cities competed for the privilege and often tried to surpass their neighbors in the magnificence of these temples. Such cities were known as "temple-keepers." Ephesus was temple-keeper of Artemis (Acts 19:35).

The step from *Dea Roma* worship to emperor worship was easily made. Julius Ceasar had claimed that he was divine and had his statue placed in the temples with the gods. An inscription in a temple in Ephesus read, "To the goddess Roma and the divine Julius." Augustus Ceasar (31

16 Henry Bettenson, ed., *Documents of the Christian Church* (London: Oxford University Press, 1947), pp. 5 f.

17 Michael Grant, *The World of Rome* (New York: The New American Library, 1960), p. 212.

B.C.–A.D. 14) did not insist on such veneration in Rome itself, but accepted the title "*Sebastos*" (worthy of reverence and worship) and exploited emperor worship in the provinces.

Caligula (A.D. 37–41) demanded this worship and even ordered that his statue be set up in the Jewish temple in Jerusalem. The furor which followed induced his advisors to persuade him to drop the plan. After this incident, Jews were exempted from the demand. Christians were safe as long as they were considered Jewish. When the church left the synagogue, Christianity became illegal. The law prohibited "new" religions.

The emperor cult was in full force during Nero's reign, but the persecution of the Christians in Rome did not appear to stem from that source. Nero sought to exploit their otherwise unpopular position and used them as scapegoats to shift responsibility from himself for the great fire.

Domitian demanded such worship and our book of Revelation is to be dated in his reign.

It should be remembered that this kind of practice was more rigidly enforced in the provinces than in Rome itself, since the distance would magnify any neglect of homage due Rome. Furthermore, the insistence on compliance would more often come from local underlings seeking to ingratiate themselves with the emperor than from the emperor himself.

Emperor-worship in the province of Asia. —Roman provinces were ruled by proconsuls who administered Roman justice, guaranteed order, and collected taxes. Local citizens were employed in these tasks and often enjoyed considerable autonomy. Religious matters were also under the control of these rulers but were delegated to priests who were in charge of the sanctuaries. Ranking priests supervised the municipal and provincial religious establishments. They, therefore, came to have considerable power in enforcing emperor worship locally if they deemed it expedient to do so.

The province of Asia excelled in Roma

and emperor worship.[18] As early as 195 B.C. Smyrna had boasted a temple to Roma. In 29 B.C. Augustus had permitted temples to Roma and Julius Caesar in Ephesus and Nicea. In the same year worship of Augustus was begun in Pergamum. In such provinces the provincials took the initiative and requested Rome's permission for such worship. The political possibilities are obvious, and Rome encouraged the practice.

Emperor worship in Revelation.—John of Patmos refers continually to the beast and its image and those who worship it (13:4,11,12,17; 14:9,11; 15:2; 16:2; 19: 20; 20:4). We know that the statue of the emperor was placed in the temple and figured in the worship. This statue must be the "image." It is obvious that the beast from the sea (13:1) is Rome and the beast from the earth which enforces worship is the imperial priesthood representing Rome (13:11 ff.). Giving breath to the image (13:15) was a trick to deceive people into worship, and the inability to buy or sell without its mark is a clear reference to economic sanctions used to enforce emperor worship (13:17).

In John's day Rome demanded that all subjects address Caesar as "Lord." To most subjects this was only an oath of allegiance to the country, but John and the Christians could address only Jesus Christ as "Lord." John evaluated the threat to be so serious that he advised martyrdom as preferable to compliance.

The theme of Revelation is the promise of victory to those who are faithful unto death.

3. Heresy in the Seven Churches. John condemned certain errors which had crept into the churches of Asia. What is a "synagogue of Satan" (2:9) or a "throne" of Satan (2:13)? Who were the Nicolaitans, and what was their error (2:6,15)? Many interpreters have seen these errors as a kind of Gnosticism.

Gnosticism matured about A.D. 135–160. Until the last century our only knowledge

[18] Frederick C. Grant, *Ancient Roman Religion* (New York: The Liberal Arts Press, 1957), p. 159 f.

of Gnosticism was gleaned from the early Christian writers who condemned it. The recent discoveries of Qumran gave some new light on Gnosticism. The discoveries in Egypt [19] have given us an extensive library of Gnostic writings. These discoveries have raised anew the question of Gnosticism's influence on the New Testament.

In general, Gnosticism designates a religious system in which salvation is achieved by means of *gnōsis* (knowledge). The system is always dualistic and maintains that the material world is hopelessly evil, fallen. A man must acquire the mystical illumination of *gnōsis* in order to be saved. Naturally, the system is esoteric and mysterious.

The origins of the system were centuries old and were located in many lands. Ancient Egypt provided one stream. Babylonian astrology and Persian dualism flowed into it. Jewish mysticism and Christian thought contributed. The diverse origins help to explain the inconsistent elements of Gnosticism.

Prior to modern discoveries, New Testament scholars frequently alluded to Gnostic, pre-Gnostic, or proto-Gnostic influence within the New Testament. Naturally, the new information has created a renewed interest in this subject. There are those who interpret the book of Revelation as an anti-Gnostic writing.[20]

There are a number of reasons for reluctance in this area. It is quite early to evaluate the new discoveries. The major ideas of the system were already understood rather clearly and remain essentially unchanged. Many New Testament scholars still maintain that Gnosticism is a second-century phenomenon and that we should refer to similar ideas of the first century as "syncretistic" or only as antecedents of Gnosticism. Even the words "Gnostic," "pre-Gnostic," or "proto-Gnostic" imply more continuity than the evidence warrants.[21]

The more traditional approach to Revelation on the grounds that it was written to combat emperor worship has provided a useful means of seeing the meaning of the book. New Testament scholars have not been able to provide a more suitable approach. For instance, Revelation contains much imagery that would be right at home in a Gnostic writing. Revelation is certainly not Gnostic. If it were intentionally anti-Gnostic, it is too much to assume that the author would have identified more clearly the errors he would have corrected?

Christian writings emerged in a syncretistic age. There are some heretical ideas and practices alluded to in the seven letters. It is possible that these form a part of later Gnosticism. But it is not yet certain that the lines were clear when John wrote.

Apocalyptic shared many ideas, motifs, and symbols with the later Gnosticism. It is likely that apocalyptic thought, which was the heir of prophecy, was a contributing source of Gnosticism. David Noel Freedman, for instance, sees Gnosticism as a "highly individualized adaptation" of apocalyptic and also its successor and heir.[22] If the errors of the seven churches were, or included, Gnostic ideas, and this may well have been the case, John did not recognize any system of thought like Gnosticism. If so, it is amazing that he did not identify more clearly the objectionable ideas.

Gnosticism may throw some light on the heresies of the Asian churches. One must exercise caution, however, lest he read back

[19] Hans Jonas, *The Gnostic Religion* (Boston: Beacon Press, 1958); W. C. van Unnik, *Newly Discovered Gnostic Writings* (Naperville: Alec R. Allenson, Inc., 1960.

[20] Barclay Newman, *Rediscovering the Book of Revelation* (Valley Forge: The Judson Press, 1968); see also his "The Fallacy of the Domitian Hypothesis," *New Testament Studies*, 10:133–39, Oct., 1963.

[21] Robert M. Grant, *Gnosticism and Early Christianity*, rev. ed., (New York: Harper & Row, 1966); Johannes Munck, "The New Testament and Gnosticism," *Current Issues In New Testament Interpretation*, William Klassen and Graydon Snyder, eds., (New York: Harper & Brothers, Publishers, 1962); R. McL. Wilson, *The Gnostic Problem*, (London: A. R. Mowbray & Co., Ltd., 1958).

[22] David Noel Freedman, "The Flowering of Apocalyptic," *Journal for Theology and the Church*, ed. Robert W. Funk, No. 6 "Apocalypticism," (New York: Herder and Herder, 1969), p. 174.

into Revelation the burdens of second-century Gnosticism.

V. Date of Composition

Scholars are almost unanimous in dating Revelation about A.D. 95 during the reign of Domitian. The discussion of "date" instead of "dates" implies that the book is a unity. In spite of several objections to the contrary, the unity of the book is assumed in this commentary.

The text has suffered in transmission and there are a number of textual variants. R. H. Charles thought he had found many interpolations and dislocations in the text which he excised or rearranged, but the result is far from convincing. Objections to the unity of the book arise from several observations. The seven letters appear to be complete in themselves and appear to be quite different from the main body of the apocalypse. Some think that there are more than one apocalypse within the book in that some of the visions seem to suggest the time of Nero rather than that of Domitian.

The integrity of the book would not be undermined even if it were established that the letters circulated independently, or that John incorporated some of his earlier apocalyptic writings without complete revision. In all fairness, however, it must be acknowledged that there is no evidence that the letters ever circulated separately. Each letter draws a part of its description of Christ from chapter one thus suggesting that it was written as a part of the whole composition. Each one makes promises which are fulfilled in the closing chapters of the book thereby suggesting that the book is a unity.

1. Date A.D. 95. The date must be late enough to allow for the existence and development of conditions as described within the seven churches of Asia. Furthermore, a date must be sought which reflects the persecution, or threat of persecution, born of the demand for Christians to yield to emperor worship. This is the occasion for which John of Patmos wrote the book.

The internal evidence seems to place the book in the reign of Domitian. Some of the seven churches did not exist prior to the sixties. Polycarp indicated that the church in Smyrna was founded after A.D. 64. The churches in Revelation had existed long enough to have suffered a loss of first enthusiasm. Also, heresies had arisen. This lapse of time would rule out a date in Nero's reign.

Persecutions of Christians took place during the reigns of both Nero (A.D. 54–68) and Domitian (A.D. 81–96). However, the Neronian persecution was limited to Rome and did not involve emperor worship at all. The persecution of Christians in the time of Domitian extended to the provinces such as Asia and was related to emperor worship.

After the death of Nero, a myth arose that he would come to life again and would lead an army of Parthians against Rome. There are references in the literature of the time to pretenders who tried to capitalize on this Nero *redivivus* myth. Two passages in Revelation appear to allude to this popular expectation (13:3; 17:8). If this is so, a date somewhat later than Nero is required.

The strange reference to the seven Roman emperors (see comment on 17:10)—of whom five had already fallen, one was, and one was yet to come—calls for a date after Nero.

There is an enigmatic reference (6:6) which states, "But do not harm oil and wine!" We know of an edict of Domitian dated A.D. 92 which aimed at increasing the grain production of the provinces by requiring a destruction of half of the vineyards. There was no mention of "oil" in Domitian's edict, but the reference to wine in the passage may reflect the edict.

The external evidence strongly favors a date in Domitian's reign. Irenaeus (*Against Heresies,* V.30) wrote (A.D. 180–190) that John, the evangelist and apostle, exiled to Patmos had written his revelation at the close of Domitian's reign. Eusebius (*Church History,* III.18) repeated Irenaeus' evidence, and the same was apparently accepted by Clement of Alexandria, Origen, and Jerome.

2. *Other Suggested Dates.* A date in the reign of Claudius (A.D. 41–54) was suggested by Epiphanius, but this date is out of question inasmuch as the churches addressed did not even exist.

A date in the time of Nero has had some notable advocates such as Westcott, Hort, and Lightfoot. The case was built on Nero's persecution and references to the temple (6:9; 11:1–2) which, it was argued, was still standing and thus required a date prior to A.D. 70.

However, we know that Nero's persecution was limited to Rome and, to our knowledge, did not extend to the provinces. Furthermore, the references to the temple may be explained as from sources from the earlier time which John used; or, better still, the temple references are not references to the literal temple in Jerusalem but are of a figurative nature.

The only dates in serious contention are those in the reigns of Nero and Domitian. The evidence strongly favors Domitian's time, about A.D. 95.

VI. Interpretation

The history of the interpretation of Revelation discloses the difficulty of our task. R. H. Charles listed nine major "methods" of interpretation, to which others have since been added. Upon closer observation, these "methods" are not really methods, but starting points. And they are not mutually exclusive. In fact, each one stresses a major emphasis or conviction which includes but subordinates some of the others.

1. *Approaches from a Historical Standpoint.* From the perspective of history, these viewpoints can be classified as preterist, continuous-historical, and futurist.

The *preterist* is also known as the contemporary-historical approach. The controlling presupposition is that John wrote for his own generation and the entire book should be interpreted accordingly. The visions and their teachings were related to

the Roman Empire and the struggle of the church with it. There is wide agreement among New Testament scholars that this is the proper starting point. This approach has many advantages. It is faithful to the historical setting. The book can be understood on this basis but faces impossible problems when removed from it.

The *continuous-historical* approach understands Revelation as a detailed forecast of history in its successive stages. Advocates of this approach tend to develop schemes of history and calendars which date the "end." Frequently, they claim that theirs is the literal approach. Needless to say, this view has led to great abuse of the book. The interpreters do not agree with each other and strangely find that their world history deals only with western civilization.

The *futurist* approach interprets the events and visions of Revelation as dealing primarily with the end of history. This eschatological view offers two options. John's message spoke entirely about an "end" he expected immediately, or about an "end" in some distant time. The former option requires the admission that John was in error since the end did not come. The latter would rob the book of its real relevance in its own generation.

These historical approaches must include in some way an understanding of the type of literature in Revelation.

2. *Approaches from a Literary Standpoint.* The *allegorical* method reflects a particular view of Scripture. When the meaning is not obvious, by allegorizing one is able to discern the hidden meaning.

The *literary-analytical* approach begins with the assumption that Revelation was composed from different sources which must be identified, and dealt with accordingly. This approach is concerned with the interpolations, dislocations, sources and their evaluation. A common fault in this method is that the interpreter often stops short of the major question, What meaning did John intend to convey?

The *literal* approach would suggest the

continuous-historical view to most readers, but McNeile [23] has used the term with a different meaning. While rejecting the continuous-historical idea of history and fully accepting the values of literary criticism, he saw Revelation as having lasting value because of principles and truths it enunciated. To McNeile, John meant to say something "quite concrete and literal." John expected literal plagues, a literal millennium, etc. to come soon upon Rome. Furthermore, he maintained that modern psychological studies throw light on such visions of ecstacy. In popular usage, the term "literal" interpretation of Revelation would assume that God has disclosed the details of future history so that Revelation is in fact a history written in advance. Literal interpretation, in its popular usage, would require that the dragon and beasts be real zoological specimens. It is regretable that scholars use this word "literal" without accenting its consequences, one of which would be the admission that John was in error inasmuch as those things did not literally happen "soon." The highly complex organization of Revelation suggests the dramatic rather than the literal approach.

The *dramatic* approach begins with the observation that Revelation is in form and content an elaborate drama which, therefore, must be interpreted as a drama (Bowman). It is interesting that this approach is not inconsistent with the preterist viewpoint, nor does it bar one from the insights of literary criticism.

3. Presuppositions in This Commentary. Certain presuppositions are already apparent and are hereby briefly acknowledged. They deal with the intention of John of Patmos.

The preterist or contemporary-historical approach is the proper starting point. John addressed the Christians of a particular area in a time of danger. He intended to encourage them to be faithful to Christ to

the death. He employed unusual visions and images to convey his message, but the point of his message is clear. We must assume that this writing had its primary meaning for the generation in which it was written, as did Galatians, 1 Corinthians, etc. Its value for subsequent generations depends on grasping its meaning for its own age.

John wrote a dramatic apocalyptic-prophecy with the formal characteristics of a pastoral letter. All these features are important. As a letter it must be understood in the light of its particular origin, destination, and purpose. As apocalyptic it confronts us with unusual images, which appeal more to the imagination than to the reason. Its visions and symbols forbid a literal interpretation in most cases (Summers, p. 48), but the noncanonical apocalyptic writings provide illumination. John intended to be writing prophecy. Prophecy maintains a cordial relationship with history and keeps the future related to the present. The interpreter must maintain the same relationship with history.

The organization of Revelation into acts and scenes which move progressively toward climactic events obliges us to see it as a drama. Recognition of this literary form in no way interferes with the visionary origin of some of the material, nor with its inspiration.

The author intended to convey a message which was Christian in its theology. He wrote in the "foreign language" of Jewish apocalyptic, but he gave us a brief glossary for use in translation. His view of Jesus Christ the Lamb is sublimely Christian. Many of his terms betray their pre-Christian and sub-Christian usage, but he intended to speak a Christian message through them. Ours is the task of translation.

An interpreter of Revelation would benefit significantly if he would read rapidly two or more of the apocalyptic works cited before beginning Revelation. If these are not available, it is recommended that the

[23] A. H. McNeile, *Introduction to the New Testament*, Sec. ed. (Oxford: The Clarendon Press, 1953), p. 253.

interpreter secure English translations with which he is not familiar and read rapidly through Daniel and Revelation without stopping to consider details. After getting this overall view, one can deal with the details with less difficulty.

VII. Plan and Outline

A glance at the outline (or the book) will reveal that John arranged his drama in a definite order of series of seven visions or events. For instance, he numbered the (1) letters to the seven churches (chs. 2—3), (2) the seven seal visions (6:1—8:5), (3) the seven trumpet visions (8:6—11:19), and (4) the seven bowl plagues (15:1—16:21). In a more subtle way, he worked in a series of seven "beatitudes" introduced by Christ's formula "Blessed . . ." (1:3; 14:13; 16:15; 19:9; 20:6; 22:7; 22:14).

In the sections between the other sevenfold series there is evidence that he is following the same plan without numbers. For instance, in his first vision of Christ he used as a formula, "I heard" or "I saw." These words, or their cognates, usually designate a new vision (12:1,3; 13:1,11; 14:1,6,14). In the section following the bowl plagues, scholars find more difficulty in identifying the series.[24] Some sections are clearly marked by the formula "And I saw" (*kai eidon*—19:11,17,19; 20:1,4,11,12). I have tried not to coerce the material into an outline, but to follow the outline as it appears in the text. John often interrupted his series with visions or explanations to prepare the reader. At points I have indicated the break by using special symbols within the sequence of arabic numerals.

After completing the introductory matters in his general letter, John told of his vision of Christ. This established his own prophetic call, mission, and authority. This first vision sets the theme for the entire book. Christ is intimately related to the churches but is also the majestic heavenly figure—divine. Christ achieved his victory

through death and resurrection; his followers will realize their victories by their faithfulness to Jesus Christ.

In his letters to the seven churches (chs. 2—3), John portrays the struggle of the earthly churches against evil powers. The churches are commended, warned, called to repentance, and assured of victory if they are faithful to Christ.

Immediately following the letters, John moved the scene to heaven and reported three visions (4:1—5:14) which show that ultimate sovereignty is God's and that Christ, who is related to the churches, is also the only one worthy to reveal man's destiny from above.

The opening of the seven seals (6:1—8:5) portrays the unfolding tragedy of human history as four horsemen ride forth bringing conquest, war, famine, and death. The fifth vision portrays the martyrs dressed in white robes under the altar in heaven. Great natural catastrophes happened on earth, but John interrupted the series to show that God's people had been marked so as to be spared. The seventh vision showed the prayers of the saints mingled with incense on heaven's altar. When this mixture was thrown on earth, thunder, lightning, and earthquake testified that heaven and earth are still related and human prayers make a difference in both places.

The seven trumpet visions (8:6—11:19) portray similar plagues directed against land, sea, fresh water, and luminaries. Three parenthetical visions declare woes on unbelievers and victory to the saints.

The visions about the great conflict (12:1—14:20) introduce the principals of the great struggle now going on and predict ultimate victory. The woman clothed with the sun is the people of God among whom the seven churches are numbered. The red dragon which attacked the woman and her child, obviously the Messiah, is identified as a dragon, Satan who had been thrown out of heaven. After he had failed to destroy the child, whom God rescued to heaven in the resurrection, the dragon attacked the

---

24 See Bowman, "Revelation, Book of," IDB, IV, 65; Leonard Thompson, "Cult and Eschatology in the Apocalypse," *Journal of Religion*, Oct. 1969, p. 332 f.

woman's offspring. This shows the contemporary Christians that their struggle is a part of a cosmic battle. The present enemy Rome is the sea beast, the dragon's agent, and the imperial cult is the land beast commissioned by the dragon to afflict God's people. However, victory was won by Christ through his faithful martyrdom and is promised to the faithful followers. The visions of the Lamb on Mount Zion, the angels in heaven, and the coming of the Son of man in judgment predict the ultimate victory.

John believed that the end could not come until great woes had come on earth. These come in the form of the seven bowls of wrath visions (ch. 16).

Prior to the final victory of the Lamb, John gave a lengthy description of Rome, which he compared to a gaudy harlot and contrasted with the Bride of Christ and the New Jerusalem. Rome's fall is predicted and mourned.

The final victory of the Lamb (19:6—20:15) is announced in heaven. The Word of God appears on a white horse; Satan is bound; the millennium shows Christ's victory on earth; the great white throne appears; the final judgment takes place.

The grand finale (21:8—22:5) is the description of the new heaven and earth, the new Jerusalem, and the joys of being with God.

Outline

I. Prologue (1:1–20)
  1. Introduction (1:1–3)
  2. Salutation (1:4–8)
  3. Call and commission (1:9–11)
  4. The vision of Christ (1:12–20)
II. Letters to the seven churches (2:1—3:22)
  1. Ephesus (2:1–7)
  2. Smyrna (2:8–11)
  3. Pergamum (2:12–17)
  4. Thyatira (2:18–29)
  5. Sardis (3:1–6)
  6. Philadelphia (3:7–13)
  7. Laodicea (3:14–22)
III. Three visions into heaven (4:1—5:14)
  1. God's throne room (4:1–11)
  2. The scroll with seven seals (5:1–5)
  3. The Lamb who opens the seals (5:6–14)

IV. The seven seal visions and two parenthetical visions (6:1—8:5)
  1. The white horse—conquest (6:1–2)
  2. The red horse—war (6:3–4)
  3. The black horse—famine (6:5–6)
  4. The pale horse—death (6:7–8)
  5. The martyrs under the altar (6:9–11)
  6. Catastrophes on earth (6:12–17)
  ¶-1. Sealing God's servants (7:1–8)
  ¶-2. The multitude in white robes (7:9–17)
  7. The golden altar of incense (8:1–5)
V. The seven trumpet visions and three parenthetical visions (8:6—11:19)
  1. The plague on the land (8:6–7)
  2. The plague on the sea (8:8–9)
  3. The plague on fresh water (8:10–11)
  4. The plague on the luminaries (8:12)
  ¶-1. The eagle vision (8:13)
  5. The demonic locust plague, the first great woe (9:1–12)
  6. The demonic cavalry from the east, the second great woe (9:13–21)
  ¶-2. The mighty angel and the little scroll (10:1–11)
  ¶-3. The two witnesses (11:1–14)
  7. The seventh trumpet—victory (11:15–19)
VI. Seven visions about the great conflict and two explanations (12:1—14:20)
  1. The pregnant woman (12:1–2, 4b–6)
  2. The red dragon (12:3–4a)
  ¶-1. The dragon cast out of heaven (12:7–12)
  ¶-2. The dragon's attack on the Christians (12:13–17)
  3. The sea beast, the Roman Empire (13:1–10)
  4. The land beast, the Roman religious establishment (13:11–18)
  5. The Lamb and his army (14:1–5)
  6. Series of angel visions (14:6–13)
  7. Visions of the harvest judgment (14:14–20)
VII. The seven bowl plagues and three introductory visions (15:1—16:21)
  ¶-1. The seven angels (15:1)
  ¶-2. The victors by the heavenly sea (15:2–4)
  ¶-3. The seven angels emerge from the tent of witness with seven bowls (15:5–8)
  1. Plague on earth (16:1–2)
  2. Death to sea life (16:3)
  3. Fresh water turned to blood (16:4–7)
  4. Plague on the sun (16:8–9)
  5. Plague of darkness (16:10–11)
  6. The call to Armageddon (16:12–16)
  7. Great calamities (16:17–21)
VIII. The fall of the great city—Rome (17:1—19:5)

¶-1. The harlot and the beast (17:1–6a)
¶-2. The mystery of the harlot (17:6b–14)
¶-3. The betrayal of the harlot (17:15–18)
1. Heaven's announcement of the fall of Rome (18:1–3)
2. Rome deserted by the Christians (18:4–8)
3. Kings lament Rome's fall (18:9–10)
4. Merchants lament Rome's fall (18:11–17a)
5. Sailors lament Rome's fall (18:17b–20)
6. The millstone vision (18:21–24)
7. Heaven's approval (19:1–5)
IX. The final victory of the Lamb (19:6—20:15)
1. Announcement of the marriage of the Lamb (19:6–10)
2. The Word of God on the white horse (19:11–16)
3. The battle of Armageddon (19:17–21)
4. The binding of Satan (20:1–3)
5. The millennium (20:4–10)
6. The great white throne (20:11)
7. The final judgment (20:12–15)
X. Eternal destiny of the victors (21:1—22:7)
1. With God in the holy city (21:1–4)
2. The consummation of salvation (21:5–8)
3. The appearance of the new Jerusalem (21:9–14)
4. Description of the holy city (21:15–21)
5. God's presence in the holy city (21:22–27)
6. Eternal life in the holy city (22:1–5)
7. The angel's final message (22:6–7)
XI. Epilogue (22:8–21)

Selected Bibliography

BARCLAY, WILLIAM. *The Revelation of John,* 2 Vols. (2nd ed.). Philadelphia: The Westminster Press, 1960.

BECKWITH, ISBON T. *The Apocalypse of John.* New York: The Macmillan Company, 1919.

BOWMAN, JOHN WICK. *The First Christian Drama.* Philadelphia: The Westminster Press, 1968.

CAIRD, G. B. *A Commentary on the Revelation of St. John the Divine.* ("Black's New Testament Commentaries.") London: Adam & Charles Black, Ltd., 1966.

CHARLES, R. H. *The Revelation of St. John.* ("The International Critical Commentary.") Two volumes. Edinburgh: T. & T. Clark, 1920.

GLASSON, T. F. *The Revelation of John.* Cambridge: The University Press, 1965.

KIDDLE, MARTIN. *The Revelation of St. John.* ("The Moffatt New Testament Commentary.") New York and London: Harper and Brothers Publishers, 1940.

McDOWELL, EDWARD A. *The Meaning and Message of the Book of Revelation.* Nashville: Broadman Press, 1951.

MINEAR, PAUL S. *I Saw a New Earth.* Washington and Cleveland: Corpus Publications, 1968.

MORRIS, LEON. *The Revelation of St. John.* ("Tyndale Bible Commentaries.") Grand Rapids: Wm. B. Eerdman's Publishing Co., 1969.

RAMSAY, W. M. *The Letters to the Seven Churches of Asia.* London: Hodder and Stoughton, 1904.

RIST, MARTIN. "Revelation," *The Interpreter's Bible,* Vol. 12. Nashville: Abingdon Press, 1957.

SUMMERS, RAY. *Worthy Is the Lamb.* Nashville: Broadman Press, 1951.

SWETE, HENRY BARCLAY. *The Apocalypse of St. John* (3rd ed.). London: Macmillan and Co., Ltd., 1909.

TENNEY, MERRILL C. *Interpreting Revelation.* Grand Rapids: Wm. B. Eerdman's Publishing Co., 1957.

TORRANCE, THOMAS F. *The Apocalypse Today.* Grand Rapids: Wm. B. Eerdmans Publishing Co., 1959.

Commentary on the Text

I. Prologue (1:1–20)

1. Introduction (1:1–3)

¹ The revelation of Jesus Christ, which God gave him to show to his servants what must soon take place; and he made it known by sending his angel to his servant John, ² who bore witness to the word of God and to the testimony of Jesus Christ, even to all that he saw. ³ Blessed is he who reads aloud the words of the prophecy, and blessed are those who hear, and who keep what is written therein; for the time is near.

The title "The Revelation to John" is an abbreviation of the actual title which is the entire statement of 1:1–2. The actual title is preferable since the shorter one is not clear as to the origin or content of the revelation. A *revelation* is an unveiling of that which has been hidden. The word is common in the New Testament, but it is used here in a specialized sense. The Greek word *apokalupsis,* translated as "revelation," is transliterated "apocalypse" (see Intr. on apocalypses).

The content of the revelation deals with *what must soon take place.* The text implies in the word *must* an urgency or necessity greater than simple futurity. John's message was not for the curious but for the committed, *the servants.* These "servants" could be taken in a technical sense to designate special ministers (cf. Amos 3:7), but the instruction that the letter be read publicly (v. 3) requires us to see servants in the inclusive sense as all Christians. The events in the book will *soon take place,* and the emphasis is repeated many times, thus requiring the interpretation that John intended his message for his own generation.

The source and transmission of the revelation establishes its authority. It is *of Jesus Christ,* which can mean from or by Jesus Christ or that he is himself the revelation. In this case there is no question since

the additional statement that *God gave him to show* the servants the things that were coming shows that the revelation is ultimately from God and intermediately from Jesus Christ, but also Christ is the essential content of the revelation. An *angel,* a customary messenger and instructor in apocalyptic, transmitted the message to John, the immediate source, who claimed to be a *witness* to the *word of God,* in the general sense, and to *the testimony of Jesus Christ,* in the specific sense. The word *witness* is also used for "martyr." John will further identify himself (1:9) by showing how his exile to Patmos resulted from his bearing this witness. Having established the authority of the word by showing its origin and transmission, John identified its nature.

John's message was both *revelation* and prophecy. The term revelation and the repeated claim that the work is a prophecy (10:11; 19:10; 22:6,7,9,10,18,19) give us help in interpretation.

Scattered at random throughout the book are seven beatitudes introduced conspicuously by the beginning words "Blessed . . . ," obviously following the pattern of Jesus' beatitudes. The first one (v. 3) pronounces a blessing upon the public reader of this prophecy and blessings upon those who *hear* and *keep* its contents. A part of this beatitude is repeated later (22:7) and shows the unity of the book. John evidently followed the pattern of the synagogue in the public reading of important writings.

Often *hear* implies also that one obeys, but John leaves no uncertainty here in that the blessing is expressly extended to those who *keep* the instructions of the book. To keep is to obey.

The promised blessing stands out even more clearly because of the urgency of the hour, *the time is near.* The *time* is the end-

257

time or the time for the fulfillment of the prophecies of the book.

2. Salutation (1:4-8)

⁴ John to the seven churches that are in Asia:

Grace to you and peace from him who is and who was and who is to come, and from the seven spirits who are before his throne, ⁵ and from Jesus Christ the faithful witness, the first-born of the dead, and the ruler of kings on earth.

To him who loves us and has freed us from our sins by his blood ⁶ and made us a kingdom, priests to his God and Father, to him be glory and dominion for ever and ever. Amen. ⁷ Behold, he is coming with the clouds, and every eye will see him, every one who pierced him; and all tribes of the earth will wail on account of him. Even so. Amen.

⁸ "I am the Alpha and the Omega," says the Lord God, who is and who was and who is to come, the Almighty.

This paragraph is the salutation of the covering letter (1:4-20) which John wrote to accompany the seven specific letters. He intended that all of the letters be read in all of the churches. Some interpreters have seen the main body as an addendum to the letters, or the letters as a preface to the revelation. Some would see the letters as fragments of previous correspondence adapted for the present use. There are no objections to this understanding provided one notes that the symmetry and careful planning so obvious throughout the book suggest that the whole work forms a literary unity.

The salutation identifies the author as **John,** so well known in Asia as to need no further identification (see the Int.). The recipients of the letter are the **seven churches** of the Roman province of Asia, but John's use of the number **seven** makes it clear that he intended to include all of the churches of which these seven are typical.

The greeting, **grace** and **peace,** is a kind of benediction. **Grace** is that unearned, freely-given favor of God known in Jesus Christ and which results in genuine peace. **Peace** is not exemption from struggle or war nor modern "peace of mind." It is an inward, calm confidence born of rightness

with God which enables the Christian to walk courageously through storm and turmoil.

The origin of the grace and peace is threefold: God, the seven spirits, and Christ. God the eternal Father is clearly meant by the description *who is and who was and who is to come.* The repetition of this formula (v. 8) precisely identifies the Lord God.

The seven spirits who are before his throne are not so easily understood. R. H. Charles regarded this an interpolation and excised it. Beckwith sees the *seven spirits* as a reference to the Holy Spirit (Beckwith, p. 424). He does so since the expression (v. 4; 3:1; 4:5; 5:6) appears in no other biblical book, and in each instance relates the seven spirits closely to Christ so as not to permit confusion with angels. The spirits are neither angels nor stars (3:1), but are the seven torches (4:5). This is strange but no stranger than Zechariah's explanation that seven lamps (4:2) are the eyes of the Lord which range through the earth (4:10) and are somehow related to the Spirit (4:6). This would be a convenient reference to the Holy Spirit but is open to objection for this very reason. It is a strange way indeed to refer to the Holy Spirit.

In Babylonian and Persian literature, the sun, moon, and five visible planets were personified into the seven spirits, angelic or divine. The Hebrews would not have these as divinities but apparently did employ them in their view of archangels (Dan. 4:13; Tobit 12:15; 1 Enoch 20:1-8). In Revelation, however, angels and spirits are different. If these are angels, they appear in John's list between Christ and God, and this would be unlikely.

John may have intended the Holy Spirit, but used his number seven in its symbolic sense of completeness.

The description of Jesus Christ is also threefold: *faithful witness, firstborn of the dead,* and *ruler of kings. Witness* is the word "martyr," but John's point is that Jesus was faithful even to the death. John did not intend Christians to seek martyrdom but rather encouraged them to be faithful even if it meant death as it did for Jesus.

Firstborn from the dead, stressing Jesus' resurrection, appears to be based on the passage in Colossians (1:18). In that epistle (Col. 4:16) there was an instruction to circulate the letter among the other churches, specifically mentioning the church of Laodicea, one of our seven churches.

The description of Christ as the *ruler of kings on earth* is a statement of praise, but it is more. Through his death, Christ had achieved his power over kings and thereby was sovereign. Jewish expectations (Psalm 89:27; Isa. 55:4) included this idea of kingly rule. John intended to contrast the weak and transient rule of Rome's kings then persecuting the church with the powerful and lasting reign of Christ, "Lord of lords and King of kings" (17:14; 19:16).[25]

John dedicated his work to Jesus Christ who *loves* (is loving) *us and freed us from our sins by his blood. Freed,* or loosed, is preferable to the variant reading "washed." John's theology agrees with Paul's that Christ's death achieved man's redemption. Old Testament sacrificial imagery is in the background but does not suggest magical power in the blood itself. Christ "died for us" or gave his life for us.

Christ's redemptive work has created a *kingdom* composed of *priests.* They will reign with him. Christians are those who know God directly and mediate their faith in him to others. This text suggests the doctrine of the priesthood of all believers. But, John uses the term *his Father* to refer to the unique relationship between Christ and the Father and in no other way (v. 6; 2:27; 3:5; 3:21; 14:1).[26]

The expectation of Christ's coming (v. 7) is of particular meaning to John's readers. His heavenly origin is indicated by *coming with the clouds* as was the case

with the son of man (Dan. 7:13), a view common in Christian expectation (Mark 13:26; 14:62; Matt. 24:30; 26:64; Luke 21:27). The universal significance of his coming is expressed in that *every eye will see him.* So far, the joyful note of expectation is dominant, but John, as is his custom, immediately turns to the negative side.

Christ's coming will be a dreadful event for those *who pierced him,* certainly not being limited to the soldiers (John 19:37) but to all who had a part in his death (cf. Zech. 12:10). The wailing of the *tribes* is not weeping in repentance but in the recognition that he is Lord and that they have rejected him. Now he will judge them.

Even so. Amen is unusual. It combines the Greek and Hebrew particles of the same meaning and gives a double emphasis "Even so! Let it be!"

John's authentication is the quotation of God identified by the double title *Lord God,* who is *Alpha* and *Omega,* the first and last letters of the Greek alphabet, hence the first and last (21:6; 22:13). These letters became important symbols in Christian art. John also preferred the title *Almighty* (1:8; 4:8; 11:17; 15:3; 16:7; 16:14; 19:6,15; 21:22), which stresses God's power; but it is used only once elsewhere in the New Testament (2 Cor. 6:18) and that in a quotation.

3. Call and Commission (1:9–11)

9 I John, your brother, who share with you in Jesus the tribulation and the kingdom and the patient endurance, was on the island called Patmos on account of the word of God and the testimony of Jesus. 10 I was in the Spirit on the Lord's day, and I heard behind me a loud voice like a trumpet 11 saying, "Write what you see in a book and send it to the seven churches, to Ephesus and to Smyrna and to Pergamum and to Thyatira and to Sardis and to Philadelphia and to Laodicea."

John's call was like that of an Old Testament prophet, and his identification of himself was like that of the apocalyptic writers (Dan. 7:28; 7:15; 8:1; 9:2; 1 Enoch 12:3). When he gave his name and reminded them that he was their *brother,* he called to their

---

25 See essays, "Sovereignties in Conflict" and "The Kings of the Earth," Paul S. Minear, in *I Saw a New Earth.*

26 Mathias Rissi, "The Kerygma of the Revelation," *Interpretation,* Jan., 1968, p. 6.

minds not only association but also oneness.

In Jesus is reminiscent of Paul's favorite way of describing the Christian's relation to the Lord as being "in Christ." John called his audience to consider a threefold experience of sharing. They were fellow-sharers in *tribulation, the kingdom,* and *patient endurance.* In Revelation the kingdom is realized only by those who develop patient endurance in their tribulation. God's kingdom is never achieved by the use of worldly power. Christ achieved by the cross; Christians must follow his way.

The vision and call came to John while he was in exile on Patmos, a small island west southwest of Miletus by 37 miles. The island is only ten miles long and six miles wide and was used by the Romans as a place of banishment. Eusebius (*Church History,* III.18) referred to this exile of John and his release after Domitian was replaced by Nerva (III.20). The vision took place on Patmos, but it is not clear whether Revelation was written at that time or later.

The exile apparently resulted from John's proclamation of the *word of God* and his *testimony of Jesus* (1:2), although we have no details of any charges. Either he referred to his preaching the gospel of Jesus or his own confession that only Jesus was Lord in face of the demand that he say "Caesar is Lord."

John the prophet was called on a Sunday, while in an ecstatic trance by hearing a *loud voice.* To be *in the Spirit* means to be caught up by the Spirit or inspired. The TEV has it stated clearly, "The Spirit took control of me."

Christians had moved from the Jewish sabbath to the first day of the week, Sunday, in commemoration of Christ's resurrection. It is possible to interpret the *Lord's day* as (1) the Day of the Lord, (2) Easter Sunday, or (3) the weekly Christian day of worship. It is unlikely that (1) is meant since it was not a day of judgment but revelation. Since the other New Testament evidence does not establish absolutely that Christians had begun to observe the first day of the week as the Lord's Day, some

case has been made for interpreting this as (2) or Easter.[27] But it seems more justifiable to look upon this as our first literary reference to the Christian day of weekly worship.[28] Deissmann theorized that since one day each month was designated "Emperor's Day," John may well have been contrasting the *Lord's day.*

The commission (v. 11) was not to speak but to *Write what you see in a book,* and to send the book to the seven churches of Asia. The seven churches are identified by the seven cities in which they are located. They were the key cities of the districts of the Roman province of Asia.

Much speculation is in print about *the seven churches.* Why these seven? There were many others in Asia. If one stood on Patmos and considered a visit to these seven, he would begin at Ephesus and would visit them along a circular route and in the order named. He would also pass through other cities in which churches were probably located. Ramsay (pp. 188–196) was probably correct in his conclusion that these cities were district centers for the distribution of mail, news, etc., and letters intended for the entire province of Asia would be disseminated from these centers. It is also probable that John knew these churches personally, but he may have known the others also. Some think that he selected these because they were representative of all churches. At any rate, the number *seven,* signifying completeness, is probably intended to include the entire Christian community of Asia, which to the author was the entire church.

4. The Vision of Christ (1:12-20)

[12] Then I turned to see the voice that was speaking to me, and on turning I saw seven golden lampstands, [13] and in the midst of the lampstands one like a son of man, clothed with a long robe and with a golden girdle round his breast; [14] his head and his hair were white as

[27] See Kenneth A. Strand, "Another Look at 'Lord's Day' in the Early Church and in Rev. 1:10," *New Testament Studies,* XIII (Jan. 1967), 174–181.
[28] See Wilfrid Stott, "A Note on the Word KYRIAKH in Rev. 1:10," *New Testament Studies,* Oct. 1965, XII, 70–75.

white wool, white as snow; his eyes were like a flame of fire, ¹⁵ his feet were like burnished bronze, refined as in a furnace, and his voice was like the sound of many waters; ¹⁶ in his right hand he held seven stars, from his mouth issued a sharp two-edged sword, and his face was like the sun shining in full strength.

¹⁷ When I saw him, I fell at his feet as though dead. But he laid his right hand upon me, saying, "Fear not, I am the first and the last, ¹⁸ and the living one; I died, and behold I am alive for evermore, and I have the keys of Death and Hades. ¹⁹ Now write what you see, what is and what is to take place hereafter. ²⁰ As for the mystery of the seven stars which you saw in my right hand, and the seven golden lampstands, the seven stars are the angels of the seven churches and the seven lampstands are the seven churches.

This vision is of great importance for the rest of the book. It stamps the apocalyptic visions which follow as "Christian." In Revelation, all depends on Christ, who is portrayed in this vision. Christ is much more awe-inspiring than Caesar.

The lampstands are heavenly symbols of the actual seven churches on earth. Christ is walking among them uniting the heavenly and the earthly. He holds them in his hand —his strong right hand—showing both his sovereignty and their security. His clothing suggests purity and royalty. His physical appearance (described in a sevenfold way) is majestic, powerful, divine, and somewhat terrifying. But his voice, though like the sound of many waters, is comforting and reassuring. It dispels John's fears, because Christ spoke of his own death and resurrection as the basis of John's and all other Christians' hope.

Christ has a two-edged sword extending from his mouth which is the symbol of his power. Though militaristic in sound and sight, the two-edged sword is his word. He conquers by speaking his word. This is the case throughout the book.

The vision of Christ displays power and security, produces confidence, and calls for adoration, reverence, and dedication.

When John turned to see the *voice,* he saw *seven golden lampstands,* which he later identified as the seven churches (1: 20). Since Christians are the light of the world, the symbol is fitting, but it also has an Old Testament origin. One of Zechariah's visions (4:2 f.) included a golden lampstand with seven lamps. His vision was related to the original golden lampstand with seven lamps which had stood in the Temple (Ex. 25:31 ff.). John's vision seems to have been of seven separate lampstands.

Christ was standing or walking among these lampstands, a significant fact itself, and he looked like *a son of man.* By the time of John this term was messianic in its meaning, with a definite connection in the Old Testament (Dan. 7:13) and supporting evidence in apocalyptic writings (1 Enoch 46:1).

His clothing consisted of a *long robe,* and a *golden girdle.* The *robe* was suggested by the high priest's clothing but may have stressed only his dignity. The *golden girdle* is a mark of dignity and appears in such apocalyptic visions (Dan. 10:5).

Significantly, John's description of Christ's physical characteristics is sevenfold: *head and hair, eyes, feet, voice, right hand, mouth,* and *face.* The whiteness of Christ's *head and hair* is compared to *wool* and *snow.* There is a positive dependence upon Daniel (7:9), who described the "ancient of days" as having hair like "pure wool" and raiment as "white as snow." The head of the Son of Man in 1 Enoch (46:1) was "white like wool."

His *eyes* appeared as flames of *fire* not only here and in other passages of Revelation (2:18; 19:12) but also in Daniel (10: 6). In that passage a man appeared in a vision with eyes like fire. Another apocalyptic vision portrayed two such men (2 Enoch 1:5).

Feet like *burnished bronze* (also Dan. 10:6); Ezek. 1:7) gleamed and sparkled as only solid metal does. In such a description, H. B. Swete (p. 17) thought the intent was to show strength, or the power to crush.

His *right hand,* symbol of power, held *seven stars,* which are the angels of the seven churches (v. 20). John probably meant to stress only that Christ had power over the churches and that they existed only as he held them. Some interpreters have seen in this passage an implication that Christ controls the astrological powers, the seven planets, and point out that Paul (Col. 1:16; 2:8–23) may have been trying to correct some faulty thinking on that subject (Rist, p. 376).

His *mouth* was described only as the source of a *sharp two-edged sword.* A painting of this would be gruesome, but in spite of the warlike nature of the symbol (2:16; 19:15), it suggests the power of his word. In Isaiah (11:4) the person described will "smite the earth" and "slay the wicked" with the "rod of his mouth." Paul described the power of Christ's word as slaying the lawless one "with the breath of his mouth" (2 Thess. 2:8). In Hebrews (4:12) the word of God is sharper than a "two-edged sword." Clearly John intends to stress not only the power of the word Christ speaks, but also that he uses no other weapons.

The brilliance of Christ's *face* points to the glory of God and Christ which is not only dazzling but also blinding *like the sun* when it shines in *full strength.*

An interpretation of the vision (vv. 17–20) is introduced by John's immediate response. The prophets responded to God's appearance in similar awe (cf. Isa. 6:1–8; Dan. 10:9; Ezek. 1:28). Reverent prostration is common in the New Testament (Matt. 17:6; Acts 26:14) and among apocalyptic writers (1 Enoch 14:14,24).

In such visionary experiences, the prophets' fear was removed only by the reassurance from God or angels (Dan. 10:10; 1 Enoch 71:2,3). Christ told John to stop being afraid. Fear is the awe-filled response of man to God's presence. Christ's claims that he is *first* and *last* (1:8), that he has been raised from death to *live evermore,* and that he has the *keys of Death and Hades,* provide a threefold basis for assurance. The first is a claim of deity. The second identifies him as Jesus the Christ known in history and resurrection. The third is the assertion of power over man's ultimate enemies.

Death and Hades appear as personifications of man's ultimate enemies. Christ is here victor over both and holds the keys to their chains. In the seal plagues, the rider of the fourth horse, the pale one, was named Death, but Hades followed near behind (6:8). When Christ's victory is complete, Death and Hades, after being forced to surrender the dead they are holding, are to be cast into the lake of fire. Not even the Christian can escape death in the old aeon, but Christ's victory destroys the fear of death.

The commission is reaffirmed. It is to *write* the content of the visions. That content is further described to include both the present, *what is,* and the future, *what is to take place hereafter.* This twofold emphasis is more prophetic than apocalyptic in outlook.

The *mystery,* hidden from others, is now made known to John's readers. The *seven stars* are the *angels of the seven churches.* On the human plane, angels are merely messengers. Therefore, these angels could be the messengers to these seven churches, or even their bishops. However, such an interpretation would ignore the customary role of angels in Revelation in particular and apocalyptic in general. Apocalyptic writers referred to angels in so many ways that we are not able to discern exactly what they thought angels really were.

II. Letters to the Seven Churches (2:1— 3:22)

The seven letters are so similar in form and content as to suggest that they were written specifically for Revelation and were not composed previously for individual occasions. However, the specific details within them are so distinctive as to require us to acknowledge that John, while intending that all be circulated to all the churches, meant to address the specific congregation with the letter bearing its name. If they are artificial literary constructions (Rist, p. 380), they appropriately convey specific messages to the individual congregations.

It is more likely that they were letters written and sent separately but revised and standardized for use in this writing (Charles, I, 43 f.).

All seven letters conform to a standard pattern which can best be seen by arranging them in parallel. The pattern is: (1) address; (2) identification of Christ; (3) commendation; (4) reprimand; (5) exhortation; and (6) promise (see Tenney for a sevenfold arrangement facing p. 68).

The address is an identical formula in every letter except for the name of the city. The identification of Christ begins in every letter with the identical phrase "The words of . . ." but thereafter employs a rich variety of terms. The commendation and reprimand always begin with Christ's assertion to the churches that he knows their works. The commendation is different in each case, with Sardis and Laodicea receiving no word of praise. The reprimand is varied, and only Smyrna and Philadelphia escape censure. The exhortations follow the pattern of calling to repentance, with a warning and/or encouragement to hold fast or be faithful. The exhortation ends in every instance with "He who has an ear, . . ." The promise(s) in every instance is "for those who conquer," and the promises vary in detail.

1. Ephesus (2:1–7)

¹ "To the angel of the church in Ephesus write: 'The words of him who holds the seven stars in his right hand, who walks among the seven golden lampstands. ² " 'I know your works, your toil and your patient endurance, and how you cannot bear evil men but have tested those who call themselves apostles but are not, and found them to be false; ³ I know you are enduring patiently and bearing up for my name's sake, and you have not grown weary. ⁴ But I have this against you, that you have abandoned the love you had at first. ⁵ Remember then from what you have fallen, repent and do the works you did at first. If not, I will come to you and remove your lampstand from its place, unless you repent. ⁶ Yet this you have, you hate the works of the Nicolaitans, which I also hate. ⁷ He who has an ear, let him hear what the Spirit says to the churches. To him who conquers I will

grant to eat of the tree of life, which is in the paradise of God.'

Address. The angel could be an earthly messenger or a bishop, but it is probably the heavenly counterpart of the earthly church just as the heavenly lampstands are representative of the earthly churches (1:20). John's apocalyptic use of angels forbids a literal interpretation of this phrase.

Ephesus, located on the coast near the mouth of the Cayster River, had been an important commercial and cultural center since Greek times. In addition to its port facilities, Roman roads terminated in the city. The city was famous as the temple keeper of Artemis (Acts 19:35), and the temple itself was one of the wonders of the ancient world.

Paul's prolonged ministry in the city (Acts 19:1–10) established the place of that church in early Christian history. Sometime after Paul's death, our author John became a revered leader there. After the destruction of Jerusalem in A.D. 70, Ephesus became one of the great Christian cities.

Christ. The author back of John's writing is identified by the introductory phrase "The words of . . ." and then with distinctive descriptions of Christ previously given (1:13,20). John implied not only Christ's presence with the churches but also implied that he is the power in which they exist.

Commendation. The commendation begins with the reminder that Christ knows what is going on in the churches, stated in the formula *I know your works.* Christ's authority to judge them is asserted, and his full competence to do so is emphasized as the enumeration of their achievements and failures continues.

The commendation of the Ephesian church is worded poetically and draws attention to three factors: accomplishment, discrimination, and endurance. The Ephesians have accomplished genuine Christian *works,* which include not only deeds or acts but life, both outward and spiritual. The *toil* suggests the heaviness of labor accomplished only by those willing to work even when weary.

Discrimination of spiritual values is a trait worthy of commendation. The recognition of *evil men* in Ephesus led to the rejection of them. The *apostles* are not "the twelve," of course, but apostles in the general sense (2 Cor. 11:13). The Ephesians were spiritually perceptive and were able to distinguish between self-styled apostles who were *false* and those itinerant witnesses of Christ who were true. However, there is no license for heresy-hunting or such cruelty as the church has known. These men were *evil* and false. The Ephesians were commended for their ability to tell the difference. There is no reference to their action.

Patient endurance is not resignation nor "putting up with it." This quality is positive and enlightened. Patience is born of strength, not weakness, and comes only to those who can distinguish the things which excel and have the stamina to wait. Endurance is perseverance. It belongs to those who can see the goal and have the motivation to achieve it. The Ephesians received double praise in that they had not even *grown weary.*

Reprimand. The reprimand is the simple but serious charge that the church noted for *love* (Acts 20:36 ff.) had abandoned it. We can only conjecture as to the specific failure of the Ephesians, but no amount of diligence, perception, or patience can fill the void when love has gone from a church. Never to have known love would have been depravity, but to have known love and to have abandoned it was apostasy.

Exhortation. The exhortation is stated in a rapid threefold command: *Remember, repent,* and *do.* God's call to man to repentance frequently begins with a call to remember what God has done in the past. Such a reminder would be the strongest motivation for repentance. To *repent* is always to return to God, and it involves a change of mind, or attitude, toward God. In loss of love, they had turned from God. In a secondary sense repentance is turning from sins, but this is possible only on the

basis of a prior change of mind toward God. The third command implies a hidden commendation, since they are given no new instructions. They are bidden to resume the praiseworthy lives they had already begun.

Christ's exhortation often has a negative side. He threatened to come in judgment and to *remove* their *lampstand* unless they repented. They had lost love for God; repentance is turning to God. The passage has to do with the witness of a church, like a lampstand which gives light and can easily be extinguished. Numerous examples could be given of once-bright churches now darkened by sin and apathy.

Almost as an afterthought, John stated a second commendation. Their hatred of the works of the *Nicolaitans* enjoyed Christ's endorsement. There is no idea of hate for the Nicolaitans. Some have tried to relate the Nicolaitans to Nicolaus of Antioch (Acts 6:5), but there is no real evidence for doing so. There is good reason for seeing a relationship between the Nicolaitans [29] and the Balaamites (2:14–16) and Jezebel (2: 20). If so, foods sacrificed to idols and immorality appear to be involved (Acts 15).

Every letter has the concluding exhortation about hearing, but with some change in order. The statement is significant for four reasons. It is clearly adapted from Jesus' statement (Mark 4:9,23; Matt. 11: 15; 13:9). It switches the emphasis from the church to individuals. It is the *Spirit* who is speaking although Christ was clearly identified as the speaker in the beginning of the letter. This relationship of Christ and Spirit is like that in Romans 8:9. The letter was singular and intended for Ephesus. Now we have the plural *churches.* The letters, if originally sent separately, have been rewritten with this insertion for the present composition to include all seven churches.

Promise. The promise is a challenge to conquer and is reflected frequently in Revelation, the theme of which is victory. The victor or the one who *conquers* does not

---

[29] Beck, "Nicolaitans," IDB, III, 547; on Nicolaus, see Irenaeus (Her., I. 26.3; III.11.1). On possible relation to "Gnosticism" see Int.

prevail over others but over evil through his faithfulness to Christ. In Revelation the true victor is the marytr. The promise is varied in the seven letters. In the Ephesian letter the promise is the privilege of eating from the *tree of life.* Both the *tree* and *paradise* are apocalyptic symbols (Ezek. 47:12; 2 Esdras 8:52; Test. Lev. 18:11; 1 Enoch 25: 4 f.) evidently taken from Eden. The symbolism implies that immortality results from eating the fruit of the tree of life. Adam was cast out of the garden and forbidden access to the tree. But the victors in Christ will be readmitted to this paradise and will eat of the tree (22:2). The promise is the promise of eternal life.

2. Smyrna (2:8–11)

⁸ "And to the angel of the church in Smyrna write: 'The words of the first and the last, who died and came to life.
⁹ " 'I know your tribulation and your poverty (but you are rich) and the slander of those who say that they are Jews and are not, but are a synagogue of Satan. ¹⁰ Do not fear what you are about to suffer. Behold, the devil is about to throw some of you into prison, that you may be tested, and for ten days you will have tribulation. Be faithful unto death, and I will give you the crown of life. ¹¹ He who has an ear, let him hear what the Spirit says to the churches. He who conquers shall not be hurt by the second death.'

Address. Smyrna (modern Izmir) competed with Ephesus in commerce, culture, and Roman influence. The city was located on the coast due north of Ephesus. It was the location of a temple to Tiberias and had observed *Roma* worship at least since 195 B.C.

The church of Smyrna is not mentioned elsewhere in the New Testament. Consequently, we do not know who founded the Christian community. Paul was near Smyrna (Acts 19:10), but we have no knowledge that he visited the city. The church received unqualified praise from John, was a significant church in the second century, and is famous because of Polycarp, bishop of Smyrna, who was burned alive in A.D. 156. Ignatius visited this church on his way to Rome and to martyr-

dom and wrote four letters while in Smyrna. Two of his letters to Smyrna have survived.

Christ. John's identification of Christ, who is represented as sending the message, is a repetition of two statements of 1:17 f. These stress his everlastingness and his resurrection from the dead.

Commendation. The commendation was somewhat vague. In three years of suffering —*tribulation, poverty,* and *slander*—they had been victorious. Indeed, they were **rich.** In the light of their sufferings, their wealth must have been in the area of spiritual achievement, blessing, and fellowship. Tribulation was some form of persecution, probably related to the opposition of the Jewish community. *Poverty* may have resulted either from mob violence against the Christians or from the Domitianic policy of confiscation of the Christians' property. This was one aspect of persecution in the early church (Heb. 10:34). The *slander* is definitely identified as Jewish in origin.

The commendation was that the Christians had remained rich in spirit even in this kind of persecution.

The Jews, according to John, were counterfeit. John, who was not above retaliation, commented that they *are not* Jews in spite of their claim. This likely reflected the early Christian interpretation that Christians are the true Israel and that circumcision is a spiritual matter (Rom. 2:28; Gal. 6:15 f.). John's second charge against the Jews was more severe. John believed that Satan was the arch-enemy of God and the author of man's dilemma. *Synagogue of Satan* links a sacred word, otherwise used to designate the assembly or congregation of the faithful, with the embodiment of evil.

There was no reprimand for the church of Smyrna.

Exhortation. The exhortation was very specific in this letter. John predicted a threefold trial: suffering, prison, and tribulation. Evidently, he anticipated a new outbreak of persecution in which all would **suffer.** John expected some of them to be imprisoned. *Tribulation* was more to be feared than simple suffering.

In this instance, it was the *devil* who was responsible for the imprisonment. John believed that Satan was the great enemy of God and man and stood behind Rome's persecution (13:1). But John's Christian theology shows in that the imprisonment is an occasion in which they may be *tested*. This should not be understood to mean that God had therefore ordained it, but that from a Christian viewpoint trial can be testing. It is also significant that John's exhortation was partly based on the limitation in time to ten days. The limit of *ten days* is apocalyptic language for a short period which can be endured. Daniel recommended testing servants for ten days (Dan. 1:12,14. On 2:11, see notes on 2:7).

The exhortation *Do not fear* was therefore presented to the Smyrnean Christians on the grounds that (1) the devil was at the back of it so the Christians must be faithful to God; (2) it was a time of testing so they must endure to prove their purity; (3) the time will be limited to a short period.

Promise. The promise is twofold. Although the tribulation was to be limited in duration, some would be killed. To *be faithful unto death* is the same as to conquer. Marytrdom was victory in John's discipleship. Christians conquer only by faithfulness to Christ—not by using the weapons of Rome.

The promise of the *crown of life* is to be fulfilled later in that they will reign forever (cf. 22:5). It is the symbol of ultimate victory and is no different really from the reward promised to the Ephesians. The promise was stated negatively in the last statement of the letter. Immunity from the *second death* (cf. 20:6,14; 21:8) will be ultimate victory—eternal life. John could not promise his readers protection against the first death, martyrdom or natural death. However, he could assure them that by faithfulness to Christ, they would be immune to danger from the second death. The term "second death" is not uncommon in the usage of the Jewish writers of the period.

3. Pergamum (2:12–17)

12 "And to the angel of the church in Pergamum write: 'The words of him who has the sharp two-edged sword.

13 " 'I know where you dwell, where Satan's throne is; you hold fast my name and you did not deny my faith even in the days of Antipas my witness, my faithful one, who was killed among you, where Satan dwells. 14 But I have a few things against you: you have some there who hold the teaching of Balaam, who taught Balak to put a stumbling block before the sons of Israel, that they might eat food sacrificed to idols and practice immorality. 15 So you also have some who hold the teaching of the Nicolaitans. 16 Repent then. If not, I will come to you soon and war against them with the sword of my mouth. 17 He who has an ear, let him hear what the Spirit says to the churches. To him who conquers I will give some of the hidden manna, and I will give him a white stone, with a new name written on the stone which no one knows except him who receives it.'

Address. Pergamum was located about 15 miles from the coast of the Aegean near the Caicus river. The city was the most important center of emperor worship in the East because of the great temple to *Roma* and Augustus which had been erected there in 29 B.C. There were temples also to Zeus, Athena, Dionysius, and Asklepios.

The city was not as important in commerce as was Ephesus, but religiously it was outstanding. Since the temple to the "divine Augustus and the goddess Roma" led all Asia in emperor worship, this is likely the reason John spoke of the city as *Satan's throne*. However, many have tried to relate this phrase to the temple of Zeus which stood on a hill about 800 feet above the city. The temple of Asklepios, the god of healing, was the headquarters of an order of medical priests whose emblem was the serpent. People came from afar to this place of healing. It was reported that patients slept in the temple to be crawled over by nonpoisonous snakes as a part of the healing process. Inasmuch as John equates Satan with the serpent of Eden, some believe this is the reason for calling Pergamum the throne of Satan, but there is a better explanation.

Christ. Christ was identified only by the single trait previously mentioned (1:16) as the one *who has the sharp two-edged sword.* Since the Roman proconsul ruled by the power of the sword, some believe John was stressing in this term that Christ really has the power of sovereignty. John was contrasting one kind of sword to another. John favored this description for Christ (see comment on 1:16; 19:21). Christ's victory over his foes depended on his word.

Commendation. Christ's statements of judgment are related to the fact that he knew the truth. In this case, the point was that the Pergamum church was located right in Satan's capital. Faithfulness was even more commendable because of the setting.

Satan's throne is probably a reference to the imperial cult which had its center in the city. Even in the shadow of this temple, these Christians still said "Jesus is Lord" and refused the oath to the emperor. To hold to his *name* was fidelity to the confession of his lordship instead of Caesar's.

The Romans offered Christians an opportunity to reject Christ and live. This took the form of cursing or denying Christ and repeating the formula of reverence to the emperor. The Christians of Pergamum were faithful *even in the days of Antipas.* The implication is that there was considerable pressure upon others even though Antipas may have been the only one put to death. There is no information available to us from contemporary sources to identify this persecution of Antipas. He may have died at the hands of the mob or by governmental decree. In the light of John's use of *faithful* and the assertion that he was *killed* we must assume the latter.

Reprimand. The condemnation of Pergamum was that the church had been too tolerant and had allowed some to remain who held to the Nicolaitan teaching. The Ephesians had been commended for recognizing and rejecting the same error. The term *Balaam* is introduced from the Old Testament story to show the error of the Nicolaitan heresy (Caird, p. 39). Balaam was the proverbial Hebrew example of the false teacher. Balaam (Num. 22–25) had counseled Balak how to ensnare Israel. The end result was that Israel committed idolatry with Baal and fornication with Moabite women (Num. 25:1–5). The false teachers, the Nicolaitans, in Pergamum were doing the same thing.

The result in Pergamum was that the Christians committed a sin which can best be understood by comparing it with the sins of Thyatira (2:20). The sins named are eating *food sacrificed to idols* and practicing *immorality.* It is likely that one sin, not two, is intended. To commit fornication in both the Old and New Testaments means either sexual immorality or religious infidelity. Idolatry and harlotry are synonymous. The offense was not the accidental eating of meat previously offered in a pagan temple and now being served on the table of a friend. Eating such meat in the religious rites of a pagan temple was at once idolatry and fornication. Furthermore, in many of the pagan rites, actual sexual immorality was also practiced in connection with the idolatrous meals (Morris, p. 67).

The sins of Pergamum are known from our record of the Jerusalem conference (Acts 15) and from Paul's letter to the Corinthians (1 Cor. 8:1; 5:1), but the severity in this passage tends to establish the sin as Christian leniency toward pagan religious practices.

Exhortation. John exhorted the Pergamene Christians to *repent,* return to God. He posed the threat that Christ would come in judgment making *war* on them with his word.

Promise. The challenge to conquer is enhanced by a twofold promise, *manna* and a *white stone.* The one who overcomes sin will receive some of the *hidden manna.* Evidently, John's thinking about food offered to an idol suggested an opposite idea in Hebrew-Christian faith—food from heaven. Moses had ordered that some of the manna be stored in the ark (Ex. 16:32–34). This heavenly food is mentioned in the New Testament (Heb. 9:4). It was believed that when the Temple fell in 586 B.C. an angel or Jeremiah had hidden the ark with its manna which would be preserved until the messianic kingdom (2 Macc. 2:4 f.; 2 Bar. 6:5–10). In Jewish apocalyptic thought, this manna would come to earth at the time of God's victory (2 Bar. 29:8). Our symbolism is different, but the meaning is identical to the promise of the tree of life (2:7). It is eternal life sustained by God.

The meaning of the *white stone* is less obvious. Two additional details fail to help much. The stone is inscribed with a *name*. And no one knows the name except the person who receives the stone. Numerous suggestions have been made. (1) Judges voted to acquit with white pebbles and to condemn with black ones. (2) Victorious athletes were given white tickets which admitted them to free meals, etc. In this case the white stone would be a ticket to the heavenly banquet and the name would be Christ's (Caird, p. 42). (3) White stones inscribed with magical names could serve as guardian amulets or charms. This draws from the world of magic. (4) It has been related to the stones on the high priest's breastplate. There is no way to determine precisely the meaning of this stone, but the context indicates that it should be understood as symbolizing in some way the ultimate victory or admission to heaven.

4. Thyatira (2:18–29)

18 "And to the angel of the church in Thyatira write: 'The words of the Son of God, who has eyes like a flame of fire, and whose feet are like burnished bronze.
19 " 'I know your works, your love and faith and service and patient endurance, and that your latter works exceed the first. 20 But I have this against you, that you tolerate the woman Jezebel, who calls herself a prophetess and is teaching and beguiling my servants to practice immorality and to eat food sacrificed to idols. 21 I gave her time to repent, but she refuses to repent of her immorality. 22 Behold, I will throw her on a sickbed, and those who commit adultery with her I will throw into great tribulation, unless they repent of her doings; 23 and I will strike her children dead. And all the churches shall know that I am he who searches mind and heart, and I will give to each of you as your works deserve. 24 But to the rest of you in Thyatira, who do not hold this teaching, who have not learned what some call the deep things of Satan, to you I say, I do not lay upon you any other burden; 25 only hold fast what you have, until I come. 26 He who conquers and who keeps my works until the end, I will give him power over the nations, 27 and he shall rule them with a rod of iron, as when earthen pots are broken in pieces, even as I myself have received power from my Father; 28 and I will give him the morning star. 29 He who has an ear, let him hear what the Spirit says to the churches.'

Address. Thyatira was about 40 miles Southeast of Pergamum near the south bank of the Lycus River on the border of Mysia. Although the city had no temple of the emperor cult, it had other temples. The trade guilds of the city were very influential. Thyatira produced an expensive purple dye which was in great demand by the fabric manufacturers of the day. Lydia was a seller of this purple dye and her coming from Thyatira suggests that there was a Jewish community in the city (Acts 16:14).

No specific information is available regarding the origin of the Christian community in the city, but Luke hinted that some of Paul's companions may have preached there during Paul's stay in Ephesus (Act 19:10).

Christ. The identification of Christ includes three details, two of which are repetitions of the description in 1:14,15. However, the term *Son of God* is not used elsewhere in Revelation but is implied (1:6; 2:27; 3:5; 3:21; 14:1). It is probable that this term is more appropriate here because Psalm 2 is in the background of other statements in this letter (2:27). In that psalm, God addressed the messianic figure as "my son." On the description of his *eyes* and *feet*, see the comment on 1:14, 15. It may be that John used the expression about his *eyes* in this letter because he wished to stress that Christ's penetrating vision can clearly see the falsity of the prophetess herein condemned.

Commendation. Christ's knowledge of the church in Thyatira is the basis of his commendation. This knowledge is stated in one area, "works," with five illustrations, love, faith, service, patient endurance, and progress.

The commendation is lavish. It is quite interesting that the praise here exceeds that given either Smyrna or Philadelphia, who received no criticism as did the Christians of Thyatira. *Love* is listed first, somewhat characteristic of John, even though Paul tended to mention faith first. Evidently, this church had not departed from love as had the church of Ephesus. The *faith* is to be understood as faithfulness. *Service* is the ministry to the needs of the brothers. *Patient endurance* is that quality already discussed (see comment on 2:2). Progress is commended. The Ephesians once had love but had lost it. The Christians of Thyatira are improving: their *latter works exceed the first*

Reprimand. The criticism of the church in Thyatira was for being too tolerant in permitting a self-appointed prophetess to beguile the local Christians into sin. The error into which she led them was the same as Nicolaitanism (2:6,14,15). R. H. Charles has argued and interpreters like Barclay [30] have conjectured that the real offense grew out of the social life of the city required of members of the guilds. Since one could not succeed in business without being in a guild, and since such involvement would require participation in the social and religious events in which both immorality and idolatry would have been included, Jezebel had persuaded the Christians that it was not wrong to participate.

Jezebel could not be the woman's real name. John has taken this epithet from the infamous wife of Ahab who had sought to introduce Baal worship to Israel. This influential woman of Thyatira is the brunt of

some severe language from John. Calling her *Jezebel* is the first blast. She called *herself a prophetess,* but John implied in his statement that he did not so recognize her. William Barclay has conjectured that she could have been the bishop's wife, since "woman" can mean wife and the angel of the church could be the "messenger" who could be the "bishop," and since some manuscripts have "your woman." [31] This ingenius conjecture has little to commend it.

The sin of the church is even more serious because this woman had been reprimanded previously (v. 21) and had refused *to repent,* and the church had been silent.

The punishment which is to come to the woman and her followers must be understood in a spiritual sense. Otherwise, it would raise insuperable problems. Her *children* must be her spiritual offspring. God would hardly kill her real children in punishment for *her* sins. The *sickbed* is in contrast to the bed of adultery, which is itself idolatry. Her lovers will enter *great tribulation* as a result of their sins. God's punishment of this woman and her followers will vindicate God's judgment and serve to announce both his knowledge of man's inmost secret and his own determination to judge man by accurate standards as *works deserve.*

Christ spoke to the *rest* of the people in the church of Thyatira, i.e., those not affected with the Nicolaitan heresy, in very complimentary terms when he refused to *lay any other burden* on them. He gave one more insight into the Nicolaitan error. The *deep things of Satan* are usually understood in one of two ways. (1) Christians knew about the "deep things of God" (1 Cor. 2:10; Rom. 11:33). Ironically, John gave the claim of these heretics a twist and referred to their knowledge as belonging to Satan. (2) In some of the Gnostic groups of the second century, there was the actual claim of knowing the *deep things of Satan.* The libertine nature of these people showed itself in their assumption that a Christian

30 William Barclay, *Letters to the Seven Churches* (Nashville: Abingdon Press, 1957), p. 59.

31 *Ibid.,* p. 58.

could take part in heathen practices outwardly and remain unaffected inwardly. In fact, by participating in these things of Satan, the Christian could show his superiority over them. It is possible that the heretics of Thyatira are showing us an early Gnostic claim (Charles, I, 73 f.; Swete, p. 45; Beckwith, p. 468 f.).

Exhortation. The exhortation is a simple charge to *hold fast* to the Christian life which they have already established. This is the same as patient endurance (cf. v. 19).

Promise. The promise is twofold: *power* to share Christ's reign *over the nations,* and the gift of the *morning star.*

The author believed the prophecy that the Messiah's followers would share his reign. Psalm 2 was understood by John and other apocalyptic writers in this way. To *rule* is "to shepherd." The *rod of iron* (cf. 12:5; 19:15) is the heavy (oak) shepherd's staff fashioned into a scepter and weapon. When it had an iron tip it was a dangerous weapon. The promise is that they will rule with him.

The smashing of *earthen pots* in *pieces* is another symbol of universal power. It is derived from a custom of Egyptian and Mesopotamian kings, in coronation rituals, who would publicly smash pottery vessels on which the names of their enemies, or all other nations, had been inscribed. The expression appeared rather often as in the description of Sargon's destruction of his enemies as vessels of clay.[32]

It is strange that sovereignty such as using a *rod of iron* and breaking *earthen pots* would be promised to a victorious Christian. When applied to the Christians, it has to mean that they will share with Christ in his reign. But it is sovereignty derived from Christ as he received *power* from his *Father.*

Several interpretations have been suggested for the *morning star.* An apocalyptic saying indicated that the righteous would

shine like the stars in heaven (Dan. 12:3; 2 Esdras 7:97; 1 Enoch 104:2). The idea is glory or brightness. The *morning star* could suggest the first resurrection. It could mean the glory Christians will know in victory. The prophetic word is like a lamp giving light until the "morning star rises in your hearts" (2 Peter 1:19). But in Revelation (22:16) Jesus himself is the "bright morning star." He marks the dawn of the new day. The other letters conclude with promises which are fulfilled in the closing chapters of the book, and they are synonymous with eternal life. This is by far the best interpretation. In spite of objections that this would make Jesus the possession of victorious Christians, the victor will receive Christ in the fullest sense. The churches are lamps, angels are stars, but Christ is the bright morning star! (Swete, p. 47).

5. Sardis (3:1–6)

[1] "And to the angel of the church in Sardis write: 'The words of him who has the seven spirits of God and the seven stars.

" 'I know your works; you have the name of being alive, and you are dead. [2] Awake, and strengthen what remains and is on the point of death, for I have not found your works perfect in the sight of my God. [3] Remember then what you received and heard; keep that, and repent. If you will not awake, I will come like a thief, and you will not know at what hour I will come upon you. [4] Yet you have still a few names in Sardis, people who have not soiled their garments; and they shall walk with me in white, for they are worthy. [5] He who conquers shall be clad thus in white garments, and I will not blot his name out of the book of life; I will confess his name before my Father and before his angels. [6] He who has an ear, let him hear what the Spirit says to the churches.'

Address. Sardis, located about 30 miles south and southeast of Thyatira, was a busy commerical and industrial town. Although the city had been much more prominent in the past, it was famous in the first century A.D. for its woolen industry. Five Roman roads served the city. Sardis had failed to get approval for the temple of Tiberias but had other temples, the most important of which was that of Cybele. The imperial

---

[32] William Klassen, "Vengeance in the Apocalypse of John," CBQ, (July, 1966) XXVIII, 307.

cult posed no serious problem for the Christians of Sardis.

The citadel of Sardis, though located on an almost impregnable hill, had fallen on at least two occasions (549 and 218 B.C.) due to lack of vigilance. Some think this historical reputation was something of the setting for John's warning about watchfulness.

Christ. Christ's identification is similar to that in the Ephesian letter. The term *seven spirits* may designate the Holy Spirit (see comment on 1:4), or may stress watchfulness since the spirits go forth to ascertain the acts of men. Christ's authority over the church is stressed in the expression *seven stars,* since Christ holds them in *his right hand* (1:16) and since the seven stars are also the seven churches (1:20).

There is no commendation for this congregation. As an afterthought, the author concedes that there are some individuals who have not *soiled their garments* with the sins which have corrupted the others.

Reprimand. The reprimand is almost as severe as that pronounced on the church of Laodicea. To less discerning eyes, the church of Sardis appeared to be alive and maintained the reputation of the past. But Christ knew and pronounced the church *dead.* He named no specific sins. Apathy born of luxury had duped the church into death.

Exhortation. The exhortation included a series of commands and a warning of judgment. *Awake* is an imperative, meaning to become vigilant. Jesus often used this figure, which implied a previous period of vigilance. Christ called them to alertness— hardly resurrection. To *strengthen* what still remained was like pulling the last few embers into a heap to rekindle the fire whose flames had long since departed and whose embers scarcely glowed. The admission that something remained goes along with the following statement that their *works* when subjected to judgment did not measure up to the standard. But they were not without works.

The call to *remember* leads to repentance (2:5). They received the Christian faith through hearing the gospel. If they *keep that* they will be approved in the judgment. *Repent* points to the turning to God based on the change of attitude resulting from remembering his gospel and their experience of faith. The warning that he would come *like a thief* if they did not act in accord with the exhortation means clearly, but only, that he would come in judgment unexpectedly.

A *few* individuals deserve consolation or encouragement because they have not soiled *their garments* with the pollution of luxury or apathy. To walk with Christ in white is a double reward. Presence with him would be enough, but the white robes in Revelation are always the attire of victory and purity. There is evidence for seeing the term as related to the resurrection bodies of Christians (2 Cor. 5:1,4). Even the "Ancient of Days" (Dan. 7:9,13) was dressed in white. These *few* were judged *worthy.* In Revelation, this is strong language meaning that they have proved through trial their enduring faithfulness and have passed the test.

Promise. The promise to the church of Sardis, like those to the other churches, is preceded by the challenge to, and condition of, victory. Only *he who conquers* will receive the threefold reward: white robes of victory, permanent listing in the book of life, and personal acknowledgment by Jesus Christ. The *white garments* are the seal of victory and hence eternal life.

The indelible record in God's book is an indisputable title to the security of heaven. No one else will be in heaven (21:27). This book had a long history before John's reference to it (cf. Ex. 32:32; Dan. 12:1). John believed that these names had been written in the book since the foundation of the world (17:8), but this predestination was conditioned upon man's faith and faithfulness since Christ could *blot* a name *out of the book.* The Christian is assured that he can depend on Christ.

The last promise is a paraphrase of Jesus'

statement (Matt. 10:32; Luke 12:8) that he would confess those in heaven who confessed him on earth. This promise assured the readers that they must *confess*, i.e., witness faithfully to Christ, in order for him to make this witness on their behalf in the presence of the Father and the angels.

6. Philadelphia (3:7–13)

7 "And to the angel of the church in Philadelphia write: 'The words of the holy one, the true one, who has the key of David, who opens and no one shall shut, who shuts and no one opens.
8 " 'I know your works. Behold, I have set before you an open door, which no one is able to shut; I know that you have but little power, and yet you have kept my word and have not denied my name. 9 Behold, I will make those of the synagogue of Satan who say that they are Jews and are not, but lie—behold, I will make them come and bow down before your feet, and learn that I have loved you. 10 Because you have kept my word of patient endurance, I will keep you from the hour of trial which is coming on the whole world, to try those who dwell upon the earth. 11 I am coming soon; hold fast what you have, so that no one may seize your crown. 12 He who conquers, I will make him a pillar in the temple of my God; never shall he go out of it, and I will write on him the name of my God, and the name of the city of my God, the new Jerusalem which comes down from my God out of heaven, and my own new name. 13 He who has an ear, let him hear what the Spirit says to the churches.'

Address. Philadelphia was not as ancient as other cities, having been built by Attalus II in the second pre-Christian century. It was about 28 or 30 miles southeast of Sardis in the province of Lydia but in the administrative district of Sardis. The city stood on a plateau near rich volcanic soil which supported rich agriculture. Philadelphia became a city rich in commerce from the grapes grown in the surrounding area, in whose villages many of the people preferred to live rather than in the city. A major reason was the fear of earthquakes, one of which had severely damaged the city in A.D. 17. Tiberias financed the rebuilding of the city, which was then given a "new name," "Neocaesarea," in his honor.

The original founding of the city was the result of the ruler's desire to spread the Greek language and civilization into the barbarous region of Phrygia, hence its location on the border. This "missionary" purpose may have been alluded to in John's "open door." [33]

Because of the grape industry, the chief deity was Dionysius, and emperor worship was not the problem as elsewhere. In Philadelphia the difficulty seems to have come largely from the Jewish community.

Christ. The identification of Christ employed the term *holy* previously reserved for God (Hab. 3:3; Isa. 40:25). Both words *holy* and *true* were used by John to describe God (6:10). In the Hebrew setting, Christ was *true* because he had kept his word and would fulfill it. The *holy one* of God was the Messiah (cf. Mark 1:24; John 6:69; Acts 4:27,30; 1 John 2:20).

To say that Christ is the one who *has the key of David* is to affirm his messianic authority to admit or exclude from the messianic kingdom. The Old Testament passage to which this refers (Isa. 22:22) indicated that Eliakim held the keys to David's house. John probably used this expression of Hebrew origin since the problem in Philadelphia stemmed from a Jewish source, and he was asserting the authority of Christ. The figure of *keys* was used elsewhere (1:18) and reference to David is at the close of the book (22:16).

Commendation. The commendation of the Christians in Philadelphia is threefold: they have an *open door* which no one can close; they are faithful in spite of their weakness; and they have not denied the name of Christ. The open door could be (1) the missionary opportunity peculiar to Philadelphia on the border of Phrygia, but this door could be closed by war, for instance. (2) It could be Christ himself, the door, but they had already entered that door. (3) It is probably the door of the messianic kingdom yet to come. Christ can guarantee these faithful Christians that no

33 Barclay, *op. cit.*, p. 80.

one can exclude them from that kingdom.

The *little power* must refer to the smallness of the congregation or their lack of wealth. Their true strength is affirmed in that they have *kept* or obeyed his *word.* When a Christian failed under such pressure, he *denied* Christ's name; whereas when he held up, he made a faithful and true testimony.

Along with the commendation of the church in Philadelphia there was a condemnation of the Jewish community, which was obviously a source of pressure upon the church as was the case in Smyrna (2:9). John followed Christian precedent in regarding Christians as the "true Israel" and clearly condemned the Jewish community as being not only false but also a *synagogue of Satan.* Attempts to exonerate John from any hint of vindictiveness have an empty sound. John gave a strange twist to the remarks of Jewish prophets that Gentiles would prostrate themselves before the Jews (Isa. 45:14; 49:23; 60:14). He portrayed these Jews as coming and bowing down before the weak Christian community in acknowledgment that the Christians were the "elect."

Through *patient endurance* these Christians have won exemption from the *hour of trial* which John expected to come soon on the whole world. This phrase is probably based on passages in which a universal cosmic suffering was expected prior to the end (Dan. 12:1; Zeph. 1:7–18). It is not clear whether the exemption will be complete, or if Christ has promised to grant adequate strength for the hour. The event is eschatological. If the Christians endure the *hour of trial,*[34] it will purify them rather than destroy them.

Those who dwell upon the earth are unregenerate mankind. In some of the plagues the physical world is afflicted, but this phrase means mankind. In every instance in Revelation it designates unbelieving man. In 6:10 it means the persecutors;

the eagle announces a triple woe upon them in 8:13; they rejoice over the death of the two prophets in 11:10; they worship the beast in 13:8; they are deceived by the beast in 13:14; their names are not included in the book of life in 17:8.

The church in Philadelphia escaped reprimand.

Exhortation. The exhortation is the simple *hold fast* what you already have. However, the urgency is heightened by the reminder that Christ will come **soon.** Victory is in their hands, but perseverance is necessary or they could still lose the victor's *crown* (see also comment on 2:10).

Promise. The destiny of the victors is in reality the same as that in the other letters —eternal life. A victor will become a *pillar* in God's temple and will be inscribed with a threefold combination of names. Of course, the term is used metaphorically since there will be no temple in God's city (21:22). The metaphor is clear in that strong men are often likened to the columns which support and remain an indispensable part of a structure. Christians longed to be with God, so the promise that the victor would never **go out** was a promise of security. Some interpreters see in this "going out" an allusion to the fear of earthquakes in Philadelphia during which the people fled the city and waited in the open country. God's city will have no such flights.

The inscriptions are three names which will be prominent later in the book. The *name of God* on a Christian would identify him and publicize God's ownership of him. The implication of God's protection is quite obvious. The servants of God were sealed with a mark on their foreheads (7:3), and the servants of the dragon were also marked or branded (14:11). Christ, the Lamb, was followed by a large army of servants who wore the names of Christ and the Father on their foreheads (14:1). The victor Christ had a name inscribed which no one else understood (19:12). In the final victory in heaven, the inhabitants will have his name "on their foreheads" (22:4). Every Christian wears his name.

---

[34] Schuyler Brown, "The Hour of Trial, Rev. 3:10," JBL (Sept. 1966) LXXXV, 308 ff.

In Philadelphia there was a practice of honoring faithful citizens of the state by inscriptions of their names on pillars in the temples.[35] Barclay believed John used the figure because his readers would understand it so well in light of that local custom.

The city, *new Jerusalem*, which will come down out of heaven (21:2) is the place of eternal life. To be inscribed with its name probably stresses permanent citizenship therein. Inasmuch as Philadelphia had received a new name, Neocaesarea, it is possible that John played on local understanding with his name of a new city.

Christ's *new name* must be the same as that inscribed on Christ which "no one knows but himself" (19:12).

This beautiful summary of three names inscribed on the faithful Christian is one of absolute security. If the believer has God's name, the name of the New Jerusalem, and Christ's new name he will surely know eternal life. All the promises to the seven churches involve aspects of eternal life. To know the name of a person is to enjoy a particular relationship with him. To know God's name (Exod. 3:14) is to know God.

7. Laodicea (3:14-22)

14 "And to the angel of the church in Laodicea write: 'The words of the Amen, the faithful and true witness, the beginning of God's creation.
15 " 'I know your works: you are neither cold nor hot. Would that you were cold or hot!
16 So, because you are lukewarm, and neither cold nor hot, I will spew you out of my mouth.
17 For you say, I am rich, I have prospered, and I need nothing; not knowing that you are wretched, pitiable, poor, blind, and naked.
18 Therefore I counsel you to buy from me gold refined by fire, that you may be rich, and white garments to clothe you and to keep the shame of your nakedness from being seen, and salve to anoint your eyes, that you may see. 19 Those whom I love, I reprove and chasten; so be zealous and repent. 20 Behold, I stand at the door and knock; if any one hears my voice and opens the door, I will come in to him and eat

with him, and he with me. 21 He who conquers, I will grant him to sit with me on my throne, as I myself conquered and sat down with my Father on his throne. 22 He who has an ear, let him hear what the Spirit says to the churches.' "

Address. Laodicea was located in the Lycus River valley along with Colossae, ten miles to the east, and Hierapolis about six miles to the north. Three Roman roads passed through Laodicea thus making the city one of commercial importance. But sheep-growing in the area was also important since the raven-black wool was in great demand. This spawned a thriving business in clothing, carpets, etc., and supported a considerable community of craftsmen. The historians of the time made numerous remarks about the wealth of Laodicea. For instance, she refused the financial aid of the emperor and used her own resources for rebuilding the city after the disastrous earthquake of A.D. 60.

In 62 B.C. the governor, Flaccus, had the Jewish contribution of twenty pounds of gold, bound for Jerusalem, seized and sent to Rome instead. It is estimated that such a gift would have represented a Jewish community of 7,000 to 7,500 in the region (Ramsay, p. 420).

The church in Laodicea probably originated from the preaching of Epaphras, whom Paul mentioned in Colossians (1:7) as having preached in the nearby Colossae and also in Laodicea and Hierapolis (Col. 4:12 f.).

Christ. The identification of Christ in this letter stresses his truthfulness, and his presence at creation. The *Amen* affirms his truthfulness (Isa. 65:16). Jesus often used the term "Truly, truly, I say . . ." employing the same word. *The faithful and true witness* and *Amen* [36] merely clarify by using a term partially introduced in the introduction of the letter (1:5) and repeated as the actual name of the victorious Christ (19:11).

The beginning of God's creation is not

---

[35] Barclay, *op. cit.*, p. 88 f.

[36] Lou H. Silberman, "Farewell to O Amhn, A Note on Rev. 3:14," JBL June, 1963, LXXXII, 214.

easy to interpret. If taken to mean that Christ was the first creature, then one has ignored the Christology of Revelation. John believed Christ was eternal (1:18; 2:8). Worship should be directed to Christ (5:13), but men must not worship beings other than God (19:10). Beckwith translated this phrase "the one from whom creation took its beginning." Another good translation is "who is the origin of all that God has created" (TEV). God is the primary source (4:11; 10:6), and Christ is the agent of creation as in John 1:3 (see Col. 1:16; Heb. 1:2). The letter to Colossae was intended by Paul for Laodicea also (Col. 4:16). He spoke of Christ as the agent of creation, and this is probably the intent of the writer of Revelation.

The church of Laodicea received no words of commendation.

Reprimand. The reprimand is the most severe in the seven letters, including charges of lukewarmness, arrogance, and blindness. Having reminded these Christians that he knew their *works,* Christ condemned them for being lukewarm in their faith. He expressed derision at their nauseating condition in the threat of rejecting them by spewing them out of his mouth.

Christ further derided them by quoting their own arrogant claims of being rich, for taking full credit for being rich, and for claiming to be completely self-sufficient. This condemnation suggests that complacency born of affluence was the primary problem of Laodicea. It is known that the community was wealthy. The claim *I have prospered* suggests that these people took full credit for their own success, thus adding a further charge against themselves. Those who are spiritually perceptive do not make such claims.

Their claims of wealth and self-sufficiency are the more ridiculous in the light of Christ's true appraisal of them. They are blind and cannot see that they are wretched, *pitiable, poor, blind,* and *naked.* All these terms describe those lacking a vital relationship with God.

Exhortation. The exhortation is quite ex-tensive but makes clear John's hope that they will repent even yet. The counsel is a challenge which sets up three spiritual gifts desirable but lacking in the Laodicean church. (1) *Gold refined by fire* is symbolic of true Christian wealth which is the patient endurance refined by suffering for Christ. (2) Nakedness was the reprimand and is here in contrast to the *white garments* given to and worn by the faithful Christians (3:5). In order to show up their nakedness, Christ dared these people to try to purchase such garments to cover their nakedness. (3) In the light of their blindness, he challenged them to buy eye salve so that they could see. Obviously, they could not make any such purchase, and their blindness made them hopeless unless they had help from God. A famous medical school in Laodicea developed and marketed an eye medicine called "Phrygian powder" (Ramsay, p. 419) to which the author may have been alluding.

Abruptly, the author changes from rebuke to a statement of affection. Quoting loosely from Proverbs 3:12, the author reminded his readers that the rebuke was a result of Christ's love. His admonition for them to be *zealous* was a call to abandon complacency which produced the lukewarmness. The command to *repent* was given to every church which had sinned (2:5; 2:16; 2:21; 3:3; 3:19).

The exhortation was concluded by a statement (v. 20) often mistakenly understood to be an individual invitation. In the context it is addressed to the church. It is as if Christ stood "outside" seeking admission by "knocking." To *hear* would be to understand and respond. When Christ reentered the church, intimate table fellowship would be resumed. Whether the Lord's Supper is intended or regular eating, the symbol is fellowship, harmony, and sustenance. This exhortation, though addressed to a church, has relevant meaning for the unbeliever.

Promise. The promise is limited to those who conquer. It is the same as that offered the Christians of Thyatira (2:26) that

Christ will share his reign with them. This is life in his Kingdom.

III. Three Visions into Heaven (4:1—5:14)

John expects severe ordeals to begin shortly (6:1—8:5). The three visions in this section build a foundation for Christian assurance. John had originally indicated that he would write about "what is" and "what is to take place hereafter" (1:19). These visions portray what already is: God is sovereign in heaven; he knows the future and has it written on the scroll; Jesus Christ is worthy to open the seals, thus revealing the future.

These visions move toward a climax in Jesus Christ, who is exalted to deity. God's throne room is filled with indescribable wonder. John's restraint shows dramatic genius. God's majesty is obvious in that angelic beings attend his throne and perpetually sing praises. Rome had no grandeur like this! The mysterious scroll with seven seals reveals both "what is" and "what is to take place hereafter." These things are already known to God but cannot happen until he permits the seals to be opened. In spite of the grimness of historical events, history has meaning and yields a kind of obedience, however stubbornly, to God.

The vision of the Lamb is the great climax. John recognized him, as all Christians will, by his wounds—those of the sacrificed Lamb. The theme of Christ's victory through suffering sets the pace for all Christian life and thought. With this vision fresh in their memory, the Christians can go forth to conquer.

1. God's Throne Room (4:1-11)

¹ After this I looked, and lo, in heaven an open door! And the first voice, which I had heard speaking to me like a trumpet, said, "Come up hither, and I will show you what must take place after this." ² At once I was in the Spirit, and lo, a throne stood in heaven, with one seated on the throne! ³ And he who sat there appeared like jasper and carnelian, and round the throne was a rainbow that looked like an emerald. ⁴ Round the throne were twenty-four thrones, and seated on the thrones were twenty-four elders, clad in white garments, with golden crowns upon their heads. ⁵ From the throne issue flashes of lightning, and voices and peals of thunder, and before the throne burned seven torches of fire, which are the seven spirits of God; ⁶ and before the throne there is as it were a sea of glass, like crystal.

And round the throne, on each side of the throne, are four living creatures, full of eyes in front and behind: ⁷ the first living creature like a lion, the second living creature like an ox, the third living creature with the face of a man, and the fourth living creature like a flying eagle. ⁸ And the four living creatures, each of them with six wings, are full of eyes all round and within, and day and night they never cease to sing,

"Holy, holy, holy, is the Lord God Almighty, who was and is and is to come!"

⁹ And whenever the living creatures give glory and honor and thanks to him who is seated on the throne, who lives for ever and ever, ¹⁰ the twenty-four elders fall down before him who is seated on the throne and worship him who lives for ever and ever; they cast their crowns before the throne, singing,

¹¹ "Worthy art thou, our Lord and God,
   to receive glory and honor and power,
   for thou didst create all things,
   and by thy will they existed and were
      created."

Scene. The location has changed from earth to *heaven*, from earthly churches in their struggles to God's throne. John's vision is clear but his visibility is limited to the throne and its immediate surroundings. We must resist the temptation of trying to sketch a diagram. The vision is introduced by the formula, *After this I looked* (lit., "After these things, I saw"), referring to previous visions.

Heaven was the vault above the earth. In early Christian thought, the universe had three levels. Earth was a flat plane; the heaven was above; the underworld was below. John apparently thought of heaven in the singular, but some writers spoke of "heavens" (2 Cor. 12:2). In one source there were seven heavens.

The *open door* allowed John to look inside. This idea is common. Some apocalyptic writers envisioned a curtain that rolled back (Ezek. 1:1) or a portal (1 Enoch 14:15) such as the one through which Enoch entered heaven (1 Enoch 14:8). John may have entered, but the equation of *Come up hither* and being *in the Spirit* suggests that he looked into heaven while in an ecstatic trance.

John's summons came by the *voice* which was as clear as a trumpet, the voice of Christ (1:10). The promise is that he will show John *what must take place after this.* Those events will begin in 6:1. John's reference to being *in the Spirit* has led to speculation that this is some kind of an intensification of inspiration since he was already in the Spirit (1:10) when he received the previous visions. Such a speculation is pointless, since he may only be reminding the readers that the source of his writing is the vision. The visions may have come on different occasions.

The Throne of God. The throne is described only in terms of its immediate surroundings. The silence about the throne itself suggests grandeur beyond description. Because the ark of the covenant was a kind of God's throne in the Old Testament, some have tried to visualize this throne as the ark. Such an interpretation would require one to see the throne room as a holy of holies, and there is no evidence for such an assumption. The *seven torches* may be appropriate near a holy of holies, but a *sea of glass* would not.

The throne stands for God's presence and power. The majestic setting included a rainbow, 24 other thrones with elders on them, seven torches, a crystal pavement, and four living creatures like cherubim.

The *rainbow* was circular in shape and surrounded the throne; it did not arch over it. It was green like an *emerald* rather than multicolored. It decorates the throne room and suggests wonder as in Ezekiel 1:28; it has no allusion to the covenant rainbow (Gen. 9:8 ff.).

The *flashes of lightning*, the *voices*, and the *peals of thunder* which intermittently punctuate the already awesome setting suggest the visible and audible manifestations of God's presence on Sinai at the giving of the law (Ex. 19:16). In Hebrew poetry, the thunderstorm suggested God's presence and majesty (1 Sam. 2:10). In general, such phenomenal natural displays are used to describe theophanies (Ezek. 1:13; Psalm 18:13 f.; Job 37:2–5). Common in Revelation (16:18) and in a different order (8:5), they are also known in 1 Enoch (14:19) where flames of fire were so bright that Enoch could not look upon them.

The *seven torches of fire* burn perpetually before the throne. Probably related to Zechariah's (4:2,10) lights which were the eyes of the Lord, these are not the seven lamps of 1:12. It is more likely that they are the seven spirits (1:4) and symbolic of the Holy Spirit. *Fire* is a fitting symbol for the Spirit's presence. *Seven* is the number of completeness.

Between John and the throne there was a flat pavement-like surface, probably semiprecious stones, which looked like a *sea of glass*, like crystal. Kings' thrones, with a degree of awesome appearance, often had such surfaces before them. They are as nothing compared to this one which is broad like the sea and reflects the flashes of lightning and the rainbow. The God of Israel had once seemed to stand on such a pavement "of sapphire stone" (Ex. 24:10). John was likely alluding to this passage and wished to stress the magnificence of the throne and the distance still remaining between him and the throne. G. B. Caird thinks the *sea of glass* (found also in (15:2) is the cosmic sea of chaos over which God claimed authority in creation. This interpretation is based on the presence of the sea monster in 13:1 and its mythological background (Caird, p. 197).

God. Although John usually shows no reluctance about using God's name, on this occasion he refers to God as *he who sat* on the throne. Although some writers suggest a human form for God, John avoids this anthropomorphism. The hint of appearance includes only that he appeared like *jasper and carnelian.* Some interpreters have found symbolic meaning in these three stones' colors (*jasper, carnelian,* and the rainbow's *emerald*), but this is weak since we are not at all certain of the colors intended. The jasper was a variety of quartz which may have been red, brown, green, gray, or opaque. Pliny understood it to be chalcedony or agate, and the LXX translated the Hebrew word as "onyx." Others identified it as opal or even the diamond. The *carnelian,* or sardius,[37] was a variety of chalcedony known in transparent red and brownish red. It was found near Sardis, hence the name, and was imported from Babylon.

The Twenty-Four Elders. In the throne room are two orders of permanent attendants: the 24 elders, and the four living creatures. The *twenty-four elders* have *twenty-four thrones* which, though undescribed, suggest both permanence and power. These elders were around the throne of God, perhaps in a circle. The number *twenty-four* suggests different interpretations: (1) the 12 patriarchs and the 12 apostles, symbolizing the two covenants of the people of God; (2) the 12 tribes of Israel represented by two elders each, one for Israel and one for the church; (3) the 24 priestly divisions of Aaron's sons (1 Chron. 24:1–19); (4) the elders of Israel, who are not numbered. Some have seen a connection with astral speculation in that there were 24 stars beyond the circle of the zodiac, 12 in the north and 12 in the south, but this is not convincing (Rist, p. 402).

The *twenty-four elders* are mentioned five other times (4:4,10; 5:8; 11:16; 19:4). The *elders* are mentioned on five occasions. (5:6,11; 7:11; 14:3), and one of them is mentioned twice (5:5; 7:13).

It is certain that the number 12 figures in understanding the elders. The most likely conjecture is that they are Israel and the church, or representatively the whole people of God. Their *thrones* and *white garments* suggest that they are kingly priests. Their *crowns* include the idea of reign. In spite of their prominence, they rank after the four living creatures whose signals to

worship they obey, and they do not appear to have a part in the final judgment. They are human—neither divine nor angelic (for a full description of the elders see R. H. Charles, I, 128 ff.).

The Four Living Creatures. Whereas the elders were primarily human beings, these are angelic or celestial beings who stand nearest God's throne and engage in acts of worship and praise. Their presence may have originally suggested the idea of guarding the throne. but such an idea is unnecessary in the case of God's throne. John was under the influence of the prophets, and we will likely find that he employed these symbols of Ezekiel and Isaiah.

Ezekiel's "four living creatures" (1:4) came out of a cloud and had human forms, but each had four faces, four wings, straight legs with feet like a calf's, and human hands under the wings. They are the "cherubim" (Ezek. 10:2) and appear to bear God's throne. Isaiah's "seraphim" (6:2–4) had six wings each and performed the same acts for God as did Revelation's living creatures.

These figures are usually considered in the category of angels,[38] but caution is in order with the equation. Cherubim guarded the tree of life in Eden (Gen. 3:24) and either guarded or supported the throne of God (Isa. 37:16). The wooden figures overlaid with gold which stood at either end of the ark of the covenant were the cherubim, who spread their wings over the mercy seat (Ex. 25:18–20).

From archaeological discoveries in the biblical world we know the sphinxes of Egypt and the winged bulls of Assyria which featured the king's heads. These impressive statues guarded the palaces of kings. They were cherubim.

The *living creatures* of Revelation bear resemblance to those of Ezekiel, but John was quite original in his use of them. The four faces on Ezekiel's cherubim were those of a man, a lion, an ox, and an eagle (1: 10). Revelations *living creatures* were like

---

[37] On the stones, see IDB or the *Westminster Dictionary of the Bible.*

[38] See "Angels" in IDB or other Bible dictionary.

a *lion*, an *ox*, a *man*, and a *flying eagle*. But John followed Isaiah 6:2 in giving each creature *six wings*. The eyes are *all around and within*, meaning that they could perceive everything in any direction. One should avoid trying to conceive of these literally. No diagram can show all these characteristics. For instance, Ezekiel's visions showed the eyes on wheels.

John's living creatures portray an order of nonhuman beings near God's throne always ready to praise God, who sits in majesty. The number four probably comes from the four points of the compass. Commentators think that the living creatures (man, a wild animal, a domestic animal, and a bird) represent all creation praising God (Swete, p. 71; Caird, p. 64; Summers, p. 132). Some think the symbolism stresses God's sovereignty over all forms of life.

Their importance is reflected in John's reference to them on fourteen different occasions. Their function is highlighted by the phrase *day and night they never cease* to sing praise to God.

The Cherubim's Doxology. There are many hymns or fragments of hymns in Revelation. Some of these are evidently derived from the Old Testament as is this one (Isa. 6:3). Others may have been common in Hebrew and Christian worship. This doxology, or threefold statement of praise to God expresses three affirmations: (1) God's holiness, (2) God's power, (3) God's eternity. R. H. Charles compared this hymn with the hymn of the elders. The hymn of the living creatures (v. 8) stresses the essential nature of God, which is holiness, omnipotence, and everlastingness; whereas the hymn of the elders (v. 11) stresses the glory of God in his works (Charles, I, 133 f.).

Holy, holy, holy stresses the biblical idea of God's otherness. God is majestic; he is not like man. Holiness in the absolute sense is the quality of God only. It is not an ethical idea. The ethical idea is derived from God's true nature. When man is enjoined to be holy, it means he is to be set apart or dedicated to God, who is true

holiness.

Lord God Almighty, used frequently in Revelation, appears nowhere else in the New Testament (see comment on 1:8). The further identification of God's eternity, *who was and is and is to come*, is customary usage (1:4).

In worship the four living creatures—who are also the highest order of angels in 1 Enoch (61:10) and never sleep (71:7)—stand before God's throne giving *glory, honor*, and *thanks* to God. *Glory* indicates brilliance, brightness, or the majesty of God. *Honor* is the divine characteristic meaning esteem, or preciousness. *Thanks* is giving to God the thanksgiving due him from his creatures because of his goodness.

Elders' Acclamation of Worthiness. The hymn of the elders' (v. 11) is a doxology also, but it is in the form of an acclamation of God's worthiness because of his creation.[39] The elders take their cue for worship from the four living creatures. Whenever these creatures *give* (the Greek tense is future but the meaning has to be present) their worship in song to God, again identified by his position on the throne, and his eternity, the elders worship. Their worship involves three acts: prostration before the throne, casting their crowns before the throne, and singing.

Prostration before God in worship is common. Casting their *crowns before the throne* is a dramatic demonstration of their acknowledgment of God's sovereignty. This is quite different from the modern sentiment, expressed in gospel songs, of desiring crowns in heaven. Creatures surrender their crowns in God's presence even when their crowns are crowns of victory as in this case. The crowns are God's gifts and are appropriately given back to him in worship.

The hymn expresses the creatures' recognition *Worthy art thou* to receive the *glory, honor*, and *power* just given by the living creatures (note "power" instead of "thanks" in this response). This acclamation is a choral response to the previous doxology.

39 John J. O'Rourke, "The Hymns of the Apocalypse," CBQ July, 1968, p. 400.

Creatures worship God just because he is God; they do not have to give reasons for worship. However, reasons can be given. In this case, God's worthiness is recognized in his creative power. The creation of *all things* and their continued existence depend on God's *will*. Some speculate that *existed* and *were created* suggest two stages, but John probably has reference only to his belief that God willed creation.

Chapter 4 is a magnificent description of God's majesty and his creatures' adoration. The only specifically Christian allusion is in the number of the elders, and that is vague. The description of God's throne and its setting could have been Hebrew, except for the forthcoming vision of the Lamb (ch. 5). This vision stresses God's holiness and the creatures' response in worship.

2. The Scroll with Seven Seals (5:1-5)

¹ And I saw in the right hand of him who was seated on the throne a scroll written within and on the back, sealed with seven seals; ² and I saw a strong angel proclaiming with a loud voice, "Who is worthy to open the scroll and break its seals?" ³ And no one in heaven or on earth or under the earth was able to open the scroll or to look into it, ⁴ and I wept much that no one was found worthy to open the scroll or to look into it. ⁵ Then one of the elders said to me, "Weep not; lo, the Lion of the tribe of Judah, the Root of David, has conquered, so that he can open the scroll and its seven seals."

Books are so numerous, available, and inexpensive today that a modern man can easily overlook the significance of this vision. In biblical times, all books were laboriously written by hand on very expensive vellum, or on papyrus which was less expensive, but costly. Only the wealthy owned books. Therefore books were held in respect. Most people saw books from a distance, only from the outside, and wondered regarding their mysterious contents.

The Scroll. John's vision was of a particularly mysterious book. Amidst all the brilliance of God's throne, God's majesty, and human and angelic attendants, suddenly all attention is drawn to a *scroll*, a book in the form of a roll. This scroll is even more awesome because it is held in

God's right hand. We have had no previous hint about the form of God, nor should this detail be used in a literal fashion. John had no other way of telling us that God holds the book. Its mysterious content is known only to him. Furthermore, this scroll was inscribed both inside and outside, contrary to the usual custom of writing only on one side and then rolling the scroll with the writing inside. Ezekiel's scroll, written also on both sides (2:9 f.), may have been John's inspiration. The greatest mystery, however, is hidden in the detail that this scroll was *sealed with seven seals.* The seal was imprinted in wax on a document, or on a binder of a document to guarantee the contents.

Obviously, the *seven seals* stress the completely hidden nature of the contents. A Roman law provided for wills to be attested by seven witnesses who affixed their seals thus guaranteeing the will. Our scroll, however, though sealed with seven seals, is opened by one person. A scroll could not be unrolled until all seals were broken, but this literal detail does not apply to the scroll in Revelation. With the breaking of each seal the drama unfolds.

Both biblical (Ezek. 2:9 ff.; Dan. 10:21; Psalm 139:16) and nonbiblical sources (1 Enoch 93:3; 106:19; 103:1-3; 4 Ezra 6: 20) speak often of mysterious books of God.

There are four suggested explanations for the scroll. (1) It may be the Lamb's book of life (3:5; 13:8; 17:8; 20:12,15; 21: 27), which would presumably reveal the names of the redeemed, but that is not the case. (2) Some think the scroll is the Old Testament. Jesus disclosed the true meaning of the Old Testament in the synagogue of Nazareth; Christ interprets the scroll of prophecy. But this view does not explain why Christ's victory through death qualified him to open it. (3) Some claim that the scroll contains a record of the events soon to take place. There is a question as to why the delay until A.D. 95 if Christ had won the right to open the seal in A.D. 29 or 30 (Caird, p. 71). (4) The scroll reveals God's redemptive plan, which was foreshadowed in the Old Testament, and as such contains the world's destiny.

The fourth possibility appears more in keeping with the whole theme. A warning is in order, however, lest we assume the apocalyptist's determinism. In Revelation there is a scroll of destiny, but there is also the constant reminder that man's response to God, obedience or rebellion, figures in determining destiny. So, the book reveals coming events, but there is no rigid determinism which rules out the importance of man's freedom.

The Angel's Question. The *strong angel* was mighty because of his *loud voice* capable of being heard all over *heaven* and *earth.* Several strong angels appear (10:1, 3; 18:21) and do mighty acts. His question asked, *Who is worthy,* playing on the word from the previous hymn, *to open* the *seals?* This question, designed to arouse suspense because all Christians were anxious about the coming events, was heard throughout the entire universe of three levels—*heaven, earth,* and *under the earth.* Paul used the same terminology to declare the universal confession of God's sovereignty (Phil. 2:10).[40]

Obviously, no one was worthy. We are not told how this was ascertained. Perhaps, John's statement indicates that there was no response to the angel's challenge. No one offered himself as worthy.

John's Response. John's unrestrained weeping, which requires the assumption that some time is involved, is due to his disappointment which stems not from idle curiosity, but from the knowledge that the promise of 4:1 cannot be kept until the seals are opened.

The Elder's Promise. An anonymous elder spoke up to assure John that there was One worthy to open the seals. *Weep not* is the equivalent of "Stop crying!" *The Lion of the tribe of Judah* is equated with the *Root of David* and identified as the victor. Judah was called a "lion's whelp" (Gen.

---

40 In the OT, there is such a division, but a third division was the sea (Ex. 20:4,11: Psalm 146:6). The meaning is to include all of creation.

49:9) and was promised the scepter until the coming of the one "to whom it belongs" (Gen. 49:10), which was taken by John to be messianic. Another Hebrew tradition spoke of a "root of Jesse" and "shoot from the stump of Jesse," which was expected to come forth "to smite the earth with the rod of his mouth," and "with his lips" to "slay the wicked" (Isa. 11:1–10).

These terms are particularly illuminating when we note that in John's usage of them they appear in bold contrast to the actual Messiah who had no characteristics of a lion, but was the opposite, a lamb. Regardless of what the Old Testament writers may have meant, the Christians saw these terms as messianic. Paul appears to have used the Isaiah passage in this way (Rom. 15:12). John quotes Christ in the final victory as speaking of himself (Rev. 22:16) in this manner.

Everything in Revelation rests on the victory which Christ won in his death. The elder explains that the "Lion" can open the seals because he *has conquered.* John has shown that the victory of Christ, won not in the conventional way by warring with weapons and power such as Rome has in abundance, can also be known by the believers. Each of the seven letters ended with a promise, a challenge to victory. The conqueror Christ can share his victory. His believers can be conquerors. This victory is portrayed in his opening the seals.

3. The Lamb Who Opens the Seals (5:6–14)

6 And between the throne and the four living creatures and among the elders, I saw a Lamb standing, as though it had been slain, with seven horns and with seven eyes, which are the seven spirits of God sent out into all the earth; 7 and he went and took the scroll from the right hand of him who was seated on the throne. 8 And when he had taken the scroll, the four living creatures and the twenty-four elders fell down before the Lamb, each holding a harp, and with golden bowls full of incense, which are the prayers of the saints; 9 and they sang a new song, saying,

"Worthy art thou to take the scroll and to open its seals,

for thou wast slain and by thy blood didst
    ransom men for God
from every tribe and tongue and people and
    nation,
10 and hast made them a kingdom and priests
    to our God,
and they shall reign on earth."
11 Then I looked, and I heard around the
throne and the living creatures and the elders
the voice of many angels, numbering myriads
of myriads and thousands of thousands,
12 saying with a loud voice, "Worthy is the
Lamb who was slain, to receive power and
wealth and wisdom and might and honor and
glory and blessing!" 13 And I heard every creature in heaven and on earth and under the
earth and in the sea, and all therein, saying,
"To him who sits upon the throne and to the
Lamb be blessing and honor and glory and
might for ever and ever!" 14 And the four living
creatures said, "Amen!" and the elders fell
down and worshiped.

This vision falls into five distinct events:
(1) the Lamb takes the scroll; (2) the four
living creatures and the elders respond in a
threefold act of worship; (3) countless
angels respond with a sevenfold acclamation of worthiness; (4) every existing creature joins in praise; (5) the "Amen!"

The Lamb Takes the Book. Without hesitation John recognizes the Lamb as the
victor by the scars of the sacrificial slaughter. He uses this designation for the crucified messiah 29 times in the book. The
other word for "lamb" appears also of Christ
in John (1:29,36) and in Acts (8:32). The
Christians interpreted Christ as Isaiah's
Suffering Servant (Isa. 53:7), and probably
applied Jeremiah's (11:19) statement of
his suffering to Jesus. One wonders how the
early Christians must have talked about the
unusual victory of Christ through death.

Christ, the Lamb, was nearer the throne
than the living creatures. He stood *among
the elders* though his presence had not
been previously noted. He was described
only by the details of *standing,* having
wounds *as though it had been slain,* and as
having *seven horns and seven eyes. Horns*
indicated power (Deut. 33:17; 1 Kings
22:11), nations or their kings (Zech. 1:18–
21), and are particularly well suited for
apocalyptic imagery (Dan. 7—8; 1 Enoch

90:37). The *seven* horns indicate complete
power. He wore the marks of his own death
and the seven horns of omnipotence. His
death was on the cross. He conquered by
his own sacrifice. John's Christology is portrayed in this death-victory. The *seven eyes*
are the *seven spirits* of God (see comment
on 1:4; 3:1) which are *sent out into all the
earth* (cf. Zech. 4:10). It is difficult to
know if John thought of the Holy Spirit or
seven separate spirits, but in any event the
seven eyes indicate the Lamb's knowledge
of all. The *seven horns* and *seven eyes* attribute omnipotence and omniscience to the
Lamb (Charles, I, 141 f.).

The Lamb *went* and *took,* or received,
the scroll directly from the hand of God
without hesitation.

Creatures and Elders Praise God. When
the Lamb took the scroll, the long-awaited
act, the permanent attendants of God's
throne room entered their threefold worship: they fell prostrate *before the Lamb;*
they presented harps and *golden bowls full
of incense;* they *sang a new song* of Christ's
worthiness. Each act is meaningful in its
own right, but together they show the
Christian belief that Christ is deserving the
same kind of worship given to God.

Harps were lyres or zithers commonly
used in worship (Psalm 33:2; Rev. 14:2).
The *golden bowls full of incense,* common
in Hebrew worship, are described as containing the *prayers of the saints* (all believers). We should think of these attendants offering their musical instruments and
bowls in worship to the Lamb. Assurance
is implied in the bowls of incense in that
the *prayers of the saints* have not been lost.
Rather, they have been preserved and given
to Christ. This assurance will be heightened
later (8:3 ff.).

The third act of worship by the elders
and cherubim was the singing of a *new
song* of acclamation, this time to Christ.
John enjoys the theme of "newness." He
speaks of a "new name" (2:17; 3:12), a
"new Jerusalem" (3:12; 21:2), a "new
heaven and a new earth" (21:1), and all
things made "new" (21:5). Even another

new song appears later (14:3). New songs were written when fresh songs of praise were needed to express gratitude for new acts of God's mercy (Psalms 33:3; 96:1). The news that the Lamb will open the seals was such an act.

The acclamation of worthiness points out three achievements of Christ: he was *slain;* he *ransomed* for God men from every tribe; he made them a *kingdom* of *priests* to God.

John's theology, like that of Paul, gives a central place to Christ's death as the atoning act. The statement *thou wast slain* refers not to accidental or unfortunate death but to Christ's victorious death on the cross.

In the second place, his *blood* was a *ransom* whereby men enslaved to sin were set free for God. The *blood* has its meaning in the sacrifice of the Old Testament. The *ransom* draws its appeal from the institution of slavery. But it has a beautiful meaning in that dark setting. One can ransom a slave and give him freedom. This is what Christ the Lamb did. He did it through struggle which involved his own death. One of the greatest theories of Christian atonement, though abused often, is the ransom theory. Gustaf Aulen has called this the classic or dramatic view and says it is the New Testament doctrine.[41]

The scope of Christ's redemptive work included all human beings regardless of *tribe, tongue, people,* or *nation.* John is sometimes accused of being Judaistic, but this emphasis is distinctively Christian.

In the third place, Christ had fashioned his followers into a *kingdom* of *priests to our God* (see comment on 1:6). Priests have direct access to God and they minister to others on God's behalf. All Christians are priests to God and for one another. But the emphasis is on kingdom. The added comment, *they shall reign,* points ahead to their complete victory, perhaps in the millennium (ch. 20) but to something more (Charles, I, 148). If Christ is victorious and reigns because of his obedient death, perhaps the Christians are already reigning

41 Gustaf Aulen, *Christus Victor* (New York: The Macmillan Company, 1951).

when they live Christlike lives and suffer for him. The term *reign* means to exercise power over others only in a corrupt society. It means to prevail or triumph. The verb *reign* is future, but many texts have a present tense making it possible that the original emphasis may have been more on the present life (Swete, p. 82).

Millions of Angels Praise God. With the adoration of the Lamb in progress, John looked and saw a new chorus of millions of angels. His term *myriads of myriads* and *thousands of thousands* simply means an infinite number (cf. Dan. 7:10). The point of John is that all the hosts of heaven join in the adoration of the Lamb. Technically, the angels are not singing but *saying* or shouting their sevenfold acclamation of the Lamb's worthiness.

The angels repeat three of the elders' terms of praise: *glory, honor,* and *power* (cf. 4:11) and add *wealth, wisdom, might,* and *blessing.* The seven terms symbolize the fullness of the praise. *Wealth* is an interesting term reminding us of Paul's statement about Christ who was rich, became poor, and made us rich (2 Cor. 8:9). Such acclamations were known in the Old Testament (1 Chron. 29:10–13).

All Creatures Join in Praise. The praise of the Lamb is now taken up *by every creature in heaven and on earth and under the earth and in the sea* (see comment on 5:3). Apart from considerations of the view of the universe and the addition of the *sea,* John simply means to indicate that every creature in all of God's creation bursts into song, praising the Lamb in his victory.

One must note, however, that the text of this hymn addresses the doxology first to God, and then *to the Lamb.* The doxology in 4:8 praises the "Lord God Almighty." The *new song* of v. 9 specifically praises the Lamb. The angels' acclamation of worthiness is to the Lamb in v. 12. The universal praise is to God *and* the Lamb, leaving no doubt as to John's intention to elevate the Lamb. John's high Christology appears often (3:21; 22:1; 7:10).

The universal praise includes four words

—*blessing, honor, glory,* and *might*—probably because there are four groups—those from *heaven, earth, under the earth,* and the *sea.*

The Amen.—How could one conclude a symphony of such magnitude? It began with the praise of the elders and creatures who remain in God's throne room. Millions of angels joined the song. Then, every creature of God's whole creation praised God and the Lamb. Dramatically, it ends with the four living creatures saying *Amen!* So be it! *And the elders fell down and worshiped.*

The three visions of these two chapters portray the majesty of God and his Christ, so that all Caesar's pomp is a shabby show; Christians must never flinch under Caesar's temporary power; they have seen into God's throne room, have seen the book of destiny, and have seen Christ who can open that book for them.

IV. The Seven Seal Visions and Two Parenthetical Visions (6:1—8:5)

This unit is the beginning of the fulfillment of John's promise to reveal the things soon to come to pass (1:1; 4:1). It is dramatically arranged in a series of seven events which happen when each of the seven seals is broken. Two explanatory visions are inserted between visions six and seven. The disclosures are not the result of reading the content of the scroll but happen as symbolic events with the breaking of the seals.

Apocalyptic thought expected a series of great woes to befall the earth prior to the end. The Synoptic Gospels preserve this expectation (Mark 13; Luke 21; Matt. 24) and cite wars, rumors of wars, earthquakes, famines, persecutions, pestilence, and unusual activity in the heavens such as changes in the sun, moon, and stars. Jesus indicated that the preaching of the gospel to all nations must precede the end (Mark 13:10). John's three series—seal visions, trumpet visions, and bowl visions—portray these events of apocalyptic horror.

Interpreters differ greatly as to whether these visions should be equated with specific historic events or should be seen in a more general sense as events which happen in many ages of history (see Int. on "Interpretation").

1. The White Horse—Conquest (6:1-2)

¹ Now I saw when the Lamb opened one of the seven seals, and I heard one of the four living creatures say, as with a voice of thunder, "Come!" ² And I saw, and behold, a white horse, and its rider had a bow; and a crown was given to him, and he went out conquering and to conquer.

The first four seal visions reveal four mysterious riders who ride forth identified by the colors of the horses, a symbol disclosing the particular purpose, and a statement or interpretation of the activity.[42] It is doubtful if any symbol in Revelation has provoked more discussion than the four horsemen, unless it is the millennium.

John was probably alluding to the four horsemen of Zechariah 1:8,11. These horses were red, sorrel, and white. They patrolled the earth. The same prophet saw a vision of four chariots drawn by horses which were red, black, white, and dappled gray respectively (Zech. 6:1-8). The number "four" may suggest the four points of the compass or the four sore punishments God sends upon sinful people. Jeremiah spoke of pestilence, sword, famine, and captivity (15:2), and "four kinds of destroyers" (15:3). Ezekiel spoke of "four sore acts of judgment, sword, famine, evil beasts, and pestilence" (14:21).

I saw marks the beginning of the vision in which the *Lamb* (see comment on 5:6) opened the first seal (see comment on 5:1). One of the cherubim commanded the first rider to *Come* in a *voice* as loud as *thunder.* Since "coming" is usually related to Christ's coming, and since Christ, as "Faithful and True," rode a white horse (19:11-16), many interpreters, including Irenaeus, take the rider on this white horse to be Christ. In this context we would have the fulfillment of the demand that the gospel be

42 Mathias Rissi, "The Rider on the White Horse," *Interpretation,* Oct. 1964, p. 408.

preached in the whole earth (Mark 13:10) before the end. But this command was to the horse, not to Christ.

The *white* designates victory. The *white horse* is military victory. The rider held a *bow.* Christ was armed not with a bow but with a two-edged sword in his mouth—the Word of God. This rider, like Christ, went forth *conquering and to conquer,* but the means of conquest was different and the consequences were greatly in contrast. This rider is followed by slaughter, famine, and death. No such sequence follows Christ's proclamation of the gospel.

In Hebrew thought, military conquests by an irreligious enemy could constitute a judgment of God (Isa. 5:26; Jer. 15) on Israel's sin. Interpreters have been tempted to relate the *white horse* to the Parthians, noted for their mounted archers, who had recently defeated the Romans in A.D. 62. In this case the *black horse* may have been the famine of the same year. While such views are attractive, one must remember the local nature of the events and the repetition of this type of event throughout history. If one identifies the white horse with the Parthians, he must deal with the fact that the end did not shortly follow.

2. *The Red Horse—War* (6:3–4)

³ When he opened the second seal, I heard the second living creature say, "Come!" ⁴ And out came another horse, bright red; its rider was permitted to take peace from the earth, so that men should slay one another; and he was given a great sword.

The horse was *bright red.* The rider was armed with a *great sword,* and his mission was armed conflict, taking *peace from the earth* and causing *men to slay one another.* The activity could be either the bloodshed which follows the conqueror or internal strife and revolution which often follow conquest. Slaying one another may suggest revolt. In either event, man's way of conquest results in bloodshed, strife, famine, and death. Christ's victory was accomplished by his own death in innocent suffering. Christian victory does not come as the

white horse, nor does it have these consequences. It follows Christ's example.

3. *The Black Horse—Famine* (6:5–6)

⁵ When he opened the third seal, I heard the third living creature say, "Come!" And I saw, and behold, a black horse, and its rider had a balance in his hand; ⁶ and I heard what seemed to be a voice in the midst of the four living creatures saying, "A quart of wheat for a denarius, and three quarts of barley for a denarius; but do not harm oil and wine!"

The ominous *black horse* bolted at the command *Come.* The rider held a *balance,* scales for weighing, in his hand symbolizing scarcity or famine. The interpretation included three sayings. The *balance* could symbolize judgment, except in this context the sayings call attention to famine. A *denarius* was equivalent to the day's wage of a laboring man. In Cicero's time it would have bought 12 quarts of wheat and 24 of barley (Kiddle, p. 115 f.). According to military records each soldier was rationed the equivalent of one quart of wheat per day. The first statement would mean that the famine would require a man to work all day for only enough food for himself. *Barley* was less expensive than wheat and less desirable. *Three quarts of barley* for a day's wage would provide enough food for a small family. These two statements indicate a famine of serious dimensions but one through which survival was to be expected.

The third saying about *oil* and *wine* is more difficult. Bread was the absolute necessity, the staff of life. *Oil* and *wine* were the two other staple items of food. Wine provided the needed sugar. Oil made possible cooking, etc. *Oil* and *wine* were not necessary, but they were not luxuries. This saying may mean that while grain is scarce, *oil* and *wine* are plentiful. But these would likely be too expensive to be purchased. We also know that in A.D. 92 Domitian issued a decree that no new vineyards be planted in Italy and that in the provinces half of them be removed so that more grain could be grown (see Int.). The famine predicted is serious but not disastrous.

4. The Pale Horse—Death (6:7-8)

7 When he opened the fourth seal, I heard the voice of the fourth living creature say, "Come!" 8 And I saw, and behold, a pale horse, and its rider's name was Death, and Hades followed him; and they were given power over a fourth of the earth, to kill with sword and with famine and with pestilence and by wild beasts of the earth.

The corpse-colored horse bears a rider named *Death*, followed by a grim companion named *Hades* (whether on horseback we do not know). Their gruesome mission was limited to a fourth of the earth, but involved killing with *sword, famine, pestilence,* and *wild beasts.* We have already noted these horrors in Ezekiel (14:21). There is no textual basis for insisting, as some scholars do, that the rider is pestilence rather than Death. *Death* is not natural death which could be welcomed by a saint in old age; this death is a horrible woe of suffering and slow death. Yet, it is limited to a *fourth of the earth.* In the later plagues, the suffering will be broader in scope.

Hades is a shadowy presence like a cloud beyond death. In this procession even Death is not the end; *Hades* follows. But Christians have no fear; *Death and Hades* fall before Christ and will be thrown into the lake of fire (20:14).

What is the relationship between these grim historical facts and Christ's victory which gave him power to open the seals? How is Christ related to the adversities of history? We should avoid an oversimplified explanation which relieves man of his responsibility for history. John intends to portray Rome's power, and all other military power, in its futile cycle of conquest, revolt, famine, and death in contrast with the ultimate victory of Christ and his saints whose triumph is through redemptive suffering.

5. The Martyrs Under the Altar (6:9-11)

9 When he opened the fifth seal, I saw under the altar the souls of those who had been slain for the word of God and for the witness they had borne; 10 they cried out with a loud voice,

"O Sovereign Lord, holy and true, how long before thou wilt judge and avenge our blood on those who dwell upon the earth?" 11 Then they were each given a white robe and told to rest a little longer, until the number of their fellow servants and their brethren should be complete, who were to be killed as they themselves had been.

The fifth seal vision provides answers for two very important questions: What has happened to those who suffered martyrdom? Why is God's final victory delayed?

No hint has been given that the scene has changed, so we must assume the vision is located in heaven. John sees the *souls* of the martyrs *under the altar.* Some would make this an earthly altar since there is no temple in heaven, but there is an altar in heaven (Rev. 8:3,5; 14:18). A popular Jewish belief indicated that souls of the righteous remained under a heavenly altar.

The martyrs are recognized by John, but we are given no hint as to how except that they had *been slain* in their faithfulness to the *word of God* and for their *witness.* Perhaps John recognizes them from their scars. Their witness involves the recognition of, and keeping, the revelation of God in Jesus Christ (Beckwith, p. 526).

The martyrs' question is also a cry for vindication. A suggestion of vindictiveness appears in the terms *how long* and *avenge our blood.* Man's pitiful cry *how long* appears often (Psalm 6:3; Isa. 6:11; Jer. 47:6; Dan. 12:6; Zech. 1:12), always reflecting his own impatient spirit, self-centeredness, and some disappointment in God. The cry for vengeance [43] is sub-Christian, when one recalls Jesus' admonition against retaliation, even though one may argue that only by such judgment of God do his own sovereignty and justice become known. The address *O Sovereign Lord, holy and true* is at once a confession of his power, holiness, and purity and a subtle reminder that he could step in and vindicate them now. *Those who dwell,* the inhabitants of earth, are the unbelievers (see comment on 3:10).

---

[43] William Klassen, "Vengeance in the Apocalypse of John," CBQ, July, 1966.

God's response to the martyrs' cry was threefold: he gave them a reward, a *white robe;* he told them *to rest a little longer;* he gave them an adequate reason for the delay—many of their *fellow servants* and *brethren* had not yet qualified for the victor's crown. The white robe is a symbol of victory and purity (3:4,5; 7:9) and as such is a kind of vindication already. Some interpreters like R. H. Charles argue that these *white robes* are resurrection bodies such as were referred to elsewhere (1 Cor. 15:35 ff.; 2 Cor. 5:1 ff.; Phil. 3:21). A resurrection would hardly take place during a waiting period or in response to impatient request.

The delay is not merely waiting; it is *rest. Rest* is qualitatively different from waiting. It has an element of victory in it. They are resting in God's presence. The *little longer* seems to indicate that John believed the time would be short (1:3; 4:1).

A good reason for the delay is simply that other martyr-candidates have not had their opportunity to win their crowns. A popular idea in Judaism was that the end of the world would not come until the number of the elect had been fulfilled (1 Enoch 47:4). G. B. Caird has offered an interesting interpretation that even God's victories come about through the faithfulness of believers (p. 87).

The vision of the martyrs under the altar shows the security of those who have already suffered, explains why God delays his final judgment, and greatly inspires John's readers to be faithful unto death and join their brethren in the company of victors. Such an encouragement is in order before the opening of the sixth seal.

6. Catastrophes on Earth (6:12–17)

12 When he opened the sixth seal, I looked, and behold, there was a great earthquake; and the sun became black as sackcloth, the full moon became like blood, 13 and the stars of the sky fell to the earth as the fig tree sheds its winter fruit when shaken by a gale; 14 the sky vanished like a scroll that is rolled up, and every mountain and island was removed from its place. 15 Then the kings of the earth and the great men and the generals and the rich and the strong, and every one, slave and free, hid in the caves and among the rocks of the mountains, 16 calling to the mountains and rocks, "Fall on us and hide us from the face of him who is seated on the throne, and from the wrath of the Lamb; 17 for the great day of their wrath has come, and who can stand before it?"

The opening of the sixth seal prompted the entire physical universe to shudder as if to fall apart. All men on earth fled looking for a place to hide and cried out under the wrath of God.

It is not surprising that these cosmic woes include seven phenomena of nature: *earthquake, sun, full moon, stars, sky, mountains,* and *islands.* Nor is it surprising that the men who were affected fell into seven groups: *kings, great men, generals, rich, strong, slave,* and *free.*

The cosmic woes expected to precede or accompany the end had a long history. Isaiah spoke of the Day of the Lord and desolation of the earth (24:3) involving the moon and sun (24:23), mountains and hills (2:12 ff.). He spoke of the failure of the sun, moon, and stars (13:10) and of men trying to escape God by hiding in caves and among rocks (2:19). Joel believed that the Day of the Lord would be accompanied or preceded by earthquakes, trembling heavens in which the sun, moon, and stars would fail (2:10). Amos spoke of the failing sun (8:9). Our Lord had more recently spoken about earthquakes, the sun being darkened, the moon failing, and the stars falling (Mark 13:8,24).

The *earthquake* is not to be equated with the local quake in Laodicea in A.D. 61. This quake shakes the whole earth and signals the beginning of the end. The failure of the *sun* is a dreadful spectacle. Instead of its brilliance, now it is as *black as sackcloth,* the black goat-hair fabric, the symbol of mourning.

The *full moon became like blood* is in keeping with the passages already cited and suggests the redness of unusual atmospheric conditions which would herald doom. The figure of stars falling like *winter fruit* in a strong *gale* is that of a trembling universe.

The sky disappeared as if split in the middle and rolled up like a scroll (Isa. 34:4). In addition to the heavenly collapse, earth's immovable mountains and islands crumble.

These woes fall indiscriminately on all classes of men which are here named in seven groups including the powerful and weak, the rich and the poor. They hid in *caves* and among the *rocks* calling for avalanches to hide them from God's judgment (Hos. 10:8; Luke 23:30). They understand these calamities to be the judgment of God, *who is seated on the throne,* and of the *Lamb,* and that it is *the great day of their wrath.* Actually, this is a preliminary woe. The great day of wrath is still in the future.

The *wrath of the Lamb* is a paradoxical term. Lambs are meek. However, the Lamb in Revelation is also the Lion of Judah, the Messiah, and the figure of judgment. Those under judgment always feel the fierceness brought about by their condemnation. These have conspired in the death of the Lamb and of his followers. Now they are facing judgment. Wrath should not be conceived in terms of arbitrary anger. Sin against God alienates the sinner, makes him an enemy of God. He cannot endure the face of God. Sinful men shield themselves from reality with human masks and deception. When God comes in judgment and tears away these camouflages, man will sense the horror of having rejected Christ.

The concluding question, *who can stand before it?* assumes that no one can. But John knows that God's people can stand the judgment and the next two visions explain why.

¶-1. Sealing God's Servants (7:1-8)

¹ After this I saw four angels standing at the four corners of the earth, holding back the four winds of the earth, that no wind might blow on earth or sea or against any tree. ² Then I saw another angel ascend from the rising of the sun, with the seal of the living God, and he called with a loud voice to the four angels who had been given power to harm earth and sea, ³ saying, "Do not harm the earth or the sea or the trees, till we have sealed the servants of our God upon their foreheads." ⁴ And I heard

the number of the sealed, a hundred and forty-four thousand sealed, out of every tribe of the sons of Israel, ⁵ twelve thousand sealed out of the tribe of Judah, twelve thousand of the tribe of Reuben, twelve thousand of the tribe of Gad, ⁶ twelve thousand of the tribe of Asher, twelve thousand of the tribe of Naphtali, twelve thousand of the tribe of Manasseh, ⁷ twelve thousand of the tribe of Simeon, twelve thousand of the tribe of Levi, twelve thousand of the tribe of Issachar, ⁸ twelve thousand of the tribe of Zebulun, twelve thousand of the tribe of Joseph, twelve thousand sealed out of the tribe of Benjamin.

Chapter seven, which interrupts the numbered seal visions, is far from parenthetic in meaning. It includes two visions and an explanation which prepare the Christians for the end expected to begin with the seventh seal opening. It also provides an encouraging answer to the question of 6:17, "Who can stand before it?" If someone objects that this chapter is out of place, as an interruption, it must be noted that the encouragement revealed in these visions is needed precisely at this time and would hardly have been understood earlier.

By far the most difficult problem in the chapter is identifying the two groups, or explaining the terminology if one group is intended. At first glance, one might assume that the 144,000 *servants* of vv. 1-8 are Jewish Christians and the great multitude of 7:9-17 are Gentile Christians. This is suggested by the naming of the twelve tribes in the first paragraph and the special emphasis in the second that the multitude is composed of all nations. Some very competent New Testament scholars so interpret the passage.[44]

A majority of recent scholars have inclined toward equating these two groups or have said that they are the same people distinguished only by their location: the 144,000 are on earth; the multitude is in heaven. In favor of the equation are several arguments. John nowhere else distinguishes between Jewish and Gentile Christians. On

---

[44] Shirley Jackson Case, *The Revelation of John* (Chicago: The University of Chicago Press, 1919), p. 271; Wilfrid J. Harrington, *The Apocalypse of St. John* (London: Geoffrey Chapman, 1969), pp. 128 ff.

the contrary, he follows other New Testament tradition (Gal. 3:29, 6:16; Phil. 3:3; Rom. 2:28 f.) which equates the Christian community with "true" Israel and sees true circumcision as an inward rather than literal identification (see Rev. 2:9; 3:9). Other New Testament writers used Jewish terminology in addressing Christians (James 1:1; 1 Peter 1:1). John's view of Christianity is cosmopolitan—all nations, etc. If the Jewish-Gentile distinction is maintained, how does one explain why the 144,000 are sealed and the multitude is not, or why the multitude has white robes but the 144,000 do not? If the 144,000 are still on earth, the seal is in order and the robes are not. The great multitude, if in heaven, would have the white robes, but would not need the sealing. Caird has argued that the 12 tribes did not exist in John's time and that the *servants* of the present vision have to be the same as the 144,000 of 14:1 who are the martyrs without racial distinction (Caird, pp. 94 f.).

Several reasons can be suggested for the two accounts if one group is intended. John may have used an apocalyptic source without revision. He may have presented two visions to give the same assurance (Kiddle, p. 139). The 144,000 are still on earth, and the multitude is already with God.[45] For a complete study of the arguments see Beckwith's commentary (Beckwith, p. 536; cf. Summers, pp. 148 ff.).

Restraint on Evil. The vision shows God's restraint on evil in that *four angels* stand at *the four corners of the earth* (cf. 20:8) holding the reins on the *four winds of the earth*, which is simply a new symbol for the four horsemen (Zech. 6:1–8). Winds could bring good rains, or evil desert siroccos, or plagues of locusts. Here, the winds are symbols of evil powers standing in restrained readiness. They are not mentioned again. They are restrained from damaging *earth, sea,* and *any tree,* which are most vulnerable to the winds. The *four corners* of the earth means the whole

45 Albertus Pieters, *The Revelation of St. John* (Grand Rapids: Wm. B. Eerdmans, 1943), p. 125.

earth (Isa. 11:12; Ezek. 7:2).

A Protecting Seal. A fifth angel emerged from the east, *the rising of the sun,* the source of light, blessing, and hope (Ezek. 43:2; Mal. 4:2). He carried the *seal of the living God,* probably like a signet ring such as Pharaoh used (Gen. 41:42). Darius used (Dan. 6:17) such a signet to seal Daniel in the lion's den. In biblical faith, *living God* boldly contrasts God with pagan idols (Josh. 3:10; Hos. 1:10; Dan. 6:26).

The angel with the seal had authority to order the four angels to restrain the winds until after the sealing of the *servants* (cf. 1:1; 2:20; 19:2,5; 22:3,6) of our God. *Our* indicates that both angels and *servants* confess the same God. The actual sealing is not described, but, obviously, the seal was placed on the *foreheads* to leave an imprint which identified the servants as belonging to God and, therefore, secure against the forthcoming evils. Seals identify, mark ownership, guarantee security. The blood on the doorposts of Egypt comes to mind. Ezekiel (9:4) used the figure. John (6:27) refers to the seal, but Paul uses the symbolism in the most beautiful way when he sees God's Holy Spirit as his seal on our lives granting identification, authentication, and security (2 Cor. 1:22; Eph. 1:13; 4:30).

The 144,000. This number is the product of multiplying the square of 12 by one thousand, which means a large number, the number of completeness. It is large but limited. Several unusual elements are in John's peculiar listing.[46] Judah is listed first, probably because Christ is the Lion of Judah. Dan is omitted, probably because tradition indicated that the antichrist would come from the tribe of Dan. Irenaeus gave this interpretation. The Testament of Dan (5:6–7) provides a literary basis for it.

¶-2. The Multitude in White Robes (7:9–17)

9 After this I looked, and behold, a great multitude which no man could number, from

46 See "Tribes, Territories of," IDB, IV, 701.

every nation, from all tribes and peoples and tongues, standing before the throne and before the Lamb, clothed in white robes, with palm branches in their hands, 10 and crying out with a loud voice, "Salvation belongs to our God who sits upon the throne, and to the Lamb!" 11 And all the angels stood round the throne and round the elders and the four living creatures, and they fell on their faces before the throne and worshiped God, 12 saying, "Amen! Blessing and glory and wisdom and thanksgiving and honor and power and might be to our God for ever and ever! Amen."

13 Then one of the elders addressed me, saying, "Who are these, clothed in white robes, and whence have they come?" 14 I said to him, "Sir, you know." And he said to me, "These are they who have come out of the great tribulation; they have washed their robes and made them white in the blood of the Lamb.
15 Therefore are they before the throne of God,
    and serve him day and night within his temple;
    and he who sits upon the throne will shelter them with his presence.
16 They shall hunger no more, neither thirst any more;
    the sun shall not strike them, nor any scorching heat.
17 For the Lamb in the midst of the throne will be their shepherd,
    and he will guide them to springs of living water;
    and God will wipe away every tear from their eyes."

The new vision introduced by, *After this I looked,* is a preview of the final heavenly state of the Christians (chs. 21—22). In substance, it says the same as the vision of the 144,000 but looks ahead until the entire heavenly company is formed.

Description of the Multitude. John used six qualifying statements to describe the great multitude. (1) The multitude is countless. This should not be contrasted with the 144,000 since that number is probably included. (2) The multitude is cosmopolitan: *every nation* is represented; no *tribes, people,* or *tongues* are absent (cf. 5:9). John gives an inspiring view of the universality of the Christian gospel. (3) The multitude is in God's presence; the throng stands before the *throne and before the Lamb.* This closeness both to God and to Christ was once reserved for the heavenly beings; now, all the Christians are

there. There is no greater victory than to be in God's presence. (4) The multitude is *clothed in white robes* signifying their purity and victory. The Christians of Sardis had been promised white robes (3:5) if they would be faithful. The promise has been kept. (5) They hold *palm branches* in their hands, another emblem of victory. Palm branches were used during the Feast of Tabernacles, in Jesus' triumphal entry (John 12:13), and on occasions of royal processions. These victors now carry palm branches not so much to celebrate their own victory as the complete victory of the Lamb.

(6) They praise God by using the word *Salvation.* This term attributed to God and to the Lamb indicates that the presence of the multitude with God is evidence of God's and the Lamb's victory. Roman emperors often used the term "Savior," but John, possibly playing on the Roman blasphemy, attributes this to God. G. B. Caird has insisted on translating this word "Victory" rather than *Salvation* because the martyrs were celebrating not their salvation but their victory through persecution (Caird, p. 100). But surely he is taking a limited view of salvation, which is really not complete until this vision becomes reality.

Angelic adoration. The *angels* appear to be in a larger circle outside the smaller circles in which were the elders and the living creatures. The angels responded to the multitude's shout of *Salvation* by falling prostrate before God and offering their praise which is essentially the same as the chorus of praise already sung (4:8; 4:11; 5:9–10; 5:12).

Identity of the Multitude. Lest John fail to identify the multitude, an elder asked two questions: *Who are these, . . . whence have they come?* John either did not know or was reluctant to reply. He said only *Sir, you know.* The elder explained not only who they were, and whence they had come, but he also stated their destiny. In fact, his answer is a poem or hymn of four strophies which the RSV prints as only three, leaving the first one in prose form.

They have come out of the *great tribulation,* meaning they have come through the great distress expected before the end. Jesus had spoken of an intense tribulation which would precede the parousia (Mark 13). Daniel had mentioned it (12:1). John expected such a time of suffering (Rev. 2:10; 3:10), and the doomed people thought it had come (6:17). Paul used this term frequently and seemed to regard suffering a necessary part of Christian living since somehow Christians filled up Christ's suffering (Col. 1:24) and suffered as members of his body (2 Cor. 1:4,5).[47]

While the imagery includes natural disaster, etc., John's major emphasis is that the Christians are engaged in a struggle with evil which may lead them to martyrdom. Their trial will be prolonged and intense, but the victors will wear white robes and will join this multitude.

The second identifying statement is that *they have washed their robes and made them white in the blood of the Lamb.* The figures are mixed. Elsewhere the robes appear to be gifts, but here the victors have actively participated in the process of cleansing. Christ's *blood* is the cleansing agent (1:5; 5:9; see also 1 Peter 1:2,19; Rom. 3:25; 5:9). Faithful Christians are now pure and wear white robes because of Christ's redemptive death.

Their third characteristic is their presence with God, *before the throne.* The longings of Israel to be with God are now realized (cf. 21:1–7). They are priests (1:6; 5:10; 20:6), uninterrupted in their worship even by darkness as in the earthly temple.

Destiny of the Multitude. The tense changes from present to future indicating the destiny of the countless multitude. Seven statements give the summary. (1) *God will shelter them with his presence* is an allusion to the Shekinah presence such as was manifested over the tabernacle, in the Temple, and in the "cloud and fire" (Isa. 4:4 ff.) symbol of his presence. The

verb suggests protective covering like a tent. For ages God's people had longed to be with God. Now it was an eternal reality. Ezekiel had written, "My dwelling place shall be with them; and I will be their God, and they shall be my people" (37:27). In this vision the dream has come true.

The next three statements suggest the desert sufferings which will be no more. They shall not (2) *hunger,* or (3) *thirst,* or be smitten by (4) the *scorching heat.* John is alluding to Isaiah (49:10). Biblical sources are rich in symbolism, such as the bread of life (John 6:51), the water of life (John 4:13 f.), and the hidden manna (Rev. 2:17).

The next promise is (5) *the Lamb . . . will be their shepherd.* The mixed figure should occasion no difficulty. John alludes probably to Psalm 23 and to Jesus "the good shepherd" of John 10:14. The symbol is that of protection and security. Promise six (6) is that he *will guide . . . to springs of living water,* fulfilling the spiritual longings of God's people. The last statement (7) portrays God, wiping *away every tear.* Heretofore, God has remained aloof and awesome while the Lamb was the comforter. Now God is displayed in the tenderest terms of caring for his children. John alludes to Isaiah (25:8) and anticipates the full joys of heaven (Rev. 21—22).

7. The Golden Altar of Incense (8:1–5)

[1] When the Lamb opened the seventh seal, there was silence in heaven for about half an hour. [2] Then I saw the seven angels who stand before God, and seven trumpets were given to them. [3] And another angel came and stood at the altar with a golden censer; and he was given much incense to mingle with the prayers of all the saints upon the golden altar before the throne; [4] and the smoke of the incense rose with the prayers of the saints from the hand of the angel before God. [5] Then the angel took the censer and filled it with fire from the altar and threw it on the earth; and there were peals of thunder, loud noises, flashes of lightning, and an earthquake.

The events which followed the opening of the six previous seals and the parenthetic

---

[47] See *"Thlipsis,"* TDNT, III, 143.

visions have led us to expect the end when the seventh seal is opened. This, however, does not take place. Instead, a series of trumpet visions is introduced. A dramatic sequence leads up to the first trumpet vision.

Silence in Heaven. The previous events have disclosed that heaven has many sounds including hymns and statements of praise. The opening of the seventh seal, which finally unrolls the entire scroll of destiny suggesting a full disclosure, is followed by an ominous *silence . . . for about half an hour.* Some have understood the delay to be an indication of delayed judgment. Everything halts in awesome silence awaiting the end. Others, however, see this silence as a dramatic suspense builder. Such a delay would be a long time in a drama but would symbolize a very short time in terms of judgment (Summers, p. 153).

The Seven Angels. These are a special group of angels who **stand before God,** as indicated by the definite article. The absence of other details suggests that the readers would have known them. The literature of the time knows of a special group of seven "Angels of the Presence" who stand before God (Tobit 12:15; 1 Enoch 81:5) and offer up the prayers of the saints. These seven archangels are named by Enoch (1 Enoch 20:1–8). Isaiah (63:9) knew of such angels and Luke knew that Gabriel was one of them (1:19).[48]

These angels received the *seven trumpets* which will figure in the next series. The trumpet is the favorite instrument of the apocalyptists since it gets men's attention for God. Trumpets figured in the fall of Jericho (Josh. 6:1–22), were blown before the ark (1 Chron. 15:24) and in the coronation of kings (1 Kings 1:34,39), and God even sounded the trumpet (Zech. 9:14). Christ calls his elect with a trumpet (Matt. 24:31); the dead are raised by a trumpet call (1 Cor. 15:52); the Lord's coming will be so announced (1 Thess. 4:16).

[48] See "Angels," IDB, I, 128 f.

Prayers of the Saints. In 6:10 the waiting martyrs had asked "How Long?" and were told to wait a little longer. Their prayers appear to have been unanswered. This account tells the Christians that their prayers are never ignored. They make a difference both in heaven and on earth.

The other *angel,* unidentified, stood before the *altar,* probably the altar of incense, as a priest would do. Swete has argued that this is the altar of incense, while the altar of 6:9 is an altar of burnt offering. R. H. Charles (I, 226 ff.) objected on the grounds that there is no altar of burnt offering in heaven. The **golden censer** was a metal ladle or shovel used in handling live coals.

In 5:8 the prayers of the saints are the same as the incense. Here *incense* is mixed with the **prayers of all the saints.** Incense (see Bible dictionary) had a long history in worship and probably in primitive times was used to get the attention of deity. The smoke rose before God conveying the offering of the saints' prayers to God. The angel should not be seen as an intermediary; the theology of John forbids it. Men are priests and approach God directly.

Earthly Effects of the Prayers. The angel had evidently laid the censer in its place because he **took** it again and filled it with burning coals which had been mingled with saints' prayers. He **threw it on the earth.** The resultant sights and sounds no longer terrify us; we are accustomed to them. But, the inhabitants of the earth are terrified by the **thunder, noises, lightning,** and **an earthquake.** The fire symbol is found in Ezekiel (10:2) and Isaiah (6:6). Here it is a picture of judgment. Many interpreters see this as an assurance to the Christians. Their prayers are not only heard in heaven, but they return to the earth in judgment on the persecutors. A note of vengeance may be in that interpretation, but one cannot overlook John's promise to the Christians that their prayers are effective in both heaven and earth. Kiddle (p. 146) has dwelt upon this theme of the prayers as judgment on earth. The prayers of the saints are the means whereby God brings doom upon the very people who persecuted the Christians. At any rate, every Christian who reads John's Revelation would get the promise that prayer makes a difference both to God and to the world.

V. The Seven Trumpet Visions and Three Parenthetical Visions (8:6—11:19)

The similarities between the seal visions and the trumpet visions are both obvious and intentional. In both series there are four brief events in quick order, two longer vision-events, and a seventh which is transitional. In both series there are interruptions, or interludes, which provide additional and needed information. The differences are also obvious. The first four seal visions bring suffering of a human origin; the first four trumpet visions bring suffering of a natural or supernatural origin. The suffering is greater in this series than in the former, but it is still limited: in 15 cases of destruction or injury, 12 limit the extent of suffering to one-third.

The plagues of Egypt appear to have been the background imagery for these natural woes, but other natural calamities may have also influenced John.

In interpreting these visions of woe, we should avoid attempting to force a chronological or some other literal scheme upon the material. For instance, the locusts of 9:4 were commanded not to harm the grass of the earth, but according to 8:7 all of the green grass had already been burned. In 8:12 a *third of the stars* were darkened, but they had already fallen from the sky in 6:13. Some interpreters attempt to reconcile these details by pointing out that the destruction of all the grass means all of it on the one-third of the land affected and therefore not in conflict with 9:4 (Beckwith, p. 556). It is more probable that John is not concerned with such details. The visions burst like flares in the sky. John sees all he can during the flash and writes it down without attempting to make all details consistent.

1. The Plague on the Land (8:6–7)

6 Now the seven angels who had the seven trumpets made ready to blow them.

7 The first angel blew his trumpet, and there followed hail and fire, mixed with blood, which fell on the earth; and a third of the earth was burnt up, and a third of the trees were burnt up, and all green grass was burnt up.

The *seven angels* with the *seven trumpets* solemnly prepared to *blow them.* Now the dreadful series of woes heralding the End is beginning.

With the blowing of the first trumpet *hail and fire* mixed with *blood* rained down on earth bringing destruction. *Hail and fire* make an unusual combination but are also mentioned in the seventh Egyptian plague (Ex. 9:24), in which the fire appears as flashing in the hail. This suggests a violent thunderstorm which could have developed the huge hailstones and would have produced much lightning. In Egypt the damage was done by the hail; in the trumpet vision the damage is done by the fire. Joel had spoken of "blood and fire" as portents in heaven (2:30), and the early Christians had used the term (Acts 2:19).

Some commentators like Charles and Swete point out that intensely red rains have fallen in Italy as late as 1901. The red color was caused by the red sands of the Sahara. Unusual natural phenomena, like sandstorms in the western United States, tend to be remembered and to become symbols of the ominous.

One thing is certain about this plague: all the injury is inflicted upon the earth. The fire destroys one-third of the *earth* and *trees* and *all the green grass* (see Zech. 13:8,9 for one-third usage). Again, it is difficult to visualize how the damage would have been distributed, but John's point is that the earth was subjected to a severe but limited destruction.

In the judgment of many, Rome's fall was aided by many natural calamities which befell her, and John here alludes to the beginning of the end of Rome (Summers, p. 156; Barclay, II, 53 f.). It takes no imagination to picture the famine which would follow such a destruction of earth's vegetation.

2. The Plague on the Sea (8:8–9)

⁸ The second angel blew his trumpet, and something like a great mountain, burning with fire, was thrown into the sea; ⁹ and a third of the sea became blood, a third of the living creatures in the sea died, and a third of the ships were destroyed.

At the sound of the trumpet, a great fiery mass resembling a *mountain* fell into the *sea*. It is possible that the recent volcanic eruption of Vesuvius in A.D. 79 could have suggested the imagery. That eruption destroyed Herculaneum and Pompeii and did great damage all the way to the coast. John's vision, however, portrays something much greater in magnitude and destructiveness. When it fell *into the sea,* it caused damage in three areas: *a third of the sea became blood;* a third of the *creatures in the sea died;* a *third of the ships* on the sea *were destroyed.* The destruction was dreadful but limited; life continued.

John's vision has to be taken as he reported it even though other literature has features which are similar. In one Egyptian plague the Nile turned to blood (Ex. 7:20 f.). Enoch spoke of stars which were "like great burning mountains" (1 Enoch 18:13). In Sibylline Book V (line 158) a burning star fell into the sea and burned it up.

3. The Plague on Fresh Water (8:10–11)

¹⁰ The third angel blew his trumpet, and a great star fell from heaven, blazing like a torch, and it fell on a third of the rivers and on the fountains of water. ¹¹ The name of the star is Wormwood. A third of the waters became wormwood, and many men died of the water, because it was made bitter.

A *great star* blazing *like a torch* fell into earth's sources of fresh water when the third angel blew the trumpet. It fell on a *third* of the *rivers* and *fountains,* or wells and springs of fresh water. The resultant pollution caused the death of many men who drank the water. This plague calls to mind the Egyptian plague which also pol-

luted the drinking water. In the case of the third trumpet plague, we would have expected that one third of men would have died, but this is not reported.

Wormwood is the *name* of the *star.* Wormwood means bitterness and is not poisonous. In the Old Testament the term is used metaphorically to designate God's judgment which is like eating bitterness (Jer. 9:15; 23:15). To Amos, wormwood is perverted justice (5:7). G. B. Caird has seen *Wormwood* as the star of Babylon to which Isaiah referred (14:12–20). This is particularly apt here because Babylon is Rome, and she has poisoned the springs with her idolatry (Caird, p. 115).

The third trumpet plague affects the fresh water to a very serious degree, but the limitation suggests that there is still time to repent.

4. The Plague on the Luminaries (8:12)

¹² The fourth angel blew his trumpet, and a third of the sun was struck, and a third of the moon, and a third of the stars, so that a third of their light was darkened; a third of the day was kept from shining, and likewise a third of the night.

In response to the fourth trumpet blast, a plague strikes all of the heavenly bodies reducing them by one-third. The ninth plague in Egypt had been one of darkness (Ex. 10:21–23). Joel spoke of the day of the Lord as a "day of darkness" (2:2). Jesus cited the darkening of the sun, moon, and stars in connection with the end (Mark 13:24).

The reference to the *third of the day* and the *third of the night* by analogy with the first three plagues suggests that John intends to convey the idea that one-third of the day was totally dark and one-third of the night lacked its usual amount of light.

¶-1. The Eagle Vision (8:13)

¹³ Then I looked, and I heard an eagle crying with a loud voice, as it flew in midheaven, "Woe, woe, woe to those who dwell on the earth, at the blasts of the other trumpets which the three angels are about to blow!"

The first four plagues were serious but much less severe than those yet to come. They attacked man's fourfold universe: earth sea, water, and sky. John, as is his habit, interrupts the sequence to arrest the attention of his readers. He does this by calling attention to an *eagle* flying high in *midheaven* crying out the woes soon to come.

Eagles were vultures and birds of prey. Apocalyptic writers used them in their imagery (Ezek. 1:10; 10:14; Dan. 7:4; 2 Baruch 77:19). The eagle had a *loud voice* and cried *Woe, woe, woe* indicative of the three other plagues to follow the trumpet blasts five, six, and seven. In two instances the text notes that the woe has passed (9:12; 11:14). However, while the demonic locust plague (9:1–12) is clearly marked as the first woe, it is not clear what John intends to be the second woe. It is probably the cavalry from the east (9:13–21), but the note does not appear until after the entire interlude of chapters 10 and 11. This could hardly mean that the third woe is 11:15–19 because that is not a woe at all. The third woe is probably the bowl series, which follows the seventh trumpet.

A horrifying suspense builds with the Eagle's scream. The tempo is increased from tragedy to disaster, from injury to torture and death.

5. The Demonic Locust Plague, the First Great Woe (9:1–12)

1 And the fifth angel blew his trumpet, and I saw a star fallen from heaven to earth, and he was given the key of the shaft of the bottomless pit; 2 he opened the shaft of the bottomless pit, and from the shaft rose smoke like the smoke of a great furnace, and the sun and the air were darkened with the smoke from the shaft. 3 Then from the smoke came locusts on the earth, and they were given power like the power of scorpions of the earth; 4 they were told not to harm the grass of the earth or any green growth or any tree, but only those of mankind who have not the seal of God upon their foreheads; 5 they were allowed to torture them for five months, but not to kill them, and their torture was like the torture of a scorpion, when it stings a man. 6 And in those days men will seek death and will not find it; they will long to die, and death will fly from them.

7 In appearance the locusts were like horses arrayed for battle; on their heads were what looked like crowns of gold; their faces were like human faces, 8 their hair like women's hair, and their teeth like lions' teeth; 9 they had scales like iron breastplates, and the noise of their wings was like the noise of many chariots with horses rushing into battle. 10 They have tails like scorpions, and stings, and their power of hurting men for five months lies in their tails. 11 They have as king over them the angel of the bottomless pit; his name in Hebrew is Abaddon, and in Greek he is called Apollyon.

12 The first woe has passed; behold, two woes are still to come.

This "first" woe is unusually severe, but a Christian theology is obvious throughout. The sovereign God is supremely in charge; the woe does not begin until he permits the star-angel to have the key; then the torment is limited. It cannot be fatal; it lasts only five months. There is the recognition that a vast reservoir of evil exists which is greater than an individual's sin or the sum of all individuals' sins. The Christian theologian, John, recognized this fact and portrayed it in terms of demonic plague. Some Christian theologians portray it as the sinful deposits in culture of billions of men forming an investment which draws compound interest at a high rate. Whatever the interpretation, evil is a cosmic whole of serious proportions evidently under clever leadership. Such evil brings suffering and torment to its depositors which so afflict human life as to make death more attractive than life. Even though John's descriptions suggest torture and vengeance, its limitations suggest that there is still time for repentance.

The Star Angel. The ancients related stars to angels, so this figure is quite clear. The star is personified and becomes an evil angel. Good and evil angels may descend or ascend; only evil angels fall. He is not Satan himself; he appears in this passage carrying out an act with God's permission. The angel did not possess the key; it was given to him for this occasion.

Opening the Pit. The abyss or bottomless

pit was conceived to be in the underworld. The three-story universe was the standard view. It is important, however, to be reminded that the view was more theological than geographical. This *bottomless pit* was the temporary dwelling place of demons, fallen spirits, etc. In its larger symbolism it is a reservoir of evil. It is not the same as hell. John mentions this pit frequently (11:7; 17:8; 20:1,3). It appears to have had a single opening at the top of a shaft which was covered by a door like a manhole cover. When the cover was removed, the *smoke* of the underworld belched forth obscuring the *sun* and filling the *air*.

The Demonic Locusts. The locusts came out of the smoke. This fearful plague has a literary tradition from the Egyptian Exodus (Ex. 10:12–20) and was the subject matter of one of the most vivid literary descriptions in ancient records (Joel 1—2). The locust plagues are still known in the biblical world [49] and are terrifying because the countless millions of flying insects arrive on the wind with a frightful noise and strip all vegetation bare leaving a swath of complete famine.

Locusts do not harm man directly. These demonic locusts had stingers like scorpions, which hide under every rock and within walls and afflict man with a very painful sting which can be fatal. These locusts were ordered to leave unharmed all vegetation and to attack all men who did not have the *seal of God upon their foreheads*.

Torment of Unbelievers. Some interpreters shy away from the idea of deliberate visitation of pain upon the unbelievers with the endorsement of God. John was not so sensitive. He seemingly thought that those who had persecuted the Christians deserved and would receive such punishment. However, John's message shows the horrible nature of existence in evil. Death would be preferable, but it cannot be found. John intends to magnify the severity of their torment with his description of

man's suffering when stung by a *scorpion*.

The torment authorization carries two limitations: it is limited to *five months*, which is the usual life span of the locust; the torment must not be fatal, which must suggest God's restraint to grant an additional opportunity for repentance.

These demonic locusts cannot harm God's servants who bear an identifying mark on their *foreheads* (cf. 7:3). Now we know that the 144,000 are God's people on earth without respect to nationality. This exemption of God's servants suggests that the torment is spiritual. Christians must endure suffering, and they confronted physical suffering in Revelation. They had no exemption. It is difficult to envision the locust-scorpions literally stinging several individuals and skipping one who was marked with the seal. For this reason, interpreters have sought such meanings as the suffering of the guilty conscience which would have afflicted unbelievers but not the servants. F. D. Maurice [50] saw superstition with all its hellish torments as the nature of this suffering. These superstitions arise from the bottomless pit of unbelief. They produce all of the spiritual agonies of conscience herein described. The torment is so great that men seek escape by death but are denied this relief.

Further Description of Locusts. Almost as an afterthought John describes the demonic locusts. He has previously dwelt on their origin and purpose. They looked like *horses arrayed for battle*. There is a vague resemblance between the head of a locust and that of a horse (see Joel 2:4). An Arab saying compares the locust's head to that of a horse, his breast to that of a lion, his feet to those of the camel, and his antennae to the hair of a maiden (Beckwith, p. 562).

The *crowns of gold* are in appearance only and probably suggest the idea of authority since locusts have no such crowns. Their faces appeared *human*, suggesting their intelligence and capacity characteristic of Revelation's demonic locusts only. The

49 Robert A. M. Conley, "Locusts: 'Teeth of the Wind,'" *National Geographic*, August, 1969, pp. 202–226.

50 F. D. Maurice, *Lectures on the Apocalypse* (London: Macmillan and Co., 1885), p. 127.

hair like women's hair is probably a reference to the appearance of the antennae. Some see a reference to the Parthian hordes whose soldiers reportedly wore long hair. Some ancient commentators like Bede saw this as a veiled suggestion of sexual abuse. One modern interpreter sees the womanish hair as midway between the human and the lion. It prepares us for the mane.[51]

The *teeth like lion's teeth* (cf. Joel 1:6) suggest insatiable appetite. The scaly *breastplates* may refer either to natural appearance or the protective shields worn by war horses. Their *noise* is like that of war chariots rushing into battle (Joel 2:5).

The terror of this plague is greater because it is a well-organized attack. The demonic locusts have a *king*. His only identification is one statement. His Hebrew name is *Abaddon;* his Greek name is *Apollyon.* Both mean destroyer. Some see an allusion to the god Apollo, but there is no basis for the idea. It may be a veiled reference to Domitian, who liked to think of himself as the incarnate Apollo.

6. The Demonic Cavalry from the East, the Second Great Woe (9:13–21)

13 Then the sixth angel blew his trumpet, and I heard a voice from the four horns of the golden altar before God, **14** saying to the sixth angel who had the trumpet, "Release the four angels who are bound at the great river Euphrates." **15** So the four angels were released, who had been held ready for the hour, the day, the month, and the year, to kill a third of mankind. **16** The number of the troops of cavalry was twice ten thousand times ten thousand; I heard their number. **17** And this was how I saw the horses in my vision: the riders wore breastplates the color of fire and of sapphire and of sulphur, and the heads of the horses were like lions' heads, and fire and smoke and sulphur issued from their mouths. **18** By these three plagues a third of mankind was killed, by the fire and smoke and sulphur issuing from their mouths. **19** For the power of the horses is in their mouths and in their tails; their tails are like serpents, with heads, and by means of them they wound.

20 The rest of mankind, who were not killed

51 Austin Farrer, *The Revelation of St. John the Divine* (Oxford: The Clarendon Press, 1964), p. 119.

by these plagues, did not repent of the works of their hands nor give up worshiping demons and idols of gold and silver and bronze and stone and wood, which cannot either see or hear or walk; **21** nor did they repent of their murders or their sorceries or their immorality or their thefts.

The sixth trumpet blast calls forth a demonic horde of cavalry invaders which brings not only great suffering but also death on a third of mankind. The passage plays on the theme of repentance; and even though earth's inhabitants did not repent, the implication is that these judgments should have brought them to repentance. One cannot overlook John's conviction, though voiced as a lament, that idolatry has a hold on man so great that he will go on worshiping the works of his own hands even while the infinite power of the true God is displayed all about him. A subtle implication in the end of the passage is that the world is just this way. John wrote to Christians to encourage them to be faithful to God even though this evil world rejects him. They must bear their witness in this world—like it is (Morris, p. 132).

The Voice from the Altar. A voice from the *horn's of the golden altar* gave the command of execution. The altar of 8:3 f. was the altar of incense on which the prayers of the saints were mingled with incense. John ties the following judgment with that vision and implies that the prayers come back from God in judgment on earth. The *horns* were decorative projections on each corner of the altar, although in early Israel horns on altars were sanctuaries of safety for those fleeing for their lives. This unidentified voice ordered the angel who had blown the trumpets to release the four angels.

The Four Angels. The *four angels* are not the same as those who restrained the four winds in 7:1. These angels are evil, since they have been *bound* and are probably the leaders of the demonic cavalry. They have been bound *at the great river Euphrates,* which was the ancient boundary between the ideal Israel and her enemies of Assyria and Babylon to the east. The eastern boundary of Rome was the Euphrates, and her enemy at this time was Parthia. The Parthians had inflicted severe defeats on the Romans and had become fearfully exaggerated in Roman legends.

The picture John paints is that of a foe standing on the border. He had been restrained; now he is released. The foe had been held for a specific time, *the hour, the day, the month, and the year;* the time had come.

Invasion from the East. John *heard* the *number of the troops*—200,000,000— which means a number beyond counting (see Psalm 68:17; Dan. 7:10). Their grim mission was to *kill a third of mankind,* more severe but still limited judgment. The horsemen bear no weapons; the horses do the killing. The riders, however, wore *breastplates* of the same colors as the *fire, smoke,* and *sulphur* fumes exhaled by the demonic horses. Some interpreters have tried to relate the colors to those of the different cavalry units, but this presupposes that John is describing the Parthians.

The demonic horses exhale *fire, smoke,* and *sulphur* and thereby inflict the deadly plagues which are fatal to one-third of mankind. Fire and brimstone are common elements in God's destruction of wicked men (14:10; 19:20; 21:8; also 1 Enoch 67:6). These three plagues from the horses' mouths are the lethal weapons, but the horses were also equipped with nonlethal serpents' heads on their tails. With these they inflicted further suffering. The legends about the Parthians indicated that their horsemen were excellent archers and did their damage both as they rode against the enemy and as they rode away from his weapons. They were able to shoot accurately to the rear. This might suggest the weapon on the tail, but this is too literal for John; he is describing a demonic cavalry. The *lions' heads* on the horses only add terror and mystery.

One is tempted to identify these invaders in some way with the Parthian hordes, but they did not destroy the Roman Empire. This invasion is much more significant than a single military operation. It portrays the fall of Rome to outside invaders as the first four plagues showed the result of natural calamities and as others will show her internal disintegration.

The Power and Folly of Idolatry. The survivors *did not repent* of their deeds. They had witnessed the judging power of God but clung tenaciously to their *idols* of *gold, silver, bronze, stone,* and *wood.* Biblical writers were amazed at the folly of men who worshiped idols which cannot *see or hear or walk* (Isa. 17:8; Psalms 115:4–7; 135:15–17). One suggestion is that they worshiped *demons.* Paul had suggested that pagans worshiped demons instead of God (1 Cor. 10:20). The difference between demon worship and idolatry is that in the former one worships an evil spirit or an imaginary one, and in the latter he worships his own handiwork.

In addition to false worship, and as a result of it, the survivors did not repent of their sins of which four are representative— *murders, sorceries, immorality,* and *thefts.* Three of the sins are violations of three of the commandments regarding killing, adultery, and stealing. Sorcery was a form of magic, trickery, or deception into evil. Biblical faith has no place for magical arts. The modern revival of such practices, common in every city and daily newspaper, comes under the severe judgment of God.

The failure of the survivors to repent is astonishing to John. The power of idolatry is illustrated both to John's readers in the first century and in the twentieth. The world crumbles because of internal decadence, wars, and the judgment of God. Man clings to his idols, his modern version of demon worship, and his sophisticated techniques for murder, sorcery, sexual immorality, and legal or illegal stealing. He still does not repent!

¶-2. The Mighty Angel and the Little Scroll (10:1–11)

¹ Then I saw another mighty angel coming down from heaven, wrapped in a cloud, with a

rainbow over his head, and his face was like the sun, and his legs like pillars of fire. ² He had a little scroll open in his hand. And he set his right foot on the sea, and his left foot on the land, ³ and called out with a loud voice, like a lion roaring; when he called out, the seven thunders sounded. ⁴ And when the seven thunders had sounded, I was about to write, but I heard a voice from heaven saying, "Seal up what the seven thunders have said, and do not write it down." ⁵ And the angel whom I saw standing on sea and land lifted up his right hand to heaven ⁶ and swore by him who lives for ever and ever, who created heaven and what is in it, the earth and what is in it, and the sea and what is in it, that there should be no more delay, ⁷ but that in the days of the trumpet call to be sounded by the seventh angel, the mystery of God, as he announced to his servants the prophets, should be fulfilled.

⁸ Then the voice which I had heard from heaven spoke to me again, saying, "Go, take the scroll which is open in the hand of the angel who is standing on the sea and on the land." ⁹ So I went to the angel and told him to give me the little scroll; and he said to me, "Take it and eat; it will be bitter to your stomach, but sweet as honey in your mouth." ¹⁰ And I took the little scroll from the hand of the angel and ate it; it was sweet as honey in my mouth, but when I had eaten it my stomach was made bitter. ¹¹ And I was told, "You must again prophesy about many peoples and nations and tongues and kings."

John interrupted his seal-vision sequence between the sixth and seventh visions to present the visions of the sealing of the 144,000 and the countless multitudes clad in white robes. That presentation heightened tension and gave the needed encouragement for events to follow. In a similar fashion, the present interlude (10: 1—11:14) breaks the sequence of trumpet-visions between six and seven. John portrays a strong angel with a little book which, after seven thunders, John was ordered to eat. Then he told of measuring the temple of God and followed with a long discussion of "Two Prophets" who are "Two Witnesses."

After the six trumpet blasts, we expect the seventh to bring the end. John holds us in suspense and intrudes into his own drama with these explanations.

The Mighty Angel. John's position has suddenly changed from heaven to earth; the strong angel came *down from heaven.* This angel is not to be identified with any other angel previously mentioned; he is not one of the seven; he is not Christ; Christ is never an angel in Revelation. This is *another* angel described in glorious terms. He wears a *cloud* as his mantle; a *rainbow* is his headdress; his *face* is brilliant *like the sun;* his *legs* are *like pillars of fire* so huge that he can stand astride the sea with one foot on land and the other on sea. His *voice* is like that of a *lion roaring.*

Clouds are the customary vehicles for heavenly beings to use in descending to earth (Dan. 7:13; Psalm 104:3). The *pillars of fire* merely add grandeur to the picture. The term could allude to the wilderness wandering. It is possible that the term was suggested to John as he stood on Patmos and saw shafts of sunlight shining through the clouds touching land and sea.

This angel is no ordinary messenger: he holds a *little scroll;* he signals the *seven thunders* to speak; he takes an oath that the delay will end soon.

The Seven Thunders. The thunders are not otherwise identified. The number seven certainly implies completeness and possibly suggests that God had spoken. In the Gospel of John (12:27 ff.), when the Father spoke to Jesus, the disciples thought it had thundered even though Jesus understood a message. John was under orders to write so he reached for papyrus and ink, but a voice from heaven forbade him to record what he had heard. Why this prohibition? Charles interpreted the messages of the seven thunders by analogy with Paul's vision into the third heaven (2 Cor. 12:2–4); the information was too sacred to be divulged. This is strange, however, for John believed in revealing the message. Earlier apocalyptists (Dan. 12:4) had sealed their messages to keep them secret until the distant future. John thought the future had come. Some see the prohibition to mean that the thunders had revealed additional woes to come, but God has canceled them (Caird, p. 126).

Other interpreters think that in the first-century setting, or in some well-known apocalypse, there were seven thunder-woes to which John alludes but indicates that God has told him not to write about them. Summers thinks that John is saying that there will be no more warnings; the six trumpet warnings are adequate; the end is coming (Summers, p. 161). Thunder is usually a warning of coming judgment (8:5; 11:19; 16:18).

The Angel's Oath. God's people have often reflected lack of patience with God in their question "How long?" The martyrs under the altar had asked this question (6:10), and God had told them to wait a little longer. Daniel had asked this question in his last recorded vision (Dan. 12:6) and had been told on the basis of an oath by "him who lives for ever" that the end would come after "a time, two times, and half a time." But, he was ordered to seal this information until the end. John, the Revealer, now portrays that the time has come. In answer to the question "How long?" he answers that it will come when the seventh trumpet is sounded (note close parallels with Dan. 12:1–13).

Overwhelming sounds and sights almost drew our attention away from John's primary purpose. The mighty angel regains attention by lifting his *right hand to heaven* in the solemn stance of taking an oath (Gen. 14:22; Deut. 32:40; Dan. 12:7). This oath is even more significant since the angel draws earth, sea, and heaven into his solemn vow. He added further weight to his oath by swearing on God's eternity and his role as Creator. John plays on these two attributes often. God is eternal; he *lives for ever and ever.* God is Creator; he created *heaven* and all it contains, *earth* and all it contains, and the *sea* and its contents. In one gesture the mighty angel touches *heaven, earth,* and *sea.*

Negatively, the angel promised that there will be *no more delay.* Positively, he indicated that the *trumpet call* of the *seventh angel* would signal the disclosure of the mystery.

Some older interpretations suggested that the passage means "time will be no more," i.e., eternity will have begun. The RSV translation is correct; the abstract idea of time is foreign to this context. To say that the seventh trumpet blast will bring fulfilment does not mean that the end will be sudden, in a moment. Time is involved in these events such as the five months in 9:5. The *mystery of God* seems to indicate the purpose of God which has been hidden, or only partially disclosed, but is soon to be revealed fully (Rom. 16:25; 1 Cor. 2:7; Eph. 3:4 ff.). In the passages cited, the prophets are mentioned and the gospel of Christ is the disclosure.

This vision ends with a new commission for John to prophesy again. God communicated his purpose and will to the prophets (Amos 3:7; Jer. 7:25; Jer. 25:4). John, the Christian prophet, has now received God's disclosure about the mystery. The following visions do not portray a sudden disappearance of earth. Rather, they deal with the Christian gospel and man's response to it. The mystery leads us to the little scroll.

John Takes the Little Scroll. The *voice* ordered John to *take* the *little scroll* and eat it. He was advised that it would taste sweet in his mouth but would be bitter in his stomach. John obeyed and reported that it tasted *sweet as honey* but was *bitter* in his *stomach.*

Ezekiel is John's prophetic example in this account. He had been ordered to take a scroll inscribed on both sides and to eat it. Its message consisted of "lamentation and mourning and woe" (Ezek. 2:8—3:3). It tasted as "sweet as honey." There was no reference to bitterness.

John's account is one of bold contrasts. The angel is mighty; the scroll is very small, a booklet. The scroll with seven seals was conspicuous for its seals; this scroll is *open.* The scroll appears to be very important; but it is never mentioned again, nor do we learn its contents. The taste of the book is sweet; its aftereffects are bitter.

Several implications are obvious. The repetition of *take* and *took* indicates that

John was not given the booklet. It was required of him that he use his initiative. The message was sweet to John, the Christian prophet, as he heard it. It probably means the Christian message or the completion of God's work. The bitterness is the fact that good news to God's people is harsh judgment when proclaimed to those who are not. John's commission to *prophesy* is related to this vision. Either he proclaims the content, or the eating of the scroll signals his commission to prophesy as God reveals his purpose to him. Barclay refers to this passage as the "Joy and Sorrow" of the messenger of God. It is joyful to know God's word, but sorrowful in that the word contains warnings and doom (Barclay, II, 68).

The final sentence restates John's prophetic mission, but it is not a call. He recorded that in the first chapter. His prophetic ministry deals with a universal audience. This mission should guide us away from such ideas as expecting the world to come to an end when the seventh trumpet sounds. John is undertaking a new prophetic mission of proclamation.

Interpretation of the Little Book. It may be futile to inquire about the content of a book which no one read before John ate it. Nevertheless, John aroused the curiosity. R. H. Charles (I, 256) saw this vision as an introduction to 11:1–13, which is a "proleptic digression" discussing Jerusalem and Jews during Antichrist's reign.

Other interpreters insist that the little scroll contained the information in the rest of Revelation. For instance, Harrington understood chapters 4—11 to be concerned with the chosen people and the rest of the book to deal with the nations. In that instance, chapter 10 would introduce the period of preaching to the Gentiles.[52] But no such distinction can be maintained; Gentiles figure in the early chapters. Furthermore, the visions of the last half of the book are introduced by the formula, "I saw," and there is never any indication that

the little scroll is related to their content.

Caird (p. 126) saw the scroll with seven seals as containing God's purposes as achieved by the Lamb; the little scroll presents a version of those purposes as they will be accomplished by the church.

The little scroll is never mentioned again. Obviously, eating it meant that John completely mastered the message. He is commissioned to prophesy about many nations. Since woes and lamentations figure in Ezekiel's vision, and since the result of eating the scroll is bitterness, we must assume that the message proclaimed includes an element of judgment and doom. Kiddle (p. 167) sees the whole intrusion (chs. 10—11) as a very special message to the church to get on with the business of publishing the gospel to the ends of the earth.

It has been suggested that the sealed scroll was the Old Testament (at least its prophetic oracles) to which Jesus supplied the key for interpretation. Then the little scroll would be the message of Jesus, open and universal.[53] But such may be much too literal for John. He never mentions the scroll again.

¶-3. The Two Witnesses (11:1–14)

[1] Then I was given a measuring rod like a staff, and I was told: "Rise and measure the temple of God and the altar and those who worship there, [2] but do not measure the court outside the temple; leave that out, for it is given over to the nations, and they will trample over the holy city for forty-two months. [3] And I will grant my two witnesses power to prophesy for one thousand two hundred and sixty days, clothed in sackcloth."

[4] These are the two olive trees and the two lampstands which stand before the Lord of the earth. [5] And if any one would harm them, fire pours from their mouth and consumes their foes; if any one would harm them, thus he is doomed to be killed. [6] They have power to shut the sky, that no rain may fall during the days of their prophesying, and they have power over the waters to turn them into blood, and to smite the earth with every plague, as often as they desire. [7] And when they have finished their testimony, the beast that ascends from the bottomless pit will make war upon them and

52 Wilfrid J. Harrington, *The Apocalypse of St. John* (London: Geoffrey Chapman, 1969), p. 150.

53 *Ibid.*, p. 148.

conquer them and kill them, 8 and their dead bodies will lie in the street of the great city which is allegorically called Sodom and Egypt, where their Lord was crucified. 9 For three days and a half men from the peoples and tribes and tongues and nations gaze at their dead bodies and refuse to let them be placed in a tomb, 10 and those who dwell on the earth will rejoice over them and make merry and exchange presents, because these two prophets had been a torment to those who dwell on the earth. 11 But after the three and a half days a breath of life from God entered them, and they stood up on their feet, and great fear fell on those who saw them. 12 Then they heard a loud voice from heaven saying to th·m, "Come up hither!" And in the sight of their foes they went up to heaven in a cloud. 13 And at that hour there was a great earthquake, and a tenth of the city fell; seven thousand people were killed in the earthquake, and the rest were terrified and gave glory to the God of heaven. 14 The second woe has passed; behold, the third woe is soon to come.

This passage is one of the most difficult in the book. Space will not permit even a summary of leading interpretations, but an attempt will be made to indicate some various views.

Although the measuring of the temple is important in its own right, it is obviously reported as an introduction to these two faithful witnesses. Measuring the temple has the same meaning as sealing the servants of God; it is for protection. Two faithful witnesses proclaim God's word during a period limited in mystical terms to 1260 days, during which time they are immune to attack. Then the beast from the bottomless pit comes and kills them. For three and one half days their corpses lie exposed in dishonor on the streets while pagans celebrate the victory of evil. The triumph is temporary; God raises the witnesses from death to heaven before the eyes of the enemy. Then a tragic earthquake brings destruction to men and indirect homage to God.

It is not accidental that these witnesses, like John on Patmos and Jesus before him, are faithful in proclaiming God's word and suffer therefor. John has seen in Christ's suffering and death his complete victory; now he sees the witnesses following Christ

in victory through death. He has constantly encouraged the Christians to live life in this manner.

There is some substance to the idea that chapter 11 introduces the major themes of the rest of the book: the beast, the Lamb, the great woes, the great city Rome, Christ, the victory, the beast's fall, and the final victory.

Measuring the Temple. The *measuring rod* was a cane-like reed used for linear measurements. John is no longer an observer; he does the measuring. His orders are to *measure the temple* (*naos*, sanctuary apart from outer courts), *those who worship there,* and to exclude *the court outside.* The exclusion of the court was made because the nations would *trample over* it for *forty-two months.* Measuring indicated the idea of rebuilding the temple in Ezekiel (40:3—42:20) and Zechariah (1:16; 2:2-8). In the present context it has the meaning of preservation. The implication is that the inner sanctuary will be preserved while the outer courts will be desecrated by the pagans.

Actually, the temple in Jerusalem had been destroyed in A.D. 70 by the Romans and has never been rebuilt. In other words it had been in ruins for 25 years when John wrote. Some have therefore assumed that he was using a source written prior to the fall in A.D. 70. In that case, the writer expected God to preserve the inner sanctuary. In fact, the Romans destroyed it all. Some preterists who hold this view insist that the two witnesses were historical individuals. Extreme futurists take it literally and assume that the temple will be rebuilt and that Antichrist will take Jerusalem, kill two famous witnesses, and leave them literally lying in the street, etc.

Paul's preoccupation with the problem of the Hebrew elect (Rom. 9—11) suggests to some that John may be dealing specifically with Jews, but John uses Israel, temple, and other Hebrew terminology in a symbolic sense to designate Christians and the church. This temple probably anticipates John's reference in 21:22. It is

God's people set in the great secular city described later (v. 8).

The period of Gentile domination is *forty-two months.* This is the same as 1260 days of v. 3 (42 months x 30 days). This span of time appears again in days (12:6) and in months (13:5). This time span appears in 12:14 as "a time, and times, and half a time," which is a year, two years, and a half-year, or three and one-half years. The mysterious time span is recorded in Daniel (7:25; 9:27; 12:7) and is equated to 1290 days (Dan. 12:11). Daniel used a week of years (7 years) of which one-half would be three and one-half years. In 1 Kings 18:1 f. the drought of Elijah lasted three years but by New Testament times had become standardized as three and one-half years (Luke 4:25). Daniel's term was used in the context of the reign of Antiochus Epiphanes, who in 168 B.C. set up a statue of Zeus in the temple in Jerusalem. Daniel called this the "abomination that makes desolate" (Dan. 11:31; 12:11; 9:27; see 1 Mac. 1:54 for history of this event).

The Two Witnesses. John gave an elaborate description of these *two witnesses.* They are prophets who *prophesy* for 1260 days immune to harmful acts. They are equated with the *two olive trees* of Zechariah (4:1–14) and the *two lampstands.* Zechariah had only one lampstand. The number *two* indicates the fact that two witnesses were necessary to establish a case in Jewish courts (Deut. 19:15; 17:6; Num. 35:30).

These witnesses enjoy God's protection during their prophetic time. Their attackers are destroyed by *fire* which *pours from their mouth and consumes their foes,* seemingly alluding to Elijah who called down fire from heaven to consume the military unit sent by King Ahaziah (2 Kings 1:9–16). In Revelation the fire comes from their mouths—not from heaven—indicating that their power, like that of the Master, was in their word. They have *power to shut the sky;* Elijah called down a long drought (1 Kings 17:1). They have *power over the waters to turn them into*

blood and to cause plagues; this suggests Moses (Ex. 7:20).

Their immunity to attack ends in 1260 days; *the beast* from the *bottomless pit* makes *war* on them, conquers them and kills them. The *war* suggests that they represent a larger group. After three and one-half days of dishonor in lying on the street, they are raised to heaven.

While Moses and Elijah are the prophets implied in the text, it is not necessary to assume that John expected them to return literally. Two Christian prophets may be seen in terms of Moses and Elijah. Some think he means to indicate the Law and the Prophets. The Law and Prophets appear to be dead, but they live on in the gospel (McDowell, p. 115). Some would equate them with Peter and Paul, the great Christian prophets, but neither lived until the time described. One suggestion is that they are the *two lampstands* against whom no criticisms were made—Smyrna and Philadelphia—but John expected all of the seven churches to witness to the earth.

There seems to be no doubt that John intends to call attention to the faithful witness of Moses and Elijah. However, John employs these visions for a purpose. He does not predict two individuals who, at that time or some later time, would make this good witness. Rather, he encouraged the entire church to make this prophetic witness (Minear, p. 99; Kiddle, p. 185).[54] The promise is that the church will enjoy God's protection long enough to achieve its mission. The enemy will slay many of the witnesses; they may lie dead in dishonor; the pagans may gloat in temporary victory; but ultimate victory belongs to those who are faithful to God. The real tragedy occurs when the church silences her own true witnesses.

In the great city, God's witnesses have a time of success and a time of defeat. They are killed and exposed. They lie in defeat and shame while evil appears triumphant. God has the final word: he raises

[54] Austin Farrer, *op. cit.,* p. 132.

them up in complete victory before their enemies.

The Beast. In the first half of Revelation John has never mentioned the beast. Now, he casually mentions *the beast that ascends from the bottomless pit.* In the second half of the book John mentions the dragon, Satan, the devil, and the beast (or beasts) almost 40 times. This personification of evil is an important figure in Jewish and Christian theology (see comment on 12: 7 ff.; 13:1–18).

The Holy City and the Great City. In the description of measuring the temple, John mentioned that the *nations* will *trample over the holy city* (v. 2). In v. 8 he tells us that the *dead bodies* of the *two prophets* will lie *in the street of the great city.* The first reference naturally suggests Jerusalem. The *great city* is further described as *Sodom* and *Egypt.* Sodom, a symbol of blind and stubborn rejection of God, was used to designate Jerusalem (Isa. 1:10). Cities such as Capernaum were considered more guilty than Sodom because they rejected Jesus (Mark 10:15; Luke 10:12; Matt. 11:24). Egypt was symbolic for the place of oppression of God's people. The city was also called the place *where their Lord was crucified,* again alluding to Jerusalem. But *what* Jerusalem did John mean? Jerusalem that killed the prophets? But Jerusalem was both *the holy city* and the *great city* in a general sense. We will miss John's point if we settle on a particular city on the map.

Prior to this chapter, John has mentioned "the city" only once—"the city of my God, the new Jerusalem" (3:12). That was in a promise of the city we shall see in the end. However, he mentions "the holy city" and "the great city" in the remainder of the book 26 times. Furthermore, he mentions Babylon six times. Specifically the "great city" is Babylon; in Revelation, Babylon is also Rome. In other words, John speaks of "two" cities which are actually only "one" city—Jerusalem the holy, Jerusalem the secular city. Actually, his reference is intended to go beyond all the cities mentioned

to a reality beyond particularity. John is concerned with the conflict between the holy city and the great wicked city. They exist together in Jerusalem, or Babylon, or Rome, or New York, or Kansas City. John saw the difference between the two in the light of the death and resurrection of Christ.[55] G. B. Caird indicates that the city is Rome, but the city, like the monster, is older than Jerusalem or Rome. Rome is merely the current embodiment of the "great city." The great city is the home of the earth inhabitants, it is the tower of Babel, the city of this world (Caird, p. 138). Against this city, the "holy city" stands in contrast. It must not be equated absolutely with Jerusalem either. We shall find its reality both in heaven and on earth as the drama continues.

Witnesses Gain Victory Through Death. The theme of Revelation is reenacted in this moving drama. The beast kills the faithful prophets. The *war* indicates a group larger than literally two. He makes war on God's witnesses of whom these two are representative. The beast conquers them. The verb is the same used of Christians when they are victorious. The beast's victory is complete. The witnesses are dead; their dead bodies lie exposed on the *street of the great city.* The magnitude of this dishonor, loathsome to Hebrews, is excelled only by the shameful rejoicing of the inhabitants *of earth.* These wicked people use the occasion for festivity—they *exchange presents.* The prophets' messages had been a *torment.* John intends to portray the complete defeat suffered in martyrdom. Jesus was actually killed and that in a very disgraceful way. Now the faithful witnesses die. Martyrdom is an ugly spectacle. Martyrs are not popular. They lie exposed to ridicule and humiliation.

After *three and a half days a breath* reentered the corpses, reminiscent of Ezekiel's valley of bones (Ezek. 37:10) and Jesus' resurrection. When they stood on their

[55] Paul S. Minear, "Ontology and Ecclesiology in the Apocalypse," *New Testament Studies,* Jan. 1966, pp. 94–98.

feet, and were raised in the *cloud,* their foes were forced to observe. This is John's way of showing the complete victory of the witnesses before the very eyes of the persecutors. The resurrection of Jesus had already happened before the witnesses saw him. This event happened right before their eyes. *The voice from heaven* called them to come up, at once showing heaven's approval of the witnesses and reminding us of the translation of Enoch and Elijah. In this passage John has made a promise of victory to every Christian who will witness faithfully for Christ. God will raise him up in victory.

Earth acknowledges their victory by the *earthquake,* which also reminds the people of God's sovereignty. The destruction was limited to a *tenth of the city* and to 7000 fatalities. The figurative nature is suggested in the number seven multiplied by the thousand. If literal Rome were intended, the fatalities would have been quite small. If literal Jerusalem were intended, the damage would have been relatively higher.

The survivors of the earthquake *gave glory to the God of heaven.* If we take the statement literally to mean "all" of the inhabitants genuinely worshiped God, then there would have been no occasion for the following woes. It is possible, however, to assume that the statement means only that the survivors who witnessed this gave glory to God. However, this is to miss the point of the passage. The real question is whether or not giving glory to God means being converted and therefore becoming witnesses, or if it means reluctantly acknowledging that God is sovereign.

There are those who believe that John was like Jonah and did not want the pagans to be converted. They think that this only means that in terror the inhabitants fall before the displayed power of God. Their response was remorse, not repentance. As in 6:15–17, they still try to hide from God. It is too late to repent. It is involuntary homage (Kiddle, p. 206). Others insist, however, that giving *glory to the God of heaven* is repentance. Fearing God and giv-

ing him glory as in 14:6,7 is related to the gospel and is the heart of worship (15:4). Refusal to do this is the ground for condemnation (16:9) (Caird, p. 139 f.; Beckwith, p. 604). On v. 14 (*the second woe*), see the comment on 8:13.

7. The Seventh Trumpet—Victory (11: 15–19)

15 Then the seventh angel blew his trumpet, and there were loud voices in heaven, saying, "The kingdom of the world has become the kingdom of our Lord and of his Christ, and he shall reign for ever and ever." **16** And the twenty-four elders who sit on their thrones before God fell on their faces and worshiped God, **17** saying,
"We give thanks to thee, Lord God Almighty,
who art and who wast,
that thou hast taken thy great power and begun to reign.
18 The nations raged, but thy wrath came,
and the time for the dead to be judged,
for rewarding thy servants, the prophets and saints,
and those who fear thy name, both small and great,
and for destroying the destroyers of the earth."
19 Then God's temple in heaven was opened, and the ark of his covenant was seen within his temple; and there were flashes of lightning, loud noises, peals of thunder, an earthquake, and heavy hail.

Now that John has shown us the little scroll and the two prophets, he returns to the trumpet visions. We have mistakenly expected the end with the blowing of the seventh trumpet; half of the book remains. John has not misled us; in a sense the end has come. The opening of the seventh seal brought silence in heaven (8:1); the blowing of the seventh trumpet brings *loud voices in heaven.* The *loud voices* announce "It has happened!" The people of God have longingly and impatiently awaited God's assertion of his kingly reign over the whole world. It has happened!

The Kingdom Has Come. The *voices* (probably the cherubim) announce that the *kingdom of the world has become the kingdom of our Lord and of his Christ.* Kingdoms of this world have always conspired against "the Lord and his anointed," but the

Lord laughed in derision. He placed a king on Zion and addressed him, "You are my son, . . ." and promised that he would rule the nations (Psalm 2). Now it has happened. Daniel spoke of him as a ruler who would come with "dominion and glory and kingdom," and that "all peoples, nations, and languages should serve him; his dominion is an everlasting dominion" (Dan. 7:14). It has happened!

Early Christians believed that Christ was this anointed one who would reign (Acts 4:26). Paul saw Christ delivering "the kingdom to God the Father after destroying every rule and every authority and power" (1 Cor. 15:24–28). It has happened! And *he shall reign for ever and ever.* So, the end has come. The goal has been reached in John's vision!

Praise of the Twenty-Four Elders. The elders prostrated themselves before God in worship. Their praise is similar to that of previous occasions (4:11; 5:9–10). The address to **Lord God almighty, who art and who wast** omits the previously-affirmed future idea "and is to come." The future, "is to come," (1:8; 4:8) is omitted here and hereafter (16:5) because he is here. The elders expressed thanksgiving to God for assuming his power and reign. He has had the power all the time but has now actively taken control. The temporary rule of the **nations** has ended in the assertion of God's **wrath** and the judgment has come. It will include the **dead.** There will be rewards for the **servants,** all of Christ's disciples, Christian prophets (10:7), and the **saints,** who are all Christians. *Those who fear thy name* are Christians in general; John does not employ the proselyte-to-Judaism idea of "God-fearers."

The negative judgment is the *destroying the destroyers* of the earth. Evildoers, and especially those with power and authority, corrupt and destroy the earth (19:2). But these destroyers are ultimately destroyed. God does not resort to brute force, however, to destroy them. They turn all of creation against themselves. The wages of destroying the earth is their own destruction.

The Ark of the Covenant. The vision of the temple in heaven must be intended in a figurative sense since John says that the heavenly city has no temple (21:22). His point here is to portray the ark of the covenant. In Solomon's temple, the ark of the covenant stood in the holy of holies as a reminder of God's covenant and presence. It was so sacred that only the high priest saw it and that only once a year. It had been destroyed (or it disappeared) by the Babylonians in 586 B.C. There was a Jewish tradition that it had been hidden and would someday be returned. Therefore, some would see this as a fulfillment. That, however, is not John's purpose. John intends to show that God, who made that covenant, remains the same yesterday, today, and forever. The symbol of his presence is John's way of showing that God has preserved the promise.

The *lightning, noises, thunder, earthquake,* and *hail* are earth's spectacular response to great announcements in heaven (8:5; 16:18).

VI. Seven Visions Concerning the Great Conflict and Two Explanations (12: 1—14:20)

These three chapters are clearly marked off as a single section by the end of the trumpet visions and the beginning of the bowl visions. There is some difference of opinion as to the division of the material. I have chosen, however, to follow the author's signs and formulas. The paragraphs concerning the war in heaven (12:7–12) and the dragon's attack on the woman and her offspring (12:13–17) do not begin with the formula "I saw," or "it appeared." So, I have outlined these as explanatory paragraphs. The other seven are clearly marked out as portents (12:1,3) which appeared, or by the formula "I saw" (13:1,11; 14:1, 6,14).

The visions answer a question, "Why has the persecution come upon us?" The answer of Revelation is that Satan is the enemy behind it all. He failed in his attack on the woman and her Son; therefore, he attacks her other children. This attack is being carried on by Satan's agents, Rome the sea beast, and the imperial cult which is the land beast. The other principal in the conflict is the Lamb who stands in readiness on Mount Zion. Angels make dramatic announcements about the coming events, and "one like a son of man" comes on a cloud in judgment.

1. The Pregnant Woman (12:1–2, 4b–6)

¹ And a great portent appeared in heaven, a woman clothed with the sun, with the moon under her feet, and on her head a crown of twelve stars; ² she was with child and she cried out in her pangs of birth, in anguish for delivery. And the dragon stood before the woman who was about to bear a child, that he might devour her child when she brought it forth; ⁵ she brought forth a male child, one who is to rule all the nations with a rod of iron, but her child was caught up to God and to his throne, ⁶ and the woman fled into the wilderness, where she has a place prepared by God, in which to be nourished for one thousand two hundred and sixty days.

A *portent* is a sign or unusual appearance which gets attention (12:3; 15:1) and points to an amazing appearance (15:1). Signs may be marvelous but deceptive acts performed by the beast (13:13,14) and demonic spirits (16:14). In this instance, the sign is a grand vision of a heavenly woman.

Her Description. Her heavenly characteristics are that she wore the **sun** as a shawl, and used the **moon** as her footstool. Her **crown** with **twelve stars,** though heavenly, has a connection with earth. The **twelve** stars relate her to the tribes of Israel. Her pregnant condition could either be heavenly or earthly, but her crying out in *pangs of birth* incline toward an earthly interpretation. Her child was a male and is to be identified with Christ, who is to **rule all the nations with a rod of iron** (see comment on 2:27; 19:15; Psalm 2:9). His rescue *up to God* is a reference to the resurrection of Jesus.

Her Identification. Interpreters point to myths from several sources as clues toward understanding this heavenly woman. (See Charles, Beckwith, Caird, Rist, etc.) It is true that there are several legends and myths which narrate stories of great heroes who were protected in birth against foes whom they later returned to destroy. In a Greek myth concerning the birth of Apollo, there are several similarities. A goddess named Leto was pregnant by Zeus. At the time of delivery a dragon named Python sought to kill her and her child. Leto was whisked away to an island refuge where she bore Apollo, who later killed the dragon. John may well have known this, or other myths, but the assumption is neither necessary nor helpful.

The pregnant woman has been identified as the virgin Mary, the Christian church, Israel, the ideal Israel, the new Israel, and the people of God. She is not the virgin Mary, because John makes it clear that the present conflict is directed toward "her offspring" (12:17). She is not the Christian church, which is the offspring and not the mother of Christ. She is not Israel, which is not the object of the present attack. She is the people of God, who as Israel in the Old Testament did produce the Messiah and as the church and new Israel is now the persecuted "offspring."

Her flight *into the wilderness* is a symbolic description of the state of the Christians. They are harassed and persecuted but protected, having been sealed by God for the limited period of suffering. The church lives in danger, hunted. The desert is the place of refuge, safety, as it was after the exodus from Egypt. This cannot refer to the dispersion of the Jews because John is concerned with the Christians. It cannot be a reference to the flight of Joseph and Mary into Egypt since John's subject is not the earthly Jesus, but the eternal Christ who came as the *offspring* of the "heavenly-earthly" woman who is the people of God.

Several biblical passages illuminate John's reference to this woman. It is very likely that the early Christians interpreted Jesus in the light of Genesis 3:15 f. In that passage, whatever its original author may have intended, the mother of the race was opposed by a serpent. In our present text, John portrays this serpent seeking to destroy a heavenly mother and her offspring. The motif of childbirth appears in Isaiah 66:7-9 and in Micah. In Micah 4:6-10 we find the "daughter of Zion, like a woman in travail" going to Babylon. A rescue will follow. Then (Mic. 5:2) Bethlehem is mentioned as the origin of a ruler in Israel, etc. Paul's reference (Gal. 4:26) to "Jerusalem above" as "our mother" shows that in New Testament times the holy city could be spoken of as a heavenly mother.

Woman Contrasted with Great Harlot. All interpreters of Revelation are fascinated by John's contrasts. Most of them see an explicit contrast between this heavenly woman and the great harlot of chapter 17.[56] The heavenly woman is clad in heavenly garb, sun, moon, stars; the harlot is dressed in the gaudy purple and scarlet, gold, jewels, pearls, etc. This woman is pregnant; the harlot holds a cup full of "abominations and impurities of her fornication." The godly woman is attacked by a red dragon; the earthly woman sits astride a "scarlet beast which was full of blasphemous names." The vulnerability of the pregnant woman is displayed in her pain and flight; the harlot enjoys the strength of her paramours, the "kings of the earth" who have "committed fornication" with her. The pregnant woman flees to the desert and lives only by the protection of God; the harlot is the "great city" and appears to possess all wealth and power. The mother brings forth a male child destined to rule; the harlot claims the power of kings, but Rome is traveling the road of Babylon. God protects the heavenly woman; the kings turn against the harlot. The heavenly woman is a mother, a bride, the holy city, and the New Jerusalem; the harlot is a barren whore, the "great city," Rome, and Babylon.

---

56 J. Edgar Burns, "The Contrasted Woman of Apocalypse 12 and 17," CBQ, Oct. 1964, pp. 459-463.

2. The Red Dragon (12:3-4a)

3 And another portent appeared in heaven; behold, a great red dragon, with seven heads and ten horns, and seven diadems upon his heads. 4 His tail swept down a third of the stars of heaven, and cast them to the earth.

The first reference in Revelation to the dragon is this *portent* in heaven. The ancient world had many stories which may have been influential in John's thought of the dragon. In *Enuma Elish,* a primeval war resulted in creation with the body of a slain deity, Tiamat, serving as the origin of matter. This struggle appeared in many settings. Babylonian myths portrayed a seven-headed dragon, and an Accadian seal of about 2500 B.C. actually pictures a monster with seven heads.

Old Testament references are striking. Leviathan was a twisting serpent (Isa. 27:1). The dragon Rahab was cut in pieces (Isa. 51:9). Leviathan has "heads" and is related to "dragons on the waters" (Psalm 74:13 f.). Jeremiah compared Nebuchadnezzar to a monster (51:34), and Ezekiel compared Pharaoh to a dragon (29:3).

In the New Testament, the dragon motif has become personified into the devil, or Satan (see comment on 12:7-17).

The fiery-red color came from the chaos monster of Babylon whose image was in Marduk's temple. The number *seven* indicates his great power. The number *ten* seems to have been related to Daniel's fourth beast (7:24). His *seven diadems* draw attention to his power and sovereignty.

The size of the dragon is emphasized in the statement that his *tail swept down a third of the stars of heaven* (cf. Dan. 8:10). A serpentine form is implied in this expression.

¶-1. The Dragon Cast Out of Heaven (12:7-12)

7 Now war arose in heaven, Michael and his angels fighting against the dragon; and the dragon and his angels fought, 8 but they were defeated and there was no longer any place for them in heaven. 9 And the great dragon was thrown down, that ancient serpent, who is called the Devil and Satan, the deceiver of the

whole world—he was thrown down to the earth, and his angels were thrown down with him. 10 And I heard a loud voice in heaven, saying, "Now the salvation and the power and the kingdom of our God and the authority of his Christ have come, for the accuser of our brethren has been thrown down, who accuses them day and night before our God. 11 And they have conquered him by the blood of the Lamb and by the word of their testimony, for they love not their lives even unto death. 12 Rejoice then, O heaven and you that dwell therein! But woe to you, O earth and sea, for the devil has come down to you in great wrath, because he knows that his time is short!"

This paragraph seeks to explain why the dragon's fury has been directed toward the earth. John believed that events in heaven and on earth were related. The dragon was defeated in war in heaven and was therefore cast down to the earth where his rage is turned against men since he cannot get at heaven in any other way because his *time is short.* The introductory statement, *Now war arose,* suggests a chronological sequence, but we must be cautious about this assumption.

If this casting of the dragon to earth followed Christ's ascension, we are unable to account for the previous evil so often attributed to Satan. If we assume this is John's retelling of some primeval "fall of Satan," we are following *Paradise Lost,* not biblical teaching. Furthermore, this passage suggests a connection between the heavenly victory of Michael over the dragon and the earthly victory *by the blood of the Lamb* (v. 11). If we press the details of the story in too literal a fashion, we are also obliged to explain why Michael, if he could defeat the dragon in heaven, cast him to earth rather than killing him. It hardly seems fair for earth. This is not the point of John's story.

John believed, as did other first-century Christians, that Satan's throne was in one of the lower heavens. In Ephesians (2:2) Satan is "the prince of the power of the air." When the "seventy" returned to the Lord after their mission, joyfully announcing that demons had yielded to them, Jesus said, "I saw Satan fall like lightning from heaven" (Luke 10:18). He was not referring to some ancient fall. In 2 Enoch (18) it is recorded that some sinful men had been sent to a second heaven where they were held in darkness by Satanail. In the *Ascension of Isaiah* (10:29; 7:9; 11:23) the firmament is called the place of the prince of this world (Beckwith, p. 617).

John also believed that at one time Satan had access to God's throne and walked in God's court. In both Job (1:6 ff.) and Zechariah (3:1 ff.), Satan appears before God as the accuser of men. Even in the New Testament there are suggestions of this accuser's or prosecutor's role. In 1 Timothy 3:6 there is a warning against falling into the "condemnation of the devil." Jude 9 speaks of Michael disputing with the devil about the body of Moses. The devil as adversary, or accuser, appears in 1 Peter 5:8.

War in Heaven. It seems unthinkable to us that God would have tolerated any kind of situation which could have resulted in war in heaven. We miss the point. The heavens included areas other than God's throneroom. Furthermore, these accounts are apocalyptic drama, and wars in heaven are commonplace in such dramas. *Michael and his angels* appear to have taken the initiative. Their foes are the *dragon and his angels* (not demons). John avoids telling the details of the battles—only the outcome.

Michael was a celestial prince or archangel, and a sort of patron saint of Israel (Dan. 10:13,21), and was expected to arise and lead Israel in her last battle against evil (Dan. 12:1). He appears only twice in the New Testament—here and in Jude 9. He appears frequently in the noncanonical literature of the period. When Satan accuses man before God's throne, Michael is man's defender.

The nature of the battle is not disclosed. No weapons were named; no fatalities were reported. Previous knowledge of Satan and Michael would indicate that the contest was verbal. Michael was victorious; the dragon was not slain as would have been expected in a literal war.

Some exegetes have seen this war as an assault on heaven in an attempt to dethrone the exalted Christ, but this would throw question on the competence of heaven's guards or the sovereignty of God. Apocalyptic uses imagery for a purpose. The purpose here is not the kind of reporting a war correspondent does. It is to tell the Christians why earth is under such devastating attack. Since *there was no longer any place for them in heaven*, the dragon and his angels were thrown out and landed on earth.

Satan's Identification. The Old Testament did not relate the serpent of Genesis to Satan. In fact, "satan" is an improper noun meaning adversary in most of its usages in the Old Testament. In only three instances can it be claimed that Satan is a proper name. In Job 1 and 2, Satan appeared as a prosecuting attorney accusing Job before God. In Zechariah 3:1–3 Satan accused Joshua the high priest before the angel of the Lord. The Chronicler (1 Chron. 21:1) reported that it was Satan who had incited David to take the census.

The literature of the New Testament era and the period immediately preceding portrays Satan as a sort of superhuman personality who reigns over a kingdom of evil.[57]

In the Septuagint, Satan was translated as *diabolos*, meaning devil. Satan (*Satanos*) appears 33 times in the New Testament and devil (*diabolos*) 32. He is the "tempter" (Matt. 4:3; 1 Thess. 3:5), the "evil one" (Matt. 13:19; 1 John 5:18), the "accuser" (Rev. 12:10), the "enemy" (Matt. 13:39), the "prince of demons" (Matt. 9:34; 12:24; Mark 3:22; Luke 11:15), the "ruler of this world" (John 12:31: 16:11), and the "prince of the power of the air" (Eph. 2:2). Paul called him "Belial" once (2 Cor. 6:15), and Jesus called him "Beelzebul" (Mark 3:22; Luke 11:15,18–19).

This figure came to be regarded as an agent of man's temptation (Luke 22:3,31;

[57] See *"Diabolos,"* TDNT, II, 72–81; "Satan," IDB, IV, 224–228; Edward Langton, *Satan, A Portrait* (London: Skeffington, 1945) and *Essentials of Demonology* (London: Epworth Press, 1948).

John 13:27; Acts 5:3), who also hinders men from accomplishing their purposes (1 Thess. 2:18). In Revelation, all of these terms and functions are pulled together. Only here is the dragon identified as the *ancient serpent,* the *Devil,* and *Satan,* and *deceiver of the whole world.*

The apocalyptic writers were dualistic. They loved this imagery of dualism. But John did not hold a metaphysical dualism. To him there was only one Eternal—God. This evil prince never threatened God; it was Michael who defeated him; God does not do business with the devil. Furthermore, John does not afford the Christians an excuse for their sins; Satan is never blamed for man's sins; man is always responsible for his own sins. Satan is a deceiver, a maligner who intends to ruin man, but man is never at his mercy. Man has a victory over evil; dualism is rejected. John has explained to the Christians only why the earth is under attack. This evil angel has been cast out of heaven and has turned his fury on God's creation.

The Victory. Michael's victory appears to have been won without weapons. The shout of victory announces that *salvation* (7:10; 12:10; 19:1), the complete work of God, has been achieved. This *salvation* is the expression of God's *power* mentioned in the doxologies (19:1; 17:13). God's *kingdom* or *reign* has come and is contrasted to kingdoms of the world. The *authority of his Christ* is now publicly manifest in contrast to the seeming defeat of Jesus in his death. John never wearies of calling attention to this contrast.

The victory is related to the *blood of the Lamb* and *the word of their testimony.* To John this is very important: the victory of Christ and his faithful Christians on earth is the basis of Michael's victory in heaven. If we take v. 11 seriously, *they* refers to the earthly victors—the martyrs who make the faithful witness. They helped win the victory in heaven because *they loved not their lives even unto death.*

Victory in heaven is the occasion for rejoicing. But *earth and sea* must prepare for *woe* because the *devil has come* down. His fury is intensified because of his expulsion from heaven.

There is no rational explanation of evil. Logically, we might question the justice of the devil's coming to earth after his expulsion from heaven. Such logic will miss John's message. His word to us is that evil is serious and cosmic. The victory of Christ over evil involves both heaven and earth. Evil may attack us and seemingly destroy us, but in Christ there is complete and eternal victory. So, prepare for battle! Be faithful unto death!

¶-2. The Dragon's Attack on the Christians (12:13–17)

13 And when the dragon saw that he had been thrown down to the earth, he pursued the woman who had borne the male child. 14 But the woman was given the two wings of the great eagle that she might fly from the serpent into the wilderness, to the place where she is to be nourished for a time, and times, and half a time. 15 The serpent poured water like a river out of his mouth after the woman, to sweep her away with the flood. 16 But the earth came to the help of the woman, and the earth opened its mouth and swallowed the river which the dragon had poured from his mouth. 17 Then the dragon was angry with the woman, and went off to make war on the rest of her offspring, on those who keep the commandments of God and bear testimony to Jesus. And he stood on the sand of the sea.

The paragraph returns to the explanation which was begun in 12:6, and answers the Christians' question, "Why the intense persecution of Christians?" The answer is that Satan, frustrated by failure to destroy Christ, defeated by Michael in a war in heaven, cast down to earth for the short time before his final destruction, attacks the woman only to fail again. His only prey left is *the rest of her offspring*, the Christians.

The Woman Rescued. The woman is the true people of God, of whom the Christians are the contemporary manifestation. The woman escaped the dragon because she was given *the two wings of the great eagle.* God's deliverance of his people is symbolized by the terminology of the parent eagle as it catches its young in the air to prevent

harm (Deut. 32:11 f.), or as being borne on eagles' wings (Ex. 19:4; Isa. 40:31).

Her flight *into the wilderness* has been identified with the flight of the Jerusalem Christians to Pella before the fall of Jerusalem in A.D. 70, but this restriction is too limited. The text hardly permits this church to be seen as the mother of Christ. Others have related this flight to the flight of Jews to Jabneh before A.D. 70, but this would have no meaning in the present context. Kiddle thinks that it symbolizes the flight of the church from "the great city," the civilized world of empire to which Christians must have no loyalties. This would make the desert the Christians' detachment from the world. Swete saw it as the church's solitary life, a policy of secrecy forced on the church by the persecution. It is probable that John has Exodus 32:11 in mind; God's deliverance is symbolized. It need not be related to one particular event.

The *time, and times, and half a time* is a repetition of the 1260 days (see comment on 11:3).

The last desperate attempt of the serpent came in the form of a flood of water *from his mouth* intended to destroy the woman. Although biblical thought includes many references to floods, etc., there is no known parallel to this diabolical scheme. The *earth* contributed to her rescue by swallowing the river. This symbol, likewise, is quite obscure. Some point out that rivers are known to flow underground. Swete cited Herodotus' statement that the Lycus River flowed underground near Colossae and the confirmation by Strabo and Pliny. This observation, however, offers no real help. It cannot be treated literally; if so, why would a river present a danger to a woman equipped with eagles' wings. Perhaps John meant to imply that the *earth* helped in the woman's rescue.

War on Woman's Offspring. The purpose of the preceding discussion about the woman was to explain the devil's hostility to the Christians. The *rest of her offspring* are the present faithful Christians who are obeying God's *commandments* and bearing their faithful *testimony to Jesus*, which was a part of the basis of victory both on earth and in heaven (12:11). Christians can be identified by their obedience and witnessing.

A textual problem appears in v. 17 (end of the verse)—in some versions appearing as v. 18. The RSV takes the correct reading to be *estathē* and translates *And he stood . . .*, which relates the statement to the preceding. The KJV follows the variant reading *estathēn*, and translates "And I stood . . ." and relates the statement to the following section. In the light of manuscript evidence and the meaning in the context, the RSV translation is preferable.

The chapter closes with the dragon, frustrated and angry, standing on the seashore ready to call up his reserves, the two terrible monsters of chapter 13.

3. The Sea Beast, the Roman Empire (13: 1–10)

¹ And I saw a beast rising out of the sea, with ten horns and seven heads, with ten diadems upon its horns and a blasphemous name upon its heads. ² And the beast that I saw was like a leopard, its feet were like a bear's, and its mouth was like a lion's mouth. And to it the dragon gave his power and his throne and great authority. ³ One of its heads seemed to have a mortal wound, but its mortal wound was healed, and the whole earth followed the beast with wonder. ⁴ Men worshiped the dragon, for he had given his authority to the beast, and they worshiped the beast, saying, "Who is like the beast, and who can fight against it?"
⁵ And the beast was given a mouth uttering haughty and blasphemous words, and it was allowed to exercise authority for forty-two months; ⁶ it opened its mouth to utter blasphemies against God, blaspheming his name and his dwelling, that is, those who dwell in heaven. ⁷ Also it was allowed to make war on the saints and to conquer them. And authority was given it over every tribe and people and tongue and nation, ⁸ and all who dwell on earth will worship it, every one whose name has not been written before the foundation of the world in the book of life of the Lamb that was slain. ⁹ If any one has an ear, let him hear:
¹⁰ If any one is to be taken captive,
    to captivity he goes;
if any one slays with the sword,
    with the sword must he be slain.

Here is a call for the endurance and faith of the saints.

Chapter 13 is not a change of subject; it is a refinement of the more general discussion of the dragon in the previous chapter. The dragon (Satan) is the foe behind earthly evil; the two beasts are the temporal manifestations which confront John's generation. The dragon is a kind of unearthly (pseudo-heavenly) embodiment of evil; the beasts are of the earth; they portray human evil in the forms of a totalitarian state and a corrupt and subservient religious establishment.

John's symbols, the beast from the sea and the beast from the land, had a long history in Jewish literature and thought (see comment on 12:3–4a,7–12). The immediate source is to be found in the apocalyptic writing of the time. Leviathan was the female monster who lived in the sea; Behemoth was the male monster who lived on the land (1 Enoch 60:7 ff.). They had been created on the fifth day and would come forth when the Messiah is revealed (2 Bar. 29:4).

Description of the Sea Beast. The grisly *beast* came up *out of the sea* as did the beasts of Daniel (Dan. 7:2–7). Most New Testament interpreters see John's sea beast as a symbol of Roman imperial power. This power came to Asia Minor by way of the sea. The annual coming of the proconsul would have symbolized this arrival. The *ten horns* and *seven heads* are also from Daniel. Daniel's leopard had four heads and the others had only one each. John has created a composite beast. Daniel's beasts were like a *lion*, a *bear*, a *leopard*, and another dreadful, almost indescribable, beast. John's was *like a leopard*, had feet like a *bear's* feet and a mouth like a *lion's mouth*. Daniel's four beasts symbolized four kingdoms—Babylonia, Media, Persia, and the Greek kingdoms—and the ten horns symbolized ten kings (Dan. 7:24) of the last kingdom. The "little horn" was Antiochus Epiphanes (IV), who was hated by the Jews most of all because he had desecrated their Temple.

John's use of Daniel's vision is obvious, but he is creative. He had made one beast out of the four, thereby attributing to Rome the combined symbolism of the four. She had the disposition of the *leopard,* which was vigilant and fierce. She had the feet of the *bear* with power to crush. The mouth *like a lion's mouth* suggested the terrifying roar so dreaded by the shepherds of Palestine (Swete, p. 162). One *mouth* for seven heads is strange, but John is concerned with the symbol, not with artists' details.

John intends that the *seven heads* be understood as Roman rulers (Rev. 17:10) and gives several clues toward identifying them (see comment on 17:10).

A *mortal wound* which had *healed* marked one of the heads. This observation is significant for two reasons: it is in contrast with the Lamb (5:6), who had scars of a fatal wound; it identifies this head with Nero (see comment on 17:10).

The blasphemous name has to be a title suggesting divinity for the emperor. Several such titles are known in the literature and on monuments: *Divus, Dominus, Kurios,* and even *Theos.* Christians used these titles only for God and Christ. Their persecution stemmed from their refusal to use these titles for the emperors. Note that the Lamb and the 144,000 on Mount Zion had "his name and his Father's name written on their foreheads" (14:1).

His Power and Authority. The beast had cosmic demonic *power* and *authority* delegated to it directly by the dragon who also provided a *throne* from which to reign. The totalitarian claims of the Roman Empire with its concentration of power appeared to John to be an earthly counterpart to Satan's kingdom of evil. Furthermore, the beast seemed to exercise universal power because *the whole earth followed it.* The beast was able to blaspheme *against God* (use divine titles for himself), *his name and his dwelling,* and get away with it; it was powerful enough to *make war on the saints* and *conquer them;* all the dwellers on earth worship it.

The beast had a magical or bewitching power—a pseudodivine power. The *whole earth* followed him in *wonder.* John spoke convincingly of the majestic power of Rome. When he spoke of her as the "great city" and the "harlot," he confessed that he too "marveled greatly" (17:6). This wonder led men to worship the beast just as they had worshiped the dragon (vv. 4,8). John was keenly aware of the demonic persuasive power of the totalitarian state which could beguile its subjects into idolatry. Modern man still falls before this persuasive power. This beast was victorious; it prevailed even over the saints. It appeared to be supreme; *Who is like the beast, and who can fight against it?* Obviously, no one can. But faithful witnesses must!

His Limitations. John knows that the beast is limited. These limitations are obvious to John for several reasons, but primarily because he never can forget that only God is omnipotent. His doxologies reverberate with words about God's power. The beast suffers from three severe limitations: his work is destructive only; his days are numbered; he will never receive the worship of that congregation listed in the heavenly register.

The beast *was given a mouth,* but he can use it only in blasphemy. The word of God is creative. The word of Christ in the testimony of believers is a victory over this destroyer (12:11). The witnessing word of faithful Christians gives victory in heaven and on earth. The beast is loud, haughty, and blasphemous, but can only destroy; he can create nothing.

His great authority is limited to *forty-two months.* John apparently sees a week of years (seven years) divided into two periods of 42 months (1260 days, three and one-half years). During the first period God's prophets were granted immunity; during the second half the beast prevailed (see comment on 11:3).

His worshipers appear to be all of mankind; but there is a limitation. Those whose *names* have been *written* in the *book of life of the Lamb* will never bend their knees to the beast. But how often today the church seems to worship the beast by endorsing and supporting the brutal state in the same name of patriotism!

Explanation of 13:8–10. There are several difficulties in this passage. The earth dwellers are unbelievers. The believers are those whose names are in the Lamb's book of life (3:5; 17:8; 20:12; 20:15; 21:27). The expression *before the foundation of the world* could mean either that the names were written in the book even before creation, or that Christ was slain for us even before creation. The former would indicate the security of election; the latter would show security in that our salvation is no afterthought with God. These ideas are taught elsewhere (Eph. 1:4; 1 Pet. 1:19–20; Rev. 17:8). Biblical faith does not explain exactly what this means, except that salvation is the eternal plan of God and the believer is secure.

The admonition (v. 9) regarding hearing is related to Jesus' warning, and signals the seriousness of what follows.

If any one is to be taken captive, to captivity . . . appears to be a quote from Jeremiah 15:2 but takes an entirely different direction when John cites Jesus' statement about using the sword (Matt. 26:52). This is not an expression of fatalism. Rather, John is indicating that the power of the beast is so great that he will overcome the faithful. One may go to captivity, as John himself had, but the Christians must not resort to the use of the sword. This is John's basic belief; victory for Christians is based on their faithfulness to Christ, who conquered by his own death. Christians must not resist the tyrant with the sword; to do so would be a denial of Christ and would deserve punishment (Swete, p. 168).

Another interpretation has been offered. Christians observe the claims of deity made by the beast, but they know that his name is not written in the book of life, so he is doomed. Calamity awaits him. He will be taken captive (19:19 f.); his own agents, now arresting the Christians, will be slain by the sword from the Messiah's mouth (19:21). So Christians can endure this last severe persecution in the knowledge of its outcome.[58]

Endurance is a great Christian virtue (1:9; 2:2; 2:19; 3:10). The call for *endurance* and *faith* (see also 14:12) is a special encouragement for a particularly difficult time. *Endurance* is not resignation but is "courageously accepting the worst life can do, and turning it into glory"[59] Christian endurance, rather than the sword, is the road to ultimate victory. *Faith* is not believing everything will work out well; it will not. *Faith* is that commitment to Jesus Christ which results in the conviction that, since he overcame through the cross, we can follow him through trial and death to ultimate victory.

John has indicated that the Roman Empire was the embodiment of evil. The totalitarian state claims the prerogatives of God and tries to become a substitute for the true God. It happened in the twentieth century, too. The ultimate victory belongs to Christ; it becomes the experience of Christians through crosslike suffering, not by using the sword.

It is customary among interpreters to regard the first beast as the Antichrist (Beckwith, Charles, Caird, Kiddle, Pieters, Barclay, Farrer, Morris). I have not used this term because it does not appear in Revelation, and because other biblical evidence does not fall into a definite concept which can properly be designated by a singular term. Antichrists appear in the plural and improper sense.

By parallel with Satan, who opposes God, Antichrist opposes Christ. He is the evil counterpart of Christ, an incarnation of the devil partaking of characteristics so religious as to deceive many into thinking he is genuine.

There are Jewish antecedents for the idea of a personal embodiment of evil. Gog and Magog (Ezek. 38—39) appear later in apocalyptic works. Antiochus Epiphanes,

---

[58] Shirley Jackson Case, *The Revelation of* John (Chicago: The University of Chicago Press, 1919), p. 314 f.

[59] Barclay, *op. cit.,* II, 127.

the most hated by the Jews, was the proto- type of Antichrist. In the *Testament of The Twelve Patriarchs* a demonic figure named Beliar appears. The Qumran scroll entitled "The War of the Sons of Light with the Sons of Darkness" features this enemy of God as Belial.

Jesus spoke of "false Christs and false prophets" who would arise in the last days and lead astray by their wonders (Mark 13: 21 f.). Paul spoke of the "lawless one" who would come with power and pretended signs and wonders; this "man of lawless- ness" is also a "son of perdition" (2 Thess. 2:3,9). Antichrist or antichrists appear in the epistles of John (1 John 2:18,22; 4:3; 2 John 7) but in a more general sense, the "spirit of antichrist."

Irenaeus identified Antichrist with a Ro- man ruler. Reformers Wyclif, Huss, Luther, Calvin, Zwingli, Knox, etc., spoke of the Papacy as the Antichrist. In more recent times Hitler was so identified. Some Chris- tians today speak of an evil personage ex- pected to come before the end. Others see Antichrist as an evil spiritual reality capable of incarnation in any age, but are cautious about identifying him with any particular historical personage.

4. The Land Beast, the Roman Religious Establishment (13:11–18)

¹¹ Then I saw another beast which rose out of the earth; it had two horns like a lamb and it spoke like a dragon. ¹² It exercises all the authority of the first beast in its presence, and makes the earth and its inhabitants worship the first beast, whose mortal wound was healed. ¹³ It works great signs, even making fire come down from heaven to earth in the sight of men; ¹⁴ and by the signs which it is allowed to work in the presence of the beast, it deceives those who dwell on earth, bidding them make an image for the beast which was wounded by the sword and yet lived; ¹⁵ and it was allowed to give breath to the image of the beast so that the image of the beast should even speak, and to cause those who would not worship the image of the beast to be slain. ¹⁶ Also it causes all, both small and great, both rich and poor, both free and slave, to be marked on the right hand or the forehead, ¹⁷ so that no one can buy or sell unless he has the mark, that is, the name of the beast or the number of its name. ¹⁸ This

calls for wisdom: let him who has understand- ing reckon the number of the beast, for it is a human number, its number is six hundred and sixty-six.

Interpreters are almost unanimous in their conclusion that the land beast is the imperial religious establishment. A pro- vincial council (in the province of Asia) composed of representatives from various towns, the *commune Asiae*, supervised em- peror worship. These council members, Asiarchs, are mentioned by Luke (Acts 19:31).

Description and Identification. The first beast, Roman imperial power, came from the sea. The second beast came from the land—was indigenous; it *had two horns like a lamb*—was religious; it *spoke like a dragon*—was deceptive. The description is simple in comparison to the portrait of the first beast. Its appearance is compared to Christ suggesting both its religious nature and the parody of Christ. Its speaking like the dragon may mean as a loud roar, or in the blasphemous things that it says.

This second beast loses its identity even before the end of the chapter in that the mark of the beast is singular. Later in the book, it is equated with the false prophet (16:13; 19:20; 20:10), forming a kind of permanent evil triumvirate which ends up in the fiery pit. The identification with the "prophet" adds further evidence as to the religious function of the land beast.

It is probable that John intends to sug- gest the Nero *redivivus* story (see Int. and comment on 17:10).

His Authority and Power. The dragon gave his power to the sea beast who in turn delegated great power and *authority* to the land beast. His power was great, coer- cive, deceptive, magical, and economic. The beast works as an agent of the first beast, *in its presence,* and commands the whole *earth* and its *inhabitants.* Coercion is its method insofar as power alone will achieve the task. This beast, however, is versatile; it uses deception and magic.

Many of the ancient religions, and per- haps modern ones, employed magic and miracles in order to enslave people. When the true prophet Moses did great signs in Egypt, the false prophets duplicated his wonders by trickery (Ex. 7:10 f.). Jesus spoke of the coming of "false Christs and false prophets" who would come and "show signs and wonders, to lead astray . . ." (Mark 13:22). Paul spoke of a "man of lawlessness" who would display the power of Satan "with all power and with pretended signs and wonders, and with all wicked deception" (2 Thess. 2:9,10).

The land beast employed magic. Three tricks are listed: it worked *great signs;* it called down *fire* from *heaven* simulating the great miracle of Elijah (2 Kings 1:10); it gave *breath to the image of the beast.* This last trick was the greatest of all. An *image of the beast which was wounded by the sword and yet lived* is a reference to the Nero myth. After building his statue, the priests somehow managed to create the illusion that it had become animated. It even spoke. When the image speaks it causes *those who would not worship the image . . . to be slain.* We know that accused Christians were forced to stand before such an image to take the oath. In this case, the animated image accused them, or convicted them for refusal to do so. Such tricks employed ventriloquism and other deception. Paul encountered a magician who stood near Sergius Paulus and prevented him from hearing the gospel until Paul announced a curse on him (Acts 13:6–12; see also Acts 16:16; 19:13 f.). Simon Magus was reported to have done the sign reported here; he brought a statue to life.[60]

The beast had universal economic power to coerce worship of the sea beast. Those who paid the proper worship to the emperor were marked (branded or tatooed) on the *right hand or the forehead.* This identifying mark was tantamount to a commercial license; those without it could neither *buy* nor *sell.* It takes but little imagination to grasp the seriousness of this economic boycott in the hands of a zealous and ambitious religious establishment.

Such marking or branding was used on slaves and captured soldiers. Both Herodotus (vii. 233) and Plutarch (Nic. 29) record such practices. Disgrace would have been one implication. In the marking of the beast, however, there is not disgrace but prestige. The power of Rome and Roman religion made it the "in" practice.

The Mark of the Beast. This mark stands in contrast to the mark of Christ on his followers (7:3). It marks identification, ownership, and loyalty. Religious worshipers may have literally worn such marks; Jews wore their phylacteries. However, the marks may not have been literal tatooes, but marks impressed on the person (Gal. 6:17).

The mark of the beast is identified by the *number of its name,* which is a *human number* (man's name) and is 666. In the Greek and Hebrew languages, characters of the alphabet were used in lieu of special symbols for numbers. For instance, in Latin X=10, C=100, M=1000. In English, we might equate A=1, B=2, C=3, etc. The numerical equivalents of the letters would then be added to get the number of the name. This art, "Gematria," was popular in ancient times. Adolf Deissmann cited such writings on the walls of Pompeii. One reads, "I love the girl whose name is 545."[61]

It is obvious that such a riddle could be worked satisfactorily only if the correct spelling in the correct language is used alongside the correct numerical key. Numerous persons have been identified as the number 666: Martin Luther, the Pope, Napoleon, Hitler, Stalin, etc. The most commonly accepted answer is Nero. We must admit, however, that we have several other reasons for identifying the beast as Nero. Nero in Greek would be *Neron Kaisar,* but this yields a number which is too large. If the name is transliterated into Hebrew, the letters will add to 666 (*nun=*

60 G. B. Caird, *op. cit.* p. 172 citing Clem. *Recog.* iii. 47; cf. Just. *Apol.* I. 26; Iren. *Haer.* i. 23; Eus. *H.E.* ii:13:1–8.

61 Adolf Deissmann, *Light from the Ancient East,* (New York: George H. Doran, 1927) p. 276.

50, *resh*=200, *waw*=6, *nun*=50, *qoph*=100, *samech*=60, *resh*=200). Some manuscripts have the reading 616 instead of 666. The Latin *Nero Kaisar* transliterated into Hebrew script gives a total of 616, which may account for the variant reading. If one begins with the English alphabet and equates A=100, B=101, C=102, etc., the name for 666 is Hitler.[62] This should be adequate reason for refraining from finding modern solutions. John almost certainly intended the reincarnated Nero as a type of the beast.

His call for *wisdom* probably means that when the evil personage appears the believers should recognize him. By using the "code" name for the reincarnate Nero, both writer and reader are safe from the charge of treason.

5. The Lamb and His Army (14:1-5)

¹ Then I looked, and lo, on Mount Zion stood the Lamb, and with him a hundred and forty-four thousand who had his name and his Father's name written on their foreheads. ² And I heard a voice from heaven like the sound of many waters and like the sound of loud thunder; the voice I heard was like the sound of harpers playing on their harps, ³ and they sing a new song before the throne and before the four living creatures and before the elders. No one could learn that song except the hundred and forty-four thousand who had been redeemed from the earth. ⁴ It is these who have not defiled themselves with women, for they are chaste; it is these who follow the Lamb wherever he goes; these have been redeemed from mankind as first fruits for God and the Lamb, ⁵ and in their mouth no lie was found, for they are spotless.

John has dramatically shown the great powers of Satanic evil embodied in the two beasts as they have forced the world into idolatry. Now he abruptly shows us a vision of the Lamb and his army standing on Mount Zion. These are the principals of the great war. The contrasts are striking. John respectively contrasts characteristics of the beasts and their followers with the Lamb and his followers: the beast versus the Lamb; standing on sand versus the

mount; every tribe and people and tongue and nation versus 144,000; the mark of the beast versus "his name and his Father's name"; the voice of blasphemy versus the voice from heaven; the idolatry of the beasts' followers versus the purity of the Lamb's; the deception of the beast versus the truthfulness of the Lamb's followers.

The new vision is introduced by the formula, *I looked*. The *Lamb* (see comment on 5:6 f.) stood majestically on *Mount Zion*, which is probably meant to be the heavenly Jerusalem (as in Heb. 12:22; Gal. 4:26). Earthly Jerusalem was seen as a counterpart of the heavenly city and symbolized security and protection (Joel 2:32; Isa. 11:9-12; 46:13). Some interpreters see this as the earthly Jerusalem and the seat of government during the millennial reign. The dragon had stood on the sand (12:17), which suggested to the Hebrews the evil and chaotic sea. In the new heaven and new earth "the sea was no more." In contrast, the Lamb stood secure and triumphant on Mount Zion.

The Lamb's Authority. In his description of the beasts, John repeatedly reminded us that the authority behind the land beast was the sea beast, who in turn had his authority and power from the dragon who was a defeated angel on borrowed time. Standing back of the Lamb was the power of the omnipotent Creator, whose *voice* was described in three similes: it was *like the sound of many waters* (see 1:15); it was like the *sound of loud thunder* (see comment on 4:5) indicating heavenly power and majesty; it was *like the sound of harpers.* The beast's voice was haughty and blasphemous.

The *name* of Christ and the *Father's name* inscribed on the foreheads of the followers indicates the close connection between this army and the power of God.

The Army of the Lamb. The Lamb's army is also in clear contrast to the whole earth which followed the beast. It is composed of 144,000 (see comment on 7:4-8) who are probably the faithful Christians comprising or representing the whole

---

[62] Thomas S. Kepler, *The Book of Revelation* (New York: Oxford University Press, 1957), p. 147.

church. The symbolism is that of completeness. This group bears the mark as the 144,000 of 7:4–8 and is probably the same. They sing a *new song* which no one else could learn (see comment on 5:9).

John described the Lamb's army as composed of men who were chaste, faithful, redeemed, dedicated, truthful, and spotless. A *literal* interpretation would exclude all women, all men except virgins, and probably all Gentiles. Several interpretations have been suggested for the difficult statement that these soldiers have not *defiled themselves with women, for they are chaste.* (1) It can mean that they were all virgins, celibates. (2) It can mean purity in worship since worshiping other gods was adultery (idolatry). (3) It may mean purity in general with the figure of chastity used in such a way as to say nothing about marriage. (4) It could be speaking of fornication and adultery in which Christians could not engage. (5) It may be a later interpolation by a monk who wanted to build a case for celibacy. (6) It may mean that they are purified for the forthcoming battle.

If literal celibacy is taught here, and some interpreters think so,[63] it is difficult to harmonize this with other New Testament passages. Jesus and Paul (Matt. 19: 12; 1 Cor. 7:25–40) both made statements which have come to us in such a way as to honor the single state. However, the overwhelming amount of New Testament evidence favors marriage (Heb. 13:4; Eph. 5:21 ff.). The term *defiled* is never used of conjugal intercourse and always carries the idea of sin which is never in Scripture associated with marriage (Beckwith, p. 649). Furthermore, if this be taken literally, the statement, *who have not defiled themselves with women,* must exclude women from the company. This is also impossible if the 144,000 are the church. It is also difficult

to explain how John could exalt celibacy, make married Christians second-class Christians at best, and then speak of the church as the bride of Christ.

Purity in worship and life is a likely interpretation in this context. Hebrews regarded idolatry as adultery (Deut. 31:16; Judg. 2:17; Hos. 9:1; Ex. 34:15). John's statement means that these 144,000 are free of any taint of idolatry.

The more likely interpretation is that of G. B. Caird (p. 179), who takes a clue from the military setting. The ancient Hebrews had rules for waging war (Deut. 20), and sexual intercourse resulted in ceremonial impurity (Lev. 15:16). David kept his soldiers away from women before battles (1 Sam. 21:5); when such impurity resulted, there were rules for purification (Deut. 23:9–10). John is portraying the church prepared for battle, and he employs a military figure to describe the church in readiness for battle. This purity is moral purity and stands in contrast to the impurity of the great harlot of chapter 17.

No more beautiful description of Christian faithfulness could be found than John's statement that they *follow the Lamb wherever he goes,* in keeping with Jesus' call, "Follow me!" They are the *redeemed;* Christ ransomed them from slavery with his own blood. They are dedicated to God and the Lamb as *first fruits* (Rom. 16:5; 1 Cor. 16:15).

Truthfulness is a great Christian virtue; it stands alongside purity. These witnesses are truthful: *in their mouth no lie was found.* By contrast, the beast maintained his power by deception. Many modern religious establishments are not known for their truthfulness. The Lamb is noted for his truthfulness (Isa. 53:9); his followers must be truthful (Eph. 4:25).

The witnesses were *spotless* (1 Peter 1:19). Such terms are borrowed from the system of sacrifice in which the animal had to be without flaw. Christians, when they give themselves to God, must become flawless (Eph. 1:4; 5:27; Col. 1:22; Phil. 2:15).

---

[63] R. H. Charles, II, p. 9 is so sure that it means literal celibacy, which to him is impossible for John, that he has concluded that it is a later interpolation by a monk arguing for celibacy.

6. *Series of Angel Visions* (*14:6–13*)

6 Then I saw another angel flying in midheaven, with an eternal gospel to proclaim to those who dwell on earth, to every nation and tribe and tongue and people; 7 and he said with a loud voice, "Fear God and give him glory, for the hour of his judgment has come; and worship him who made heaven and earth, the sea and the fountains of water."

8 Another angel, a second, followed, saying, "Fallen, fallen is Babylon the great, she who made all nations drink the wine of her impure passion."

9 And another angel, a third, followed them, saying with a loud voice, "If any one worships the beast and its image, and receives a mark on his forehead or on his hand, 10 he also shall drink the wine of God's wrath, poured unmixed into the cup of his anger, and he shall be tormented with fire and brimstone in the presence of the holy angels and in the presence of the Lamb. 11 And the smoke of their torment goes up for ever and ever; and they have no rest, day or night, these worshipers of the beast and its image, and whoever receives the mark of its name."

12 Here is a call for the endurance of the saints, those who keep the commandments of God and the faith of Jesus.

13 And I heard a voice from heaven saying, "Write this: Blessed are the dead who die in the Lord henceforth." "Blessed indeed," says the Spirit, "that they may rest from their labors, for their deeds follow them!"

The Angel with the Eternal Gospel. The beasts and their legions stand in battle array; the Lamb and his 144,000 stand on Mount Zion; the final conflict appears to be imminent. But, God halts the movement of time until *another angel* flies across the sky at the zenith, in *midheaven* (cf. 8:13; 19:17) so as to be seen by all, and speaks with a *loud voice* so as to be heard by all. He gives one last call to repentance: *Fear God and give him glory; for the hour of his judgment has come; and worship him.*

Scholars disagree as to whether this gospel is a call to repentance and salvation or simply an announcement of doom. The angel brings *an eternal gospel,* and some maintain that the lack of the definite article means it is other than "the" gospel. It is directed specifically to the unbelieving world of earth dwellers. Furthermore, it

does announce the *hour of judgment.* The gospel is "eternal," meaning that it has always existed or will be everlastingly valid. It is, however, as stated here, without a specific allusion to Christ. But to *fear God and give him glory* is similar to Paul's preaching in Lystra (Acts 14:15), and is not at variance with the Christian gospel.

Jesus had preached an urgent message for men to repent for the kingdom of God had come (Mark 1:15). The early church believed that the gospel would "be preached throughout the whole world" before the end (Matt. 24:14). John may be alluding to this belief. It has been done; now before the end, there is one final proclamation.

The message here must be a call to repentance. *Gospel* means "good news" even without the article. The statements *give glory, worship him,* and *fear God* mean nothing unless they mean repent. John's belief is Christian. Even at this late date, the mercy of God waits. Christ's gospel of forgiveness is still valid; the door is still open. It is meaningless to call men to repentance unless they can repent. God forgives them when they do repent.

Angel Announcing Fall of Babylon. The second angel to fly across the sky announced the fall of *Babylon the great* as if it had already happened. John is using Isaiah's statement (21:9) about Babylon, proverbial as the wicked, powerful, and seductive city. But in John's time Rome had replaced Babylon and had exceeded her in wickedness. In later New Testament times Rome was called "Babylon" (16:19; 17:5; 18:2,10,21; 1 Peter 5:13). Noncanonical literature made the same equation (2 Bar. 11:1; Sibyl. V, 143 ff.). Rome, like Babylon before her, had used her power and wealth to seduce the nations. She had acted like a temple prostitute who intoxicated her victims before seducing them. Even this warning seems to imply a call to repentance.

Angel Announcing Doom on Beast Worshipers. The first angel called men to repentance; the second announced the fall of Rome; the third announces the doom of all who worship the beast. This announcement of doom is also a warning to Christians not to turn away from God.

Christians were subject to coercion, persecution, economic boycott, and even death for refusing to worship the statue of the emperor; each man who worshiped him and wore his *mark* on the *forehead* or *hand* will suffer a twofold punishment: (1) he will *drink the wine of God's wrath* undiluted; (2) he will be *tormented with fire and brimstone* forever. These severe punishments are permanent. If they seem too severe, one must recall that the doomed people have refused many calls to repentance—one just previously stated. They are not casual sinners; they have confirmed their rejection of God by worshiping the beast and wearing his mark.

Their punishment is intensely severe. They drink the wine of God's *wrath* (*thumos*) *poured unmixed* (undiluted) *into the cup of his anger* (*orgē*). Wrath (*thumos*) alone would have been sufficient. It is God's hot anger or passion. *Orgē* speaks of his reaction to man's sins. This double emphasis is like "the fury of the wrath of God." The statement is derived from the Old Testament (Jer. 25:15–17,27 ff.; Psalm 60:3; 75:8; Job 21:20; Isa. 51:17), where the punishment man has brought on himself by his sin is compared to drinking the bitter wine of God's anger.

The *torment* of the beasts' worshipers involves four assertions: they will burn in *fire and brimstone* which is the awful fate of the beast and false prophet (19:20), the devil (20:10), and all who fail to conquer whether through weakness or wickedness (21:8); their torment will take place *in the presence* (full view) *of the Lamb* and *holy angels;* the *smoke of their torment,* reminiscent of Sodom and Gomorrah (Gen. 19:28), will never cease; they, in contrast to the righteous (14:13), will never have *rest, day or night.*

The greatest problem of interpretation in this passage is the apparent vindictiveness. Christian interpreters have regarded it as sub-Christian reflecting the stress of the time but impossible to reconcile with the teaching of Jesus. Some reject its obvious implications since such endless and horrible suffering could serve no good purpose and offer no prospect of release (Glasson, p. 86). Others see the language as dealing with ultimate realities and prefer a literal interpretation. Their case merely points out that man has brought this judgment on himself. Others believe that if there are those who resist God's love finally, they, with Hades and Death, will be thrown into the lake of fire (20:14 ff.), which is "extinction and total oblivion" (Caird, p. 187).

Call to Endurance, Obedience, and Faith. In the midst of the preceding doom and forboding thoughts, John's Christian orientation speaks. He speaks often of the patient *endurance* (cf. 1:9; 2:2,19; 3:10) so necessary for Christian victory. *Saints* prove their steadfastness by obedience to God's commandments (John 6:29). The beasts' worshipers had certainly broken the first commandment. The *faith* of Jesus is the faithful witness to Jesus.

John's Second Beatitude: Blessed Are the Dead in Christ. This beatitude (one of seven, 1:3; 14:13; 16:15; 19:9; 20:6; 22:7; 22:14) comes at an opportune time and provides needed encouragement. John, as did Paul in his letter to the Thessalonians, deals with the question, What about the dead? If they died *in the Lord,* they are truly *blessed;* they are resting *from their labors* (contrasted with v. 11, *no rest*); *their deeds follow them!* Their endurance, obedience, and faith come along as evidence on their behalf.

7. Visions of the Harvest Judgment (14:14-20)

14 Then I looked, and lo, a white cloud, and seated on the cloud one like a son of man, with a golden crown on his head, and a sharp sickle in his hand. 15 And another angel came out of the temple, calling with a loud voice to him who sat upon the cloud, "Put in your sickle, and reap, for the hour to reap has come, for the harvest of the earth is fully ripe." 16 So he who sat upon the cloud swung his sickle on the

earth, and the earth was reaped.

17 And another angel came out of the temple in heaven, and he too had a sharp sickle. 18 Then another angel came out from the altar, the angel who has power over fire, and he called with a loud voice to him who had the sharp sickle, "Put in your sickle, and gather the clusters of the vine of the earth, for its grapes are ripe." 19 So the angel swung his sickle on the earth and gathered the vintage of the earth, and threw it into the great wine press of the wrath of God; 20 and the wine press was trodden outside the city, and blood flowed from the wine press, as high as a horse's bridle, for one thousand six hundred stadia.

After the portrayal of the principals of the great conflict, John shows us the future judgment (chs. 19—20) by using two familiar symbols from the Old Testament: grain harvest and grape harvest. Joel had written: "Put in the sickle, for the harvest is ripe. Go in, tread, for the wine press is full. The vats overflow, for their wickedness is great" (Joel 3:13). From this statement John's sickle, grain harvest, vintage, and judgment motifs are derived.

The Reapers. We are accustomed to thinking of angels as reapers (Matt. 13:39), but in this passage the first reaper is *one like a son of man,* the identical terminology used to describe Christ in 1:13. Since this reaper takes orders from an angel, and since Christ is the exalted Judge in Revelation, some think this *son of man* is an angel (Morris, Glasson, etc.). However, since this term is used distinctively of Christ, and since Christ appears in Revelation in different roles—martyr, Lamb, warrior, etc.—most interpreters see him as Christ the Judge (Beckwith, Swete, Charles, Summers, Barclay, Rist). The problem of Christ's taking orders from the angel is explained by pointing out that the angel bears the message from God. He came *out of the temple.* The statement *for the hour to reap has come* is taken to allude to Christ's own statement that no one but the Father knew the hour (Mark 13:32).

The *white cloud* is the usual vehicle for Christ's coming (Matt. 24:30; 26:64) and going (Acts 1:9) and returning (Acts 1:11). He wears a *golden crown,* prob-

ably to identify him as victor and to contrast him with the beast who also wore a crown.

The angel reapers are not identified in detail. The angel (see 8:5 for fire angel; 16:5 for water angel; 7:1 for wind angel) gave the order to harvest the grapes.

The Harvest. Both grain and grape harvests illustrate the single event of coming judgment. Some would make the grain harvest include only the righteous and the vintage only the wicked, but this cannot be substantiated. The grain harvest, as the end of the world (Mark 4:29; Matt. 13:30; Jer. 51:33; Hos. 6:11), appears to include both righteous and wicked. John uses the two symbols to describe the single judgment which is going to happen soon. The *sickle* is the usual tool used in harvesting grain (Mark 4:29), but it is not a customary symbol for judgment except in Revelation.

In both illustrations, the grain and the grapes were pronounced ready for harvest because they were *ripe.* Evidently all conditions had been met, such as preaching the gospel to all nations. Everything is in readiness. *Put in your sickle!*

The Judgment. Inasmuch as the grapes are thrown into the great *wine press of the wrath of God,* some interpreters (Swete) see this judgment as of the wicked only. The grain was the righteous and was gathered by the Son of man; an angel reaped the grapes. Others point out that in the parable of the tares angels reap both righteous and wicked and that the distinction cannot be sustained. Wine has been used as a symbol of seductive evil (14:8), but it is also symbolic of Christ's redeeming blood.

John's picture of judgment reflects Isaiah 63:3, in which God's vengeance on Edom is described in terms of his treading the wine press and trampling the people in anger until their blood soiled his garments. Such symbolic language of judgment is not strange, but in this instance there is a river of *blood* 200 miles long and deep enough to reach a horse's bridle. The number *one thousand six hundred stadia* (about 200 miles) would not match with any significant measurement we know. Palestine is not that long. Some think it is 4 x 4 x 100 having symbolic significance, but this is very obscure.

In Enoch (1 Enoch 100:1–3) men slay one another until the "streams flow with their blood" and horses walk "up to the breast in the blood of sinners."

God's judgment over Israel's enemies took place outside the city (Zech. 14:4; Dan. 11:45; Joel 3:2,12). Jesus was crucified outside Jerusalem, and John may have been suggesting some significant relationship, but this is not clear. The *city* here is symbolic Jerusalem, the great city, even Rome. Caird has an interesting, though uncertain, interpretation on this point. Since those who remain in the city in a later chapter are the ones who are condemned, these are the martyrs. Judgment would take place in the city. Martyrdom takes place *outside the city.* Protection and safety are found outside the city (12:6; 18:4; Heb. 13:12–13). The blood of the martyrs is related to the cup of vintage God forces on the nations (14:10). In short, the blood of the martyrs would be a part of God's work in the judgment of Rome (Caird, pp. 192 f.).

VII. The Seven Bowl Plagues and Three Introductory Visions (15:1—16:21)

John has already shown two series of seven events of judgment on men. The forthcoming series is similar to the trumpet series but much more severe. These plagues will be the last; they are a part of the end. But John introduces them with three other visions (15:1–8).

¶-1. The Seven Angels (15:1)

¹ Then I saw another portent in heaven, great and wonderful, seven angels with seven plagues, which are the last, for with them the wrath of God is ended.

The *portent* (sign) in heaven marks a momentous announcement (12:1,3). It stirs wonder. *Seven angels* bear *seven plagues.*

These are the *last,* and mark the end of God's wrath (on God's wrath see comment on 14:10,19). Some commentators wonder how John saw the angels who appear later as coming out of the temple (15:6).

¶-2. The Victors by the Heavenly Sea (15:2–4)

² And I saw what appeared to be a sea of glass mingled with fire, and those who had conquered the beast and its image and the number of its name, standing beside the sea of glass with harps of God in their hands. ³ And they sing the song of Moses, the servant of God, and the song of the Lamb, saying,
"Great and wonderful are thy deeds,
  O Lord God the Almighty!
Just and true are thy ways,
  O King of the ages!
⁴ Who shall not fear and glorify thy name, O Lord?
For thou alone art holy.
All nations shall come and worship thee,
for thy judgments have been revealed."

Prior to the opening of the seventh seal (8:1 ff.) which introduced the seven trumpet woes, John portrayed the security of God's faithful by telling of the sealing of the 144,000 and the great multitude in white robes. Now he portrays the safety of God's victors before telling of the bowl plagues. However, his narrative portrays more than their safety; it proclaims their victory because they know the new "Exodus." They stand by the heavenly Red Sea and sing the *song of Moses;* they have been delivered.

A sea like glass. John saw this sea in 4:6. It surrounds God's throne (see comment on 4:6); it appears to be *mingled with fire.* The red color suggests the fire through which the martyrs had come, or the blood they had shed in martyrdom. The earthly sea has connotations of evil (12:17; 21:1); this heavenly sea suggests deliverance because it alludes to the Exodus. Several details of the story suggest Egypt: the plagues, the sea, the Song of Moses, the tent of witness, and the destruction of the enemy who had persecuted God's people. Other New Testament writers have seen a new "Exodus" in the Christian experience (1 Cor.

5:7; 1 Cor. 10:1–11; 2 Cor. 3:6).

The Victors. They are *those who had conquered the beast,* its *image,* and *number*—three ways of saying the same thing. These victors stand delivered by the sea holding *harps of God* (zithers). The inclusion of this detail and the omission of others indicate only that they are about to sing. They are victors, not because they survived, but because they overcame the beast through their suffering. They were probably put to death (13:15) because they would not worship the beast, its image, or wear its mark. Christ had overcome through his death on the cross; these had overcome through their faithful endurance even to death.

Their Song. Their song is described by two phrases: the *song of Moses* and *the song of the Lamb.* The *song of Moses* points us to Exodus 15 or Deuteronomy 32. It is doubtful if distinction is intended between two songs. Moses' song of victory followed the deliverance from Egypt and was sung by the Red Sea. This song, probably a Christian hymn adapted from the Old Testament, is sung after deliverance and is sung by the heavenly "Red Sea." Beckwith strongly disagrees, claiming that there is no evidence for associating this song with the Exodus (pp. 676 ff.). The message of this song is one of praise to God.[64]

In 14:3 the 144,000 sang a "new song" which no one else knew. In this song God is praised because of his power, justice, truthfulness, holiness, and just judgments. His deeds are *great and wonderful* because he has won victory over the beast. John uses the term *Almighty* nine times in Revelation. God's power is the Christians' confidence for victory. God's ways are just

64 The Old Testament sources of the hymn can be seen in the following list, arranged by the number of lines in the RSV. (1) Psalms 92:5; 111:2; 98:1; 139:14; 1 Chron. 16:9; (2) Amos 4:13; (3) Psalm 145:17; Deut. 32:4; (4) Jer. 10:7; (5) Jer. 10:7; Mal. 1:11; Psalm 86:9; (6) 1 Sam. 2:2; Psalm 99:3; (7) Psalm 86:9; (8) Psalm 98:2. On the songs in Revelation see comment on 4:8,11; 5:9; 14:3.

and true in contrast to the beasts', which were coercive, deceitful, and false. The Roman emperors lived for a short time; God is *King of the ages.* No one can resist God; everyone will *fear and glorify* his name, because he is *holy.* Only God is holy; he is different from creation. The coming of all nations is a problem to some since nations are scheduled for destruction. Some see the statement as a part of a hymn unrevised to fit his theology. It is more likely that it is a hymn of praise voicing hope or conviction that men from every nation will come. John is not interested in the kind of *fear* and *worship* which would be only the reluctant acknowledgment by defeated sinners that God is. He wants no last minute confession before the execution. Fearing God and worshiping him involve decision, faith, and endurance. God is to be praised because his *judgments,* now revealed, prove him to be just.

¶-3. The Seven Angels Emerge from the Tent of Witness with Seven Bowls (15:5–8)

5 After this I looked, and the temple of the tent of witness in heaven was opened, 6 and out of the temple came the seven angels with the seven plagues, robed in pure bright linen, and their breasts girded with golden girdles. 7 And one of the four living creatures gave the seven angels seven golden bowls full of the wrath of God who lives for ever and ever; 8 and the temple was filled with smoke from the glory of God and from his power, and no one could enter the temple until the seven plagues of the seven angels were ended.

I looked marks the new vision which signals the beginning of the seven bowl plagues.

The Tent of Witness. The author alludes not to Solomon's Temple but to the prior tabernacle or tent of testimony (Num. 9:15). This tabernacle of the wilderness journeys was the prototype of the Temple, and was itself built according to instructions from heaven (Ex. 25:40). In 11:19, God's temple had been opened to disclose the ark of the covenant within. John employs the early Old Testament imagery to emphasize the nearness of God.

The Seven Angels. These angels, clothed in celestially bright clothing emerge from the opened tent. Their *linen* clothing would suggest whiteness or brightness. A variant reading suggests "stones" instead of linen, which would likely refer to the kind of stones worn by the high priests. Their *golden girdles* probably symbolize royalty. We are not sure if these are the same as the seven angels of the Presence of 8:2.

The Seven Golden Bowls. The text implies that the angels emerged from the tent with *the plagues* (v. 6), but clearly states in the following verse that *one of the four living creatures* distributed the bowls to them after their exit. A golden censer had been used to hold incense and the saints' prayers (8:3,5). Judgment has been described as drinking the "wine of God's wrath, poured unmixed into the cup of his anger" (14:10). The *golden bowls* should be conceived as containers larger than cups, perhaps like incense bowls filled with this deadly anger or wrath of God. By analogy with the saints' prayers of 8:3, we may think of God's wrath accumulating in these seven bowls. Inasmuch as the people have not repented, God now judges earth by having the angels return this human deposit in God's anger back to earth.

The Glory of God. Smoke frequently symbolized the presence of God. Mount Sinai, wrapped in smoke, concealed God's presence (Ex. 19:18). Smoke indicated God's presence in Isaiah's vision (Isa. 6:4). Both the cloud and the glory were present in Ezekiel's vision (10:4). Cloud and smoke prevented Moses from entering the tent (Ex. 40:35). John, influenced by these passages, declares that no one can enter the temple until after the plagues.

John's major emphasis is on the holiness and glory of God. God's presence, manifested in fire and smoke, inspires awe. However, the awesome majesty of God does not permit familiarity; it demands reverence; one removes his shoes in God's presence. To the unbeliever, God's glory and holiness appear as consuming wrath; the unbeliever cannot stand before God.

1. The Plague on Earth (16:1–2)

¹ Then I heard a loud voice from the temple telling the seven angels, "Go and pour out on the earth the seven bowls of the wrath of God."
² So the first angel went and poured his bowl on the earth, and foul and evil sores came upon the men who bore the mark of the beast and worshiped its image.

The first four plagues of the bowl series are similar to the trumpet woes. Both series afflict earth, sea, fresh water, and the luminaries. There are several differences. The bowl plagues move along more quickly; they are much more severe, they attack only unbelievers; there is less thought of repentance. The severity of the plagues and the unrepentant nature of the afflicted suggest the need for justifying God's action, which is done by the water angel.

The *loud voice* is identified only as coming *from the temple;* it gives the expected order of execution to *pour out* the *bowls of wrath.* The *bowls of wrath* can be conceived by comparison with the censer which contained the prayers of the saints.

Wrath from the first bowl, when poured *on the earth,* caused *foul and evil sores* on the beast's followers. The sixth Egyptian plague consisted of sores on both men and animals (Ex. 9:10–11).

2. Death to Sea Life (16:3)

³ The second angel poured his bowl into the sea, and it became like the blood of a dead man, and every living thing died that was in the sea.

The second bowl of wrath turned the *sea* into coagulated blood and killed *every living thing* in the sea. The first Egyptian plague affected only the Nile River (Ex. 7:17–21). The present plague was an attack upon nature, producing unbelievable stench and death, but was not fatal to men. The sea was the origin and home of the dragon; perhaps John's purpose is to show the destruction of its base, the chaotic sea. The second trumpet woe had resulted in the death of one-third of the life in the sea; this plague causes complete destruction.

3. Fresh Water Turned to Blood (16:4–7)

⁴ The third angel poured his bowl into the rivers and the fountains of water, and they became blood. ⁵ And I heard the angel of water say,
"Just art thou in these thy judgments,
   thou who art and wast, O Holy One.
⁶ For men have shed the blood of saints and prophets,
   and thou hast given them blood to drink.
It is their due!"
⁷ And I heard the altar cry,
"Yea, Lord God the Almighty,
   true and just are thy judgments!"

The third bowl plague turned all of earth's sources of fresh water into blood. This plague is more similar to the first Egyptian plague than was the second bowl plague. In the third trumpet plague, the fresh water was turned bitter by the falling of the star Wormwood and caused some fatalities (cf. 8:10–11). In the present instance, John implies that all fresh water was turned into *blood.* Not only is this a terrifying thought from the standpoint of leaving no drinking water, but it is unusually horrible to one with Hebrew background to think of drinking blood, even if one could survive thereby.

John accepted, or at least employed, the commonly believed notion that guardian angels watched over the elements of nature. He has spoken of a "wind angel" (7:1) and a "fire angel" (14:18); now he speaks of a "water angel." One might have assumed that the "water angel" would have reacted negatively to God's judgment on his domain as a means of judging earth's inhabitants. The opposite is the case; he proclaims God's justice.

Water Angel's Justification. This saying of the angel is similar to the song of 15:3–4. It draws attention to God's nature as eternal (*thou who art and wast*) and holy, and to his *judgments* as *just.* The angel anticipates complaints against God and gives the reason for God's harsh judgment. The earth inhabitants had shed the blood of the *saints* (Christians in general) and *prophets* (a special class of saints) in their persecution of them. Consequently, according to the *lex talionis,* they deserve to be forced to drink blood. *It is their due!*

John usually intends a much more serious interpretation than the literal one would allow. Conceivably people could go on living by drinking blood. John intends to show in this passage that human evil has its consequences. Man reaps what he sows (Gal. 6:7). G. B. Caird (p. 202) has pointed out that John has combined the three great "principles of God's providential ordering of history enunciated in the Book of Wisdom." This book, known as The Wisdom of Solomon, is to be dated between 50 B.C. and A.D. 10.[65] Its author stated that (1) God "shall make the whole creation his weapons for vengeance on his enemies" (Wis. of Sol. 5:17); (2) "that by what things a man sinneth, by these he is punished" (Wis. of Sol. 11:16); (3) and "by what things their foes were punished, by these they in their need were benefited" (Wis. of Sol. 11:5).

It is quite easy to see that creation serves as God's judgment and that man reaps in kind for his sins. It is less easy to see how these punishments on God's enemies bring any benefits to God's people.

The water angel's declaration that earth's inhabitants deserve their punishment may be illustrated in modern times. We have used our knowledge of nature to create devastating nuclear bombs; we must live in terror of them and breathe and eat the deadly fallout left by their testing. We have impoverished the world in the manufacture of conventional weapons; we must live with that burden of heavy taxes, unfed poor, inadequate housing, etc. The passage has a vindictive sound, but the biblical writers, in spite of their tendency to attribute even disaster to God, are pointing out

---

65 R. H. Charles, *Apoc. and Pseud.* I, 521.

the eternal truth that man receives back from nature the due penalty for his misuse of it. God's creation girds itself in protest to human mistreatment of other men. It rains back its condemnation on the oppressor.

Heaven's Confirmation. The water angel stated earth's acknowledgment that God's judgment was just. Lest there be any question from any other quarter, John reports that the *altar* cried out affirming heaven's approval that the judgment is *true* and *just* (see comment on 15:3).

4. Plague on the Sun (16:8–9)

⁸ The fourth angel poured his bowl on the sun, and it was allowed to scorch men with fire; ⁹ men were scorched by the fierce heat, and they cursed the name of God who had power over these plagues, and they did not repent and give him glory.

The fourth trumpet plague had affected the sun by reducing its power by one-third (8:12). The fourth bowl plague affects the sun, but the result is the opposite. The contents of the bowl caused the intensity of the sun's heat to be increased so that men were *scorched by the fierce heat.* This event was not prompted by an Egyptian plague, but stands in contrast to the lot of the redeemed. The redeemed shall not hunger or thirst; "the sun shall not strike them, nor any scorching heat" (7:16).

The terror of this plague, apparently limited to unbelievers, needs no explanation. Biblical and nonbiblical literature portray fire as the means of punishment on the wicked. The amazing fact in this account is the response of the afflicted; they *curse* (lit., blaspheme) *the name of God.* The word blaspheme is stronger than *curse.* It harks back to the beast's blaspheming the name of God (13:6). John is amazed that the people *did not repent and give him glory.* Their hearts, like Pharaoh's, grew harder under punishment. The depth of their degradation is obvious; sensitive souls would have repented. Does John mean to imply that they could have been saved at this late date? Probably, since *repent and*

give him glory usually means the genuine worship of God.

5. Plague of Darkness (16:10–11)

¹⁰ The fifth angel poured his bowl on the throne of the beast, and its kingdom was in darkness; men gnawed their tongues in anguish ¹¹ and cursed the God of heaven for their pain and sores, and did not repent of their deeds.

The contents of the fifth bowl were poured directly on the beast's *throne,* which is almost certainly Rome. The immediate result is *darkness,* which may be an allusion to the ninth Egyptian plague (Ex. 10:21–23). If so, however, how do we explain the intense suffering which caused men, in convulsions of pain, to gnaw *their tongues?* Inasmuch as their *pain and sores* are mentioned, we may assume that these plagues are cumulative or that they happen in such quick succession that the sores have not healed. R. H. Charles has interpreted this plague in parallel to the fifth trumpet plague, which was also the "first woe" (9:1–11). In that woe, a cloud of smoke from the pit became a cloud of scorpion-like locusts which tortured men. This would account both for the darkness and the suffering (Charles, II, 45). Caird has seen the first four plagues as "natural" plagues and the last three as "political" plagues. Then, this darkness would be the political chaos which followed Nero's suicide. The doubts, fears, suspicions, and hysteria would have been the suffering. He thinks that even the natural plagues indicate spiritual rather than physical suffering (Caird, p. 204 f.).

The response of the afflicted is again spotlighted. Since they curse God, we must assume that they blame God for their suffering. If they think that he is, and that he is powerful enough to bring about these conditions, why do they refuse to repent and acknowledge him? Obviously, John's amazement illustrates the illogical nature of human evil. Their guilt is compounded by their acknowledgment, even in cursing him, that God is. Man's depravity is so deeply ingrained that even the wrath of

God does not turn man from sin. Faith is not the grudging assent that God is; neither is it the intellectual affirmation of God. This is the reason John believed in hell. He believed that men could say no to God forever.

6. The Call to Armageddon (16:12–16)

12 The sixth angel poured his bowl on the great river Euphrates, and its water was dried up, to prepare the way for the kings from the east. 13 And I saw, issuing from the mouth of the dragon and from the mouth of the beast and from the mouth of the false prophet, three foul spirits like frogs; 14 for they are demonic spirits, performing signs, who go abroad to the kings of the whole world, to assemble them for battle on the great day of God the Almighty. 15 ("Lo, I am coming like a thief! Blessed is he who is awake, keeping his garments that he may not go naked and be seen exposed!") 16 And they assembled them at the place which is called in Hebrew Armageddon.

Several separate events follow the pouring of the sixth bowl contents, but these all center around the assembling of all nations to the great battleground of Armageddon. Evidently, Rome is the true target of the battle.

The Euphrates Dries Up. The first result of the pouring was that the Euphrates River dried up to permit the kings from the east to move their armies on Rome. The Euphrates was the eastern boundary of Rome. Beyond the river were unknown kingdoms and the Parthians, who inspired great fear in Rome. The Nero redivivus myth is probably implied in that he was expected to lead the Parthians against Rome (see Int. and comment on 13:3; 17:12–14). In the sixth trumpet plague, the second woe (9:13–21), four angels, previously bound at the Euphrates, had been released to lead 200,000,000 troops of cavalry against mankind. Now, the river is dried up to permit passage of all the armies of the east.

In the Exodus God dried up the Red Sea to permit the Israelites to gain their freedom (Ex. 14:21). Joshua passed over the Jordan in a similar deliverance (Josh. 3:17). Prophets spoke of such deliverances (Isa.

11:16; Jer. 51:36; Zech. 10:11). Herodotus (History 1.191) recorded that Cyrus had been able to capture Babylon because he had dried up the flow of the Euphrates for a short time by building dams. This event is preparatory; no immediate suffering is recorded.

Three Foul Spirits. The agents for calling the nations together for the battle are the three foul spirits like frogs. John may have intended some contrast with the "seven spirits of God sent out into all the earth" (Rev. 5:6). Frogs conveyed an evil connotation. They figured in the plagues of Egypt. In Zoroastrian thought, frogs were related to the evil spirit; Ahriman preferred to take the form of a frog (Rist, p. 485).

The origin of the foul spirits is the mouths of the dragon, the beast, and the false prophet respectively. This is the first mention of the false prophet, but he is identical with the second beast of 13:11 (19:20; 20:10; 13:14; on the dragon see comment on 12:3 ff.; on the beast see comment on ch. 13). John intended to convey the idea that the spoken word of the dragon, beast, and false prophet is the means of his deceptive power. Swete sees a play on the words "spirit" and "breath" since in Greek pneuma means both. These spirits would be the evil influence of these three enemies. Glasson has seen in this evil triumvirate a trinity of evil. The Dragon stands against God; the beast opposes Christ; the false prophet is a counterpart of the Holy Spirit. The Holy Spirit inspires the true prophets; this false prophet does the opposite (Glasson, p. 93).

By nature the three foul spirits are unclean demonic spirits who can perform signs. Egyptian magicians "did" signs to match those of Moses; the second beast did a marvelous sign in animating the statue; these evil spirits do miracles to arouse the kings to battle.

The mission of the foul spirits is to assemble the kings of the whole world for battle, the long-expected day of judgment. The great day was spoken of by the prophets (cf. Joel 2:11) as the time of God's judgment. New Testament writers related it to Christ's coming (2 Thess. 1:10) or the Day of the Lord (1 Cor. 1:8; 1 Thess. 5:2). John expects all nations, not just Rome, to assemble for battle and be defeated by God's forces, or he alludes to this expectation to suggest the great battle between evil and God. The evil spirits, playing on demonic-type greed, fear, hatred, ambition, false religious claims, and other motivations that call nations to war, unwittingly accomplish God's summons to judgment.

John's third beatitude. John's third beatitude (see 1:3; 14:13, etc.) appears quite unexpectedly, warning that Christ's coming will be unexpected *like a thief* (see comment on 3:3) and stating the blessedness of the one who is *awake,* i.e., alert and watchful, ready. Readiness is described as *keeping his garments* at hand. To be *naked* and *exposed* would be the humiliation of the lack of spiritual preparation (see comment on 3:18). This has nothing to do with resurrection bodies; these would not be in man's province to keep.

Armageddon. The text indicates that the kings gather for battle at a *place* called in *Hebrew Armageddon.* It is to be regretted that John did not give the Greek equivalent as he did in the case of Abaddon (9:11). No such place is known on the maps of the ancient world. The word does not appear elsewhere in Hebrew, suggesting that John has used a name which would have a symbolic meaning. Some texts have a variant reading which could mean the mountain of Megiddo, but this is uncertain.

Inasmuch as John is portraying a battle between God's forces and the forces of evil, it may allude to Megiddo, one of the fortress cities of Solomon near which had been several memorable battles. Megiddo stood on the ridge south of the plain of Esdraelon. It overlooked and guarded the plain through which the armies from Africa and Asia marched to battle one another. Megiddo was mentioned in connection with Deborah and Barak's overthrow of Sisera

(Judg. 5:19-21); Ahaziah was wounded nearby and died in Megiddo (2 Kings 9:27); Pharaoh Neco killed King Josiah at Megiddo (2 Kings 23:29). If John intended to locate the battle at or near Megiddo, it was surely to stress some idea such as the "battleground of the nations."

There are several possibilities for interpretation: (1) the city Megiddo; (2) the land of Megiddo; (3) Mount Megiddo, which would mean the portion of the mountain on which Megiddo was located; (4) a corruption of a Hebrew phrase meaning "mount of assembly," "city of desire," or "his fruitful mountain," which would be Mount Zion.[66] Bowman favors this last interpretation.

Ezekiel located the last battle with Gog and Magog in the "mountains of Israel," (Ezek. 38:8,21; 39:2,4,17), but there is no known reason for equating this with Megiddo. Nevertheless, it is possible that John is here influenced by Ezekiel. If a geographical location is intended, Megiddo has the best case. Summers is probably correct in his statement that Armageddon has "no location on the maps of the world" (Summers, p. 190). Others insist that whatever else may have been intended, John did not expect a final battle in Palestine but at Rome (Caird, p. 207). But this battle is not the kind that can be located on a map like Waterloo or Iwo Jima.

One of the greatest commentaries ever written on Revelation concludes about Armageddon that, "it is then an imaginary name for designating the scene of the great battle between Antichrist and the Messiah" (Beckwith, p. 685).

7. Great Calamities (16:17-21)

¹⁷ The seventh angel poured his bowl into the air, and a great voice came out of the temple, from the throne, saying, "It is done!" ¹⁸ And there were flashes of lightning, loud noises, peals of thunder, and a great earthquake such as had never been since men were on the earth, so great was that earthquake. ¹⁹ The great city was split into three parts, and

⁶⁶ John Wick Bowman, "Armageddon," IDB, I, 226 f.

the cities of the nations fell, and God remembered great Babylon, to make her drain the cup of the fury of his wrath. ²⁰ And every island fled away, and no mountains were to be found; ²¹ and great hailstones, heavy as a hundredweight, dropped on men from heaven, till men cursed God for the plague of the hail, so fearful was that plague.

The bowl contents were poured *into the air*, the habitat of demons. Since all men depend on the air, this plague would reach all men. It is much more serious even than the plagues upon the sea, the fresh water, the earth, or the sun. Its repercussions are far more serious than those from the seventh trumpet blast, which included lightning, thunder, earthquake, and hail (11:19).

The *great voice* which came from the *temple* was one of great authority if it was not God's voice. It announced the completion of the plagues—*It is done!* This means that the plague which has just begun is the very last. The forces of nature respond to the voice. The *earthquake* was greater than had ever been before, and the first century A.D. was a century of earthquakes.

So terrible was the earthquake that the *great city* (see comment on 14:8; 17:18) was *split into three parts*. The *great city* is not only Babylon and Rome, but man's civilization. Other *cities* fell indicating the worldwide nature of this catastrophe. *God remembered great Babylon* calls to mind the prediction of 14:10 and 19, in which his wrath is portrayed as a cup of wine to be drunk. Now he forces her to *drain the cup* [of the wine] *of the fury of his wrath*. For some reason, the RSV omitted the words "of the wine." The earthquake does not exhaust God's furious wrath which will be drunk in the coming chapters.

Islands of the sea shuddered and sank into the depths. Mountains crumbled into the valleys (see 6:14). *Hail* had destroyed crops and had killed some men and animals during the seventh Egyptian plague (Ex. 9:22–26). Joshua had won one battle when *hail* fell on the enemy (Josh. 10:11). The *hailstones* of this bowl plague were as

heavy as a hundredweight. This weight varied from 66 pounds to as much as 138 pounds.[67] Of greater wonder to John than the great hailstones was the observation that men *cursed God* because of the hail. Implied is his expectation that they would have repented.

VIII. The Fall of the Great City—Rome (17:1—19:5)

John's imagery is flexible, complex, and provocative. We have noted that the ultimate enemy is the dragon or Satan; the power of the dragon has been delegated to the sea beast (13:1), which is identified as the Roman Empire. While no literal distinction should be made between Rome and the Roman Empire, it seems that John, in this section, is dealing more specifically with the city Rome, the great city. But again, one will go astray if he draws a sharp and literal line of distinction. Definitely, John intends to contrast this woman with the woman of chapter 12. He intends a contrast between the "holy city" and this "great city." He also intends to suggest a contrast between this harlot and the bride of Christ. But the great city is more than Rome; it is the city of man.

¶-1. The Harlot and the Beast (17:1–6a)

¹ Then one of the seven angels who had the seven bowls came and said to me, "Come, I will show you the judgment of the great harlot who is seated upon many waters, ² with whom the kings of the earth have committed fornication, and with the wine of whose fornication the dwellers on earth have become drunk." ³ And he carried me away in the Spirit into a wilderness, and I saw a woman sitting on a scarlet beast which was full of blasphemous names, and it had seven heads and ten horns. ⁴ The woman was arrayed in purple and scarlet, and bedecked with gold and jewels and pearls, holding in her hand a golden cup full of abominations and the impurities of her fornication; ⁵ and on her forehead was written a name of mystery: "Babylon the great, mother of harlots and of earth's abominations." ⁶ And I saw the woman, drunk with the blood of the saints and the blood of the martyrs of Jesus.

⁶⁷ O. R. Sellers, "Weights and Measures," IDB, IV, 828 ff.

The Angel's Introduction of the Harlot.
One of the angels which had poured out
the bowls of wrath became John's interpreter. He promised John that he would
show him the *judgment of the great harlot,* and this is the subject of the whole
section. It is God's *judgment* even though
God does not directly "do" it. Actually, it
is brought about by internal forces; the
beast who had supported the harlot be-
trayed and destroyed her.

The *great harlot,* though called Babylon,
is equated with the city of Rome. Anyone
familiar with ancient descriptions of Rome
on seven hills would recognize John's identification (17:9). But John means more
than the real estate of seven hills and the
people who resided there. The city of Rome
had given birth to the Empire. She had
been deified as Roma. Roma had become
a mother goddess to whom temples were
erected in the provinces. John speaks of
more than the capital city; he speaks of
Roma who had become an object of worship. John's reference to Rome as a harlot
may appear to show lack of respect and
patriotism, but it is not lacking in historical
precedent. Nahum called Nineveh (Nah.
3:4) a harlot; Isaiah so designated Tyre
(Isa. 23:17); and even Jerusalem was
called a whore (Isa. 1:21).

Rome was seated upon *many waters.*
This phrase could have reference to Rome's
location near the water, or to her powerful
maritime commerce. Jeremiah (51:13) had
used this term in describing ancient Babylon, which was located by the Euphrates
and had an elaborate system of canals
around it. John could have taken the description of the contemporary Babylon,
Rome, without any modification. It is more
likely that he is following Old Testament
precedent in referring to streams of water
as peoples. He pointedly identifies the
phrase as the numerous nations, tongues,
and peoples (Rev. 17:15) which give Rome
her power.

God's *judgment* of Rome is grounded on
two of her crimes: she has *committed fornication* with the *kings of the earth* (Minear,

pp. 235–246); she has seduced the subjects
of the kings (*dwellers on earth*) by intoxi-
cating them with the *wine* of her *fornication.* The great city has power to corrupt
her kings and their subjects. The reference
may be to the idolatry of emperor worship;
it may refer to the materialistic seduction
of men in which they turn away from God.

The Description of the Harlot. John was
carried away *in the Spirit,* which means an
ecstatic trance or state of inspiration (1:10;
4:2; 21:10), to the *wilderness.* The wilderness was the location of the vision of the
woman clothed with the sun (12:1); God
cared for her in the desert. The desert is a
more likely place for man to meet God;
Moses met God in the desert (Ex. 3);
Elijah and John the Baptist met God in the
wilderness. It may appear strange that John
is taken into the wilderness to see his vision
of the great harlot. Perhaps, it is in the
wilderness that one can best see the great
city for what it really is.

The harlot is in striking contrast with
the woman of chapter 12 (see comment on
12:1–6,13–17). She sat on a *scarlet* beast.
The dragon (12:3) was fiery red, but no
color was indicated for the beast (13:1)
with which comparison is made in this description. The beast (ch. 13) had a blasphemous name on its heads; this beast is
full of blasphemous names. These *names*
were probably titles of deity ascribed to
Roman emperors.

Purple and *scarlet* clothing suggest the
magnificence and luxury of imperial Rome.
No hidden meaning is couched in the *gold
and jewels and pearls;* they designate only
her wealth. The *golden cup* shows wealth
and suggests the harlot's habit of seducing
her victims by getting them drunk. John
appears to be alluding to Jeremiah's statement, "Babylon was a golden cup in the
Lord's hand, making all the earth drunken"
(Jer. 51:7).

The *cup* was full of *abominations,* which
probably means idolatrous requirements
Rome exacted from her subjects, and *impurities of her fornication.* Both terms suggest desecration and idolatry.

The Name of the Harlot. Roman harlots wore headbands on their brows with their names exposed. The great harlot wore such a band which identified her as *Babylon* and *mother of harlots.* The *mystery* is that John calls her Babylon but identifies her as Rome so that his readers would understand the mystery. Harlotry and idolatry were abominable to God and his people; Rome is the mother of such evils.

The woman clothed in the sun (12:1–6, 13–17) was the mother of the Messiah, and all Christians were her offspring. Roma was the mother of harlots.

The great harlot was drunk from drinking the *blood of the saints.* John may have been thinking of the blood bath during Nero's time or the persecutions of Domitian's reign.

The great city has powers of corruption even beyond its own knowledge. When one stands outside the cultural setting (in the wilderness) he can see the seductive power of the great secular city more clearly than he can when he is a part of it. Rome is every city.

¶-2. The Mystery of the Harlot (17:6b–14)

When I saw her I marveled greatly. **7** But the angel said to me, "Why marvel? I will tell you the mystery of the woman, and of the beast with seven heads and ten horns that carries her. **8** The beast that you saw was, and is not, and is to ascend from the bottomless pit and go to perdition; and the dwellers on earth whose names have not been written in the book of life from the foundation of the world, will marvel to behold the beast, because it was and is not and is to come. **9** This calls for a mind with wisdom: the seven heads are seven hills on which the woman is seated; **10** they are also seven kings, five of whom have fallen, one is, the other has not yet come, and when he comes he must remain only a little while. **11** As for the beast that was and is not, it is an eighth but it belongs to the seven, and it goes to perdition. **12** And the ten horns that you saw are ten kings who have not yet received royal power, but they are to receive authority as kings for one hour, together with the beast. **13** These are of one mind and give over their power and authority to the beast; **14** they will make war on the Lamb, and the Lamb will conquer them, for he is **Lord of lords and King of kings,** and

those with him are called and chosen and faithful."

Marvelous in Appearance. John unabashedly confessed that he *marveled greatly* on seeing the great harlot. She was bewitching in her charm. Who has not marveled at the amazing beauty, complexity, and personality of a great city? Who has not stood on the verge of reverence when he observes the efficient war machine of a totalitarian state, or the amazing complex of a modern industrialized state? Does not modern man respond with a mood approaching reverence when an astronaut steps on the moon as the result of the great effort of a modern state? John understood the temptation to idolize the temporal state, but the angel guide warned against this response; he explained the mystery of the *woman, and of the beast.*

Mistress of the Beast. Most of the explanation deals with the beast, and this is as it should be. The harlot is not only intimately related to the beast; she is dependent on it. John sees the ungodly worldly power-combines which try to stand against God as resting on the power of Satan's agents.

Identification of the Evil Powers. John took considerable liberty in his use of terms and symbols. For instance, the beast may be the entire Roman Empire or, on other occasions, a single king. Some interpreters explain these inconsistencies on the ground that John used sources without modification. Apocalyptic writers were not greatly concerned about such apparent flaws in their compositions.

The *beast* on which the woman sat is the real subject in this explanation of the mystery. Both the red dragon (12:3) and the sea beast (13:1) had *seven heads and ten horns.* The dragon was equated with Satan (12:9); the sea beast was Satan's agent and was equated with the Roman Empire (see comment on 13:1–10,18). John repeats the belief that the beast (or one of its heads) had been alive, is dead, but is expected to return. This is the *eighth* who is also of *the seven.* There is little doubt but that he alludes to the Nero *redivivus myth* (see comment on ch. 13, and in Int.), even though he equates the beast with one of its heads.

The *dwellers on earth* are the followers of the beast. Throughout Revelation these earth inhabitants are the unregenerate people. They are not listed in the *book of life;* they are capable of worshiping God since they bear his image; but they do not worship God, and they fall into worship of the beast. They are seduced by the beast because it awakens wonder in them. They are particularly deceived by the fact that *it was and is not and is to come.* They have rejected Christ, who truly was, was dead, and is alive forever more (1:18), but have believed a myth about a wicked Caesar.

In true apocalyptic style, John interprets the *seven heads* as the *seven hills* on which the woman was seated and as *seven kings.* Any schoolboy would have identified Rome by the seven hills. Latin literature abounds with references to the city on seven hills; a festival celebrated the enclosure of the seven hills within the walls (Caird, p. 216). In this case, the reference is to the city Rome, or *Dea Roma,* rather than to the whole empire.

There is no doubt but that John intended the *seven heads* to suggest *seven kings.* It is less certain as to which seven he intended. His clues are two: *five* have already *fallen;* the *eighth* king is one of *the seven.* This would suggest that the sixth king was reigning when John wrote; he states that the seventh would reign only for a *little while;* since the *eighth* is of *the seven,* he must be the reincarnated Nero, or a king like Nero. The Roman rulers are as follows:

*Julius Caesar	Died in 44 B.C.	
*Augustus	31 B.C.—A.D. 14	
Tiberius	A.D. 14—37	
Caligula (Gaius)	A.D. 37—41	
*Claudius	A.D. 41—54	
Nero	A.D. 54—68	
Galba	A.D. 68—69	
Otho	A.D. 69	
Vitellius	A.D. 69	
*Vespasian	A.D. 69—79	

*Titus	A.D. 79—81
Domitian	A.D. 81—96

There are several difficulties which prevent a certain solution. Only those marked by the asterisk were deified by the Roman Senate, but we do not know if this mattered to John. Julius Caesar did not officially have the title "Emperor." Augustus was the first to wear the title. Then, shall we begin with Augustus? Galba, Otho, and Vitellius were only pretenders; should they be omitted? John may have ignored these three whose combined reigns added only to a year and a half.

If we begin with Augustus and omit the three pretenders, Nero was the fifth, Vespasian the sixth who *is,* Titus fits as seven who reigns only a *little while,* and Domitian would be the eighth, the reincarnated Nero. This is not a difficult solution. It requires that the author (though writing in Domitian's time) transfer himself to the reign of Vespasian (Swete, p. 220 f.; Charles, p. 69; Barclay, p. 190; Morris, p. 210). The preceding interpretation enjoys wide acceptance, but does require that John used earlier sources without revision or projected himself back from the time of Domitian to that of Vespasian.

There are many commentators who reject the approach which tries to identify these kings. They point out that John often used the number seven in the sense of completeness and did not intend it to be taken literally (Rist, p. 495; Beckwith, p. 708; Caird, p. 218), that similar riddles (Dan. 11:2) often cannot be identified, and that often the apocalyptic explanations are just as mysterious as the original statements.

The *ten horns* are identified as *ten kings* who have not yet come to *power;* they will reign only for *one hour* (a very short time); they are in alliance with the *beast* and serve him; they will *make war on the Lamb* and be defeated by him. We are accustomed to the ten horns from previous usage (12:3; 13:1). The symbol was developed in the Old Testament. Strong bulls pushed with their horns; horns became symbolic for political power (Psalm 132:17; Jer.

48:25) and then designated kings (Dan. 7:8,11,21; Zech. 1:18;19). John's use of the *ten horns* as *ten kings* is very similar to Daniel's ten kings but less easily identified.

Whereas the seven Roman rulers reigned in succession, these ten kings appear to reign in different kingdoms at the same time. They willingly serve the beast. Perhaps they are rulers of kingdoms not controlled by Rome. Suggestions for identifying them are numerous. (1) They may be ten Persian satraps who return with Nero (reincarnated) to fight Rome. (2) They may be ten governors of the Roman provinces who incidentally reigned only for one year, the *one hour*. (3) They could be ten future kings who will join Nero, but are otherwise unidentified. (4) Possibly they are to be seen as demonic powers since Nero is a beast from the abyss. (5) They may be eschatological figures expressing the totality of powers aligned against the Lamb (Beckwith, p. 700).

The Inevitable Conflict with the Lamb. It is very strange that John in describing the harlot and the beast and the evil coalition of ten kings should forget Rome for the moment and speak of war on the Lamb. These kings of earth submit to the beast in their feverish quest for worldly power. Rome had unscrupulously enlisted religion as an aid in subjecting the people. She had usurped prerogatives belonging only to God. She had claimed the totality of man's loyalty corrupting man's religions by allowing them to continue in a secondary role. All power structures of earth which overstep their bounds inevitably make war on the Lamb. They join the beast, become beastly, but they are doomed ultimately.

The *Lamb will conquer them,* and that for two good reasons: he is no second-rate king who thinks he can get power by surrendering it, but he is *Lord of lords and King of kings;* his followers are not earth's opportunists dazed by temporary splendor, but they are *called and chosen and faithful.* Roman emperors used pretentious titles for themselves, but John knew who was

Lord of all and King (19:16). He does not fight with frail weapons; he speaks in power.

The Lamb's followers contribute to his victory not because of their military or economic prowess but precisely because of who they are and what they are. The *called* and the *chosen* are usually the same, but in the parable of the wedding garment (Matt. 22:14) they were different. The *called* were the "invited"; the *chosen* were the "elect." The word elect is a little stronger in that it implies both the invitation and the acceptance. The Lamb's followers recognized the true authority which *called* them and they chose to be *chosen.* God took the initiative; they responded. God took the initiative with the earth dwellers, too, but they were seduced and chose the beast.

Followers called *faithful* have been truly praised. Jesus Christ is the *faithful* One (1:5; 3:14; 19:11). The martyrs were *faithful* (2:10,13).

¶-3. The Betrayal of the Harlot (17:15–18)

15 And he said to me, "The waters that you saw, where the harlot is seated, are peoples and multitudes and nations and tongues. 16 And the ten horns that you saw, they and the beast will hate the harlot; they will make her desolate and naked, and devour her flesh and burn her up with fire, 17 for God has put it into their hearts to carry out his purpose by being of one mind and giving over their royal power to the beast, until the words of God shall be fulfilled. 18 And the woman that you saw is the great city which has dominion over the kings of the earth."

A Reminder of Rome's Power. Before telling of her betrayal, John reminds us of the great influence she had known. He introduced her as one *seated upon many waters* (see comment 17:1). Now he explains that these *waters* are the *peoples and multitudes and nations and tongues.* Most of the world was subservient to Rome.

Prediction of Rome's Fall. The woman of chapter 12 was attacked by the dragon, but God preserved her in the wilderness. The woman of chapter 17 (Rome, the great city) has been the lover of the beast; she derived her power for a time from him and his evil cohorts. The *ten* kings and the *beast* will turn on the woman; there will be no one to protect her. John's perception is very clear. Worldly combines of power grounded in evil are fickle alliances indeed; the allies turn on one another and become the enemies. Her luxurious clothing will be no more; they will leave her *desolate and naked.* This is a horrible but accurate description of the harlot when her lovers are through with her. The term *devour her flesh* is a symbol of complete destruction (Jer. 10:25; Mic. 3:3; Zeph. 3:3). To *burn her up with fire* may allude to Nero's burning of Rome, but more probably points to the utter destruction of great cities burned by their captors.

Her Fall Is God's Jugdment. In the Old Testament God punished Israel by permitting her enemies (Assyria, Babylon, etc.) to attack her. This did not remove responsibility from the cruel nations; they acted out of greed, aggression, and will to power. John is following the Old Testament interpretation. Even though Rome's fall is the result of the hatred of her own kind, the beast and the ten kings, it can be called a judgment of God. John, believing in the complete sovereignty of God, plainly believed that God would employ these wicked evil powers to punish Rome. In God's world, evil may prevail for a time, but it perpetuates its own power of destruction. God is not mocked! Man reaps what he sows! Harlot Rome was allied with the beast; there was a temporary advantage; the beast turned on Rome and destroyed her; but the beast, also, will come to judgment.

A Reminder of the Woman's Identity. She had paraded in pomp and wealth. Kings were her paramours; earth dwellers drank her wine; the world bowed before her. John closes the chapter with the reminder of her former glory in contrast to her predicted desolation.

Rome is Babylon; Babylon is Babel; Babel is the symbol of sinful man's attempt to build his own tower to heaven, to seize

God. Babel was filled with pride; Babel sought to take God by force; Babel worships this world; Babel goes on without God in utter confusion. Egypt, Assyria, Babylon, Persia, Greece, Rome, and modern states perpetuate Babel's error. They all depend on the wrong kind of power, suffer from undiluted pride and egoism, and think they have hold of the ultimate. They employ a pseudo-religious grasp on people as a means of power. That was the role of the beast from the land. In the United States, there are many confessing Christians who neither know nor care about the difference between Christian faith and a patriotic feeling toward God and America. John predicted the fall of all of this.

1. Heaven's Announcement of the Fall of Rome (18:1-3)

¹ After this I saw another angel coming down from heaven, having great authority; and the earth was made bright with his splendor. ² And he called out with a mighty voice,
"Fallen, fallen is Babylon the great!
  It has become a dwelling place of demons,
  a haunt of every foul spirit,
  a haunt of every foul and hateful bird;
³ for all nations have drunk the wine of her
    impure passion,
  and the kings of the earth have committed
    fornication with her,
  and the merchants of the earth have grown
    rich with the wealth of her wantonness."

The Messenger. The angel which came from heaven with the message was distinguished from the angel of 17:1,7. His *great authority* is either in his appearance or in his *mighty voice.* The angel glowed brightly because he had recently been in God's presence (Ezek. 43:2), and now reflected some of God's splendor to the earth.

Babylon in Ruins. Although the author has clearly indicated that he speaks of Rome, he continued the symbolism of Babylon by quoting Isaiah (21:9). He is so certain of his prediction that he states the fall as if it were an accomplished fact.

The site will be abandoned by men and will be a dwelling place for *demons* and a *haunt* for *every foul spirit* and *hateful bird.* Isaiah had so described the fall of Babylon.

He wrote that wild beasts would roam its site, howling creatures would inhabit its abandoned houses, and jackals would live in its forsaken palaces (Isa. 13:21–22).

Three charges constitute the case against Rome and justify her predicted fall: (1) she seduced the nations into drinking her wine; (2) she seduced the kings of earth into fornication, idolatry (see comment on 17:2); and (3) the economic boom created by luxury-loving Rome encouraged the rise of a mercantile class which had *grown rich* at the expense of the peoples of the world. Wealth is power; those who hold it have more power than generals with armies. John could see the corrupting power of wealth; men worshiped material wealth as they bowed to Roma.

2. Rome Deserted by the Christians (18: 4–8)

4 Then I heard another voice from heaven saying,
"Come out of her, my people,
    lest you take part in her sins,
    lest you share in her plagues;
5 for her sins are heaped high as heaven,
    and God has remembered her iniquities.
6 Render to her as she herself has rendered,
    and repay her double for her deeds;
    mix a double draught for her in the cup she
        mixed.
7 As she glorified herself and played the wanton,
    so give her a like measure of torment and
        mourning.
Since in her heart she says, 'A queen I sit,
    I am no widow, mourning I shall never see,'
8 so shall her plagues come in a single day,
    pestilence and mourning and famine,
    and she shall be burned with fire;
    for mighty is the Lord God who judges her."

After the heavenly announcement of Rome's forthcoming fall, an unidentified *voice* calls the Christians out of the city.

Christians Called Out of Rome. The address *my people* suggests that God is speaking, but the reference to God in the third person indicates that it is another's *voice.* The call from God to his people to "come out" appears frequently in the Bible. Sometimes the call is for a literal departure as in the case of Abraham (Gen. 12:1), but more

often it is a call for God's people to separate themselves from worldly living (Eph. 5:7–11).

John appears to be following Jeremiah (51:45), who so instructed the people in connection with Babylon's fall. We are also reminded of the Christians' flight from Jerusalem before its destruction by Titus in A.D. 70. A literal flight from Rome surrounded by armies may have been impossible. To move out of the city before the armies came would either mean moving to another city with the same characteristics, or living a nomadic existence. It is unlikely that John intended such an instruction. To separate oneself from all involvement in the cultural, economic, and political life of the city would be irresponsible at best. John does not mean a literal migration from the city before an actual destruction by armies. He means for Christians to live in relationship to God and not to surrender themselves to the great city.

Reasons for Deserting Rome. John sees four good reasons for the Christians to desert the totalitarian claims of Rome. (1) There is always the danger of taking *part in her sins.* The culture of the great city has alluring charm. (2) Participation in her sins would lead to sharing *in her plagues.* (3) Rome had accumulated a pile of sins which stood as high as the architects in Babel had hoped to build their tower. When one buys stock in the great secular city, he accepts her liabilities as well as her assets. (4) Punishment is inevitable; God forgives, and hence forgets the sins of repenting sinners; but, God remembers *iniquities* for which no repentance is made; they cry out like Abel's blood; God cannot ignore sin.

Instructions Concerning Rome's Treatment. The text does not indicate that the statements following (v. 6 f.) are intended for someone other than Christians, but the context does. R. H. Charles calls them the "ministers of God's wrath"; Beckwith spoke of them as "spirits of vengeance"; Caird sees them as "angelic agents of retribution." The Christians are not the agents of judgment.

While the translation sounds vindictive, the term *Render to her as she herself has rendered* means only that her punishment is in keeping with her sin. God's judgment is just; it is meted out on the basis of what the accused has done (Jer. 50:15,29; 51:24,56). Jesus said, "The measure you give will be the measure you get" (Matt. 7:2). The *double* repayment for *deeds* is not an arbitrary severity; sins such as persecuting the Christians have an accumulative seriousness; they result in other sins and sufferings; they multiply their harmful effects. The *double draught* is based on the fact that Rome had made the nations drunk (14:8, 10), and now she receives the same punishment.

Justification for Rome's Punishment. Our author sees three reasons for Rome's severe punishment: (1) *she glorified herself;* (2) she claimed to be a self-sufficient *queen,* supreme even over the future; (3) the Lord God is the judge of all.

Human sin is the inordinate love of self which results in the subordination of God; it is pride. Man is God's creature; he must glorify God. There is no greater sin than self-glory. Rome—as all other human collectives whether political, economic, or ecclesiastical are tempted on inclined to do—became enamored with herself even while she was *wanton;* she deserved *torment* and *mourning.*

Isaiah's oracle concerning the doom of Babylon appears to have been in John's present description of Rome. Babylon was a "mistress of kingdoms"; she boasted, "I shall be mistress for ever"; she sat securely thinking herself supreme; she said "I shall not sit as a widow"; her ruin and widowhood came "in one day" (Isa. 47:5–11). Now, Rome repeats the same vain claim of self-sufficiency and perpetuity. Her complete destruction shall come suddenly, *in a single day.*

The Lord God has given freedom to his creatures, but he is responsible and expects them to be. They will all stand before God and be judged. Man makes history; it appears at times to be meaningless and un-directed; but history comes under the judgment of God. Rome, in all her power, stands naked and alone before God to answer for her deeds. Modern kingdoms, with their overweening pride and haughtiness, must also stand before God.

3. The Kings Lament Rome's Fall (18:9-10)

⁹ And the kings of the earth, who committed fornication and were wanton with her, will weep and wail over her when they see the smoke of her burning; ¹⁰ they will stand far off, in fear of her torment, and say,
"Alas! alas! thou great city,
thou mighty city, Babylon!
In one hour has thy judgment come."

Those who benefited most from their contracts with Rome—allied kings, merchants, and mariners—successively mourn her sudden fall. Their dirges are simultaneously sad and beautiful; Rome was beautiful; Rome was truly a great city; even in her fall the grandeur showed. Regardless of their profit motive, they betray a deep love for Rome. John reveals an incredible appreciation for the great city; this genuine regard tempers his feelings against her.

The *kings of the earth* are not the Parthians or the ten horns (17:14) who destroy Rome; they are the kings who joined Rome and shared her wealth at the expense of their own integrity. They loved luxury as she did; they *committed fornication* with her. Their weeping and wailing *over her* was genuine; ironically, they stood at a safe distance watching the column of smoke which marked her burning. She was abandoned by her adulterous lovers in the loneliness of her judgment.

The kings' dirge correctly acknowledges that Babylon and Rome were truly *great* and mighty cities. From *far off* and in great *fear,* the kings note that all of her greatness has collapsed in *one hour,* which is the length of time allotted to the kings who make war on the Lamb (17:12–14).

The kings' lamentation should be compared to that of the princes who mourned the fall of Tyre (Ezek. 26:15–18).

4. The Merchants Lament Rome's Fall (18:11–17a)

11 And the merchants of the earth weep and mourn for her, since no one buys their cargo any more, 12 cargo of gold, silver, jewels and pearls, fine linen, purple, silk and scarlet, all kinds of scented wood, all articles of ivory, all articles of costly wood, bronze, iron and marble, 13 cinnamon, spice, incense, myrrh, frankincense, wine, oil, fine flour and wheat, cattle and sheep, horses and chariots, and slaves, that is, human souls.
14 "The fruit for which thy soul longed has gone from thee,
and all thy dainties and thy splendor are lost to thee, never to be found again!"
15 The merchants of these wares, who gained wealth from her, will stand far off, in fear of her torment, weeping and mourning aloud,
16 "Alas, alas, for the great city
that was clothed in fine linen, in purple and scarlet,
bedecked with gold, with jewels, and with pearls!
17 In one hour all this wealth has been laid waste."

Rome was the business capital of the world. She was the dominant maritime power. Her merchant marine brought goods from every part of the known world. Rome derived great wealth from this trade. Ancient Tyre had been the middleman of the Mediterranean world. Ezekiel (27) had portrayed Tyre's commerce and had listed most of the imports which are listed here by John. The Roman port, Ostia, was one of the greatest trading centers in history.

The Merchants of Earth. The businessmen of the ancient world were heartless, too. John described the *kings of earth* in more charitable terms; they had committed adultery with Rome; they stood *far off* when she burned; but they were moved; they cared. The *merchants of earth* wept over Rome's fall for only one reason: *no one* bought *their cargo any more.* John is ruthless in his description of them. They looked upon Rome's fall and noted with *mourning* that *all this wealth has been laid waste.* Their hearts were not moved by the fall of a great city; no emotions or sentiments were stirred except those based on economic greed.

Warring kings and adulterous lovers are gifted with a degree of companionship and understanding when compared to the *merchants of earth.* Some merchants will sell weapons to both sides in a war and weep when one destroys the other only because a better balance would have prolonged the market. Some will advertise dishonestly to sell merchandise which is actually harmful to its buyers. Some live on the profits of selling products to people who do not need them and cannot afford them. A warring king takes risks and "feels" something even for the vanquished; an adulterous lover, even in desertion, has known an involvement and has some care; the merchant dominated completely by the profit motive is incapable of a true lamentation; he must look for another market.

The Cargo. John listed 28 separate import items. His reason is to show the luxury of Rome. There is no hidden meaning, but there are many interesting details and implications in his list (see Bible dictionary on each item.) Since the first eight fall naturally into two groups of four, many efforts have been made to group all of them according to some scheme (Charles, II, 102; Beckwith, p. 715 ff.).

It is obvious that (1) *gold, silver, jewels,* and *pearls* are precious metals and stones for jewelry. (2) Fine *linen, purple, silk,* and *scarlet* are for luxurious clothing. (3) *Scented wood, ivory,* and *costly wood* are used in expensive and ornate furniture. (4) *Bronze, iron,* and *marble* may continue the furniture line or designate building materials. (5) *Cinnamon, spice, incense, myrrh,* and *frankincense* are probably perfume-type cosmetics. (6) *Wine, oil, fine flour,* and *wheat* would be staple food items unless *fine* suggests luxury. (7) Regrettably, *slaves* who are *human souls,* were imported along with *cattle, sheep, horses,* and *chariots.* Modern dehumanization is economic, political, military, and religious as it was in Rome.

The *fruit* is that which ripens in late summer or early autumn. This lamentation points out that the fruit for which the *soul* has *longed* is gone; it will not ripen in the autumn. The *dainties* (*lipara*) and the *splendor* (*lampra*) form a play on similar words. The dainties are probably the rich and dainty foods; the splendor probably means the gay attire and costly furniture which came as a result of Rome's conquests and national policy (Swete, p. 235). One could expect the fruit in a later season, but there is no hope for Rome. Her hopes are gone forever, *never to be found again!*

The Lamentation. No patriotic love nor filial respect marks the merchants' dirge. It is motivated by their loss of wealth (v. 15); its statements are concerned with the symbols of Rome's wealth now lost (v. 16); they stand at a safe distance, *far off.* The *kings of earth* had recognized Rome's fall as *judgment;* the *merchants of earth* overlook any meaning; they see only *wealth* which has *been laid waste.*

5. Sailors Lament Rome's Fall (18:17b–20)

And all shipmasters and seafaring men, sailors and all whose trade is on the sea, stood far off [18] and cried out as they saw the smoke of her burning,
"What city was like the great city?"
[19] And they threw dust on their heads, as they wept and mourned, crying out,
"Alas, alas, for the great city
    where all who had ships at sea grew rich by her wealth!
In one hour she has been laid waste.
[20] Rejoice over her, O heaven,
    O saints and apostles and prophets,
    for God has given judgment for you against her!"

The Mariners. The *shipmasters* were the captains in command of the ships and were distinguished from the ship owners (Acts 27:11), who may not have been aboard. The *seafaring men* were all travelers by sea—crewmen, businessmen, tourists, passengers, etc. *Sailors* were the crewmen who manned the ships.

The Mariners' Lamentation. From afar these seafaring people watch the smoke of the burning city. Their grief, though profit is involved, appears to be genuine. They cry that *the great city* had no equals; they *threw dust on their heads* showing deep grief; they *wept* and *mourned* as did the mariners when Tyre fell (Ezek. 27:29–34); they paid tribute to the city to whose port *all* sea lanes led; they lamented the suddenness of her fall *in one hour.*

The Judgment of Rome. The RSV has placed v. 20 in quotes also as if the mariners address God's hosts with the announcement of his judgment. The poet and apocalyptic writer certainly has the freedom to do this, but the change is abrupt. Interpreters ask on what basis the mariners could address *heaven, saints, apostles,* and *prophets* with such a theological interpretation. R. H. Charles therefore deleted the passage. Caird sees it as an introduction to the following paragraph, but this ignores the obvious change in the next statement. The angel has been speaking since 18:4; whether this is the angel's interpretation or the mariners' interpretation related by the angel is not crucial. It is obviously in contrast with the preceding statement and appears to be in contrast with the rejoicing of 11:10. In that passage, earth inhabitants rejoiced at the death of the two witnesses. Now, God's faithful are told to rejoice, but not primarily because Rome has fallen, but because God has given his judgment against Rome and *for* his faithful ones.

6. The Millstone Vision (18:21–24)

[21] Then a mighty angel took up a stone like a great millstone and threw it into the sea, saying,
"So shall Babylon the great city be thrown down with violence,
    and shall be found no more;
[22] and the sound of harpers and minstrels, of flute players and trumpeters,
    shall be heard in thee no more;
and a craftsman of any craft
    shall be found in thee no more;
and the sound of the millstone
    shall be heard in thee no more;
[23] and the light of a lamp
    shall shine in thee no more;
and the voice of bridegroom and bride
    shall be heard in thee no more;
for thy merchants were the great men of the earth,
    and all nations were deceived by thy sorcery.

24 And in her was found the blood of prophets
and of saints,
and of all who have been slain on earth."

The Symbolic Act. A mighty angel (see comment on 5:2; 10:2) threw a *great millstone* into the *sea* and pronounced the fall of *Babylon.* The symbolic act shows the suddenness and finality of the fall. It is not to be understood literally; Jeremiah had used the figure of a stone cast into the Euphrates to symbolize the fall of Babylon (Jer. 51:63). The act may allude to Jesus' statement about the judgment on one who caused "little ones to sin" (Luke 17:2).

The Angel's Interpretation of the Meaning. The fall of Rome is portrayed in a deeply moving way by four terms: violence, permanence, silence, and darkness. The *violence* is only mentioned in this passage; the permanence appears in the statement that she *shall be found no more.* John displays genuine poetic imagination in his description of the fallen city in terms of its silence and darkness. He does so by pointing out those sounds and sights which give a city its character.

The sounds and the sights of the city may be taken for granted until the city lies in ruins. With little imagination one can feel the dreadful loneliness of the quiet and dark city. John could have chosen many sounds to describe the city. He selected three: they are music, the sounds of working craftsmen, and the *voice of bridegroom and bride.* A great city knows the joy, gaiety, and music (see Bible dictionary on musical terms). How could one describe more clearly the utter desolation of a city than to point out the absence of music?

In the city one hears the saw and hammer, as craftsmen build houses; he hears the distinctive ringing rhythm of the blacksmith shop; he hears the noise of the factory. After Rome's fall, these sounds will be heard no more—only the deathly silence of the ghost town. In the living city one hears the joyful voices from the wedding party; in fallen Rome these cheerful voices are heard no more.

John cites only one illustration that appeals to sight—the *lamp* which lights the city. The lights in the homes and on the streets give a city its charm and friendliness. A blackout during a war is a cold and lonely experience. Rome will be clothed in darkness.

The desolation is final; the sounds of arts, crafts, and family are heard no more; the concert hall, the blacksmith shop, and the church are silent; the sounds of joy, and work, and home are heard no more.

Justification of Rome's Fall. The angel concludes his statement with three reasons why Rome has fallen: (1) Rome had the world's power; her merchants were *the great men.* Possession of power in the world grants opportunity and demands responsibility. Rome had used her power for her own exaltation. (2) She *deceived* nations by her *sorcery;* the black arts curse those who use them as well as the victims; power corrupts. Rome had earned her punishment. (3) Rome had killed the *prophets* and *saints;* their *blood* cried out to God; Christians had been taught to endure and not to retaliate; Rome had confused love with weakness. The nation which kills its prophets and saints plots its own ruin.

7. Heaven's Approval (19:1-5)

1 After this I heard what seemed to be the mighty voice of a great multitude in heaven, crying,
"Hallelujah! Salvation and glory and power
belong to our God,
2 for his judgments are true and just;
he has judged the great harlot who corrupted the earth with her fornication,
and he has avenged on her the blood of his
servants."
3 Once more they cried,
"Hallelujah! The smoke from her goes up for
ever and ever."
4 And the twenty-four elders and the four living creatures fell down and worshiped God who is seated on the throne, saying, "Amen. Hallelujah!" 5 And from the throne came a voice crying,
"Praise our God, all you his servants,
you who fear him, small and great."

Commentaries differ as to the paragraph divisions in this section. I have chosen to divide after v. 5 because it appears that these statements are praises to God for the judgment on Rome; beginning with v. 6, though the praise continues, the direction is changed to the future; the subject matter is the coming marriage of the Lamb.

The spirit and movement of this passage have been captured by the "Hallelujah Chorus" of Handel's great oratorio, *The Messiah,* which drew from this passage and from Revelation 11:15. We shall understand these statements more clearly if we think of *The Messiah.*

Praise of the Multitude. Rome's destruction is now complete (in anticipation); the hosts of heaven burst into a *Hallelujah* chorus. Although we may have expected the praise to have come first from *saints, apostles,* and *prophets* (18:20), the *multitude* is much more inclusive, probably the great multitude of 7:9 or the angelic host of 5:11. *Hallelujah* is a Hebrew word used frequently in the Psalms to introduce or conclude a song, and is translated "Praise the Lord." It appears in noncanonical writings, but appears in the New Testament only in this chapter.

The first "Hallelujah" consists of four lines, each of which makes a distinct affirmation: (1) God is to be praised because now men recognize his *salvation, glory,* and *power.* His salvation and power appeared in 12:10; his glory and power were joined in 4:11. Salvation belongs to God (7:10); man does not earn or possess it; man enters God's salvation by faith. Salvation is more than the deliverance of the saints; it includes God's safeguarding them and bringing them and his whole cause to final victory. (2) Then, the multitude affirms that God's *judgments are true and just.* Previously, the altar had made this affirmation (16:7); the servants had lived by faith in this affirmation and the hope it expressed (15:3); now their faith has been vindicated; they know by experience that it is true. (3) The third affirmation justifies the second by citing his judgment on Rome, *the great harlot.* The angel had promised that he would judge her (17:1); God kept the promise so he is *true.* His judgment is *just*

for two reasons: she deserved the judgment because she was a harlot; she multiplied her guilt by corrupting *the earth with her fornication.* (4) Finally, the *servants* had been taught to be faithful unto death; they had been true and had suffered; God *avenged* their blood thus proving his trustworthiness.

The second "Hallelujah" points out the visible evidence of God's judgment; the *smoke* ascending is perpetual evidence that God's judgment is sure. One should not push the term *for ever and ever* or should not interpret it in relationship to the smoke. The idea of a new heaven and earth would make it unlikely that a spiral of smoke from Rome's ruins would be seen eternally.

Praise by Elders and Cherubim. The permanent attendants of God's throne proclaim their approval of God's judgment. Earlier in the drama they led the worship (4:9-10; 5:8; 5:14; 7:11; 14:3). This is their last appearance in Revelation. The *Amen* is merely an affirmation of "truly" or "verily." They only say, in effect, "Amen, Praise God!"

The Voice from the Throne. The fourth "Hallelujah" exhorts all *servants* to praise God. Hallelujah is translated *Praise our God.* The use of *our God* suggests that Christ is the speaker. In an earlier round of praising God, the participants praised God in a sequence which started at the throne and worked outward—cherubim and elders, angelic hosts, then all creatures. In this round the order is reversed.

IX. The Final Victory of the Lamb (19:6—20:15)

1. Announcement of the Marriage of the Lamb (19:6-10)

6 Then I heard what seemed to be the voice of a great multitude, like the sound of many waters and like the sound of mighty thunderpeals, crying,
"Hallelujah! For the Lord our God the Almighty reigns.
7 Let us rejoice and exult and give him the glory,
for the marriage of the Lamb has come, and his Bride has made herself ready;

8 it was granted her to be clothed with fine linen, bright and pure"—
for the fine linen is the righteous deeds of the saints.

9 And the angel said to me, "Write this: Blessed are those who are invited to the marriage supper of the Lamb." And he said to me, "These are true words of God." **10** Then I fell down at his feet to worship him, but he said to me, "You must not do that! I am a fellow servant with you and your brethren who hold the testimony of Jesus. Worship God." For the testimony of Jesus is the spirit of prophecy.

A change in the direction of the drama is indicated by *Then I heard*. The preceding hallelujah chorus was sung in the light of the fall and judgment of the harlot; this praise is to God because of what is now envisioned as coming. It is already present by anticipation. The *great mutitude* may be the same as that in 19:1. The description that it sounded like a roaring waterfall or *mighty thunderpeals* may or may not indicate another multitude (see 1:15; 14:2).

The Almighty Reigns. The call to praise God is based on the affirmation that the *Almighty reigns*. This is John's favorite term for God. The statement should not be understood as implying that he had not been sovereign before. During the time of man's sinfulness, God's world has been abused; God's people have been oppressed; now God has actively asserted control. His kingdom, promised and known partially by those in faith, has now come in its fullness.

The Marriage Predicted. In this symbol, John brings together several symbolic ideas: the reign of God as a feast, Israel as the bride of Yahweh, and the clean garments of purity. The call to rejoicing and glorifying God is justified by the promise of the forthcoming marriage. This is a prediction of the final consummation which takes place in 21:11–22:5.

The Old Testament writers employed the metaphor of marriage to indicate the bond of love between God and Israel (Isa. 54:5, 6; Ezek. 16:8–14; Hos. 2:19–20). The metaphor appears in several adaptations in the New Testament to portray the love of Christ for his faithful followers. Christ used it, and it is used of him in the Gospels

(Matt. 22:1–14; 25:1–13; Mark 2:19–20; John 3:29). After the resurrection the term is used to describe the relationship between Christ and the church (2 Cor. 11:2; Eph. 5:22–27).

The Readiness of the Bride. In Revelation, the Bride is the general or universal church sometimes called the holy city and the new Jerusalem (21:2). There can be no doubt as to John's intention for this Bride to be in contrast to the great harlot (ch. 17). Apart from the woman Jezebel (2:20), John mentions only three women in Revelation: the mother of chapter 12, the harlot of chapter 17, and the Bride. We noted that the heavenly mother was the heavenly or ideal Israel who bore the messiah. The harlot Babylon was Rome or the great city of man. The Bride is the church of earth which awaits the coming of Christ. There is no reason for confusion in the fact that John uses both symbols, mother and bride. John's use of symbols is not pedantic or literal.

Joy is the dominant theme suggested by the readiness of the Bride. The bridal gown is *bright and pure* in contrast to the purple and scarlet of the great harlot. White garments are always the symbol of purity. The harlot was gaudily bedecked with "gold and jewels and pearls," but the Bride had no need of such artificial ornaments. The Bride wears the *fine linen* which John makes symbolic of the *righteous deeds of the saints*. She is adorned with living deeds of righteousness. Some authorities, thinking this statement (v. 8*b*) is awkward, delete it as a gloss. It makes good sense as it is since the victorious Christians are attired in white and since their faithfulness is a part of heaven's victory over evil.

The Fourth Beatitude. The angel is evidently the guiding angel who explained the visions of chapter 17. His command to write is a reminder of the importance of what follows. This beatitude (see 1:3; 14:13; 16:15; 20:6; 22:7; 22:14) pronounces *Blessed* (happy or to-be-congratulated) are those *invited* to the *marriage supper*. The term "invited" is a form of the verb call but does not have the same significance as the terms "called" and "chosen" (17:14). The kingdom of heaven has included the idea of a marriage feast (Matt. 22:1–14; 25:1–13). A messianic banquet was anticipated in connection with the coming of the Messiah. John combines these ideas into the *marriage supper of the Lamb*. In one sense, those invited are the same as the church, the Bride. In another sense, one must consider the wedding banquet as something very special, not to be assumed, but for the invited. Happy indeed are those who are invited to the feast. In 3:20 Christ stands at the door and knocks; table fellowship is offered to those who respond. This promise has been fulfilled in that Christ now invites followers to his marriage feast.

John sometimes makes oath-like assurances regarding the truthfulness of his statements (21:5; 22:6). The angel authenticated this section (17:1—19:9) by his statement *These are true words of God*.

Prohibition of Angel Worship. Although the angel had been speaking for some time, John was awestruck at the reference to the true word of God. He *fell down* as if *to worship* the angel. The angel rebuked him and insisted that he was a *fellow servant*. When Peter arrived at the house of Cornelius, the centurion fell down before Peter, who rebuked him for it (Acts 10:25). In Lystra, Paul and Barnabas were mistaken for deities; Paul rebuked men for attempting to worship other men (Acts 14:15). It is strange that John made this mistake after his close association with the angel; it is doubly strange that he made the same mistake twice (22:8). Perhaps John is trying to correct the angel-worship known to have prevailed in Asia (Col. 2:18), but he did not specifically refer to it in the letters to the seven churches.

The angel's insistence that he was a fellow servant means that all creatures, human and angelic, worship only God.

The *testimony of Jesus* is the witness he bore in life and death which became the basis of victory over evil (1:5; 3:14). To *hold the testimony of Jesus* is to stand faith-

fully on Jesus' principle of life which is the giving of self in faithfulness to God. John considered his exile to have been the result of his testimony to Jesus (1:1,9). The dragon was angry with the offspring of the woman for their "testimony to Jesus" (12: 17). This witnessing is the identifying mark of discipleship. It has nothing to do with a verbal statement of faith; it involves a life committed to Jesus in such a way that one gives himself.

2. The Word of God on the White Horse (19:11–16)

¹¹ Then I saw heaven opened, and behold, a white horse! He who sat upon it is called Faithful and True, and in righteousness he judges and makes war. ¹² His eyes are like a flame of fire, and on his head are many diadems; and he has a name inscribed which no one knows but himself. ¹³ He is clad in a robe dipped in blood, and the name by which he is called is The Word of God. ¹⁴ And the armies of heaven, arrayed in fine linen, white and pure, followed him on white horses. ¹⁵ From his mouth issues a sharp sword with which to smite the nations, and he will rule them with a rod of iron; he will tread the wine press of the fury of the wrath of God the Almighty. ¹⁶ On his robe and on his thigh he has a name inscribed, King of kings and Lord of lords.

This new vision, introduced by *I saw*, appears to John through the open doors of heaven. Some call this the most detailed and vivid description of the return of Christ found in the New Testament and compare it with 1 Thessalonians 4:16–18 (Glasson, p. 109). The text, however, does not indicate a return to earth at this time; it is a description of Christ in heaven. The magnitude of the event to be described is indicated by the expression *heaven opened* (Ezek. 1:1; Matt. 3:16). The heavenly Christ is now ready for the great battle.

His Description. John describes the coming Lord with seven identifying terms. (1) He rode a *white horse* which is symbolic of the conquerer, victory. This horse must not be confused with the horse of 6:2; that horse symbolized conquest; its rider carried a bow; it was followed by bloodshed. This white horse bears a rider who is Christ.

(2) His *eyes are like a flame of fire* (see comment on 1:14; 2:18). (3) He wears *many diadems* on his head in contrast to the dragon which wore seven diadems (12:3) and the sea beast which had ten (13:1). (4) He has a secret *name* inscribed which only he understands. Since another name is inscribed on his robe, it is likely that this name is on his head or diadems. (5) He wore a *robe dipped in blood.*

There are three leading interpretations of the blood: it is the blood of the Lamb; it is the blood of Christ's enemies; it is the blood of the martyrs. Since Christ here appears as the warrior, not the Lamb, and since John usually specifies the blood of the Lamb when he intends it (5:9; 7:14; 12:11), many assume it cannot be the blood of Christ himself. However, if it were so, it would give a meaningful contrast with the white robes of his followers cleansed by his blood.

Many commentators prefer to interpret the blood as that of Christ's enemies (so Charles, Swete, Beckwith, *et al.*). The figure appears to be related to Isaiah 63: 1–4, in which God punished Edom and returned with his apparel red from treading "the wine press . . . their lifeblood . . . stained [his] raiment." Charles sees the blood as that of the Parthian kings (17:14); others interpret the blood as that from the enemies yet to be slain. G. B. Caird, assuming that some connection with the vintage of 14:18–20 is definitely implied, argues that the blood on Christ's garment symbolizes the blood of the martyrs (Caird, p. 243). In the light of John's free use of symbols, it is entirely possible that he means to symbolize Christ's own sacrifice, the blood of the Lamb, or his judgment in victory, the blood of his enemies, or the blood of the martyrs. This last interpretation requires us to assume that the faithful witness of the Christians is a part of Christ's own victory.

(6) Christ's mouth held a *sharp sword* which protruded like a tongue. This strange symbol has already appeared (see comment on 1:16; 2:12,16); its meaning is that Christ's only weapon is his word. Isaiah had written that God would "smite the earth with the rod of his mouth" (11:4) and that God's mouth was "like a shorp sword" (49: 2). Paul had referred to the "sword of the Spirit, . . . the word of God" (Eph. 6:17). In Hebrews 4:12 "The word of God is . . . sharper than any two-edged sword, . . ." Christ will smite the nations with this word (19:15); he has no other weapons. Swete sees this as the power of the gospel as it sweeps across the world (Swete, p. 254).

(7) *His robe* and *his thigh* bore an inscription *King of kings and Lord of lords.* Christ appears in great majesty on the white horse of victory, eyes flaming, diadems in abundance, a secret name, a robe stained with blood, his word ready to smite, and wearing the supreme title of sovereignty.

His Names. John employs four different names for Christ in this passage. (1) He is called *Faithful and True* (see comment on 1:5; 3:7,14). (2) John speaks of a secret *name inscribed* which *no one knows* but Christ. R. H. Charles (II, 132) argued that this statement breaks the train of thought, is actually contradicted by the giving of the name later, and should be excised as an interpolation. The interpretation is unnecessary. Knowing the name of God is important as it was in the case of Moses' call (Ex. 3:14). To know his name is to be in fellowship with him, to be able to pray to him. The name of Jesus was used in healing diseases. There was a current belief that hidden names had marvelous power; by this name Christ could subdue his foes (Beckwith, p. 732). This name of Jesus is related to the name written on the stone and given to the Christian who conquers (2:17); Christ's own "new name" will be inscribed on the Christian victor (3:12); this name was inscribed on the Lamb's followers (14: 1). Rist believes the name is simply "Jesus," in spite of the objection that it is too obvious. He points out that if one follows the same cryptography which identifies the Antichrist with 666, he will see that Jesus is 888. This would be an ideal foil to the secret name of the Antichrist (Rist, p. 513).

(3) Another name is *The Word of God,* but this is not necessarily a translation of the secret name. In the Old Testament, God's word was powerful, dependable, and seemed to have a tangible existence beyond its original verbalization (Isa. 55:11). God had created the world by speaking his word (Gen. 1). John's gospel (John 1:1–14) interprets Jesus as the Word of God who was "in the beginning . . . with God . . . and . . . was God, and . . . became flesh." The same idea is present elsewhere (1 John 1:1; Heb. 1:2). Theologically, there is no name with more significance than "The Word of God." God who spoke in the Old Testament days in various ways had now spoken his clearest message to man in Jesus Christ, *The Word of God.*

(4) The name *King of kings and Lord of lords* was on his robe and thigh. In the prediction of his battle with the kings (17:14), he has the same title but the terms are reversed. His complete sovereignty is pictured in the name.

His Army. The *armies of heaven* are understood by some to be angelic hosts, by others to be composed of the martyrs. Their *white horses* suggest victory. Legions of angels were mentioned as available to help Christ if called upon (Matt. 26:53), but this is a symbolic way of speaking about God's protection. These troops are not in battle dress; they wear robes of *fine linen, white and pure.* The description suggests the martyrs who follow Christ (14:4). The Christians had been promised (2:26–27) that if they overcame they would share Christ's rule. Christ's followers when attacked by the ten kings were described as "called," "chosen," and "faithful" (17:14); this would not fit the angels. The two passages are further related by the use of the term *King of kings and Lord of lords.* The martyrs had been victorious in life and now share in Christ's ultimate victory.

His Mission. Messianic hope included the expectation that the Messiah would execute judgment and make war upon the enemies of God and his people. The threefold mis-sion of judging, making war, and reigning is now accomplished. The militaristic sound of making war should be understood in the light of Christ's only weapon—his word—and the reminder that his followers bore no arms. He accomplished his victory over his foes not in a conventional war. His word is more powerful than any human weapon. (On *rod of iron* see 2:27; on *fury of the wrath of God* see comment on 14:19–20 and 16:19.)

3. The Battle of Armageddon (19:17–21)

[17] Then I saw an angel standing in the sun, and with a loud voice he called to all the birds that fly in midheaven, "Come, gather for the great supper of God, [18] to eat the flesh of kings, the flesh of captains, the flesh of mighty men, the flesh of horses and their riders, and the flesh of all men, both free and slave, both small and great." [19] And I saw the beast and the kings of the earth with their armies gathered to make war against him who sits upon the horse and against his army. [20] And the beast was captured, and with it the false prophet who in its presence had worked the signs by which he deceived those who had received the mark of the beast and those who worshiped its image. These two were thrown alive into the lake of fire that burns with brimstone. [21] And the rest were slain by the sword of him who sits upon the horse, the sword that issues from his mouth; and all the birds were gorged with their flesh.

The only biblical reference to the name Armageddon is in Revelation 16:16 (see comment), in which there is only the prediction of the battle. John presents the fulfillment of that prediction in this paragraph. It is of great significance that he portrays not the battle itself but only the summons, the adversaries, and a view of the defeat with its gruesome carnage. This paragraph is very similar to Ezekiel 39:17–20, in which God commanded the birds to be summoned to a sacrificial feast at which he would serve the flesh and blood of Gog's princes and mighty men. The birds and beasts would eat and drink in gluttony and drunkenness. John apparently has used this grim carnage to describe the fall of evil. In true apocalyptic fashion, it is gruesome and cruel. It is in contrast to the marriage feast of the

Lamb (19:9).

The Summons to Battle. In keeping with John's belief that even evil somehow answered to God's sovereignty, an *angel* issued the summons. The angel stood *in the sun* and spoke *with a loud voice* so that every eye would see and every ear hear. The call was to the *great supper of God* (cf. Ezek. 39:17) to eat the flesh of men and animals. All divisions of men are named. Perhaps, one could think of a defeat in war as an evidence of God's judgment, but the gruesome details of this supper are incompatible with the nature of the Lamb and his sacrifice. It must be seen symbolically.

The Army of Evil. The evil forces were led by the *beast* (see comment on ch. 13); his forces included the *kings of the earth* (see comment on 6:15; 16:14; 17:2) and their armies. John intends us to envision all of earth's evil powers in coalition under the power of the beast attacking Christ and his followers.

The Defeat of Evil. John makes no statement about the battle which is evidence that he does not intend to describe an earthly military campaign but a spiritual struggle. He portrays only the result—defeat. The *beast* is captured along with his chief lieutenant, the *false prophet,* who has been identified as the Roman religious cult (13:11–18). He had used deceptive *signs* to deceive people. (On the *mark of the beast* and its *image,* see comment on 13: 17; 14:9,11; 16:2.) These leaders were thrown into the *lake of fire* (see below).

The followers of the beast, *the rest,* were slain by the *sword that issues from* Christ's *mouth.* This conveys in the foreign language of apocalyptic the idea that Christ's word defeats or slays the wicked. The hideous picture of total disaster is that of a battlefield strewn with corpses being eaten by vultures.

Charles thinks the slaughter should be taken quite literally; Christ killed the captives and sent their spirits to Hades. Swete understands it spiritually since the sword of his mouth is not a literal or lethal weapon. It is unthinkable that Christ would line up the captives and literally slaughter them. There is no textual problem to explain the difficulty. Revelation is apocalyptic; the language is strange. This confronts the interpreter in many passages. Christ rejected a kingdom of this world based on military power; taken literally, this passage portrays him as establishing his kingdom in the manner he rejected during the incarnation. It is more Judaistic than Christian. This favors an interpretation of the war as the struggle of evil forces against God, who finally overthrows them.

The Lake of Fire. Revelation does not use the word "hell"; it speaks of the *lake of fire* (19:20; 20:10,14,15; 21:8). Both biblical and nonbiblical sources have a considerable amount of indefiniteness about the terms for the future age. In the Old Testament, Sheol was the dark and cheerless realm of the dead. In Greek translations Sheol appears as "Hades," the abode of the dead. Evidently, because of its destructive nature, the fiery element developed during the intertestamental period.

Jesus referred to the abode of the dead, places of suffering and blessing, and the final states of man in a traditional manner. In the story of the rich man and Lazarus (Luke 16:19–31) we have distinctions between the temporary abode of the wicked and the righteous. Abraham's bosom is pleasant; Hades, formerly the abode of the dead, now has fire in it. Even though this scene is this side of the final judgment, it has a note of permanence in the great gulf. The term hell (Gehenna) draws some of its imagery from the valley outside Jerusalem (Hinnom), which was used for the city dump. Its burning continuously reflected waste, judgment, and rejection. In Matthew 25:41 the Son of man will consign the wicked to "the eternal fire prepared for the devil and his angels."

In Revelation, the abyss or "bottomless pit" is a preliminary abode for fallen angels, demons, the beast, and the false prophet (9:1,2,11; 11:7; 17:8; 20:1,3). The temporary nature is seen in 17:8 in contrast to "perdition."

The *lake of fire* is John's term for Gehenna or hell. It is a permanent abode. It is for the beast, the devil, the dragon, the false prophet (19:20; 20:10). Death and Hades will be placed there (20:14); all whose names are not in the book of life will go to the lake of fire (20:15); all wicked people will go to this permanent punishment (21:8).

Numerous references to this place of hell appear in the other apocalyptic works (1 Enoch 54:1-6; 90:24-27; 108:1-6). The "lake of torment" is in contrast to the "place of rest," and the "furnace of the Pit" to the "paradise of joy" (2 Esdras 7:36).

In spite of moral protests to the contrary such as the assertion that punishment without hope of correction and release is contrary to the nature of God, John sees the *lake of fire* as an eternal place of punishment. But it is punishment in a kind of existence which men have chosen—without God.

4. The Binding of Satan (20:1-3)

¹ Then I saw an angel coming down from heaven, holding in his hand the key of the bottomless pit and a great chain. ² And he seized the dragon, that ancient serpent, who is the Devil and Satan, and bound him for a thousand years, ³ and threw him into the pit, and shut it and sealed it over him, that he should deceive the nations no more, till the thousand years were ended. After that he must be loosed for a little while.

John had exhorted the Christians to be faithful to God during their persecution by Rome; many had been faithful to the death. John had promised them victory through suffering; it has come. In the previous chapters he showed how Satan's agents, Rome, the imperial cult, etc., had been overthrown. The beast and the false prophet had been cast into the lake of fire. Now, it is time for Satan to be bound. This is a cosmic victory, the removal of evil's king.

The new vision is marked by the formula, *I saw*. The *angel* from *heaven* is probably the same one which fell like a star (9:1) since he holds the *key of the bottomless pit.*

His origin in heaven and possession of the key suggest that the bottomless pit is under the ultimate jurisdiction of heaven. John employs four symbols to portray Satan's limitation: the key, the chain, the pit, and the seal on its door. The security of the pit is guaranteed by the fact that the *key* is kept in heaven; the *great chain* would hinder Satan's activity during his confinement; the *pit* is secure in itself; the angel *sealed it,* presumably with God's seal, thus preventing any tampering.

The sovereignty of God is implied in the simple assertion that the angel *seized* the dragon; there is no hint of struggle; God gives the orders. (On the identification of the *dragon* with the *serpent*, the *Devil*, and *Satan*, see comment on 12:9.)

Satan's purpose had been to *deceive the nations;* he will do this no more for a *thousand years.* Satan had accomplished his deception through his subordinates, the beasts who had been captured. Now the victory is complete in that Satan is bound; but, it is temporary; he must *be loosed for a little while.* The difficulty of these phrases offers us a clue for their understanding. If the struggle between God and Satan were a literal one, why merely throw him into the bottomless pit? Why not destroy him completely? Or, why release him after the thousand years? What claim does Satan have on God? Obviously, these questions miss the point. John is not writing about Satan's destiny or rights; he is portraying the Christian victory.

Satan's power had seemed so great to the Christians; really, it is as nothing. John had repeatedly portrayed the temporary character of evil's victories. He used terms such as three and one-half years, "a time, times, and half a time," 42 months, and 1260 days. The kings had authority for only "one hour" (17:12). Rome's ruin came in "one hour." In all of these terms, John stresses the brevity of evil's power. By contrast, Christ's power will involve a reign of a thousand years (see comment on 20:4-10).

No good reason can be offered for the loosing of Satan unless it is the belief that his evil influence is necessary to sift or test the Christians converted during the period.

5. The Millennium (20:4–10)

4 Then I saw thrones, and seated on them were those to whom judgment was committed. Also I saw the souls of those who had been beheaded for their testimony to Jesus and for the word of God, and who had not worshiped the beast or its image and had not received its mark on their foreheads or their hands. They came to life, and reigned with Christ a thousand years. 5 The rest of the dead did not come to life until the thousand years were ended. This is the first resurrection. 6 Blessed and holy is he who shares in the first resurrection! Over such the second death has no power, but they shall be priests of God and of Christ, and they shall reign with him a thousand years.

7 And when the thousand years are ended, Satan will be loosed from his prison 8 and will come out to deceive the nations which are at the four corners of the earth, that is, Gog and Magog, to gather them for battle; their number is like the sand of the sea. 9 And they marched up over the broad earth and surrounded the camp of the saints and the beloved city; but fire came down from heaven and consumed them, 10 and the devil who had deceived them was thrown into the lake of fire and brimstone where the beast and the false prophet were, and they will be tormented day and night for ever and ever.

The Thousand-Year Reign. The first ten verses of chapter 20 of Revelation include all of the specific biblical teaching on the thousand-year reign of Christ. In spite of volumes which have been written on the subject, John gave only a few specific details. During the millennium Satan will be bound; the faithful Christian martyrs will be raised from the dead at the beginning of the reign; they will sit on thrones and will share Christ's reign on earth; their state is blessed because they have no fear of the second death and they serve God and Christ as priests.

Not only is the millennium unique to the book of Revelation, but also the idea is of secondary importance in the paragraphs which present it. John's introduction of the millennium (20:3) is incidental to his discussion of the binding of Satan; the second paragraph which gives most of the informa-

tion (vv. 4–6) is actually dealing with the first resurrection and the joy of the martyrs who share it; the third paragraph (vv. 7–10) mentions the millennium only in connection with the loosing of Satan for a short period.

It must be asserted, however, that John is deeply convinced of Christ's coming to establish his sovereignty. John had written about the temporary triumph of evil in the work of the dragon and its beasts; Christians had died in the struggle. John proclaims that Jesus Christ will reign on earth, the scene of evil's short victory.

Furthermore, Christ's victory will be a long reign—a thousand years. The triumph of evil had been very brief. The two witnesses of God (11:3 ff.) had been killed and had lain exposed in dishonor on the street "three days and a half." God raised them from the dead. The dragon had attacked the mother of the Messiah, but his power was limited to three and one-half years (12:14). Christ will reign for a thousand years. The ten kings had power for only "one hour" (17:12); Christ will reign for a thousand years. Satan will be loosed for a "little while," but Christ will reign for a thousand years.

It also seems likely that John intends to stress that the reign of Christ will be on the earth. Interpreters differ greatly in their understanding of the millennium. Some see it as a future event expected to happen literally on earth with Christ ruling the world of believers and unbelievers. Others see it in spiritual terms as the "reign" which may have begun even in Christ's resurrection.

The First Resurrection. In Daniel's vision (Dan. 7) there are many features which are repeated in Revelation; one is a kingdom in which God's people share the reign by sitting on *thrones.* In this passage, the martyrs are raised from the dead in the first resurrection to share Christ's reign and judgment in keeping with an expectation encouraged by Jesus (Matt. 19:28).

This first resurrection includes only the martyrs who had been *beheaded* because of their faithful *testimony.* Additional evidence of their faithfulness is seen in the notation that they do not have the beast's mark on their *foreheads* and *hands.* John reemphasizes that only the martyrs are raised in the first resurrection by asserting that the *rest of the dead* were not raised until after the thousand years (Beckwith, p. 740; Rist, p. 520). Some interpreters think it possible that faithful Christians who resisted emperor worship but were not slain may have been included (Swete, p. 262; Barclay, II, 246; these would have been the "Confessors" of the later church). No other biblical evidence supports the idea that martyrs will be raised separately or prior to others.

The Fifth Beatitude. This special blessing (20:6) is pronounced on the martyrs of the first resurrection. They will no longer fear; the *second death* cannot harm them. They are further blessed in that they are *priests* and will reign with Christ *for a thousand years.* How blessed indeed! Their patient endurance was for such a short time by comparison.

The Loosing of Satan. John indicates that Satan has been bound in chains in the bottomless pit throughout the thousand years (20:3). This is *his* prison prepared for him. John, however, leaves us in the dark as to why Satan should be released. One could argue that God should have destroyed him. Such an assumption can be based only on a too literal reading of the text. John's thought is dualistic, but stops short of dualism. He never sees Satan as a threat to God or God's sovereignty. Satan appears to possess some kind of power on earth, but there is no satisfactory explanation as to why he should be released. Perhaps, his temptation would guarantee the genuineness of the faith of those who had believed during the millennium. Or possibly, John cannot think of earthly existence apart from evil power.

Satan's purpose is to *deceive the nations* of the whole earth by leading them into their last battle.

Gog and Magog. Evil seems always to fight against God. The battle of Armageddon was not enough; after a thousand years these evil nations prepare for battle under the prodding of Satan.

Gog and *Magog* are from Ezekiel (38–39). Magog was listed in the table of nations (Gen. 10:2) among the sons of Japheth (see also 1 Chron. 1:5), but no real country is known with that name. A king named *Gog* from Magog was incited to fight against Israel. In this passage God is reported to have brought about a terrible destruction on Gog and his nations so that the birds and beasts gorged themselves on the carcasses; people were still burying corpses seven months later.

By the time John wrote Revelation, there were popular stories that Gog and Magog would appear during, or after, the messianic reign. It is possible that Ezekiel's description alluded to the Scythian invasions, but John intends no national distinction.

These nations are innumerable; they cover the whole earth; they surround the *saints* and their *beloved city,* which would have to be Jerusalem if a literal city is intended. There is no battle, however. Many interpreters are disappointed in that they want God's people to arm themselves and destroy Satan's forces with weapons. This does not happen.

The End of Satan. The *devil* is now judged and thrown into the *lake of fire* to join his cohorts, the *beast* and the *false prophet.* This is Satan's final judgment; he will be tormented forever (see comment on 19:20).

Interpretation of the Millennium. John's interim kingdom appears to have grown out of the Old Testament prophetic hope, which insisted that God would establish his kingdom on earth, and the messianic and apocalyptic thought of a later time.[68] The prophets expected God to judge evil in his world; they expected the Day of the Lord. God would come and set up his kingdom on earth. As messianic thought developed,

---

[68] See "Millennium," IDB, Vol. 3, 381 f.

it became related to the Day of the Lord. Apocalyptic thought added the idea that the world was so evil that God's kingdom would have to break in from the outside. The conflict led to the idea of an interim or temporal reign prior to God's final kingdom. However, our sources reflect no uniformity, or even general agreement, about such a kingdom or messianic hope.

Several nonbiblical writings of the New Testament period give some light. In 2 Esdras (7:26–30, which is the same as 4 Ezra), there is a temporal messianic kingdom of 400 years in which the messiah reigns. After the 400 years he dies. Following a period of seven days of silence, there is a resurrection. In 2 Enoch (32:2—33:2) an apocalyptic view of the present world presents a scheme of history in which time is divided into periods of a thousand years each. The eighth period of one thousand years is the eternal age. Although no messiah is mentioned, the seventh period may have been the parallel to the millennial messianic reign. In 2 Baruch (39—40) a messiah is expected to be revealed at the end of the last kingdom of a series of four. The fourth period is noted for wickedness. The messiah will judge the evil and will reign as long as corruption lasts in the world.

Numerous New Testament passages portray the expectation of Christ's return, but we must not confuse this hope with the millennial hope. They are not the same. Only one passage suggests an interregnum on earth. In 1 Corinthians (15:23–28) Paul writes that at Christ's coming, he will deliver the kingdom to God after he has established sovereignty over all things, but this may not be an interim reign. The other passages speak of Christ's return, resurrection, and judgment, but never allude to any kind of millennium (Mark 13; 1 Thess. 4:13–18; 2 Thess. 2:1–12; 2 Peter 3:1–12).

The term "thousand years" (Gk. *chilia etē*, Latin *millennium*) may suggest only completeness, or perfection in Revelation. In Psalm 90:4) a thousand years with God is only as yesterday; in the New Testament a thousand years to God are as one day (2 Peter 3:8). It is not at all likely that John intended the thousand years to be taken any more literally than the seven-headed beast with ten horns. It is the indefinitely long reign of the Messiah.

Millennial hope has appeared many times in the life of the church but never with any uniformity. Some interpreters have tried to interpret it literally; others like Origen and Augustine allegorized it. The Reformers cherished the hope. Modern groups such as Irvingites, Mormons, Seventh Day Adventists, and Jehovah's Witnesses have made it a major theme. Other Christian groups have exaggerated the idea far beyond the importance suggested by the scarcity of biblical information on the subject.

In general, there are three major interpretations: premillennialism, postmillennialism, and nonmillennialism (amillennialism).

Premillennialists are so called because they believe that Christ will return before the millennium. They believe their view is the literal view taught in Scripture. Christ will reign on earth (probably in Jerusalem) for a literal thousand years. The promises made to Israel will be fulfilled. This view is Judaistic in outlook; it has special provisions for the Jews. It features several resurrections, judgments, etc.[69] Many differing views appear within Premillennialism, but all of them labor under the burden of placing Christ on the throne of an earthly kingdom such as the one he rejected during his lifetime.

Postmillennialism is that position held by those who expect Christ's return after the millennium. They expect a thousand years of peace and righteousness to precede the return of Christ. This view prospered in the optimistic climate of liberal theology in which the kingdom of God appeared to be coming in response to man's righteousness. Two World Wars and the degradation of the century have all but destroyed this

---

69 See C. C. Ryrie, *The Basis of the Premillennial Faith* (New York: Loizeaux Brothers, 1953).

view.[70]

The Amillennialists understand the millennium to designate the reign of Christ in a spiritual sense. They do not reject the idea of Christ's return, judgment, resurrection of men, etc. They rather reject the idea of a literal reign of Christ on this earth. Many of them see the reign of Christ to have begun in the life or resurrection of Christ. Christ's return could happen at any time. Only one resurrection and one judgment will mark the end of history. They do not expect an interim reign between history and eternity.[71]

6. The Great White Throne (20:11)

[11] Then I saw a great white throne and him who sat upon it; from his presence earth and sky fled away, and no place was found for them.

The throne is probably not the same as that of 4:2 since it was in heaven, and it is unlikely that the wicked would be admitted to heaven even for judgment. This throne is identified only in terms of the One who sat thereon. Although judgment has been given to Christ the Son (John 5:22; 2 Cor. 5:10) in some instances, it is the Father who sits upon the throne (5: 1,7,13).

God is so majestic that *earth and sky fled* from his presence. The *sky* is the heaven; the fleeing of earth and heaven makes room for the new earth and heaven soon to come (21:1). This dissolution of the heaven and earth is also reflected in 2 Peter (3:10).

7. The Final Judgment (20:12-15)

[12] And I saw the dead, great and small, standing before the throne, and books were opened. Also another book was opened, which

[70] See A. H. Strong, *Systematic Theology* (Philadelphia: The Judson Press, 1907), p. 1013.
[71] See Ray Summers, *The Life Beyond* (Nashville: Broadman Press, 1959), pp. 209–216, for charts of the three positions; see his *Worthy Is the Lamb* (Nashville: Broadman Press, 1951), pp. 204–206, for his amillennial position. On millennialism see Shirley Jackson Case, *The Millennial Hope* (Chicago: University of Chicago Press, 1918); D. H. Kromminga, *The Millennium in the Church* (Grand Rapids: Wm. B. Eerdmans, 1945); Loraine Boettner, *The Millennium* (Philadelphia: The Presbyterian and Reformed Publishing Company, 1957).

is the book of life. And the dead were judged by what was written in the books, by what they had done. [13] And the sea gave up the dead in it, Death and Hades gave up the dead in them, and all were judged by what they had done. [14] Then Death and Hades were thrown into the lake of fire. This is the second death, the lake of fire; [15] and if any one's name was not found written in the book of life, he was thrown into the lake of fire.

The growing tension of 20 chapters reaches its climax in the judgment scene. Man's eternal destiny hangs in the balance. The account is surprisingly brief. We have noted that the scene of the judgment is before the great white throne; God himself is the judge.

The Defendants. The first resurrection featured only the martyrs; this general resurrection includes all the dead; nothing is said about the living. John portrays the inclusiveness by citing the *dead* of all classes, the dead in the *sea* and the *dead* who had been held captive by **Death** and **Hades.** Death at sea was fearful; denial of burial was a serious threat to man. John says that in this final judgment the dead from the sea as well as from the graves will be raised. Death and Hades (see comment on 6:8) are personified here. They are man's enemies. **Death** is related to man's sin and estrangement from God; **Hades** was thought to be the prison in which the dead were held. They surrender their prisoners for this final judgment.

The Books of Evidence. The two books are distinguished in that one contains the records of peoples' deeds in life; the other is the *book of life* in which the redeemed are listed. The book of life (see comment on 17:8) is very important to John and is also called the "Lamb's book of life" (21: 27). Other biblical writers spoke of this book (Phil. 4:3; Dan. 12:1; Ex. 32:32) and of names being written in heaven (Luke 10:20; Heb. 12:23). If one's name is written in the book of life, he is guaranteed admission to God's presence; if his name is not in the book of life, he will certainly be rejected (3:5; 13:8; 20:15; 21:27). Numerous references in nonbiblical sources of the time indicate that this idea of a book of life was commonly accepted (1 Enoch 104:1; Jubilees 30:22).

Other record books in heaven are opened in the judgment. They contain the record of men's deeds. The references to records in heaven's books to be used in judgment are common in biblical (Dan. 7:10; Mal. 3:16) and nonbiblical sources (2 Esdras 6:20; 2 Baruch 24:1; 1 Enoch 47:3).

The Basis of Judgment. The brevity and simplicity of John's account of the final judgment is startling. Men are judged on two grounds: by *what they had done* in life, and whether their names were recorded in the book of life. The first standard simply stresses the stewardship of life: man is judged on the basis of what he did with what he had in life. The second standard involves all the faith and decision through which one goes in declaring himself for God. The Christians chose God, refused the beast's identification and accepted Christ's identity. Then, in one sense, man judges himself by the record he sends ahead and by his faith to be identified with Christ and his followers.

The Second Death. Being cast into the lake of fire is the *second death.* Death means more than cessation of the life process. To live is to be with God; death is separation from God. *Second death* is final and complete separation from God (on the *lake of fire* see comment on 19:20). Again, John's restraint is dramatically impressive. Briefly, he states the sorrowful end of the condemned; he then moves on to a lengthy and joyful description of the redeemed.

X. Eternal Destiny of the Victors (21:1— 22:7)

John has described in great detail the travail of human history and the suffering role of God's people. Now he looks beyond earth's final judgment and sees the destiny of the Christians. This entire section, though consisting of seven paragraphs, actually presents three controlling ideas: (1) there will be a new creation; (2) a new city

will be man's abode; (3) God's presence will be known in a new fullness. Of these, God's presence is determinative in spite of the obvious fact that John devotes more space to the description of the holy city.

1. With God in the Holy City (21:1-4)

¹ **Then I saw a new heaven and a new earth; for the first heaven and the first earth had passed away, and the sea was no more.** ² **And I saw the holy city, new Jerusalem, coming down out of heaven from God, prepared as a bride adorned for her husband;** ³ **and I heard a great voice from the throne saying, "Behold, the dwelling of God is with men. He will dwell with them, and they shall be his people, and God himself will be with them;** ⁴ **he will wipe away every tear from their eyes, and death shall be no more, neither shall there be mourning nor crying nor pain any more, for the former things have passed away."**

The paragraph is an introductory description in which the three themes are briefly outlined; subsequent paragraphs deal specifically with each. The introductory nature is obvious in the repeated statement about the new Jerusalem *coming down* (21:2,10), and the additional description of the holy city.

A New Creation. In biblical faith, God's creation is good; biblical writers did not subscribe to the dualism which maintained that matter was by nature evil; they, rather, saw man's sin as corrupting God's good creation. Consequently, they tended to think of God's redemptive work as bringing about a renovation of his creation. They spoke of a *new heaven and a new earth* and the dissolution of the former earth. Their point is not whether God transforms the old heaven and earth, or creates a new one "out of nothing."

Isaiah spoke of such a new creation of heaven and earth (Isa. 65:17). Jesus spoke of a "new world" which would be related to the kingdom of the Son of man (Matt. 19:28). Paul employed the theme of the new creation when describing the transformation of men who believed in Christ (2 Cor. 5:17; Gal. 6:15; see Eph. 2:15; 4:24). In 2 Peter (3:10) the old heavens and earth are to be destroyed and replaced by new ones (3:13).

Nonbiblical sources of the period also reflect the belief in the new heaven and earth (2 Baruch 32:6; 44:12; 48:50; 51:3; 1 Enoch 91:16; 2 Esdras 7:30).

John believed that the new creation would have no *sea.* Customarily, biblical writers divided man's natural environment into heavens, earth, and sea. John's aversion to the sea suggests a threefold explanation. (1) Before the day of safe ships and reliable navigation aids, men had a deep fear of the sea. (2) In the mythological background, the sea symbolized evil. The biblical dragon, Rahab, Leviathan (Isa. 27:1, 51:9; Job 26:12), and John's dragon came from the sea (Rev. 13:1). (3) From his exile on Patmos John could see the mainland, but was separated from his flock by the sea. Heaven will have no sea.[72]

A New City. Revelation includes several distinctive ideas related to man's habitation in the city. The great city stood in contrast to the holy city. John could hardly think of man's existence apart from life in a city. This city is *holy* and *new.* It is a recreated *Jerusalem* which had its origin in heaven; it comes *down out of heaven.* Earthly Jerusalem, the holy city, had a long tradition and many fond memories for God's people; but, Jerusalem stoned the prophets and crucified Christ. The *new Jerusalem* should be thought of as a new creation of God. The name draws upon the best of Jerusalem's history; it is not related to Jerusalem's geography as such. John has previously referred to the Bride and the forthcoming marriage (19:7–8); now he describes the new holy city as a beautiful bride *adorned for her husband.*

God's Presence in a New Fullness. By faith the Christians had already known God's presence; in heaven they will know his presence without hindrance. Heaven could be described in terms of "where God is." John describes the new Jerusalem at great length, but it is obvious that in heaven all eyes focus on God, who alone gives life and meaning to the new city.

The *voice* is probably that of the throne angel (16:17; 19:5) since God does not speak until later (21:5). God's presence had been symbolized by the tabernacle and temple; now God will be personally present. This age-old hope (Ezek. 37:27) is finally realized. The covenant will be fully known: God will be *with them and they shall be his people. God himself* is intended to stress the direct presence of God, and not a mediated or partial presence.

God's presence is described in terms of the comfort it brings and the evils it dispels. The awesomeness of God, noted previously, gives way to tenderness in his wiping away the tears *from their eyes.* The Christians had known the threat of *death* and the human experience of *mourning, crying,* and *pain;* these evils, results of human sin, cannot survive in God's presence. They are a part of the old order or the *former things* which have passed away forever.

2. The Consummation of Salvation (21: 5–8)

5 And he who sat upon the throne said, "Behold, I make all things new." Also he said, "Write this, for these words are trustworthy and true." 6 And he said to me, "It is done! I am the Alpha and the Omega, the beginning and the end. To the thirsty I will give water without price from the fountain of the water of life. 7 He who conquers shall have this heritage, and I will be his God and he shall be my son. 8 But as for the cowardly, the faithless, the polluted, as for murderers, fornicators, sorcerers, idolaters, and all liars, their lot shall be in the lake that burns with fire and brimstone, which is the second death."

The New Creation. In the initial creation, God said, "Let there be . . . and it was so." It is fitting that God should speak the new creation into existence. After proclaiming that he is making *all things new,* he commands John to record his message which is *trustworthy and true* (3:14; 19:11; 22:6).

---

[72] It is interesting that in this section John lists seven evils which will be "no more" (the "sea" 21:1; "death, mourning, crying, and pain" in 21:4; "anything accursed" in 22:3; and "night" in 22:5).

The Consummation. God's proclamation *It is done!* marks the consummation of all that had been predicted and promised throughout the book. The end has come! Lest there be any question of the authority back of the message, God authenticates his message; it is from him who alone can be called *Alpha and Omega* (1:8; 22:13).

God's Promise. It is obvious that John is still dealing with a future event in that God states a promise to the *thirsty* and those who conquer. The *thirsty* are those with a longing for God and a thirst for righteousness (Matt. 5:6; John 4:14; 7:37). God's presence satisfies the thirst; John uses the symbolic language of the *fountain* (v. 6) and the *river* (22:1). The thirst appears in contrast to the abundance of the source of water and its freeness (*without price*, 22:17).

The victor (*he who conquers*) is John's term for the faithful Christian who conquers evil and temptation. He faithfully overcomes the beast by being faithful to Christ. Only the victors will receive the inheritance of God's sons (see Gal. 4:7; Rom. 8:17). The terminology stresses the intimate family relationship which will be known by faithful Christians.

God's Warning. God's proclamation includes a stern warning to all who are not victors that they will go to the *lake of fire* (see comment on 19:20 and 20:14). This warning must be seen in the light of the previous promise or misunderstanding will result. The *cowardly* are not timid or meek people; they are those who recanted in the face of persecution. These fearful people cringed when challenged to live for God; fear is the opposite of faith; faith has an element of courage in it. The *faithless* are those who were unfaithful in their trial. Living without faith in God is adequate ground for condemnation. The *polluted* are the abominable ones who partook of the impurities of the harlot (17:4). *Murderers* and *fornicators* are two common classes of criminals, but may also be those who helped kill the Christians and those who participated in the idolatry of em-

peror worship. *Sorcerers* are those idolaters who help to deceive people into false worship (22:15; 9:21; 18:23). *Idolaters* worshiped substitute gods. The book of Revelation is severe in its condemnation of *liars* and all forms of falsity (2:2; 3:9; 14:5; 21:8,27; 22:15).

3. The Appearance of the New Jerusalem (21:9–14)

⁹ Then came one of the seven angels who had the seven bowls full of the seven last plagues, and spoke to me, saying, "Come, I will show you the Bride, the wife of the Lamb." ¹⁰ And in the Spirit he carried me away to a great, high mountain, and showed me the holy city Jerusalem coming down out of heaven from God, ¹¹ having the glory of God, its radiance like a most rare jewel, like a jasper, clear as crystal. ¹² It had a great, high wall, with twelve gates, and at the gates twelve angels, and on the gates the names of the twelve tribes of the sons of Israel were inscribed; ¹³ on the east three gates, on the north three gates, on the south three gates, and on the west three gates. ¹⁴ And the wall of the city had twelve foundations, and on them the twelve names of the twelve apostles of the Lamb.

Finally, the goal comes into view. Pilgrims who had made the long journey to Jerusalem would never forget the joy when they first saw the holy city in the distance. This scene is filled with indescribable joy. John and the persecuted Christians have traveled a long and difficult journey; victory is now in sight.

The guiding angel is *one of the seven angels who had the seven bowls* of wrath; a relationship to the vision of the harlot is suggested (17:1). John intends that we contrast the two.

The Invitation to John. The angel's invitation employs the same words, *Come, I will show you* (see 17:1). The *Bride* is in clear contrast to the harlot. John has previously referred to those invited to the wedding feast (19:9) and has just mentioned the adorned Bride. The time has come; he speaks of the Bride, proleptically, as the *wife of the Lamb.* But the following description is that of a city rather than a woman. The city, however, is personified and joins with the Spirit in issuing the final invitation of the book (22:17).

In the Spirit designates a trance-like vision. The *great high mountain* from which he saw the vision is not a particular mountain on the map; mountains have symbolic meaning in such visions. In Assyrian, Babylonian, and Hebrew literature mountains are associated with the heavens or the throne of God (1 Enoch 18:8; 24:1–3; 25:3; see Isa. 2:2; Mic. 4:1). The high mountain suggests a contrast with the wilderness whence he saw the harlot vision.

Vision of the City. The *holy city* appears to be descending from heaven to earth. This is not as strange as it sounds. The martyrs from earth have been waiting in heaven; the earth has been under the dominion of evil. While it may be claiming too much to claim that the heavenly city will be located on earthly terrain, it is not too much to note that this vision reunites heaven and earth. It marks complete victory in God's redemption.

As previously indicated, this descent of the holy city was introduced in 21:2. This does not mean that it descended twice, or that John saw it twice.[73] Such a view is too literal. The first reference is preparatory.

Several promises appeared in the earlier chapters of the book which are fulfilled in these last two chapters. For instance, the Philadelphian Christians had been promised a part in this "new Jerusalem which comes down from my God" (3:12). The Ephesian Christians had been promised that if they were faithful they would eat of the "tree of life" which was located in the "paradise of God" (2:7). The fulfillment is near (22:2).

John's first impression when seeing the holy city was that it was gloriously and

radiantly beautiful. The phrase *glory of God* always suggests brilliance and light. We will learn later that the city needs no luminaries since "the glory of God is its light" (21:23). The entire city glowed like a *most rare jewel.* John adds illustrations suggesting the appearance of *jasper* and *crystal,* but they are eclipsed by the brilliance already flashed before us.

After the initial shock from the glory of the city, John notes other factors in its external appearance. Any description of a city would likely include walls and gates, but John appears to have been following Ezekiel (48:30–35), who described a city which was named "The Lord is there." That city had four high walls and three gates on each side which were named for the 12 tribes. The city in Revelation has *twelve angels* stationed one at each gate. They are watchmen (cf. Isa. 62:6).

The *twelve gates* are inscribed with the names of the 12 *sons of Israel,* indicating the completeness of God's people. In addition to the names of the tribes, as in Ezekiel's city, this city wall is built on *twelve foundations* (probably huge stones) on which were inscribed the names of the *twelve apostles of the Lamb.* This last statement indicates the completeness of the church and suggests a metaphorical meaning such as that found in Ephesians (2:20).

4. Description of the Holy City (21:15–21)

15 And he who talked to me had a measuring rod of gold to measure the city and its gates and walls. 16 The city lies four-square, its length the same as its breadth; and he measured the city with his rod, twelve thousand stadia; its length and breadth and height are equal. 17 He also measured its wall, a hundred and forty-four cubits by a man's measure, that is, an angel's. 18 The wall was built of jasper, while the city was pure gold, clear as glass. 19 The foundations of the wall of the city were adorned with every jewel; the first was jasper, the second sapphire, the third agate, the fourth emerald, 20 the fifth onyx, the sixth carnelian, the seventh chrysolite, the eighth beryl, the ninth topaz, the tenth chrysoprase, the eleventh

---

[73] R. H. Charles argued that since John saw the vision twice, it must have happened twice. Therefore he assumed it was misplaced and placed it before the millennium. Caird prefers to think of the descent as a "permanent characteristic" of the city. In other words, John would not have missed it if he had arrived a few minutes earlier or later.

jacinth, the twelfth amethyst. ²¹And the twelve gates were twelve pearls, each of the gates made of a single pearl, and the street of the city was pure gold, transparent as glass.

John's favorite way of describing a city is to "measure" it. He had measured the temple (11:1), but only an angel would be capable of measuring a city as large as this one. John's measuring rod had been a common reed; the angel used a measuring rod of gold. The description is given in very literal terms which deal with the shape, dimensions, and building materials used in the building of the city. It is probable, however, that John intends these only to suggest a greatness beyond actual measurement and description.

The Shape of the City. A quadrangular city would not be strange, but this one is cubical. The shape was probably dictated by the shape of the holy of holies in Solomon's Temple (1 Kings 6:20). Inasmuch as the walls are much lower than the stated height of the city, we must not think of the city as "box-shaped." If one conceives of the city literally, he should think of the buildings reaching into the heavens and the much lower wall surrounding it.

The Dimensions of the City. Its *length, breadth,* and *height* are *equal;* each dimension was measured at *twelve thousand stadia* or 1500 miles. The walls were only *one hundred and forty-four cubits,* about 216 feet. A cubit was originally a unit of measure the length of a man's arm from elbow to the tip of his middle finger, about 18 inches. John's reference to a *man's measure* and an *angel's* is not intended to give the size of angel's arms. His point is only that the standard of measurement is man's cubit even though an angel is measuring the walls. John did not specify whether the measurement of the wall was its height or thickness. One would usually think of the height, but Ezekiel speaks of the thickness of the wall at its base (40:5). The measurement of the base could be made at the gate and some interpreters believe this is intended (Beckwith, p. 761), but John is probably speaking of height.

The Building Materials. Although given in literal terms, John appears to mean that the city defies description; its beauty and magnificence are boundless. The precious stones are probably to be seen as adornment on the foundation stones since the verb means "to build into" rather than to build "out of" (Swete, p. 290).

The jewels or stones adorning the foundations retain the symbolism of *twelve* and may allude to the stones on the breastplate of the high priest (Ex. 28:17–21; 39:10–14). The king of Tyre wore such adornment (Ezek. 28:12–19). Job (28:12–19) and Isaiah (54:12) were familiar with such stones. It is possible that the stones on the high priest's breastplate had some early connection with the signs of the zodiac.[74]

There are two other significant details deserving comment. The gates were made of huge pearls, one pearl per gate (in Isa. 54:11–12 gates are made of carbuncles). Post-Christian Jewish writings speak of city gates made of single pearls. Another amazing statement is that the city is made of *pure gold* and that it is *transparent as glass.* The term stresses magnificence and not suitability for building materials. The Temple had been world-famous for the gold overlay on the eastern façade. God's holy city will be much more magnificent. The transparency suggests its purity.

5. God's Presence in the Holy City (21: 22–27)

²² And I saw no temple in the city, for its temple is the Lord God the Almighty and the Lamb. ²³ And the city has no need of sun or moon to shine upon it, for the glory of God is its light, and its lamp is the Lamb. ²⁴ By its light shall the nations walk; and the kings of the earth shall bring their glory into it, ²⁵ and its gates shall never be shut by day—and there shall be no night there; ²⁶ they shall bring into it the glory and the honor of the nations. ²⁷ But nothing unclean shall enter it, nor any one who practices abomination or falsehood, but only those who are written in the Lamb's book of life.

---

[74] See "Jewels and Precious Stones," in IDB, II, 898–905; for discussion of the stones, their arrangement, and relation to Ex. 28, etc., see R. H. Charles, II, 165–169.

John's preoccupation with describing the city leads to amazement when he looks inside the city. Though presented briefly, John leaves no room for uncertainty as to the meaning of the Christian's destiny. All that is meant by the holy city can be summed up by saying (1) God is there, and (2) the faithful of earth, *written in the Lamb's book of life*, are there with God. John's description of the inside of the holy city follows two lines: notable presences and notable absences.

Notable Presences in the Holy City. God, who is now present with his people on a full and enduring basis (21:3-4), is the "All in All" of heavenly life. The Temple had once symbolized God's presence and worked its way into the language of faith (2 Cor. 6:16). Now God is present with his people in such a way that no temple is necessary. The *Lord God* is the center of life in the holy city; the *Lamb* is associated with the *Almighty*. John knows God the Almighty through the work of the Lamb.

The presence of God casts a brilliant glory over the city alleviating the need for luminaries; God is the *light* and *lamp*. This glory of God attracts the *nations* and *the kings of earth*. A difficulty appears at first since we have been told of their destruction (13:7 ff.; 19:21). The complexity of this problem suggested to R. H. Charles (II, 144 ff.) two cities from heaven instead of one. He rearranged the text in chapters 20—22 and assumed that John died after writing 20:3; someone else wrote the rest by using John's notes. The reconstruction is not convincing and seems to demand a consistency which neither John foresaw nor Charles accomplished. It is unnecessary to treat the text so rigidly. John sees a fulfillment of the hope that the Gentiles would respond to God (Isa. 60:3; 66:18-19; Zech. 2:11; 8:23; Dan. 7:14; 1 Enoch 10:21). John mentions the "healing of the nations" even in the last chapter (22:2).

The *kings of earth* are very significant in Revelation. They hold the power of man's political structures and as such contribute significantly to the revolt against

God (10:11; 16:14; 17:2; 17:18; 18:3; 19:18, 19). But Christ is the ruler of earth's kings (1:5), "Lord of lords, and King of kings" (17:14; 19:16). It is reasonable to conclude that in this final victory Christ will receive the homage due him from the kings of earth.

Man will be present in the holy city. The faithful witnesses whose names are in the book of life will be present with God in this new habitation.

Notable Absences in the Holy City. John's presentation of the holy city's true nature revealed the presence of God Almighty and redeemed man. It also presents negatively what these "presences" exclude.

The *temple* is absent. Even John's promises (3:12; 7:15) and hopes included the imagery of the temple, but when he looks inside the holy city he notes that God's presence makes a temple unnecessary.

The *sun* and *moon* are absent. God's glory is the only source of light. This *lamp* is adequate.

There are no locked gates in this city. The gates are *never* shut *by day* and there is *no night there*. Gates usually exclude; they keep intruders out. Heaven's gates are never closed. John had seen an "open door" in heaven (4:1); "an open door" stood before the church of Philadelphia which "no one is able to shut" (3:8); but, there is one locked door in Revelation (3:20) before which Christ stands and knocks. It was locked from the inside; even Christ could not force entry. Men must open their hearts to God; he does not coerce faith. But heaven's doors remain open!

No night will be in that city. This statement seems to reflect Isaiah 60:19-20, but is important to John for he repeats it (22:5). Night and darkness are terms suggesting fear, insecurity, and evil in the Johannine literature. In God's city there will be perennial peace, security, light, and joy. When the great wicked city fell, darkness resulted; "the light of a lamp shall shine in thee no more" (18:23); by contrast the holy city will never know night or darkness.

No kind of evil will be in this city. The *unclean* thing will never enter; sinful men, those practicing *abomination* and *falsehood,* are excluded. The wicked city (the harlot) held in her hand a "cup full of abominations and the impurities of her fornication" (17:4). She was the "mother of harlots and of earth's abominations" (17:5). The holy city (the Bride) is pure. *Falsehood* is especially reprehensible to John (21:8; 22:15); it had been used to deceive people into idolatry (13:14); it will be excluded from the holy city.

6. Eternal Life in the Holy City (22:1–5)

¹ Then he showed me the river of the water of life, bright as crystal, flowing from the throne of God and of the Lamb ² through the middle of the street of the city; also, on either side of the river, the tree of life with its twelve kinds of fruit, yielding its fruit each month; and the leaves of the tree were for the healing of the nations. ³ There shall no more be anything accursed, but the throne of God and of the Lamb shall be in it, and his servants shall worship him; ⁴ they shall see his face, and his name shall be on their foreheads. ⁵ And night shall be no more; they need no light of lamp or sun, for the Lord God will be their light, and they shall reign for ever and ever.

The final vision of the holy city affords a brief but beautiful view of the Christian hope—eternal life with God. Five themes are woven together: (1) the river of the water of life; (2) the tree of life; (3) God and the Lamb are the center and source of all; (4) God's children worship and share the reign forever; (5) all evil fruits will be absent.

The River of the Water of Life. The dry climate of the biblical world with its desert or semidesert existence contributed to the religious symbols of the Bible. *Water* and the *tree* are meaningful symbols in biblical faith. Water means life; the *river of the water of life* symbolizes the source of eternal life.

Obviously, John follows Old Testament imagery. There was a river in the Garden of Eden (Gen. 2:10). The psalmist (46:4) spoke of a "river whose streams make glad the city of God." Immediately in John's mind was the vision of Ezekiel (47:1–2) in which a river flowed from the temple ever increasing in size and depth until it brought life even to the Dead Sea. In its depths fish grew in abundance. Zechariah (14:7–8) looked forward to a future in which water would flow from Jerusalem in two rivers—one to the east, one to the west.

The symbol of water as spiritual life is found in the Gospel of John (4:14; 7:38). This *water* is related to eternal life in Revelation (7:17; 21:6; 22:17). The plagues struck at the sources of fresh water (8:10; 16:4); in the new city there will be an abundance of living water.

The *river* in the new Jerusalem is absolutely pure, **bright as crystal.** It flows not from the temple as did Ezekiel's river; there is no temple in this city; this river flows from the **throne of God and of the Lamb** indicating its boundless supply. The river flows **through** the main street of the new city. Artists have been undecided as to whether it divided the street into two streets by flowing through its **middle** or whether it filled the street thus making it a canal. Such literal thinking spoils John's imagery. The river points to eternal life from God.

The Tree of Life. This is another symbol of eternal life. John promised the Ephesian Christians that they would "eat of the tree of life which is in the paradise of God" (2:7) if they were faithful. To eat of the tree is to have eternal life (22:2; 22:14); to be denied the tree of life is to lose eternal life (22:19).

Ezekiel (47:12) had written of trees by the side of the river which bore fruit every month for food and for healing. Although John speaks of the **tree of life,** one gets the idea of a grove or a row of trees flanking each side of the river. John specifies **twelve kinds of fruit** rather than the same kind of fruit 12 times yearly, but this is not certain. His point is the abundant and regular supply.

The **healing** of the **nations** creates a problem. There is no problem about the *healing;* this was also stated by Ezekiel. The problem arises from previous statements regarding the defeat, judgment, and destruction of the nations (19:21; 20:7; 20:15). R. H. Charles, for instance, sees such a conflict in this statement that he rearranges the material. G. B. Caird, on the other hand, has insisted that the great redemptive work of God is not limited to a handful of martyrs; rather, the *nations of* 21:24 and 22:2 may also be redeemed. Even though they have trampled the holy city, have followed the whore, and have been defeated, they finally bring their willing tribute into God's city as they had once taken their trade to Rome (Caird, p. 279). They receive healing for their wounds. This interpretation is attractive, but John probably means the nations which have responded in obedience as in 7:9, and the "glory and the honor" which are possessed by the nations and freely given to God (21:26).

God and the Lamb Are Central. John ever returns to his theme that "heaven is where God is," and that speaking of God requires speaking of the Lamb. The *river* flows from the *throne* of *God* and the *Lamb;* the ultimate source is God. The *tree of life,* by the river, has its life from God. The assertion that God's throne is in the city is adequate proof that all evil and sorrow have been excluded. The justification for saying that there is no light from the sun is that *the Lord will be their light.* In short, all the Christian hope of eternal life can be summed up in the simple statement that we shall be "with God" completely.

Worship and Reign. John says little about the activities of men in this heavenly city, but it seems clear that he expects men to worship God unceasingly, and to share in God's reign. They *shall worship him;* they will look on his *face,* see him in a new fullness; they continue to wear his *name on their foreheads* in constant confession of his ownership, their identity and security. Reigning *for ever and ever* is to be understood by comparison with the millennial

reign, long but limited; this reign is without end. We do not know clearly what such a reign would be. Evidently, God is sovereign; man would not want any of God's sovereignty for himself. The idea of kingdom is very important to John (1:6; 5:10; 2:26–27; 3:21). John had promised the victorious Christians that they would share in this reign. Now it is fulfilled. Swete (p. 302) sees this reign as being partly realized in the present life of the church.

Absences in the City. God's presence automatically excludes evil and its fruits. The first Eden had come under a curse because of man's sin; there will *no more be anything accursed* in the new Eden. Night, with its darkness and uncertainty, is a symbol of evil; sinful men loved darkness rather than light (John 3:19); redeemed men live forever in the light of the *Lord God* (see comment on 21:25).

7. The Angel's Final Message (22:6–7)

6 And he said to me, "These words are trustworthy and true. And the Lord, the God of the spirits of the prophets, has sent his angel to show his servants what must soon take place. 7 And behold, I am coming soon."
Blessed is he who keeps the words of the prophecy of this book.

The prophecy has ended. The guiding angel or Christ gives his authentication to the preceding message. The promise *I am coming soon* suggests that the speaker is Christ himself. Beckwith has seen four distinct messages in these two verses. (1) The angel sanctions the truth of the book. (2) The writer solemnly affirms that it is God who gave this prophecy. (3) Christ himself gave the assurance that his coming would be soon; this is the central theme of the book. (4) There is a warning to heed the prophetic truth in the book (Beckwith, p. 774).

The *spirits of the prophets* suggest relationship with the spirit of prophecy (19:10). John, the prophet, has received this revelation from Christ that Christ is coming soon; God reveals his actions to his prophets. John looks upon his book as a prophecy (1:3).

The Sixth Beatitude. This *Blessed* is an abbreviated form of the first beatitude (1:3), stressing only the keeping of the prophecy.

XI. Epilogue (22:8–21)

The remaining verses are filled with authentications, promises, warnings, and instructions. They are loosely tied together suggesting misplacement to many. Efforts to rearrange them have yielded disappointing results. It will be helpful to the interpreter to compare these statements with those in the prologue. There are many parallels suggesting that the author in the conclusion is looking back at his introduction.

God authenticates the prophecy (1:1; 22:16); Jesus endorsed it (1:1; 22:6); angels mediated it (1:1; 22:16); it is prophecy (1:3; 22:6,9); John identifies himself and authenticates the writing (1:1,4,9; 22:8); the author claims to be a prophet (1:1,9–11; 22:8,10); he instructs that the book be read in the churches (1:3,11; 22:16); it brings encouragement to the faithful (1:3; 22:7,12,14); it brings warnings to the wicked (1:7; 22:11); Jesus is coming soon (1:3; 22:7,10,12,20).

1. John's Authentication (22:8–9)

⁸ I John am he who heard and saw these things. And when I heard and saw them, I fell down to worship at the feet of the angel who showed them to me; ⁹ but he said to me, "You must not do that! I am a fellow servant with you and your brethren the prophets, and with those who keep the words of this book. Worship God."

John repeats his name and the basis or authority upon which he has written his prophecy (see comment on 1:9 ff.). It is strange that he would repeat the reference to his attempt at worshiping the angel (see comment on 19:10) since he was rebuked for so doing. Evidently, he wishes to re-emphasize that man must *Worship God* and no one else. Angel worship is forbidden.

2. Prohibition Against Sealing the Book (22:10–11)

¹⁰ And he said to me, "Do not seal up the words of the prophecy of this book, for the time is near. ¹¹ Let the evildoer still do evil, and the filthy still be filthy, and the righteous still do right, and the holy still be holy.

Apocalyptic writers frequently sealed their writings until some distant future when they would be opened (Dan. 8:26; 12:4,9). John was ordered not to seal his book, *for the time is near.* John, in this instance, is more of a prophet than an apocalyptist. He hides nothing; he makes public what God has disclosed. This statement places a heavy burden on the futuristic view of Revelation.

The translation of v. 11 suggests the most deterministic sounding statement in Revelation. It is difficult. Obviously, it was suggested by Daniel 12:10, which is John's Old Testament source for sealing the book. Possibly, John means that the *evildoer,* the *filthy,* the *righteous,* and the *holy* have made their choices which are irrevocable. The "fixed" connotation sounded in this verse is quite incompatible with John's frequent insistence that men should repent.

3. Promise and Warning (22:12–15)

¹² "Behold, I am coming soon, bringing my recompense, to repay every one for what he has done. ¹³ I am the Alpha and the Omega, the first and the last, the beginning and the end."
¹⁴ Blessed are those who wash their robes, that they may have the right to the tree of life and that they may enter the city by the gates. ¹⁵ Outside are the dogs and sorcerers and fornicators and murderers and idolaters, and every one who loves and practices falsehood.

The promise *I am coming soon* requires that Christ be the speaker. He promises reward on the basis of what man has done (see comment on 20:12). The authentication *I am the Alpha and the Omega* requires that God the Father be the speaker (see comment on 1:8 and 21:6). However, the close association of the Lamb with God has minimized the distinction.

The Seventh Beatitude. This last beatitude (see comment on 1:3; 14:13; 16:15;

19:9; 20:6; 22:7) pronounces blessing on those whose purity gains them admission to eternal life and the means by which they have achieved it. Their robes are white and pure because of the cleansing power of Christ (7:14). The present verse stresses their active part in this process; they *wash their robes.* Some early manuscripts have "do his commandments"; the meaning is identical. The purity of Christ's redemption is prerequisite to admission to the *city by the gates* and to the *tree of life* (see comment on 22:2) which symbolize eternal life.

Contrast with the Wicked. The blessedness of the righteous is seen more clearly in John's contrast with those outside. *Outside* does not mean that the wicked are milling around the exterior of the walls of the holy city. It means that they will never be inside the city; they are in the lake of fire (20:15). The term could have some reference to life in the present world; the righteous already know a habitation with God; the wicked are already outside.

All of the terms designating the wicked have been discussed previously (see comment on 21:8) except the *dogs.* This term was used in derision to point to the base, despised, and rejected. It often designated the Gentiles in the sense of being the rejected or unclean (see Matt. 7:6; 15:26,27; Mark 7:27,28; Phil. 3:2).

4. Jesus' Final Authentication (22:16)

16 "I Jesus have sent my angel to you with this testimony for the churches. I am the root and the offspring of David, the bright morning star."

The whole book is "the revelation of Jesus Christ" (1:1); Jesus Christ was the authorization of John's prophecy as he appeared in the first vision; it is fitting that Jesus speak again at the close of the book indicating his endorsement of it. Jesus authenticates the book by referring to the *angel* which he sent, the *testimony* which has been mentioned many times in the book, and to the *churches,* and by his own claim to be the *offspring of David* (see

3:7; 5:5) and the *bright morning star* (see 2:28).

5. A Concluding Invitation (22:17)

17 The Spirit and the Bride say, "Come." And let him who hears say, "Come." And let him who is thirsty come, let him who desires take the water of life without price.

The interpreters tend to understand this verse as a response to Christ's promise to come soon. In that event, *the Spirit* (probably the Spirit of prophecy) *and the Bride* (the church composed of the saints) join in a prayer for Christ to come quickly. The other statements make this interpretation very difficult. John appears to be witnessing for Christ; he is writing about the future; it is not too late yet. John says, after the other attestations of the book's truthfulness, that the Holy Spirit and the Bride join in issuing an invitation for all hearers of the gospel to *Come* and to repeat the invitation for others to *Come.* The *thirsty* are those in need of eternal life; it is abundant and free. Come! *take the water of life without price.*

6. John's Warning (22:18–19)

18 I warn every one who hears the words of the prophecy of this book: if any one adds to them, God will add to him the plagues described in this book, 19 and if any one takes away from the words of the book of this prophecy, God will take away his share in the tree of life and in the holy city, which are described in this book.

Ancient writers safeguarded their works by appending warnings or curses upon those who would tamper with them (Deut. 4:2; 12:32). These appear frequently in the Apocrypha and Pseudepigrapha. John is not addressing the scribe who may inadvertently make an error while copying the manuscript. He is speaking to all who *hear* his *prophecy.* His warning is like a curse. In neat parallel, the one who *adds to them* will be afflicted with the plagues of the book and the one who *takes away* will lose eternal life, the *tree of life.*

John spoke only of the prophecies in his own book. He had no way of knowing that

Revelation would stand at the end of the canon of Scripture. Certainly, the entire Bible deserves our utmost respect in understanding and interpreting it, but the present verse applies only to Revelation.

7. Conclusion of the Letter (22:20–21)

20 He who testifies to these things says, "Surely I am coming soon." Amen. Come, Lord Jesus!
21 The grace of the Lord Jesus be with all the saints. Amen.

The Apocalypse, in spite of its organization as a drama, begins and ends as a pastoral letter. Christ the Author, who *testifies*, repeats his promise *Surely, I am coming soon*. John, the author, responds *Amen. Come, Lord Jesus!* John's response is the translation of the earliest Christian confession "Marana tha."

The epistolary conclusion is a benediction of *Grace* which word has not been used since the beginning of the letter (1:4).

John has looked into heaven and has written his long apocalyptic prophecy about the things soon to come. He has seen the grandeur of heaven and the terror of the lake of fire. He has seen the final victory of the Lamb. But, he ends his letter on a very human plane as a man in exile with all of the danger before him and his churches.

What else could he say other than *The grace of the Lord Jesus be with all the saints. Amen.*

General Articles

Worship in the Bible

Charles A. Trentham

Martin Luther said, "To have a God is to worship him." The ancient Hebrew, banished from his homeland and his traditional place of worship, sat down by the waters of Babylon and sobbed: "If I forget you, O Jerusalem, let my right hand wither" (Psalm 137:5). He saw that nothing was going right with him since his worship was out of order.

The renewal of the soul is essential if we are to perform well in the social arena. Our age has placed proper emphasis upon Jesus as "the man for others," but it has often forgotten Jesus, the man from God. Our secularizing of the sacred has given us a clear goal to live for, but it has not given us resources to live from. Jesus constantly reminded his followers that his good deeds were done in a power that was not his own. He often turned to God for the renewal of that power. Apart from worship, faith dies, moral power degenerates, and the prophetic word is lost. Apart from the vision of the holy city of God, the dream of a righteous and happy city on earth will perish. If we see worship as a mirror of reality in which we perceive God and ourselves at the deepest level, it becomes an enlarging of our consciousness and an awareness without which we can only pretend to live.

For the ancient Hebrew, worship was the awareness of God. It was drawing near to God. It was also something he did to implement that awareness. "O come, let us worship and bow down: let us kneel before the Lord, our Maker" (Psalm 95:6). Worship was also his means of proclaiming the unique worth of his God (v. 3).

Israel's awareness of and response to God came out of the nation's experience in history. Memorable events determined the shape of her worship, and it, in turn, influenced the worship patterns of the *new* Israel.

I. Worship in the Old Testament

1. Among the Patriarchs. The earliest reference to any act of worship in the Bible appears in Genesis 4:3–4, the offerings of Cain and Abel, and that chapter's last verse probably refers to the beginning of worship generally. But the book does not tell why the rituals began; that was assumed at the time of writing. By Noah's time, animal sacrifice must have been recognized as *the* acceptable worship form (Gen. 8:20).

The worship of the patriarchs was different from that of their pagan neighbors in that it was based not on agriculture or fertility rites but on visits of God to the patriarchs. They built their altars and places of worship where God or God's representatives had appeared (Gen. 12:7, 28:18; Ex. 17:15). God's promise to Abraham was repeated to Isaac, and he responded in a similar manner in Genesis 26:24–25. Jacob's vision of God caused him to name the meeting place "Bethel" (house of God) and to make his memorable vow. After Jacob's reconciliation with Esau, God called him to make an altar and perform a ritual of purification and changing of garments (Gen. 35:1–4).

This event reveals the family aspect of worship in this period. However primitive it may appear, worship among the patriarchs was personal and familial and was linked inseparably with righteous behavior before God. These men believed that God was very near and real to them (Gen. 18:1).

2. From Egypt to Canaan. That sense of immediate awareness of God's presence is shown in Moses' experience with the burning bush (Ex. 3:1–6). It prepared him for his confrontation with Pharaoh, and the need for worship was the basis of his demand that the Israelites be freed (Ex. 5:1–3).

The climactic experience of deliverance

from Egyptian slavery was celebrated in the Feast of the Passover (Ex. 12:11; 34:25). It was also known as the Feast of Unleavened Bread and became the most important of Israel's worship festivals. While it may have been related to pre-Israelite observances, its relation to God's act in Egypt made it central in Yahweh worship. We know much more about its celebration from the New Testament than from the Old.

After crossing the Red Sea, Moses and the people of Israel sang unto the Lord the song in Exodus 15:1–19. It was characteristic of Israel to ascribe praise to God for his mighty works. Not only did they sing, but Miriam took her timbrel and led the women in dancing.

The period of encampment at Mount Sinai was also the occasion of memorable worship experiences. The people were instructed to wash their garments and to avoid at all cost any contact with the mountain after Moses consecrated them (Ex. 19:10–14). Then they trembled before the dramatic demonstration of God's presence before the Decalogue was given to Moses. Afterward, covenant acts of worship were performed (Ex. 24:3–8).

Before the people left the foot of Sinai, the Lord instructed Moses to have them "make me a sanctuary, that I may dwell in their midst" (Ex. 25:8). This large tent and its furnishings are described in Exodus 25—27. It provided altars for burnt offerings and incense, but its most revered object was the ark of the covenant in a separate tent shelter called the holy of holies. This gold-covered chest probably contained the Decalogue or some other list of covenant requirements. At each end of its solid gold lid was a cherub with its wings stretched toward the other, and between the cherubim was the mercy seat, and the dwelling place of Yahweh was just above it.

Sacrifices, offerings, and observances of Mosaic times are described in Exodus 29:38—31:17. After the tabernacle had been built, it became a center also for individual communion with God (Ex. 33:7–11) as well as the national focus of worship. According to the book of Numbers men of the tribe of Levi were selected "to do service at the tent of meeting" (8:15). Thus, Israelite worship was a matter of development acording to need and divine command.

Israel's entrance into Canaan and the fall of Jericho can be viewed as religious pageantry as much as military processions. When Israel camped at Gilgal, on the eastern border of Jericho, twelve stones of remembrance were carried out of the Jordan to remind their children that God carried his people over Jordan as he did across the Red Sea "so that all peoples of the earth may know that the hand of the Lord is mighty" (Josh. 4:24).

It is probable that Gilgal was the site of Israel's first worship in the Promised Land. Thus, it became a prominent sanctuary; many years later Saul was crowned there. As Israel possessed the land, she also captured the sanctuaries of the Canaanites. Every village of any size had its own "high place." Other notable sanctuaries of this period were at Dan, Beersheba, Shechem, and Shiloh. Pagan practices began to affect both worship and morality of the Israelites, but after the third distribution of conquered territory, the people "assembled at Shiloh, and set up the tent of meeting there" (Josh. 18:1).

3. Worship in the Early Monarchy. Contending with the pagans was difficult both in politics and in religion. The book of Judges reveals how much Baal-worship undermined Israelite belief and behavior. By the time of Samuel the ark of the covenant was used in vain as a fetish in Israel's attempt to defeat the Philistines. When the ark was captured, Shiloh lost its significance as the sanctuary of God. Regular worship at a central place is not mentioned from Joshua through 1 Samuel.

Then in 2 Samuel a revival of the worship of Yahweh began under the leadership of David. He brought the ark to Jerusalem (2 Sam. 6:15) and placed it in a special tent. Later, he purchased Araunah's threshing floor as the site for an altar to God—and eventually for Solomon's Temple. Some scholars feel that David combined several religious traditions to help the faith of Israel speak to its times. However that may be, "he worked out the principles, the spirit, and some of the forms" (Davies, p. 880) and was primarily responsible for the development of music in Israelite worship (2 Sam. 6:5; 1 Chron. 24—26)—a development of tremendous spiritual potential.

4. In the Temple. Just as Israel achieved a climactic and distinctive level in its national life in Solomon's reign, so did Solomon's Temple mark a new era in the nation's worship. It was the most attractive and permanent place of worship the people had known. Scholars are convinced that it borrowed some art and architectural features from Canaan, Phoenicia, and Egypt (1 Kings 5:6; 7:14), but it certainly embodied the distinctiveness of Israel's worship in the central symbols of early Yahwism. Seven years in construction, the Temple was a significant advance beyond the primitive setting and forms of Israel's early worship. It is not accurate to claim that Solomon's concept of a sacred *place* was an innovation; Israel had always given prominence in her worship to a sacred place (i.e., Mount Sinai, varied locations for the tabernacle and ark, and later sanctuaries like Gilgal and Shiloh).

Israel's worship calendar focused on three major festivals of agricultural origins but religious significance. The Passover, observed in the spring, was also called the Feast of Unleavened Bread (Ex. 12:1—13:16). In midsummer came the Feast of Weeks (Lev. 23:9–21), which is called Pentecost in the New Testament. The third festival, the Feast of Booths, emphasized harvest thanksgiving; it was a joyous weeklong celebration recalling the wilderness wanderings and the need for renewing the covenant with God (Lev. 23:39–43).

Of course, the book of Psalms, in various stages of development, became the prayer and praise book of the Temples; its Hebrew title means "songs of praise." It was a rich resource for both public and private worship, and it has continued in that role for both Jew and Christian.

The Temple was supremely the place where worshipers rejoiced before their God. They brought their offerings, tithes, and sacrifices. Their worship included music, solos, anthems, dancing, processions accompanied by a variety of musical instruments. Incense burning symbolized the ascending prayers of the people. Simple preaching and many kinds of oracles proclaimed peace and reassurance. The hero stories of Israel's fathers and soldiers were recited. Prayers were offered; vows and vigils were observed. The recitation of creeds, the offering of confession, sacred meals and washings, and the lighting of sacred fires were all a part of Israel's worship. It had rich variety and called forth a multitude of sacred memories as the people thought of God's manifold mercies and mighty deliverances.

5. Judged by the Prophets. Because Israel herself was so morally wrong, said the prophets, her worship was wrong. She tried to substitute sacrifices for mercy, but God would not receive them (Isa. 1:13). This does not mean, however, that the prophets condemned the whole structure of worship and sacrifice. Not even the most solemn of them (Amos or Jeremiah) could find fault with Israel's spontaneous rejoicing before God. Amos denounced her excessive feasts (5:21–24) and those acts of worship which ignored repentance (4:4–6). The prophets criticized hypocritical worship, the kind that went through the motions correctly but did not lead to self-examination, repentance, and right living.

However, Israel did not heed the warnings of the eighth-century prophets. Religious practices from neighboring countries were brought into the Temple, and worship was broadened to include idols as well as Yahweh. The most significant reform was led by Josiah when he suppressed idolatry and tried to purify worship in Jerusalem (2 Kings 23:4–25). But even his influence lasted only through his reign. Within about forty years Jerusalem was overrun by

Nebuchadnezzar, the Temple was burned, and its furnishings became the spoils of war. For many in Judah this was the ultimate catastrophe; how could they worship without the Temple?

6. Worship After the Exile. During the years of captivity, the sacrificial practices were discontinued. The regular feasts could not be observed, but one scholar has suggested that their seasons may have been celebrated as memorials, when the mercies of God would be recalled and hopes rekindled for the future. The sabbath became the chief and regular day of worship.

Also during this period the synagogue may have been started as a substitute for the Temple and as a local center of study and worship. Deprived of the Temple cultus, the people more and more gloried in the law of God, of which they were the sole custodians. As the place for reading and studying the law, the synagogue was primarily an institution of learning. But worship there consisted of prayer, reading the Law and Prophets, singing the Psalms, and teaching. We may safely assume that synagogue worship both reflected and contributed to the intense spirit of nationalism, extreme zeal for rabbinical interpretations of the law, growing eschatological expectation, and concepts of religious devotion more ceremonial than moral—all of which characterized developing Judaism. The literature of the late Old Testament period and implications clearly seen in the teaching of Jesus reflect this insight about the worship of this period.

After the exile the people who had maintained their distinctiveness through decades of foreign captivity continued their main feasts but made some changes in worship patterns. Cultic prophets probably became choirs of Temple singers, using different collections of psalms. The Feast of Tabernacles was enlarged and divided into three festivals: New Year's Day, Day of Atonement, and Feast of Tabernacles.

We have assumed that the second Temple did not measure up to Solomon's in size or beauty (Hag. 2:3), but it required several years to build and lasted nearly five centuries. Although its holy of holies contained no ark, the Temple was still the center of Israel's worship and the symbol of her commitment to God.

7. Role of the Book of Psalms. Beginning probably with David's efforts in behalf of corporate worship, a collection of psalms was used as a resource for worship. After Solomon's Temple was built and its worship leaders were increased, various collections of psalms came into use. Then after the Exile, these were probably brought together and edited. Certainly by the last quarter of the third century B.C. the book had reached its present size and organization. Thus, the Psalter had a continuing influence on Hebrew worship in the days of both the first and the second Temple. The Levites sang Psalms 24, 48, 81, 82, 92—94 every week in Temple services. Psalms 113—118 (Hallel) were used as part of the liturgy of the great annual feasts of Israel. Synagogue worship also included the singing of psalms.

A remarkable feature of the Psalms is their personal appeal although probably being intended primarily for corporate worship.

Even as modern hymnals are arranged to point the direction to God and to enrich and enlarge the soul, so was the Psalter. Every phrase of the spiritual pilgrimage and response to God is graphically described: (1) thanksgiving is given (Psalms 23; 30—32; 34; 66; 92; 107; 116; 138—139; 146); (2) the cry for protection, justice, and vindication from those who are oppressed and unjustly accused is heard (Psalms 7; 11; 26; 42; 43; 52; 54; 56; 64; 70; 120; 140; 142); (3) the mentally disturbed are called to find therapy in prayer, sleep, and meditation in the sanctuary (Psalms 3—5; 17; 57; 59; 143); (4) the sick, whose afflictions are augmented by a sense of personal guilt and injustice, are called to listen to others who have known these experiences and have been helped by God (Psalms 13; 22; 28; 31:9-24; 35; 38; 41; 69; 71; 86; 102; 109); (5) many prayers for the sick appear (Psalms 6; 39; 62; 83); (6) prayers of the penitent are found (Psalms 51; 130); (7) the call to unfaltering trust in God steadies the soul of the psalmist and offers stability to others (Psalms 16; 91; 131).

II. Worship in the New Testament

Since the first Christians were Jews who were faithful in their worship at the Temple and the synagogue, it was natural for them to use familiar forms as they moved into the Christian context. Psalms, prayers, Scripture reading and interpretation continued as the ways of worship, but they were transformed in the light of the Christian message. Of course, Christians abandoned the sacrificial system because Christ's death had spelled its end.

We are not given a clear picture of early Christian worship in the New Testament. Only one account of the observance of the Lord's Supper appears—and that the lamentable perversion of this meaningful ordinance as it was practiced by the church in Corinth. The baptism of converts is recorded without specific description of its being related to private or corporate worship. It needs to be said, however, that each ordinance, so full of theological content for worship, was a dramatic act of involvement for participants and believing witnesses. These—together with preaching—made up the heart of early Christian worship, all magnifying Jesus the Christ as risen Redeemer and living Lord.

Without a detailed portrayal of content, liturgy, and form of New Testament worship, we may be certain that the teaching of Jesus, interpreted and complemented by the teaching of the apostles, made the most telling contribution to both concepts and practices of worship. The Lord had said, "God is spirit, and those who worship him must worship in spirit and truth" (John 4: 24). That statement, though not reported in the Gospel till almost the end of the New Testament period, would surely have left its unforgettable impact on the apostles and, through their teaching, on the early church.

This became an even more meaningful reality for the believers through the coming of the Holy Spirit. God is not localized. God in Christ through the Spirit is everywhere. He can be worshiped anywhere. He must be worshiped in reality, without the vanity of pretense or the mockery of hypocrisy through unfaithfulness. Worship is involvement with the Father and the living Lord through the Spirit in the wonder of reverential praise, penitent confession, self-giving, and expectant hope.

While of necessity remembering the immaturity of the early Christian community and the impact of both Hebrew and pagan concepts on the developing life of the church, the worship of the believers was surely marked by dynamic conviction as to the reality of the resurrection of Jesus and excited expectation of his return. As the fires of persecution increased toward the end of the first century, scattering Christians and creating small groups bound together by their confession, "Jesus is Lord," their worship became the source of consolation and courage and the motivation for sharing their goods with one another, giving their witness to pagans, and remaining faithful even unto death. To persons of such devotion and hope the worship scenes in the book of Revelation would speak with tremendous force and comfort.

1. Influence of Judaism. The Christian movement began within Judaism and in its early years was vitally related to it. When at twelve Jesus became a son of the Law, he joined his elders on the Passover pilgrimage to Jerusalem and the Temple (Luke 2:41–47). Later at the peak of his ministry Jesus showed his deep feeling for the Temple when he drove out the money-changers (Mark 11:15–17). His practice of regular worship in the synagogues is revealed in his experience at Nazareth (Luke 4:16–17) and Capernaum (John 6:59).

The earlier believers among the Jews also revealed a similar commitment to both the Temple and the synagogue. Even after the crucifixion and resurrection they went daily to the Temple "teaching and preaching

Jesus as the Christ" (Acts 5:42). Years later despite the threat against his life, Paul identified himself with Temple requirements (Acts 21:26). Meanwhile, he had not hesitated to worship and preach in the synagogues of Asia Minor (Acts 13:13–16).

Of course, the Scriptures for Christian worship in New Testament times were the Jewish Law and Prophets, plus the Writings, including the book of Psalms. According to the four Gospels, Jesus quoted from various Old Testament books, especially Deuteronomy, Isaiah, and Psalms. In his last recorded teaching session with his disciples he said, "Everything written about me in the law of Moses and the prophets and the psalms must be fulfilled" (Luke 24:44).

Even when the break came between Judaism and Christianity, believers adapted the synagogue order of service for their own needs and continued to search the Scriptures.

2. Gentile Influence. When Christianity moved into the Gentile world, some words were borrowed from non-Jewish culture to clarify ideas strange to Gentile ears. With the possible exception of some marriage customs and funeral feasts, however, no positive elements in Christian worship can be traced directly to non-Jewish sources.

Some scholars have tried to link Christianity with the dying and rising gods of the mystery religions and with sacred meals in which the life of the gods was supposed to be imparted (for example, the rites of initiation into the cult of Attis and the communal meal of Mithraism). In form there were similarities, but the essence of the Christian meal can be accounted for only in the last supper of Jesus, which had its root in the Passover meal of Israel.

Three basic differences marked Christian worship from the mystery religions: Christianity claimed uniqueness while the mystery cults were admittedly syncretic. Again, Christianity shouted her mystery from the housetops (Rom. 16:25), but the ethnic cults carefully concealed their secrets. Preaching was a basic part of Christian worship and Christian mission. Finally,

Christianity proclaimed a resurrection which was primarily a triumph over sin accomplished by God incarnate in an actual person who willingly laid down his life in love to deliver his people from both sin and death.

3. Christian Distinctives. Although worship in the New Testament was closely related to that of Judaism, some differences appeared at once and others developed as Christianity moved away from Judaism. Franklin Segler (pp. 27–28) cites some of these from Phifer: (1) The writings of some Christian leaders began to supplement and eventually to precede the Law and the Prophets. (2) In addition to the book of Psalms new hymns were supplied by Christian writers to enrich their worship. (3) Baptism and the Lord's Supper became distinctive features. (4) Because of Christ's resurrection and his promise of the Spirit, a spontaneous zeal quickened the worship with a sense of God's presence. (5) A new time and place also made their worship different.

At first, Jewish Christians continued their worship at the Temple and/or synagogue on the seventh day; then they gathered on the first day to memorialize the resurrection. Of course, Gentile believers had no commitment to the sabbath unless they had been Jewish proselytes. Ultimately, the first day as the Lord's Day became *the* day of Christian worship.

The site of this first-day worship moved from home to home (Acts 2:46). As the synagogues proved inhospitable to the Christian witness, private homes and occasionally some public building became the center of worship. Jesus had promised his presence when two or three were gathered in his name (Matt. 18:20), and he had shown his disciples that God could be worshiped in other places than Temple and synagogue. Neither he nor they repudiated buildings for worship; since it was a spiritual experience, the committed community itself was just more important.

Although the features of the synagogue service influenced early Christian worship, the New Testament does not reveal a specific order. Segler lists some worship elements that are mentioned at various places in the New Testament: music had a central place; the Scriptures were read; prayer was important; the worshipers said "Amen" to express their approval; a sermon or exposition of Scripture had an important part; exhortation seemed to be essential; offerings were customary; open confession of either sin or faith was practiced; and both baptism and the Lord's Supper were observed (pp. 29–31).

4. Baptism. Christian baptism arose in part from Jewish proselyte baptism, the purification ceremony prior to entering the holy place, and the baptism practiced by John the Baptist. When a Gentile was converted to Judaism, he was required to immerse himself in water in the presence of two witnesses. From this bath he came forth as a "newborn child," symbolizing his renunciation of his pagan past and his new relationship of being accepted by God.

John's baptism differed from Jewish proselyte baptism for it declared that even the Jews, God's chosen people, needed purification. It was distinctive also in its strong eschatological emphasis. John was proclaiming a preparation for a new age in which God would cleanse and recreate the whole world. John's baptism, therefore, symbolized in each participant what God would soon accomplish for all mankind through the Messiah. Each repentant person who was baptized of John was, therefore, submitting to God's judgment upon this evil world (Luke 3:16–17). Could this have been the clue to the meaning of our Lord's baptism?

For all of its rich ceremonial background, Christian baptism found its uniqueness in the example and mission of Jesus. His baptism was a decisive commitment to his unique relationship to God and to his role as the Suffering Servant who would fulfill his mission in the cross and the resurrection. He would personally suffer for men the baptism of fire (Luke 12:49–50). His mission was not one of judgmental destruction but one of the personal suffering which brings

life through his death on the cross.

Early Christians regarded the church as the community of the Spirit. For them this was first manifested when Jesus was anointed as the Messiah in his baptism (Acts 10:37–38). They, therefore, associated the water baptism of Jesus with the coming of the Holy Spirit. Therefore, the entrance into the community of the Spirit was symbolized by baptism and became a requirement for church membership.

The form of Christian baptism was like that of John's but it was filled with the new meaning that Christ brought. It portrayed not only the washing away of sin through repentance but also the receiving of the Holy Spirit as Jesus had (Acts 2:38). To enter the church one must be baptized in the name of Jesus. This was a means of publicly proclaiming Jesus as the Messiah and confessing him as Lord. It also symbolized the entrance into the saving body of Christ himself.

With all the discussion concerning ceremonies in the New Testament, it seems strange that no passage ever describes a controversy over baptism. It appears to be a firmly established custom of which Paul writes: "One Lord, one faith, one baptism" (Eph. 4:5).

Some believe that the Ethiopian's question to Philip was the customary liturgical question asked by each candidate. The administrator would reply, "If you believe with all your heart, you may." Then the candidate would make this profession of faith: "I believe that Jesus Christ is the Son of God" (Acts 8:36–39). Other confessions of faith are also connected with baptism such as "Jesus is Lord" (1 Cor. 12:3), which is, perhaps, the earliest. Others may appear in John 2:22; Romans 1:3–6; 8:34; 10:9–10; 1 Corinthians 15: 3 ff.; 1 Timothy 3:16; 6:13–14; 2 Timothy 2:8; 1 Peter 3:18–22.

The earliest form of baptism was the single immersion in water (running water was preferred) of one who personally confessed, "I believe that Jesus Christ is the Son of God." It marked the beginning of a new life in the new messianic community of the risen Lord.

5. The Lord's Supper. Aside from the accounts of the institution of the Lord's Supper found in the Gospels (Matt. 26:26–30; Mark 14:22–26; Luke 22:19–20) and implied references in the book of Acts (2:42; 10:41; 20:11), Paul's instruction to the Corinthians (1 Cor. 10—11) provides the material bearing on the observance of the Lord's Supper as an aspect of worship by the early church.

Very briefly, a few observations may be suggestive for understanding and appreciation. (1) It was the intention and command of Jesus that the Supper should be observed by Christians as an impressive and continuing reminder of his sacrifice for the remission of sins, this observance seemingly being designed to become a worship ritual to dramatize the truth of redemption in the most meaningful way possible and to inspire the holiest desire to be involved in the sufferings of Christ through penitence, thanksgiving, and commitment. (2) The observance of the Supper was to be declarative of personal faith in the sacrifice of Christ as the means of redemption, of corporate unity in the body of Christ, and of expectation in his coming again. (3) The observance of the Supper calls for spiritual self-examination in the light of the meaning of the death of Christ and his lordship over life. Such self-examination, together with the symbolism of the elements and the theological content of the ordinance, should make worship through the Supper the means of blessed renewal, cleansing, and dedication.

The Supper seems to have been celebrated daily or at least quite frequently. As with the regular worship services, it was held in the homes of believers (Acts 2:46) with each person responsible for his own food or bringing something for the common table. Prayers, psalms, Scripture reading, and eventually preaching had their part in the joyful service.

6. Extrabiblical Sources. Two documents of the second century throw more light on early Christian worship. One is a letter (*ca.* 113 A.D.) from Pliny, governor of Bithynia, to the Emperor Trajan based on information from some who had once been Christians.

They contended that the sum of their guilt or error had lain in this, that they were accustomed on a special day to assemble before daylight and to sing antiphonally a hymn to Christ as if he were a god, and to bind themselves by an oath not for any wrong purpose, but not to commit theft or robbery or adultery, not to break their word or to deny a deposit when asked for. After this it was their custom to depart, and to meet together again to take food, but ordinary and harmless food.

The second document is known as the First Apology of Justin Martyr, written about 150 A.D. and addressed to the Emperor Hadrian and others. Three long paragraphs near the end deal with Christian worship. The service was held on Sunday and began immediately with the reading of the Scriptures, both the Septuagint and the Gospels. Then came the sermon by the bishop delivered from his chair. Afterward, the congregation arose and with outstretched arms offered their common prayers. A deacon would propose a special object of prayer. This request would be followed by an interval of silent individual intercession. Then the bishop would sum up the prayers of the congregation in the "collect." These prayers were extemporaneous and were intoned in a chant halfway between speaking and singing; they were concluded with a loud "amen" by the congregation. The word Justin used meant "shout in applause." This word meant not only "so be it," but it also gathered up the great expectation of the congregation that God would answer. The expectation was based upon the fulfilment which was already present in Christ. This may explain what Paul meant when he said, "For all the promises of God find their Yes in him. That is why we utter the Amen through him, to the glory of God" (2 Cor. 1:20).

At the close of the common prayers the kiss of peace was conferred, which was an oriental practice comparable to our shaking of hands (Luke 7:45). Each Christian then brought his offering of bread and wine, which the deacons placed on the table for the bishop's prayer of consecration. This extemporaneous prayer was concluded with the congregational "amen." Then the deacons served the people. No benediction nor other kind of devotion was offered because the Lord's Supper was itself in its entirety the climax of the service.

III. Implications for Contemporary Worship

1. Sense of God's Nearness. Israel's joy was rooted in her awareness of God. The Hebrew patriarchs believed that God was very near and real to them. He not only controlled the world but was near as a friend is near. Worship for them was drawing near to God. They could do that because he had already drawn near to them. When God visited his people, the place of his visit was marked by an altar.

The structure of the tabernacle marked the degrees of the nearness of God. The holy of holies, where only the high priest could go, was the nearest place of all. The tabernacle itself was a constant reminder of the tabernacling presence of God. Jesus himself became God's final tabernacle; he "dwelt [tabernacled] among us" (John 1:14). Meaningful worship includes a mystical awareness of the nearness of God.

2. Offerings. When Israel went up before God, she carried offerings: tithes, first-fruits and firstlings, and sacrifices. When Moses received the offering for the tabernacle, the people were so generous that he had to restrain them (Ex. 36:6). The early church also placed great stress upon benevolent giving. Paul even stressed that the thief should stop stealing and work with his hands, not that he might be able to provide for himself but that he might have something to give to the needy (Eph. 4:28).

3. Sacrifices. One way of access to God for Israel was by sacrifice and peace offerings. These were not attempts to buy divine favor. Rather, they were God's own provision for reconciliation. Those who sacrificed were practicing the humility and obedience

which God required. The blood poured out on the altar was life which only God can give. It is always God who provides for atonement. The blood is the symbol of life. It represents self, time, and property which are being surrendered to God.

With the levitical priesthood and sacrifices in her background, the *new* Israel came to see in Christ not only the tabernacling presence of God but their great High Priest who is himself the final sacrifice for sin, making all bloody altars obsolete. He was offered once for all for sin (Heb. 9:28).

4. Purification and Consecration. The Day of Atonement was the most solemn of all days when purification was made annually for the Temple, priests, and all people (Lev. 16). The worship of Israel placed heavy emphasis upon purification, washing of garments (Ex. 19:10–13), and consecration. This attitude became a vital part of the worship of the early church (Rom. 12) and should always mark the believer's worship. God's demand for reconciliation includes cleansing and renewal.

5. Social Concern. Worship in Israel made her aware of her relation not only to God but to all whom God had created, especially the needy, the oppressed, the fatherless, the infirm, those who could not care for themselves. Many were the promises of God to those who cared for the poor, and many were his warnings against those who oppressed the poor.

6. Inspiration and Hope. The singing, preaching, teaching, praying, and fellowship of the church are intended to bring inspiration to the worshiper that he may bear his burden and his affliction in the strength of God. Worship should rekindle hope and confidence in the final triumph of God and his goodness. The fellowship of worship reminds us that we are not alone. We are all members of the body of Christ in whose love we were born, in whose strength we bear our burdens, in whose grace we find forgiveness and life eternal.

7. Ecstasy in Worship. Ecstasy is a part of Christian worship. The church experienced ecstasy when the wind, fire, and tongues gave evidence of the presence of the Holy Spirit. Those exalted feelings followed much prayer and strong conviction. Peter's prayer brought an ecstatic vision. Stephen's vision also had elements of ecstasy (Acts 7:55). Paul's conversion included ecstasy (Acts 9:22). When he was caught up in the third heaven, he heard unutterable things and did not know whether he was in the body or out of the body (2 Cor. 12:2–4). John was "in the Spirit on the Lord's day" (Rev. 1:10); in his state of ecstasy he heard a voice and saw a vision.

The New Testament described these experiences but assigns a higher value to *living* in the Spirit as the normal pattern of Christian experience.

8. Vital Participation. Biblical patterns show us that worship involves vital participation. Many people over thirty leave a worship service asking, "What did he say?" They are accustomed to verbal forms of perception. But those under thirty are asking, "What happened?" They are accustomed to perception that comes from participation. They want a service which is a "happening." Ancient worship had that quality. Too often our worship is reduced to a second-hand description of reality instead of an event in which God is actually encountered. The church must again draw on the infinite variety of form and substance to quicken worship and give us again our sacred excitement.

9. Duty and Privilege. A significantly important admonition related to worship is found in Hebrews 10:25. Its context would have been widely applicable to the experience of Christians in New Testament times and equally so now. Meeting together for corporate worship is a duty not to be treated lightly. The urgent spiritual needs of Christians, so richly satisfied through meaningful worship, involve an obligation on their part to seek the enrichment of heart and mind and renewal of purpose and hope that would come from worship. The communion with God through response to his grace and

truth and through the instruction and sanctifying work of his Spirit cleanses and consecrates the life of his people. Further such worship equips the people of God with vision and compassion to become the servants of God in the world. What worship contributes to the Christian makes it a duty too sacred to neglect.

As worthy as a sense of duty may be, the sense of privilege is the compulsion that should capture the response of the Christian. Again the Hebrews passage (10:19–26) is eloquent with persuasive appeal. The redeemed people of God have a living way of direct access to God—the Holy One, the Almighty, the God of glory and grace—through the living Mediator, who gained this access for everyone by the shedding of his blood. On this basis, all are invited to draw near to God with full assurance of faith, that is, full confidence of acceptance into the very presence and life of God himself. Christian worship is the privilege of ascribing praise to the eternal God, bowing in devotion before the Lord of heaven and earth, declaring love and gratitude for the Saviour, and receiving the forgiveness and joy and strength of life in the Spirit.

For Further Reading

BUTTRICK, GEORGE A. *Prayer.* Nashville: Abingdon Press, 1942.

DAVIES, G. HENTON. "Worship in the Old Testament," *The Interpreter's Dictionary of the Bible,* Vol. R-Z. Ed. GEORGE A. BUTTRICK. Nashville: Abingdon Press, 1962.

HEILER, FRIEDRICH. *Prayer.* London: Oxford University Press, 1932.

PEAKE, A. S., Ed. *The People and the Book,* "Worship and Ritual." Nashville: Abingdon Press, 1925.

"Public Worship," *Review and Expositor,* Vol. LXII, No. 3. Louisville, Kentucky: Southern Baptist Theological Seminary, Summer, 1965.

RICHARDSON, C. C. "Worship in New Testament Times, Christian," *The Interpreter's Dictionary of the Bible,* Vol. R-Z. Ed. GEORGE A. BUTTRICK. Nashville: Abingdon Press, 1962.

SEGLER, FRANKLIN M. *Christian Worship: Its Theology and Practice.* Nashville: Broadman Press, 1967.

Ethics in the Bible

William M. Pinson, Jr.

Asking "What is the right thing to do?" calls for a consideration of ethics. Ethics is concerned with standards, values, and duties for human conduct. It seeks to determine what *ought* to be done and how to do it—in individual action, interpersonal relations, family life, and society.

The biblical writers gave a great deal of attention to ethics. After a thorough study of ethics in the Bible, T. B. Maston concluded: "The ethical is a significant phase of practically every book of both testaments and is the central theme or dominant interest of a number of the books" (p. 281).

I. Basic Approaches

Most biblical scholars agree that ethical emphases are a significant part of the Bible, but they disagree on how these relate to life today. Some dismiss biblical ethics as outdated and irrelevant, but most consider the ethics in the Bible as in some way applicable to our situation.

One approach is to view the Bible as a rule book or code for human conduct, accepting both the laws of the Old Testament and the precepts of the New Testament as authoritative for today. Advocates of this position turn to the Bible for specific answers for all moral problems.

A number of shortcomings have been pointed out concerning the rule book approach to biblical ethics. For example, many modern issues such as birth control, drug abuse, heart transplants, and atomic warfare are not specifically dealt with in the Bible. On the other hand, numerous rules in the Bible were so related to the times in which they were given that they have little meaning today (Lev. 25:44–46). Certain biblical commands are contrary to current laws (Lev. 20:10–16). Finally, even very explicit commands can leave uncertainties. For example, does the command "Thou shalt not kill" apply to abortion or not?

A second approach to biblical ethics insists that no commandment or teaching in the Bible is absolutely binding. The exception is love, the only absolute; by it all attitudes and actions are to be judged. Exponents of this position believe that a person cannot know what he ought to do apart from a concrete situation. A person is to do the loving and responsible thing in each situation. Advocates of this position claim that the Bible is helpful in at least three ways: It shows that God deals with men according to their situation, not by rules or codes (Matt. 12:1–8). It points to the primacy of love in human relations (Matt. 22:34–40). It helps develop and motivate the kind of character necessary for making adequate ethical decisions (2 Tim. 3:16–17).

A number of objections have been raised against this approach. It does not take the Bible seriously enough; for example, it slights the numerous specific guidelines for ethical action set forth by Jesus, Paul, and others in the Bible. It is too optimistic about man's ability to know what is the loving thing to do; love often needs concrete instruction. It stresses too much the uniqueness of situations; most situations have universal qualities. In spite of its criticism of moral principles and laws, it sets up its *own* list of guidelines and rules.

A third approach emphasizes the principles and ideals of the Bible. Many of these are explicitly stated; others are implied in rules which are not directly applicable today. Efforts are made to determine the basic principles behind these specific commandments (Ex. 21:1–11; Lev. 19:27). It is believed that such principles are abidingly relevant although certain specific commands might not be. Principles must be applied to concrete decisions and current issues. This calls for the use of sound biblical interpretation and the exercise of reason enlightened by the Holy Spirit.

Criticism has been directed to the principle approach to biblical ethics: It can harden into legalism. It sometimes values principles more than persons. It is difficult to determine which principle should take priority when in a particular situation several seem to conflict. It is often next to impossible to know whether an ethical command in the Bible is a basic principle or an application of a principle in a specific situation.

Any approach to biblical ethics calls for interpretation and application. Even the most devout Christians do not follow literally all the ethical teachings of the Bible. For example, many Christians eat pork, allow women to speak in church, refrain from stoning adulterers to death, and wear jewelry all of which violate specific biblical commands or teachings (cf. Lev. 11:7–8; 20:10; 1 Tim. 2:9–14; 1 Cor. 14:34–35). Obviously some precepts are considered more authoritative than others.

One basic method of interpretation used by many Christians is to evaluate the Old Testament in the light of the New and all ethical emphases in both Testaments in the light of the life and teachings of Jesus. This method is based on the belief that in Christ God has revealed himself most completely (Heb. 1:1–2). Therefore, whenever Jesus' life or teaching seems to conflict with an Old Testament command, Jesus' word is to be taken as authoritative (Ex. 21:23 and Matt. 5:38–39; Lev. 20:10 and John 8:1–11).

Christians disagree on the general relation of the ethical teachings of the Old Testament to those of the New. Some believe that Old Testament emphases are not authoritative unless specifically cited in the New. Others contend that Old Testament precepts are binding unless specifically set aside in the New Testament. Many insist that although the so-called ceremonial and civil law in the Old Testa-

ment is not binding, the moral law is still authoritative.

Interpretation is necessary also to determine what the Bible teaches about specific issues. It is not enough to know what the Bible says. We must also understand what it means and how it applies to us today.

For example, the Bible says many things about divorce (Lev. 27:7,14; Deut. 24: 1–4; Mal. 2:16; Matt. 5:31–32; 19:3–12; Mark 10:1–12; Luke 16:18; 1 Cor. 7:1–15). Taking into account these specific statements as well as basic principles for Christian living, a Christian must determine what the Bible means for Christians to do in regard to divorce. Of course, a Christian should accept the Bible as authoritative. But he must still *interpret* the ethical teachings in the Bible and apply them to his life in order to determine what he ought to do. Such an approach calls for depth understanding of the nature of biblical ethics.

II. General Characteristics

A number of characteristics are evident in the ethics of the Bible. An awareness of them will aid in interpretation and application.

Religious.—The ethical emphases of the Bible are rooted in religious experience. Many ethical systems in the world are built on reason or tradition and have little or nothing to do with religion. Such approaches to ethics have man as their starting point and reason as their basic method. Biblical ethics, on the other hand, is centered in God and depends primarily upon revelation.

Theology and ethics go hand in hand in the Bible. Divine conduct is related to human conduct. A religion which is concerned only with doctrine and ritual is displeasing to God. God requires righteousness, justice, love, and mercy from his people. The Ten Commandments (Ex. 20:1–17) and Jesus' Great Commandment (Matt. 22:34–40) are vivid examples of the interrelatedness in the Bible of the vertical and horizontal, the religious and ethical.

The close relation of religion and ethics is also seen in the concepts of God, man, and sin. God is a moral Person. He reveals his nature and will to man. Man is created capable of knowing and responding to God's revelation. His failure to do so is sin. Sin, therefore, is more than violation of religious taboos. It has an ethical dimension.

Salvation also is related to ethics. The Bible clearly indicates that although salvation does not come by works, good works are an evidence or purpose of salvation (Eph. 2:8–10). Faith is adequate only when it results in God-pleasing attitudes and conduct (Matt. 7:15–23; Rom. 6:1–4).

Varied.—The Bible contains varying degrees and levels of ethical emphases. Genesis, Exodus, Leviticus, Deuteronomy, Proverbs, Amos, Micah, Isaiah, Hosea, the Synoptic Gospels, the latter portions of Romans, Galatians, Ephesians, and Colossians, the epistles to Timothy and Titus, 1 Corinthians, 1 John, and James contain a great deal of ethical material.

The scope of ethics in the Bible includes both inner attitudes (Matt. 5:21–30; Gal. 5:22–23) and outer action (Rom. 13:1–7; 1 Cor. 7:1–24). Personal conduct is considered as well as social institutions. (See "Areas of Concern" below.)

Different parts of the Bible present distinct ethical emphases. The Old Testament is primarily, but not exclusively, concerned with specific commands, law, outward conduct, negative injunctions, and standards for the Hebrew people and nation. The New Testament is devoted more to general principles, grace, inner attitudes, motivation, and standards for individuals and churches.

In addition there is great variety within both the Old and the New Testament. The Pentateuch is devoted mainly to laws and rules related to the covenant. The prophets stress that religious activity apart from righteous living is displeasing to God. The wisdom literature urges men to live by the dictates of godly wisdom.

In the New Testament the teachings of Jesus stress loving service, inner attitude, the kingdom of God, the expectations of a loving heavenly Father, and the proper relation of religion and ethics. In comparison with Jesus, Paul is more specific, negative, and church-centered. He deals extensively with issues such as the relation of law and grace, Gentile and Jew, church and world, which Jesus said little about. John's teachings are general and stress love in action while James' are specific and relate faith and work.

In spite of the variety and diversity there is an amazing unity to the ethics in the Bible. This unity is largely due to the fact that all ethical emphases are related to God, the central character and unifying factor in the Bible.

Relevant.—The ethics in the Bible are relevant and authoritative for men today. The ethical teachings speak to man's present problems. Part of the reason for the Bible's up-to-date quality is that man has not changed essentially since the Bible was written.

Not all the ethical teachings of the Bible are equally relevant. Those portions which are the least related to historical circumstances are in general the most abidingly relevant. Statements of basic principles and ideals are often more relevant than specific codes of conduct. Many of these are ideals of perfection. They are beyond man's capacity to attain. "They are the ideals that create the dynamic tension at the heart of our Christian faith which is the secret of its creativity" (Maston, p. 287).

That there is some type of progress or refinement in the ethics of the Bible is obvious. Such progress is particularly noticeable when one moves from the Old Testament to the New, especially the life and teachings of Jesus. The New Testament is more thoroughly relevant than the Old. The climax of God's revelation came in his Son, Jesus Christ. Jesus made clear the supreme authority of his ethical teachings when in the Sermon on the Mount he declared, "You have heard that it was said to the men of old. . . . But I say to you."

To say that an ethical teaching is less relevant than another does not mean that it is not inspired or helpful. Even those portions which, in the light of Jesus' teachings, are clearly not applicable to us can still be informative. Ethical teachings not directly related to our times frequently contain basic principles which are abidingly relevant. Instructions on what to do when you find your neighbor's ox loose (Deut. 22:1–2) are not particularly useful to the modern city dweller. Yet behind the specific instructions are principles of honesty and of concern for persons and property which apply to city life in the twentieth century.

Unique.—Many of the percepts and principles in the Bible can be found in the writings of other religions. The uniqueness of biblical ethics is primarily in the person and work of Jesus Christ. Although much of Jesus' ethical teachings can be found elsewhere, he presents a unique selection and combination of teachings found nowhere else. Because of the incarnation he provides authoritative standards in his life and teachings. By his crucifixion he makes possible our freedom to follow his way. As a result of the resurrection he can empower the believer by living through him. In the promise of his coming again he offers encouragement to be faithful in spite of difficulties because ultimate victory is assured.

III. Major Emphases

Efforts have been made to systematize biblical ethics around one theme, but it is artificial to force the ethics of the Bible into such a mold. A number of emphases are prominent in the ethics of the Bible.

Will of God.—A major theme is that men are to do the will of God. The Old Testament is filled with commands from God to his people. Clearly he expected them to do his will. When the prophets thundered, "Thus saith the Lord," they were also stressing that God's will was to be done. Jesus undergirded this theme in his ministry (cf. Matt. 7:21). His concept of the kingdom of God called for radical obedience to God's will. The Bible is the primary, although not exclusive, resource for finding God's will.

Godlikeness.—The Bible states that man is made in the image of God (Gen. 1:26–27). However marred by sin, man is still in God's image (Gen. 9:6). Whatever else the image of God may mean it certainly indicates that man was created to be like God insofar as human limitation permits. The character of God is to be the pattern for the character of man.

This theme is sounded in both testaments. Leviticus records God's command, "You shall be holy; for I the Lord your God am holy" (Lev. 19:2). And Jesus declared, "You, therefore, must be perfect, as your heavenly Father is perfect" (Matt. 5:48). The biblical writers indicate that God is loving, just, merciful, righteous, and forgiving. Therefore, men are also to display these characteristics in their lives.

Love.—Because God is love, his people are to love. Love is one of the most significant themes in biblical ethics. It is the supreme virtue. Love for God and love for neighbor were stressed in the Old Testament (Lev. 19:18; Deut. 6:5). Jesus indicated that love for God and neighbor summarize the entire Law and Prophets (Matt. 22:34–40). New Testament writers often emphasize the importance of love (Rom. 13:8,10; Gal. 5:14; James 2:8; 1 John 3:11).

The New Testament uses a special word for Christian love, agape. Agape as described by the Bible is no bland virtue (Matt. 22:34–40; 1 Cor. 13); it involves forgiveness, compassion, and ministering to the needs of one's neighbors. Love is to be extended to others without regard to their merit or thought of their response. Love for God involves trust, adoration, and obedience. Love for neighbor is benevolent good will in action. Love for God and love for neighbor go together.

Covenant.—The biblical ethic could properly be called a covenant ethic. In the covenant instituted at Sinai (Ex. 19;

Deut. 5) God set forth specific obligations for his people. When they agreed to the terms of the covenant, they promised to obey these rules. God in turn promised to protect them if they obeyed. The requirements were both religious and moral in nature. In the "new covenant" (Jer. 31:31–34; Matt. 26:28; Heb. 8:6–13) Jesus called men to follow him and to obey God's will in all of life.

Each covenant is a work of God's grace. The response of faith to that grace involves obedience to the source of the grace, the author of the covenant—God. The covenant people are to be the instruments of God's redemptive purpose. As such they are expected to live up to certain requirements which are largely ethical in nature.

Community.—Both the old and the new covenant were instituted with groups of people—Israel and the New Israel. The ethical requirements are for a community of persons, not merely individuals. They are intended for the people of God. It is not that the ethical requirements of the Bible have no bearing on other people; but they are especially designed by God for those who know him, love him, and pledge to do his will. For example, the Law was primarily for the nation Israel, and Paul's ethical teaching primarily for the churches.

Within the fellowship of faith God's people make ethical decisions. It is in the context of Christian community, prayer, worship, sharing, and study of the Word of God that believers live and act. The emphasis on community is so important in the ethics of the Bible that some scholars use the descriptive phrase "koinonia ethics."

Lordship of Christ.—Jesus, according to the Bible, is to be not only Saviour but also Lord. The lordship of Christ means, among other things, that Christians are to follow his example and obey his teachings.

Closely related to the theme of "Be like God" is the New Testament emphasis "Be like Christ." Such stress on being like Christ is in keeping with the biblical em-phasis that God was in Christ and that Christ reveals the Father. Since we are to be like God and since Jesus reveals most fully what God is like, we are to be like Jesus. New Testament writers often stress that theme (Mark 8:34; John 13:34; 1 Cor. 11:1; Phil. 2:5–11; 1 Peter 2:21–23).

Another aspect of the lordship of Christ is obedience to his teachings. Jesus told his followers, "Go therefore and make disciples of all nations . . . teaching them to observe all that I have commanded you" (Matt. 28:19–20). He also said, "If you love me, you will keep my commandments" (John 14:15). A large part of Jesus' teachings have to do with ethics.

In many ways the life and the teachings of Jesus reinforced one another. Jesus taught that the disciples' life was to be characterized by love, self-denial, cross bearing, forgiveness, humility, servanthood, and care for the total needs of men. Jesus by his life demonstrated each of these characteristics.

Kingdom of God.—One of Jesus' chief emphases in his teaching was the kingdom of God. According to Jesus the kingdom is not developed by men but rather is established by God. Men enter the kingdom by turning from their own way to live in obedience to the will of God. The kingdom concept, therefore, is a blend of the religious and the ethical. It deals with the reign of God in all of life.

Spirit-led Life.—The New Testament stresses that Christians are to follow the leadership of the Holy Spirit. Jesus promised that the Spirit would enlighten (John 16:13–15), comfort (John 14:16), and empower the disciples (Acts 1:8).

Acts is a record of the early church under the leadership of the Spirit. For example, the Spirit led the church to understand that God is no respector of persons, that prejudice is wrong, and that a church is to be open to persons of any race.

Paul more clearly than anyone else sets forth the moral dimensions of the Spirit-led life. He urges believers to "walk by the Spirit" (Gal. 5:16). Paul indicates that the Spirit empowers and strengthens the Christian (Eph. 3:16). He describes the fruit of the Spirit in ethical terms (Gal. 5:22). He states that the Spirit delivers Christians from sin (Rom. 8:2) and helps them in the battle with evil (Eph. 6:17). Paul declares that the Spirit brings unity in the church in spite of national, sexual, or racial differences (1 Cor. 12:13). Sins against the body are wrong because the body is "a temple of the Holy Spirit" (1 Cor. 6:19).

IV. Areas of Concern

In discovering what the Bible teaches about particular areas of life, it is important to keep in mind the need for careful interpretation. To consult all passages dealing with a particular topic does not necessarily lead to an understanding of what the Bible teaches. All the basic themes of biblical ethics must also be related to the subject.

Individual.—Much of the Bible's ethical teaching is concerned with the individual —his health, well-being, attitudes, and personal conduct. Large portions of the Old Testament law are devoted to health measures. Diet and sanitation are emphasized (Lev. 11—15). The New Testament teachings on health are less extensive, but they are no less significant. The Christian is to care for his body primarily because it belongs to God (1 Cor. 6:13), is a living sacrifice (Rom. 12:1), and is the temple of the Holy Spirit (1 Cor. 6:19).

The individual's mental and emotional well being are also of concern to God. The Christian is to have the mind of Christ and to set his mind on things above (Phil. 2:5; Col. 3:2). He is to rejoice, be filled with hope, trust in God, reject anxiety, and let the peace of Christ rule in his heart. (Matt. 6:25–34; John 14:27; Col. 3:15; 1 Tim. 4:10).

Virtues to be cultivated and vices to be eliminated are part of the ethical emphases of the Bible. In the Old Testament

Psalms 1, 15, and 24, Job 31, Ezekiel 18, and portions of Isaiah, Micah, Hosea, and Amos set forth qualities pleasing or displeasing to God. Portions of the New Testament also set forth virtues and vices (Gal. 5:16–25; Eph. 4:1—5:20; Col. 3:1–17; and others).

Interpersonal Relations.—Many of the virtues and vices discussed in the Bible apply not only to individual character but also to relations between individuals. In the Law many pages are devoted to interpersonal relations. The Ten Commandments indicate that each person's rights are to be respected. A person is not to take away another's life, wife, property, or good name—or even ponder such an act (Ex. 20:13–17).

Both Testaments clearly indicate that all men are to be treated with dignity and respect regardless of race, nationality, religion, or social standing. Several reasons are given for such treatment. All men are created in the image of God (Gen. 1:26–27). God loves all men and provides for the unjust as well as the just (Matt. 5:45), Christ died for all men (Rom. 5:18). God is not partial to any persons (Acts 10:34). Despite persistent efforts to justify racial discrimination and segregation on the basis of Scripture, no adequate exegesis supports such interpretations.

The Bible declares that persons in need are to be cared for and that person-damaging social structures are to be corrected. The demands of love include justice in the social order. The Old Testament law makes special provision for the poor and the powerless (Ex. 22:25–27; Lev. 14:21–32; Deut. 15:1–11.) The prophets called for both individuals and the nation to care for the poor, the widows, the orphans, and others in need. They promised judgment on those who did not seek justice for the oppressed (Isa. 1:1–31; Amos 5:11–12).

Jesus spent considerable time ministering to the needy; he was concerned about the whole man. He fed the hungry, comforted the sorrowing, healed the sick, made men whole, and dealt with sin. He announced his ministry and offered evidence of being the Messiah in terms of caring for total human need (Matt. 11:2–6; Luke 4:18). He indicated that men would be judged on the basis of whether or not they ministered to persons in need (Matt. 25:31–46).

The early churches followed Jesus' pattern. Jesus' disciples healed the sick, fed the hungry, and cared for the poor. New Testament writers stressed bearing one another's burdens (Gal. 6:2), doing good to all men (Gal. 6:10), helping the weak (1 Thess. 5:14; James 1:27), and caring for persons in need (1 John 3:17–18).

Family Life.—The Bible indicates that the nature of marriage is a union of male and female (Gen. 2:24). Marriage as such has been established and blessed by God (Gen. 1:27–28; 2:18–24) and is honorable (Heb. 13:4). Those with a gift for celibacy may refrain from marriage in order to devote themselves more fully to service in the kingdom of God (Matt. 19:10–12; 1 Cor. 7:7,25–27). But celibacy is not more pleasing to God than marriage.

The marriage union is to be an exclusive one (Matt. 19:4–6; 1 Cor. 7:10). There is to be no adultery, polygamy, or continued dependence on parents. Furthermore, the union is to last a lifetime (1 Cor. 7:39). Divorce, Jesus indicated, was not part of God's original plan for marriage (Matt. 19:3–12). The New Testament *possibly* allows divorce and remarriage in the case of sexual infidelity or desertion by an unbelieving mate (Matt. 5:31–32; 19:3–12; 1 Cor. 7:15). Mark 10:2–12 and Luke 16:18 do not provide any grounds for divorce and remarriage.

The Bible indicates that there is a threefold purpose for marriage. One purpose is to provide intimate companionship for a man and a woman (Gen. 2:18,22; Matt. 19:4–6). Another is to provide a constructive expression for sexual desire (1 Cor. 7:2–6; Heb. 13:4). The Bible views sex as a good gift from God which can bring happiness when used in the way God intended. The Bible indicates that sexual intercourse, an expression of the one flesh union, is only for a man and woman married to each other. Homosexuality, incest, bestiality, as well as fornication and adultery are forbidden (Ex. 20:14; Lev. 18: 6–23; Matt. 5:27–30; 19:9; Rom. 1:26–27).

A third purpose for marriage is procreation (Gen. 1:28.). However, the Bible does not indicate that procreation should be an intended aspect of every act of sexual intercourse (1 Cor. 7:1–5). Conception control when practiced for worthy reasons does not violate biblical teachings. In the light of the population explosion, it may be a Christian obligation.

The Bible sets forth guidelines for family relations. Between husband and wife the key terms are love, fidelity, respect, and consideration for each other's needs (Eph. 5:21–33; 1 Cor. 7:1–5). Children are to obey and honor their parents (Deut. 5:16; Eph. 6:1–4). Parents are to love, discipline, nurture, provide for the physical needs of, and give religious instruction to their children (Ex. 12:26–27; Col. 3:21; Titus 2:4).

Economics and Daily Work.—The Bible contains no blueprint for an economic system, but it does contain guidelines for economic activity. The Old Testament sets forth many rules for such things as slavery, harvesting of crops, loaning money, and ownership of land (Ex. 15:1–18; Lev. 19). Private ownership of property is recognized in the Bible but is never considered absolute (e.g. Lev. 19:9–10; 25:23). The land and all that is on it belong to God (Ex. 19:5; Psalm 24:1; Isa. 66:2). Man should not abuse or pollute God's land.

God gives the power to gain wealth (Deut. 8:17,18); no one is a "self-made man." Wealth is to be gained by honest labor and not by theft, dishonesty, or oppressive tactics (Prov. 21:6; Mark 12:40; Eph. 4:28). In both the Old and New Testament it is recognized that the poor are to be provided for and not taken advantage of (Job 31:16–33; Isa. 58:7–8, Amos 2:6–7).

The New Testament contains several warnings about the potential danger of wealth. Wealth can be an obstacle to entering into the kingdom of God (Matt. 19:23). It is deceitful, creating a false sense of security (Luke 12:16-21). The love of money is the root of all kinds of evil (1 Tim. 6:9-10). Material treasures are not as valuable as spiritual ones (Matt. 6:17-21). Concern for material possessions can choke spiritual growth (Matt. 13:22); therefore, men should not be anxious about material things (Matt. 6:24-34).

Jesus' life and teachings indicate that the material possessions gained by honest work are to be used in several ways: to care for one's self and family (Matt. 7:11; 15:1-6), to aid the needy (Matt. 25), to support religious leaders and institutions (Matt. 17:24-27; Mark 12:42), and to pay taxes (Matt. 22:15-22).

Paul taught that a person is to work to earn a living if possible (1 Thess. 4:11; 2 Thess. 3:10). If for some reason a person is unable to work, he is to be cared for. Income from work is to be used to provide for one's family (1 Tim. 5:8), to contribute to the support of religious leaders (1 Cor. 9:14), to pay taxes (Rom. 13:6-7), and to provide for persons in special need (Rom. 12:8,13; 2 Cor. 8:1-5).

State and Citizenship.—The Bible provides no outline for a form of government. It does indicate, however, something about the nature of government and of the responsibility of citizens. It recognizes government as a valid institution. Jesus accepted government, operated within its framework, acknowledged the right of taxation, and submitted to the authority of the state (Matt. 17:24-25; 22:15-22). Paul taught that government is ordained of God and exists to protect the righteous, punish evildoers, and advance the welfare of the citizens (Rom. 13:1-7). The right of the state to make and enforce laws as well as to punish criminals is recognized in both testaments.

The Bible indicates that government officials should be men of upright character who will carry out the legitimate functions of the state. They should be honest and accept no bribes (Ex. 23:8). They should fear God, keep his commandments (Deut. 17:18-20; Psalm 2:10-11), and recognize that their power comes from God (John 19:11; Rom. 13). They should not get drunk (Prov. 31:4,5), act unjustly, or show favoritism (Lev. 19:15; Deut. 16:19). Jesus and the prophets were severely critical of government leaders who abused their position (2 Sam. 12:1-10; Isa. 1:23; Amos 5:7,12; Mark 8:15; Luke 13:32).

According to the New Testament, Christians are to honor government officials (Rom. 13:7; 1 Peter 2:17), pay taxes (Matt. 22:21), obey laws (Rom. 13:1-7), and pray for officials (1 Tim. 2:1-2). They are not to submit to the state, however, when to do so would be contrary to God's will (Acts 5:29).

War and military force play a large role in the Bible. Although the ideal of God is peace (Psalm 46:9; Isa. 2:4; 11:1-10), the horror of war is realistically presented (2 Sam. 2:26; Psalm 79:1-2; Jer. 16:4; Isa. 1:7-8). Yet the Old Testament pictures God as sometimes allowing, even commanding, war (Lev. 26:7-8; Deut. 7:1-2; 20:1-20; 2 Sam. 22:35; 1 Chron. 5:22). It should be noted that these wars were unique, however; they were the wars which gained God's people the promised land.

In the New Testament there are no direct teachings about war. Some of Jesus' actions and teachings have been used to approve war. He taught that wars and rumors of wars would persist but would not necessarily indicate his return (Matt. 24:6). He accepted the role of military men (Luke 14:31) and praised the faith of one (Luke 7:1-9).

Other of Jesus' teachings are used to support pacifism. Jesus praised peacemakers (Matt. 5:9) and called for his disciples to love their enemies, practice non-resistance, and do good to those who harmed them (Matt. 5:38–48). He taught that those who take the sword will perish by the sword and commanded Peter to put up his weapon (Matt. 26:52).

The New Testament is practically silent on such issues as revolution, Christian participation in political action, and church-state relations. Direct Christian political action, apart from revolution, was hardly a live option for Christians under the Roman dictatorship. But it can be assumed that responsible Christian citizenship in a democracy calls for involvement in political action. Biblical insight and historical evidence tend to support separation as the best relation of church and state.

V. *Motivation for Action*

The Bible sets forth not only what is right for men but also why they are to do the right. The Scriptures contain appeals and encouragement for moral living as well as suggestions on how to appropriate available help.

Appeals.—Most appeals in the Bible for ethical conduct are centered in the nature and acts of God. To glorify God because of who he is and because of what he has done is a frequent biblical appeal (Rom. 15:6,9; 1 Cor. 6:20; 2 Cor. 9:13). In the Old Testament the reason often given for following commands is that God is the Lord (Lev. 19:1–37). In other cases appeals are made on the basis of God's grace —his unmerited love and care for his people.

A common theme in the New Testament is that believers should obey God because of what he has done for them (Rom. 12:1–2; 1 Cor. 6:20; Gal. 5:1; Eph. 3:20–24; Col. 3:1–17; 1 John 3:1–10). For example, they are to love one another because God had first loved them (Eph. 5:2; 1 John 4:11,19), and to forgive one another because God in Christ had forgiven them (Eph. 4:32).

God's loving acts are most frequently described in relation to Christ—his life, sacrifice, and concrete expressions of love. Jesus specifically commanded his disciples to love one another as he had loved them (John 15:12). New Testament writers appealed for action on the basis of Christ's actions: Because Jesus sacrificed, we are to be willing to sacrifice (1 Peter 4:12, 12–19). Because of Jesus' generosity, we are to be generous (2 Cor. 8:1–9).

In a similar vein, Christians are to conduct themselves so as to be worthy of the gospel (Phil. 1:27). Because of the blessings they have received in Christ, they should be willing to follow him (Phil. 3:8–11). A related appeal is to live godly lives in order to bear witness and prove false the defaming statements of unbelievers (1 Peter 2:15; 3:1–3).

Other motives for conduct are on a different level. Rather than appeals for godly living on the basis of gratitude for what God has done, they are on the basis of what God can do. For example, men are urged to live up to God's standards so that their prayers will be answered (2 Chron. 7:14; James 5:16). The New Testament frequently states that right conduct brings reward and wrong actions result in suffering and punishment (Matt. 25:31–46). The Old Testament contains several vivid passages depicting reward for obedience and punishment for disobedience (Lev. 26:14–39; Isa. 1:1–31). In the New Testament the final judgment, the Day of the Lord, and the second coming of Christ all are discussed in terms of ethical action (Matt. 25:31–46; 1 Thess. 5:2–11; 1 Peter 4:7–11; Rev. 2:5–8).

Enabling.—How can people find power to overcome temptation, live up to God's standards, and do God's will? The New Testament insists that only in Christ can men hope to find such strength. The Christian life is not so much imposed from without as expressed from within. The living Christ dwells with the believer to guide and strengthen him (Gal. 2:20; Phil. 4:13). As T. W. Manson said, "The living Christ still has two hands, one to point the way, and the other held out to help us along" (p. 68).

Christians can draw on power from God,

the living Christ, and the indwelling Spirit through worship, prayer, and Christian fellowship (Rom. 15:16; Gal. 2:20; 5:16– 6:5; Eph. 4:11–16; Col. 1:9–14; 3:16–17; 4:2–4). As Christians resist temptation and draw near to God, he will draw near to them (James 4:7–8).

What if a person falls short and fails to live up to the biblical standards? For the unbeliever the answer is to turn from his sin and to walk God's way by faith in Christ. For the believer the response is confession to God, acceptance of forgiveness, and renewed effort with God's help.

The Bible's answer for falling short does not mean failure is to be taken lightly. The effect of neglecting God's standards continues even after confession and forgiveness have taken place. But the Christian is not to brood over past sin. He is to go on to new achievements with God in Christ.

VI. Conclusion

The nature of biblical ethics calls for openness and obedience. The Bible speaks with authority concerning ethical issues. Yet devout Christians differ on what the Bible teaches about subjects such as abortion, conception control, capital punishment, and war. Differences exist primarily because the ethical emphases in the Bible must be interpreted and applied by fallible human beings. Each of us should be open to insights from others while we pursue our own understanding of ethics in the Bible.

The person who really believes the Bible will apply it in all areas of his life—in work, family, recreation, and politics as well as in church-related activity. Failure to care for the poor, minister to the prisoner, and feed the hungry indicates lack of commitment to the biblical revelation. A person who neglects his family, discriminates against persons because of race, or avoids payment of taxes obviously does not take the Bible seriously. The ethical teachings of the Bible demand obedience as well as study. The Christian is not only to believe the truth of God's Word but also to do it.

For Further Reading

BARNETTE, HENLEE H. *Introducing Christian Ethics*. Nashville: Broadman Press, 1961.

BRUCE, W. S. *The Ethics of the Old Testament*. Edinburgh: T. and T. Clark, 1909.

CAVE, SYDNEY. *The Christian Way: A Study of New Testament Ethics in Relation to Present Problems*. New York: Philosophical Library, Inc., 1949.

DEWAR, LINDSAY. *An Outline of New Testament Ethics*. London: Hodder and Stoughton, 1949.

GARDNER, E. CLINTON. *Biblical Faith and Social Ethics*. New York: Harper & Row, Publishers, 1960.

KNOX, JOHN. *The Ethic of Jesus in the Teaching of the Church*. New York: Abingdon Press, 1961.

LILLIE, WILLIAM. *Studies in New Testament Ethics*. Philadelphia: Westminster Press, 1961.

MANSON, T. W. *Ethics and the Gospel*. New York: Charles Scribner's Sons, 1960.

MARSHALL, L. H. *The Challenge of New Testament Ethics*. London: Macmillan and Co., Ltd., 1960.

MASTON, T. B. *Biblical Ethics: A Survey*. Waco: Word Books, Inc., 1967.

MUILENBURG, JAMES. *The Way of Israel*. New York: Harper and Row, 1961.

RAMSEY, PAUL. *Basic Christian Ethics*. New York: Charles Scribner's Sons, 1950.

The Mission of the People of God   E. Luther Copeland

The unfolding revelation of the Bible has to do with the redemptive purpose of the one God, encompassing the whole world, crucially involving the witness of the covenant people of God, and centering in the person and work of the Messiah. This statement suggests four major constituents of the Biblical understanding of mission: (1) the constitution of the people of God through election and covenant; (2) the monotheistic faith of Israel; (3) the universal reference of Israel's vocation; (4) the expectation of a messianic salvation.

These sub-themes can be traced throughout the Old Testament and the New. They do not appear full-grown in the early stages of Israel's history. Rather, they undergo development and encounter threatened eclipses as well as progressive enrichment.

I. The Mission of the People of God in the Old Testament (Covenant)

The missionary witness of the Old Testament is an unfolding one and in a profound sense an ambiguous and incomplete one. It waits upon the eschatological event of the messianic salvation which could be known beforehand only in poetic and prophetic visions and metaphors. In fact, mission, in the strict sense of being sent forth to the nations to win them to faith in God, is almost entirely absent in the Old Testament.

1. Ambiguities in Understanding Mission

Perhaps the ambivalent character of the missionary understanding of the Old Testament may be demonstrated by a brief look at each of the sub-themes suggested above as corollaries to the missionary dimension of the Bible.

With regard to election and covenant, the very events by which Yahweh had manifested his choice of Israel as his own people were themselves harsh judgments upon other nations. Egypt was scourged and defeated in order that Israel might be freed; and the nations occupying Canaan were plundered, slaughtered, and displaced so that Israel might possess the land. Therefore, the universal context and reference of Israel's covenant was obscured by harsh attitudes toward other nations.

The monotheistic faith of Israel, so essential to her missionary understanding, was subject to development and to testing. Israel was constantly tempted to conform to the religions of her pagan neighbors, thus debasing her great vision of God and forsaking her mission. At the same time, in her revulsion to paganism, she was prone to make of her God a kind of tribal deity, acknowledged officially as God of the whole earth but for all practical purposes concerned with Israel alone.

And what of the universalism of Israel's vocation? At best, she had a kind of threefold function *vis-à-vis* the nations. As *prophet,* Israel was God's witness to the nations. Through her the judging and saving word of God was to go forth. As *priest,* Israel stood before God as responsible for the nations and before the nations as responsible for mediating to them God's revelation. Likewise, through her attitude toward *kingship*—the insistence that God was her king, though she also had human kings—she was to live out in her national life the meaning of God's kingship over the universe. Yet the very uniqueness of her holy vocation as the people of God implied separation from the nations, not the mingling and identification with them which are essential to mission.

As for messianic eschatology, Israel hoped for a coming salvation which often appeared quite nationalistic—salvation for Israel but harsh judgment upon the nations or their subservience to Israel. Even when an equal sharing of the nations and Israel is envisioned as the future redemption, the direction was centripetal, not a centrifugal mission from Israel to the nations but an eschatological gathering of the nations to Zion accomplished by God and his Messiah. How Israel could contribute to this final event was by no means clear.

Taking these factors of ambiguity into account, it is remarkable that the Old Testament has so much to contribute to the understanding of mission.

2. The Missionary Understanding of the Constitution of Israel as a Nation

In the Pentateuch the historical events are recounted by which Israel is constituted as the people of God. Key passages are Genesis 12:1–3 and Exodus 19:3–6. The setting for the particular election and call of Israel, however, is a plane of sweeping universalism. The Bible begins with a "prologue to the drama of redemption" (Genesis 1–11). Elements in this prologue are (1) the sole creatorship, sovereignty, and unity of God; (2) the unity of the human race; (3) the tragic and universal need for redemption; and (4) the divine concern for man.

With Genesis 12 the searchlight of salvation history comes to focus upon one individual, Abram. The call of Abram, as recounted in Genesis 12:1–3, is deeply significant for the understanding of God's redemptive mission. It is noteworthy that this scriptural passage and its understanding of Israel's vocation are identified by scholars as within the most ancient strand of Pentateuchal tradition.

What important facets of the understanding of Israel's vocation are found in this account of Abram's call? (1) God's choice of Abram was actually the choice of a people, not merely an individual. (2) Abram was required to break the closest cultural and social ties and take the way of faith and pilgrimage; as such, he was the forerunner of all missionaries. (3) Abram was to be blessed, not as a mere favorite of God, but as a medium of God's blessing:

"I will bless you, . . . so that you will be a blessing." (4) As the mediator of God's blessing in the world, Abram and his heirs become the criterion for God's blessing and judgment; that is, the attitude once expresses toward the chosen medium of God's revelation inevitably reflects his attitude toward God himself. (5) Thus, Abram and his heirs serve a universal purpose; through them "all the families of the earth will bless themselves"—will participate in God's blessing, obviously some special kind of blessing, because the families of mankind receive the ordinary blessings of God independently of Abram and his descendants.

Another key passage in the Pentateuch expressive of Israel's significance as the people of God is Exodus 19:3–6. At Mount Sinai by God's election, some scattered tribes with no status and with a background of slavery have become God's own people. The covenant by which Israel is constituted as the people of God is based upon the grace of Yahweh, manifested in the deliverance from Egyptian bondage. By election and covenant, Yahweh has invested Israel with a holy vocation which has universal significance. In the context of "all peoples" and "all the earth," Israel is God's "own possession," something "withdrawn from the general property as a special donation." [1]

As a "kingdom of priests" the new nation was, on the one hand, a community of priests serving in the court of the divine King as his retinue and, on the other hand, priests standing before the King of all the earth representing the whole of mankind (de Dietrich). As "holy nation" Israel was to manifest in her national life the holy character of Yahweh: "You shall be holy; for I the Lord your God am holy" (Lev. 19:2).

The one place in all the world, then, where God's holy character as king of the earth was to be manifested was in the life of this nation of former slaves who recog-

---

[1] Suzanne de Dietrich, The Witnessing Community, p. 54, following Martin Buber, Moses (London: East and West Library, 1946), pp. 105–106.

nized him as king. Thus Israel was the medium of God's revelation in the world.

3. Mission in the Liturgy of Israel's Worship

The worship of the people of God in the Old Testament, as expressed in the Psalms, offers considerable witness to missionary themes. However, by no means all of the psalms in the book of Psalms can be said to be "missionary" even in the incomplete sense in which mission is understood in the Old Testament. At times, also, universalism in the psalms is contradicted or seriously qualified by nationalism which views the nations as subservient to Israel or under the destructive judgment of God.

(1) In the Psalms there is the recurring theme of Israel's ethical monotheism, the foundation of any biblical sense of mission. God is declared to be the sole creator and sovereign of the universe, equitable in judgment and rich in mercy.

(2) The Psalms often interpret religion in universal terms, transcending locale and cult. To claim that "the sacrifice acceptable to God is a broken spirit" (Psalm 51:17), for example, is to express religion in inward and ethical terms not dependent upon a particular cult.

(3) Frequently, there appears in the Psalms a vision of a kingdom, universal and eternal, often depicted as mediated by the ideal king who is God's son and his anointed ("Messiah"). so monotheism and universalism are joined with messianic eschatology.

(4) Several psalms describe the sufferings of the righteous; and at least one (Psalm 22) seems to relate the suffering of some righteous Israelite to the accomplishing of God's missionary purpose. After the suffering of this righteous one, he witnesses to his own people (v. 22), and the ultimate result is the conversion of the nations (v. 27).

(5) In the Psalms, the worship of the one God is assumed to be the only worthy expression of the religious life. Not only are idols denounced (e.g., Psalm 135:15–

18), but all that exists, including even the natural phenomena, is expected to show forth God's praise (e.g., Psalm 148).

(6) Therefore, there is the recurring call to all the peoples of the earth, and indeed to "everything that breathes," to praise the Lord. This is missionary liturgy, the universal invitation in Israel's worship.

And in at least one psalm, the covenant purpose of God as expressed in Genesis 12:1–3 and Exodus 19:3–6 is splendidly articulated in Israel's address to the covenant God in worship. In Psalm 67:1–4 Israel's claim to God's blessing is grounded in her mediation of God's redemptive revelation to the nations.

4. Mission in the Ministry of the Prophets

It has been aptly said that the prophet was a peculiar work of God in Israel. He was not provided for in the national organization as were priest and king. He was a charismatic; he knew himself as one directly in touch with God and commissioned by God. Thus, the prophet was in a peculiarly advantageous position to interpret God's character and purpose and Israel's vocation without a prosaic slavery to tradition.

(1) In general, the prophets recognize the instrumental character of Israel's election. God has a purpose for Israel, and Israel in loyalty to the covenant must seek to understand and fulfill that purpose. To be disloyal and disobedient is to run the risk of rejection by God (cf. Hosea 4:6).

(2) In remarkable measure, the prophets are convinced of God's sovereignty over all nations in judgment and mercy. Thus, they pronounce judgment upon the nations for their treatment of Israel or for their general depravity; but they also at times have a message of mercy for the nations— and sometimes harsh judgment upon Israel.

(3) In a sense, therefore, the prophetic vocation is a missionary vocation. God "sends" the prophets to address Israel and often to address the nations, too. Jeremiah, for example, is appointed "a prophet to the nations" (Jer. 1:5).

(4) Even more emphatically than the psalmists, the prophets understand religion in terms of inward and ethical dimensions which transcend and sometimes oppose cult (*cf.* Micah 6:6–8; Amos 5:21–24).

(5) Likewise, the continuing revelation through the prophets serves to develop Israel's monotheistic faith and bring it to its most exalted heights.

(6) In certain of the prophets there is an accentuation of eschatological expectation. The "day of the Lord" comes into focus, often as a day of judgment upon the nations. Frequently, however, the end time is seen in terms of a redeemed world, with the nations gathered to Zion to participate in the revelation in and through Israel.

(7) Closely related is the development of themes or figures expressing the (messianic) instrumentality by which the coming redemption is to be realized: the messianic King, the Branch, the Son of Man, the Servant of Yahweh, etc.

(8) The prophets' own vocation as witness, proclaimer of the word of God, helped them to understand that God's people had the vocation of witnessing to the nations. This is probably the basic import of the book of Jonah. Israel (Jonah) has a vocation to speak God's indiscriminate word of judgment and mercy to the nations—even to the hated Ninevites. But (post-exilic) Israel was turned inward upon herself and felt fiercely exclusive toward the nations.

The prophetic understanding of Israel's mission comes to its apex in Deutero-Isaiah (Isa. 40 ff.). By this great prophet of the exile the vocation of Israel is understood in terms of the servant of Yahweh, and there seems to be a progressive interpretation of the servant's role and identity.

First of all, we are introduced to the servant identified with Israel as a whole (*cf.* Isa. 41:8 ff.). Second, the vocation of the servant, Israel, is a mission to the nations. This mission seems to include a kingly function to establish justice by law (42:1–4), as well as a prophetic function

of witness which also has liberating consequences (42:6 ff., 18–20; 43:10–13). God has given Israel as a "covenant to the people," presumably a promise that what God means to Israel he will mean to the whole world; and as a "light to the nations," a pledge that the revelation which Israel has received will be shared with the nations.

Third, a tragic vitiation of Israel's vocation is noted: when God calls the blind and deaf nations to hear and see by means of his servant, alas, the servant himself is even more blind and deaf! (42:18–20). Fourth, the identity of the servant seems to pass from the whole of Israel to a remnant group or individual. The servant's mission is both to the nations and to Israel herself (49:5–6).

Finally, the profound truth is dramatically expressed that the universal mission of the servant can be accomplished only through the priestly function of vicarious suffering (52:13—53:12). The figures of the servant as prophet and king are merged with that of the priest who "makes himself an offering for sin" (53:10), thus making the "many" righteous by bearing their iniquities (53:11).

Do these servant passages mean to recapitulate the narrowing process of God's electing purpose in history? From Israel in her wholeness, to Israel decimated through apostasy and judgment and reduced to the southern kingdom, to a remnant of Judah after the exile? It appears that in the thought of the great prophet of the exile God's servant Israel is identified ever more narrowly until the focus is upon one remnant group or individual who uniquely suffers and thus effects salvation for the larger Israel and for the nations.

5. Summary

We can summarize the missionary understanding of the Old Testament people of God as follows:

(1) The Old Testament understanding of mission is ambiguous and incomplete; it waits upon a fulfillment which will

clarify, focus, and empower the universal witness.

(2) This understanding of mission revolves around the ideas of election-covenant, monotheistic faith, universal vocation, and messianic eschatology.

(3) The direction of mission is almost entirely centripetal: Zion is the center of God's revelation in Torah and people, where the nations are to be gathered to learn of God and participate in his salvation.

(4) Therefore, there is little if any awareness of a need to *go* as witnesses but rather to *be* witnesses. Not *going* but *being;* God in the midst of his people, and his people in the midst of the nations.

(5) Israel looks to the future for her full redemption and that of the world. The relation of her vocation as God's royal community, his priest, and his prophet to the coming messianic vocation is not very clear.

(6) Mission is best expressed, however indirectly, in liturgy (the Psalms) and in prophetic oracle. In charismatic utterance, the salvation of the nations is announced and all peoples are invited to come and participate in the knowledge and worship of the true God. But Israel does not go out to the nations on mission. God was enacting in Israel a drama of redemption for the whole world. Or, in Israel God was addressing an open letter to the nations.

II. *The Mission of the People of God in the New Testament* (Covenant)

When we cross over from the Old Testament to the New, we find the conviction that the missionary or proto-missionary themes of the Old Testament have been strikingly fulfilled. The new age of messianic redemption has dawned in the mighty redemptive acts of God in Jesus of Nazareth. A "new covenant" is enacted and a "new covenant" people emerge, continuous but in a sense discontinuous with Israel. This new people of God, the church of Christ, has a mission to all nations. Mission is no longer merely centripetal but also centrifugal. The center to which the

nations are now being gathered is not the physical temple in Zion but the risen Christ himself. Since the center is universalized, the mission is mobile, free to extend to the farthest corners of the earth.

1. *The Mission of Jesus*

From the very first, the church understood her mission as grounded in the mission of Jesus, her Lord. As he is the center and touchstone in all other matters of Christian revelation, so also in mission. This fact is nowhere better expressed than in the missionary commission attributed to the risen Christ in the Gospel of John: "As the father has sent me, even so I send you" (John 20:21). The mission of the church, then, is the continuation of the mission of the Christ.

This brief article can do no more than summarize the mission of Jesus, crucially important though it is, and cannot enter into the critical problems of the Gospel testimony.[2]

(1) In creative fashion, Jesus clarified and brought into truly universal focus the missionary purpose of God which was seen in the Old Testament only in incompleteness and ambiguity. In his sense of messianic vocation, he combined the dawn of the messianic kingdom, the reconstitution of the "covenant" people, the gathering of the Gentiles, and the disparate messianic images.

(2) Jesus saw his mission as, first of all, a mission to Israel for the sake of the world. The promises to the fathers must be fulfilled. He must reconstitute Israel as the covenant people of God, as the community of eschatological expectation, as participants in and witnesses to the new age of universal redemption. Therefore, with some exceptions, he confined his ministry to "the lost sheep of the house of Israel."

It is important to note, however, that Jesus rejected the identity of God's people according to cult or physical lineage. God's

2 See Ferdinand Hahn, *Mission in the New Testament,* especially pp. 26–46; and Joachim Jeremias, *Jesus' Promise to the Nations.*

people included tax collectors and outcasts as well as respectable Pharisees. In fact, anyone doing the will of God was brother, sister, and mother to Jesus (Matt. 12:50). Thus the way was prepared for the recognition that in Christ there is neither Jew nor Gentile.

(3) In Jesus there was a tension between the messianic kingdom already present in him and his works and thus already challenging the demonic powers of darkness, and an absolutely crucial denouement with these powers which was yet to come —in his cross.

(4) Jesus understood his suffering and death as essential elements in the eschatological redemption of the world: "The time of the Gentiles must follow the Cross" (Jeremias, p. 72).

(5) His few exceptional ministries to Gentiles stand in the early eschatological dawn as significant foregleams, proofs before the time, of the messianic kingdom soon to come fully and universally to light by means of his death and resurrection.

(6) The accomplishment of the mission of Jesus in his earthly ministry and passion was the essential foundation of his continuing universal mission, through his church, as the exalted Christ.

2. The Great Commission

If the followers of Jesus understood their own mission as continuous with the messianic ministry of Jesus which culminated in his passion and resurrection, it was the resurrection which convinced them that he was indeed the Messiah, that his death was the messianic sacrifice for the sins of the world, and that he had initiated the "last days," the "time of the Gentiles." And the summation of these insights is located in the Great Commission.

Though the term "Great Commission" usually refers to the words of the risen Lord in Matthew 28:18–20, there is a different version of this commission in each of the four Gospels (Mark 16:15–18; Luke 24:45–49 complemented by Acts 1:8; and

John 20:21–23). Although the conclusion of Mark's Gospel as we have it today has been shown by textual criticism to be a later addition to this earliest Gospel, nevertheless, its commission is ancient.

There are several critical problems relating to these commissions, though they can receive only the briefest mention here.[3] These problems center around the differences in the commissions as found in the four Gospels, the reflections in some terminology of a later theological and liturgical development of the church, the absence of references to the commissions in other New Testament literature, and the apparent time-lag between these commands to a universal mission and the actual execution of the Gentile mission.

To conclude that because of these problems, the risen Christ never issued such a commission, the Gospel writers having simply read back into the record the later developed conviction of the church, is unwarranted. On the other hand, there is no reason to expect verbatim quotations from the risen Lord. No doubt the language and ideas of the commission reflect both the vivid memories of the first community of disciples and the insights received through the Holy Spirit in the years between the event and its being recorded in writing.

It is noteworthy, also, that although the four versions of the commission vary in language and ideas, there is significant agreement among them: (1) All four commissions witness to the near-incredible reality of the resurrection of Jesus. (2) Each in its particular context and mode of expression testifies to the authority of the risen Christ, expressed most vividly in the enthronement language of Matthew's version. (3) Each version represents the risen Jesus as sending the disciples on a mission bounded only by the ends of the earth and the end of time. (4) Each commission conveys the assurance to the dis-

[3] See E. Luther Copeland, "The Great Commission and Mission," Southwestern Journal of Theology, IX:2 (Spring, 1967), pp. 79–89.

ciples of the continued presence of the risen Lord, or the Holy Spirit, as they fulfill the commission.

The import of the missionary commissions, therefore, is that the universal mission of the church is based on the reality of the resurrection of Jesus Christ, including, of course, his sacrificial death for the sins of the world as the culmination of his own ministry. It was the great eschatological event of cross-resurrection which marked the beginning of the promised age of messianic redemption in which the Gentiles are to be gathered to God and the universal sovereignty of God in Christ is to be manifested.

3. Pentecost

If the incarnation, cross, and resurrection initiated the new age of universal redemption, Pentecost confirmed the fact. Pentecost is the first sovereign act of the risen, exalted Lord. So closely is it related to the resurrection that John's Gospel simply merges Easter and Pentecost (John 20:21–23). In Acts 2 the meaning of Pentecost is explained in terms of the prophecy of Joel (Joel 2:28–32), depicting a universal outpouring of the Spirit of God "in the last days" resulting in prophesying by all of God's people, accompanied by many "wonders . . . and signs" and by a universal salvation.

Pentecost is the great dynamic and charismatic empowering of the whole church for universal witness. In the Old Testament, the vision of God was given only to a few such as Moses. A veil, as it were, stood between man and God; and prophet, priest, and cult mediated God's word and presence. Now, in the freedom of the Spirit, "We all, with unveiled face, beholding the glory of the Lord, are being changed into his likeness" (2 Cor. 3:18). So all are priests and prophets, fulfilling the covenant language of Exodus 19:3–6, a "kingdom of priests" and a "holy nation." The emphasis of Acts 2 is upon witness which is identified with prophecy. Thus, by the power of the Holy Spirit all Christians are equipped to witness to what God has done and is doing in Jesus Christ.

Moreover, Pentecost blends the centripetal missionary emphasis of the Old Testament with a new centrifugal direction. There is a parallel here with the ancient story of the tower of Babel. There, primeval men, through the sin of presumptuous pride, became alienated from each other and unable to communicate. In Pentecost, God's scattered people are gathered in Jerusalem in humble submission to God, and a miracle of communication occurs. The Spirit breaks through the language barriers and a new reconciliation results.

Thus the Old Testament theme of a gathering in Zion is fulfilled—or its fulfillment begins. Significantly, however, this eschatological gathering, though in Jerusalem, is not at the Temple, just as the appearances of the risen Lord had not been there. The disciples "were all together in one place" (Acts 2:1), but the place is not identified except as "a house where they were sitting" (Acts 2:2), probably the "upper room" of Acts 1:13. The Temple is replaced, then, by the flesh and blood community of "living stones" of which the risen Christ himself is the living cornerstone "chosen and precious" (1 Peter 2:4). So the center to which the world's people are to be gathered is universalized. Wherever the disciples gather together, there is Christ in their midst. And wherever Christ is present, in the person of a disciple on mission (Matt. 28:20), or in the face of one of the least of his brothers in need (Matt. 25:40), there is the center to which the church is gathered.

Therefore, the mission is both centripetal and centrifugal. Each center which the gospel reaches is supposed to become a hub from which it extends to new centers. Thus the witness is to encompass ever-enlarging circles from Jerusalem as the first center to "all Judea and Samaria and to the end of the earth" (Acts 1:8).

4. "The Early Struggle for an Unhindered Gospel" [4]

The Acts of the Apostles records this kind of expansion as the gospel overleaps barriers of cult and race and of the limited understanding of the disciples. The Holy Spirit thrusts them out in these ever-enlarging circles of witness:

(1) At first the gospel operates among Jews and Jewish proselytes gathered in Jerusalem for the feast of Pentecost (Acts 2:5–11)—still, therefore, within the bounds of Judaism.

(2) In the Christian community, however, Hellenists come into prominence in universalizing the understanding of the Church's mission (Acts 6:1 ff.). These are not Greeks ("Hellenes") but Jews who have been subjected to Hellenistic (Greek) influences, and who presumably, therefore, have more of a cosmopolitan influence than the Palestinian Jews. The "seven men" of Acts 6:3–6 seem to have been Hellenists: they have Greek names and one of them is a proselyte. Two of these seven who did not stick to serving at tables helped to broaden the church's understanding of the gospel: Stephen by his preaching and martyrdom (Acts 6:8—7:60) and Philip by his missionary itineration (Acts 8:5–40).

(3) In Philip's preaching in Samaria, the gospel reached a new circle, the hated Samaritans—not Jews but not Gentiles, a people of mixed race and garbled religion. Before this episode was over, Samaritan believers had been baptized and had received the Holy Spirit, and two of the apostles, Peter and John, were preaching the gospel in the Samaritan villages.

(4) Through Philip the gospel crossed another barrier when he witnessed to an Ethiopian eunuch. This man was in some sense a proselyte and thus related to Judaism. But he was a Gentile of the black race, and it is likely that his physical handicap as a eunuch kept him from full status as a proselyte. He believed the gospel, however, and nothing was found to "prevent" his baptism (Acts 8:36–38).

(5) A further circle was reached and a further barrier overleaped as Peter preached the gospel to Romans (Acts 10:1—11:18). These people of Cornelius' household were "God-fearers," meaning those who had accepted the monotheistic faith of the Jews but had not gone all the way to accept circumcision and the observance of the Mosaic law as proselytes. Even so, it took a vision from heaven to send Peter into this Gentile home and to break down his scruples against interdining. Again, no one was found to "forbid" the baptism of these Gentiles and their acceptance in the new covenant people of God (Acts 10:47–48).

(6) Next, the gospel moved to the full inclusion of the Gentiles (Acts 11:19–26). Jewish Christians from Cyprus and Cyrene came to Antioch in Syria and preached to Greeks, and a large number of these Greeks were converted. Thus a new dimension was reached and Antioch became a new center for a mission to the Gentile world.

Now a troublesome question had to be faced, provoked by a strict party of Jewish Christians who insisted that Gentile converts to Christian faith had to be circumcised and observe the Mosaic law in order to be saved (Acts 15:1). The fundamental question was, what is the relation of the Jesus Christ movement to Judaism?

(7) The result was a conference in Jerusalem described in Acts 15 and Galatians 2.[5] The agreement arrived at was that the Gentiles did not need to be circumcised. Rather, according to Galatians 2:1–10, the Jewish Christians associated with Jerusalem would give major attention to evangelizing the Jews while the Hellenist Jewish Christians at Antioch would give major attention to the Gentile mission. Also, a collection should be taken for the poor in Jerusalem. According to Acts 15, a further agreement was reached which was some-

---

[4] Subtitle to the book by Frank Stagg, *The Book of Acts* (Nashville: Broadman Press, 1955).

[5] Hahn claims that there were two conferences, the two being merged together in the account in Acts 15; *op. cit.*, pp. 77–86.

thing of a compromise. Gentile Christians not only were expected to abstain from the glaring sexual immorality ("unchastity") of the Gentile world but also to observe certain delicacies which were designed to make inter-dining possible between Jewish and Gentile Christians without offense to Jewish sensitivities.

So the gospel, under the impulse of the Spirit of the risen Lord, had overleaped the barriers of race and cult and was operating freely in the world of universal man.

5. The Israel of the New Covenant

Meanwhile, the nature of the church as the missionary people of God was understood with increasing richness and variety of expression. Perhaps the most completely developed statement of the church's identity as the Israel of God is 1 Peter 2:4-10. Here the figures used are all from the Old Testament, and the covenant language of Exodus 19:3-6 is expressly applied to the church.

There is, first of all, the figure of the messianic stone. Three passages in the Old Testament in which this figure is used are brought together (Isa. 28:16; Psalm 118:22; Isa. 8:14-15). The composite picture thus constructed is of the builders (leaders) of Israel at work on the house of the covenant, coming to the one stone essential to their building, setting the stone aside as unfit, and then stumbling and falling upon it. The picture, then, is of official Israel's rejection of the Messiah and the consequent judgment upon Israel (cf. Matt. 21:42-43 and parallels; Acts 4:11).

The implication is that there is discontinuity between the old (rejected) Israel and the new. That the judgment upon the old Israel is irrevocable, however, is not implied. It is possible that it is assumed (as in Rom. 9—11) that old Israel is doomed to a tragic incompleteness, frustration, lack of fulfillment, until she recognizes the one stone which will complete the building of God within her—just as the church is under judgment when she forsakes her foundation stone. Thus, as there is one Mes-

siah, so there will be one Israel.

In any case, a miracle occurs! The rejected stone, an inanimate thing as such, comes alive! And by this resurrection it gathers to itself other living stones and a "spiritual house" emerges, a temple, a "holy priesthood," an altar where spiritual sacrifices are offered to God through Jesus Christ (1 Peter 2:4-5).

The church, therefore, is constructed out of those who, as living stones, gather in faith (the mode of address is exhortation: "Come to him . . . and . . . be yourselves built") to him who is the cornerstone (cf. Eph. 2:17-22). In faith they assent to God's judgment upon the Christ: "In God's sight chosen and precious" (1 Peter 2:4), now also to those "who believe, he is precious" (2:7).

There is now applied to the church all the rich covenant language of Israel (2:9). The term "a chosen race" is from Isaiah 43:20 and is used only once in the Old Testament. The word "race" means "nation" but with the emphasis upon origin. The church, like Israel, is called from out of the world of nations for service to the nations. She is "called out of the world . . . to proclaim the great acts of God in the world." [6] The church does well to remember, also, that she is "chosen" only in Christ. Neither the church corporately nor any of its members individually has any right to claim election except as joined to the "chosen and precious" One in faith and obedience. There must be no presumption upon election.

The other terms, "a royal priesthood, a holy nation, God's own people," are taken from Exodus 19:3-6 with only a slight change in the form of the last phrase. The meaning is the same as that applied to Israel: The church as "royal priesthood" is the people who serve God as king, sharing something of his royal character, and who stand before him as responsible for the whole world in priestly function. The one place in the whole world, then, where

6 Johannes Blauw, *The Missionary Nature of the Church*, p. 129.

the kingship of God, who is sovereign of the universe, is to be seen unmistakably is the church. She is a "holy nation," set apart from all other peoples with the vocation of living out in her corporate life the holy character and purposes of God. She is "God's own people," recognizing that out of all the universe which is his property he has chosen her. If all others ignore or reject his right to possession of the world, she will witness to his ownership and relate to the world as steward and priest.

But what had to be perceived from the meaning of the terms in Exodus 19:3–6 is made explicit in this passage: "that you may declare the wonderful deeds of him who called you out of darkness into his marvelous light" (2:9). To "declare" or show forth what God has done is more than mere telling. It embraces all the rich meanings of the convenantal titles with which the church has been named. Coupled with the new covenant understanding of mission, it means that the church's purpose both by *being* and *going* is to communicate the gospel.

Therefore, the Christian mission is inevitably an ethical mission. To be God's people means, as the prophets understood it, "to do justice, and to love kindness." As Jesus himself expressed it (quoting Isaiah), it means "to preach good news to the poor . . . to set at liberty those who are oppressed" (Luke 4:18). The gospel is to be communicated not just by *telling* but by *doing* the works of God in Christ.

And if the covenant with Israel in the past was based on a miraculous deliverance in the historical event of the Exodus, the New Covenant with Israel (the church) is based on the mighty deliverance wrought through the cross and resurrection of Jesus Christ. So the church is to keep vivid the consciousness that the blood of God's covenant with her is not that of animals but the precious blood of the Messiah himself,

"like that of a lamb without blemish or spot" (1 Peter 1:19). So she has been called "out of darkness into his marvelous light." Once a "no people," she is now "God's people." Once without mercy, she has now received mercy (2:10).

At her best, then, the church knows that although God has made her to share in his kingly glory, she has no merit of her own. She is content to exalt her king and serve him as she serves the world. After all, her Lord himself, being "in the form of God" took "the form of a servant" (Phil. 2:6–7). And the church knows that only as she fulfills her mission to the ends of the earth and the end of the world, does she have any right to claim the exalted titles which God, in the mystery of his electing grace, conferred upon Israel.

For Further Reading

BLAUW, JOHANNES. *The Missionary Nature of the Church.* New York: McGraw-Hill, 1962.

BOER, HARRY R. *Pentecost and Missions.* Grand Rapids: Wm. B. Eerdmans Publishing Co., 1961.

CARVER, WILLIAM OWEN. *The Bible a Missionary Message.* New York: Fleming H. Revell Company, 1921.

DE DIETRICH, SUZANNE. *The Witnessing Community.* Philadelphia: The Westminster Press, 1958.

GOERNER, H. C. *Thus It Is Written.* Nashville: Broadman Press, 1944.

HAHN, FERDINAND. *Mission in the New Testament.* London: SCM Press, Ltd., 1965.

JEREMIAS, JOACHIM. *Jesus' Promise to the Nations.* London: SCM Press, Ltd., 1958.

LOVE, JULIAN PRICE. *The Missionary Message of the Bible.* New York: The Macmillan Company, 1941.

MARTIN-ACHARD, ROBERT. *A Light to the Nations.* Edinburgh: Oliver and Boyd, 1962.

RETIF, A., and P. LAMARCHE. *The Salvation of the Gentiles and the Prophets.* Baltimore: Helicon Press, Inc., 1966.

ROWLEY, H. H. *The Biblical Doctrine of Election.* 3rd ed. London: Lutterworth Press, 1953.

⸻. *The Missionary Message of the Old Testament.* London: The Carey Kingsgate Press, Ltd., 1944.